The Definitive Guide to SWT and JFace

ROB WARNER
WITH
ROBERT HARRIS

Apress®

The Definitive Guide to SWT and JFace
Copyright © 2004 by Rob Warner with Robert Harris

ISBN (pbk): 1-59059-325-1

Printed and bound in the United States of America 9 8 7 6 5 4 3

Trademarked names may appear in this book. Rather than use a trademark symbol with every occurrence of a trademarked name, we use the names only in an editorial fashion and to the benefit of the trademark owner, with no intention of infringement of the trademark.

Lead Editor: Steve Anglin

Technical Reviewer: Gábor Lipták

Editorial Board: Steve Anglin, Dan Appleman, Ewan Buckingham, Gary Cornell, Tony Davis, Jason Gilmore, Jonathan Hassell, Chris Mills, Dominic Shakeshaft, Jim Sumser

Project Manager: Tracy Brown Collins

Copy Edit Manager: Nicole LeClerc

Copy Editors: Susannah Pfalzer, Kim Wimpsett

Production Manager: Kari Brooks

Production Editor: Ellie Fountain

Compositor: Linda Weidemann, Wolf Creek Press

Proofreader: Patrick Vincent

Indexer: Kevin Broccoli

Cover Designer: Kurt Krames

Manufacturing Manager: Tom Debolski

Distributed to the book trade in the United States by Springer-Verlag New York, Inc., 233 Spring Street, 6th Floor, New York, NY 10013 and outside the United States by Springer-Verlag GmbH & Co. KG, Tiergartenstr. 17, 69112 Heidelberg, Germany.

In the United States: phone 1-800-SPRINGER, e-mail orders@springer-ny.com, or visit http://www.springer-ny.com. Outside the United States: fax +49 6221 345229, e-mail orders@springer.de, or visit http://www.springer.de.

For information on translations, please contact Apress directly at 2560 Ninth Street, Suite 219, Berkeley, CA 94710. Phone 510-549-5930, fax 510-549-5939, e-mail info@apress.com, or visit http://www.apress.com.

The information in this book is distributed on an "as is" basis, without warranty. Although every precaution has been taken in the preparation of this work, neither the author(s) nor Apress shall have any liability to any person or entity with respect to any loss or damage caused or alleged to be caused directly or indirectly by the information contained in this work.

The source code for this book is available to readers at http://www.apress.com in the Downloads section.

To my son Tyson, age 10, who proclaimed this to be
"some dumb computer book about Java, divided by 27."

—ROB WARNER

For Charlie, Mallory, Alison, and mom.

—ROBERT HARRIS

Contents at a Glance

Contents

Chapter 10 Graphics *369*

Chapter 11 Displaying and Editing Text................. *435*

Chapter 12 Advanced Topics.............................. *497*

Part III   Using JFace

Chapter 13 Your First JFace Application *543*

Chapter 14 Creating Viewers.............................. *551*

Chapter 19 Miscellaneous Helper Classes 773

Chapter 20 Creating Wizards 793

Index 825

About the Authors

Rob Warner graduated from Brigham Young University in December 1993 with a degree in English, then immediately took a job in the technology industry. He has developed software in various languages for the transportation, banking, and medical industries during his career. Now president and CEO of Interspatial, Inc., he designs and develops Java-based solutions using both Eclipse and its derivative, WebSphere Studio Application Developer. He has used SWT and JFace on several projects, including an executive information system for a religious organization, a password-retrieval Eclipse plug-in, and various other applications and utilities. Rob lives in Jacksonville, Florida with his wife Sherry and their five children: Tyson, Jacob, Mallory, Camie, and Leila.

Robert Harris is a software engineer focused on distributed object computing. Since earning his master's of science degree from the University of Florida, he has been designing and implementing flexible, resilient solutions in the telecommunications, transportation, and medical industries. His personal interests include speaking French with his seven-year-old daughter Mallory, catching bugs with his six-year-old son Charlie, and infuriating his wife Alison (age withheld).

About the
Technical Reviewer

Gábor Lipták is an independent consultant with more than ten years of industry experience, mostly in object-oriented environments with Smalltalk, C++, and Java. Gábor has written multiple technical articles and has served as technical reviewer for several books. Gábor is now working on a Java e-commerce project and can be reached at gliptak@hotmail.com.

Acknowledgments

I THANK MY beautiful wife and my wonderful children for their patience. This book represents hours not spent with them, and I thank them for this opportunity. You can now have your husband and father back. I also thank my extended family for their continual effort to fill the holes I kept leaving behind. I appreciate all your service.

I thank the wonderful folks at Apress for all their hard work in bringing this book to fruition. Tracy Brown Collins kept the focus and kept this book moving forward. I thank her for her patient prodding. Susannah Pfalzer and Kim Wimpsett helped clarify our thoughts and saved us from some embarrassing typos. Ellie Fountain and Steve Anglin took us through the final stretch. Finally, Gábor Lipták provided essential insights to keep the book technically correct, and kept us on our toes.

Thanks also to my colleague and now fellow author, Joseph Schmuller, for showing me the possibilities. Another colleague, Keith Barrett, provided essential guidance during the formative years of my career, for which I'm grateful. I also thank a dear friend, Ryan Smith, for giving me my first IDE and introducing me to programming.

During most of the time I was writing this book, I worked (in my day job) with a group of wonderful folks on the ShipCSX team. I miss working with you, and I hope all is well.

Finally, thanks to the Eclipse team for producing such a wonderful IDE, widget set, and abstraction library. It has been a pleasure immersing myself in Eclipse, and I continually find new capabilities in this amazing tool. Thanks, too, for opening the source, which proved essential for understanding how to leverage SWT and JFace. This book wouldn't have been possible without the open source.

—Rob Warner

WITHOUT THE FAMILY with which I have been blessed, neither this book nor anything would be possible. I would therefore like to thank my mother Marian and brothers Michael and David.

Over the years, I have had the opportunity to work with an amazing array of professionals, from whom I have learned this wonderful and rewarding trade. A few that come to mind are Noam Kedem, Matthew Dragiff, Eyal Wirzansky, Jim Simak, Bob Moriarty, Anish Mehra, Krishna Sai, Sreedhar Pampati, and James Earl Carter.

Also, a special thanks to Robert A. White, who has taught me many things, the first of which was "how to right."

I can't forget to mention Brenda Star, Bernie and Ruth Nachman, Landon Walker, Mike and Tammy Shumer, and Clark Morgan. Thanks, guys.

—Robert Harris

Introduction

WHEN THE ECLIPSE.ORG TEAM built their namesake product, Eclipse, they necessarily released the new graphical user interface (GUI) libraries that composed its interface: SWT and JFace. Though Eclipse utterly depends on these libraries, the converse isn't true: neither SWT nor JFace depends on Eclipse, and developers can freely use these open source libraries in their own applications.

While most available information regarding these compelling libraries focuses on using them to extend the Eclipse tool, *The Definitive Guide to SWT and JFace* takes a different tack: it explains how to use the libraries in standalone applications. These libraries, which rely on native widgets, boast native look and feel and native performance. This means that not only will Java applications built using these libraries run on all major environments, but also that they'll run at native or near-native speeds. Java can finally shed the "too slow and ugly" label of its adolescence, having matured into a worthy desktop competitor.

What to Expect from This Book

This book doesn't teach you Java. It also doesn't teach you how to use Eclipse, nor does it teach you how to build Eclipse plug-ins. You can find a number of other books that teach Java or Eclipse, many of them excellent and deserving of your time and study. This book ignores specific tools, however, and instead focuses on the SWT and JFace libraries to help you build independent desktop applications.

After reading this book, you'll be able to design, develop, and deploy fully operational, cross-platform desktop applications that use either SWT alone, or SWT combined with JFace. You'll understand how to leverage these libraries to create a range of simple to intricate user interfaces that look, feel, and perform like the rest of the applications your users run. You can use whatever development tools you choose to accomplish that.

This book uses SWT and JFace 3.0, which was still under development during this book's writing. As such, you may find a wart or two, or a changed API. We apologize, but accept this as a necessary evil in order to give you the most current information available. Check the Apress Web site for any errata or code changes.

This book serves as both tutorial and reference guide. We hope that, after your initial read, you keep this book handy, ready to resolve your questions and problems with SWT and JFace. May it become soiled and dog-eared through frequent use!

Who Should Read This Book

If you're new to SWT and JFace, or even if you've used them but want to learn more, this book contains the information you'll need to become an SWT and JFace expert. This book expects you to know how to program in Java, though you don't have to be an expert. It does, however, assume that you know the meanings of terms such as "compiler," "classpath," and "inheritance."

This book requires no knowledge or understanding of SWT or JFace, or even of GUI programming in general. It targets the gamut of the SWT and JFace experience, from people who have never heard of SWT or JFace, to developers who have worked with these libraries extensively, but want to fill in the gaps of what they know and use.

How This Book Is Organized

This book comprises three sections. The first section, which includes Chapters 1 and 2, explains both the history of Java desktop toolkits and the need for SWT and JFace, and helps you set up your computer's environment for the rest of the book. If history doesn't excite you, feel free to skim these chapters. Make sure, however, to glean from them the information necessary to set up your environment for building SWT applications.

Chapters 3 through 12 make up the second section. They guide you through SWT, from the obligatory "Hello World" program to advanced topics such as printing and Web browsing. The chapters build on each other, lending themselves to sequential study. Type in the examples, compile them, and run them to see how SWT works. Feel free to tinker with the code to produce new results.

Finally, the third section (Chapters 13 through 20) explores JFace. Again, these chapters build on each other, so we recommend taking them step by step. If you have no plans to use JFace in your applications, and instead rely exclusively on SWT, you may skip this section. However, you'll ignore a library that can help you build SWT applications much more quickly.

What You Need

To run the examples in this book, you must have a computer with a Java development environment version 1.4 or later installed. Your computer must run an operating environment that SWT supports, which includes (among others) Microsoft Windows 98 or later, Mac OS X, Linux, and various UNIX platforms. See more information about supported platforms in Chapter 2.

The examples in this book don't require that you run Eclipse, or even have it installed on your computer. However, you must have the SWT libraries installed to run the SWT examples in Chapters 3 through 12. To run the JFace examples in Chapters 13 through 20, you must also have the JFace libraries installed. Chapter 2 explains how to install these libraries.

Whether you use Eclipse, some other integrated development environment (IDE), or command-line tools, you must have some way to edit text and compile the examples. We provide Ant build scripts to compile and run the examples; to use them, you must have Ant (http://ant.apache.org) installed on your computer. However, compiling and running the examples doesn't require that you use Ant. Chapter 2 explains how to set up various development environments to compile and run the examples.

The examples in this book have been tested on Microsoft Windows, Linux, and Mac OS X. Except where otherwise noted, they should run fine not only on these platforms, but also on all other SWT-supported platforms. Let us know if you have any problems.

Source Code

You can download all the source code, the Ant scripts, and the images used in the examples in this book from the Apress Web site, packaged as a single ZIP file. To download, use your Web browser to go to this URL:

```
http://www.apress.com/book/download.html
```

Select *The Definitive Guide to SWT and JFace* from the list, and then follow the prompts to download the ZIP file containing the code.

How to Contact Us

Please send any questions or comments regarding the book or the source code to the authors, at the e-mail addresses listed below.

Rob Warner: rwarner@interspatial.com

Robert Harris: rlharris@comcast.net

Part I

Getting Ready

CHAPTER 1

Evolution of Java GUIs

WHEN JAVA WAS FIRST RELEASED in the spring of 1995, it included a library, the Abstract Windowing Toolkit (AWT), for building graphical user interfaces (GUIs) for applications. Java's ambitious claim—"write once, run anywhere"—promised that an application laden with drop-down menus, command buttons, scroll bars, and other familiar GUI "controls" would function on various operating systems, including Microsoft Windows, Sun's own Solaris, Apple's Mac OS, and Linux, without having to be recompiled into platform-specific binary code.

Revolutionary at the time, Java's claim, and albeit nascent support for true operating-system–independent application development, led to both an explosion of Java applets (applications designed to run inside a Web browser) and plans to port leading desktop applications to Java (Corel's WordPerfect Office suite and Netscape's Navigator, a.k.a. "Javagator," to name two).

Although most of the efforts to create desktop applications have faded since then, the GUI capabilities of Java have conversely grown stronger. Tracking the evolution of GUIs in Java takes us through three major windowing toolkits: AWT, Swing, and the Standard Widget Toolkit (SWT). We examine each of these in this chapter, as well as a fourth library, JFace, that's not a windowing toolkit, but rather an abstraction layer built atop SWT.

AWT

Much of the excitement surrounding the introduction of Java was based on *applets*, a new technology by which programs could be distributed via the Internet and executed inside of a browser. Users and developers alike embraced the new paradigm, which promised to simplify multiplatform development, maintenance, and distribution—some of the most challenging issues in commercial software development.

To facilitate the creation of GUIs in Java, Sun had originally created a graphics library with a distinctive, Java-based look and feel on all platforms. Netscape, Sun's primary partner in the applet technology strategy, argued that applets should maintain the look and feel of the runtime system. They hoped that applets would appear and behave just like every other application on the platform. Netscape's views held sway, and Sun abandoned its Java look.

To achieve the Netscape "native look and feel" goal, AWT was created in the final development stages of the first version of the Java Development Kit (JDK). The default implementation of AWT used a "peer" approach, in which each Java GUI widget had a corresponding component in the underlying windowing system.

For example, each `java.awt.Button` object (AWT's "push" button) would create a dedicated button in the underlying native windowing system. When a user clicked the button, the event would flow from the native implementation's library into the Java Virtual Machine (JVM), and eventually to the logic associated with the `java.awt.Button` object. The implementation of the peer system and the communication between the Java component and the peer was hidden inside the low-level implementation of the JVM; the Java-level code stayed identical across platforms.

However, to remain faithful to the "write once, run anywhere" promise, compromises had to be made. Specifically, a "lowest common denominator" approach was adopted in which only features offered by *all* of the native windowing systems would be available in AWT. This required developers to develop their own high-level widgets for more advanced features (such as a tree view), and left users with varied experiences.

Other issues slowed the acceptance of applets as well. Applets ran inside of a security "sandbox" that prevented malicious applets from misusing resources such as the file system and network connection. Although the sandbox prevented security breaches, it neutered applications. After all, what good is an application that can't make a connection or save a file? Java GUIs were also not as responsive as native applications. This was due in some part to the then-current level of hardware performance and the interpretive nature of Java.

As a consequence, applications developed with AWT lacked many of the features of a modern GUI, while still not attaining the goal of appearing and behaving like applications developed using native windowing toolkits. Something better was needed for Java GUIs to succeed.

Swing

Announced at the JavaOne conference in 1997 and released in March 1998, the Java Foundation Classes (JFC) included a new windowing toolkit for Java. Code-named Swing, these new GUI components offered an appreciable upgrade to AWT, and seemed poised to help Java take over the computing world. Times were heady for Java: downloadable applets would be the software of the future, people would switch from other operating systems to JavaOS and from traditional computers to thin-client network computers called JavaStations, and Microsoft would finally be dethroned as the unchallenged player in the desktop arena. Although this vision was never realized, Swing has nonetheless flourished as a GUI for Java applets and applications.

The Swing Architecture

Although "Swing" was just the code name for the new components, the name stuck and persists to this day. Perhaps the name was too appropriate to jettison; the new windowing toolkit attempted to swing the proverbial pendulum in several ways:

- Whereas AWT relied on a peer architecture, with Java code widgets wrapping native widgets, Swing used no native code and no native widgets.

- AWT left screen painting to the native widgets; Swing components painted themselves.

- Because Swing didn't rely on native widgets, it could abandon AWT's least-common-denominator approach and implement every widget on every platform, creating a much more powerful toolkit than AWT could ever achieve.

- Swing, by default, would adopt the native platform's look and feel. However, it wasn't limited to that, and introduced "pluggable look and feels" so that a Swing application could look like a Windows application, a Motif application, or a Mac application. It even had its own look and feel, dubbed "Metal," so that a Swing application could completely ignore the operating environment it ran on, and just look like itself—a defiant blot on a humdrum, conforming desktop. Imagine the hubris!

However, Swing components moved beyond simple widgets, and embraced the emerging design patterns and best practices. With Swing, you didn't just get a handle to a GUI widget and stuff data into it; you defined a model to hold the data, a view to display the data, and a controller to respond to user input. In fact, most Swing components are built on the model-view-controller (MVC) design pattern, which makes application development cleaner and maintenance more manageable.

Where Did It Fall Short?

Though Swing improved tremendously on AWT, it still failed to catapult Java forward as the tool of choice for creating desktop applications. Its proponents will point quickly to successful Swing applications such as jEdit, an open-source text editor (http://www.jedit.org/), or Together, a Unified Modeling Language (UML) modeling tool from Borland (http://www.borland.com/), but Swing applications continue to be rarities on computing desktops. Sun posts "Swing Sightings" (http://java.sun.com/products/jfc/tsc/sightings/), a running log of available Swing applications, proof positive that their advents are noteworthy. We've yet to see Web pages devoted to "C++ Sightings" or "Visual Basic Sightings."

Why hasn't Swing fulfilled its promise? The reasons probably boil down to

- Speed, or, more specifically, the lack thereof

- Look and feel

Swing devotees bristle at the suggestion that Swing applications struggle with speed. Admittedly, later iterations of Swing, just-in-time (JIT) compilers, JVMs, and the Java language itself have significantly narrowed the gap between Swing applications and their native counterparts. However, Swing continues to have a somewhat sluggish and less responsive feel than native applications. As desktop computers become faster and users' expectations rise along with the speed improvements, any perceived lethargy becomes both frustrating and intolerable.

The howling you hear is from Swing developers outraged by the assertion that look and feel is an issue with Swing. After all, they scream, Swing has all kinds of pluggable look and feels, and can look like virtually anything. Java 2 Platform, Standard Edition (J2SE) 1.4.2 even added Windows XP and GTK+ support, so that a Swing application on those platforms automatically picks up their look and feel.

However, therein lies the issue: Swing will always be a step behind the latest GUIs, because support for the GUI must be written explicitly into the Java library. A Swing application running on Windows XP still looks like a Windows 98 application if it's running under J2SE 1.4.1 or earlier. Also, users are increasingly imprinting their personalities on their desktops using "skins," or alternative graphical look and feels, using software such as XP themes or WindowBlinds (http://www.stardock.net/). Swing doesn't pick up the skins, defying not only the operating system, but now the user preferences, too.

In short, Swing applications still don't perform as well as native applications, and don't quite look like them, either. For Java to shrug off its perennial understudy position and command a starring role in desktop application development, its GUI demands improvement.

Model-View-Controller

The MVC architecture segregates the data (model), the presentation of the data (view), and the manipulation of the data (controller). For example, suppose that you have an application that keeps track of your favorite color. The application must

- Know the color you've selected and store it in memory

- Display the currently selected color

- Allow you to change the color

- Persist the color

The selected color represents the model. It might be stored as a Java Color object, a binary RGB value, or a String holding the HTML representation.

The way the currently selected color is displayed represents the view. It might display the RGB values as numbers, the HTML value as a single string, the name of the color, or a color swatch.

The controller contains both the method for changing the color and the mechanism for persisting the data. You might click the desired color in a color wheel, type in the name of the color, type in the HTML value for the color, or move a set of sliders representing RGB values. To persist the color, the application might store it in a database, write it to an XML file, or save it using the Java preferences API.

The way to display or select the color shouldn't have any impact on the color itself. The color selected shouldn't change the storage mechanism. Adhering to the design allows you to change one component without having to change the others. For example, if colorblind users complain that they can't determine what color they've selected from the color swatch shown, you can change the view to show the name, but leave the model and the controller alone.

The MVC pattern has proven itself a powerful, and now indispensable, way to build applications.

SWT

When the Eclipse.org consortium set out to build Eclipse, they realized that Swing and AWT were both inadequate for building real-world commercial applications. Consequently, they decided to build a new GUI toolkit to use for the Eclipse interface, borrowing heavily from libraries in VisualAge SmallTalk. They called the new toolkit the Standard Widget Toolkit (SWT). Recognizing that native performance requires native widgets, SWT's designers adopted AWT's peer architecture, falling back on Java implementations only when native widgets didn't exist (for example, tree controls on Motif). Thus, SWT takes the "best of both worlds" approach between AWT and Swing: native functionality when available, Java implementation when unavailable. This guarantees that widgets look and respond comparably to native widgets.

SWT was released in 2001, integrated with the Eclipse Integrated Development Environment (IDE). Since that initial release, it has evolved and become an independent release. It's available for numerous operating systems including Microsoft Windows, Mac OS X, and several flavors of Unix, among others. At the time of this writing, the current official release is version 2.1.3. Version 3.0 is in beta, and is also available for download. This book uses SWT 3.0.

Another important advantage of SWT is that its source code is freely available under an open-source license that has no viral repercussions. This means you can use SWT in your applications and release them under any licensing scheme. The availability of source code is also essential to understanding the library's lower-level functionality or debugging applications. Open-source software also tends to be updated more frequently than commercially released software.

JFace

Building on top of SWT, JFace offers the power of SWT with the ease of the MVC pattern. SWT provides the raw widgets with a straightforward API—for example, you create a table widget and insert the rows and columns of data you want to display. JFace provides an abstraction layer on top of SWT, so instead of programming directly to the API, you program to the abstraction layer and it talks to the API. Think of the difference between programming to the native C interface of widgets vs. using a C++ GUI class library, or between using AWT vs. using Swing. These analogies help to illustrate the difference between SWT and JFace. For example, to use a table in JFace, you still create the table widget, but you don't put data into it. Instead, you give it your content (or model) provider class and your display (or view) provider class. The table then calls your provider classes to determine both content and how to display that content.

JFace doesn't completely abstract the breadth of SWT. Even in applications written in JFace, SWT and its lower-level API peek their heads through often. After stepping you through SWT in the second section of this book to build the proper foundation, we explore the power of JFace in the third section.

Summary

From its outset, Java has provided libraries for writing cross-platform, windowed, GUI applications, through AWT, Swing, and now SWT and JFace. Initial toolkits were underpowered, but subsequent offerings have addressed previous generations' shortcomings and effected great advances. SWT and JFace position Java as not only a viable, but also an advantageous platform for developing desktop applications. Whereas attempts to embrace the portability and strength of Java in times past necessarily meant accepting its GUI deficiencies, today that downside has disappeared. Java can finally command its place on desktop computers.

The next chapter introduces you to Eclipse, the Java IDE that begat SWT and JFace, and shows you how to prepare your system to build SWT and JFace applications.

CHAPTER 2

Getting Started with Eclipse

IN NOVEMBER 2001, a consortium of technology companies formed to "create better development environments and product integration," according to an Eclipse.org press release.[1] The consortium includes (among others):

- IBM

- Merant

- Borland

- Rational

- Red Hat

- SUSE LINUX

Dubbed Eclipse.org, the consortium soon released its flagship product, Eclipse: an open source, extensible IDE for building Java applications.

The development community quickly took notice of Eclipse. When version 2.1 was released in March 2003, seven million copies were downloaded in the first two days. Three lively Usenet newsgroups teem with Eclipse users. Web sites have sprung up to supplement the main Eclipse Web site, `http://www.eclipse.org`. Articles have appeared on various Web sites, including IBM's developerWorks site (`http://www.ibm.com/developerworks/`), detailing how to use this exciting tool. IBM has even built its Web development IDE, WebSphere Studio Application Developer, as an extension of Eclipse. Both Rational and Borland have released their UML modeling tools as plug-ins for Eclipse. SlickEdit's Visual SlickEdit, an industry-leading source-code editor, is now available as an Eclipse plug-in. The Eclipse community has responded with hundreds of other plug-ins, from the truly useful (Telnet clients, J2EE environments, profilers) to the merely fun (MP3 players and Tetris clones). See the Eclipse Plugin Central Web site (`http://www.eclipseplugincentral.com/`) for more details on available plug-ins.

---

1. Eclipse.org press release, "Eclipse.org Consortium Forms to Deliver New Era Application Development Tools," `http://www.eclipse.org/org/pr.html`.

Why all the fuss about another Java IDE? For one thing, the tool is free, both in the monetary sense (free as in beer, to use the open source community's jargon) and in the reusable-code sense (free as in speech). For another, it affords incredible opportunities for extension, and many individuals and companies have already written plug-in tools for Eclipse.

Eclipse is written in Java, yet looks and performs as if it were a native program. Perhaps most important, it includes a windowing toolkit—SWT—that is freely usable to build other Java applications that also look and perform as if they were native programs. This toolkit, the focus of this book, can be used outside of Eclipse as well.

This chapter introduces you to Eclipse and shows you how to get started building SWT and JFace applications. It also presents some alternatives to using Eclipse to build SWT and JFace applications. However, it doesn't go into depth on using Eclipse—other texts do that. In fact, we rarely mention Eclipse after this chapter. Beyond this chapter, all of the code and instructions are IDE agnostic, and you can use your favorite development tools as you learn SWT and JFace. By the end of this chapter, you'll understand how to use SWT and JFace in whatever Java development environment you use.

Installing Eclipse

The Eclipse.org download site distributes the entire Eclipse system, including SWT and JFace. The main download site is `http://www.eclipse.org/downloads`. Several mirror sites, linked from the main download page, are also available for downloading Eclipse. You can download Eclipse in either binary or source code form. Source code is available either as a ZIP file or from CVS; binaries are platform-specific ZIP archives.

Eclipse supports most major platforms. Binary downloads are available for these platforms:

- Windows 98/Me/2000/XP

- Linux (both Motif and GTK 2)

- Solaris 8

- QNX

- AIX

- HP-UX

- Mac OS X

You can also download SWT for Windows CE, but not Eclipse.

Most operating systems have only one corresponding distribution file. However, on Linux the distribution is also windowing-system dependent: you choose between the Motif and GTK versions, though nothing prevents you from downloading and installing both. Select the appropriate link for your system and download the installation file to a temporary directory.

NOTE   *Eclipse doesn't include a Java Runtime Environment (JRE). You must first install a 1.4.1 or higher JRE or JDK before running Eclipse.*

Eclipse offers no fancy installers or setup routines. To install Eclipse, simply unzip the downloaded file to the desired parent directory (for example, `c:\` on Windows or `/usr/local` on Linux or Unix). A directory called `eclipse` is created inside the selected parent directory, and all Eclipse files are copied to their appropriate locations beneath that directory. You launch Eclipse by running the appropriate program for the operating system (for example, `eclipse.exe` or `eclipse`). You can also create a desktop icon for launching Eclipse. Figure 2-1 shows the properties for a desktop icon on Windows.

Figure 2-1. Eclipse desktop shortcut properties

When you launch Eclipse for the first time, Eclipse completes the installation process and creates a workspace.

Passing arguments to the Eclipse launch command, whether from the command line or inside the shortcut, changes Eclipse's default behavior during that run of the program. The defaults are reasonable, but if you're adventurous, you can try some of the more useful command-line options shown in Table 2-1.

Table 2-1. Eclipse Command-Line Arguments

Argument	Explanation
-data <directory>	Specifies <directory> as the working directory in which Eclipse both loads current projects and creates new ones. By default, the working directory is called workspace and resides below the Eclipse installation directory—unless you don't have write permissions, in which case it's created in your home directory.
-debug	Starts Eclipse in debug mode
-nosplash	Turns off (doesn't display) the splash screen
-vm <javaVM>	Specifies <javaVM> as the JVM for Eclipse to use. You must either have a JVM in your execution path or specify the location of one with the -vm command.
-vmargs <arguments>	Specifies arguments to pass to the JVM

Creating Your First Program

When you launch Eclipse, you see your workspace, which is a container for your projects. Your initial workspace doesn't contain any projects, and looks something like Figure 2-2.

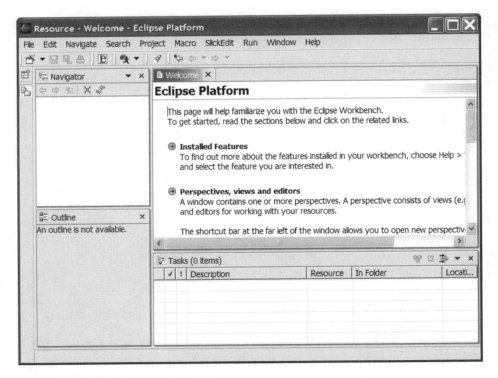

Figure 2-2. The Eclipse main window

You can't do much without a project, so select File ➤ New ➤ Project from the menu. You should see a dialog box like the one shown in Figure 2-3.

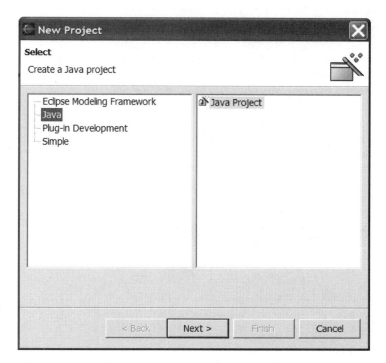

Figure 2-3. The New Project window

Select Java in the left pane, Java Project in the right, and click Next. Type **Test** in the Project name field (see Figure 2-4).

Click Finish. When prompted to switch to the Java Perspective; click Yes, which returns you to the Eclipse main window. The Package Explorer window on the left should now show your new Test project.

Perspectives in Eclipse

Perspectives in Eclipse are task-specific views of your workspace. They define the window layout, menu options, and available toolbars. You can edit your code in any perspective, but using the perspective appropriate to your present task makes your work easier.

Eclipse installs a few useful perspectives, including Debug, which displays tools and options for debugging your code, and Java Browsing, which is optimized for browsing through your Java code. You can customize these perspectives to suit your needs, and even save the customized perspectives. Don't be afraid to experiment—you can always restore a perspective to its default layout by selecting Window ➤ Reset Perspective from the main menu.

Some Eclipse plug-ins install new perspectives. For example, a profiling plug-in installs a Profiling perspective that contains tools and views for profiling your programs. Source Control perspectives allow you to browse through source control archives.

Perspectives offer powerful ways to accomplish the various tasks associated with software development. Learn to leverage their capabilities to increase your development productivity.

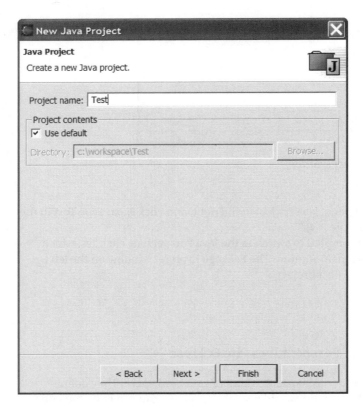

Figure 2-4. Select a project name.

Next, add code to your project. Right-click the Test project and select New ➤ Class from the popup menu. The dialog box should look like Figure 2-5.

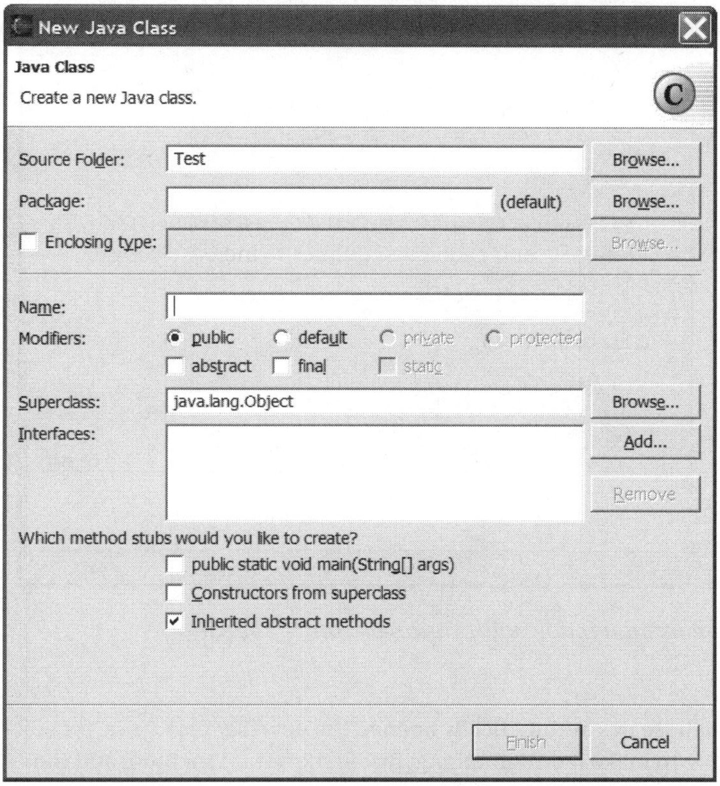

Figure 2-5. The New Java Class window

Type **test** in the Name field, select the checkbox by the "public static void main(String[] args)" option in the "Which method stubs would you like to create?" section, and click Finish. Eclipse creates your new source code file and returns you to the main window, which should now look like Figure 2-6.

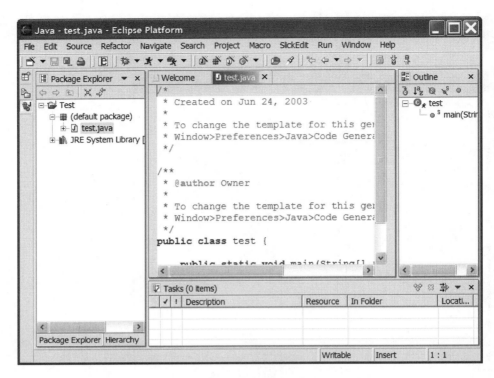

Figure 2-6. The Eclipse main window with your new source code file

You can see that Eclipse has automatically opened the new file, test.java, for editing. Let's add some code to make it do something; inside the main() method, add the code:

```
System.out.println("Hello from Eclipse");
```

Click File ➤ Save, which both saves the file and compiles it. You should now have a program ready to run. If you've made any mistakes, the Tasks window at the bottom of the Eclipse main window will show an error icon and a description of the problem, similar to Figure 2-7. Click the Task entry to jump to the offending code.

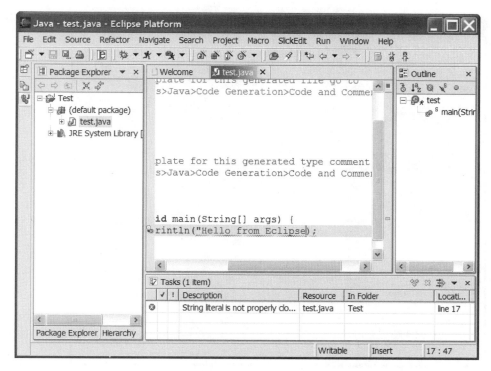

Figure 2-7. A syntax error in the Tasks window

Correct the error and click File ➤ Save again. Correct all errors until the Tasks window has no entries.

To run the program, select Run ➤ Run from the main menu. You should see a dialog that looks something like Figure 2-8.

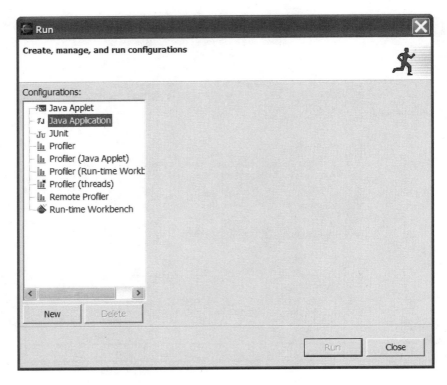

Figure 2-8. The Run dialog

Select Java Application and click the New button. Eclipse automatically deter-mines that you want to run your `test` class, and populates the dialog to look like Figure 2-9.

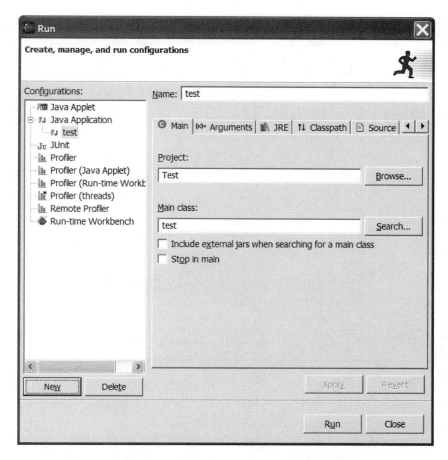

Figure 2-9. The Run dialog with your test class ready to run

Click the Run button. The program runs, and prints "Hello from Eclipse" in the console window at the bottom of the Eclipse main window. You might have to scroll up to see it, but your Eclipse main window should now be greeting you (see Figure 2-10).

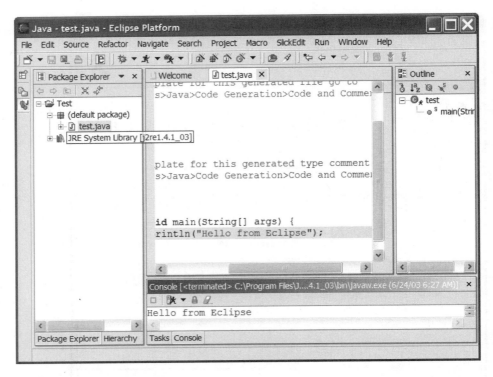

Figure 2-10. Hello from Eclipse

Congratulations! You're now up and running in Eclipse.

This was a simple application that required no external JAR files or libraries. In the next section, we tackle a more complex example where you must edit the Eclipse compile and runtime environments.

Including the SWT Libraries

To create SWT programs in the Eclipse environment, you must configure the Java build path (or classpath) so that it includes the SWT JAR file (swt.jar). To demonstrate the correct configuration of your environment for building SWT applications, you'll create a simple program based on SWT that opens a window.

Add a new class to the project you created earlier by right-clicking your project's name in the Package Explorer window and choosing New ➤ Class from the context menu. Enter **BlankWindow** for the class name and click Finish. Your new class is created and its code appears in the editor window. Enter the code in Listing 2-1 into the editor window.

Listing 2-1. `BlankWindow.java`

```java
import org.eclipse.swt.widgets.*;

public class BlankWindow
{
 public static void main (String[] args)
 {
  Display display = new Display();
  Shell shell = new Shell(display);
  shell.open();
  while (!shell.isDisposed())
  {
   if (!display.readAndDispatch())
   {
    display.sleep();
   }
  }
  display.dispose();
 }
}
```

When you save this file, you get indications of errors in the file (check the Tasks window). To compile the program, add the SWT JAR file to the Java build path of the project. The build path is configured in the Properties window, which you can open by right-clicking the project name in the Package Explorer tab of Eclipse and selecting Properties from the context menu. Choose Java Build Path on the left, and select the Libraries tab on the right. Click the button labeled Add External JARs to bring up a file selection dialog box. Use the file selection box to add `swt.jar`; its location is operating system, windowing system, and Eclipse version dependent. In general, it's located in here:

```
<eclipse_install_directory>/
  plugins/
    org.eclipse.swt.<windowing_system>_<eclipse_version_number>/
      ws/
        <windowing_system>/
         swt.jar
```

For example, Eclipse 3.0 on Windows places `swt.jar` in `plugins\`
`org.eclipse.swt.win32_3.0.0\ws\win32` beneath the Eclipse installation directory; on Linux Motif, in `plugins/org.eclipse.swt.motif_3.0.0/ws/motif`; and on Mac OS X, in `plugins/org.eclipse.swt.carbon_3.0.0/ws/carbon`. Figure 2-11 shows the SWT JAR added to the Java Build Path.

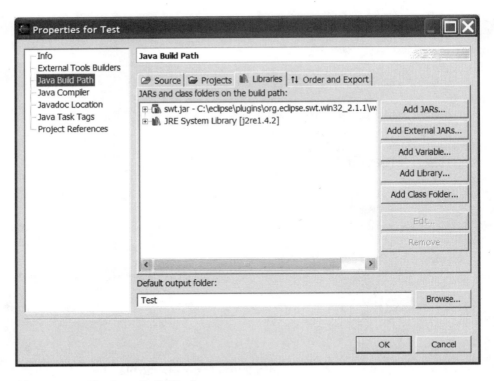

Figure 2-11. The Java Build Path

NOTE   *The GTK version also requires* swt-pi.jar, *found in the same directory as* swt.jar, *to be in the Java Build Path.*

The errors should now disappear from the Tasks window. You have now successfully saved and compiled your first program. However, you must configure one more parameter before you can run the program. As SWT depends on Java Native Interface (JNI) implementations for the windowing system functionality, you must configure the runtime environment so that it can locate the libraries in which the local implementations are stored. Again, this configuration is dependent upon your operating and windowing systems.

To set up the native libraries, select Run ➤ Run from the main menu of Eclipse to open the Run dialog box. Click the New button, which creates a configuration called BlankWindow with BlankWindow as the Main class. Click the Arguments tab, and in the "VM arguments" section enter an argument to add the directory containing the library to the Java library path. The argument to define is **-Djava.library.path**. The library's parent directory structure is generally like this:

```
<eclipse_install_directory>/
  plugins/
    org.eclipse.swt.<windowing_system>_<eclipse_version_number>/
      os/
        <operating_system>/
        <processor_architecture>
```

For Windows, it's plugins\org.eclipse.swt.win32_3.0.0\os\win32\x86 inside the Eclipse installation directory. For Mac OS X, it's plugins/org.eclipse.swt.carbon_3.0.0/ os/macosx/ppc. See Figure 2-12 for an example of what you enter on Windows.

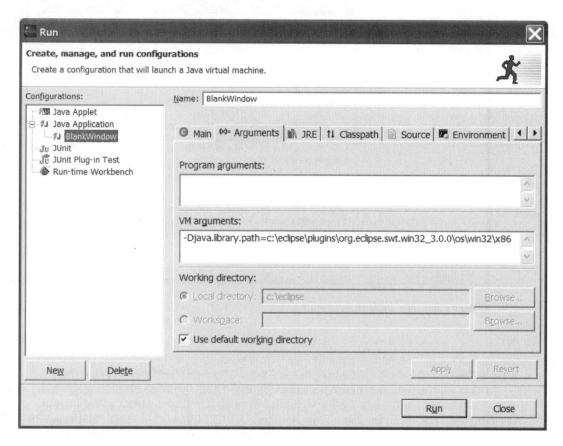

Figure 2-12. The Run dialog with the SWT library added

Click the Run button, and your blank window should appear. You're now ready to build more meaningful SWT and JFace applications.

Getting Help

Eclipse installs extensive online documentation, including overviews, tutorials, and Javadocs of the SWT and JFace libraries. To access the help, select Help ➤ Help Contents from the main menu. The help window appears, and should look like Figure 2-13.

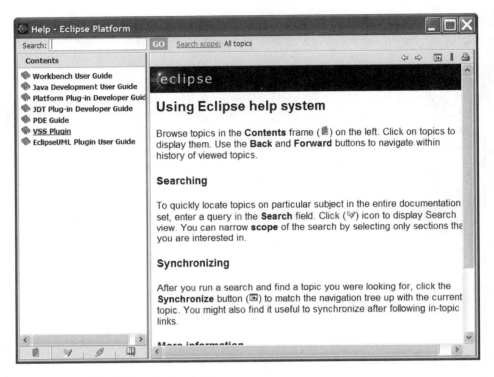

Figure 2-13. The Eclipse help window

Eclipse uses an internal Web server to display the help, so you might have problems viewing the help from behind a firewall. If you cannot see the help, check your proxy settings and make sure you aren't going through the proxy for local addresses.

The left pane is a navigable tree; click through it to find the topic you want, and the text appears on the right pane. Help for SWT and JFace is hidden in "Platform Plug-in Developer Guide." The section titled "Programmer's Guide" contains prose concerning SWT and JFace; "Reference" contains the Javadoc documentation; and "Examples Guide" explains how to install and run the example code.

You can also search through the help text by entering a search string in the provided text field and clicking Go. Suggested matches appear in the left pane; clicking them displays their text on the right.

Eclipse's main Web site (http://www.eclipse.org) offers articles, discussion forums, news, and code examples to help you with Eclipse. You can also sign up on the Web site for access to the available Eclipse newsgroups, which are hosted on news.eclipse.org.

The groups are password protected, so be sure to sign up. These are the available groups in the Eclipse Project:

- `eclipse.platform.swt`: SWT User Forum

- `eclipse.tools.jdt`: Java Development Tools User Forum

- `eclipse.platform`: Eclipse Project Tool Builders Forum

- `eclipse.tools`: Retired Eclipse Project Tool Builders Forum that was split into the preceding three newsgroups; it's read-only, and stays available for its archive

The Web site provides instructions for configuring your news reader for these newsgroups.

 NOTE *You must have a user ID and password to access the Eclipse newsgroups.*

Alternatives to Eclipse

So, do you think that IDEs are for wimps, and that real programmers use only Emacs or vi? Or do you love IntelliJ IDEA and loathe the thought of switching to a different IDE? Perhaps you have no money, no hard drive space, little memory, and are determined to do all development in Windows Notepad. Maybe you never leave Visual SlickEdit or CodeWright. Can SWT accommodate you?

The answer, happily, is yes. Although Eclipse is built on SWT and can't run without it, the converse isn't true: SWT runs fine without Eclipse. You can develop, build, and deploy SWT applications without Eclipse—you just need the SWT libraries.

Obtaining the SWT Libraries

Eclipse provides a separate download for SWT, available from the Web site. The download contains all the files—JAR file or files and native library—necessary to build SWT applications. The JAR file or files must be in your classpath, and the native library must be in your library path. Note that the native library contains a version number, which changes as SWT is updated, and you must use the JAR file packaged with the native library. See the sections on setting up your libraries earlier in this chapter to determine how to set them up on your platform.

Obtaining the JFace Libraries

JFace, which is covered in the last section of this book, isn't yet available as a separate download, though the Eclipse community continues to clamor for this. The only way to obtain the JFace libraries currently is to download and install Eclipse. The libraries are all contained in Java class files, and are found in your eclipse\plugins directory. They are

- `org.eclipse.jface_<version_number>\jface.jar`

- `org.eclipse.jface.text_<version_number>\jfacetext.jar`

- `org.eclipse.osgi_3.0.0_<version number>\osgi.jar`

- `org.eclipse.text_<version number>\text.jar`

- `org.eclipse.core.runtime_<version_number>\runtime.jar`

These files must all be in your classpath. Because JFace is built on top of SWT, it requires that the swt.jar file be in your classpath and the SWT native libraries be in your library path as well.

Once you have downloaded and installed Eclipse, you can copy these files to other locations and remove Eclipse. Just be sure to use the new locations when defining your classpath.

Using an Alternate IDE or Text Editor

Those not wanting to leave the familiarity of their current IDE—NetBeans, JBuilder, IDEA, or some other IDE—should have no problems developing SWT and JFace applications. There are two crucial configuration steps for your IDE:

- Add swt.jar to your classpath

- Add the native library to your library path

For example, in NetBeans 3.5, add swt.jar to the classpath by right-clicking FileSystems, selecting Mount ➤ Archive Files, and navigating to and selecting swt.jar. To add the native library to the library path, do the following:

1. Select Tools ➤ Options from the main menu.

2. Select Debugging and Executing ➤ Execution Types ➤ External Execution.

3. Select External Process and click the ellipses.

4. Add the argument right before the {classname} entry (Djava.library.path=<path containing the native library>).

The details for configuring other IDEs differ slightly, but the steps are the same: add the swt.jar file to the classpath and the native library to the library path.

The same principles hold true for using a text editor; if your text editor supports configuring classpaths and launching your applications with VM arguments, you can code, build, and test your SWT or JFace application from within your editor. Consult your editor's documentation for how to configure your classpath and library path.

If your editor doesn't support those configuration features, or you don't wish to bother with them, you must pass the arguments on the command line when you compile and run. To compile BlankWindow.java from the command line, you type this code:

```
javac -classpath <full path of swt.jar> BlankWindow.java
```

To run the application, you type this code:

```
java -classpath <full path of swt.jar> -Djava.library.path=
  <full path containing native library> BlankWindow
```

Whether you work in Eclipse, some other IDE, or a text editor, you'll be able to compile and run SWT and JFace applications.

> **NOTE** *For Visual SlickEdit users who want to use Eclipse without leaving their favorite editor behind, Visual SlickEdit is available as an Eclipse plug-in. See the SlickEdit Web site (*http://www.slickedit.com/*) for details. It works in Eclipse 2.x, and the company pledges to support Eclipse 3.0 when it's released. For vi key mapping, you can also use viPlugin from* http://www.satokar.com/viplugin/index.php.

Summary

In this chapter, you've seen that Eclipse.org has provided the Java community with a tremendous tool with its flagship product, Eclipse. Capable as a Java development IDE, it also contains everything you need to develop standalone applications using the included open source libraries, SWT and JFace. You've also discovered that SWT and JFace impose no Eclipse usage requirement—you can continue to use your favorite development tools to build SWT and JFace applications.

In the next chapter, you begin exploring SWT, and develop your first SWT application.

Part II

Using SWT

CHAPTER 3

Your First SWT Application

BURGEONING PROGRAMMERS yearn to greet the world in code; this chapter guides you through creating your first application in SWT—the inescapable "Hello, World." It explains how SWT works, and leads you through the major objects you'll deal with when using SWT. It discusses the lifecycle of SWT widgets as well.

"Hello, World" in SWT

You must apply a few minor changes to your BlankWindow program from the previous chapter to convert it into the canonical "Hello, World" application. More specifically, you must create an instance of an org.eclipse.swt.widgets.Label object, set its text to the preferred message, and add the label to your form. The following code reflects these changes.

```
import org.eclipse.swt.widgets.Display;
import org.eclipse.swt.widgets.Shell;
import org.eclipse.swt.widgets.Label;
import org.eclipse.swt.SWT;

public class HelloWorld
{
 public static void main(String[] args)
 {
  Display display = new Display();
  Shell shell = new Shell(display);
  Label label = new Label(shell, SWT.CENTER);
  label.setText("Hello, World");
  label.setBounds(shell.getClientArea());
  shell.open();
  while (!shell.isDisposed())
  {
   if (!display.readAndDispatch())
   {
    display.sleep();
   }
  }
```

```
    display.dispose();
  }
}
```

Compiling and Running the Program

Compiling HelloWorld.java should work similarly to the compile command from the previous chapter. From this point forward, we won't explicitly give instructions on the compilation or run steps, unless they vary from those examples presented in the previous chapter.

Compiling and running your programs from the command line soon becomes tedious and error prone. To address this issue, we provide an Ant build configuration file that you can use for the programs you develop in this book. To compile and run your programs, copy build.xml to the same directory as your source code and run Ant, specifying your main class name as the value for the property main.class. For example, to compile and run your HelloWorld program, type this:

```
ant -Dmain.class=HelloWorld
```

To just compile your program, you may omit the main.class property, and you must specify the compile target, like this:

```
ant compile
```

Listing 3-1 contains the Ant build file you'll use throughout the SWT portion of this book.

Listing 3-1. build.xml

```xml
<?xml version="1.0" encoding="ISO-8859-1"?>
<project name="GenericSwtApplication" default="run" basedir=".">
 <description>
  Generic SWT Application build and execution file
 </description>

 <property name="main.class" value=""/>
 <property name="src"        location="."/>
 <property name="build"      location="."/>

 <!-- Update location to match your eclipse home directory -->
 <property name="ecl.home"  location="c:\eclipse"/>

 <!-- Update value to match your windowing system (win32, gtk, motif, etc.) -->
 <property name="win.sys"    value="win32"/>
```

```
<!-- Update value to match your os (win32, linux, etc.) -->
<property name="os.sys"    value="win32"/>

<!-- Update value to match your architecture -->
<property name="arch"      value="x86"/>

<!-- Update value to match your SWT version -->
<property name="swt.ver"   value="3.0.0"/>

<!-- Do not edit below this line -->
<property name="swt.subdir"
 location="${ecl.home}/plugins/org.eclipse.swt.${win.sys}_${swt.ver}"/>
<property name="swt.jar.lib" location="${swt.subdir}/ws/${win.sys}"/>
<property name="swt.jni.lib" location="${swt.subdir}/os/${os.sys}/${arch}"/>

<path id="project.class.path">
 <pathelement path="${build}"/>
 <fileset dir="${swt.jar.lib}">
  <include name="**/*.jar"/>
 </fileset>
</path>

<target name="compile">
 <javac srcdir="${src}" destdir="${build}">
  <classpath refid="project.class.path"/>
 </javac>
</target>

<target name="run" depends="compile">
 <java classname="${main.class}" fork="true" failonerror="true">
  <jvmarg value="-Djava.library.path=${swt.jni.lib}"/>
  <classpath refid="project.class.path"/>
 </java>
</target>
</project>
```

You must update your copy of the build.xml file as indicated in the file, updating the Eclipse home directory, the windowing system, the operating system, the architecture, and the SWT version.

What is Ant?

Ant, part of the Apache Jakarta project (http://jakarta.apache.org/), is a Java-specific "make" utility. Winner of the *Java Pro* 2003 Readers' Choice Award for Most Valuable Java Deployment Technology, it simplifies the build process for Java applications, and has become the Java industry standard build utility.

Rather than using traditional "make" files, Ant uses XML configuration files for building applications. To build a Java application, then, you create an XML file that specifies your files, dependencies, and build rules, and then run Ant against that XML file. By default, Ant searches for a file called `build.xml`, but you can tell Ant to use other file names. You can specify targets and properties for Ant as well.

For more information, and to download Ant, see the Ant Web site at `http://ant.apache.org/`.

Running this program displays a window that greets the world, as seen in Figure 3-1.

Figure 3-1. "Hello, World" in SWT

Understanding the Program

These lines give you the proper imports for the class:

```
import org.eclipse.swt.widgets.Display;
import org.eclipse.swt.widgets.Shell;
import org.eclipse.swt.widgets.Label;
import org.eclipse.swt.SWT;
```

Most classes that use SWT import the SWT object and pieces of the swt.widgets package.
These lines create the Display object and the Shell object:

```
Display display = new Display();
Shell shell = new Shell(display);
```

At a high level, the Display object represents the underlying windowing system. The Shell object is an abstraction that represents a top-level window when created with a Display object, as this one is. A more detailed introduction to the Display and Shell classes is presented later in this chapter.

Next, you create your label widget with this code:

```
Label label = new Label(shell, SWT.CENTER);
label.setText("Hello, World");
label.setBounds(shell.getClientArea());
```

The Label object is capable of displaying either simple text, as you use it here, or an image. The widget is constructed with a reference to a Shell object, which is an indirect descendant of the Composite class. Composite classes are capable of containing other controls. When SWT encounters this line, it knows to create the underlying windowing system's implementation of the label widget on the associated Composite object.

To make your window display, you call this:

```
shell.open();
```

This indicates to the underlying system to set the current shell visible, set the focus to the default button (if one exists), and make the window associated with the shell active. This displays the window and allows it to begin receiving events from the underlying windowing system.

The main loop of your application is this:

```
while (!shell.isDisposed())
{
 if (!display.readAndDispatch())
 {
  display.sleep();
 }
}
```

You'll have a loop similar to this in each of your SWT applications. In this loop, you first check to make sure that the user hasn't closed your main window. Because the window is still open, you next check your event queue for any messages that the windowing system or other parts of your application might have generated for you. If no events are in the queue, you sleep, waiting for the next event to arrive. When the next event arrives, you repeat the loop, ensuring first that the event didn't dispose your main window.

Finally, you call:

```
display.dispose();
```

Because your window has been disposed (by the user closing the window), you no longer need the resources of the windowing system to display the graphical components. Being good computing citizens, you now return these resources back to the system.

Understanding the Design Behind SWT

As you learned in Chapter 1, SWT uses the native widget library provided by the under-lying OS, providing a Java veneer for your application to talk to. The lifecycle of the wid-get's Java object mirrors the lifecycle of the native widget it represents; when you create the Java widget, the native widget is created, and when the Java widget is destroyed the native widget is also destroyed. This design avoids issues with calling methods on a code object when the underlying widget hasn't yet been created, which can occur in other toolkits that don't match the lifecycles of the code widget and the native widget.

For example, compare the two-step creation process of the Microsoft Foundation Classes (MFC). If you want to create a button, you write code such as this:

```
CButton button; // Construct the C++ object on the stack
button.Create(<parameters>); // Create the Windows widget
```

Say you were to insert code between the construction of the C++ object and the native Windows widget that relied on the existence of the Windows widget; for exam-ple, code such as this:

```
CButton button; // Construct the C++ object on the stack
CString str = _T("Hi"); // Create a CString to hold the button text
button.SetWindowText(str); // Set the button text--PROBLEM!
button.Create(<parameters>); // Creates the Windows widget
```

The code compiles without complaint, but doesn't run as expected. The debug version of the code causes an assertion, and the behavior of the release version is undefined.

Parenting Widgets

Most GUIs require you to specify a parent for a widget before creating that widget, and the widget "belongs" to its parent throughout its lifecycle. The lifetime of the parent component constrains the lifetime of the child component. In addition, many native widgets have particular characteristics, or "styles," that you must set on their creation. For example, a button might be a push button or a checkbox. Because an SWT widget creates its corresponding native widget when it's constructed, it must have this infor-mation passed to its constructor. SWT widgets in general take two parameters: a parent and a style. The parent is typically of type `org.eclipse.swt.widgets.Widget` or one of its subclasses. The styles available are integer constants defined in the SWT class; you can pass a single style, or use bitwise ORs to string several styles together. We'll introduce the styles available to a particular widget throughout this book as we discuss that widget.

Disposing Widgets

Swing developers will scoff at the information in this section, taking it as proof of SWT's inferiority. Java developers in general will likely feel a certain amount of distaste or discomfort here, for the message of this section is: you have to clean up after yourself. This notion, anathema to Java developers, flouts Java's garbage collection and returns a responsibility to developers that they'd long ago left behind.

Why do you have to dispose objects? Java's garbage collection manages memory admirably, but GUI resource management operates under heavier constraints. The number of available GUI resources is much more limited and, on many platforms, is a system-wide limitation. Because SWT works directly with the native underlying graphic resources, each SWT resource consumes a GUI resource, and timely release of that resource is essential not only for your SWT application's well-being, but also for the well-being of all other GUI programs currently running. Java's garbage collection carries no timeliness guarantees, and would make a poor manager of graphic resources for SWT. So, instead, you as programmer must assume the responsibility.

How onerous is the task? Actually, it's not much work at all. In their series of articles on SWT, Carolyn MacLeod and Steve Northover describe two simple rules to guide your disposal efforts:[1]

- If you created it, you dispose it.

- Disposing the parent disposes the children.

Rule 1: If You Created It, You Dispose It

In the section "Understanding the Design Behind SWT" earlier in this chapter, you learned that native resources are created when an SWT object is created. In other words, when you call the SWT object's constructor, the underlying native resource is created. So, if you code this, you've constructed an SWT Color object, and thus have allocated a color resource from the underlying GUI platform:

```
Color color = new Color(display, 255, 0, 0); // Create a red Color
```

Rule 1 says you created it, so you must dispose it when you are done using it, like this:

```
color.dispose(); // I created it, so I dispose it
```

---

1. Carolyn MacLeod and Steve Northover, *SWT: The Standard Widget Toolkit—Part 2: Managing Operating System Resources*, www.eclipse.org/articles/swt-design-2/swt-design-2.html.

However, if you don't call a constructor to get a resource, you must not dispose the resource. For example, consider the following code:

```
Color color = display.getSystemColor(SWT.COLOR_RED); // Get a red Color
```

Once again, you have a Color object that contains a red Color resource from the underlying platform, but you didn't allocate it. Rule 1 says you must not dispose it. Why not? It doesn't belong to you—you've just borrowed it, and other objects might still be using it or will use it. Disposing such a resource could be disastrous.

Rule 2: Disposing the Parent Disposes the Children

Calling dispose() on every SWT object created with new would quickly become tedious, and would doom SWT to a marginalized existence. However, SWT's designers realized that, and created a logical cascade of automatic disposal. Whenever a parent is disposed, all its children are disposed. This means that when a Shell is disposed, all the widgets belonging to it are automatically disposed as well. In fact, when any Composite is disposed, all its children are automatically disposed. You'll notice that you never call label.dispose() in your "Hello, World" program, even though you create a new Label object using a constructor. When the user closes the Shell, the Label object is automatically disposed for you.

You might be thinking that you'll never need to call dispose(), and that this entire section was a waste of space. Indeed, you'll likely write many applications in which all resources have a parent, and they'll all automatically be disposed for you. However, consider the case in which you want to change the font used in a Text control. You'd code something like this:

```
Text text = new Text(shell, SWT.BORDER); // Create the text field
Font font = new Font(display, "Arial", 14, SWT.BOLD); // Create the new font
text.setFont(font); // Set the font into the text field
```

The Font object you've created has no parent, and thus won't be automatically disposed, even when the Shell is closed and the Text object using it is disposed. You might chafe at the added burden of having to dispose of font yourself, but realize that text has no business disposing it—it doesn't own it. In fact, you might be using the same Font object for various other controls; automatic disposal would cause you serious problems.

Ignoring Disposed Objects

Astute readers will have noticed a hole in the mirrored lifecycle discussed in this chapter: what happens in the case where the Java object wrapping a native widget is still in scope, but the Shell object to which it belongs has been disposed? Or what about a widget that has had its dispose method invoked manually? Won't the native widget have been disposed? Can't you then call a method on the Java object when the underlying native widget doesn't exist?

The answer is indeed yes, and you can get yourself into a bit of trouble if you call methods on a widget whose native widget has been disposed. Once a widget has been disposed, even if it is still in scope, you shouldn't try to do anything with it. Yes, the Java object is still available, but the underlying peer has been destroyed. If you do try to do anything with a disposed widget, you'll get an SWTException with the text "Widget has been disposed." Consider the code in Listing 3-2.

Listing 3-2. Broken.java

```
import org.eclipse.swt.*;
import org.eclipse.swt.layout.*;
import org.eclipse.swt.widgets.*;
public class Broken
{
 public static void main(String[] args)
 {
   Display display = new Display();
   Shell shell = new Shell(display);
   shell.setLayout(new RowLayout());
   Text text = new Text(shell, SWT.BORDER);
   shell.open();
   while (!shell.isDisposed())
   {
    if (!display.readAndDispatch())
    {
     display.sleep();
    }
   }
   System.out.println(text.getText()); // PROBLEM!
   display.dispose();
 }
}
```

The code compiles and runs, but after the main window is closed the console prints a stack trace that looks like this:

```
org.eclipse.swt.SWTException: Widget is disposed
 at org.eclipse.swt.SWT.error(SWT.java:2332)
 at org.eclipse.swt.SWT.error(SWT.java:2262)
 at org.eclipse.swt.widgets.Widget.error(Widget.java:385)
 at org.eclipse.swt.widgets.Control.getDisplay(Control.java:735)
 at org.eclipse.swt.widgets.Widget.isValidThread(Widget.java:593)
 at org.eclipse.swt.widgets.Widget.checkWidget(Widget.java:315)
 at org.eclipse.swt.widgets.Text.getText(Text.java:705)
 at Broken.main(Version.java:24)
```

What's more, when you run this on Windows XP, you get a dialog telling you that `javaw.exe` has encountered a problem, needs to close, and would you like to send Microsoft an error report?

The lesson is simple: once an object is disposed, whether its `dispose()` method has been explicitly invoked or its parent has been disposed, leave it alone.

Understanding the Display Object

The `Display` object represents the connection between the application-level SWT classes and the underlying windowing system implementation. The `Display` class is windowing-system dependent and might have some additional methods in its API on some platforms. Here we'll discuss only the part of the API that's universally available.

In general, each of your applications will have one, and only one, `Display` object (this is a limitation of some lower-level windowing systems). The thread that creates the `Display` object is, by default, the thread that executes the event loop and is known as the user-interface thread. You can call many of the member functions of widgets only from the user-interface thread. Other threads accessing these members will result in an `SWT.ERROR_THREAD_INVALID_ACCESS` type of exception.

One of the most important tasks of this class is its event-handling mechanism. The `Display` class maintains a collection of registered event listeners, reads events from the lower-level operating-system event queue, and delivers these events to the appropriate implementations of registered listener logic.

There are two levels to the event-handling mechanism in SWT. At the lowest level, Listeners are registered via the `Display` object with an identifier specifying the type of associated event. When the associated event occurs, the Listener's `handleEvent()` method is called. This system isn't as elegant as the alternative event handling mechanism; however, it's more efficient.

At a higher level, "typed" implementations of `EventListeners` are notified of the occurrence of the event. The classes that are registered to listen for these events implement subinterfaces of `EventListener`. This system is more elegant, granular, and object-oriented, at the expense of being more demanding on the system.

You typically construct a `Display` object with no arguments; you can construct one from a `DeviceData` object, which might be useful for debugging. See Table 3-1 for descriptions of the `Display` constructors.

Table 3-1. `Display` *Constructors*

Constructor	Description
`public Display()`	Creates a new `Display` object and sets the current thread to be the user-interface thread. You'll almost always use either this constructor or `Display.getDefault()` in your application.
`public Display(DeviceData data)`	Creates a new `Display` object, setting the `DeviceData` member of the `Display`. You use `DeviceData` for some lower-level debugging and error configuration.

Display also has several methods, some of which can be profitably ignored (beep(), anyone?). Table 3-2 lists Display's methods.

Table 3-2. Display *Methods*

Method	Description
void addFilter(int eventType, Listener listener)	Adds a listener that's notified when an event of the type specified by eventType occurs.
void addListener(int eventType, Listener listener)	Adds a listener that's notified when an event of the type specified by eventType occurs.
void asyncExec(Runnable runnable)	Gives non-user-interface threads the ability to invoke the protected functions of the SWT widget classes. The user-interface thread performs the code (invokes the run() method) of the runnable at its next "reasonable opportunity." This function returns immediately. See syncExec().
void beep()	Sounds a beep.
void close()	Closes this display.
void disposeExec(Runnable runnable)	Registers a Runnable object whose run() method is invoked when the display is disposed.
static Display findDisplay(Thread thread)	Given a user-interface thread, this function returns the associated Display object. If the given thread isn't a user-interface thread, this method returns null.
Widget findWidget(int handle)	Returns the widget for the specified handle, or null if no such widget exists.
Shell getActiveShell()	Returns the currently active Shell, or null if no shell belonging to the currently running application is active.
Rectangle getBounds()	Returns this display's size and location.
Rectangle getClientArea()	Returns the portion of this display that's capable of displaying data.
static Display getCurrent()	If the currently running thread is a user-interface thread, this thread returns the Display object associated with the thread. If the thread isn't a privileged user-interface thread, this method returns null.
Control getCursorControl()	If the mouse or other pointing device is over a control that's part of the current application, this function returns a reference to the control; otherwise, it returns null.
Point getCursorLocation()	Returns the location of the on-screen pointer relative to the top left corner of the screen.
Point[] getCursorSizes()	Returns the recommended cursor sizes.
Object getData()	Returns the application-specific data set into this display.
Object getData(String key)	Returns the application-specific data for the specified key set into this display.

Table 3-2. Display *Methods (continued)*

Method	Description
static Display getDefault()	Returns the default display of this application. If one hasn't yet been created, this method creates one and marks the current thread as the user-interface thread. The side effect of becoming the user-interface thread obligates the use of the current thread as the event loop thread for the application.
int getDismissalAlignment()	Returns the alignment for the default button in a dialog, either SWT.LEFT or SWT.RIGHT.
int getDoubleClickTime()	Sets the maximum amount of time that can elapse between two mouse clicks for a double-click event to occur.
Control getFocusControl()	Returns the control that currently has the focus of the application. If no application control has the focus, returns null.
int getIconDepth()	Returns the depth of the icons on this display.
Point[] getIconSizes()	Returns the recommended icon sizes.
Monitor[] getMonitors()	Returns the monitors attached to this display.
Monitor getPrimaryMonitor()	Returns the primary monitor for this display.
Shell[] getShells()	Returns an array of the active shells (windows) that are associated with this Display.
Thread getSyncThread()	If the user-interface thread is executing code associated with a Runnable object that was registered via the syncExec() method, this function will return a reference to the thread that invoked syncExec() (the waiting thread). Otherwise, this function returns null.
Color getSystemColor(int id)	Returns the matching system color as defined in the SWT class. If no color is associated with id, this method returns the color black. Remember this is a system color—you shouldn't dispose it when you're finished with it.
Font getSystemFont()	Returns a reference to a system font (it shouldn't be disposed), which is appropriate to be used in the current environment. In general, widgets are created with the correct font for the type of component that they represent and you should rarely need to change this value to maintain the correct system appearance.
Thread getThread()	Returns the user-interface thread of this Display. The thread that created this Display is the user-interface thread.
Point map(Control from, Control to, int x, int y)	Maps the point specified by x, y from the from control's coordinate system to the to control's coordinate system.
Rectangle map(Control from, Control to, int x, int y, int width, int height)	Maps the rectangle specified by x, y, width, height from the from control's coordinate system to the to control's coordinate system.

Table 3-2. Display *Methods (continued)*

Method	Description
Point map(Control from, Control to, Point point)	Maps the specified point from the from control's coordinate system to the to control's coordinate system.
Point map(Control from, Control to, Rectangle rectangle)	Maps the specified rectangle from the from control's coordinate system to the to control's coordinate system.
boolean readAndDispatch()	This is the main event function of the SWT system. It reads events, one at a time, off the windowing system's event queue. After receiving the event, it invokes the appropriate methods on the listener objects that have registered interest in this event. If no events are on the event queue, readAndDispatch() executes any requests that might have been registered with this display via syncExec() or asyncExec(), notifying any syncExeced threads on completion of the request. This method returns true if there are more events to be processed, false otherwise. Returning false allows the calling thread to release CPU resources until there are more events for the system to process via the sleep() method.
void removeFilter(int eventType, Listener listener)	Removes the specified listener from the notification list for the specified event type.
void removeListener(int eventType, Listener listener)	Removes the specified listener from the notification list for the specified event type.
static void setAppName (String name)	Sets the application name.
void setCursorLocation (int x, int y)	Moves the on-screen pointer to the specified location relative to the top left corner of the screen.
void setCursorLocation (Point point)	Moves the on-screen pointer to the specified location relative to the top left corner of the screen.
void setData(Object data)	Sets the application-specific data.
void setData(String key, Object data)	Sets the application-specific data for the specified key.
void setSynchronizer (Synchronizer synchronizer)	Sets the synchronizer for this display.
boolean sleep()	Allows the user-interface thread to relinquish its CPU time until it has more events to process or is awakened via another means; for example, wake(). This allows the system to process events much more efficiently, as the user-interface thread only consumes CPU resources when it has events to process.
void syncExec(Runnable runnable)	Like asyncExec(), this method gives non-user-interface threads the ability to invoke the protected functions of the SWT widget classes. The user-interface thread performs this code (invokes the run method) of runnable at its next "reasonable opportunity." This function returns after the run method of the Runnable object returns.

Table 3-2. Display *Methods (continued)*

Method	Description
void timerExec(int milliseconds, Runnable runnable)	Registers a Runnable object that the user-interface thread runs after the specified time has elapsed.
void update()	Causes all pending paint requests to be processed.
void wake()	Wakes up the user-interface thread if it's in sleep(). Can be called by any thread.

Although a Display object forms the foundation for your GUI, it doesn't present any graphical components to the screen. In fact, the Display by itself displays nothing at all. You must create a window, represented by a Shell object. This leads us to our next section, which discusses Shells.

Understanding the Shell Object

The Shell object represents a window—either a top-level window or a dialog window. It contains the various controls that make up the application: buttons, text boxes, tables, and so on. It has six constructors; two of them aren't recommended for use, and future releases might not support them. Construction follows the SWT pattern of passing a parent and a style (or multiple styles bitwise-ORed together), though some constructors allow default values for either or both parameters. Table 3-3 lists the constructors.

Table 3-3. Shell *Constructors*

Constructor	Description
public Shell()	Empty constructor, which is equivalent to calling Shell((Display) null). Currently, passing null for the Display causes the Shell to be created on the active display, or, if no display is active, on a "default" display. This constructor is discouraged, and might be removed from a future SWT release.
public Shell(int style)	This constructor, too, isn't recommended for use, as it calls Shell((Display) null, style), so also might be removed from SWT.
public Shell(Display display)	Constructs a shell using display as the display, null for the parent, and SHELL_TRIM for the style, except on Windows CE, where it uses NONE (see Table 3-4).
public Shell(Display display, int style)	Constructs a shell using display as the display, null for the parent, and style for the style. See Table 3-4 for appropriate Shell styles.
public Shell(Shell parent)	Constructs a shell using the parent's Display as the display, parent for the parent, and DIALOG_TRIM for the style, except on Windows CE, where it uses NONE (see Table 3-4).
public Shell(Shell parent, int style)	Constructs a shell using the parent's Display as the display, parent for the parent, and style for the style. See Table 3-4 for appropriate Shell styles.

Internally, all the constructors call a package-visible constructor that sets the display, sets the style bits, sets the parent, and then creates the window. If the Shell has a parent, it's a dialog; otherwise, it's a top-level window. Table 3-4 lists the appropriate styles for a Shell object; note that all style constants, as you'll see in the next section, are static members of the SWT class. Also, realize that the style you set is treated as a hint; if the platform your application is running on doesn't support the style, it's ignored.

Table 3-4. Shell *Styles*

Style	Description
BORDER	Adds a border.
CLOSE	Adds a close button.
MIN	Adds a minimize button.
MAX	Adds a maximize button.
NO_TRIM	Creates a Shell that has no border and can't be moved, closed, resized, minimized, or maximized. Not very useful, except perhaps for splash screens.
RESIZE	Adds a resizable border.
TITLE	Adds a title bar.
DIALOG_TRIM	Convenience style, equivalent to TITLE | CLOSE | BORDER.
SHELL_TRIM	Convenience style, equivalent to CLOSE | TITLE | MIN | MAX | RESIZE.
APPLICATION_MODAL	Creates a Shell that's modal to the application. Note that you should specify only one of APPLICATION_MODAL, PRIMARY_MODAL, SYSTEM_MODAL, or MODELESS; you can specify more, but only one is applied. The order of preference is SYSTEM_MODAL, APPLICATION_MODAL, PRIMARY_MODAL, then MODELESS.
PRIMARY_MODAL	Creates a primary modal Shell.
SYSTEM_MODAL	Creates a Shell that's modal system-wide.
MODELESS	Creates a modeless Shell.

Most of the time, you won't specify a style when you create a Shell, as the default settings usually produce what you want. Feel free to experiment with the styles, though, so you understand what each of them does.

Shell inherits a number of methods from its extensive inheritance tree, and adds a few methods of its own (see Table 3-5 for a full listing of Shell-specific methods). However, the two methods you'll use most are open(), which opens (displays) the Shell, and, to a lesser degree, close(), which closes the Shell. Note that the default operating platforms' methods for closing a Shell (for example, clicking the close button on the title bar) are already implemented for you, so you might never need to call close().

Table 3-5. Shell *Methods*

Method Name	Description
void addShellListener (ShellListener listener)	Adds a listener that's notified when operations are performed on the Shell.
void close()	Closes the Shell.
void dispose()	Disposes the Shell, and recursively disposes all its children.
void forceActive()	Moves the Shell to the top of the z-order on its Display and forces the window manager to make it active.
Rectangle getBounds()	Returns the Shell's size and location relative to its parent (or its Display in the case of a top-level Shell).
Display getDisplay()	Returns the Display this Shell was created on.
boolean getEnabled()	Returns true if this Shell is enabled, and false if not.
int getImeInputMode()	Returns this Shell's input-method editor mode, which is the result of bitwise ORing one or more of SWT.NONE, SWT.ROMAN, SWT.DBCS, SWT.PHONETIC, SWT.NATIVE, and SWT.ALPHA.
Point getLocation()	Returns the location of this Shell relative to its parent (or its Display in the case of a top-level Shell).
Region getRegion()	Returns this Shell's region if it's nonrectangular. Otherwise, returns null.
Shell getShell()	Returns a reference to itself.
Shell[] getShells()	Returns all the Shells that are descendants of this Shell.
Point getSize()	Returns this Shell's size.
boolean isEnabled()	See getEnabled().
void open()	Opens (displays) this Shell.
void removeShellListener (ShellListener listener)	Removes the specified listener from the notification list.
void setActive()	Moves the Shell to the top of the z-order on its Display and asks the window manager to make it active.
void setEnabled(boolean enabled)	Passing true enables this Shell; passing false disables it.
void setImeInputMode (int mode)	Sets this Shell's input-method editor mode, which should be the result of bitwise ORing one or more of SWT.NONE, SWT.ROMAN, SWT.DBCS, SWT.PHONETIC, SWT.NATIVE, and SWT.ALPHA.
void setRegion(Region region)	Sets the region for this Shell. Use for nonrectangular windows.
void setVisible(boolean visible)	Passing true sets this Shell visible; passing false sets it invisible.

The SWT Class—Constants and Methods

The SWT class contains a repository of class-level constants and methods to simplify SWT programming.

Curiously, nothing prevents you from creating an SWT object, though no harm is done by creating one. The SWT class derives from java.lang.Object and has no constructors defined so that the default constructor can be invoked. However, an SWT object has no state beyond what it inherits from java.lang.Object, and is essentially useless.

The SWT class provides a few convenience methods, all of which, as mentioned earlier, are static. Most applications will have no need to use these; they're listed in Table 3-6.

Table 3-6. SWT *Methods*

Method Name	Description
static void error(int code)	Throws an exception based on code. It's the same as calling static void error(int code, (Throwable) null).
static void error(int code, Throwable throwable)	Throws an exception based on code. throwable should either be null or the Throwable that caused SWT to throw an exception. code is one of the error constants defined in SWT.
static String getMessage (String key)	Gets the appropriate National Language Support (NLS) message as a String for key. See java.util.ResourceBundle for more information on NLS. The resource bundle is found in org.eclipse.swt.internal.SWTMessages .properties; see Table 3-7 for the supported keys and corresponding messages.
static String getPlatform()	Gets the SWT platform name (for example, "win32," "gtk," "carbon").
static int getVersion()	Gets the SWT library version number.

Enter this code on Windows XP and Eclipse 2.1.1:

```
System.out.println("Platform: " + SWT.getPlatform());
System.out.println("Version: " + SWT.getVersion());
```

The code prints:

```
Platform: win32
Version: 2135
```

Table 3-7. SWT Message Keys and Values

Key	Value
SWT_Yes	Yes
SWT_No	No
SWT_OK	OK
SWT_Cancel	Cancel
SWT_Abort	Abort
SWT_Retry	Retry
SWT_Ignore	Ignore
SWT_Sample	Sample
SWT_A_Sample_Text	A Sample Text
SWT_Selection	Selection
SWT_Current_Selection	Current Selection
SWT_Font	Font
SWT_Color	Color
SWT_Extended_style	Extended style
SWT_Size	Size
SWT_Style	Style
SWT_Save	Save
SWT_Character_set	Character set
SWT_ColorDialog_Title	Colors
SWT_FontDialog_Title	Fonts
SWT_Charset_Western	Western
SWT_Charset_EastEuropean	East European
SWT_Charset_SouthEuropean	South European
SWT_Charset_NorthEuropean	North European
SWT_Charset_Cyrillic	Cyrillic
SWT_Charset_Arabic	Arabic
SWT_Charset_Greek	Greek
SWT_Charset_Hebrew	Hebrew
SWT_Charset_Turkish	Turkish
SWT_Charset_Nordic	Nordic
SWT_Charset_Thai	Thai
SWT_Charset_BalticRim	Baltic Rim
SWT_Charset_Celtic	Celtic
SWT_Charset_Euro	Euro
SWT_Charset_Romanian	Romanian
SWT_Charset_SimplifiedChinese	Simplified Chinese
SWT_Charset_TraditionalChinese	Traditional Chinese
SWT_Charset_Japanese	Japanese

Table 3-7. SWT Message Keys and Values (continued)

Key	Value
SWT_Charset_Korean	Korean
SWT_Charset_Unicode	Unicode
SWT_Charset_ASCII	ASCII
SWT_InputMethods	Input Methods

Summary

An SWT-based program connects to the underlying windowing system through its Display object. Windows, widgets, and events are built upon and travel through this crucial object. The windows you create in your applications are all Shells. This chapter built your obligatory "Hello, World" SWT program and explained the design behind SWT. You now know how to create widgets with parents, to clean up after yourselves, and not to touch things that don't belong to you.

In the next chapter, you learn how to place your widgets on windows where you want them.

CHAPTER 4

Layouts

AWT INTRODUCED LAYOUTS to an unsuspecting, and soon befuddled, programming audience. Most programmers had learned to lay out controls by using drag-and-drop GUI builders or by editing resource files; with AWT, they had to write code. After a time, Java IDEs began to incorporate custom layout managers that allowed developers to drag and drop controls, but early adopters had to do without GUI builders. More puzzling, however, was the "layout" abstraction itself; many programmers (read: Windows programmers) were accustomed to specifying exact locations and sizes for each control. Aside from screen resolution technicalities, developers knew all they needed to know about the target machines when building applications, so absolute positioning made absolute sense. However, the cross-platform nature of Java demanded the abstraction; Java applications could be running on a variety of operating systems, on a variety of hardware. Developers no longer knew enough about all the target machines: what fonts were available, how large a text box would be to fit text vertically, how many pixels the decoration of a button would occupy, and so forth. Layouts handled the relative positioning and sizing of controls; as programmers learned how to harness their power, enthusiasm for layouts quickly grew.

SWT continues with layouts, offering five layout classes: FillLayout, RowLayout, GridLayout, FormLayout, and StackLayout. This chapter discusses each of these layouts, explains how to build your own layout class, and shows you how to place controls without using a layout. Finally, it discusses some of the GUI builders available for SWT.

Discussing layouts presents a chicken-and-egg problem: how do you teach layouts without having taught controls, so you have controls to lay out? Conversely, how do you teach controls without having taught layouts, so you have some way of placing and sizing controls for display? Our solution to this dilemma is to teach layouts using a single control—a regular push button—and then teach controls in the next chapter. For now, all you need to know about controls is that this code creates a button:

```
Button button = new Button(shell, SWT.PUSH);
```

You can set the button's text by calling its setText() method:

```
button.setText("My Button");
```

Alternatively, you can create and set text in one line:

```
new Button(shell, SWT.PUSH).setText("My Button");
```

The button is created and added to the parent window, so that the layout can place and size it appropriately.

When a Shell is first displayed, it assumes a default size assigned by the windowing system, without accounting for what size it should be to contain its controls properly. Calling pack() causes the Shell to calculate its proper size and resize itself accordingly. In many of the examples, you call pack() just before you call open(). One more thing to understand before we delve into layouts is that composites are containers, both for controls and for other composites. They're represented in SWT by the Composite object. The Shell object subclasses Composite, and thus can contain controls and other composites; you can create and nest composites, each of which can hold both controls and other composites. Create composites by calling this constructor, where parent is the parent composite, or the container for the composite you're creating:

```
Composite composite = new Composite(parent, SWT.NONE);
```

Understanding Layouts

Layouts provide a decoupling layer between the controls in a composite and the composite itself; they define where to place the composite's controls. They usually do this in a platform-independent manner, and often in a way that maintains relative sizing when the parent window is resized. You set a layout into the composite using the composite's setLayout() method.

All the layout classes available in SWT derive from org.eclipse.swt.widgets.Layout, which is an abstract class that currently has no implementation (and yes, it's in the widgets package, not the layout package—this is so composites, which reside in the same package, can call the protected methods on the layout class). It has no public API; you create the layout class and associate it with the composite, and the SWT framework calls the necessary methods to use the layout.

Although each composite can have only one layout, you can have multiple composites in a window, each with its own layout. You can even nest the composites. Because each composite has its own layout object, independent from all other composites, you can use any and all layout classes in the same window to achieve the overall layout you wish.

Using FillLayout

FillLayout is the simplest of the layout classes; it places all controls in either a single column or a single row, and makes them all the same size. It has a public property, type, that determines whether to place the controls in column or a row. You can pass type to the constructor, or you can set it after construction. See Table 4-1 for the FillLayout constructors.

Table 4-1. `FillLayout` *Constructors*

Constructor	Description
`public FillLayout()`	Constructs a `FillLayout` and sets type to `SWT.HORIZONTAL`.
`public FillLayout(int type)`	Constructs a `FillLayout` and sets type to the passed type.

The possible values for type are `SWT.HORIZONTAL`, which then lays the controls out in a single row, and `SWT.VERTICAL`, which lays the controls out in a single column.

 NOTE `FillLayout` *does no validation for the type you specify, so you can pass any* int *value. Although* `FillLayout` *defaults to* `SWT.HORIZONTAL`, *if you specify a type that isn't* `SWT.HORIZONTAL` *or* `SWT.VERTICAL`, *it will use* `SWT.VERTICAL`.

To create a horizontal `FillLayout` and set it into a `Shell`, you use this code:

```
FillLayout layout = new FillLayout();
layout.type = SWT.HORIZONTAL;
shell.setLayout(layout);
```

You can trim a line of code by passing the type in the constructor; you create a vertical `FillLayout` with this code:

```
FillLayout layout = new FillLayout(SWT.VERTICAL);
shell.setLayout(layout);
```

If you don't need to retain a reference to your layout after setting it into the `Shell`, you can construct and set in one step:

```
shell.setLayout(new FillLayout(SWT.VERTICAL));
```

Let's look at an example of `FillLayout`. In the following code, you create a `Display` and a `Shell`, then you create a horizontal `FillLayout` and set it as the layout for the `Shell`. You then add three buttons, labeled one, two, and three, and you enter your main event loop. This code should show three buttons in a row, filling the window (see Figure 4-1).

To compile and run this code, create a file called `FillLayoutHorizontal.java` in the directory structure `examples/ch4` beneath a parent directory. Type the code shown in Listing 4-1 into the file and save it. Then, open a command prompt or a shell and navigate to the parent directory. Copy the `build.xml` file you created in Chapter 3 into the parent directory and type this:

```
ant -Dmain.class=examples.ch4.FillLayoutHorizontal
```

Notice the full package name for your main class. The class should compile and run, and you should see the window shown in Figure 4-1.

Figure 4-1. A horizontal FillLayout

We won't repeat these instructions throughout the book; as we introduce new code, follow the preceding steps, substituting the fully qualified name of the appropriate class for main.class.

Listing 4-1. FillLayoutHorizontal.java

```java
package examples.ch4;

import org.eclipse.swt.widgets.*;
import org.eclipse.swt.layout.FillLayout;
import org.eclipse.swt.SWT;

public class FillLayoutHorizontal {
  public static void main(String[] args) {
    Display display = new Display();
    Shell shell = new Shell(display);
    shell.setLayout(new FillLayout(SWT.HORIZONTAL));
    new Button(shell, SWT.PUSH).setText("one");
    new Button(shell, SWT.PUSH).setText("two");
```

```
    new Button(shell, SWT.PUSH).setText("three");
    shell.open();
    while (!shell.isDisposed()) {
      if (!display.readAndDispatch()) {
        display.sleep();
      }
    }
    display.dispose();
  }
}
```

If you pass SWT.VERTICAL instead to your FillLayout constructor, so that the line reads as follows, the buttons are aligned vertically (see Figure 4-2):

```
shell.setLayout(new FillLayout(SWT.VERTICAL));
```

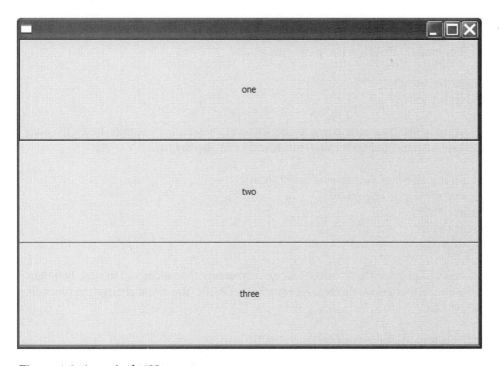

Figure 4-2. A vertical FillLayout

FillLayouts can't do more than relatively simple layouts, so you'll likely reserve them for nested composites. For complex layouts, you'll need to use one of the more advanced layout classes.

Using RowLayout

RowLayout is similar to FillLayout: it places all controls in a single column or row. However, it doesn't force all contained controls to the same size. It also can wrap controls to a new row or column if it runs out of space.

RowLayout uses instances of the RowData class to determine initial widths and heights for its controls. You associate a RowData object to a control by passing the RowData to the control's setLayoutData() method; the layout retrieves the RowData from the control to determine sizing and placement.

 CAUTION   *The* Widget *class, from which SWT controls derive, has a method called* setData() *that, like* setLayoutData(), *takes an* Object *as a parameter. If you're setting a layout data instance into a control, and it's not behaving as you'd expect, make sure you aren't inadvertently calling* setData() *instead of* setLayoutData().

The RowData class has two public members:

```
public int height
public int width
```

You can set these after constructing a RowData object. For example, here's the code to create a Button and set it to 100 pixels wide and 50 pixels tall:

```
Button button = new Button(shell, SWT.PUSH);
RowData rowData = new RowData();
rowData.height = 50;
rowData.width = 100;
button.setLayoutData(rowData);
```

RowData provides two convenience constructors that allow you to specify height and width, either as two discrete integers or as a Point. You could change the preceding code to this:

```
Button button = new Button(shell, SWT.PUSH);
button.setLayoutData(new RowData(100, 50)); // width, height
```

Alternatively, you could change the code to this:

```
Button button = new Button(shell, SWT.PUSH);
button.setLayoutData(new RowData(new Point(100, 50))); // width, height
```

RowLayout, like FillLayout, has a public attribute type that contains either SWT.HORIZONTAL or SWT.VERTICAL to configure the layout as a row or a column, respectively. RowLayout has several other configurable attributes as well (see Table 4-2).

Table 4-2. `RowLayout` *Attributes*

Attribute	Description
`boolean justify`	If `true`, justifies the entire row or column; it doesn't change the size of the controls, but rather spaces them evenly to fill the space. Think of a line of text in a newspaper story that has excess space between letters to preserve the justification of the column. The default is `false`.
`int marginBottom`	The size of the bottom margin, in pixels, for the layout. The default is 3.
`int marginLeft`	The size of the left margin, in pixels, for the layout. The default is 3.
`int marginRight`	The size of the right margin, in pixels, for the layout. The default is 3.
`int marginTop`	The size of the top margin, in pixels, for the layout. The default is 3.
`boolean pack`	If `true`, tells all controls to use their preferred size. The default is `true`.
`int spacing`	The size of the space, in pixels, between neighboring controls. The default is 3.
`int type`	The type of the layout; if it's `SWT.HORIZONTAL` (the default), the layout will use rows. If it's `SWT.VERTICAL`, the layout will use columns. Current implementations will use `SWT.VERTICAL` if an invalid value is specified.
`boolean wrap`	If `true`, will wrap the controls to the next row or column if the current row or column is out of space. The default is `true`.

`RowLayout` has two constructors: an empty constructor, and one that takes a single parameter for the `type` value.

Consider the following code:

```
package examples.ch4;

import org.eclipse.swt.widgets.*;
import org.eclipse.swt.layout.RowLayout;
import org.eclipse.swt.SWT;

public class RowLayoutHorizontal {
  public static void main(String[] args) {
    Display display = new Display();
    Shell shell = new Shell(display);
    shell.setLayout(new RowLayout(SWT.HORIZONTAL));
    new Button(shell, SWT.PUSH).setText("one");
    new Button(shell, SWT.PUSH).setText("two");
    new Button(shell, SWT.PUSH).setText("three");
    new Button(shell, SWT.PUSH).setText("four");
    new Button(shell, SWT.PUSH).setText("five");
    new Button(shell, SWT.PUSH).setText("six");
    new Button(shell, SWT.PUSH).setText("seven");
    shell.open();
    while (!shell.isDisposed()) {
      if (!display.readAndDispatch()) {
        display.sleep();
```

```
        }
      }
      display.dispose();
    }
}
```

This code creates a horizontal row layout, accepting all the default values for the row layout's attributes. If you compile and run this code, you'll see a window that looks like Figure 4-3.

Figure 4-3. A default RowLayout

Because you've accepted the default value for wrap, which is true, resizing the window causes the controls to wrap to a second row (see Figure 4-4).

Figure 4-4. A default RowLayout *after resizing*

By manipulating the various values of the row layout, and using RowData objects for some controls, you can alter the behavior of the layout significantly. See Listing 4-2 for some of the things you can do.

Listing 4-2. RowLayoutTest.java

```java
package examples.ch4;

import org.eclipse.swt.widgets.*;
import org.eclipse.swt.layout.RowLayout;
import org.eclipse.swt.layout.RowData;
import org.eclipse.swt.SWT;

public class RowLayoutTest {
  public static void main(String[] args) {
    Display display = new Display();
    Shell shell = new Shell(display);
    RowLayout layout = new RowLayout(SWT.VERTICAL);
    layout.marginLeft = 12;
    layout.marginTop = 0;
    layout.justify = true;
    shell.setLayout(layout);
    new Button(shell, SWT.PUSH).setText("one");
    new Button(shell, SWT.PUSH).setText("two");
    new Button(shell, SWT.PUSH).setText("three");
    new Button(shell, SWT.PUSH).setText("four");
    new Button(shell, SWT.PUSH).setText("five");
    new Button(shell, SWT.PUSH).setText("six");
    Button b = new Button(shell, SWT.PUSH);
    b.setText("seven");
    b.setLayoutData(new RowData(100, 100));
    shell.open();
    while (!shell.isDisposed()) {
      if (!display.readAndDispatch()) {
        display.sleep();
      }
    }
    display.dispose();
  }
}
```

This code creates a vertical row layout, changes the top and left margins, and justifies the controls. It also uses a RowData object to set the size of your button labeled "seven." Compiling and running the code displays a window that looks like Figure 4-5.

Figure 4-5. A RowLayout *with some changed properties*

You'll see that a vertical row layout looks exactly like what you'd call a column layout; the columnar capability of RowLayout was added in SWT 2.0. Rather than create a new class and duplicate a lot of code, SWT's developers reused RowLayout and added the vertical attribute. For purists (and we've met a few), you could create a new class called ColumnLayout that extends RowLayout and sets type to SWT.VERTICAL—if that would make you feel better. The rest of you can just accept the name mismatch.

RowLayout's abilities supersede FillLayout's, but still don't suffice for complex layouts. GridLayout, the subject of our next section, takes layouts a leap forward.

Using GridLayout

If you plan to learn only one layout, make it GridLayout. Packing the most power for the learning effort required, GridLayout works from the simple to the complex. As its name implies, GridLayout lays out controls in a grid. By using Composites to nest GridLayouts within GridLayouts, you can give structure and aesthetics to complex layouts. GridLayout has two constructors, listed in Table 4-3.

Table 4-3. GridLayout *Constructors*

Constructor	Description
public GridLayout()	Constructs a default GridLayout.
public GridLayout(int numColumns, boolean makeColumnsEqualWidth)	Constructs a GridLayout with numColumns columns. If makeColumnsEqualWidth is true, all columns will have the same width.

GridLayout has six public data members, listed in Table 4-4. Perhaps the most important of these is numColumns, which controls the structure of this layout. This member holds the number of columns this layout uses; controls are laid out left to right, one per column, wrapping to the next row when the columns are filled.

Table 4-4. GridLayout *Data Members*

Attribute	Description
int horizontalSpacing	The amount of horizontal space, in pixels, between adjacent cells.
boolean makeColumnsEqualWidth	If true, forces all columns to be the same width.
int marginHeight	The size of the margin, in pixels, along the top and bottom edges of the layout.
int marginWidth	The size of the margin, in pixels, along the left and right edges of the layout.
int numColumns	The number of columns for the layout.
int verticalSpacing	The amount of vertical space, in pixels, between adjacent cells.

You can further tune your GridLayout by setting GridData instances into your controls. GridData objects, which you shouldn't reuse among controls, fine-tune how the layout treats the GridData's associated controls. They have two constructors, as seen in Table 4-5.

Table 4-5. GridData *Constructors*

Constructor	Description
public GridData()	Constructs a default GridData.
public GridData(int style)	Constructs a GridData, setting member data values according to the values specified in style.

As with the other layout data classes, GridData has public members to control its state. It also provides various constants that you can pass to the constructor; these constants set combinations of public members to achieve certain effects. You can chain several constants together using bitwise ORs. Table 4-6 lists the data members; Table 4-7 lists the constants, and what effect they have.

Table 4-6. GridData *Members*

Attribute	Description
boolean grabExcessHorizontalSpace	If true, instructs the cell to fill the excess horizontal space in the layout. The default is false.
boolean grabExcessVerticalSpace	If true, instructs the cell to fill the excess vertical space in the layout. The default is false.
int heightHint	The minimum height, in pixels, for the row. The default is SWT.DEFAULT.
int horizontalAlignment	The horizontal alignment for the cell; possible values are BEGINNING, CENTER, END, and FILL, for left justified, centered, right justified, and justified, respectively. The default is BEGINNING, which will also be used if an invalid value is set.
int horizontalIndent	The size of the horizontal indent, in pixels, on the left of the cell. The default is zero.
int horizontalSpan	The number of columns the cell should occupy. The default is one.
int verticalAlignment	The vertical alignment for the cell; possible values are BEGINNING, CENTER, END, and FILL, for top justified, centered, bottom justified, and justified, respectively. The default is CENTER, although BEGINNING will be used if an invalid value is set.
int verticalSpan	The number of rows the cell should occupy. The default is one.
int widthHint	The minimum width, in pixels, for the column. The default is SWT.DEFAULT.

Table 4-7. GridData *Constants*

Constant	Description
BEGINNING	Not used for style; alignment constant that left aligns when specifying horizontal alignment and top aligns when specifying vertical alignment.
CENTER	Not used for style; alignment constant that centers the control in the cell, whether horizontally or vertically.
END	Not used for style; alignment constant that right aligns when specifying horizontal alignment and bottom aligns when specifying vertical alignment.
FILL	Not used for style; alignment constant that fully justifies the control in the cell, whether horizontally or vertically.
FILL_BOTH	Sets both horizontalAlignment and verticalAlignment to FILL. Sets both grabExcessHorizontalSpace and grabExcessVerticalSpace to true.
FILL_HORIZONTAL	Sets horizontalAlignment to FILL and grabExcessHorizontalSpace to true.
FILL_VERTICAL	Sets verticalAlignment to FILL and grabExcessVerticalSpace to true.

Table 4-7. GridData *Constants (continued)*

Constant	Description
GRAB_HORIZONTAL	Sets grabExcessHorizontalSpace to true.
GRAB_VERTICAL	Sets grabExcessVerticalSpace to true.
HORIZONTAL_ALIGN_BEGINNING	Sets horizontalAlignment to BEGINNING.
HORIZONTAL_ALIGN_CENTER	Sets horizontalAlignment to CENTER.
HORIZONTAL_ALIGN_END	Sets horizontalAlignment to END.
HORIZONTAL_ALIGN_FILL	Sets horizontalAlignment to FILL.
VERTICAL_ALIGN_BEGINNING	Sets verticalAlignment to BEGINNING.
VERTICAL_ALIGN_CENTER	Sets verticalAlignment to CENTER.
VERTICAL_ALIGN_END	Sets verticalAlignment to END.
VERTICAL_ALIGN_FILL	Sets verticalAlignment to FILL.

Be careful when specifying combinations of constants, as no check is done for conflicting values.

To create a 2×2 grid, you write code like this:

```
GridLayout layout = new GridLayout();
layout.numColumns = 2;
shell.setLayout(layout);
new Button(shell, SWT.PUSH).setText("one");
new Button(shell, SWT.PUSH).setText("two");
new Button(shell, SWT.PUSH).setText("three");
new Button(shell, SWT.PUSH).setText("four");
```

This produces a window that looks like Figure 4-6. Notice that the buttons have different widths, depending on the length of their text. You might think that adding a line of code to set the makeColumnsEqualWidth to true makes the buttons the same width:

```
layout.makeColumnsEqualWidth = true;
```

However, compiling and running this code demonstrates that this isn't the case (see Figure 4-7). The makeColumnsEqualWidth data member forces the columns to have equal width, but doesn't affect the size of the controls within the columns. You use GridData instances to do that.

Figure 4-6. A 2×2 GridLayout

Figure 4-7. A 2×2 GridLayout *with equal column widths*

Let's say you decide that you want the buttons to fill the horizontal and vertical excess space. You create a GridData object with the FILL_BOTH style:

```
GridData data = new GridData(GridData.FILL_BOTH);
```

This sets horizontalAlignment and verticalAlignment to FILL, and sets grabExcessHorizontalSpace and grabExcessVerticalSpace to true. Because you want all your buttons to have this same style, you might think you can save object creation by reusing the GridData object:

```
Button one = new Button(shell, SWT.PUSH);
one.setText("one");
one.setLayoutData(data);

Button two = new Button(shell, SWT.PUSH);
two.setText("two");
two.setLayoutData(data);

Button three = new Button(shell, SWT.PUSH);
three.setText("three");
three.setLayoutData(data);

Button four = new Button(shell, SWT.PUSH);
four.setText("four");
four.setLayoutData(data);
```

However, when you compile and run this, you see that some buttons are missing (see Figure 4-8).

Figure 4-8. Trying to reuse GridData *objects*

That's when you remember that GridData objects cannot be reused, and that each GridData must belong to only one control. Here's the corrected code:

```
package examples.ch4;

import org.eclipse.swt.widgets.*;
import org.eclipse.swt.layout.GridData;
import org.eclipse.swt.layout.GridLayout;
import org.eclipse.swt.SWT;

public class GridLayout2x2 {
  public static void main(String[] args) {
    Display display = new Display();
    Shell shell = new Shell(display);
    GridLayout layout = new GridLayout();
    layout.numColumns = 2;
    layout.makeColumnsEqualWidth = true;
    shell.setLayout(layout);

    GridData data = new GridData(GridData.FILL_BOTH);
    Button one = new Button(shell, SWT.PUSH);
    one.setText("one");
    one.setLayoutData(data);

    data = new GridData(GridData.FILL_BOTH);
    Button two = new Button(shell, SWT.PUSH);
    two.setText("two");
    two.setLayoutData(data);

    data = new GridData(GridData.FILL_BOTH);
    Button three = new Button(shell, SWT.PUSH);
    three.setText("three");
    three.setLayoutData(data);

    data = new GridData(GridData.FILL_BOTH);
    Button four = new Button(shell, SWT.PUSH);
    four.setText("four");
    four.setLayoutData(data);

    shell.pack();
    shell.open();
    while (!shell.isDisposed()) {
      if (!display.readAndDispatch()) {
        display.sleep();
      }
    }
    display.dispose();
  }
}
```

Compiling and running this class produces the window seen in Figure 4-9.

Figure 4-9. A GridLayout *with all buttons set to fill horizontally and vertically*

Now that you understand the fundamentals of GridLayout, you can nest GridLayouts within other GridLayouts to produce more complex layouts. For example, to produce the layout shown in Figure 4-10, you would write the code in Listing 4-3.

Listing 4-3. GridLayoutComplex.java

```
package examples.ch4;

import org.eclipse.swt.widgets.*;
import org.eclipse.swt.layout.GridData;
import org.eclipse.swt.layout.GridLayout;
import org.eclipse.swt.SWT;

public class GridLayoutComplex {
  public static void main(String[] args) {
    Display display = new Display();
    Shell shell = new Shell(display);
    GridLayout layout = new GridLayout();
    layout.numColumns = 3;
    layout.makeColumnsEqualWidth = true;
    shell.setLayout(layout);

    // Create the big button in the upper left
    GridData data = new GridData(GridData.FILL_BOTH);
    data.widthHint = 200;
    Button one = new Button(shell, SWT.PUSH);
    one.setText("one");
    one.setLayoutData(data);

    // Create a composite to hold the three buttons in the upper right
    Composite composite = new Composite(shell, SWT.NONE);
    data = new GridData(GridData.FILL_BOTH);
```

```
      data.horizontalSpan = 2;
      composite.setLayoutData(data);
      layout = new GridLayout();
      layout.numColumns = 1;
      layout.marginHeight = 15;
      composite.setLayout(layout);

      // Create button "two"
      data = new GridData(GridData.FILL_BOTH);
      Button two = new Button(composite, SWT.PUSH);
      two.setText("two");
      two.setLayoutData(data);

      // Create button "three"
      data = new GridData(GridData.HORIZONTAL_ALIGN_CENTER);
      Button three = new Button(composite, SWT.PUSH);
      three.setText("three");
      three.setLayoutData(data);

      // Create button "four"
      data = new GridData(GridData.HORIZONTAL_ALIGN_BEGINNING);
      Button four = new Button(composite, SWT.PUSH);
      four.setText("four");
      four.setLayoutData(data);

      // Create the long button across the bottom
      data = new GridData();
      data.horizontalAlignment = GridData.FILL;
      data.grabExcessHorizontalSpace = true;
      data.horizontalSpan = 3;
      data.heightHint = 150;
      Button five = new Button(shell, SWT.PUSH);
      five.setText("five");
      five.setLayoutData(data);

      shell.pack();
      shell.open();
      while (!shell.isDisposed()) {
        if (!display.readAndDispatch()) {
          display.sleep();
        }
      }
      display.dispose();
    }
  }
```

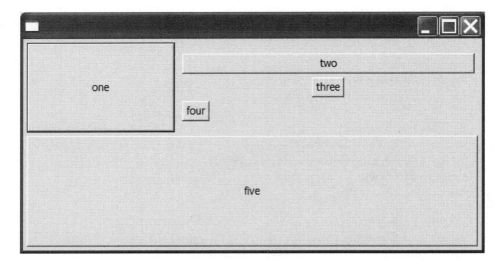

Figure 4-10. A complex GridLayout

You might be tempted to skip the rest of this chapter, thinking that the layouts we've discussed so far afford all the layout power you'll need. True, you can accomplish extremely complex layouts with what you've learned so far, and as long as you make your windows a fixed size, you shouldn't have any problems. Look at what happens, though, if you resize the complex grid layout you just created—some of the buttons disappear (see Figure 4-11).

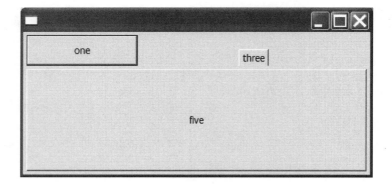

Figure 4-11. A resized complex grid layout

If you want more control over how your controls respond to resizing, you need to use FormLayout, which we discuss in the next section.

Using FormLayout

Looming as the most difficult layout to learn and understand is FormLayout, but rewards come to those who invest the time to learn it. As testimony to its complexity, it, unlike the other layouts, affords no simple explanation or one-sentence overview. However, FormLayout does offer the most control over intricate layouts, and merits a place in your arsenal. Consider it the GridBagLayout of SWT.

Like other layout classes, FormLayout uses a layout data class: FormData. FormData, in turn, uses an additional class to control widget sizing and placement: FormAttachment. Up to four instances of FormAttachment are set into the FormData object for the control; each FormAttachment instance corresponds to one side of the control (top, bottom, left, and right). FormAttachment defines how widgets position themselves with respect to the parent composite or to other controls within that composite. More specifically, a FormAttachment defines how the side of the control it belongs to positions and sizes itself with respect to the thing it's attached to, be it the parent or another control.

For those of you whose dexterity in math fueled a career in computer programming, and if you now find yourself grabbing data from a database and throwing it on a screen without doing so much as simple arithmetic, you need to dust off a few of those math skills now. FormAttachment uses this algorithm to determine sizing and placement:

```
y = ax + b
```

You'll recognize this as the standard linear equation, in which y is the value of the y coordinate, x is the value of the x coordinate, a is the slope, and b is the offset. In FormAttachment terms, y is the height, x is the width, a is a percentage of the attached-to object, and b is the offset. FormAttachment instances hold these values in member data (see Table 4-8).

Table 4-8. FormAttachment *Member Data*

Attribute	Description
int alignment	Specifies the alignment of the side of the control that this FormAttachment belongs to, relative to the control it's attached to. For attachments belonging to the top or bottom side, possible values are SWT.TOP, SWT.CENTER, and SWT.BOTTOM. For left or right attachments, possible values are SWT.LEFT, SWT.CENTER, and SWT.RIGHT. The side belonging to this FormAttachment is attached to the side of the attached control indicated by alignment. The default is to attach to the adjacent side.
Control control	Specifies the control this FormAttachment attaches to.
int denominator	Specifies the denominator of the a value of the equation. The default value is 100.
int numerator	Specifies the numerator of the a value of the equation.
int offset	Specifies the offset in pixels of the corresponding side from the attached composite or control.

FormAttachment specifies five constructors, none of which are empty, to help set its member data. They're listed in Table 4-9.

Table 4-9. FormAttachment *Constructors*

Constructor	Description
FormAttachment(Control control)	Constructs a FormAttachment attached to the specified control.
FormAttachment(Control control, int offset)	Constructs a FormAttachment attached to the specified control, with the specified offset.
FormAttachment(Control control, int offset, int alignment)	Constructs a FormAttachment attached to the specified control, with the specified offset and alignment.
FormAttachment(int numerator)	Constructs a FormAttachment with the specified numerator, a denominator of 100, and no offset.
FormAttachment(int numerator, int offset)	Constructs a FormAttachment with the specified numerator and offset, and a denominator of 100.
FormAttachment(int numerator, int denominator, int offset)	Constructs a FormAttachment with the specified numerator, denominator, and offset.

FormData contains up to four instances of FormAttachment, one for each side of the corresponding control. In addition, FormData can specify a width and a height. Table 4-10 lists the member data for FormData.

Table 4-10. FormData *Member Data*

Attribute	Description
FormAttachment bottom	The FormAttachment corresponding to the bottom side of the control.
int height	The desired height, in pixels, for the control.
FormAttachment left	The FormAttachment corresponding to the left side of the control.
FormAttachment right	The FormAttachment corresponding to the right side of the control.
FormAttachment top	The FormAttachment corresponding to the top side of the control.
int width	The desired width, in pixels, for the control.

When you construct a FormData object, you can optionally pass the width and height. Otherwise, use the default (empty) constructor. If you specify no FormAttachment objects, the control will attach to the top and left edges of the parent composite. If you define multiple controls this way, they'll be layered on top of each other, all in the upper-left corner of the parent.

FormLayout itself has two data members, marginHeight and marginWidth, specifying sizes, in pixels, for the margins that surround the composite's content. marginHeight corresponds to the top and bottom margins, and marginWidth corresponds to the left and right margins. However, only an empty constructor is available, so you must specify any margin values after constructing the FormLayout. The margin values default to zero.

The simplest usage of FormLayout would be a window with one button and no FormData (see Listing 4-4).

Listing 4-4. FormLayoutSimple.java

```java
package examples.ch4;

import org.eclipse.swt.widgets.*;
import org.eclipse.swt.layout.FormLayout;
import org.eclipse.swt.SWT;

public class FormLayoutSimple {
  public static void main(String[] args) {
    Display display = new Display();
    Shell shell = new Shell(display);
    shell.setLayout(new FormLayout());
    new Button(shell, SWT.PUSH).setText("Button");
    shell.pack();
    shell.open();
    while (!shell.isDisposed()) {
      if (!display.readAndDispatch()) {
        display.sleep();
      }
    }
    display.dispose();
  }
}
```

This code produces a window with a single button in the upper-left corner (see Figure 4-12).

Figure 4-12. A simple FormLayout

You can change the margins by retaining a reference to your FormLayout object and setting its marginHeight and marginWidth properties, so that the code would look something like this:

```java
FormLayout layout = new FormLayout();
layout.marginHeight = 5;
layout.marginWidth = 10;
shell.setLayout(layout);
```

The resulting window would look like Figure 4-13.

Figure 4-13. A simple FormLayout *with margins set*

However, until you use FormData and FormAttachment, you can't do much else.

Try using a FormData, but still no FormAttachments. FormData has the public properties height and width; you set those to change the size of the button:

```
Button button = new Button(shell, SWT.PUSH);
button.setText("Button");
FormData data = new FormData();
data.height = 50;
data.width = 50;
button.setLayoutData(data);
```

Now your window looks like Figure 4-14.

Figure 4-14. A FormLayout *with a* FormData *set for the button*

The button occupies a static position on the window; resizing this window has no effect on the button. Let's say, though, that you always want the button to extend within 50 pixels of the right edge of the window; you must add a FormAttachment to the FormData object you created earlier. Because you want to attach the right side of the button to the parent window, you set the right property of the FormData. When attaching to the side of the parent composite, you set the numerator to zero for the top and left edges, and 100 for the bottom and right edges, for 0% and 100% of the parent composite, respectively. You use the constructor that takes the numerator, which you set to 100, and the offset, which you set to –50. You don't need to set the denominator, because the default of 100 is what you want. The code looks like this:

```
data.right = new FormAttachment(100, -50);
```

Now when you compile and run your program, the button appears with its right edge exactly 50 pixels from the right edge of the window, as seen in Figure 4-15. Resizing the window keeps the button's right edge 50 pixels from the right edge of the window, as seen in Figure 4-16.

Figure 4-15. A button attached to the right edge of the window, offset by 50 pixels

Figure 4-16. Resizing the window

Notice that the entire button has moved to maintain its right edge 50 pixels from the right edge of the window. Hmm. What you really wanted was for the button to stay in the same place, but stretch to fill the space. To accomplish this, you must attach the left side of the button to its location, so you set the FormData's left property:

```
data.left = new FormAttachment(0, 10);
```

Passing zero for the numerator attaches the left edge of the button to the left side of the window (yes, it's also possible to attach the left edge of the button to the right edge of the window—try it to see what happens). Passing 10 for the offset maintains the left edge of the button 10 pixels from the left edge of the window. The initial window doesn't look much different from your initial window before, but resizing the window demonstrates that the left edge of the button is now anchored to the left edge of the window, as seen in Figure 4-17.

Figure 4-17. Left and right sides of the button attached to the left and right sides of the window, respectively

Notice that the FormAttachment settings trump the width you set on the FormData, so you remove that line of code.

You seem to be getting the hang of this. Now, attach the top of the button to the top of the window. However, instead of attaching it to a precise pixel offset, you'll place it at the position that's 25% of the height of the window down from the top of the window. Just for fun, you'll express it as ¼, rather than setting the numerator to 25 and leaving the denominator at the default of 100. You set the offset to zero. You add the following code.

```
data.top = new FormAttachment(1, 4, 0);
```

Now the button keeps its top edge one-fourth of the way down from the top of the window, no matter how often you resize the window (see Figure 4-18).

Figure 4-18. Top edge of the button anchored to a point 25% down from the top of the window

Let's add a button below this button. You'll anchor the bottom of the button to the bottom of the window, the top of the button to the bottom of your existing button (with five pixels of spacing between them), and the left and right edges of the button to the left and right edges, respectively, of your existing button. You start by creating your button:

```
Button button2 = new Button(shell, SWT.PUSH);
button2.setText("Button 2");
```

You then create a FormData object, and set its bottom data member that attaches to the very bottom of the window. You set the numerator to 100 and the offset to zero:

```
data = new FormData();
button2.setLayoutData(data);
data.bottom = new FormAttachment(100, 0);
```

To attach the top edge of your button to the existing button, you must use a FormAttachment constructor that takes a Control as an argument, so you can pass the existing button. Because you also want five pixels' space between the two buttons, you'll use the constructor that takes a Control and an offset:

```
data.top = new FormAttachment(button, 5);
```

You didn't have to specify that you wanted to attach to button's bottom edge; by default, edges are attached to adjacent edges when you set Control. Because you're specifying a FormAttachment for the top of the new button, and you're attaching to an existing button that was added before this one, your new button's top edge is adjacent to the existing button's bottom edge, and the two are attached.

You might be tempted to use the same constructor to attach the new button's left edge to the existing button's left edge, or even use the constructor that just takes a Control object, because the offset will be zero, so you use this code:

```
data.left = new FormAttachment(button);
```

However, this code attaches the left edge of your new button to the right edge of your existing button, as Figure 4-19 shows. Because you haven't specified which edge of button to attach to, the adjacent edge, the right, is assumed. You must explicitly attach to the left edge by passing SWT.LEFT for alignment:

```
data.left = new FormAttachment(button, 0, SWT.LEFT);
```

You complete the task by attaching the right edge of the new button to the right edge of button:

```
data.right = new FormAttachment(button, 0, SWT.RIGHT);
```

Compiling and running demonstrates that you've achieved your desired results, as shown in Figure 4-20.

Figure 4-19. Left edge of Button 2 erroneously attached to right edge of Button

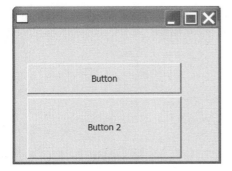

Figure 4-20. Two buttons attached

Listing 4-5 shows the entire code listing.

Listing 4-5. FormDataFormAttachment.java

```
package examples.ch4;

import org.eclipse.swt.widgets.*;
import org.eclipse.swt.layout.FormAttachment;
import org.eclipse.swt.layout.FormData;
import org.eclipse.swt.layout.FormLayout;
import org.eclipse.swt.SWT;

public class FormLayoutFormAttachment {
  public static void main(String[] args) {
    Display display = new Display();
    Shell shell = new Shell(display);
    FormLayout layout = new FormLayout();
    layout.marginHeight = 5;
    layout.marginWidth = 10;
    shell.setLayout(layout);
    Button button = new Button(shell, SWT.PUSH);
    button.setText("Button");
    FormData data = new FormData();
    data.height = 50;
    data.right = new FormAttachment(100, -50);
    data.left = new FormAttachment(0, 10);
    data.top = new FormAttachment(1, 4, 0);
    button.setLayoutData(data);

    Button button2 = new Button(shell, SWT.PUSH);
    button2.setText("Button 2");
    data = new FormData();
    button2.setLayoutData(data);
    data.bottom = new FormAttachment(100, 0);
    data.top = new FormAttachment(button, 5);
    data.left = new FormAttachment(button, 0, SWT.LEFT);
    data.right = new FormAttachment(button, 0, SWT.RIGHT);

    shell.pack();
    shell.open();
    while (!shell.isDisposed()) {
      if (!display.readAndDispatch()) {
        display.sleep();
      }
    }
    display.dispose();
  }
}
```

CAUTION *Don't create circular attachments (for example, attaching the bottom of one control to the top of another, and then attaching the top of that control to the bottom of the first). The results are undefined.*

Now that you understand the fundamentals of FormLayout, FormData, and FormAttachment, let's tackle anew the layout you created when we discussed GridLayout. This time, you want the following:

- A button in the upper left, filling the left-upper quarter of the window

- Three buttons that collectively fill the in the right-upper quarter of the window

- A button filling the bottom half of the window

- Five pixels of space between adjacent edges

You start with the upper-left button; you attach the top and left edges to the window, offsetting by five pixels:

```
Button one = new Button(shell, SWT.PUSH);
one.setText("One");
FormData data = new FormData();
data.top = new FormAttachment(0, 5);
data.left = new FormAttachment(0, 5);
data.bottom = new FormAttachment(50, -5);
data.right = new FormAttachment(50, -5);
one.setLayoutData(data);
```

To create the upper-right three buttons, you reason that you can put them all in a composite with a grid layout, and attach the composite to your first button:

```
Composite composite = new Composite(shell, SWT.NONE);
GridLayout gridLayout = new GridLayout();
gridLayout.marginHeight = 0;
gridLayout.marginWidth = 0;
composite.setLayout(gridLayout);
Button two = new Button(composite, SWT.PUSH);
two.setText("two");
GridData gridData = new GridData(GridData.FILL_BOTH);
two.setLayoutData(gridData);
Button three = new Button(composite, SWT.PUSH);
three.setText("three");
gridData = new GridData(GridData.FILL_BOTH);
three.setLayoutData(gridData);
```

```
Button four = new Button(composite, SWT.PUSH);
four.setText("four");
gridData = new GridData(GridData.FILL_BOTH);
four.setLayoutData(gridData);
data = new FormData();
data.top = new FormAttachment(0, 5);
data.left = new FormAttachment(one, 5);
data.bottom = new FormAttachment(50, -5);
data.right = new FormAttachment(100, -5);
composite.setLayoutData(data);
```

You attach the bottom button to the upper-left button and the window:

```
Button five = new Button(shell, SWT.PUSH);
five.setText("five");
data = new FormData();
data.top = new FormAttachment(one, 5);
data.left = new FormAttachment(0, 5);
data.bottom = new FormAttachment(100, -5);
data.right = new FormAttachment(100, -5);
five.setLayoutData(data);
```

The window displays the layout as you expect, even after resizing (see Figure 4-21).

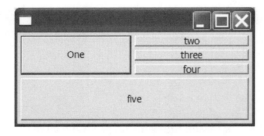

Figure 4-21. A complex FormLayout

Listing 4-6 shows the complete code listing for your complex FormLayout.

Listing 4-6. FormLayoutComplex.java

```
package examples.ch4;

import org.eclipse.swt.widgets.*;
import org.eclipse.swt.layout.FormAttachment;
import org.eclipse.swt.layout.FormData;
import org.eclipse.swt.layout.FormLayout;
import org.eclipse.swt.layout.GridData;
```

```
import org.eclipse.swt.layout.GridLayout;
import org.eclipse.swt.SWT;

public class FormLayoutComplex {
  public static void main(String[] args) {
    Display display = new Display();
    Shell shell = new Shell(display);
    FormLayout layout = new FormLayout();
    shell.setLayout(layout);
    Button one = new Button(shell, SWT.PUSH);
    one.setText("One");
    FormData data = new FormData();
    data.top = new FormAttachment(0, 5);
    data.left = new FormAttachment(0, 5);
    data.bottom = new FormAttachment(50, -5);
    data.right = new FormAttachment(50, -5);
    one.setLayoutData(data);

    Composite composite = new Composite(shell, SWT.NONE);
    GridLayout gridLayout = new GridLayout();
    gridLayout.marginHeight = 0;
    gridLayout.marginWidth = 0;
    composite.setLayout(gridLayout);
    Button two = new Button(composite, SWT.PUSH);
    two.setText("two");
    GridData gridData = new GridData(GridData.FILL_BOTH);
    two.setLayoutData(gridData);
    Button three = new Button(composite, SWT.PUSH);
    three.setText("three");
    gridData = new GridData(GridData.FILL_BOTH);
    three.setLayoutData(gridData);
    Button four = new Button(composite, SWT.PUSH);
    four.setText("four");
    gridData = new GridData(GridData.FILL_BOTH);
    four.setLayoutData(gridData);
    data = new FormData();
    data.top = new FormAttachment(0, 5);
    data.left = new FormAttachment(one, 5);
    data.bottom = new FormAttachment(50, -5);
    data.right = new FormAttachment(100, -5);
    composite.setLayoutData(data);

    Button five = new Button(shell, SWT.PUSH);
    five.setText("five");
    data = new FormData();
    data.top = new FormAttachment(one, 5);
    data.left = new FormAttachment(0, 5);
```

```
        data.bottom = new FormAttachment(100, -5);
        data.right = new FormAttachment(100, -5);
        five.setLayoutData(data);

        shell.pack();
        shell.open();
        while (!shell.isDisposed()) {
          if (!display.readAndDispatch()) {
            display.sleep();
          }
        }
        display.dispose();
      }
    }
```

Using StackLayout

We discuss StackLayout last, not because it's the most complex, but because it's the only SWT layout that isn't in package org.eclipse.swt.layout. Instead, it's in org.eclipse.swt.custom, which is a loose collection of various customized controls bolted onto SWT. It implements what amounts to be a flipchart: all controls are the same size and are put in the same location. As the name of the layout intimates, they're all stacked atop each other, and only the topmost control is visible.

StackLayout has only an empty constructor, and has a public data member called topControl that determines which control is on top of the stack and visible. This member is of type Control and defaults to null, so no controls are visible in the layout until you set this data member. Note that changing the value of topControl doesn't move the control to the top of the stack until layout() on the container is called, either explicitly or in response to some event (such as resizing the window).

See Table 4-11 for a full list of the StackLayout data members.

Table 4-11. StackLayout *Data Members*

Attribute	Description
int marginHeight	The size of the margin, in pixels, along the top and bottom edges of the layout.
int marginWidth	The size of the margin, in pixels, along the left and right edges of the layout.
Control topControl	The control to place on top of the stack and display. Default is null.

In Listing 4-7, you create a StackLayout and add three buttons to it. You also add an event handler, so that clicking the top button cycles through the three buttons, bringing the next one to the top. (We discuss events in Chapter 6.) Notice the call to shell.layout() near the bottom of the listing; try removing that line and rerunning the application.

Listing 4-7. StackLayoutTest.java

```java
package examples.ch4;

import org.eclipse.swt.events.*;
import org.eclipse.swt.widgets.*;
import org.eclipse.swt.custom.StackLayout;
import org.eclipse.swt.SWT;

public class StackLayoutTest {
  public static void main(String[] args) {
    Display display = new Display();
    Shell shell = new Shell(display);
    StackLayout layout = new StackLayout();
    shell.setLayout(layout);
    StackLayoutSelectionAdapter adapter = new StackLayoutSelectionAdapter(shell,
        layout);
    Button one = new Button(shell, SWT.PUSH);
    one.setText("one");
    one.addSelectionListener(adapter);
    Button two = new Button(shell, SWT.PUSH);
    two.setText("two");
    two.addSelectionListener(adapter);
    Button three = new Button(shell, SWT.PUSH);
    three.setText("three");
    three.addSelectionListener(adapter);
    layout.topControl = one;
    shell.open();
    while (!shell.isDisposed()) {
      if (!display.readAndDispatch()) {
        display.sleep();
      }
    }
    display.dispose();
  }
}

class StackLayoutSelectionAdapter extends SelectionAdapter {
  Shell shell;
  StackLayout layout;

  public StackLayoutSelectionAdapter(Shell shell, StackLayout layout) {
    this.shell = shell;
    this.layout = layout;
  }
```

```
public void widgetSelected(SelectionEvent event) {
  Control control = layout.topControl;
  Control[] children = shell.getChildren();
  int i = 0;
  for (int n = children.length; i < n; i++) {
    Control child = children[i];
    if (child == control) {
      break;
    }
  }
  ++i;
  if (i >= children.length)
    i = 0;
  layout.topControl = children[i];
  shell.layout();
  }
}
```

Run the program and click the button repeatedly to see the buttons cycle among one, two, and three (see Figures 4-22 and 4-23).

Figure 4-22. A StackLayout

Figure 4-23. The StackLayout *after clicking the button once*

We've covered all the layouts provided by SWT; what if none of these meet your needs? In that case, you have two options: create your own layout class or abandon layouts altogether. We cover these options in the next two sections.

Creating Your Own Layout

Unless you require convoluted layout logic, creating a layout is relatively simple. You subclass org.eclipse.swt.widgets.Layout and provide implementations for its two abstract methods:

```
protected abstract Point computeSize(Composite composite, int wHint, int hHint,
  boolean flushCache)
protected abstract void layout(Composite composite, boolean flushCache)
```

Both methods are declared protected, so you never call them directly. A composite calls computeSize() on its associated layout to determine the minimum size it should occupy, while still holding all its child controls at their minimum sizes. In your implementation, you typically will iterate through the container's controls to determine the minimum size they'll use in your layout. The composite parameter contains the Composite object for which the layout will compute the size; wHint and hHint are width and height hints, respectively, that can constrain the composite's size even further. Different layouts treat these hints differently. The flushCache parameter tells the layout whether to flush any cached layout values; for layouts that must make expensive computations, caching those values and respecting a false value for this parameter can increase responsiveness.

You might notice that computeSize() returns a Point object. How, you might ask, can a Point object, which is one dimensional, hold two-dimensional size information? The returned Point object is the lower-right corner of the composite's bounding rectangle; the upper-left corner is at point (0, 0), so the Point that computeSize() returns is an offset from (0, 0), and thus provides the composite's size.

The layout() method does the work of laying out the controls. It calculates the positions and sizes for the children of the passed Composite, then places them accordingly by calling setBounds() on each one. In your implementation, you typically will iterate through the container's controls, determining where to place and how to size each, then call the control's setBounds() method using the values you've calculated. Again, the flushCache parameter determines whether to flush any cached layout values; respect it if it makes sense for your layout.

If your layout requires some additional data per control, create a class to hold that data; users of your control can create instances and set them into their controls using setLayoutData(). Convention dictates that the name of your layout data class mimic the name of your layout, substituting Data for Layout, but that naming convention isn't required. setLayoutData() takes a java.lang.Object as a parameter, so you can derive your layout data class from anything.

In this section, you create a new layout called BorderLayout. AWT users will remember this layout, which places controls directionally (north, south, east, west, and center). You determine the following requirements:

- You can add multiple controls for any given direction; we'll just show the last control added for that direction.

- It isn't necessary that any direction have an associated control.

- A control need not have a direction; if no direction is specified, you assume "center" for the direction.

In the AWT BorderLayout, you specified the direction when you added the control to its container:

```
Panel panel = new Panel(); // Create the container
panel.setLayout(new BorderLayout()); // Create and set the layout
panel.add(new Button("Hello"), BorderLayout.NORTH);
```

Because SWT differs significantly (remember that you add a control to a parent by passing the parent to the control's constructor), you can't reuse this API. Instead, you'll create a data object to be used in conjunction with your BorderLayout called BorderData. Because you know exactly how many directions you must account for (five), you'll create all the possible BorderData objects as static constants of the class, and prevent users from creating new BorderData objects. Clients will reuse the five BorderData instances. Listing 4-8 shows your BorderData class.

Listing 4-8. `BorderData.java`

```java
package examples.ch4;

/**
 * Each control controlled by a BorderLayout
 * can have a BorderData attached to it, which
 * controls its placement on the layout.
 * Notice that the constructor is private;
 * we don't want people creating new BorderData
 * objects. We have the entire set of possibilities
 * in the public static constants.
 */
public class BorderData {
  /** North */
  public static final BorderData NORTH = new BorderData("North");

  /** South */
  public static final BorderData SOUTH = new BorderData("South");

  /** East */
  public static final BorderData EAST = new BorderData("East");

  /** West */
  public static final BorderData WEST = new BorderData("West");

  /** Center */
  public static final BorderData CENTER = new BorderData("Center");

  private String name;

  private BorderData(String name) {
    this.name = name;
  }
}
```

You can see that you use a TypeDef Enum pattern to create five BorderData objects, one for each direction. You make the constructor private to prevent someone from clumsily creating a new BorderData, which you wouldn't know how to handle anyway. You superfluously give each BorderData a name, though you don't do anything with it.

You're now ready to create your BorderLayout class. In your implementation of computeSize(), you iterate through the parent's controls to determine which control, if any, to use for each of the directions. Remember that we decided that you would show the last control added for a given direction. Because the presence and size of controls for each direction can have an impact on the sizing and placement of controls for other directions, you can't approach this problem linearly. For example, the first control in the array might be the "west" control, which you should place in the upper-left corner if no "north" control exists; otherwise, it should go directly below the "north" control on the left. However, the "north" control might be the last control in the list, so trying to determine size and placement for each control as you go through the list would be difficult. Instead, you create five member variables, one for each control:

```
private Control north;
private Control south;
private Control east;
private Control west;
private Control center;
```

You then create a helper method to fill the controls, which you call from computeSize(). This method, called getControls(), iterates through the parent's controls, determining the direction for each control. It sets the appropriate member variable to that control, overlaying any previous value the member variable had. It looks like this:

```
protected void getControls(Composite composite) {
  // Iterate through all the controls, setting
  // the member data according to the BorderData.
  // Note that we overwrite any previously set data.
  // Note also that we default to CENTER
  Control[] children = composite.getChildren();
  for (int i = 0, n = children.length; i < n; i++) {
    Control child = children[i];
    BorderData borderData = (BorderData) child.getLayoutData();
    if (borderData == BorderData.NORTH)
      north = child;
    else if (borderData == BorderData.SOUTH)
      south = child;
    else if (borderData == BorderData.EAST)
      east = child;
    else if (borderData == BorderData.WEST)
      west = child;
    else
      center = child;
  }
}
```

Note that this method will throw a ClassCastException if the control's layout data is something other than a BorderData object. You would discover this during development, and it's the behavior you want.

Once computeSize() knows which controls will actually display on the window, it can compute the minimum size for the parent. The width is the maximum of the widths of these controls:

- The north control

- The south control

- The west control plus the center control plus the east control

- The wHint passed to computeSize()

Any of these controls that are null don't factor into the size. The height is the maximum of the heights of these:

- The north control plus the maximum height among the west, center, and east controls, plus the south control

- The hHint passed to computeSize()

You create a helper method for determining the size of the control, which calls the control's computeSize() method, passing in SWT.DEFAULT for both width and height; it looks like this:

```
protected Point getSize(Control control, boolean flushCache)
{
  return control.computeSize(SWT.DEFAULT, SWT.DEFAULT, flushCache);
}
```

Your implementation of computeSize() looks like this:

```
protected Point computeSize(Composite composite, int wHint, int hHint,
  boolean flushCache) {
  getControls(composite);
  int width = 0, height = 0;

  // The width is the width of the west control
  // plus the width of the center control
  // plus the width of the east control.
  // If this is less than the width of the north
  // or the south control, however, use the largest
  // of those three widths.
  width += west == null ? 0 : getSize(west, flushCache).x;
  width += east == null ? 0 : getSize(east, flushCache).x;
  width += center == null ? 0 : getSize(center, flushCache).x;
  if (north != null) {
    Point pt = getSize(north, flushCache);
    width = Math.max(width, pt.x);
  }
  if (south != null) {
    Point pt = getSize(south, flushCache);
    width = Math.max(width, pt.x);
  }
```

```
// The height is the height of the north control
// plus the height of the maximum height of the
// west, center, and east controls
// plus the height of the south control.
height += north == null ? 0 : getSize(north, flushCache).y;
height += south == null ? 0 : getSize(south, flushCache).y;

int heightOther = center == null ? 0 : getSize(center, flushCache).y;
if (west != null) {
    Point pt = getSize(west, flushCache);
    heightOther = Math.max(heightOther, pt.y);
}
if (east != null) {
    Point pt = getSize(east, flushCache);
    heightOther = Math.max(heightOther, pt.y);
}
height += heightOther;

// Respect the wHint and hHint
return new Point(Math.max(width, wHint), Math.max(height, hHint));
}
```

For your layout() method, which places and sizes the controls in the parent container, you face the same issue of determining the actual controls to lay out. To solve this, you reuse the getControls() method you created earlier. Once you have the controls, you get the area of the parent on which to lay out the controls with this line of code:

```
Rectangle rect = composite.getClientArea();
```

Then, you just go through your controls one at a time, reusing your getSize() method to get their sizes and calling setBounds() to place them appropriately. Your layout() implementation, then, is this:

```
protected void layout(Composite composite, boolean flushCache) {
    getControls(composite);
    Rectangle rect = composite.getClientArea();
    int left = rect.x, right = rect.width, top = rect.y, bottom = rect.height;
    if (north != null) {
        Point pt = getSize(north, flushCache);
        north.setBounds(left, top, rect.width, pt.y);
        top += pt.y;
    }
    if (south != null) {
        Point pt = getSize(south, flushCache);
        south.setBounds(left, rect.height - pt.y, rect.width, pt.y);
        bottom -= pt.y;
    }
    if (east != null) {
```

```
      Point pt = getSize(east, flushCache);
      east.setBounds(rect.width - pt.x, top, pt.x, (bottom - top));
      right -= pt.x;
    }
    if (west != null) {
      Point pt = getSize(west, flushCache);
      west.setBounds(left, top, pt.x, (bottom - top));
      left += pt.x;
    }
    if (center != null) {
      center.setBounds(left, top, (right - left), (bottom - top));
    }
  }
}
```

Your BorderLayout class is now complete; the full listing appears in Listing 4-9.

Listing 4-9. BorderLayout.java

```
package examples.ch4;

import org.eclipse.swt.SWT;
import org.eclipse.swt.graphics.Point;
import org.eclipse.swt.graphics.Rectangle;
import org.eclipse.swt.widgets.Composite;
import org.eclipse.swt.widgets.Control;
import org.eclipse.swt.widgets.Layout;

/**
 * This class contains a BorderLayout, which is loosely
 * patterned after the old AWT BorderLayout.
 * It uses the <code>BorderData</code> class to determine
 * positioning of controls. To position controls,
 * call <code>control.setLayoutData()</code>, passing
 * the <code>BorderData</code> of your choice.
 *
 * For example:
 *
 * <code>
 *   shell.setLayoutData(new BorderLayout());
 *   Button button = new Button(shell, SWT.PUSH);
 *   button.setLayoutData(BorderData.NORTH);
 * </code>
 *
 * Note that you can add as many controls to the
 * same direction as you like, but the last one
 * added for the direction will be the one displayed.
 */
public class BorderLayout extends Layout {
```

```
private Control north;
private Control south;
private Control east;
private Control west;
private Control center;

/**
 * Computes the size for this BorderLayout.
 * @param composite the composite that contains the controls
 * @param wHint width hint in pixels for the minimum width
 * @param hHint height hint in pixels for the minimum height
 * @param flushCache if true, flushes any cached values
 * @return Point
 * @see org.eclipse.swt.widgets.Layout#computeSize(
 *   org.eclipse.swt.widgets.Composite, int, int, boolean)
 */
protected Point computeSize(Composite composite, int wHint, int hHint,
  boolean flushCache) {
 getControls(composite);
 int width = 0, height = 0;

 // The width is the width of the west control
 // plus the width of the center control
 // plus the width of the east control.
 // If this is less than the width of the north
 // or the south control, however, use the largest
 // of those three widths.
 width += west == null ? 0 : getSize(west, flushCache).x;
 width += east == null ? 0 : getSize(east, flushCache).x;
 width += center == null ? 0 : getSize(center, flushCache).x;

 if (north != null) {
   Point pt = getSize(north, flushCache);
   width = Math.max(width, pt.x);
 }
 if (south != null) {
   Point pt = getSize(south, flushCache);
   width = Math.max(width, pt.x);
 }

 // The height is the height of the north control
 // plus the height of the maximum height of the
 // west, center, and east controls
 // plus the height of the south control.
 height += north == null ? 0 : getSize(north, flushCache).y;
 height += south == null ? 0 : getSize(south, flushCache).y;
```

```
   int heightOther = center == null ? 0 : getSize(center, flushCache).y;
   if (west != null) {
     Point pt = getSize(west, flushCache);
     heightOther = Math.max(heightOther, pt.y);
   }
   if (east != null) {
     Point pt = getSize(east, flushCache);
     heightOther = Math.max(heightOther, pt.y);
   }
   height += heightOther;

   // Respect the wHint and hHint
   return new Point(Math.max(width, wHint), Math.max(height, hHint));
}


/**
 * This does the work of laying out our controls.
 * @see org.eclipse.swt.widgets.Layout#layout(
 *    org.eclipse.swt.widgets.Composite, boolean)
 */
protected void layout(Composite composite, boolean flushCache) {
  getControls(composite);
  Rectangle rect = composite.getClientArea();
  int left = rect.x, right = rect.width, top = rect.y, bottom = rect.height;
  if (north != null) {
    Point pt = getSize(north, flushCache);
    north.setBounds(left, top, rect.width, pt.y);
    top += pt.y;
  }
  if (south != null) {
    Point pt = getSize(south, flushCache);
    south.setBounds(left, rect.height - pt.y, rect.width, pt.y);
    bottom -= pt.y;
  }
  if (east != null) {
    Point pt = getSize(east, flushCache);
    east.setBounds(rect.width - pt.x, top, pt.x, (bottom - top));
    right -= pt.x;
  }
  if (west != null) {
    Point pt = getSize(west, flushCache);
    west.setBounds(left, top, pt.x, (bottom - top));
    left += pt.x;
  }
  if (center != null) {
    center.setBounds(left, top, (right - left), (bottom - top));
  }
}
```

```
    protected Point getSize(Control control, boolean flushCache) {
      return control.computeSize(SWT.DEFAULT, SWT.DEFAULT, flushCache);
    }

    protected void getControls(Composite composite) {
      // Iterate through all the controls, setting
      // the member data according to the BorderData.
      // Note that we overwrite any previously set data.
      // Note also that we default to CENTER
      Control[] children = composite.getChildren();
      for (int i = 0, n = children.length; i < n; i++) {
        Control child = children[i];
        BorderData borderData = (BorderData) child.getLayoutData();
        if (borderData == BorderData.NORTH)
          north = child;
        else if (borderData == BorderData.SOUTH)
          south = child;
        else if (borderData == BorderData.EAST)
          east = child;
        else if (borderData == BorderData.WEST)
          west = child;
        else
          center = child;
      }
    }
  }
```

To test your new layout, you create a window with controls in each direction. You create a BorderLayout and set it into your Shell object. You create five buttons and set the appropriate BorderData for each using the setLayoutData() method. Your code looks like Listing 4-10.

Listing 4-10. BorderLayoutTest.java

```
package examples.ch4;

import org.eclipse.swt.widgets.*;
import org.eclipse.swt.SWT;

public class BorderLayoutTest {
  public static void main(String[] args) {
    Display display = new Display();
    final Shell shell = new Shell(display);
    shell.setLayout(new BorderLayout());
    Button b1 = new Button(shell, SWT.PUSH);
    b1.setText("North");
    b1.setLayoutData(BorderData.NORTH);
    Button b2 = new Button(shell, SWT.PUSH);
```

```
    b2.setText("South");
    b2.setLayoutData(BorderData.SOUTH);
    Button b3 = new Button(shell, SWT.PUSH);
    b3.setText("East");
    b3.setLayoutData(BorderData.EAST);
    Button b4 = new Button(shell, SWT.PUSH);
    b4.setText("West");
    b4.setLayoutData(BorderData.WEST);
    Button b5 = new Button(shell, SWT.PUSH);
    b5.setText("Center");
    b5.setLayoutData(BorderData.CENTER);
    shell.pack();
    shell.open();
    while (!shell.isDisposed()) {
      if (!display.readAndDispatch()) {
        display.sleep();
      }
    }
    display.dispose();
  }
}
```

Compiling and running produces a window that looks like Figure 4-24.

Figure 4-24. Your BorderLayout *in action*

Try using BorderLayout in different scenarios, adding controls for only some directions, or adding multiple controls for the same direction, to see how the layout handles those situations.

The built-in layouts will likely handle most of your layout needs, but when they don't, don't hesitate to build your own layout class. With only two methods to implement (computeSize() and layout()), layouts are simple to build, and offer you ultimate control over the presentation of your windows.

Not Using a Layout

If you've read this far and can't stomach the thought of using layouts, rest assured that layouts aren't mandatory. You can place controls absolutely, without using a layout, though you'll lose the benefits that layouts offer, including platform transparency and automatic resizing and redistribution of your controls. You also assume the work of placing your controls, so you haven't gained any benefit, but we'll show you how to shun layouts nonetheless.

You might naively think you can just create a Shell and add controls to it, so you code this:

```
Shell shell = new Shell(display);
new Button(shell, SWT.PUSH).setText("No layout");
shell.open();
```

Then you compile and run it, and you don't see your button; all you have is a blank window. One of the things a layout does for you is call setBounds() on your controls to size and place them; because you aren't using a layout, you must do it yourself. So, you code this:

```
package examples.ch4;

import org.eclipse.swt.widgets.*;
import org.eclipse.swt.SWT;

public class NoLayoutSimple {
  public static void main(String[] args) {
    Display display = new Display();
    Shell shell = new Shell(display);
    Button button = new Button(shell, SWT.PUSH);
    button.setText("No layout");
    button.setBounds(5, 5, 100, 100);
    shell.pack();
    shell.open();
    while (!shell.isDisposed()) {
      if (!display.readAndDispatch()) {
        display.sleep();
      }
    }
    display.dispose();
  }
}
```

Compiling and running this program shows your button (see Figure 4-25).

Figure 4-25. A window with no layout

The org.eclipse.swt.widgets.Control superclass has two public setBounds()
implementations, as shown in Table 4-12.

Table 4-12. Control.setBounds() *Implementations*

Method	Description
public void setBounds(int x, int y, int width, int height)	Sets the bounds on the control; x is the *x* coordinate for the upper-left corner; y is the *y* coordinate for the upper-left corner; width is the width of the control; and height is the height of the control.
public void setBounds(Rectangle rect)	Sets the bounds on the control; rect is type org.eclipse.swt.graphics.Rectangle, which has four data members: x, y, width, height. It has a constructor that takes all four as parameters.

You could also have used the setBounds() method that takes a Rectangle to achieve
the same effect:

```
button.setBounds(new Rectangle(5, 5, 100, 100));
```

Be sure to import org.eclipse.swt.graphics.Rectangle if you take this approach.

You must call setBounds() on each control or composite you add to the window
for it to appear. You can make the screen as complex as you wish, and even resize your
controls yourself by using event handlers (we discuss events in Chapter 6). However,
we expect that you'll soon realize that leveraging layouts is much easier than avoiding
them.

GUI Builders for SWT

If you're aching for a drag-and-drop tool to build your GUIs visually, rather than worm-
ing your way through code, you have some options. First, Eclipse itself offers a tool
with its plug-in examples (available as a separate download) that provides rudimentary
layout building. To obtain it, use Eclipse's Update Manager, or download it from the
Eclipse downloads site (http://www.eclipse.org/downloads). You can find complete
instructions in the Eclipse help, under Platform Plug-in Developer Guide ➤ Examples
Guide ➤ Installing the examples. After installing, select Window ➤ Show View ➤ Other,
and in the resulting pop-up window, select SWT Examples ➤ SWT Layouts. A new window is added to your Eclipse window (see Figure 4-26).

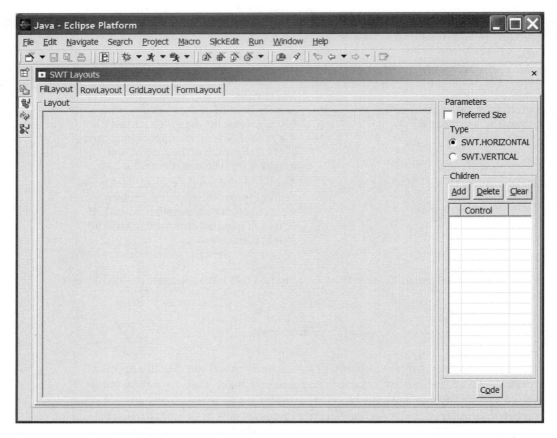

Figure 4-26. The SWT Layouts plug-in

Use this plug-in to create FillLayouts, RowLayouts, GridLayouts, and FormLayouts (StackLayouts aren't provided, presumably because they're in a different package). Select the tab of the layout you wish to create, set the properties for the layout using the controls provided, and add controls to the layout by clicking the Add button. You can change controls by selecting their type in the list and choosing a new type from the dropdown. You can change control properties as well, and proper layout data objects are generated for you. When you're finished, click the Code button at the bottom to see the generated code.

Admittedly, this isn't a full-featured GUI builder, and you'll probably want to alter control names from the generated "button0," "button1" ilk. You also must be using Eclipse to run this tool. The tool is a one-way generator only; you can't change the code to update the layout or import code into the layout. However, think of the SWT Layouts plug-in as a quick-and-dirty mockup tool that alleviates much of the drudgery of creating layouts, and you'll probably find it useful.

A company called Instantiations (http://www.instantiations.com/) has released an SWT GUI builder called SWT Designer, which comes in both a free (limited) version and a commercial professional version. Using SWT Designer, you can drag and drop controls to create your interface. You can find more information about the tool at http://www.swt-designer.com/.

Another SWT GUI builder comes from the Eclipse project. Called Visual Editor Project, it's still in its early stages, but shows some promise. At the time of this writing, it supports building GUIs in Swing only, though version 1.0.0 promises to support SWT. You can read about it at http://www.eclipse.org/vep/. Other SWT GUI builder tools are sprouting up as developers rush to fill a niche. Check out the Eclipse Plug-in Central site (http://www.eclipseplugincentral.com/) to find more tools.

The Apache Jakarta project offers another tool for creating SWT GUIs called JellySWT, which is a subset of the Jelly Jakarta project (http://jakarta.apache.org/commons/jelly/index.html). JellySWT is a Jelly library to create SWT interfaces. It provides no drag-and-drop or graphical layout capabilities, but rather allows you to create XML documents that render SWT front ends. A sample JellySWT script—one that creates a blank window—looks something like this:

```
<?xml version="1.0"?>
<j:jelly xmlns:j="jelly:core" xmlns="jelly:swt" xmlns:log="jelly:log">
  <shell text="JellySWT" var="shell" style="border, close, min, max, resize,
    title">
  </shell>

  ${shell.pack()}
  ${shell.open()}

  <j:set var="display" value="${shell.display}"/>

  <j:while test="${!shell.isDisposed()}">
    <j:if test="${display.readAndDispatch()}">
      <j:set var="foo" value="${display.sleep()}"/>
    </j:if>
  </j:while>
  ${display.dispose()}
</j:jelly>
```

Using JellySWT alleviates none of the manual coding burden; it just changes the language you write the code in. It certainly makes clear the separation of the view from the model and controller, and allows SWT to ride the XML wave. For more information, see the JellySWT Web site (http://jakarta.apache.org/commons/jelly/jellyswt.html).

Summary

Layouts assume the responsibility of placing and sizing your controls, even when their containing window is resized, and display controls properly on all platforms. SWT offers five layouts, which you can mix and match to create sophisticated layout aggregations. You can also create your own layout class that has whatever custom behavior you deem appropriate. Embracing layouts in your SWT GUIs makes them easier to create. You can choose to eschew layouts, and slog through placing your controls yourself, but we don't recommend it.

You have a few options to writing Java code when creating your layouts, including graphical builder tools and an XML solution. Experiment with these tools and incorporate the ones that help into your toolset.

Now that you know how to lay out controls, you're ready to learn about the controls available for laying out in your application. The next chapter covers all of the basic controls that SWT provides; combined with the information in this chapter, you're ready to create professional-looking cross-platform GUIs.

CHAPTER 5

Widgets

ALAS, MAN CAN'T LIVE by buttons alone. Building useful and elegant user interfaces depends on a rich set of graphical components or widgets. This chapter covers the basic widgets offered by SWT: Label, Button, Text, List, Combo, Slider, Group, ScrollBar, ProgressBar, and Menu. First, however, it discusses the base classes underlying the widgets: Widget and Control.

Introducing Widget

SWT's Widget class forms the base of all windowing components. The Widget class provides generic low-level event handling, creation and destruction semantics, and some convenience methods for finding certain values associated with widgets. Although an abstract class, Widget has no abstract methods and isn't intended to be subclassed by application developers. Table 5-1 describes Widget's methods.

Table 5-1. Widget *Methods*

Method	Description
void addListener(int eventType, Listener listener)	Adds a listener for the event type specified by eventType to the notification list. Chapter 6 covers events and listeners.
void addDisposeListener (DisposeListener listener)	Adds a listener that's notified when this Widget is disposed.
void dispose()	Releases any resources associated with this Widget and all its child Widgets.
Object getData()	Returns the application-specific data associated with this Widget.
Object getData(String key)	Returns the application-specific data associated with this Widget for the specified key.
Display ·getDisplay()	Returns the Display used to create this Widget. If null, returns the Display associated with this Widget's parent.
int getStyle()	Returns the style constants associated with this Widget.
boolean isDisposed()	Returns true if this Widget or its parent has been disposed.
void notifyListeners(int eventType, Event event)	Notifies registered listeners for the event type specified by eventType that an event has occurred.
void removeListener(int eventType, Listener listener)	Removes the specified listener from the notification list for the event type specified by eventType.

Table 5-1. Widget *Methods (continued)*

Method	Description
void removeDisposeListener (DisposeListener listener)	Removes the specified listener from the notification list.
void setData(Object data)	Sets the application-specific data for this Widget.
void setData(String key, Object value)	Sets the application-specific data associated with this Widget for the specified key.

Introducing Control

The abstract class Control subclasses Widget, and each Control wraps a native widget. Known as a "peer," the native widget ties its lifetime to its associated Control. All the basic widget classes in this chapter except ScrollBar and Menu directly subclass Control. The two exceptions directly subclass Widget and have no associated native peers.

A few styles, described in Table 5-2, apply to all Control classes. These styles, as well as any widget-specific styles, represent hints to the underlying environment. You have no guarantee that the windowing system will comply with your style requests.

NOTE   *Many styles represent hints that might or might not affect the realized component. Some operating or windowing systems might not support particular styles and will ignore them. You can determine the applied styles for a created widget by calling* Widget*'s* getStyle() *method. Also note that some styles may have different effects based on the layout manager.*

Table 5-2. Control *Styles*

Style	Description
SWT.BORDER	Draws a border around this Control
SWT.LEFT_TO_RIGHT	Orients this Control from left to right
SWT.RIGHT_TO_LEFT	Orients this Control from right to left

Control provides methods that control its display and behavior, including size, colors, fonts, popup menus, and tool tips. It also supports common events and listeners, discussed in greater depth in Chapter 6. Table 5-3 describes Control's methods.

Table 5-3. Control *Methods*

Method	Description
void addControlListener (ControlListener listener)	Adds a listener that's notified when this Control is moved or resized.
void addFocusListener (FocusListener listener)	Adds a listener that's notified when this Control gains or loses the focus.
void addHelpListener (HelpListener listener)	Adds a listener that's notified when the user requests help, typically by pressing the F1 key.
void addKeyListener (KeyListener listener)	Adds a listener that's notified when this Control receives an event from the keyboard.
void addMouseListener (MouseListener listener)	Adds a listener that's notified when the user presses or releases a mouse button on this Control.
void addMouseTrack Listener(MouseTrack Listener listener)	Adds a listener that's notified when the mouse enters, exits, or hovers over this Control.
void addMouseMove Listener(MouseMove Listener listener)	Adds a listener that's notified when the mouse moves over the area of this Control.
void addPaintListener (PaintListener listener)	Adds a listener that's notified when this Control is painted.
void addTraverseListener (TraverseListener listener)	Adds a listener that's notified when events such as the arrow, Escape, or Tab keys are struck while this Control has the keyboard focus..
Point computeSize(int wHint, int hHint)	Computes the size of this Control using the width and height hints specified by wHint and hHint, respectively. Returns the size in a Point object.
Point computeSize(int wHint, int hHint, boolean changed)	Computes the size of this Control using the width and height hints specified by wHint and hHint, respectively. Returns the size in a Point object. If changed is true, this Control shouldn't use cached data from any previous computations to compute the size.
boolean forceFocus()	Causes this Control to assume the keyboard focus. Returns true if this Control successfully assumes focus. Otherwise, returns false.
Accessible getAccessible()	Returns this Control's Accessible instance.
Color getBackground()	Returns the current background color of this Control.
int getBorderWidth()	Returns the width in pixels of this Control's border.
Rectangle getBounds()	Returns the Rectangle that bounds this Control.
boolean getEnabled()	Returns true if this Control is enabled or false if it's disabled. Enabled Controls appear normal and allow users to interact with them. Disabled Controls appear "grayed out" on most systems and don't allow user interaction. Though the enabled state of a Control might be true, it might still be disabled because of the state of its parent.
Font getFont()	Returns the font used to display text on this Control.
Color getForeground()	Returns the current foreground color of this Control.
Object getLayoutData()	Returns the layout data associated with this Control.

Table 5-3. Control *Methods (continued)*

Method	Description
`Point getLocation()`	Returns this `Control`'s location relative to its parent.
`Menu getMenu()`	Returns the popup menu associated with this `Control` or null if no associated popup menu exists.
`Monitor getMonitor()`	Returns this `Control`'s `Monitor`.
`Composite getParent()`	Returns this `Control`'s parent.
`Shell getShell()`	Returns this `Control`'s parent `Shell`.
`Point getSize()`	Returns this `Control`'s size as a `Point`.
`String getToolTipText()`	Returns this `Control`'s tool tip text.
`boolean getVisible()`	Returns `true` if this `Control` is visible. Otherwise, returns `false`. Note that though a `Control`'s visible state may be `true`, it might still not be visible if its parent isn't visible.
`boolean isEnabled()`	Returns `true` if this `Control` and all of its ancestors are enabled. Otherwise, returns `false`.
`boolean isFocusControl()`	Returns `true` if this `Control` currently has the focus of keyboard events. Otherwise, returns `false`.
`boolean isReparentable()`	Returns `true` if the lower-level operating system allows this `Control` to be associated with a different parent than the one with which this `Control` was created. Otherwise, returns `false`.
`boolean isVisible()`	Returns `true` if this `Control` and all its ancestors are currently visible. Otherwise, returns `false`.
`void moveAbove(Control control)`	Moves this `Control` on top of the specified `Control`, obscuring the specified `Control`. If `control` is null, this `Control` will appear on top of all other colocated `Controls`.
`void moveBelow(Control control)`	Moves this `Control` beneath the specified `Control` so this `Control` can't be seen. If `control` is null, this `Control` hides beneath all other colocated `Controls`.
`void pack()`	Resizes this `Control` and all its children to their preferred sizes.
`void pack(boolean changed)`	Resizes this `Control` and all its children to their preferred sizes. If `changed` is `true`, this `Control` shouldn't use cached data from any previous computations to compute the sizes.
`void redraw()`	Marks this `Control` for redraw.
`void redraw(int x, int y, int width, int height, boolean all)`	Marks the area of this `Control` specified by `x`, `y`, `width`, and `height` for redraw. If `all` is `true`, children that either wholly or partly occupy the given rectangle are also marked for redraw.
`void removeControlListener (ControlListener listener)`	Removes the specified listener from the notification list.
`void removeFocusListener (FocusListener listener)`	Removes the specified listener from the notification list.
`void removeHelpListener (HelpListener listener)`	Removes the specified listener from the notification list.
`void removeKeyListener (KeyListener listener)`	Removes the specified listener from the notification list.

Table 5-3. Control *Methods (continued)*

Method	Description
void removeMouseTrack Listener(MouseTrack Listener listener)	Removes the specified listener from the notification list.
void removeMouseListener (MouseListener listener)	Removes the specified listener from the notification list.
void removeMouseMove Listener(MouseMove Listener listener)	Removes the specified listener from the notification list.
void removePaintListener (PaintListener listener)	Removes the specified listener from the notification list.
void removeTraverse Listener(Traverse Listener listener)	Removes the specified listener from the notification list.
void setBackground(Color color)	Sets this Control's background color. If color is null, sets the background color to the default color for this Control.
void setBounds(int x, int y, int width, int height)	Sets the bounds of this Control to the specified values.
void setBounds(Rectangle rect)	Sets the bounds of this Control to the specified Rectangle.
void setCapture(boolean capture)	If capture is true, this Control captures all mouse events. Otherwise, this Control ignores mouse events.
void setCursor(Cursor cursor)	Sets the cursor (for example, hourglass or arrow) to display when the mouse pointer lies within the bounds of this Control. If cursor is null, sets the cursor to the default Cursor for this Control.
void setEnabled(boolean enabled)	If enabled is true, enables this Control. Otherwise, disables this Control.
boolean setFocus()	Causes this Control to assume the keyboard focus. Returns true if this Control successfully assumes focus. Otherwise, returns false.
void setFont(Font font)	Sets this Control's font.
void setForeground(Color color)	Sets this Control's foreground color.
void setLayoutData(Object layoutData)	Sets this Control's layout data.
void setLocation(int x, int y)	Sets the location of this Control relative to the upper-left corner of its parent.
void setLocation(Point location)	Sets the location of this Control relative to the upper-left corner of its parent.
void setMenu(Menu menu)	Sets the popup menu associated with this Control.
boolean setParent (Composite parent)	If the underlying system supports reparenting controls, sets this Control's parent. Returns true if setting the parent succeeds. Otherwise, returns false.
void setRedraw(boolean redraw)	If redraw is false, prevents this Control from being redrawn when paint events occur. Otherwise, allows redrawing to occur.

Table 5-3. Control *Methods (continued)*

Method	Description
void setSize(int width, int height)	Sets the size of this Control.
void setSize(Point size)	Sets the size of this Control.
void setToolTipText (String string)	Sets this Control's tool tip text.
void setVisible(boolean visible)	If visible is true, displays this Control. Otherwise, hides this Control. Note that a visible Control won't display if its parent is hidden or if it's obscured by a call to moveAbove() or moveBelow().
Point toControl(int x, int y)	Converts the specified coordinates from Display-relative to Control-relative.
Point toControl(Point point)	Converts the specified Point from Display-relative to Control-relative.
Point toDisplay(int x, int y)	Converts the specified coordinates from Control-relative to Display-relative.
Point toDisplay(Point point)	Converts the specified Point from Control-relative to Display-relative.
boolean traverse(int traversal)	Performs the specified traversal. Returns true if the traversal succeeds. Otherwise, returns false.
void update()	Forces processing of all outstanding paint requests.

The rest of this chapter focuses on specific widgets provided by SWT. Take the time to familiarize yourself with these widgets. Experiment with them. Understand their basic creation pattern. You'll see these widgets throughout the rest of this book.

Introducing Label

In its basic form, a Label displays unselectable, uneditable text. You often use them to communicate the role of other widgets. For example, you might place a Label displaying the text "Name:" beside a text field used to enter a name. Beyond this traditional Label usage, the SWT Label class also serves two additional purposes: to display images and to provide a graphical separator that divides other GUI components. This section explores all three Label uses.

To create a Label, use its only constructor:

```
Label(Composite parent, int style)
```

parent specifies the Composite to house the Label, and style specifies the style bits to apply to the Label. Table 5-4 describes the applicable styles. You can combine them using the bitwise OR operator, though some are mutually exclusive. For example, you can specify only one alignment constant (SWT.LEFT, SWT.CENTER, or SWT.RIGHT).

Table 5-4. Label *Styles*

Style	Description
SWT.SEPARATOR	Creates a visual divider.
SWT.HORIZONTAL	Used with SWT.SEPARATOR to create a horizontal separator.
SWT.VERTICAL	Used with SWT.SEPARATOR to create a vertical separator. This is the default.
SWT.SHADOW_IN	Used with SWT.SEPARATOR to draw a separator that appears recessed.
SWT.SHADOW_OUT	Used with SWT.SEPARATOR to draw a separator that appears extruded.
SWT.SHADOW_NONE	Used with SWT.SEPARATOR to draw a separator that appears unshadowed.
SWT.CENTER	Orients the text or image in the center of this Label.
SWT.LEFT	Orients the text or image to the left of this Label.
SWT.RIGHT	Orients the text or image to the right of this Label.
SWT.WRAP	Creates a Label that can wrap. Support for wrapped labels depends on the layout manager and is spotty.

Many of the styles have an effect only when creating separators, as Table 5-4 indicates. Separators divide the visual area of your applications into sections, which can make your interfaces more intuitive. They can run horizontally or vertically and can display extruded, intruded, or flat. How they display depends on the underlying windowing system.

Table 5-5 lists Label's interesting methods. Note that separators display neither text nor images.

Table 5-5. Label *Methods*

Method	Description
int getAlignment()	Returns the alignment constant associated with this Label (SWT.LEFT, SWT.CENTER, or SWT.RIGHT).
Image getImage()	Returns this Label's Image.
String getText()	Returns this Label's text.
void setAlignment(int alignment)	Sets this Label's alignment. alignment should be one of SWT.LEFT, SWT.CENTER, or SWT.RIGHT.
void setImage(Image image)	Sets this Label's Image.
void setText(String string)	Sets this Label's text.

Labels display either text or an image, but not both. If you call both setText() and setImage() on the same Label, the last one you call trumps. Chapter 10 discusses how to create images, as well as which image formats SWT supports.

For example, to create a left-aligned Label that displays the text "This is a Label," use this code:

```
new Label(parent, SWT.LEFT).setText("This is a Label");
```

The LabelExample program, shown in Listing 5-1, demonstrates Label. Figure 5-1 shows this program's window.

Listing 5-1. LabelExample.java

```java
package examples.ch5;

import org.eclipse.swt.*;
import org.eclipse.swt.widgets.*;
import org.eclipse.swt.layout.*;
import org.eclipse.swt.graphics.*;

/**
 * This class demonstrates Labels
 */
public class LabelExample {
  public static void main(String[] args) {
    Display display = new Display();
    Shell shell = new Shell();
    shell.setLayout(new GridLayout(1, false));

    // Create a label
    new Label(shell, SWT.NONE).setText("This is a plain label.");

    // Create a vertical separator
    new Label(shell, SWT.SEPARATOR);

    // Create a label with a border
    new Label(shell, SWT.BORDER).setText("This is a label with a border.");

    // Create a horizontal separator
    Label separator = new Label(shell, SWT.HORIZONTAL | SWT.SEPARATOR);
    separator.setLayoutData(new GridData(GridData.FILL_HORIZONTAL));

    // Create a label with an image
    Image image = new Image(display, "interspatial.gif");
    Label imageLabel = new Label(shell, SWT.NONE);
    imageLabel.setImage(image);

    shell.open();
    while (!shell.isDisposed()) {
      if (!display.readAndDispatch()) {
        display.sleep();
      }
    }
    display.dispose();
  }
}
```

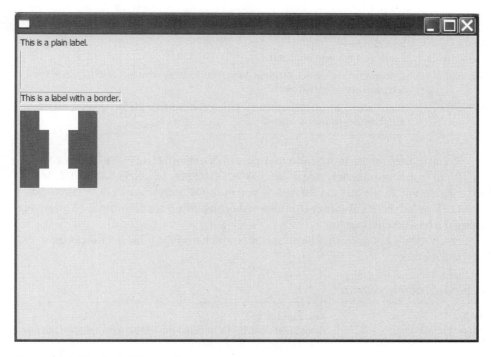

Figure 5-1. The LabelExample program

Introducing Button

When users want your application to do something, they often look for buttons to click. SWT uses the Button class to represent standard push buttons. In addition, SWT uses Button to represent checkboxes, toggle buttons, and radio buttons. You determine the type of widget that Button creates by the style constants you pass to Button's constructor, which looks like this:

Button(Composite parent, int style)

Table 5-6 describes applicable styles for Button.

Table 5-6. Button *Styles*

Style	Description
SWT.ARROW	Creates a push button that displays an arrow.
SWT.CHECK	Creates a checkbox.
SWT.PUSH	Creates a push button.
SWT.RADIO	Creates a radio button.
SWT.TOGGLE	Creates a push button that preserves its pushed or nonpushed state.
SWT.FLAT	Creates a push button that appears flat.
SWT.UP	When combined with SWT.ARROW, displays an upward-pointing arrow.
SWT.DOWN	When combined with SWT.ARROW, displays a downward-pointing arrow.

Table 5-6. Button *Styles (continued)*

Style	Description
SWT.CENTER	Centers the associated text.
SWT.LEFT	Left-aligns the associated text. When combined with SWT.ARROW, displays a leftward-pointing arrow.
SWT.RIGHT	Right-aligns the associated text. When combined with SWT.ARROW, displays a rightward-pointing arrow.

Think of these styles in sets: You may pass only one of SWT.LEFT, SWT.CENTER, or SWT.RIGHT. You may pass only one of SWT.ARROW, SWT.CHECK, SWT.PUSH, SWT.RADIO, or SWT.TOGGLE. Finally, if you pass SWT.ARROW, you may pass only one of SWT.UP, SWT.DOWN, SWT.LEFT, or SWT.RIGHT. You may combine style constants from different sets, however, using the bitwise OR operator.

Use Button's API to control its appearance and behavior. Table 5-7 describes Button's methods.

Table 5-7. Button *Methods*

Method	Description
void addSelection Listener(Selection Listener listener)	Adds a listener that's notified when the user selects (pushes, checks, and so on) this Button.
int getAlignment()	Depending on the type of this Button, returns either the orientation of the text (SWT.LEFT, SWT.RIGHT, or SWT.CENTER) or the direction of the arrow (SWT.LEFT, SWT.RIGHT, SWT.UP, or SWT.DOWN).
Image getImage()	Returns this Button's Image or null if this Button has no associated Image.
boolean getSelection()	For SWT.CHECK, SWT.RADIO, or SWT.TOGGLE buttons, returns true if this Button is selected. Otherwise, returns false.
String getText()	Returns this Button's text.
void removeSelection Listener(Selection Listener listener)	Removes the specified listener from the notification list.
void setAlignment(int alignment)	Sets this Button's alignment. For arrow buttons, you can pass one of SWT.LEFT, SWT.RIGHT, SWT.UP, or SWT.DOWN. For all other button types, you can pass one of SWT.LEFT, SWT.RIGHT, or SWT.CENTER.
void setImage(Image image)	Sets this Button's Image.
void setSelection(boolean selected)	If selected is true, selects this Button. Otherwise, deselects this Button. Valid for SWT.TOGGLE, SWT.RADIO, or SWT.CHECK types only.
void setText(String string)	Sets this Button's text.

The ButtonExample program in Listing 5-2 demonstrates creating the various button types (see Figure 5-2).

Listing 5-2. `ButtonExample.java`

```java
package examples.ch5;

import org.eclipse.swt.SWT;
import org.eclipse.swt.layout.*;
import org.eclipse.swt.widgets.*;

/**
 * This class demonstrates Buttons
 */
public class ButtonExample {
  public static void main(String[] args) {
    Display display = new Display();
    Shell shell = new Shell(display);
    shell.setLayout(new GridLayout(3, true));

    // Create three push buttons
    new Button(shell, SWT.PUSH).setText("Push 1");
    new Button(shell, SWT.PUSH).setText("Push 2");
    new Button(shell, SWT.PUSH).setText("Push 3");

    // Create three checkboxes
    new Button(shell, SWT.CHECK).setText("Checkbox 1");
    new Button(shell, SWT.CHECK).setText("Checkbox 2");
    new Button(shell, SWT.CHECK).setText("Checkbox 3");

    // Create three toggle buttons
    new Button(shell, SWT.TOGGLE).setText("Toggle 1");
    new Button(shell, SWT.TOGGLE).setText("Toggle 2");
    new Button(shell, SWT.TOGGLE).setText("Toggle 3");

    // Create three radio buttons
    new Button(shell, SWT.RADIO).setText("Radio 1");
    new Button(shell, SWT.RADIO).setText("Radio 2");
    new Button(shell, SWT.RADIO).setText("Radio 3");

    // Create three flat buttons
    new Button(shell, SWT.FLAT).setText("Flat 1");
    new Button(shell, SWT.FLAT).setText("Flat 2");
    new Button(shell, SWT.FLAT).setText("Flat 3");

    // Create three arrow buttons
    new Button(shell, SWT.ARROW);
    new Button(shell, SWT.ARROW | SWT.LEFT);
    new Button(shell, SWT.ARROW | SWT.DOWN);
```

```
    shell.pack();
    shell.open();
    while (!shell.isDisposed()) {
      if (!display.readAndDispatch()) {
        display.sleep();
      }
    }
    display.dispose();
  }
}
```

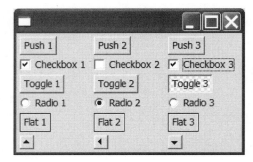

Figure 5-2. The ButtonExample program

Introducing Text

Reading labels, clicking buttons, and selecting checkboxes suffices for rudimentary interactions but falters when users or applications require more expressive communications. Applications should encourage users to say what they think, or at least type what they think, and they must be able to accept typed input. SWT offers the Text class for text-entry fields that allow users to input data using the keyboard. To create a Text widget, call its constructor, passing the parent and the desired style constants together using the bitwise OR operator:

```
Text(Composite parent, int style)
```

You can constrain Text instances to a single line of text or allow them to display multiple lines. You determine single line vs. multiple line upon construction by passing the appropriate style. Table 5-8 describes the styles that Text supports.

Table 5-8. Text *Styles*

Style	Description
SWT.MULTI	Creates a multiple-line text field.
SWT.SINGLE	Creates a single-line text field. This is the default. You may specifiy only one of SWT.MULTI or SWT.SINGLE.
SWT.READ_ONLY	Creates a text field with uneditable contents.
SWT.WRAP	With multiple-line text fields, causes text to wrap.
SWT.BORDER	Draws a border around the text field. Note that this style isn't set by default, and your text fields will look funny without it.
SWT.CENTER	Centers the text in this text field.
SWT.LEFT	Left-aligns the text in this text field. This is the default.
SWT.RIGHT	Right-aligns the text in this text field. You may specify only one of SWT.CENTER, SWT.LEFT, or SWT.RIGHT.
SWT.PASSWORD	Creates a text field suitable for password entry—it doesn't display the actual characters the user types, but rather it displays asterisks.
SWT.H_SCROLL	Creates a horizontal scrollbar to scroll this text field.
SWT.V_SCROLL	Creates a vertical scrollbar to scroll this text field.

To create a single-line Text with a border and left-aligned text, for example, use this code:

```
Text text = new Text(parent, SWT.BORDER); // SWT.SINGLE | SWT.LEFT set by default
```

You can configure the Text objects you create using Text's methods, described in Table 5-9.

Table 5-9. Text *Methods*

Method	Description
void addModifyListener (ModifyListener listener)	Adds a listener that's notified when the text in this Text changes.
void addSelectionListener (SelectionListener listener)	Adds a listener that's notified when the user presses Enter while this Text has focus. Note that notifications occur only for single-line Texts.
void addVerifyListener (VerifyListener listener)	Adds a listener that's notified when the text in this Text is about to change. This listener can veto the change.
void append(String string)	Appends the specified text to the text in this Text.
void clearSelection()	Deselects any text in this Text.
void copy()	Copies the selected text to the clipboard.
void cut()	Cuts the selected text to the clipboard.

Table 5-9. Text *Methods (continued)*

Method	Description
int getCaretLineNumber()	Returns the zero-based line number of the current caret position within this Text.
Point getCaretLocation()	Returns the coordinates of the caret's location.
int getCaretPosition()	Returns the zero-based offset of the current caret position from the beginning of the text.
int getCharCount()	Returns the number of characters in this Text.
boolean getDoubleClick Enabled()	Returns true if double-clicking is enabled. Otherwise, returns false.
char getEchoChar()	Returns the character displayed for each character the user types.
boolean getEditable()	Returns true if the content of this text component can be edited. Otherwise, returns false.
int getLineCount()	Returns the number of lines of text in this Text.
String getLineDelimiter()	Returns the line delimiter used between lines of text in a multiple-line Text.
int getLineHeight()	Returns the height in pixels of a line of text in this Text.
int getOrientation()	Returns this Text's orientation (SWT.LEFT_TO_RIGHT or SWT.RIGHT_TO_LEFT).
Point getSelection()	Returns the range of the selected text. The x component contains the zero-based index of the first selected character, and the y component contains the number one higher than the zero-based index of the last selected character.
int getSelectionCount()	Returns the number of characters in the current selection.
String getSelectionText()	Returns the selected text in this Text.
int getTabs()	Returns the number of tab stops, which defaults to 8.
String getText()	Returns the text in this Text.
String getText(int start, int end)	Returns the range of text in this Text specified by start and end. start specifies the zero-based index of the first character in the range, and end specifies the zero-based index of the last character in the range.
int getTextLimit()	Returns the number of characters this Text can hold.
int getTopIndex()	Returns the zero-based line number of the line currently displayed at the top of this Text.
int getTopPixel()	Returns the top pixel of the line currently displayed at the top of this Text.
void insert(String string)	Inserts the specified text at the current caret position, shifting any following text.
void paste()	Pastes the contents of the clipboard into this Text, replacing any currently selected text.
void removeModifyListener (ModifyListener listener)	Removes the specified listener from the notification list.

Table 5-9. Text *Methods (continued)*

Method	Description
void removeSelection Listener(SelectionListener listener)	Removes the specified listener from the notification list.
void removeVerifyListener (VerifyListener listener)	Removes the specified listener from the notification list.
void selectAll()	Selects all the text in this Text.
void setDoubleClickEnabled (boolean doubleClick)	If doubleClick is true, enables double-click notifications. Otherwise, disables them.
void setEchoChar(char echo)	Sets the character that's displayed when the user enters text. Use this to hide user input–like passwords.
void setEditable(boolean editable)	If editable is true, makes the text in this Text editable. Otherwise, makes it read-only.
void setFont(Font font)	Sets the font used to display the text in this Text.
void setOrientation(int orientation)	Sets this Text's orientation (SWT.LEFT_TO_RIGHT or SWT.RIGHT_TO_LEFT).
void setRedraw(boolean redraw)	If redraw is false, suspends redrawing this Text. Otherwise, resumes redrawing this Text.
void setSelection(int start)	Moves the caret to the zero-based offset specified by start.
void setSelection(int start, int end)	Selects the range of text specified by start and end. start specifies the zero-based index of the first character to select, and end specifies the number one higher than the zero-based index of the last character to select.
void setSelection(Point selection)	Selects the range of text specified by the x and y members of the specified Point. x specifies the zero-based index of the first character to select, and y specifies the number one higher than the zero-based index of the last character to select.
void setTabs(int tabs)	Sets the number of tab stops for this Text.
void setText(String string)	Sets this Text's text.
void setTextLimit(int limit)	Sets the maximum number of characters this Text will hold.
void setTopIndex(int index)	Scrolls the line at the specified zero-based index to the top of this Text.
void showSelection()	Scrolls the text as necessary to display the current selection.

The TextExample program creates an array of Text widgets to demonstrate the possibilities. It creates a left-aligned Text, a right-aligned Text, a password Text, a read-only Text, and a multiple-line Text. You can find the code in Listing 5-3. Figure 5-3 shows the program's main window.

Listing 5-3. TextExample.java

```java
package examples.ch5;

import org.eclipse.swt.SWT;
import org.eclipse.swt.layout.*;
import org.eclipse.swt.widgets.*;

/**
 * This class demonstrates text fields
 */
public class TextExample {
  public static void main(String[] args) {
    Display display = new Display();
    Shell shell = new Shell(display);
    shell.setLayout(new GridLayout(1, false));


    // Create a single-line text field
    new Text(shell, SWT.BORDER);

    // Create a right-aligned single-line text field
    new Text(shell, SWT.RIGHT | SWT.BORDER);

    // Create a password text field
    new Text(shell, SWT.PASSWORD | SWT.BORDER);

    // Create a read-only text field
    new Text(shell, SWT.READ_ONLY | SWT.BORDER).setText("Read Only");

    // Create a multiple-line text field
    Text t = new Text(shell, SWT.MULTI | SWT.BORDER | SWT.WRAP | SWT.V_SCROLL);
    t.setLayoutData(new GridData(GridData.FILL_BOTH));

    shell.open();
    while (!shell.isDisposed()) {
      if (!display.readAndDispatch()) {
        display.sleep();
      }
    }
    display.dispose();
  }
}
```

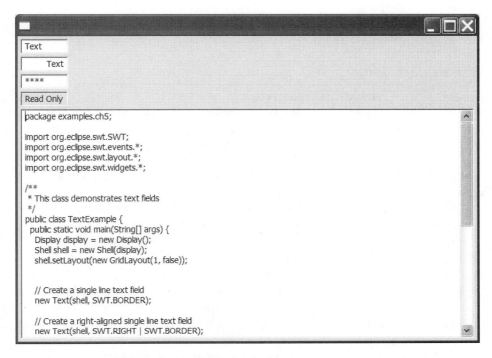

Figure 5-3. The TextExample program

Introducing List

List boxes display lists of strings and allow users to select one or more of them. SWT uses the List class to implement list boxes. To create a List, call its constructor, passing the parent and desired style constants:

```
List(Composite parent, int style)
```

You can combine style constants using the bitwise OR operator. Table 5-10 describes the applicable style constants for List.

Table 5-10. List *Styles*

Style	Effect
SWT.BORDER	Draws a border around this List.
SWT.SINGLE	Creates a List that allows selection of only one item at a time. This is the default.
SWT.MULTI	Creates a List that allows selection of multiple items at a time. You may specify only one of SWT.SINGLE or SWT.MULTI.
SWT.H_SCROLL	Creates a horizontal scrollbar to scroll this List.
SWT.V_SCROLL	Creates a vertical scrollbar to scroll this List.

The methods that List offers focus on adding, selecting, and removing items. Table 5-11 describes List's methods.

Table 5-11. List *Methods*

Method	Description
void add(String string)	Adds the specified string as the last item in this List.
void add(String string, int index)	Adds the specified string as the item at the specified zero-based index in this List, shifting all following items down.
void addSelectionListener (SelectionListener listener)	Adds a listener that's notified when an item in this List is selected.
void deselect(int index)	Deselects the item at the specified zero-based index.
void deselect(int[] indices)	Deselects the items at the specified zero-based indices.
void deselect(int start, int end)	Deselects the items between the specified zero-based indices, inclusive.
void deselectAll()	Deselects all items in this List.
int getFocusIndex()	Returns the zero-based index of the item in this List that currently holds the focus or -1 if no item has the focus.
String getItem(int index)	Returns the text of the item at the specified zero-based index.
int getItemCount()	Returns the number of items in this List.
int getItemHeight()	Returns the height in pixels of one item in this List.
String[] getItems()	Returns the text of all the items in this List.
String[] getSelection()	Returns the text of all the selected items in this List.
int getSelectionCount()	Returns the number of selected items in this List.
int getSelectionIndex()	Returns the zero-based index of the first selected item in this List or -1 if no items are selected.
int[] getSelectionIndices()	Returns the zero-based indices of the selected items in this List.
int getTopIndex()	Returns the zero-based index of the item displayed at the top of this List.
int indexOf(String string)	Returns the zero-based index of the first item in this List that matches the specified string or -1 if no items match.
int indexOf(String string, int start)	Returns the zero-based index of the first item at or after the index specified by start in this List that matches the specified string or -1 if no items match.
boolean isSelected(int index)	Returns true if the item at the given index is selected. Otherwise, returns false.
void remove(int index)	Removes the item at the specified zero-based index.
void remove(int[] indices)	Removes the items at the specified zero-based indices.
void remove(int start, int end)	Removes the items between the specified zero-based indices, inclusive.
void remove(String string)	Removes the first item in this List that matches the specified string.
void removeAll()	Removes all the items from this List.

Table 5-11. List *Methods (continued)*

Method	Description
void removeSelectionListener (SelectionListener listener)	Removes the specified listener from the notification list.
void select(int index)	Selects the item at the specified zero-based index.
void select(int[] indices)	Selects the items at the specified zero-based indices.
void select(int start, int end)	Selects the items between the specified zero-based indices, inclusive.
void selectAll()	Selects all items in this List.
void setFont(Font font)	Sets the font used by this List.
void setItem(int index, String string)	Sets the text of the item at the specified zero-based index to the specified string.
void setItems(String[] items)	Sets the contents of this List to the specified strings.
void setSelection(int index)	Deselects all currently selected items, and selects the item at the specified zero-based index.
void setSelection(int[] indices)	Deselects all currently selected items, and selects the items at the specified zero-based indices.
void setSelection(int start, int end)	Deselects all currently selected items, and selects the items between the specified zero-based indices, inclusive.
void setSelection(String[] items)	Deselects all currently selected items, and selects the specified items.
void setTopIndex(int index)	Scrolls this List so that the item at the specified zero-based index appears at the top of this List.
void showSelection()	Scrolls this List so that the selected item displays.

The ListExample program shown in Listing 5-4 creates two Lists, side by side. The List on the left allows a single selection, and the List on the right allows multiple selections. The program fills both Lists with the same items, using two different approaches. The program then selects some items in each list. Figure 5-4 shows the program.

Listing 5-4. ListExample.java

```
package examples.ch5;

import org.eclipse.swt.SWT;
import org.eclipse.swt.layout.*;
import org.eclipse.swt.widgets.*;

/**
 * This class demonstrates Lists
 */
public class ListExample {
```

```java
      // Strings to use as list items
      private static final String[] ITEMS = { "Alpha", "Bravo", "Charlie", "Delta",
        "Echo", "Foxtrot", "Golf", "Hotel", "India", "Juliet", "Kilo", "Lima", "Mike",
        "November", "Oscar", "Papa", "Quebec", "Romeo", "Sierra", "Tango", "Uniform",
        "Victor", "Whiskey", "X-Ray", "Yankee", "Zulu"
      };

      public static void main(String[] args) {
        Display display = new Display();
        Shell shell = new Shell(display);
        shell.setLayout(new FillLayout());

        // Create a single-selection list
        List single = new List(shell, SWT.BORDER | SWT.SINGLE | SWT.V_SCROLL);

        // Add the items, one by one
        for (int i = 0, n = ITEMS.length; i < n; i++) {
          single.add(ITEMS[i]);
        }

        // Select the fifth item
        single.select(4);

        // Create a multiple-selection list
        List multi = new List(shell, SWT.BORDER | SWT.MULTI | SWT.V_SCROLL);

        // Add the items all at once
        multi.setItems(ITEMS);

        // Select the 10th through 12th items
        multi.select(9, 11);

        shell.open();
        while (!shell.isDisposed()) {
          if (!display.readAndDispatch()) {
            display.sleep();
          }
        }
        display.dispose();
      }
    }
```

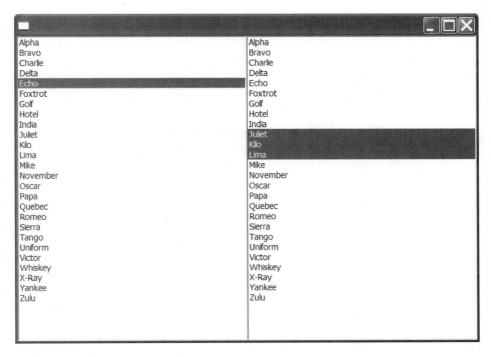

Figure 5-4. The ListExample program

Introducing Combo

The Text widget provides users the flexibility to enter what they want, but at a price—users assume the onus of authoring the entire input. The List widget removes this onus by listing all available options and allowing users to select one or more, but it doesn't allow the user to enter anything not listed. Combo boxes, also known as dropdowns, combine the strengths of Text and List, erasing their shortcomings. They present a list of items from which users can select but also allow users to type their own input.

SWT uses the Combo class to represent combo boxes. It offers one constructor:

```
Combo(Composite parent, int style)
```

The applicable style constants, described in Table 5-12, control Combo's behavior. A Combo can selectively show or hide its list of options, appearing to make the list "drop down" below the text-input field. Alternatively, it can always display its list of items and provide no mechanism for hiding the list. It can also force selection from the list, not allowing users to type their own inputs.

Table 5-12. Combo *Styles*

Style	Description
SWT.DROP_DOWN	Creates a Combo whose list "drops down."
SWT.READ_ONLY	Disallows typing input. Only SWT.DROP_DOWN Combos can be read-only.
SWT.SIMPLE	Creates a Combo whose list always displays.

Since a Combo acts somewhat like a Text and somewhat like a List, its API supports both Text-like operations and List-like operations. Some methods apply to a Combo's text field, and some apply to its list. Table 5-13 describes Combo's methods.

Table 5-13. Combo *Methods*

Method	Description
void add(String string)	Adds the specified string to the end of this Combo's list.
void add(String string, int index)	Adds the specified string as the item in this Combo's list at the specified zero-based index, shifting all following items down.
void addModifyListener (ModifyListener listener)	Adds a listener that's notified when the text in this Combo's text field changes.
void addSelectionListener (SelectionListener listener)	Adds a listener that's notified when the user selects an item in this Combo's list.
void clearSelection()	Clears any selection in the text field of this Combo.
void copy()	Copies the selected text in this Combo's text field to the clipboard.
void cut()	Cuts the selected text in this Combo's text field to the clipboard.
void deselect(int index)	Deselects the item at the specified zero-based index in this Combo's list.
void deselectAll()	Deselects all items in this Combo's list.
String getItem(int index)	Returns the item at the specified zero-based index in this Combo's list.
int getItemCount()	Returns the number of items in this Combo's list.
int getItemHeight()	Returns the height in pixels of a single item in this Combo's list.
String[] getItems()	Returns the items in this Combo's list.
int getOrientation()	Returns this Combo's orientation (SWT.LEFT_TO_RIGHT or SWT.RIGHT_TO_LEFT).
Point getSelection()	Returns the zero-based indices of the current selection in this Combo's text field. The returned Point's x member contains the beginning of the range, and the y member contains the end of the range.
int getSelectionIndex()	Returns the zero-based index of the selected item in this Combo's list or -1 if no items are selected.
String getText()	Returns the text in this Combo's text field.
int getTextHeight()	Returns the height in pixels of this Combo's text field.

Table 5-13. Combo *Methods (continued)*

Method	Description
int getTextLimit()	Returns the maximum number of characters this Combo's text field holds.
int indexOf(String string)	Returns the zero-based index of the first item in this Combo's list that matches the specified string or -1 if no items match.
int indexOf(String string, int start)	Returns the zero-based index of the first item at or after the index specified by start in this Combo's list that matches the specified string or -1 if no items match.
void paste()	Pastes from the clipboard into this Combo's text field.
void remove(int index)	Removes the item at the specified zero-based index from this Combo's list.
void remove(int start, int end)	Removes the items between the specified zero-based indices, inclusive, from this Combo's list.
void remove(String string)	Removes the first item in this Combo's list that matches the specified string.
void removeAll()	Removes all the items from this Combo's list.
void removeModifyListener (ModifyListener listener)	Removes the specified listener from the notification list.
void removeSelectionListener (SelectionListener listener)	Removes the specified listener from the notification list.
void select(int index)	Selects the item in this Combo's list at the specified zero-based index.
void setItem(int index, String string)	Sets the text of the item in this Combo's list at the specified zero-based index to the specified string.
void setItems(String[] items)	Sets the contents of this Combo's list to the specified strings.
void setOrientation(int orientation)	Sets this Combo's orientation (SWT.LEFT_TO_RIGHT or SWT.RIGHT_TO_LEFT).
void setSelection(Point selection)	Selects the range of text in this Combo's text field specified by the x and y members of the specified Point. x specifies the zero-based index of the first character to select, and y specifies the number one higher than the zero-based index of the last character to select.
void setText(String string)	Sets the text of this Combo's text field.
void setTextLimit(int limit)	Sets the maximum number of characters this Combo's text field will hold.

The ComboExample program shown in Listing 5-5 creates three Combos: a dropdown Combo, a read-only dropdown Combo, and a simple Combo. Figure 5-5 shows ComboExample's window.

Listing 5-5. ComboExample.java

```java
package examples.ch5;

import org.eclipse.swt.SWT;
import org.eclipse.swt.layout.*;
import org.eclipse.swt.widgets.*;

/**
 * This class demonstrates Combo
 */
public class ComboExample {
  // Strings to use as list items
  private static final String[] ITEMS = { "Alpha", "Bravo", "Charlie", "Delta",
    "Echo", "Foxtrot", "Golf", "Hotel", "India", "Juliet", "Kilo", "Lima", "Mike",
    "November", "Oscar", "Papa", "Quebec", "Romeo", "Sierra", "Tango", "Uniform",
    "Victor", "Whiskey", "X-Ray", "Yankee", "Zulu"
  };

  public static void main(String[] args) {
    Display display = new Display();
    Shell shell = new Shell(display);
    shell.setLayout(new GridLayout(2, true));

    // Create a dropdown Combo
    Combo combo = new Combo(shell, SWT.DROP_DOWN);
    combo.setItems(ITEMS);

    // Create a read-only Combo
    Combo readOnly = new Combo(shell, SWT.DROP_DOWN | SWT.READ_ONLY);
    readOnly.setItems(ITEMS);

    // Create a "simple" Combo
    Combo simple = new Combo(shell, SWT.SIMPLE);
    simple.setItems(ITEMS);

    shell.open();
    while (!shell.isDisposed()) {
      if (!display.readAndDispatch()) {
        display.sleep();
      }
    }
    display.dispose();
  }
}
```

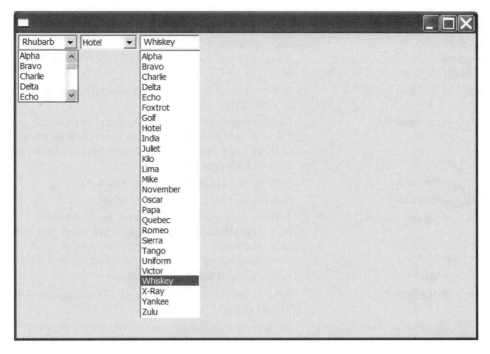

Figure 5-5. The ComboExample program

Introducing Slider

Sliders allow users to select a value within a given range by sliding a "thumb" across the range to the desired value. Users can change the selected value by clicking and dragging the thumb with the mouse, pressing the arrow keys on the keyboard, clicking the arrow buttons at the ends of the slider, or clicking between the arrow buttons and the thumb. You can create both horizontal and vertical sliders. SWT uses the Slider class to represent sliders.

To create a slider, use its constructor:

```
Slider(Composite parent, int style)
```

You can pass either SWT.HORIZONTAL or SWT.VERTICAL for style to create a horizontal or a vertical slider, respectively. You can't combine the styles.

To customize Sliders, use the methods described in Table 5-14.

Table 5-14. Slider *Methods*

Method	Description
void addSelectionListener (SelectionListener listener)	Adds a listener that's notified when users select this Slider.
boolean getEnabled()	Returns true if this Slider is enabled. Otherwise, returns false.
int getIncrement()	Returns the increment value: the number by which the selected value changes when users click the arrow buttons at the ends of this Slider or press the arrow keys on the keyboard.
int getMaximum()	Returns this Slider's maximum value.
int getMinimum()	Returns this Slider's minimum value.
int getPageIncrement()	Returns the page increment value: the number by which the selected value changes when users click the areas between the thumb and the arrow buttons or press the page up or page down keys on the keyboard.
int getSelection()	Returns this Slider's current value.
int getThumb()	Returns the size of this Slider's thumb, relative to this Slider's range.
void removeSelectionListener (SelectionListener listener)	Removes the specified listener from the notification list.
void setEnabled(boolean enabled)	If enabled is true, enables this Slider. Otherwise, disables this Slider.
void setIncrement(int value)	Sets the increment value: the number by which the selected value changes when users click the arrow buttons at the ends of this Slider or press the arrow keys on the keyboard.
void setMaximum(int value)	Sets this Slider's maximum value.
void setMinimum(int value)	Sets this Slider's minimum value.
void setPageIncrement(int value)	Sets the page increment value: the number by which the selected value changes when users click the areas between the thumb and the arrow buttons or press the page up or page down keys on the keyboard.
void setSelection(int value)	Sets this Slider's value.
void setThumb(int value)	Sets the size of this Slider's thumb, relative to this Slider's range.
void setValues(int selection, int minimum, int maximum, int thumb, int increment, int pageIncrement)	Sets this Slider's value, minimum, maximum, thumb size, increment value, and page increment value as specified.

The SliderExample program, shown in Listing 5-6, demonstrates sliders. It creates a horizontal slider and a vertical slider, as shown in Figure 5-6.

Listing 5-6. SliderExample.java

```java
package examples.ch5;

import org.eclipse.swt.SWT;
import org.eclipse.swt.layout.*;
import org.eclipse.swt.widgets.*;

/**
 * This class demonstrates Sliders
 */
public class SliderExample {
  public static void main(String[] args) {
    Display display = new Display();
    Shell shell = new Shell(display);
    shell.setLayout(new GridLayout(1, false));

    // Create a horizontal Slider, accepting the defaults
    new Slider(shell, SWT.HORIZONTAL);

    // Create a vertical Slider and set its properties
    Slider slider = new Slider(shell, SWT.VERTICAL);
    slider.setMinimum(0);
    slider.setMaximum(100);
    slider.setIncrement(5);
    slider.setPageIncrement(20);
    slider.setSelection(75);

    shell.open();
    while (!shell.isDisposed()) {
      if (!display.readAndDispatch()) {
        display.sleep();
      }
    }
    display.dispose();
  }
}
```

Figure 5-6. The SliderExample program

Introducing Group

Whether through using a personal digital assistant (PDA) or a traditional day planner, people strive to organize their lives. Through organization, challenges that would otherwise overwhelm people instead become both manageable and conquerable. Breaking life's tasks into discrete chunks has proven to be a winning strategy.

This divide-and-conquer approach applies to user interface design as well. Windows wadded with widgets erect usability barriers. The group widget, represented in SWT by the Group class, provides visual organization and structure. Surprisingly simple—it consists of a thin rectangular outline that surrounds its contained controls—it nonetheless can offer the user an orderly interface that reinforces relationships among widgets.

Since a Group derives from Composite, it can contain other widgets. To add widgets to a Group, and thus cause them to display within the Group's boxy embrace, pass the Group as the widget's parent in the widget's constructor. Radio buttons, for example, typically rest inside a Group, counting on the Group to clue the user in that only one of the radio buttons can be selected at a time. Use Groups to demarcate any set of widgets. To create a Group, pass the parent and the desired style constants to the constructor:

```
Group(Composite parent, int style)
```

Although Group purports to support several styles that affect its line display, it emphatically reminds you that styles merely provide hints about your wishes to the underlying windowing system. None of the "shadow" styles have any effect on Microsoft Windows, for example. Table 5-15 describes the supported styles.

Table 5-15. Group Styles

Style	Description
SWT.SHADOW_ETCHED_IN	Creates a Group with the "etched in" shadow style.
SWT.SHADOW_ETCHED_OUT	Creates a Group with the "etched out" shadow style.
SWT.SHADOW_IN	Creates a Group with the "in" shadow style, which isn't necessarily popular.
SWT.SHADOW_OUT	Creates a Group with the "out" shadow style.
SWT.SHADOW_NONE	Creates a Group with no shadow style.
SWT.NO_RADIO_GROUP	If this Group contains radio buttons, removes the default single-selection behavior of radio buttons. It allows selection of multiple radio buttons within this Group.

A Group can optionally display some text along its top, specified by the setText() method. Group's spartanly equipped API, described in Table 5-16, reminds you that it offers little beyond visual organizational clues.

Table 5-16. Group Methods

Method	Description
Rectangle computeTrim(int x, int y, int width, int height)	Computes the bounding Rectangle necessary to hold the client area specified by x, y, width, and height
Rectangle getClientArea()	Returns the bounding Rectangle of this Group's client area
String getText()	Returns this Group's optional title text
void setText(String string)	Sets this Group's optional title text

The GroupExample program in Listing 5-7 creates two Groups, each holding radio buttons. The second group has the SWT.NO_RADIO_GROUP style, so you can select multiple radio buttons inside it (see Figure 5-7).

Listing 5-7. GroupExample.java

```
package examples.ch5;

import org.eclipse.swt.SWT;
import org.eclipse.swt.layout.*;
import org.eclipse.swt.widgets.*;
```

```
/**
 * This class demonstrates Groups
 */
public class GroupExample {
  public static void main(String[] args) {
    Display display = new Display();
    Shell shell = new Shell(display);
    shell.setLayout(new GridLayout());

    // Create the first Group
    Group group1 = new Group(shell, SWT.SHADOW_IN);
    group1.setText("Who's your favorite?");
    group1.setLayout(new RowLayout(SWT.VERTICAL));
    new Button(group1, SWT.RADIO).setText("John");
    new Button(group1, SWT.RADIO).setText("Paul");
    new Button(group1, SWT.RADIO).setText("George");
    new Button(group1, SWT.RADIO).setText("Ringo");

    // Create the second Group
    Group group2 = new Group(shell, SWT.NO_RADIO_GROUP);
    group2.setText("Who's your favorite?");
    group2.setLayout(new RowLayout(SWT.VERTICAL));
    new Button(group2, SWT.RADIO).setText("Barry");
    new Button(group2, SWT.RADIO).setText("Robin");
    new Button(group2, SWT.RADIO).setText("Maurice");

    shell.open();
    while (!shell.isDisposed()) {
      if (!display.readAndDispatch()) {
        display.sleep();
      }
    }
    display.dispose();
  }
}
```

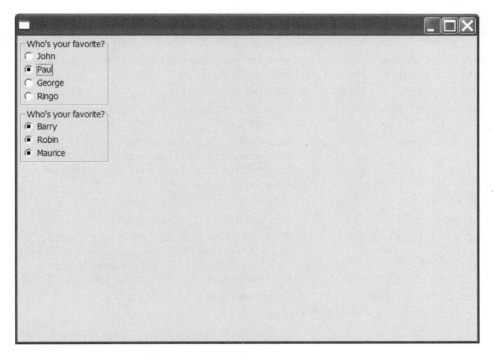

Figure 5-7. The GroupExample program

Introducing ScrollBar

Scrollbars, represented by SWT's ScrollBar class, appear and function much like Sliders. However, you don't create ScrollBars directly. In fact, you have no access to ScrollBar's only constructor. Instead, you create a ScrollBar by passing one of the scrolling style constants described in Table 5-17 to the constructor of a Scrollable-derived widget, and it creates the ScrollBar. You can then retrieve a reference to the scrollable widget's ScrollBar by calling getHorizontalBar() or getVerticalBar() for horizontal or vertical ScrollBars, respectively. Table 5-18 describes methods you can call on your retrieved ScrollBar reference.

ScrollBars, like Sliders, display a movable thumb that represents the ScrollBar's current position. They also have clickable arrow buttons that move the thumb. Also, you can click the ScrollBar between the thumb and an arrow button to increment or decrement the ScrollBar by a full page.

Table 5-17. Scrollable *Styles*

Style	Description
SWT.H_SCROLL	Creates a horizontal ScrollBar (passes the SWT.HORIZONTAL style to ScrollBar's constructor)
SWT.V_SCROLL	Creates a vertical ScrollBar (passes the SWT.VERTICAL style to ScrollBar's constructor)

Table 5-18. `ScrollBar` *Methods*

Method	Description
void addSelectionListener (SelectionListener listener)	Adds a listener that's notified when the user scrolls this `ScrollBar`.
void dispose()	Disposes this `ScrollBar`.
boolean getEnabled()	Returns `true` if this `ScrollBar` is enabled. Otherwise, returns `false`.
int getIncrement()	Returns the increment value: the number by which the selected value changes when users click the arrow buttons at the ends of this `ScrollBar` or press the arrow keys on the keyboard.
int getMaximum()	Returns this `ScrollBar`'s maximum value.
int getMinimum()	Returns this `ScrollBar`'s minimum value.
int getPageIncrement()	Returns the page increment value: the number by which the selected value changes when users click the areas between the thumb and the arrow buttons or press the page up or page down keys on the keyboard.
Scrollable getParent()	Returns this `ScrollBar`'s parent.
int getSelection()	Returns this `ScrollBar`'s current value.
Point getSize()	Returns this `ScrollBar`'s size. The x component of the returned `Point` represents the width in pixels. The y coordinate represents the height in pixels.
int getThumb()	Returns the size of this `ScrollBar`'s thumb, relative to this `ScrollBar`'s range.
boolean getVisible()	Returns `true` if this `ScrollBar` is visible. Otherwise, returns `false`.
boolean isEnabled()	Returns `true` if this `ScrollBar` and all its ancestors are enabled. Otherwise, returns `false`.
boolean isVisible()	Returns `true` if this `ScrollBar` and all its ancestors are visible. Otherwise, returns `false`.
void removeSelectionListener (SelectionListener listener)	Removes the specified listener from the notification list.
void setEnabled(boolean enabled)	If `enabled` is `true`, enables this `ScrollBar`. Otherwise, disables this `ScrollBar`.
void setIncrement(int value)	Sets the increment value: the number by which the selected value changes when users click the arrow buttons at the ends of this `ScrollBar` or press the arrow keys on the keyboard.
void setMaximum(int value)	Sets this `ScrollBar`'s maximum value.
void setMinimum(int value)	Sets this `ScrollBar`'s minimum value.
void setPageIncrement(int value)	Sets the page increment value: the number by which the selected value changes when users click the areas between the thumb and the arrow buttons or press the page up or page down keys on the keyboard.
void setSelection(int value)	Sets this `ScrollBar`'s value.
void setThumb(int value)	Sets the size of this `ScrollBar`'s thumb, relative to this `ScrollBar`'s range.

Table 5-18. ScrollBar *Methods (continued)*

Method	Description
void setValues(int selection, int minimum, int maximum, int thumb, int increment, int pageIncrement)	Sets this ScrollBar's value, minimum, maximum, thumb size, increment value, and page increment value as specified.
void setVisible(boolean visible)	If visible is true, shows this ScrollBar. Otherwise, hides it.

The ScrollBarExample program shown in Listing 5-8 creates a List with a vertical ScrollBar. The program adds several items to the List and then selects the last item and scrolls it into view. Finally, it retrieves a reference to the List's ScrollBar, determines its scroll value, and adds an item to the List that reports the value (see Figure 5-8).

Listing 5-8. ScrollBarExample.java

```
package examples.ch5;

import org.eclipse.swt.SWT;
import org.eclipse.swt.layout.*;
import org.eclipse.swt.widgets.*;

/**
 * This class demonstrates ScrollBars
 */
public class ScrollBarExample {
  public static void main(String[] args) {
    Display display = new Display();
    Shell shell = new Shell(display);
    shell.setLayout(new FillLayout());

    // Create a List with a vertical ScrollBar
    List list = new List(shell, SWT.V_SCROLL);

    // Add a bunch of items to it
    for (int i = 0; i < 500; i++) {
      list.add("A list item");
    }

    // Scroll to the bottom
    list.select(list.getItemCount() - 1);
    list.showSelection();

    // Get the ScrollBar
    ScrollBar sb = list.getVerticalBar();
```

```
    // Add one more item that shows the selection value
    list.add("Selection: " + sb.getSelection());

    shell.open();
    while (!shell.isDisposed()) {
      if (!display.readAndDispatch()) {
        display.sleep();
      }
    }
    display.dispose();
  }
}
```

Figure 5-8. The ScrollBarExample program

Introducing ProgressBar

A well-written GUI constantly conveys its state. When your application performs a long-running process during which the application might not be responsive, you should communicate as much as possible about the process's progress. Designed for just this purpose, progress bars display, as their name implies, incremental progress. They display an empty bar (either horizontal or vertical) that incrementally fills with color. For example, most Web browsers display a progress bar to track the progress of large file downloads.

SWT uses the `ProgressBar` class to implement progress bars. To create a `ProgressBar`, pass the parent and style constants to the constructor:

```
ProgressBar(Composite parent, int style)
```

Table 5-19 describes the supported styles.

Table 5-19. `ProgressBar` *Styles*

Style	Description
SWT.SMOOTH	Creates a progress bar that displays a continuous bar as its indicator. The default is to display a distinctly divided bar.
SWT.HORIZONTAL	Creates a horizontal progress bar.
SWT.VERTICAL	Creates a vertical progress bar.
SWT.INDETERMINATE	Creates a progress bar that constantly cycles, indicating continuous work.

A `ProgressBar` has a minimum value, a maximum value, and a current value, and `ProgressBar`'s API provides getters and setters for these values (see Table 5-20). Before beginning your work, you should set the minimum and maximum values to numbers that reflect the work you're going to perform and then update the current value periodically to show progress. You can avoid this minutia by using the `SWT.INDETERMINATE` style, but that gives users much less useful feedback: the operation is happening but doesn't know when it'll finish.

Table 5-20. `ProgressBar` *Methods*

Method	Description
int getMaximum()	Returns this `ProgressBar`'s maximum value
int getMinimum()	Returns this `ProgressBar`'s minimum value
int getSelection()	Returns this `ProgressBar`'s current value
void setMaximum(int value)	Sets this `ProgressBar`'s maximum value
void setMinimum(int value)	Sets this `ProgressBar`'s minimum value
void setSelection(int value)	Sets this `ProgressBar`'s current value

The ProgressBarExample program shown in Listing 5-9 shows two `ProgressBars`: a smooth one and a divided one. The divided one carries the `SWT.INDETERMINATE` style, so it cycles constantly. The program spawns a thread that runs 30 seconds, incrementing the smooth `ProgressBar` every second. Figure 5-9 shows the program's window.

Listing 5-9. `ProgressBarExample.java`

```
package examples.ch5;

import org.eclipse.swt.SWT;
import org.eclipse.swt.layout.*;
```

```java
import org.eclipse.swt.widgets.*;

/**
 * This class demonstrates ProgressBar
 */
public class ProgressBarExample {
  public static void main(String[] args) {
    Display display = new Display();
    Shell shell = new Shell(display);
    shell.setLayout(new GridLayout());

    // Create a smooth ProgressBar
    ProgressBar pb1 = new ProgressBar(shell, SWT.HORIZONTAL | SWT.SMOOTH);
    pb1.setLayoutData(new GridData(GridData.FILL_HORIZONTAL));
    pb1.setMinimum(0);
    pb1.setMaximum(30);

    // Create an indeterminate ProgressBar
    ProgressBar pb2 = new ProgressBar(shell, SWT.HORIZONTAL | SWT.INDETERMINATE);
    pb2.setLayoutData(new GridData(GridData.FILL_HORIZONTAL));

    // Start the first ProgressBar
    new LongRunningOperation(display, pb1).start();

    shell.open();
    while (!shell.isDisposed()) {
      if (!display.readAndDispatch()) {
        display.sleep();
      }
    }
  }
}

/**
 * This class simulates a long-running operation
 */
class LongRunningOperation extends Thread {
  private Display display;
  private ProgressBar progressBar;

  public LongRunningOperation(Display display, ProgressBar progressBar) {
    this.display = display;
    this.progressBar = progressBar;
  }
```

```
public void run() {
  // Perform work here--this operation just sleeps
  for (int i = 0; i < 30; i++) {
    try {
      Thread.sleep(1000);
    } catch (InterruptedException e) {
      // Do nothing
    }
    display.asyncExec(new Runnable() {
      public void run() {
        if (progressBar.isDisposed()) return;

        // Increment the progress bar
        progressBar.setSelection(progressBar.getSelection() + 1);
      }
    });
  }
}
}
```

Figure 5-9. The ProgressBarExample program

Introducing Menus

The component listed third in the Windows-Icons-Menus-Pointers (WIMP) interface, menus wrench computing from the exclusive grasp of the elite and hand it over to the masses. Interacting with computers used to mean memorizing and typing cryptic commands to accomplish tasks. The domain knowledge rested with the user. For example, people using vi had to type ":%s/this/that/g" (after first ensuring they were in command mode) to replace all instances of "this" with "that" in the current file. MS-DOS users copied directory trees with "xcopy /s /e . newDir." WordPerfect users, at least, could purchase paper overlays to place on their keyboards around the function keys so they could scan the overlay before pressing Shift+F7 to print the current document.

Menus transfer that domain knowledge to the party better at memorization: the computer. To replace all instances of "this" with "that," users using programs with menus select a command such as Edit ➤ Replace from a menu. They copy directory trees by selecting the directory to copy, selecting Copy from a menu, selecting the destination, and selecting Paste from a menu. They print by selecting, again from a menu, File ➤ Print. Menus eliminate the need to memorize and type obscure commands, making program interaction available to average users.

Creating Menus

To create a menu, use SWT's Menu class, which offers the four constructors described in Table 5-21. Menus come in the following three types:

- Bar menus, which typically display across the top of the parent window.

- Dropdown menus, which drop down from a bar, a popup, or another dropdown menu.

- Popup menus, which display at the mouse cursor location and disappear after the user selects an item.

SWT uses style constants for these types, described in Table 5-22. You may specify only one of SWT.BAR, SWT.DROP_DOWN, or SWT.POP_UP for a single menu. You can add a style to each of these menu types (using the bitwise OR operator), SWT.NO_RADIO_GROUP, to remove support for radio groups in the menu. You shouldn't subclass Menu.

Table 5-21. Menu *Constructors*

Constructor	Description
Menu(Control parent)	Constructs a popup menu as a child of the specified parent. Automatically uses the SWT.POP_UP style.
Menu(Decorations parent, int style)	Constructs a menu, with the specified style, as a child of the specified parent. Chapter 8 covers Decorations, but you typically pass the parent Shell object.
Menu(Menu parentMenu)	Constructs a dropdown menu as a child of the specified parent menu's parent. Automatically uses the SWT.DROP_DOWN style.
Menu(MenuItem parentItem)	Constructs a dropdown menu as a child of the specified parent item's parent menu. Automatically uses the SWT.DROP_DOWN style.

Table 5-22. Menu *Styles*

Style	Description
SWT.BAR	Creates a horizontal menu used as the main menu for the window
SWT.DROP_DOWN	Creates a menu that drops down from another menu, either a bar menu or another dropdown menu
SWT.POP_UP	Creates a menu that pops up at a given location and isn't a child of a bar menu
SWT.NO_RADIO_GROUP	Creates a menu that doesn't support radio groups

What you consider to be a single menu for an application actually comprises, in SWT, several Menu objects. Consider, for example, the menu shown in Figure 5-10. In SWT, this uses several Menu objects: a bar (shown by itself in Figure 5-11) and dropdowns (such as the one shown—the vertical menu that drops down from the bar) for each of the items in the bar. Popup menus, too, can consist of several Menu objects cascading from each other.

Figure 5-10. Two menus (a bar and a dropdown)

File Edit Format View Help

Figure 5-11. A bar menu

The following code, for example, creates a bar menu:

```
Menu menu = new Menu(shell, SWT.BAR);
```

and this code creates a popup menu:

```
Menu menu = new Menu(composite, SWT.POP_UP);
```

Adding Items to Menus

Menus must have items to be useful. File, from Figure 5-10, is a menu item. So is Exit. Without menu items, the menu would have nothing to select and couldn't respond to user input in any meaningful way.

SWT uses the MenuItem class to represent items in the menu. It offers two constructors:

```
MenuItem(Menu parent, int style)
MenuItem(Menu parent, int style, int index)
```

where parent is the menu this item belongs to, style is the style for the menu item, and index is the zero-based index of the menu item, relative to the other items in the parent menu. You shouldn't combine styles, and you shouldn't subclass MenuItem. Support for the styles depends on the underlying environment. The SWT.PUSH style, for example, has no effect in Windows. Table 5-23 describes the supported styles.

Table 5-23. MenuItem *Styles*

Style	Description
SWT.CHECK	Creates a menu item that can be toggled on and off. When on, it displays a check mark beside it.
SWT.CASCADE	Creates a menu item that can have a set of submenu items.
SWT.PUSH	Creates a menu item that can be pushed.
SWT.RADIO	Creates one item within a group that can be toggled on and off. Only one item in the group can be on. When on, it displays a check mark beside it.
SWT.SEPARATOR	Creates a separator item.

Traditional menu items, such as those in Figure 5-10 that do something when you click them, use the style SWT.NONE. The following code creates a traditional menu item:

```
MenuItem item = new MenuItem(menu, SWT.NONE);
```

and this code creates a check menu item:

```
MenuItem item = new MenuItem(menu, SWT.CHECK);
```

Creating a Bar Menu with Dropdowns

Most applications have a traditional menu, which consists of a bar menu and several dropdown menus. To create such a menu, use these steps:

1. Create a bar menu.

2. Add several menu items of type `SWT.CASCADE`.

3. Set the text of each menu item using `MenuItem.setText()`.

4. Create each dropdown menu by calling either `new Menu(shell, SWT.DROP_DOWN)` or `new Menu(barMenu)`.

5. Set each dropdown into the appropriate bar menu item by calling `MenuItem.setMenu(dropdownMenu)`.

6. Create items for each dropdown menu.

7. Set the bar menu as the main menu for the shell by calling `setMenuBar(menu)`.

For example, to create the menu shown in Figure 5-10 (without displaying the accelerator keys), use the code shown in Listing 5-10.

Listing 5-10. Creating a Bar Menu with Dropdowns

```
// Create the bar menu
Menu menu = new Menu(shell, SWT.BAR);

// Create all the items in the bar menu
MenuItem fileItem = new MenuItem(menu, SWT.CASCADE);
fileItem.setText("File");
MenuItem editItem = new MenuItem(menu, SWT.CASCADE);
editItem.setText("Edit");
MenuItem formatItem = new MenuItem(menu, SWT.CASCADE);
formatItem.setText("Format");
MenuItem viewItem = new MenuItem(menu, SWT.CASCADE);
viewItem.setText("View");
MenuItem helpItem = new MenuItem(menu, SWT.CASCADE);
helpItem.setText("Help");

// Create the File item's dropdown menu
Menu fileMenu = new Menu(menu);
fileItem.setMenu(fileMenu);

// Create all the items in the File dropdown menu
MenuItem newItem = new MenuItem(fileMenu, SWT.NONE);
newItem.setText("New");
```

```
MenuItem openItem = new MenuItem(fileMenu, SWT.NONE);
openItem.setText("Open...");
MenuItem saveItem = new MenuItem(fileMenu, SWT.NONE);
saveItem.setText("Save");
MenuItem saveAsItem = new MenuItem(fileMenu, SWT.NONE);
saveAsItem.setText("Save As...");

// Create the first separator
new MenuItem(fileMenu, SWT.SEPARATOR);

MenuItem pageSetupItem = new MenuItem(fileMenu, SWT.NONE);
pageSetupItem.setText("Page Setup...");
MenuItem printItem = new MenuItem(fileMenu, SWT.NONE);
printItem.setText("Print...");

// Create the second separator
new MenuItem(fileMenu, SWT.SEPARATOR);

MenuItem exitItem = new MenuItem(fileMenu, SWT.NONE);
exitItem.setText("Exit");

// Set the bar menu as the menu in the shell
shell.setMenuBar(menu);
```

This code creates only one dropdown menu—the one for the File bar menu item—but you can mimic that dropdown menu to create dropdown menus for each of the other bar menu items.

Creating a Popup Menu

Popup menus languished in obscurity until Microsoft discovered the right mouse button (the secondary button in politically correct terminology) and made it an integral part of Windows 95. Now, users expect to be able to right-click virtually anything to see a menu describing the actions the user can perform on the selected object. As the name suggests, a popup menu "pops up" when the appropriate platform-specific mouse button or key sequence is pressed. Like bar menus, popup menus can have cascading items and dropdown menus. They can have all types of menu items and can do anything a bar menu can.

For example, to create a popup menu for a composite that looks like Figure 5-12, use the code shown in Listing 5-11.

Listing 5-11. Creating a Popup Menu

```
// Create the popup menu
Menu menu = new Menu(composite);
```

```
// Create all the items in the popup menu
MenuItem newItem = new MenuItem(menu, SWT.CASCADE);
newItem.setText("New");
MenuItem refreshItem = new MenuItem(menu, SWT.NONE);
refreshItem.setText("Refresh");
MenuItem deleteItem = new MenuItem(menu, SWT.NONE);
deleteItem.setText("Delete");

// Create the New item's dropdown menu
Menu newMenu = new Menu(menu);
newItem.setMenu(newMenu);

// Create the items in the New dropdown menu
MenuItem shortcutItem = new MenuItem(newMenu, SWT.NONE);
shortcutItem.setText("Shortcut");
MenuItem iconItem = new MenuItem(newMenu, SWT.NONE);
iconItem.setText("Icon");

// Set the popup menu as the popup for the composite
composite.setMenu(menu);
```

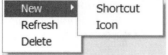

Figure 5-12. A popup menu

Creating a No Radio Group

Radio groups allow only one item within the group to be selected at a time. You can create menu items as part of a radio group using the SWT.RADIO style. You can even create multiple radio groups in the same menu by separating sets of radio menu items using a separator menu item. For example, Listing 5-12 creates two radio groups, each of which can have only one selected item.

Listing 5-12. Creating a No Radio Group

```
// Create the first radio group
MenuItem item1 = new MenuItem(menu, SWT.RADIO);
item1.setText("Radio One");
MenuItem item2 = new MenuItem(menu, SWT.RADIO);
item2.setText("Radio Two");
MenuItem item3 = new MenuItem(menu, SWT.RADIO);
item3.setText("Radio Three");

new MenuItem(menu, SWT.SEPARATOR);
```

```
// Create the second radio group
MenuItem itema = new MenuItem(menu, SWT.RADIO);
itema.setText("Radio A");
MenuItem itemb = new MenuItem(menu, SWT.RADIO);
itemb.setText("Radio B");
MenuItem itemc = new MenuItem(menu, SWT.RADIO);
itemc.setText("Radio C");
```

Figure 5-13 shows the menu created by Listing 5-12, with one item from each group selected.

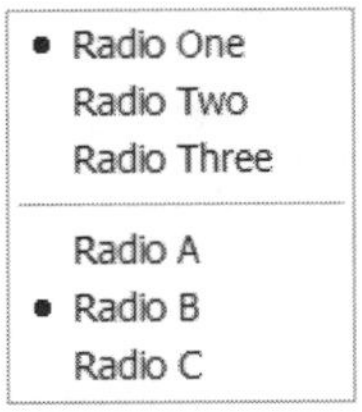

Figure 5-13. A menu with two radio groups

Sometimes, however, you might want the radio look and selection functionality, but you want users to be able to select each option individually and have multiple options within the group selected. To achieve this, create the menu with the SWT.NO_RADIO_GROUP style, using the bitwise OR operator to add the style to any other style you specify. You can't use any of the Menu constructors that don't allow the specification of a style, so your code will look something like this:

```
Menu popUp = new Menu(shell, SWT.POP_UP | SWT.NO_RADIO_GROUP);
Menu dropDown = new Menu(shell, SWT.DROP_DOWN | SWT.NO_RADIO_GROUP);
```

Menus created with this style enforce no radio group restrictions, and users can select and deselect multiple radio items as if they were created with the SWT.CHECK style. Figure 5-14 shows a no radio group menu with all three options selected.

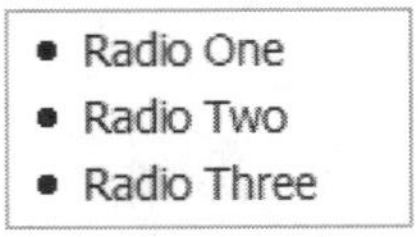

Figure 5-14. A no radio group menu

Manipulating Menus and MenuItems

In many cases, you'll create your application's menu as previously shown, add event handlers to it (covered in Chapter 6), and not worry about the menu again. Sometimes, however, you'll want to customize how the menu and its items behave. Both Menu and MenuItem have a set of methods to enable you to do that. Table 5-24 describes Menu's methods, and Table 5-25 describes MenuItem's methods.

Table 5-24. Menu *Methods*

Method	Description
void addHelpListener (HelpListener listener)	Adds a listener that's notified when the user requests help, usually by pressing F1.
void addMenuListener (MenuListener listener)	Adds a listener that's notified when a menu is either hidden or shown.
MenuItem getDefaultItem()	Returns the default menu item or null if none has been set.
boolean getEnabled()	Returns true if this menu is enabled and false if it isn't.
MenuItem getItem(int index)	Returns the menu item at the specified zero-based index.
int getItemCount()	Returns the number of items in this menu.
MenuItem[] getItems()	Returns the items in the menu.
Decorations getParent()	Returns this menu's parent.
MenuItem getParentItem()	Returns this menu's parent menu item or null if has no parent item.
Menu getParentMenu()	Returns this menu's parent menu or null if it has no parent menu.
Shell getShell()	Returns the Shell to which this menu belongs.
boolean getVisible()	Returns true if this menu is visible and false if it's invisible.
int indexOf(MenuItem item)	Returns the zero-based index of the specified menu item or -1 if the item does not exist in this menu.
boolean isEnabled()	Returns true if this menu and all its ancestors are enabled or false if it or any of its ancestors isn't enabled.
boolean isVisible()	Returns true if this menu and all its ancestors are visible or false if it or any of its ancestors isn't visible.
void removeHelpListener (HelpListener listener)	Removes the specified listener from the notification list.
void removeMenuListener (MenuListener listener)	Removes the specified listener from the notification list.
void setDefaultItem (MenuItem item)	Sets the specified menu item as the default item for this menu.
void setEnabled(boolean enabled)	If enabled is true, enables this menu. Otherwise, disables this menu.
void setLocation(int x, int y).	Sets this menu's location relative to the display
void setLocation(Point location)	Sets this menu's location relative to the display.
void setVisible(boolean visible)	If visible is true, shows this menu. Otherwise, hides this menu.

Table 5-25. `MenuItem` *Methods*

Method	Description
void addArmListener (ArmListener listener)	Adds a listener that's notified when the item is about to be selected ("armed").
void addHelpListener(Help Listener listener)	Adds a listener that's notified when the user requests help, usually by pressing F1.
void addSelectionListener (SelectionListener listener)	Adds a listener that's notified when this item is selected.
int getAccelerator()	Returns this item's accelerator key.
boolean getEnabled()	Returns true if this item is enabled or false if it's not enabled.
Image getImage()	Returns this item's image or null if it has no image.
Menu getMenu()	Returns the dropdown menu associated with this item (if this item is a cascade menu) or null if it has no associated menu.
Menu getParent()	Returns this item's parent menu.
boolean getSelection()	Returns true if this item is selected or false if it's not selected.
String getText()	Returns this item's text.
boolean isEnabled()	Returns true if this item and all its ancestors are enabled or false if it or any of its ancestors isn't enabled.
void removeArmListener (ArmListener listener)	Removes the specified listener from the notification list.
void removeHelpListener (HelpListener listener)	Removes the specified listener from the notification list.
void removeSelection Listener(SelectionListener listener)	Removes the specified listener from the notification list.
void setAccelerator(int accelerator)	Sets this item's accelerator key.
void setEnabled(boolean enabled)	If enabled is true, enables this item. Otherwise, disables this item.
void setImage(Image image)	Sets this item's image.
void setMenu(Menu menu)	Sets this item's dropdown menu.
void setSelection(boolean selected)	If selected is true, selects this item. Otherwise, deselects this item.
void setText(String text)	Sets this item's text.

One method that you'll use virtually every time you create a menu item is its setText() method. Otherwise, the item will be blank, and users will have no idea what they're selecting. You'll use setMenu() to associate a dropdown menu with its parent. You can enable and disable menu items and entire menus by calling the appropriate setEnabled() method, and you can show and hide both menus and menu items by calling setVisible().

Selecting Menu Items

Both check and radio menu items can be selected, both by the user and by the program. MenuItem offers the setSelection() method to select and deselect an item. For example, to create a check menu item and select it, use the following code:

```
MenuItem item = new MenuItem(menu, SWT.CHECK);
item.setText("My Check Item");
item.setSelection(true);
```

The next bit of code creates a radio menu item and deselects it:

```
MenuItem item = new MenuItem(menu, SWT.RADIO);
item.setText("My Radio Item");
item.setSelection(false);
```

Adding Images

Menu items can display images, which can make them easier to identify. When facing a long list of textual menu items, users will appreciate an unambiguous image that directs them to their desired menu item choice at a glance. You add the image to the item by calling its setImage() method. This code shows you how:

```
MenuItem item = new MenuItem(menu, SWT.NONE);
item.setText("My Menu Item");
item.setImage(myImage);
```

Images can adorn menu items of all types and, when used judiciously, can make your menus easier to navigate. Figure 5-15 shows a menu with images.

Figure 5-15. A menu with images

Seeing Menus in Action

The Menus application listed in Listing 5-13 shows the various types of menus and menu items. It has a bar menu across the top, with a dropdown menu attached to the File menu item. The left half of the window has a popup menu with a cascading drop-down menu, a check menu item, a push menu item, and two radio groups. It also has images associated with some of the items. The right half of the window has a no radio group popup menu. Experiment with both the code and the application to see what menus can do for you.

Listing 5-13. `Menus.java`

```java
package examples.ch5;

import org.eclipse.swt.*;
import org.eclipse.swt.graphics.*;
import org.eclipse.swt.layout.*;
import org.eclipse.swt.widgets.*;

/**
 * This class demonstrates menus
 */
public class Menus {
  private Image star;
  private Image circle;
  private Image square;
  private Image triangle;

  /**
   * Runs the application
   */
  public void run() {
    Display display = new Display();
    Shell shell = new Shell(display);
    shell.setText("Menus");
    createContents(shell);
    shell.open();
    while (!shell.isDisposed()) {
      if (!display.readAndDispatch()) {
        display.sleep();
      }
    }
    if (circle != null) circle.dispose();
    if (star != null) star.dispose();
    if (square != null) square.dispose();
    if (triangle != null) triangle.dispose();
    display.dispose();
  }
```

```
/**
 * Creates the main window's contents
 *
 * @param shell the main window
 */
private void createContents(Shell shell) {
  shell.setLayout(new FillLayout());
  createBarMenu(shell);
  createPopUpMenu(shell);
  createNoRadioGroupPopUpMenu(shell);
}

/**
 * Creates the bar menu for the main window
 *
 * @param shell the main window
 */
private void createBarMenu(Shell shell) {
  // Create the bar menu
  Menu menu = new Menu(shell, SWT.BAR);

  // Create all the items in the bar menu
  MenuItem fileItem = new MenuItem(menu, SWT.CASCADE);
  fileItem.setText("File");
  MenuItem editItem = new MenuItem(menu, SWT.CASCADE);
  editItem.setText("Edit");
  MenuItem formatItem = new MenuItem(menu, SWT.CASCADE);
  formatItem.setText("Format");
  MenuItem viewItem = new MenuItem(menu, SWT.CASCADE);
  viewItem.setText("View");
  MenuItem helpItem = new MenuItem(menu, SWT.CASCADE);
  helpItem.setText("Help");

  // Create the File item's dropdown menu
  Menu fileMenu = new Menu(menu);
  fileItem.setMenu(fileMenu);

  // Create all the items in the File dropdown menu
  MenuItem newItem = new MenuItem(fileMenu, SWT.NONE);
  newItem.setText("New");
  MenuItem openItem = new MenuItem(fileMenu, SWT.NONE);
  openItem.setText("Open...");
  MenuItem saveItem = new MenuItem(fileMenu, SWT.NONE);
  saveItem.setText("Save");
  MenuItem saveAsItem = new MenuItem(fileMenu, SWT.NONE);
  saveAsItem.setText("Save As...");
  new MenuItem(fileMenu, SWT.SEPARATOR);
  MenuItem pageSetupItem = new MenuItem(fileMenu, SWT.NONE);
```

```java
        pageSetupItem.setText("Page Setup...");
        MenuItem printItem = new MenuItem(fileMenu, SWT.NONE);
        printItem.setText("Print...");
        new MenuItem(fileMenu, SWT.SEPARATOR);
        MenuItem exitItem = new MenuItem(fileMenu, SWT.NONE);
        exitItem.setText("Exit");

        // Set the bar menu as the menu in the shell
        shell.setMenuBar(menu);
    }

    /**
     * Creates the left-half of the popup menu
     *
     * @param shell the main window
     */
    private void createPopUpMenu(Shell shell) {
        // Create a composite that the popup menu will be
        // associated with
        Label label = new Label(shell, SWT.BORDER);
        label.setText("Pop-up Menu");

        // Create the popup menu
        Menu menu = new Menu(label);

        // Create the images
        star = new Image(shell.getDisplay(), this.getClass().getResourceAsStream(
            "/images/star.gif"));
        circle = new Image(shell.getDisplay(), this.getClass().getResourceAsStream(
            "/images/circle.gif"));
        square = new Image(shell.getDisplay(), this.getClass().getResourceAsStream(
            "/images/square.gif"));
        triangle = new Image(shell.getDisplay(), this.getClass().getResourceAsStream(
            "/images/triangle.gif"));

        // Create all the items in the popup menu
        MenuItem newItem = new MenuItem(menu, SWT.CASCADE);
        newItem.setText("New");
        newItem.setImage(star);
        MenuItem refreshItem = new MenuItem(menu, SWT.NONE);
        refreshItem.setText("Refresh");
        refreshItem.setImage(circle);
        MenuItem deleteItem = new MenuItem(menu, SWT.NONE);
        deleteItem.setText("Delete");

        new MenuItem(menu, SWT.SEPARATOR);
```

```
    // Add a check menu item and select it
    MenuItem checkItem = new MenuItem(menu, SWT.CHECK);
    checkItem.setText("Check");
    checkItem.setSelection(true);
    checkItem.setImage(square);

    // Add a push menu item
    MenuItem pushItem = new MenuItem(menu, SWT.PUSH);
    pushItem.setText("Push");

    new MenuItem(menu, SWT.SEPARATOR);

    // Create some radio items
    MenuItem item1 = new MenuItem(menu, SWT.RADIO);
    item1.setText("Radio One");
    item1.setImage(triangle);
    MenuItem item2 = new MenuItem(menu, SWT.RADIO);
    item2.setText("Radio Two");
    MenuItem item3 = new MenuItem(menu, SWT.RADIO);
    item3.setText("Radio Three");

    // Create a new radio group
    new MenuItem(menu, SWT.SEPARATOR);

    // Create some radio items
    MenuItem itema = new MenuItem(menu, SWT.RADIO);
    itema.setText("Radio A");
    MenuItem itemb = new MenuItem(menu, SWT.RADIO);
    itemb.setText("Radio B");
    MenuItem itemc = new MenuItem(menu, SWT.RADIO);
    itemc.setText("Radio C");

    // Create the New item's dropdown menu
    Menu newMenu = new Menu(menu);
    newItem.setMenu(newMenu);

    // Create the items in the New dropdown menu
    MenuItem shortcutItem = new MenuItem(newMenu, SWT.NONE);
    shortcutItem.setText("Shortcut");
    MenuItem iconItem = new MenuItem(newMenu, SWT.NONE);
    iconItem.setText("Icon");

    // Set the popup menu as the popup for the label
    label.setMenu(menu);
}
```

```
/**
 * Creates the no radio group popup menu
 *
 * @param shell the main window
 */
private void createNoRadioGroupPopUpMenu(Shell shell) {
    // Create a composite that the popup menu will be
    // associated with
    Label label = new Label(shell, SWT.BORDER);
    label.setText("No Radio Group Menu");

    // Create the popup menu with the no radio group style
    Menu menu = new Menu(shell, SWT.POP_UP | SWT.NO_RADIO_GROUP);
    label.setMenu(menu);

    // Create all the items in the popup menu
    MenuItem item1 = new MenuItem(menu, SWT.RADIO);
    item1.setText("Radio One");
    MenuItem item2 = new MenuItem(menu, SWT.RADIO);
    item2.setText("Radio Two");
    MenuItem item3 = new MenuItem(menu, SWT.RADIO);
    item3.setText("Radio Three");

    // Set the popup menu as the popup for the label
    label.setMenu(menu);
}

/**
 * The application entry point
 *
 * @param args the command line arguments
 */
public static void main(String[] args) {
    new Menus().run();
}
}
```

Either create the necessary images or download them with the source codes, and copy them to a directory called images that's a peer to the examples directory.

Running this application produces the window shown in Figure 5-16. Right-click (or use your platform's appropriate mouse button or keystroke) the left half of the window to see the popup menu, and right-click the right half to see the no radio group menu. Click the File menu item in the bar menu to show its dropdown menu.

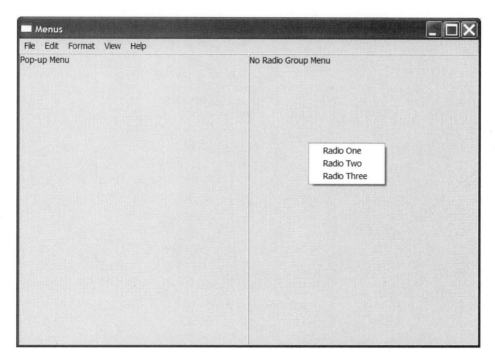

Figure 5-16. The Menus application

Summary

The extensive palette of widgets that SWT offers allows you to build user interfaces that range from the simple to the complex. The wide variety of controls accommodates many types of programs, and the widgets conform to a common usage pattern. By using a peer system, wrapping Java code around native widgets, SWT guarantees that the widgets you use in your applications look and behave as users expect.

CHAPTER 6

Events

DISPLAYING A USEFUL SET of graphical components, however elegantly and dynamically laid out, garners neither accolades nor loyalty if your applications don't respond to user input. When users click buttons or select menu items, for example, your applications better do something in response. Users quickly lose interest in applications that ignore them.

The scheme that a windowing system uses to deliver events into application code is known as the "event model." SWT communicates events using the Observer design pattern, in which listeners implement a well-known interface and register their interest with sources. When an event occurs, the source broadcasts the event to its list of registered listeners. The listeners then choose how to respond to the event.

Understanding Untyped vs. Typed Listeners

SWT offers two types of listeners: untyped and typed. Though less friendly to code with, untyped listeners can lead to smaller, though potentially uglier, code. Typed listeners lead to more modular designs and also make clear which events a particular widget supports. Either typed or untyped widgets work equally well in running code.

Introducing Untyped Listeners

The untyped listener interface, represented by the `Listener` interface, contains one method:

```
void handleEvent(Event event)
```

It resides in the `org.eclipse.swt.widgets` package, as does the `Event` object it receives. `Event` offers an amalgam of public members, described in Table 6-1, that contains data relevant to the particular event. Note that members irrelevant to a particular event contain garbage. Use the member data to determine how to respond to the event.

Table 6-1. Event *Members*

Member	Description
`int button`	The one-based index of the button that was clicked or released.
`char character`	The character that was typed.
`int count`	The number of pending paint events.
`Object data`	Application-specific data.
`int detail`	A detail constant from the SWT class that contains details about the event.

Table 6-1. Event *Members (continued)*

Member	Description
Display display	The display where the event occurred.
boolean doit	A flag indicating whether to process this event. Not supported for all events.
int end	The end of the range of modified text.
GC gc	The graphics context associated with this event.
int height	The height in pixels of the rectangle that needs painting.
Widget item	The widget where the event occurred.
int keyCode	The key code of the key that was typed.
int start	The beginning of the range of modified text.
int stateMask	The mask describing the state of the modifier keys at the time of the event.
String text	The text to insert.
int time	The event's time.
int type	The type of the event. This is the field to switch on to handle the various event types.
Widget widget	The widget that issued the event.
int width	The width in pixels of the rectangle that needs painting.
int x	Either the x offset of the rectangle that needs painting or the x coordinate of the mouse pointer at the time of the event, depending on the event.
int y	Either the y offset of the rectangle that needs painting or the y coordinate of the mouse pointer at the time of the event, depending on the event.

Using the untyped event mechanism can result in an untamed morass of spaghetti code if you're not careful. You can also freely add listeners to widgets for events that the widgets don't support. The compiler won't complain, and the program won't throw exceptions at run time. The program will blithely ignore your listeners, however, and might inflict frustrating debugging sessions as you wonder why your listeners aren't being called. Consider yourself warned.

To add an untyped listener to a widget, call addListener() on it. Its signature looks like this:

```
void addListener(int eventType, Listener listener)
```

eventType contains one of the event type constants from the SWT class, described in Table 6-2. Each type constant corresponds to an event that can occur in your programs. The Listener class represented by the listener parameter can be named or anonymous and can be inner or outer, though you'll usually use an anonymous inner class. To add a listener to a button, for example, that reacts when the button is clicked, use code like this:

```
button.addListener(SWT.Selection, new Listener() {
  public void handleEvent(Event e) {
    switch (e.type) {
    case SWT.Selection:
      System.out.println("Button pressed");
      break;
    }
  }
};
```

Table 6-2. Event *Types*

Type	Description
SWT.Activate	Triggered when the widget becomes the active window
SWT.Arm	Triggered when the widget is armed
SWT.Close	Triggered when the widget is closed
SWT.Collapse	Triggered when a tree node is collapsed
SWT.Deactivate	Triggered when the widget is no longer the active window
SWT.DefaultSelection	Triggered when the default selection occurs
SWT.Deiconify	Triggered when the widget is restored from being minimized
SWT.Dispose	Triggered when the widget is disposed
SWT.DragDetect	Triggered when the widget is dragged
SWT.Expand	Triggered when a tree node is expanded
SWT.FocusIn	Triggered when the widget gains focus
SWT.FocusOut	Triggered when the widget loses focus
SWT.HardKeyDown	Triggered when a special hardware key, such as on a Pocket PC device, is pressed
SWT.HardKeyUp	Triggered when a special hardware key, such as on a Pocket PC device, is released
SWT.Help	Triggered when the user requests help
SWT.Hide	Triggered when the widget is hidden
SWT.Iconify	Triggered when the widget is minimized
SWT.KeyDown	Triggered when the user presses a key
SWT.KeyUp	Triggered when the user releases a key
SWT.MenuDetect	Triggered when a menu is selected
SWT.Modify	Triggered when the text of a widget is modified
SWT.MouseDoubleClick	Triggered when the mouse is double-clicked
SWT.MouseDown	Triggered when the mouse button is clicked
SWT.MouseEnter	Triggered when the mouse pointer enters the widget
SWT.MouseExit	Triggered when the mouse pointer exits the widget
SWT.MouseHover	Triggered when the mouse pointer hovers over the widget
SWT.MouseMove	Triggered when the mouse pointer moves through the widget

Table 6-2. Event Types (continued)

Type	Description
SWT.MouseUp	Triggered when the mouse button is released
SWT.Move	Triggered when the widget is moved
SWT.None	Null event
SWT.Paint	Triggered when the widget is painted
SWT.Resize	Triggered when the widget is resized
SWT.Selection	Triggered when the widget is selected
SWT.Show	Triggered when the widget is shown
SWT.Traverse	Triggered when the user tabs through the controls
SWT.Verify	Triggered when the text for the widget is about to change, allowing you to veto the change

Introducing Typed Listeners

Typed listeners live in a different package—org.eclipse.swt.events—as if to distance themselves from the taint of untyped listeners. Instead of relying on generic methods, listeners, and events, typed listeners use classes and interfaces specific to each possible event. For instance, to listen for a button click, you register a SelectionListener implementation with the button using the button's addSelectionListener() method. SelectionListener contains a method called widgetSelected() that's called when the button is pressed. Its signature is as follows:

```
void widgetSelected(SelectionEvent event)
```

You can see that the method to add the listener specifies what type of listener to add. The listener itself has a specific type. The method called when the event triggers also shuns the generic handleEvent(). Finally, the event itself carries a specific type. No trace of the untyped event model's blandness remains.

All typed events ultimately derive from a common class: TypedEvent. This class contains the public members common to all the typed events described in Table 6-3. Each event class potentially contains other members that carry further data specific to the event. For example, many event classes have a boolean member called doit that you can set to false to cancel the processing of that event.

Table 6-3. TypedEvent Members

Member	Description
Object data	Contains application-specific data
Display display	The display where the event occurred
int time	The time at which the event occurred
Widget widget	The source of the event

Implementations of the typed listener interfaces must define each method declared by the interface. For interfaces that define only one method, this presents no hardship. Interfaces that define more than one method, however, can make you do more work than you had planned. For example, the SelectionListener interface mentioned previously has a second method—widgetDefaultSelected()—that you must implement whether you have any response for it. To alleviate this burden, SWT provides implementations of every listener interface that has more than one method. The names of these classes end in Adapter.

Table 6-4 describes each typed listener with its associated event class and adapter, if applicable.

Table 6-4. Typed Listeners

Listener	Description	Event	Adapter
ArmListener	Listens for arm events	ArmEvent	None
ControlListener	Listens for move and resize events	ControlEvent	ControlAdapter
DisposeListener	Listens for dispose events	DisposeEvent	None
FocusListener	Listens for focus gained and lost events	FocusEvent	FocusAdapter
HelpListener	Listens for help requests	HelpEvent	None
KeyListener	Listens for key presses and releases	KeyEvent	KeyAdapter
MenuListener	Listens for menu events	MenuEvent	MenuAdapter
ModifyListener	Listens for text modifications	ModifyEvent	None
MouseListener	Listens for mouse button presses	MouseEvent	MouseAdapter
MouseMoveListener	Listens for mouse movements	MouseEvent	None
MouseTrackListener	Listens for when the mouse enters, exits, or hovers over a control	MouseEvent	MouseTrackAdapter
PaintListener	Listens for paint events	PaintEvent	None
SelectionListener	Listens for selection events (for example, button clicks)	SelectionEvent	SelectionAdapter
ShellListener	Listens for shell events	ShellEvent	ShellAdapter
TraverseListener	Listens for traverse events	TraverseEvent	None
TreeListener	Listens for tree events	TreeEvent	TreeAdapter
VerifyListener	Listens for, and potentially intercepts, text modifications	VerifyEvent	None

The balance of this chapter examines a representative sample of the typed listeners through code.

Using SelectionListener and DisposeListener

If buttons or menus form any part of your application's interface, you'll surely create SelectionListeners to respond when users click the buttons or select the menus. The DisposeListenerExample program demonstrates SelectionListener (see Listing 6-1). It also demonstrates DisposeListener, which is notified on the associated widget's disposal. It creates two shell windows, one a child of the other. The parent shell displays a message. The child shell displays a message and a button. Clicking the button or closing the child shell changes the message on the main shell.

Listing 6-1. DisposeListenerExample.java

```java
package examples.ch6;

import org.eclipse.swt.SWT;
import org.eclipse.swt.events.*;
import org.eclipse.swt.layout.*;
import org.eclipse.swt.widgets.*;

/**
 * This class demonstrates SelectionListener and DisposeListener
 */
public class DisposeListenerExample {
  /**
   * The application entry point
   *
   * @param args the command line arguments
   */
  public static void main(String[] args) {
    Display display = new Display();

    // Create the main window
    Shell mainShell = new Shell(display);
    mainShell.setLayout(new FillLayout());
    mainShell.setText("Big Brother");
    final Label mainMessage = new Label(mainShell, SWT.LEFT);
    mainMessage.setText("Don't even think about it");

    // Create the child shell and the dispose listener
    final Shell childShell = new Shell(mainShell);
    childShell.addDisposeListener(new DisposeListener() {
      public void widgetDisposed(DisposeEvent event) {
        // When the child shell is disposed, change the message on the main shell
        mainMessage.setText("Gotcha");
      }
    });
    childShell.setLayout(new FillLayout());
    childShell.setText("little brother");

    // Put a message on the child shell
    new Label(childShell, SWT.LEFT)
        .setText("If you dispose me, my big brother's gonna get you!");
```

```
    // Add a button and a listener to the child shell
    Button button = new Button(childShell, SWT.PUSH);
    button.setText("Close Me!");
    button.addSelectionListener(new SelectionAdapter() {
      public void widgetSelected(SelectionEvent event) {
        // When the button is clicked, close the child shell
        childShell.close();
      }
    });

    // Open the shells
    mainShell.open();
    childShell.open();

    while (!mainShell.isDisposed()) {
      if (!display.readAndDispatch()) {
        display.sleep();
      }
    }
    display.dispose();
  }
}
```

Using ControlListener

A ControlListener listens for resize or move events. The ControlListenerExample program displays a whimsical image in a window (see Listing 6-2). If you resize the window so that the image doesn't fit inside it, the image disappears and a message displays. Resize the window large enough, and the image reappears.

Listing 6-2. ControlListenerExample.java

```
package examples.ch6;

import org.eclipse.swt.SWT;
import org.eclipse.swt.events.*;
import org.eclipse.swt.graphics.*;
import org.eclipse.swt.layout.*;
import org.eclipse.swt.widgets.*;

/**
 * This class demonstrates ControlListeners
 */
public class ControlListenerExample {
  /**
```

```
 * Runs the application
 */
public void run() {
  Display display = new Display();
  Shell shell = new Shell(display);
  Image image = new Image(display, "happyGuy.gif");
  createContents(shell, image);
  shell.pack();
  shell.open();

  while (!shell.isDisposed()) {
    if (!display.readAndDispatch()) {
      display.sleep();
    }
  }
  if (image != null) image.dispose();
  display.dispose();
}

/**
 * Creates the main window's contents
 *
 * @param shell the main window
 * @param image the image
 */
private void createContents(Shell shell, Image image) {
  shell.setLayout(new GridLayout());

  // Create a label to hold the image
  Label label = new Label(shell, SWT.NONE);
  label.setLayoutData(new GridData(GridData.VERTICAL_ALIGN_BEGINNING));
  label.setImage(image);
  shell.setData(label);

  // Add the listener
  shell.addControlListener(new ControlAdapter() {
    public void controlResized(ControlEvent event) {
      // Get the event source (the shell)
      Shell shell = (Shell) event.getSource();

      // Get the source's data (the label)
      Label label = (Label) shell.getData();

      // Determine how big the shell should be to fit the image
      Rectangle rect = shell.getClientArea();
      ImageData data = label.getImage().getImageData();
```

```
      // If the shell is too small, hide the image
      if (rect.width < data.width || rect.height < data.height) {
        shell.setText("Too small.");
        label.setText("I'm melting!");
      } else {
        // He fits!
        shell.setText("Happy Guy Fits!");
        label.setImage(label.getImage());
      }
    }
  });
}


/**
 * Application entry point
 *
 * @param args the command line arguments
 */
public static void main(String[] args) {
  new ControlListenerExample().run();
}
}
```

Figure 6-1 shows the application's window sized large enough to hold the image, and Figure 6-2 shows the window sized too small.

Figure 6-1. The window showing the image

Figure 6-2. The window when too small

Using FocusListener

FocusListener is informed when a control gains or loses the focus. The Focus-
ListenerExample program displays six buttons (see Listing 6-3). It creates a
FocusListener that changes the button's text when it gains or loses focus and adds
the listener to each button. Tab through or click the buttons to see the text change.

Listing 6-3. FocusListenerExample.java

```
package examples.ch6;

import org.eclipse.swt.SWT;
import org.eclipse.swt.events.*;
import org.eclipse.swt.layout.*;
import org.eclipse.swt.widgets.*;

/**
 * This class demonstrates FocusListener
 */
public class FocusListenerExample {

  /**
   * The application entry point
   *
   * @param args the command line arguments
   */
  public static void main(String[] args) {
    // Create the shell
    Display display = new Display();
    Shell shell = new Shell(display);
    shell.setLayout(new GridLayout(3, true));
    shell.setText("One Potato, Two Potato");
```

```
    // Create the focus listener
    FocusListener listener = new FocusListener() {
      public void focusGained(FocusEvent event) {
        Button button = (Button) event.getSource();
        button.setText("I'm It!");
      }

      public void focusLost(FocusEvent event) {
        Button button = (Button) event.getSource();
        button.setText("Pick Me!");
      }
    };

    // Create the buttons and add the listener to each one
    for (int i = 0; i < 6; i++) {
      Button button = new Button(shell, SWT.PUSH);
      button.setLayoutData(new GridData(GridData.FILL_HORIZONTAL));
      button.setText("Pick Me!");
      button.addFocusListener(listener);
    }

    // Display the window
    shell.pack();
    shell.open();
    while (!shell.isDisposed()) {
      if (!display.readAndDispatch()) {
        display.sleep();
      }
    }
    display.dispose();
  }
}
```

Figure 6-3 shows the program's window with the focus on the bottom-right button. Notice that its text differs from the other buttons' text.

Figure 6-3. The FocusListenerExample program

Using MouseListener, MouseMoveListener, and MouseTrackListener

SWT divides mouse-related activity into three separate listener interfaces for performance reasons. One advantage of SWT's event model is that when an event occurs that has no registered listeners, the event drops out early in the event-handling process. For events that happen infrequently, passing an event all the way into application-specific code, just to be ignored, has little impact on performance. Events that occur frequently, however, would waste valuable resources to deliver a large quantity of events into application code where they'll ultimately be ignored. To avoid burning CPU cycles, SWT divides mouse event handling into logical categories based on their frequency.

At the lowest frequency, the MouseListener interface receives notification of mouse click events. MouseTrackListener, at the middle frequency, receives notification when the mouse enters, exits, or hovers over the associated widget. Finally, at the highest frequency, MouseMoveListener receives notification each time the mouse moves. The MouseEventExample program implements all three interfaces, displaying information any time one of them receives mouse events (see Listing 6-4).

Listing 6-4. MouseEventExample.java

```
package examples.ch6;

import org.eclipse.swt.SWT;
import org.eclipse.swt.events.*;
import org.eclipse.swt.layout.*;
import org.eclipse.swt.widgets.*;

/**
 * This class demonstrates mouse events
 */
public class MouseEventExample implements MouseListener, MouseMoveListener,
    MouseTrackListener {

  // The label to hold the messages from mouse events
  Label myLabel = null;

  /**
   * MouseEventExample constructor
   *
   * @param shell the shell
   */
  public MouseEventExample(Shell shell) {
    myLabel = new Label(shell, SWT.BORDER);
    myLabel.setText("I ain't afraid of any old mouse");
    shell.addMouseListener(this);
    shell.addMouseMoveListener(this);
    shell.addMouseTrackListener(this);
  }
```

```
/**
 * The application entry point
 *
 * @param args the command line arguments
 */
public static void main(String[] args) {
  // Create the window
  Display display = new Display();
  Shell shell = new Shell(display);
  shell.setLayout(new GridLayout());
  shell.setSize(450, 200);
  shell.setText("Mouse Event Example");

  // Create the listener
  MouseEventExample myMouseEventExample = new MouseEventExample(shell);

  // Display the window
  shell.open();
  while (!shell.isDisposed()) {
    if (!display.readAndDispatch()) {
      display.sleep();
    }
  }
  display.dispose();
}

/**
 * Called when user double-clicks the mouse
 */
public void mouseDoubleClick(MouseEvent e) {
  myLabel.setText("Double Click " + e.button + " at: " + e.x + "," + e.y);
}

/**
 * Called when user clicks the mouse
 */
public void mouseDown(MouseEvent e) {
  myLabel.setText("Button " + e.button + " Down at: " + e.x + "," + e.y);
}

/**
 * Called when user releases the mouse after clicking
 */
public void mouseUp(MouseEvent e) {
  myLabel.setText("Button " + e.button + " Up at: " + e.x + "," + e.y);
}
```

```
/**
 * Called when user moves the mouse
 */
public void mouseMove(MouseEvent e) {
  myLabel.setText("Mouse Move at: " + e.x + "," + e.y);
}


/**
 * Called when user enters the shell with the mouse
 */
public void mouseEnter(MouseEvent e) {
  myLabel.setText("Mouse Enter at: " + e.x + "," + e.y);
}


/**
 * Called when user exits the shell with the mouse
 */
public void mouseExit(MouseEvent e) {
  myLabel.setText("Mouse Exit at: " + e.x + "," + e.y);
}


/**
 * Called when user hovers the mouse
 */
public void mouseHover(MouseEvent e) {
  myLabel.setText("Mouse Hover at: " + e.x + "," + e.y);
}
}
```

Figure 6-4 shows the program's window after the release of the first button.

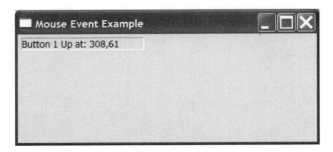

Figure 6-4. The MouseEventExample program

Using Several Listeners

The MultipleListenersExample program uses three listeners—ModifyListener,
VerifyListener, and HelpListener—to present a temperature conversion utility (see
Listing 6-5). It displays two text fields, one for Fahrenheit temperatures and one for

Celsius temperatures. Type a temperature in one field to see the appropriate converted value in the other. Press F1 while the cursor is in one of the text fields to display context-sensitive help.

The application uses ModifyListener to detect when the text in one of the text fields changes, so it can calculate the converted value and display it in the other text field. It uses VerifyListener to prevent the user from typing invalid characters (for example, letters) into the temperature fields. Finally, it uses HelpListener to display the help.

Listing 6-5. MultipleListenersExample.java

```java
package examples.ch6;

import org.eclipse.swt.SWT;
import org.eclipse.swt.events.*;
import org.eclipse.swt.layout.*;
import org.eclipse.swt.widgets.*;

/**
 * This class demonstrates various listeners
 */
public class MultipleListenersExample implements HelpListener, VerifyListener,
    ModifyListener {

  // Constants used for conversions
  private static final double FIVE_NINTHS = 5.0 / 9.0;
  private static final double NINE_FIFTHS = 9.0 / 5.0;

  // Widgets used in the window
  private Text fahrenheit;
  private Text celsius;
  private Label help;

  /**
   * Runs the application
   */
  public void run() {
    Display display = new Display();
    Shell shell = new Shell(display);
    shell.setText("Temperatures");
    createContents(shell);
    shell.pack();
    shell.open();
    while (!shell.isDisposed()) {
      if (!display.readAndDispatch()) {
        display.sleep();
      }
    }
    display.dispose();
  }
```

```java
/**
 * Create the main window's contents
 * @param shell the main window
 */
private void createContents(Shell shell) {
  shell.setLayout(new GridLayout(3, true));

  // Create the label and input box for Fahrenheit
  new Label(shell, SWT.LEFT).setText("Fahrenheit:");
  fahrenheit = new Text(shell, SWT.BORDER);
  GridData data = new GridData(GridData.FILL_HORIZONTAL);
  data.horizontalSpan = 2;
  fahrenheit.setLayoutData(data);

  // Set the context-sensitive help
  fahrenheit.setData("Type a temperature in Fahrenheit");

  // Add the listeners
  fahrenheit.addHelpListener(this);
  fahrenheit.addVerifyListener(this);
  fahrenheit.addModifyListener(this);

  // Create the label and input box for Celsius
  new Label(shell, SWT.LEFT).setText("Celsius:");
  celsius = new Text(shell, SWT.BORDER);
  data = new GridData(GridData.FILL_HORIZONTAL);
  data.horizontalSpan = 2;
  celsius.setLayoutData(data);

  // Set the context-sensitive help
  celsius.setData("Type a temperature in Celsius");

  // Add the listeners
  celsius.addHelpListener(this);
  celsius.addVerifyListener(this);
  celsius.addModifyListener(this);

  // Create the area for help
  help = new Label(shell, SWT.LEFT | SWT.BORDER);
  data = new GridData(GridData.FILL_HORIZONTAL);
  data.horizontalSpan = 3;
  help.setLayoutData(data);
}

/**
 * Called when user requests help
 */
public void helpRequested(HelpEvent event) {
```

```
  // Get the help text from the widget and set it into the help label
  help.setText((String) event.widget.getData());
}

/**
 * Called when the user types into a text box, but before the text box gets
 * what the user typed
 */
public void verifyText(VerifyEvent event) {
  // Assume you don't allow it
  event.doit = false;

  // Get the character typed
  char myChar = event.character;
  String text = ((Text) event.widget).getText();

  // Allow '-' if first character
  if (myChar == '-' && text.length() == 0) event.doit = true;

  // Allow zero to nine
  if (Character.isDigit(myChar)) event.doit = true;

  // Allow backspace
  if (myChar == '\b') event.doit = true;
}

/**
 * Called when the user modifies the text in a text box
 */
public void modifyText(ModifyEvent event) {
  // Remove all the listeners, so you don't enter any infinite loops
  celsius.removeVerifyListener(this);
  celsius.removeModifyListener(this);
  fahrenheit.removeVerifyListener(this);
  fahrenheit.removeModifyListener(this);

  // Get the widget whose text was modified
  Text text = (Text) event.widget;

  try {
    // Get the modified text
    int temp = Integer.parseInt(text.getText());

    // If they modified Fahrenheit, convert to Celsius
    if (text == fahrenheit) {
      celsius.setText(String.valueOf((int) (FIVE_NINTHS * (temp - 32))));
    } else {
```

```
      // Convert to Fahrenheit
      fahrenheit.setText(String.valueOf((int) (NINE_FIFTHS * temp + 32)));
    }
  } catch (NumberFormatException e) { /* Ignore */ }

  // Add the listeners back
  celsius.addVerifyListener(this);
  celsius.addModifyListener(this);
  fahrenheit.addVerifyListener(this);
  fahrenheit.addModifyListener(this);
}

/**
 * The application entry point
 * @param args the command line arguments
 */
public static void main(String[] args) {
  new MultipleListenersExample().run();
}
}
```

Figure 6-5 shows the window with a temperature entered and some help text displayed.

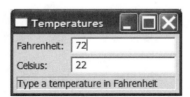

Figure 6-5. Converting temperatures

Summary

In contrast to poker, which rewards stoicism, applications must react to their surroundings. Specifically, they must react appropriately and expectedly to user input. Whether you opt for the massive switch statement approach offered by untyped listeners or the modular approach of typed listeners, you can receive notifications for virtually anything that happens to your applications. If you opt for the typed approach, be sure to take advantage of the adapter classes, where applicable, to save yourself from implementing empty methods for events that don't interest you.

CHAPTER 7

Dialogs

Users interact with applications primarily through the applications' main windows.
For example, in a word processor, users type their documents in the main window,
change font styles and sizes using the menu housed by the main window, and print
using the print button on the main window's toolbar. Often, users never leave the main
application window for the duration of their interaction with the application.

Sometimes, however, the main application window doesn't have sufficient space
to handle all necessary user interactions. Perhaps the application must display an informational message related to a temporary state, or ask for confirmation before performing a destructive operation. Reserving perpetual space in the main application window
for this interaction would unnecessarily clog the main window. Instead, the main window delegates these sorts of tasks to dialog windows that pop up, accomplish the specific task, and disappear.

SWT provides wrapper classes for six common dialogs:

- Message box

- Color Selection dialog

- Directory Selection dialog

- File Open/File Save dialog

- Font Selection dialog

- Print dialog

This chapter discusses five of the six common dialogs, deferring discussion of the
Print dialog to Chapter 12, which covers printing. It also explains how to create and use
your own dialog classes.

Using the Dialogs

The common dialog classes in SWT descend from SWT's abstract `Dialog` class
(`org.eclipse.swt.widgets.Dialog`). A dialog's parent, which is passed to the constructor, is always a `Shell` object. Dialogs can be modal, which means they disallow
input to other windows until they're dismissed, or modeless. "Modeless" means they
allow input to all other windows while they're displayed. Different levels of modality

are available, each of which disallows input to different sets of windows. Not all platforms support all modalities; this is a restriction of the underlying platforms, not SWT. The parent and mode, expressed by constants and combined with any other appropriate style, are passed to the constructor. Table 7-1 lists the mode constants.

Table 7-1. Mode Constants

Constant	Description
SWT.APPLICATION_MODAL	Modal to the application; input is blocked to other windows in the application, but input to other applications isn't blocked.
SWT.PRIMARY_MODAL	Modal to the parent window of the dialog; input is blocked to the parent of the dialog only, but input to other dialogs in the application, or to any windows in other applications, isn't blocked.
SWT.SYSTEM_MODAL	Input is blocked to all other windows of all applications until the dialog is dismissed.
SWT.NONE	Modeless (the default).

NOTE   *All the common dialogs default to primary modal, though you change the modality by passing the appropriate style to the constructor. Your custom dialogs can use any of the offered modalities.*

The `Dialog` class provides methods to get and to set the text in the title bar:

```
String getText() // Gets the title bar text
void setText(String text) // Sets the title bar text
```

When creating your own dialog classes, discussed at the end of this chapter, you derive from `Dialog`; you never subclass any of the common dialog classes, however much you are tempted to do so. The SWT documentation mentions this design intention, which is neither arbitrary nor mean spirited. The SWT common dialog classes wrap common dialogs provided by the various platforms that SWT supports, and these common dialogs vary widely across the several platforms. Because the common dialogs can differ from platform to platform in look, widget placement, and features, trying to change behavior that might or might not exist across platforms would be problematic at best, and catastrophic at worst. For example, your common dialog subclass might work perfectly on Windows, and work with some glitches on Linux GTK+, but fizzle miserably on Mac OS X. If the common dialogs don't meet your requirements, don't subclass them; write your own dialogs from scratch.

CAUTION   *Don't subclass SWT's common dialog classes!*

Whenever you use one of SWT's dialog classes (or one you've created yourself), you follow a pattern:

1. Instantiate the dialog, passing the parent Shell and any pertinent style constants.

2. Set any pertinent data into the dialog.

3. Call the dialog's open() method, which displays the dialog, receives the user input, and returns the selected data when the user dismisses the dialog.

4. Do something with the returned data.

In code, this procedure looks something like this:

```
<DialogType> dlg = new <DialogType>(shell);
dlg.setSomeData(data);
<ReturnType> returnValue = dlg.open();
if (returnValue == null) {
  // User clicked cancel
} else {
  // Do something with returnValue
}
```

Message boxes, implemented by the class MessageBox, deviate slightly from this pattern: their open() methods return an int, not an Object, so testing for null doesn't compile. The int that open() returns is the style value of the button used to dismiss it. The next section covers message boxes.

Displaying Messages

Marriage counselors harp on the importance of communication; your applications must heed the same advice and communicate to your users. You commonly need to display information and get simple responses, whether merely acknowledgments that the user has read the presented information or answers to questions that affect processing. For example, an application might alert users that an entered value is out of range, or might ask users if they really want to delete a file. Use the MessageBox class for these communications, when all you need to do is display some simple text or ask a question, and receive one of the following responses:

- OK

- Yes

- No

- Cancel

- Retry

- Abort

- Ignore

Displaying a Message Box

To display a message box, create a `MessageBox` object and call its `open()` method, like this:

```
MessageBox messageBox = new MessageBox(shell);
messageBox.open();
```

This creates a default message box, seen in Figure 7-1. Of course, this empty message box wouldn't impress users. You must do a little more work to customize the message box and make it useful.

Figure 7-1. A default message box

A message box contains four customizable pieces of information:

- The text in the title bar

- The text message displayed within the dialog

- The icon displayed within the dialog

- The buttons displayed within the dialog

As with the other dialog classes, call `setText()` to change the text in the title bar. For example, write this to display the text "Important Message!" in the message box's title bar:

```
messageBox.setText("Important Message!");
```

The text message displays within the window of the dialog, above any buttons. It usually contains the information you're presenting or the question you're posing. Call setMessage() to change the text message:

```
messageBox.setMessage("Are you sure you want to delete the file?");
```

The icons and buttons are determined at construction by the style bits passed to the constructor. Combine the desired icon style with the desired buttons into an int using the bitwise OR operator. Table 7-2 lists the icon styles, and Table 7-3 lists the button styles.

Table 7-2. The Icon Styles for MessageBox

Style	Description
SWT.ICON_ERROR	Displays the error icon
SWT.ICON_INFORMATION	Displays the information icon
SWT.ICON_QUESTION	Displays the question icon
SWT.ICON_WARNING	Displays the warning icon
SWT.ICON_WORKING	Displays the working icon

Only one icon displays in the message box, so you should pass only one of the icon styles to the constructor. Passing more than one produces undefined behavior.

Table 7-3. The Button Styles for MessageBox

Style	Description
SWT.OK	Displays an OK button
SWT.OK | SWT.CANCEL	Displays an OK and a Cancel button
SWT.YES | SWT.NO	Displays a Yes and a No button
SWT.YES | SWT.NO | SWT.CANCEL	Displays a Yes, a No, and a Cancel button
SWT.RETRY | SWT.CANCEL	Displays a Retry and a Cancel button
SWT.ABORT | SWT.RETRY | SWT.IGNORE	Displays an Abort, a Retry, and an Ignore button

For example, to display a message box with the question icon, a button labeled Yes, a button labeled No, and a simple question, use this code:

```
MessageBox messageBox = new MessageBox(shell, SWT.ICON_QUESTION | SWT.YES |
   SWT.NO);
messageBox.setMessage("Is this question simple?");
int rc = messageBox.open();
```

Clicking one of the buttons closes the dialog and returns the int value of the selected button to the calling application. For example, if the user clicked the button labeled Yes in the message box created by this code, rc would equal SWT.YES.

NOTE *You might try to create different combinations of buttons by mixing the button constants, such as* SWT.YES *and* SWT.ABORT. *However, SWT ignores all but the listed combinations.*

Table 7-4 lists MessageBox's methods. Figures 7-2 through 7-7 display various button and icon combinations for message boxes on Windows. Icons differ across platforms.

Table 7-4. MessageBox *Methods*

Method	Description
String getMessage()	Returns the text message displayed within the message box
int open()	Opens the message box and returns the style constant corresponding to the button clicked to dismiss the message box
void setMessage(String string)	Sets the text message displayed within the message box

Figure 7-2. An informational message box

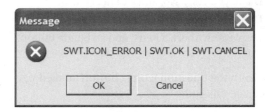

Figure 7-3. An error message box

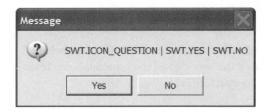

Figure 7-4. A yes/no question message box

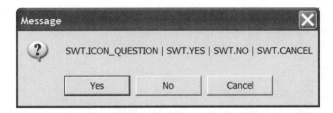

Figure 7-5. A yes/no/cancel question message box

Figure 7-6. A warning message box

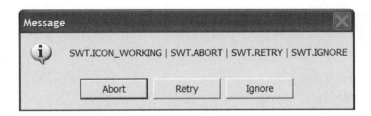

Figure 7-7. An abort/retry/ignore message box

Customizing a Message Box

The ShowMessageBox program in Listing 7-1 allows you to type a message, select an icon and button style, and click the Show Message button to display a message box with your information. It displays the return value of the message box's open( ) method, which is the style constant of the selected button. Figure 7-8 shows its main window.

Listing 7-1. ShowMessageBox.java

```
package examples.ch7;

import org.eclipse.swt.*;
import org.eclipse.swt.events.*;
import org.eclipse.swt.layout.*;
import org.eclipse.swt.widgets.*;
```

```java
/**
 * This class demonstrates the MessageBox class
 */
public class ShowMessageBox {
  // Strings to show in the Icon dropdown
  private static final String[] ICONS = { "SWT.ICON_ERROR",
      "SWT.ICON_INFORMATION", "SWT.ICON_QUESTION", "SWT.ICON_WARNING",
      "SWT.ICON_WORKING"};

  // Strings to show in the Buttons dropdown
  private static final String[] BUTTONS = { "SWT.OK", "SWT.OK | SWT.CANCEL",
      "SWT.YES | SWT.NO", "SWT.YES | SWT.NO | SWT.CANCEL",
      "SWT.RETRY | SWT.CANCEL", "SWT.ABORT | SWT.RETRY | SWT.IGNORE"};

  /**
   * Runs the application
   */
  public void run() {
    Display display = new Display();
    Shell shell = new Shell(display);
    shell.setText("Show Message Box");
    createContents(shell);
    shell.pack();
    shell.open();
    while (!shell.isDisposed()) {
      if (!display.readAndDispatch()) {
        display.sleep();
      }
    }
    display.dispose();
  }

  /**
   * Creates the main window's contents
   *
   * @param shell the parent shell
   */
  private void createContents(final Shell shell) {
    shell.setLayout(new GridLayout(2, false));

    // Create the dropdown to allow icon selection
    new Label(shell, SWT.NONE).setText("Icon:");
    final Combo icons = new Combo(shell, SWT.DROP_DOWN | SWT.READ_ONLY);
    for (int i = 0, n = ICONS.length; i < n; i++)
      icons.add(ICONS[i]);
    icons.select(0);
```

```
// Create the dropdown to allow button selection
new Label(shell, SWT.NONE).setText("Buttons:");
final Combo buttons = new Combo(shell, SWT.DROP_DOWN | SWT.READ_ONLY);
for (int i = 0, n = BUTTONS.length; i < n; i++)
  buttons.add(BUTTONS[i]);
buttons.select(0);

// Create the entry field for the message
new Label(shell, SWT.NONE).setText("Message:");
final Text message = new Text(shell, SWT.BORDER);
message.setLayoutData(new GridData(GridData.FILL_HORIZONTAL));

// Create the label to show the return from the open call
new Label(shell, SWT.NONE).setText("Return:");
final Label returnVal = new Label(shell, SWT.NONE);
returnVal.setLayoutData(new GridData(GridData.FILL_HORIZONTAL));

// Create the button and event handler
// to display the message box
Button button = new Button(shell, SWT.PUSH);
button.setText("Show Message");
button.addSelectionListener(new SelectionAdapter() {
  public void widgetSelected(SelectionEvent event) {
    // Clear any previously returned value
    returnVal.setText("");

    // This will hold the style to pass to the MessageBox constructor
    int style = 0;

    // Determine which icon was selected and
    // add it to the style
    switch (icons.getSelectionIndex()) {
    case 0:
      style |= SWT.ICON_ERROR;
      break;
    case 1:
      style |= SWT.ICON_INFORMATION;
      break;
    case 2:
      style |= SWT.ICON_QUESTION;
      break;
    case 3:
      style |= SWT.ICON_WARNING;
      break;
    case 4:
      style |= SWT.ICON_WORKING;
      break;
    }
```

```java
// Determine which set of buttons was selected
// and add it to the style
switch (buttons.getSelectionIndex()) {
case 0:
  style |= SWT.OK;
  break;
case 1:
  style |= SWT.OK | SWT.CANCEL;
  break;
case 2:
  style |= SWT.YES | SWT.NO;
  break;
case 3:
  style |= SWT.YES | SWT.NO | SWT.CANCEL;
  break;
case 4:
  style |= SWT.RETRY | SWT.CANCEL;
  break;
case 5:
  style |= SWT.ABORT | SWT.RETRY | SWT.IGNORE;
  break;
}

// Display the message box
MessageBox mb = new MessageBox(shell, style);
mb.setText("Message from SWT");
mb.setMessage(message.getText());
int val = mb.open();
String valString = "";
switch (val) // val contains the constant of the selected button
{
case SWT.OK:
  valString = "SWT.OK";
  break;
case SWT.CANCEL:
  valString = "SWT.CANCEL";
  break;
case SWT.YES:
  valString = "SWT.YES";
  break;
case SWT.NO:
  valString = "SWT.NO";
  break;
case SWT.RETRY:
  valString = "SWT.RETRY";
  break;
case SWT.ABORT:
```

```
                valString = "SWT.ABORT";
                break;
            case SWT.IGNORE:
                valString = "SWT.IGNORE";
                break;
            }
            returnVal.setText(valString);
        }
    });
}


/**
 * Application entry point
 *
 * @param args the command line arguments
 */
public static void main(String[] args) {
    new ShowMessageBox().run();
}
}
```

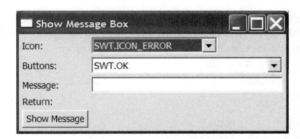

Figure 7-8. The ShowMessageBox application

Experiment with the ShowMessageBox application. Notice the various icons used on your platform. Understand the return values from the open() method. You'll use message boxes time and again in your applications to communicate with users.

Choosing a Color

The color selection dialog displays the spectrum of available screen colors, allowing users to select one by clicking it. Chapter 10, which covers graphics, discusses color much more in depth. For the purposes of this chapter, you need only understand that colors on a computer screen comprise the following three components.

- Red

- Green

- Blue

These are stored as integers, each ranging from zero to 255. The union of red, green, and blue is commonly abbreviated to RGB. SWT provides a class called RGB that stores RGB values. Its sole constructor takes three int parameters, one for each color component:

```
public RGB(int red, int green, int blue)
```

Note that the RGB class holds the data that can represent a color, but does not itself represent a color—a subtle, yet important, distinction. SWT provides a class called Color that represents an actual color, and can be instantiated by passing both the device the color will be displayed on and an RGB object to its constructor, like this:

```
RGB rgb = new RGB(255, 0, 0); // pure red
Color color = new Color(display, rgb);
```

NOTE *You manage the* Color *objects you create, and therefore you must dispose them when you're through using them by calling* dispose(). RGB *objects are merely data and represent no operating system resources, so therefore aren't disposed.*

Displaying the Color Selection Dialog

ColorDialog offers the standard two SWT constructors: one that takes a parent, and one that takes a parent and a style. The parent is always a Shell, so the two constructors look like this:

```
public ColorDialog(Shell parent)
public ColorDialog(Shell parent, int style)
```

Because no styles apply to ColorDialog, you'll usually call the single-argument constructor.

Table 7-5 lists the methods for ColorDialog. The open() method displays the color selection dialog and returns an RGB object containing the appropriate values for the selected color, or null if the dialog was cancelled. You can use this RGB object to create a Color object for use anywhere in your applications. Here's the syntax for using ColorDialog to have users select a color and then for creating a Color object to match the selected color:

```
ColorDialog dlg = new ColorDialog(shell);
RGB rgb = dlg.open();
if (rgb != null) {
  Color color = new Color(shell.getDisplay(), rgb);
  // Do something with color
  // Remember to call color.dispose() when your application is done with color
}
```

 CAUTION   *Don't dispose a color while your application is still using it.*

Table 7-5. ColorDialog *Methods*

Method	Description
RGB getRGB()	Returns the RGB object containing the red, green, and blue values for the color selected, or null if no color was selected
RGB open()	Displays the color selection dialog and returns the RGB object containing the red, green, and blue values for the color selected, or null if no color was selected
void setRGB(RGB rgb)	Selects the color whose red, green, and blue values match those of the passed RGB object

Customizing the Color Selection Dialog

You can change the text in the title bar of the color dialog by calling setText(), passing a String containing the new text. However, you'll usually leave the default text intact. What you'll usually customize, though, is the color that's initially selected, matching it to any previously selected color. To select a color, call setRGB(), passing an RGB object that contains the red, green, and blue values for the color you want selected. For example, to display a color selection dialog with the color blue selected, you use this code:

```
ColorDialog dlg = new ColorDialog(shell);
dlg.setRGB(new RGB(0, 0, 255));
dlg.open();
```

The ChooseColor program in Listing 7-2 demonstrates ColorDialog. It displays a color and a button. Click the button to show the standard color selection dialog. Choose a color to change the color display in the main application window.

Listing 7-2. ChooseColor.java

```java
package examples.ch7;

import org.eclipse.swt.*;
import org.eclipse.swt.events.*;
import org.eclipse.swt.graphics.*;
import org.eclipse.swt.layout.*;
import org.eclipse.swt.widgets.*;

/**
 * This class demonstrates the ColorDialog class
 */
public class ChooseColor {
  private Color color;

  /**
   * Runs the application
   */
  public void run() {
    Display display = new Display();
    Shell shell = new Shell(display);
    shell.setText("Color Chooser");
    createContents(shell);
    shell.pack();
    shell.open();
    while (!shell.isDisposed()) {
      if (!display.readAndDispatch()) {
        display.sleep();
      }
    }
    // Dispose the color we created for the Label
    if (color != null) {
      color.dispose();
    }
    display.dispose();
  }

  /**
   * Creates the window contents
   *
   * @param shell the parent shell
   */
  private void createContents(final Shell shell) {
    shell.setLayout(new GridLayout(2, false));
```

```
    // Start with Celtics green
    color = new Color(shell.getDisplay(), new RGB(0, 255, 0));

    // Use a label full of spaces to show the color
    final Label colorLabel = new Label(shell, SWT.NONE);
    colorLabel.setText("                              ");
    colorLabel.setBackground(color);

    Button button = new Button(shell, SWT.PUSH);
    button.setText("Color...");
    button.addSelectionListener(new SelectionAdapter() {
      public void widgetSelected(SelectionEvent event) {
        // Create the color-change dialog
        ColorDialog dlg = new ColorDialog(shell);

        // Set the selected color in the dialog from
        // user's selected color
        dlg.setRGB(colorLabel.getBackground().getRGB());

        // Change the title bar text
        dlg.setText("Choose a Color");

        // Open the dialog and retrieve the selected color
        RGB rgb = dlg.open();
        if (rgb != null) {
          // Dispose the old color, create the
          // new one, and set into the label
          color.dispose();
          color = new Color(shell.getDisplay(), rgb);
          colorLabel.setBackground(color);
        }
      }
    });
  }

  /**
   * The application entry point
   *
   * @param args the command line arguments
   */
  public static void main(String[] args) {
    new ChooseColor().run();
  }
}
```

Figure 7-9 shows the main window for the application, while Figure 7-10 shows the standard color selection dialog on Windows.

Figure 7-9. *The ChooseColor application's main window*

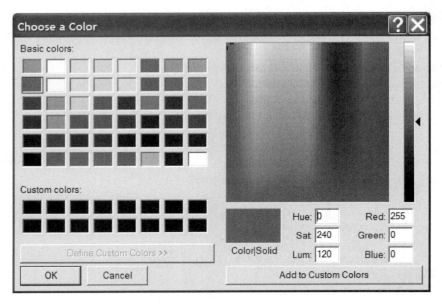

Figure 7-10. *The standard color selection dialog on Windows*

Browsing Directories

One of the raging questions clogging message boards when Windows 95 appeared was how to present a standard directory-selection dialog. Windows 95, and all subsequent 32-bit Windows operating systems, do offer a directory selection dialog, but it's somewhat confusing to program. It involves memory structures, item identifier lists, and shell programming; a typical use in C++ might look like this:

```
BROWSEINFO bi;
ZeroMemory(&bi, sizeof(BROWSEINFO));
bi.hwndOwner = AfxGetMainWnd()->m_hWnd;
bi.ulFlags = BIF_RETURNONLYFSDIRS;
LPITEMIDLIST pidl = SHBrowseForFolder(&bi);
if (pidl != NULL) {
  CString strDir;
  LPTSTR szPath = strDir.GetBuffer(MAX_PATH + 1);
  SHGetPathFromIDList(pidl, szPath);
  strDir.ReleaseBuffer();
  // Do something with the selected directory, now in strDir
}
```

SWT's DirectoryDialog class is, thankfully, simpler to use, yet provides all the same functionality as SHBrowseForFolder()—and is, of course, cross platform. You'll use this class whenever your applications require a user-selected directory, whether it's for an installation location, a location to store the MP3 files users (legally) rip using your CD recording software, or for any other situation requiring a directory.

Displaying the Directory Selection Dialog

As with the other dialog classes, DirectoryDialog must have a Shell as its parent. It has no applicable styles, and provides, in addition to the standard parent-and-style constructor, a constructor that takes only a parent:

```
public DirectoryDialog(Shell parent, int style)
public DirectoryDialog(Shell parent)
```

Table 7-6 lists DirectoryDialog's methods. The open() method opens the dialog, allows the user to navigate through the file system to select a directory, and returns the selected directory as a String. Here's the syntax for creating the dialog and retrieving the selected directory:

```
DirectoryDialog dlg = new DirectoryDialog(shell);
String selectedDirectory = dlg.open();
```

This code displays the dialog seen in Figure 7-11. Note that in the preceding code, selectedDirectory contains null if the dialog is dismissed via its Cancel button. Otherwise, it contains the selected directory.

Table 7-6. DirectoryDialog *Methods*

Method	Description
String getFilterPath()	Returns the selected directory
String getMessage()	Returns the message displayed within the dialog
String getText()	Returns the text displayed in the dialog's title bar
String open()	Displays the dialog and returns the full path to the selected directory, or null if the user cancels the dialog
void setFilterPath(String string)	Sets the initial directory to select and display
void setMessage(String string)	Sets the message to display within the dialog
void setText(String string)	Sets the text to display in the dialog's title bar

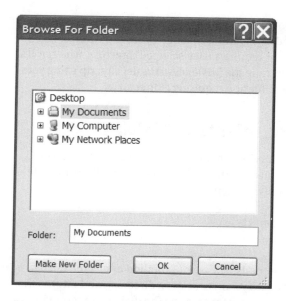

Figure 7-11. The standard DirectoryDialog

Customizing the Directory Selection Dialog

You have a few options for customizing the dialog. You can change these:

- The text displayed in the title bar

- The text displayed as a message

- The initially selected and displayed directory

Call setText(), passing the desired text, to change what's displayed in the title bar. Call setMessage(), passing your custom message, to change the message text. Finally, call setFilterPath(), passing in the desired initial directory as a String. If the path doesn't exist, it will be ignored.

The ShowDirectoryDialog program in Listing 7-3 provides a text box for directory entry, and a button labeled Browse that displays a DirectoryDialog. Selecting a directory in the dialog updates the text box in the main window with the full path of the selected directory. The code looks like this:

Listing 7-3. ShowDirectoryDialog.java

```
package examples.ch7;

import org.eclipse.swt.*;
import org.eclipse.swt.events.*;
import org.eclipse.swt.layout.*;
import org.eclipse.swt.widgets.*;
```

```java
/**
 * This class demonstrates the DirectoryDialog class
 */
public class ShowDirectoryDialog {
  /**
   * Runs the application
   */
  public void run() {
    Display display = new Display();
    Shell shell = new Shell(display);
    shell.setText("Directory Browser");
    createContents(shell);
    shell.pack();
    shell.open();
    while (!shell.isDisposed()) {
      if (!display.readAndDispatch()) {
        display.sleep();
      }
    }
  }

  /**
   * Creates the window contents
   *
   * @param shell the parent shell
   */
  private void createContents(final Shell shell) {
    shell.setLayout(new GridLayout(6, true));
    new Label(shell, SWT.NONE).setText("Directory:");

    // Create the text box extra wide to show long paths
    final Text text = new Text(shell, SWT.BORDER);
    GridData data = new GridData(GridData.FILL_HORIZONTAL);
    data.horizontalSpan = 4;
    text.setLayoutData(data);

    // Clicking the button will allow the user
    // to select a directory
    Button button = new Button(shell, SWT.PUSH);
    button.setText("Browse...");
    button.addSelectionListener(new SelectionAdapter() {
      public void widgetSelected(SelectionEvent event) {
        DirectoryDialog dlg = new DirectoryDialog(shell);

        // Set the initial filter path according
        // to anything they've selected or typed in
        dlg.setFilterPath(text.getText());
```

```
    // Change the title bar text
    dlg.setText("SWT's DirectoryDialog");

    // Customizable message displayed in the dialog
    dlg.setMessage("Select a directory");

    // Calling open() will open and run the dialog.
    // It will return the selected directory, or
    // null if user cancels
    String dir = dlg.open();
    if (dir != null) {
      // Set the text box to the new selection
      text.setText(dir);
    }
  }
});
}

/**
 * The application entry point
 *
 * @param args the command line arguments
 */
public static void main(String[] args) {
  new ShowDirectoryDialog().run();
}
}
```

The main window for the application looks like Figure 7-12. Click the button labeled Browse to display the directory selection dialog, shown in Figure 7-13. Experiment with the application to see the interaction.

Figure 7-12. The ShowDirectoryDialog main window

Figure 7-13. A customized DirectoryDialog

Selecting Files for Open or Save

The lifeblood of most applications, files typically contain all the data that users have painstakingly and laboriously entered into your programs. If your applications can't open and save files properly, users will be streaking to uninstall them. The interface for opening and saving files must be simple and painless. Luckily for you, you don't have to design or implement a solution; SWT's FileDialog displays the common open and save file dialogs your users are accustomed to.

Displaying the Open or Save File Dialog

FileDialog offers two constructors:

```
public FileDialog(Shell parent, int style)
public FileDialog(Shell parent)
```

The parent must be a Shell, and style designates whether the dialog is for opening a single file, opening multiple files, or saving a file. The style constants are listed in Table 7-7. If you specify both SWT.OPEN and SWT.SAVE, the results are undefined.

Table 7-8 lists FileDialog's methods. To open an Open FileDialog, use this code:

```
FileDialog dlg = new FileDialog(shell, SWT.OPEN);
String fileName = dlg.open();
if (fileName != null) {
  // Open the file
}
```

Table 7-7. FileDialog *Constants*

Constant	Description
SWT.OPEN	Creates a dialog for opening a single file. This is the default.
SWT.MULTI	Creates a dialog for opening multiple files.
SWT.SAVE	Creates a dialog for saving a file.

Table 7-8. FileDialog *Methods*

Method	Description
String getFileName()	Returns the name of the selected file relative to the filter path. When multiple files are selected, returns the name of the first selected file relative to the filter path.
String[] getFileNames()	Returns the names of all selected files, relative to the filter path.
String[] getFilterExtensions()	Returns the filter extensions used by the dialog.
String[] getFilterNames()	Returns the filter names used by the dialog.
String getFilterPath()	Returns the filter path used by the dialog.
String getText()	Returns the title bar text.
String open()	Displays the file dialog and returns the full path of the selected file.
void setFileName(String string)	Sets the name of the file to select initially when the dialog appears.
void setFilterExtensions (String[] extensions)	Sets the filter extensions the user can choose from to filter the files the dialog displays.
void setFilterNames (String[] names)	Sets the filter names the user can choose from to filter the files the dialog displays.
void setFilterPath(String string)	Sets the filter path.
void setText(String text)	Sets the title bar text.

Specifying File Types and Extensions

Both Open and Save file dialogs allow you to specify the types of files your applications can open and save, both by description and by extension. These types you specify are commonly called filters, because they filter which files are displayed in the dialog. FileDialog provides methods for setting these filter descriptions and extensions:

```
setFilterNames(String[] names);
setFilterExtensions(String[] extensions);
```

The filter names and extensions are passed in parallel arrays of Strings. You'll typically use static data, either hard-coded or read from a resource bundle. Convention dictates that the filter names show their corresponding filter extensions in parentheses, but this is entirely optional and has no bearing on which files are filtered. If you pass more filter names than filter extensions, the extraneous names are ignored. However, if you pass more filter extensions than filter names, the extra filter extensions are retained, and are used as the filter names as well. For example, a program that opens tabular data from various other programs might set its filter names and extensions like this:

```
dlg.setFilterNames(new String[] {
  "OpenOffice.org Spreadsheet Files (*.sxc)",
  "Microsoft Excel Spreadsheet Files (*.xls)",
  "Comma Separated Values Files (*.csv)",
  "All Files (*.*)"
});
dlg.setFilterExtensions(new String[] {
  "*.sxc", "*.xls", "*.csv", "*.*"
};
```

Figure 7-14 shows the Open dialog using these names and extensions, and Figure 7-15 shows the Save dialog.

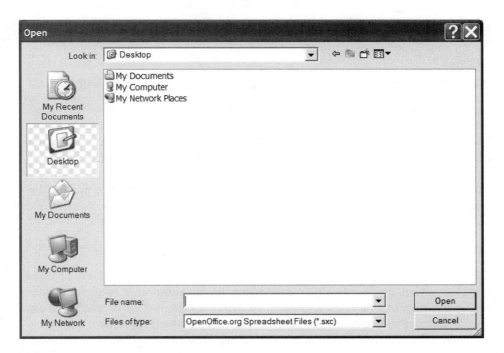

Figure 7-14. The File Open dialog

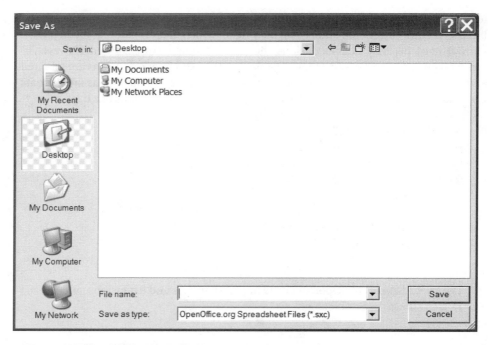

Figure 7-15. The File Save dialog

Specifying the Starting Directory and File Name

Users appreciate applications that remember where they like to open and save files, without having to navigate through the directory tree every time. FileDialog's setFilterPath() method allows you to specify the initial directory for the dialog. You can retrieve this information by calling getFilterPath(), and store it in the user's preferences for future use.

Some applications suggest a file name to use for saving a file by prefilling the entry field in the Save dialog box. You can do the same by calling setFileName(), passing the suggested file name, before calling the open() method.

Getting the Selected File or Files

Usually you'll save the return value from calling open(), which contains the full path of the selected file (or null if the user cancelled the dialog). However, in some situations you'll want more or different information. Perhaps you want just the file name, without the path, or you've allowed selection of multiple files. The getFileName() method returns just the selected file's name, without the path information. The getFilterPath() method returns just the path information. You can stitch the two together to get the full path to the file.

When you're dealing with multiple files, you must stitch the paths and file names together to get full path names to the selected files. The getFileNames() method returns an array of Strings containing just the selected files' names, without path information.

Use the getFilterPath() method to get the path to prepend. For example, to store the full path names for all selected files into a collection called files, write code like this:

```
FileDialog dlg = new FileDialog(shell, SWT.MULTI);
Collection files = new ArrayList();
if (dlg.open() != null) {
  String[] names = dlg.getFileNames();
  for (int i = 0, n = names.length(); i < n; i++) {
    StringBuffer buf = new StringBuffer(dlg.getFilterPath());
    if (buf.charAt(buf.length() - 1) != File.separatorChar)
      buf.append(File.separatorChar);
    buf.append(names[i]);
    files.add(buf.toString());
  }
}
```

Using the File Dialogs

The example application in Listing 7-4, ShowFileDialog, demonstrates how to use FileDialog. It displays three buttons: Open Multiple, Open, and Save. Clicking a button displays the file dialog in the requested mode. The text box in the main application window displays any selected files. Figure 7-16 shows the application.

Figure 7-16. The ShowFileDialog application

Listing 7-4. ShowFileDialog.java

```
package examples.ch7;

import java.io.File;
import org.eclipse.swt.*;
import org.eclipse.swt.events.*;
import org.eclipse.swt.layout.*;
import org.eclipse.swt.widgets.*;

/**
 * This class demonstrates FileDialog
 */
```

```
public class ShowFileDialog {
  // These filter names are displayed to the user in the file dialog. Note that
  // the inclusion of the actual extension in parentheses is optional, and
  // doesn't have any effect on which files are displayed.
  private static final String[] FILTER_NAMES = {
      "OpenOffice.org Spreadsheet Files (*.sxc)",
      "Microsoft Excel Spreadsheet Files (*.xls)",
      "Comma Separated Values Files (*.csv)", "All Files (*.*)"};

  // These filter extensions are used to filter which files are displayed.
  private static final String[] FILTER_EXTS = { "*.sxc", "*.xls", "*.csv", "*.*"};

  /**
   * Runs the application
   */
  public void run() {
    Display display = new Display();
    Shell shell = new Shell(display);
    shell.setText("File Dialog");
    createContents(shell);
    shell.pack();
    shell.open();
    while (!shell.isDisposed()) {
      if (!display.readAndDispatch()) {
        display.sleep();
      }
    }
    display.dispose();
  }

  /**
   * Creates the contents for the window
   *
   * @param shell the parent shell
   */
  public void createContents(final Shell shell) {
    shell.setLayout(new GridLayout(5, true));

    new Label(shell, SWT.NONE).setText("File Name:");

    final Text fileName = new Text(shell, SWT.BORDER);
    GridData data = new GridData(GridData.FILL_HORIZONTAL);
    data.horizontalSpan = 4;
    fileName.setLayoutData(data);

    Button multi = new Button(shell, SWT.PUSH);
    multi.setText("Open Multiple...");
```

```
multi.addSelectionListener(new SelectionAdapter() {
  public void widgetSelected(SelectionEvent event) {
    // User has selected to open multiple files
    FileDialog dlg = new FileDialog(shell, SWT.MULTI);
    dlg.setFilterNames(FILTER_NAMES);
    dlg.setFilterExtensions(FILTER_EXTS);
    String fn = dlg.open();
    if (fn != null) {
      // Append all the selected files. Since getFileNames() returns only
      // the names, and not the path, prepend the path, normalizing
      // if necessary
      StringBuffer buf = new StringBuffer();
      String[] files = dlg.getFileNames();
      for (int i = 0, n = files.length; i < n; i++) {
        buf.append(dlg.getFilterPath());
        if (buf.charAt(buf.length() - 1) != File.separatorChar) {
          buf.append(File.separatorChar);
        }
        buf.append(files[i]);
        buf.append(" ");
      }
      fileName.setText(buf.toString());
    }
  }
});

Button open = new Button(shell, SWT.PUSH);
open.setText("Open...");
open.addSelectionListener(new SelectionAdapter() {
  public void widgetSelected(SelectionEvent event) {
    // User has selected to open a single file
    FileDialog dlg = new FileDialog(shell, SWT.OPEN);
    dlg.setFilterNames(FILTER_NAMES);
    dlg.setFilterExtensions(FILTER_EXTS);
    String fn = dlg.open();
    if (fn != null) {
      fileName.setText(fn);
    }
  }
});

Button save = new Button(shell, SWT.PUSH);
save.setText("Save...");
save.addSelectionListener(new SelectionAdapter() {
  public void widgetSelected(SelectionEvent event) {
    // User has selected to save a file
    FileDialog dlg = new FileDialog(shell, SWT.SAVE);
```

```
        dlg.setFilterNames(FILTER_NAMES);
        dlg.setFilterExtensions(FILTER_EXTS);
        String fn = dlg.open();
        if (fn != null) {
           fileName.setText(fn);
        }
     }
  });
}


/**
 * The application entry point
 *
 * @param args the command line arguments
 */
public static void main(String[] args) {
  new ShowFileDialog().run();
}
}
```

Warning Before Overwriting Existing Files

Before you become too smug about how simply you can get file names for opening and saving, try this: in the ShowFileDialog sample application, select to save a file, and in the ensuing File dialog box, select an existing file and click OK. Don't you expect a warning, saying that the file already exists, and do you want to overwrite it? No such warning displays, and the file name is returned to the application without any indication that you've selected an existing file. For the ShowFileDialog application, this presents no problem, as no files are saved and no overwriting happens. However, if your applications overwrite users' files without seeking confirmation, your users won't use them for long. Users expect applications to request confirmation before performing destructive actions.

Scanning FileDialog's documentation reveals no method call or style setting to address this problem, nor does the source code. The omission seems curious, until you remember that not only is SWT cross platform, but also that it uses each operating environment's native dialogs. Not all Save dialogs offer built-in support for warning before overwriting files. SWT doesn't address this problem directly; you must solve it yourself.

Following object-oriented principles would lead you to subclass FileDialog and provide your own implementation for the open() method. However, SWT warns against subclassing its dialog classes, so shun that solution. Instead, create a façade that wraps FileDialog, passing all method calls but open() to the underlying FileDialog instance. The code samples accompanying this book include the full source of an example class—SafeSaveDialog. You can find the code samples in the Downloads section of the Apress Web site (http://www.apress.com). SafeSaveDialog has a private FileDialog member:

```
private FileDialog dlg;
```

This member is constructed in the SafeSaveDialog constructor:

```
public SafeSaveDialog(Shell shell) {
  dlg = new FileDialog(shell, SWT.SAVE);
}
```

SWT provides wrapper methods for the entire FileDialog API that simply pass the request to the dlg member variable. However, the open() method is different, and looks like this:

```
public String open() {
  // Store the selected file name in fileName
  String fileName = null;

  // The user has finished when one of the
  // following happens:
  // 1) The user dismisses the dialog by pressing Cancel
  // 2) The selected file name does not exist
  // 3) The user agrees to overwrite existing file
  boolean done = false;

  while (!done) {
    // Open the File Dialog
    fileName = dlg.open();
    if (fileName == null) {
      // User has cancelled, so quit and return
      done = true;
    }
    else {
      // User has selected a file; see if it already exists
      File file = new File(fileName);
      if (file.exists()) {
        // The file already exists; asks for confirmation
        MessageBox mb = new MessageBox(dlg.getParent(),
          SWT.ICON_WARNING | SWT.YES | SWT.NO);

        mb.setMessage(fileName + " already exists. Do you want to replace it?");

        // If they click Yes, drop out. If they click No,
        // redisplay the File Dialog
        done = mb.open() == SWT.YES;
      } else {
        // File does not exist, so drop out
        done = true;
```

```
            }
         }
      }
   }
   return fileName;
}
```

If the user selects an existing file from within SafeSaveDialog, a message box appears asking for confirmation. If the user selects not to overwrite the existing file, the file dialog reappears, and will continue reappearing until the user cancels the File dialog, selects a file name that doesn't represent an existing file, or answers Yes to the warning.

Choosing a Font

With early word processors, users were tickled enough that they could edit the content on screen before printing their documents onto paper. No longer shackled to the irreversibility of typewriters, few cared whether the typeface or font on screen matched the one on the printed documents. Word processors tracked typefaces by codes or markers embedded in the text. However, as operating environments moved from text-based displays to graphical-based displays, users became more exacting about the relationship between the computer screen and the printed page. The shift to What You See Is What You Get (WYSIWYG) meant that the fonts displayed on the screen had to match the fonts printed on paper. Interfaces to allow users to select fonts evolved into today's common Font Selection dialog.

SWT provides the FontDialog class to display the common font selection dialog. FontDialog's open() method returns a FontData object (or null if the user cancels the dialog), which you can use to create a Font. Chapter 11 delves deeper into fonts; this chapter offers only enough to understand how to use FontDialog.

SWT uses two classes to represent fonts: Font, which represents the onscreen font, and FontData, which represents the data used to construct the onscreen font. You saw this paradigm earlier in the chapter, with Color representing an onscreen color and RGB representing the data used to create the color. Like Color objects, Font objects represent operating system resources, and you must dispose any you create. FontData objects contain only data, and aren't operating system resources, so they aren't disposed.

Fonts can be displayed in many colors, but neither Font nor FontData store any color information. In order to display fonts in colors other than black, controls carry both font properties and color properties, wedding them for the display. However, the common Font dialog allows color selection, as seen in Figure 7-17.

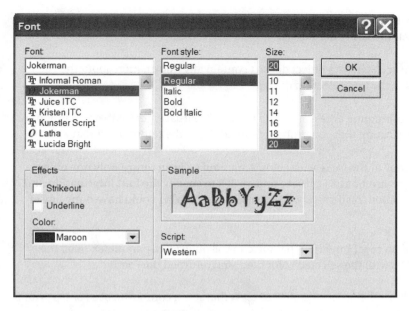

Figure 7-17. The common Font dialog

Displaying the Font Selection Dialog

To display the Font Selection dialog, create a `FontDialog` instance and call its `open()` method. The `open()` method returns a `FontData` object containing all the data necessary to create the selected font, or `null` if the user cancelled the dialog. The code looks like this:

```
FontDialog dlg = new FontDialog(shell);
FontData fontData = dlg.open();
if (fontData != null) {
  Font font = new Font(shell.getDisplay(), fontData);
  // Do something with font
  // Remember to call font.dispose() when your application is done with font
}
```

 CAUTION *Don't dispose a font while your application is still using it.*

Though using `FontDialog` seems as straightforward as using the other common dialogs, two factors muddy the waters:

- The returned `FontData` object doesn't contain any information about the color selected in the font selection dialog.

- The corresponding accessor for the returned `FontData`, `getFontData()`, is deprecated, indicating that you probably shouldn't use the returned `FontData`.

First, let's look at the issue with color. A method call can return only one object, so `open()` can't return both a `FontData` and an `RGB` to specify the font information and the color information, respectively. To solve this, `FontDialog` could have done any of the following:

- Provided an `open()` method that took an `RGB` object as a parameter, filled the passed `RGB` with the selected color data, and returned the `FontData`

- Cobbled together a `FontDataAndRGB` class that was a composite of a `FontData` and an `RGB`, and had `open()` return a `FontDataAndRGB` instance

- Returned the `FontData` containing the information about the selected font, and provided a method call to retrieve the color information

SWT's designers opted for the last option, which seems the most straightforward. So, you call `FontDialog.getRGB()` to retrieve the selected color's information. To use the font selection dialog to change both the font and the color of a label, write code that looks like this:

```
FontDialog dlg = new FontDialog(shell);
FontData fontData = dlg.open();
if (fontData != null) {
  Font font = new Font(shell.getDisplay(), fontData);
  Color color = new Color(shell.getDisplay(), dlg.getRGB());
  myLabel.setFont(font);
  myLabel.setForeground(color);
}
```

That solves the color problem. Now, why is `getFontData()` deprecated? On most platforms, a single `FontData` suffices to create the selected font. However, the X Window System can require multiple `FontData` objects to create a font. SWT 2.1 added a `Font` constructor that takes an array of `FontData` objects instead of just a single `FontData`. SWT 2.1.1 deprecated `FontDialog`'s `getFontData()` and `setFontData()` methods, and added `getFontList()` and `setFontList()` to deal with `FontData` arrays. Because changing the `open()` method to return `FontData[]` would break existing code, you're stuck with a return value you probably shouldn't use, except perhaps to determine whether the user clicked OK or Cancel.

Rewriting the preceding code to use getFontList() produces the following:

```
FontDialog dlg = new FontDialog(shell);
if (dlg.open() != null) {
  Font font = new Font(shell.getDisplay(), dlg.getFontList());
  Color color = new Color(shell.getDisplay(), dlg.getRGB());
  myLabel.setFont(font);
  myLabel.setForeground(color);
}
```

Table 7-9 lists FontDialog's methods.

Table 7-9. FontDialog *Methods*

Method	Description
FontData getFontData()	This method is deprecated; use getFontList() instead.
FontData[] getFontList()	Returns an array of FontData objects that contain the information about the selected font.
RGB getRGB()	Returns the red, green, and blue values as an RGB object for the selected color.
String getText()	Gets the title bar text for the dialog.
FontData open()	Displays the dialog and returns a FontData object representing the selected font, or null if the user cancelled the dialog.
void setFontData(FontData fontData)	This method is deprecated; use setFontList() instead.
void setFontList(FontData[] fontData)	Sets the information for the font to display as selected in the dialog.
void setRGB(RGB rgb)	Sets the RGB values for the color to display as selected in the dialog.
void setText(String text)	Sets the title bar text for the dialog.

Customizing the Font Selection Dialog

Besides changing the title bar text of the font selection dialog by calling setText(), you can set the font and color that are initially selected when the dialog appears. Call setFontList(), passing the array of FontData objects that represents the font you want to select. The Font class provides a method called getFontData that returns its array of FontData objects. Call setRGB(), passing the RGB that represents the color you want to select. The ChooseFont program in Listing 7-5 demonstrates how to do that. Its main window displays the text "The Selected Font" and a button for displaying the font selection dialog. Click the button, and the font selection dialog displays with the main window's font already selected. Figure 7-18 shows the application's main window.

Listing 7-5. ChooseFont.java

```java
package examples.ch7;

import org.eclipse.swt.*;
import org.eclipse.swt.events.*;
import org.eclipse.swt.graphics.*;
import org.eclipse.swt.layout.*;
import org.eclipse.swt.widgets.*;

/**
 * This class demonstrates the FontDialog class
 */
public class ChooseFont {
  private Font font;
  private Color color;

  /**
   * Runs the application
   */
  public void run() {
    Display display = new Display();
    Shell shell = new Shell(display);
    shell.setText("Font Chooser");
    createContents(shell);
    shell.pack();
    shell.open();
    while (!shell.isDisposed()) {
      if (!display.readAndDispatch()) {
        display.sleep();
      }
    }
    // Dispose the font and color we created
    if (font != null) font.dispose();
    if (color != null) color.dispose();

    display.dispose();
  }

  /**
   * Creates the window contents
   *
   * @param shell the parent shell
   */
  private void createContents(final Shell shell) {
    shell.setLayout(new GridLayout(2, false));
```

```
    final Label fontLabel = new Label(shell, SWT.NONE);
    fontLabel.setText("The selected font");

    Button button = new Button(shell, SWT.PUSH);
    button.setText("Font...");
    button.addSelectionListener(new SelectionAdapter() {
      public void widgetSelected(SelectionEvent event) {
        // Create the color-change dialog
        FontDialog dlg = new FontDialog(shell);

        // Prefill the dialog with any previous selection
        if (font != null) dlg.setFontList(fontLabel.getFont().getFontData());
        if (color != null) dlg.setRGB(color.getRGB());

        if (dlg.open() != null) {
          // Dispose of any fonts or colors we have created
          if (font != null) font.dispose();
          if (color != null) color.dispose();

          // Create the new font and set it into the label
          font = new Font(shell.getDisplay(), dlg.getFontList());
          fontLabel.setFont(font);

          // Create the new color and set it
          color = new Color(shell.getDisplay(), dlg.getRGB());
          fontLabel.setForeground(color);

          // Call pack() to resize the window to fit the new font
          shell.pack();
        }
      }
    });
  }

  /**
   * The application entry point
   *
   * @param args the command line arguments
   */
  public static void main(String[] args) {
    new ChooseFont().run();
  }
}
```

Figure 7-18. The ChooseFont application

Creating Your Own Dialogs

As helpful as the common dialogs are, they don't cover all, or even most, situations. You'll often need to create your own custom dialogs to accommodate your applications' needs. Custom dialogs can contain the gamut of widgets that main windows can. They can use all the same layout classes. They can be modal or modeless. They can have a fixed size, or be resizable. They're essential to most nontrivial applications.

Create dialogs to show and allow editing of preferences, to display an About box for your application, or for any other situation in which you need input from the user and don't want to (or can't) devote main window space to that input.

Creating a Dialog Class

To create your own dialog, you do the following:

1. Create a class that subclasses org.eclipse.swt.widgets.Dialog.

2. Implement a method named open() that returns an object appropriate to your dialog's purpose.

3. In open(), create the window, create the controls and event handlers (including controls and event handlers to dismiss the dialog), and display the window.

4. Provide getters and setters for any data.

For example, suppose you must implement a dialog that requests a line of text from the user. It must do the following:

- Display a customizable message that defaults to "Please enter a value:"

- Provide a text box to receive the user's input

- Provide an OK button to dismiss the dialog and return the text the user typed

- Provide a Cancel button to dismiss the dialog and return no text

Begin by creating a class that extends SWT's Dialog class:

```
public class InputDialog extends Dialog
```

Add two member variables, one to hold the customizable message and one to hold the input:

```
private String message;
private String input;
```

Add a getter and a setter for each variable, and set the default value for message in the constructor.

The bulk of your work lies in the development of the open() method, which must do the following:

1. Create a Shell object to house the dialog.

2. Create the controls (one Label, one Text, and two buttons).

3. Create event handlers for the buttons that dismiss the dialog and set the appropriate value into input (the text in the text box for the OK button, or null for the Cancel button).

4. Return the value of input.

Listing 7-6 shows the complete class.

Listing 7-6. InputDialog.java

```
package examples.ch7;

import org.eclipse.swt.*;
import org.eclipse.swt.events.*;
import org.eclipse.swt.layout.*;
import org.eclipse.swt.widgets.*;

/**
 * This class demonstrates how to create your own dialog classes. It allows users
 * to input a String
 */
public class InputDialog extends Dialog {
  private String message;
  private String input;

  /**
   * InputDialog constructor
   *
   * @param parent the parent
   */
```

```java
public InputDialog(Shell parent) {
  // Pass the default styles here
  this(parent, SWT.DIALOG_TRIM | SWT.APPLICATION_MODAL);
}

/**
 * InputDialog constructor
 *
 * @param parent the parent
 * @param style the style
 */
public InputDialog(Shell parent, int style) {
  // Let users override the default styles
  super(parent, style);
  setText("Input Dialog");
  setMessage("Please enter a value:");
}

/**
 * Gets the message
 *
 * @return String
 */
public String getMessage() {
  return message;
}

/**
 * Sets the message
 *
 * @param message the new message
 */
public void setMessage(String message) {
  this.message = message;
}

/**
 * Gets the input
 *
 * @return String
 */
public String getInput() {
  return input;
}

/**
 * Sets the input
```

```
 *
 * @param input the new input
 */
public void setInput(String input) {
  this.input = input;
}

/**
 * Opens the dialog and returns the input
 *
 * @return String
 */
public String open() {
  // Create the dialog window
  Shell shell = new Shell(getParent(), getStyle());
  shell.setText(getText());
  createContents(shell);
  shell.pack();
  shell.open();
  Display display = getParent().getDisplay();
  while (!shell.isDisposed()) {
    if (!display.readAndDispatch()) {
      display.sleep();
    }
  }
  // Return the entered value, or null
  return input;
}

/**
 * Creates the dialog's contents
 *
 * @param shell the dialog window
 */
private void createContents(final Shell shell) {
  shell.setLayout(new GridLayout(2, true));

  // Show the message
  Label label = new Label(shell, SWT.NONE);
  label.setText(message);
  GridData data = new GridData();
  data.horizontalSpan = 2;
  label.setLayoutData(data);

  // Display the input box
  final Text text = new Text(shell, SWT.BORDER);
  data = new GridData(GridData.FILL_HORIZONTAL);
```

```
        data.horizontalSpan = 2;
        text.setLayoutData(data);

        // Create the OK button and add a handler
        // so that pressing it will set input
        // to the entered value
        Button ok = new Button(shell, SWT.PUSH);
        ok.setText("OK");
        data = new GridData(GridData.FILL_HORIZONTAL);
        ok.setLayoutData(data);
        ok.addSelectionListener(new SelectionAdapter() {
          public void widgetSelected(SelectionEvent event) {
            input = text.getText();
            shell.close();
          }
        });

        // Create the cancel button and add a handler
        // so that pressing it will set input to null
        Button cancel = new Button(shell, SWT.PUSH);
        cancel.setText("Cancel");
        data = new GridData(GridData.FILL_HORIZONTAL);
        cancel.setLayoutData(data);
        cancel.addSelectionListener(new SelectionAdapter() {
          public void widgetSelected(SelectionEvent event) {
            input = null;
            shell.close();
          }
        });

        // Set the OK button as the default, so
        // user can type input and press Enter
        // to dismiss
        shell.setDefaultButton(ok);
      }
    }
```

Figure 7-19 shows the InputDialog.

Figure 7-19. The InputDialog

Using Your Dialog Class

You use your dialog class the same way you use the common dialogs:

- Construct an instance, passing the parent Shell.

- Perform any customizations by calling setters.

- Call open(), saving the return value.

- Test the return value for null. If non-null, use the value.

Here's a simple usage of the InputDialog class you created:

```
InputDialog dlg = new InputDialog(shell);
String input = dlg.open();
if (input != null) {
  // Do something with input
}
```

You can also customize the dialog by changing its title bar text and message before calling open():

```
dlg.setText("Name");
dlg.setMessage("Please enter your name:");
```

The ShowInputDialog program in Listing 7-7 uses the InputDialog class. It contains a place to display some text, and a button that says Push Me (see Figure 7-20). Pushing the button pops up the dialog. Enter some text and click OK, and the text you entered appears in the main window.

Listing 7-7. ShowInputDialog.java

```java
package examples.ch7;

import org.eclipse.swt.*;
import org.eclipse.swt.events.*;
import org.eclipse.swt.layout.*;
import org.eclipse.swt.widgets.*;

/**
 * This class demonstrates the custom InputDialog class
 */
public class ShowInputDialog {
  public void run() {
    Display display = new Display();
    Shell shell = new Shell(display);
```

```
      createContents(shell);
      shell.pack();
      shell.open();
      while (!shell.isDisposed()) {
        if (!display.readAndDispatch()) {
          display.sleep();
        }
      }
      display.dispose();
    }

    private void createContents(final Shell parent) {
      parent.setLayout(new FillLayout(SWT.VERTICAL));

      final Label label = new Label(parent, SWT.NONE);

      Button button = new Button(parent, SWT.PUSH);
      button.setText("Push Me");
      button.addSelectionListener(new SelectionAdapter() {
        public void widgetSelected(SelectionEvent event) {
          // Create and display the InputDialog
          InputDialog dlg = new InputDialog(parent);
          String input = dlg.open();
          if (input != null) {
            // User clicked OK; set the text into the label
            label.setText(input);
            label.getParent().pack();
          }
        }
      });
    }

    public static void main(String[] args) {
      new ShowInputDialog().run();
    }
  }
```

Figure 7-20. The ShowInputDialog program

Summary

Dialogs break out of the confines of the main application window, offering rich opportunities for user interaction without hogging main window space. Avail yourself of the power and ease of the standard dialog classes, whether to show error messages, allow color selection, provide file system navigation to open files, or any of the other common dialog functions. With only a few lines of code, you can incorporate proven dialogs into your applications.

Creating your own dialogs is only marginally more difficult. By adhering to the pattern that the common dialogs use, you can make your own dialogs as easy to use as the common dialogs are. Use dialogs to offload user interaction that doesn't merit a permanent place in your main application windows.

CHAPTER 8

Advanced Controls

MANY APPLICATIONS RUN admirably using only the standard controls discussed in Chapter 5, adequately presenting all application data and sufficiently handling user interaction. However, as applications become more advanced in the kinds of data they consume, process, and display, they become starved for more powerful widgets. This chapter discusses the advanced controls that SWT offers: decorations, tabs, toolbars, coolbars, sashes, tables, and trees. Using them expands the realm of problems your applications can solve.

Decorations

Decorations objects (that's not a typo; the class indeed is named Decorations, not Decoration) represent windows inside a main window. They're neither main windows (Shells) nor dialog boxes (Dialogs); they're always contained within a top-level window. They exhibit much of the same look and behavior as Shell objects, but are wholly contained inside them. Depending on how they're created, you can maximize, minimize, move, resize, and close them. They could almost fool you into thinking they'd be useful for Multiple Document Interface (MDI) applications, but they're too crippled to meaningfully stand in for full MDI windows, as this chapter explains.

The Eclipse team claims that the Decorations class was supposed to be abstract (it's the superclass of Shell), but somehow it slipped through as concrete in SWT 1.0.[1] Because changing it would break others' extant code, the Eclipse team has left it concrete and available. They warn, however (though the Javadoc documentation makes no mention of it), that the implementation is partial, and that you use it at your own risk. After reading this section, you might come to the same conclusions.

 CAUTION *The Eclipse team recommends that you not use the* Decorations *class.*

What can you use for developing MDI applications, then, if Decorations can't do MDI? SWT doesn't yet include full MDI support, though it's planned for some undetermined future release. Because the Eclipse IDE doesn't use MDI, adding the support

---

1. https://bugs.eclipse.org/bugs/show_bug.cgi?id=29891

hasn't yet risen high enough on the priority list to be implemented in SWT. Until MDI support appears, you can try to limp along with Decorations objects, or you can use tabbed interfaces to present multiple documents instead. See the section on tabs in this chapter for more information.

Creating Decorations

The appearance and behavior of Decorations objects depend on three factors:

- The constants passed to the Decorations constructor

- The capabilities of the host window manager

- The layout of the parent

Decorations has a single constructor:

```
public Decorations(Composite parent, int style)
```

Table 8-1 lists the available constants for style. You can combine multiple styles using the bitwise OR operator. Understand that the specified constants are hints to the underlying window manager, and don't provide behaviors that the window manager doesn't natively provide. For example, the SWT.ON_TOP style currently has no effect on Windows. You shouldn't subclass Decorations.

Table 8-1. Decorations *Styles*

Constant	Description
SWT.BORDER	Creates a window with a nonresizable border.
SWT.CLOSE	Creates a window that can be closed. For most window managers, this means creating a title bar with a close button.
SWT.MIN	Creates a window that can be minimized. For most window managers, this means creating a title bar with a minimize button.
SWT.MAX	Creates a window that can be maximized. For most window managers, this means creating a title bar with a maximize button.
SWT.NO_TRIM	Creates a window with no border, title bar, or any other kind of trim.
SWT.RESIZE	Creates a window with a resizable border.
SWT.TITLE	Creates a window with a title bar.
SWT.ON_TOP	Creates a window at the top of the z-order within the parent composite.
SWT.TOOL	Creates a window with a thin tool border.
SWT.SHELL_TRIM	Convenience constant that combines SWT.CLOSE, SWT.TITLE, SWT.MIN, SWT.MAX, and SWT.RESIZE.
SWT.DIALOG_TRIM	Convenience constant that combines SWT.CLOSE, SWT.TITLE, and SWT.BORDER.

Even if you never directly use the Decorations class, it's worth familiarizing yourself with its methods. Because Shell subclasses Decorations, you'll use many of these methods when working with Shells. Table 8-2 lists the methods.

Table 8-2. `Decorations` *Methods*

Method	Description
`Rectangle computeTrim(int x, int y, int width, int height)`	Returns the bounding rectangle required to hold the client area specified by the arguments.
`Rectangle getBounds()`	Returns the bounding rectangle for this `Decorations`.
`Rectangle getClientArea()`	Returns the bounding rectangle for the client area only.
`Button getDefaultButton()`	Returns the default button, or `null` if none has been set.
`Image getImage()`	Returns the image associated with this `Decorations`, or `null` if no image has been set.
`Image[] getImages()`	Returns the images associated with this `Decorations`, or `null` if no images have been set.
`Point getLocation()`	Returns this `Decorations`' location relative to its parent.
`boolean getMaximized()`	Returns `true` if this `Decorations` is maximized, or `false` if it isn't.
`Menu getMenuBar()`	Returns this `Decorations`' menu bar, or `null` if no menu bar has been set.
`boolean getMinimized()`	Returns `true` if this `Decorations` is minimized, or `false` if it isn't.
`Point getSize()`	Returns this `Decorations`' size.
`String getText()`	Returns the text this `Decorations` displays in its title bar (if it has one).
`boolean isReparentable()`	Returns `true` if the underlying windowing system supports changing the parent of this `Decorations`, or `false` if it doesn't.
`void setDefaultButton(Button button)`	Sets the default button for this `Decorations`.
`void setImage(Image image)`	Sets the image for this `Decorations`.
`void setImages(Image[] images)`	Sets the images for this `Decorations`.
`void setMaximized(boolean maximized)`	If maximized is `true`, maximizes this `Decorations`.
`void setMenuBar(Menu menu)`	Sets the menu bar for this `Decorations`.
`void setMinimized(boolean minimized)`	If minimized is `true`, minimizes this `Decorations`.
`void setText(String string)`	Sets the text that this `Decorations` displays in its title bar.
`void setVisible(boolean visible)`	If visible is `true`, shows this `Decorations`. If visible is `false`, hides it.

SWT places and sizes `Decorations` objects within the parent composite's layout just as it does for other controls. For example, if the parent composite's layout is a `GridLayout`, a child `Decorations` will initially occupy its cell in the grid, obeying all `GridData` set into it. See Chapter 4 for more information on layouts. However, once the

Decorations is initially sized and placed, it isn't confined by the layout. Resizable Decorations can be resized, and movable ones can be moved, beyond the bounds specified by the layout. However, resizing the parent window enforces anew the layout, and the child Decorations instances jump back to their initial size and position in the layout. Because this behavior will likely disconcert users, keep it in mind when designing your applications.

Displaying Decorations

The DecorationsExample program in Listing 8-1 displays nine Decorations objects, one for each distinct style. It labels each Decorations with the style used to create it. Run the application and try manipulating the Decorations objects—see which can be resized, which can be closed, which can be minimized, and which can be maximized. Remember that results will vary depending on the underlying window manager.

Listing 8-1. DecorationsExample.java

```java
package examples.ch8;

import org.eclipse.swt.*;
import org.eclipse.swt.layout.*;
import org.eclipse.swt.widgets.*;

/**
 * This application shows the various styles of Decorations
 */
public class DecorationsExample {
  /**
   * Runs the application
   */
  public void run() {
    Display display = new Display();
    Shell shell = new Shell(display);
    shell.setText("Decorations Example");
    createContents(shell);
    shell.open();
    while (!shell.isDisposed()) {
      if (!display.readAndDispatch()) {
        display.sleep();
      }
    }
    display.dispose();
  }

  /**
   * Creates the various Decorations
   *
```

```
 * @param composite the parent composite
 */
public void createContents(Composite composite) {
  // There are nine distinct styles, so create
  // a 3x3 grid
  composite.setLayout(new GridLayout(3, true));

  // The SWT.BORDER style
  Decorations d = new Decorations(composite, SWT.BORDER);
  d.setLayoutData(new GridData(GridData.FILL_BOTH));
  d.setLayout(new FillLayout());
  new Label(d, SWT.CENTER).setText("SWT.BORDER");

  // The SWT.CLOSE style
  d = new Decorations(composite, SWT.CLOSE);
  d.setLayoutData(new GridData(GridData.FILL_BOTH));
  d.setLayout(new FillLayout());
  new Label(d, SWT.CENTER).setText("SWT.CLOSE");

  // The SWT.MIN style
  d = new Decorations(composite, SWT.MIN);
  d.setLayoutData(new GridData(GridData.FILL_BOTH));
  d.setLayout(new FillLayout());
  new Label(d, SWT.CENTER).setText("SWT.MIN");

  // The SWT.MAX style
  d = new Decorations(composite, SWT.MAX);
  d.setLayoutData(new GridData(GridData.FILL_BOTH));
  d.setLayout(new FillLayout());
  new Label(d, SWT.CENTER).setText("SWT.MAX");

  // The SWT.NO_TRIM style
  d = new Decorations(composite, SWT.NO_TRIM);
  d.setLayoutData(new GridData(GridData.FILL_BOTH));
  d.setLayout(new FillLayout());
  new Label(d, SWT.CENTER).setText("SWT.NO_TRIM");

  // The SWT.RESIZE style
  d = new Decorations(composite, SWT.RESIZE);
  d.setLayoutData(new GridData(GridData.FILL_BOTH));
  d.setLayout(new FillLayout());
  new Label(d, SWT.CENTER).setText("SWT.RESIZE");

  // The SWT.TITLE style
  d = new Decorations(composite, SWT.TITLE);
  d.setLayoutData(new GridData(GridData.FILL_BOTH));
  d.setLayout(new FillLayout());
  new Label(d, SWT.CENTER).setText("SWT.TITLE");
```

```
    // The SWT.ON_TOP style
    d = new Decorations(composite, SWT.ON_TOP);
    d.setLayoutData(new GridData(GridData.FILL_BOTH));
    d.setLayout(new FillLayout());
    new Label(d, SWT.CENTER).setText("SWT.ON_TOP");

    // The SWT.TOOL style
    d = new Decorations(composite, SWT.TOOL);
    d.setLayoutData(new GridData(GridData.FILL_BOTH));
    d.setLayout(new FillLayout());
    new Label(d, SWT.CENTER).setText("SWT.TOOL");
  }

  /**
   * The entry point for the application
   *
   * @param args the command line arguments
   */
  public static void main(String[] args) {
    new DecorationsExample().run();
  }
}
```

The program's display should look like Figure 8-1. Figure 8-2 shows the application with a few windows moved, one resized, and one minimized (see the lower-left corner of the main window).

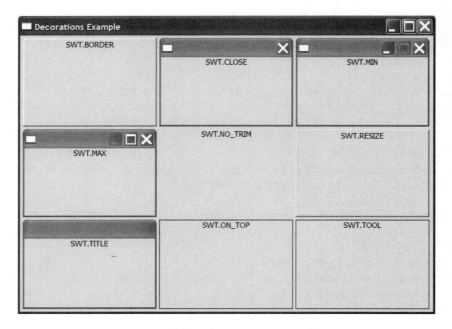

Figure 8-1. Decorations *in their applicable styles*

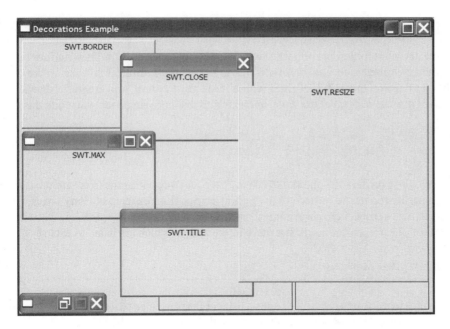

Figure 8-2. Moving, resizing, and minimizing Decorations

Remember the caveat about resizing the parent window, that it will lay out anew the Decorations objects? This can particularly become a problem if any Decorations objects have been closed. For example, GridLayouts will throw an ArrayIndexOutOfBoundsException if the parent window is resized after a child Decorations has been closed, because they will try to position a control that no longer exists. Extensively test any of your applications that use Decorations, and don't forget to note the effects of resizing the parent.

Tabs

When controls run amok in a congested GUI, often the best solution involves splitting them among several windows. To maintain cohesion, GUI designers invented tabs, which allow several windows or "pages" of forms to be stacked on top of each other. Selecting a tab brings the corresponding page of controls to the fore, much as selecting a physical tab in a notebook flips directly to a specific page in the notebook. OS/2's properties notebooks pushed tabs toward the mainstream, and Microsoft's Windows 95, with its Properties pages, popularized tabs into a mainstay of desktop GUIs.

Tabs continue to grow their domain. Spreadsheets come together in "workbooks," providing tabs for navigation among them. Configuration screens separate categories of options into separate tabs. The latest Web browsers, including Mozilla, Netscape, and Opera, offer "tabbed browsing," displaying each Web page in its own tab. Tabs have largely displaced the MDI model for presenting multiple views in a window, and are essential to solving the information overload computers present.

Creating Tabs

SWT divides its tab implementation into two classes: TabFolder and TabItem, neither of which should be subclassed. TabFolders, which aren't visible, contain TabItems. To create a tabbed interface, create a TabFolder with a Shell as its parent, and create TabItems as children of the TabFolder. For example, to create and display a single tab, you code this:

```
TabFolder tabFolder = new TabFolder(shell, SWT.NONE);
TabItem item = new TabItem(tabFolder, SWT.NONE);
```

Pass SWT.TOP (the default) or SWT.BOTTOM to TabFolder's constructor to create tabs that run along the top or the bottom of the parent composite, respectively. Any styles passed to TabItem's constructor are ignored.

TabFolder offers a few methods, the more interesting of which are listed in Table 8-3.

Table 8-3. TabFolder *Methods*

Method	Description
void addSelectionListener (SelectionListener listener)	Adds a listener that's notified when any of the tabs in the tab folder is selected.
TabItem getItem(int index)	Returns the tab at the specified zero-based index.
int getItemCount()	Returns the number of tabs in this tab folder.
TabItem[] getItems()	Returns an array containing all the tabs in this tab folder.
TabItem[] getSelection()	Returns an array containing all the selected tabs in this tab folder, or an empty array if no tabs are selected.
int getSelectionIndex()	Returns the index of the selected tab.
int indexOf(TabItem tabItem)	Returns the zero-based index of the specified tab.
void removeSelectionListener (SelectionListener listener)	Removes the specified selection listener from the notification list.
void setSelection(int index)	Selects the tab at the specified zero-based index.
void setSelection(TabItem[] items)	Selects the tabs specified. Passing null throws an exception; passing an empty array deselects all tabs. The algorithm selects each tab, starting with the last tab in the array and moving backward to the first. This means that for implementations that can have only one selected tab, like Windows, the first tab in the array is selected.

However, most programs will ignore this API and not call any of these methods, because the tab paradigm works as you'd expect without any help from you. You click a tab, and the tab and its contents come to the front. You just create the TabFolder and the TabItems it contains.

Adding Content to Tabs

The simple example in the previous section created a TabFolder and a TabItem, but the displayed tab was blank (see Figure 8-3). The only thing less interesting than a blank tab is a set of blank tabs; tabs should have content. They should also have labels. TabItem provides methods to do that, as well as other functions necessary for using tabs. Table 8-4 lists TabItem's methods.

Figure 8-3. A lone, anonymous tab

Table 8-4. TabItem *Methods*

Method	Description
void dispose()	Closes the tab, recursively disposing all its contained widgets.
Control getControl()	Returns the contents—the widgets displayed—of this tab. The returned Control can be a single control, or it can be a composite that contains other controls.
Image getImage()	Returns the image associated with this tab.
TabFolder getParent()	Returns this tab's parent.
String getText()	Returns this tab's label.
String getToolTipText()	Returns the tool tip text for this tab.
void setControl(Control control)	Sets the contents—the widgets displayed—of this tab. control can be a single control, or it can be a single composite that contains other controls.
void setImage(Image image)	Sets the image for this tab.
void setText(String text)	Sets the label for this tab.
void setToolTipText(String toolTipText)	Sets the tool tip text for this tab.

Create a tab with a label, an image, a tool tip, and a control, using code such as this:

```
TabItem tabItem = new TabItem(tabFolder, SWT.NONE);
tabItem.setText("My Tab");
tabItem.setToolTipText("This is my tab");
tabItem.setImage(myImage);
// Notice the control's parent: tabFolder, not tabItem or shell
tabItem.setControl(new Text(tabFolder, SWT.BORDER | SWT.MULTI | SWT.WRAP));
```

This code creates a tab labeled My Tab. Hovering over the tab displays the tool tip "This is my tab." The tab has an image (the image contained in myImage) and displays a multiline edit field.

Because setControl() takes a single control, you might think that you're limited to displaying a single widget per tab, rendering tabs not very useful. You can display as many widgets as memory and resources permit; you create a Composite, and stuff the controls into it. You then pass the Composite to the tab's setControl() method. The code might look like this:

```
TabItem tabItem = new TabItem(tabFolder, SWT.NONE);
tabItem.setText("My Tab");
tabItem.setToolTipText("A tab with multiple widgets");
Composite composite = new Composite(tabFolder, SWT.NONE);
composite.setLayout(new FillLayout());
new Button(composite, SWT.PUSH).setText("Button One");
new Button(composite, SWT.PUSH).setText("Button Two");
new Button(composite, SWT.PUSH).setText("Button Three");
tabItem.setControl(composite);
```

This creates a tab with three buttons on it. You can nest composites within composites to create whatever layouts and widgets you wish.

The TabComplex program in Listing 8-2 illustrates the abilities of tabs. It creates four tabs, each containing a label and an image. Three of the tabs have associated controls (the fourth tab stays empty, demonstrating that you don't have to put controls on a tab). You can copy the images from the downloaded code, or open your favorite graphics editor and create your own images. Put them in a directory called images that's a peer to your examples directory.

Listing 8-2. TabComplex.java

```
package examples.ch8;

import java.io.*;

import org.eclipse.swt.SWT;
import org.eclipse.swt.events.*;
import org.eclipse.swt.graphics.Image;
import org.eclipse.swt.layout.*;
import org.eclipse.swt.widgets.*;
```

```
/**
 * Creates a tabbed display with four tabs, and a few controls on each page
 */
public class TabComplex {
  private static final String IMAGE_PATH = "images"
      + System.getProperty("file.separator");

  private Image circle;
  private Image square;
  private Image triangle;
  private Image star;

  /**
   * Runs the application
   */
  public void run() {
    Display display = new Display();
    Shell shell = new Shell(display);
    shell.setLayout(new FillLayout());
    shell.setText("Complex Tabs");
    createImages(shell);
    createContents(shell);
    shell.open();
    while (!shell.isDisposed()) {
      if (!display.readAndDispatch()) {
        display.sleep();
      }
    }
    display.dispose();
  }

  /**
   * Creates the contents
   *
   * @param shell the parent shell
   */
  private void createContents(Shell shell) {
    // Create the containing tab folder
    final TabFolder tabFolder = new TabFolder(shell, SWT.NONE);

    // Create each tab and set its text, tool tip text,
    // image, and control
    TabItem one = new TabItem(tabFolder, SWT.NONE);
    one.setText("one");
    one.setToolTipText("This is tab one");
    one.setImage(circle);
    one.setControl(getTabOneControl(tabFolder));
```

```
            TabItem two = new TabItem(tabFolder, SWT.NONE);
            two.setText("two");
            two.setToolTipText("This is tab two");
            two.setImage(square);
            two.setControl(getTabTwoControl(tabFolder));

            TabItem three = new TabItem(tabFolder, SWT.NONE);
            three.setText("three");
            three.setToolTipText("This is tab three");
            three.setImage(triangle);
            three.setControl(getTabThreeControl(tabFolder));

            TabItem four = new TabItem(tabFolder, SWT.NONE);
            four.setText("four");
            four.setToolTipText("This is tab four");
            four.setImage(star);

            // Select the third tab (index is zero-based)
            tabFolder.setSelection(2);

            // Add an event listener to write the selected tab to stdout
            tabFolder.addSelectionListener(new SelectionAdapter() {
              public void widgetSelected(org.eclipse.swt.events.SelectionEvent event) {
                System.out.println(tabFolder.getSelection()[0].getText() + " selected");
              }
            });
        }

        /**
         * Creates the images
         *
         * @param shell the parent shell
         */
        private void createImages(Shell shell) {
          try {
            circle = new Image(shell.getDisplay(), new FileInputStream(IMAGE_PATH
                + "circle.gif"));
            square = new Image(shell.getDisplay(), new FileInputStream(IMAGE_PATH
                + "square.gif"));
            star = new Image(shell.getDisplay(), new FileInputStream(IMAGE_PATH
                + "star.gif"));
            triangle = new Image(shell.getDisplay(), new FileInputStream(IMAGE_PATH
                + "triangle.gif"));
          } catch (IOException e) {
            // Images not found; handle gracefully
          }
        }
```

```java
/**
 * Disposes the images
 */
private void disposeImages() {
  if (circle != null)
    circle.dispose();
  if (square != null)
    square.dispose();
  if (star != null)
    star.dispose();
  if (triangle != null)
    triangle.dispose();
}

/**
 * Gets the control for tab one
 *
 * @param tabFolder the parent tab folder
 * @return Control
 */
private Control getTabOneControl(TabFolder tabFolder) {
  // Create a composite and add four buttons to it
  Composite composite = new Composite(tabFolder, SWT.NONE);
  composite.setLayout(new FillLayout(SWT.VERTICAL));
  new Button(composite, SWT.PUSH).setText("Button one");
  new Button(composite, SWT.PUSH).setText("Button two");
  new Button(composite, SWT.PUSH).setText("Button three");
  new Button(composite, SWT.PUSH).setText("Button four");
  return composite;
}

/**
 * Gets the control for tab two
 *
 * @param tabFolder the parent tab folder
 * @return Control
 */
private Control getTabTwoControl(TabFolder tabFolder) {
  // Create a multiline text field
  return new Text(tabFolder, SWT.BORDER | SWT.MULTI | SWT.WRAP);
}

/**
 * Gets the control for tab three
 *
 * @param tabFolder the parent tab folder
 * @return Control
 */
```

```
        private Control getTabThreeControl(TabFolder tabFolder) {
          // Create some labels and text fields
          Composite composite = new Composite(tabFolder, SWT.NONE);
          composite.setLayout(new RowLayout());
          new Label(composite, SWT.LEFT).setText("Label One:");
          new Text(composite, SWT.BORDER);
          new Label(composite, SWT.RIGHT).setText("Label Two:");
          new Text(composite, SWT.BORDER);
          return composite;
        }

        /**
         * The entry point for the application
         *
         * @param args the command line arguments
         */
        public static void main(String[] args) {
          new TabComplex().run();
        }
    }
```

Compile and run to see a window with four tabs, with the third tab selected (see Figure 8-4). Select the various tabs, one by one, and bring each to the forefront. Figure 8-5 shows the window with the first tab selected. Notice that as you select the tabs, a line is written to the console indicating which tab is selected.

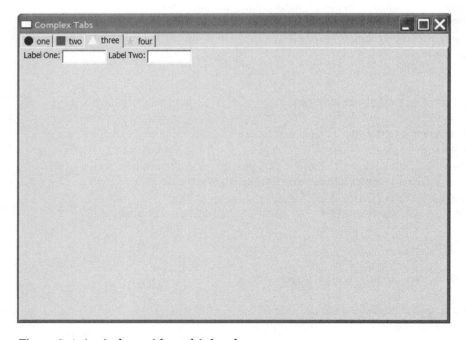

Figure 8-4. A window with multiple tabs

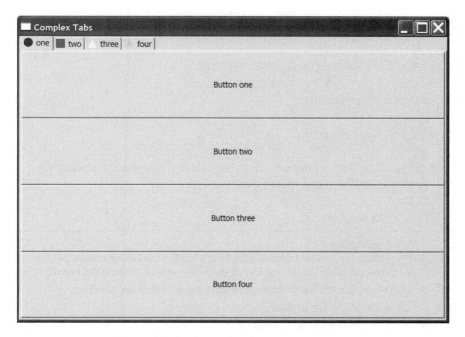

Figure 8-5. A window with the first tab selected

`TabFolder` and `TabItem` should meet your typical tabbing needs. Chapter 9 discusses `CTabFolder`, from the SWT custom package, which adds more power and flexibility to tabs.

Toolbars

A Windows word processor called Ami, produced by a small company called Samna, introduced toolbars in 1988.[2] Ami was subsequently bought by Lotus and renamed Ami Pro. It continued to outpace its competitors (Microsoft Word and WordPerfect) in usability. Contemporary trade magazines heralded this upstart word processor, and Ami Pro cultivated a devout following. Sadly, Ami Pro stagnated, came late to the 32-bit party, swapped its friendly moniker for Word Pro, and disappeared from public consciousness, usage, and hard drives (though it's still available; see `http://www.lotus.com/ products/smrtsuite.nsf/wPages/wordpro`). Fortunately, however, its competitors aped its advances, including its toolbar, and today almost all applications have toolbars. SWT makes adding toolbars to your applications easy.

Creating Toolbars

The `ToolBar` class implements a container for toolbar items—buttons or dropdowns—displaying images, text, or both. This class should not be subclassed. A toolbar can be

---

[2] `http://www.zisman.ca/Articles/1991-92/OCP_AmiPro.html`

horizontal or vertical, which is determined at construction. This code creates a horizontal toolbar:

```
ToolBar toolBar = new ToolBar(shell, SWT.HORIZONTAL);
```

This code creates a vertical toolbar:

```
ToolBar toolBar = new ToolBar(shell, SWT.VERTICAL);
```

The target platform determines whether a particular alignment (horizontal or vertical) is available. Table 8-5 lists other styles and their effects.

Table 8-5. ToolBar *Constants*

Constant	Description
SWT.FLAT	Makes the toolbar items flat; only the button under the mouse pointer appears raised. If not specified, the items will be perpetually raised.
SWT.WRAP	Wraps the toolbar buttons; this style has no effect on Windows.
SWT.RIGHT	Right aligns the toolbar.
SWT.HORIZONTAL	Draws a horizontal toolbar.
SWT.VERTICAL	Draws a vertical toolbar.
SWT.SHADOW_OUT	Causes a shadow to be drawn around the toolbar that makes the toolbar look as if it's protruding from the screen.

You can use these styles alone or in combinations using the bitwise OR operator. ToolBar has a few methods worth noting; Table 8-6 lists them.

Table 8-6. ToolBar *Methods*

Method	Description
ToolItem getItem(int index)	Returns the toolbar item for the zero-based index.
ToolItem getItem(Point point)	Returns the toolbar item beneath the specified point (or null if no item exists beneath that point).
int getItemCount()	Returns the number of items in this toolbar.
ToolItem[] getItems()	Returns all the items in this toolbar.
int getRowCount()	Returns the number of rows occupied by this toolbar (used when the toolbar wraps).
int indexOf(ToolItem item)	Returns the zero-based index of the specified ToolItem.

Plugging in ToolItems

A toolbar without any toolbar items can't do much. The ToolItem class implements the items that appear in a toolbar. These items can be any of the following:

- Regular push buttons

- Stateful push buttons ("toggle" buttons)

- Grouped stateful push buttons (only one in the group can be selected at a time)

- Dropdowns

You can also create separators, which enforce gaps between items. You determine the type of a `ToolItem` by passing its corresponding constant to the constructor (see Table 8-7 for the constants). You shouldn't combine constants using bitwise OR operators; the results of doing that are undefined.

Items in the toolbar can display text, images, both, or neither. All items in the toolbar adopt the same size for the dimension perpendicular to the alignment, but maintain their natural sizing for the dimension parallel to the alignment. In other words, items in a horizontal toolbar have the same height but varying widths, depending on their contents, while the items in a vertical toolbar have the same width but varying heights.

Table 8-7. Constants for Creating Tool Items

Constant	Description
`SWT.CHECK`	Creates a stateful push button ("toggle" button).
`SWT.DROP_DOWN`	Creates a dropdown.
`SWT.PUSH`	Creates a traditional push button.
`SWT.RADIO`	Creates a grouped stateful push button (only one in the group may be selected at a time).
`SWT.SEPARATOR`	Creates a separator.

For example, to create a push button you use this code:

```
ToolItem item = new ToolItem(toolBar, SWT.PUSH);
```

You can mix and match the different types on the same toolbar. For example, the following code creates a toolbar with two push buttons, two check buttons, two radio buttons, and two dropdowns, with separators dividing dissimilar types:

```
ToolBar toolBar = new ToolBar(shell, SWT.HORIZONTAL);
ToolItem item = new ToolItem(toolBar, SWT.PUSH);
item.setText("Button One");
item = new ToolItem(toolBar, SWT.PUSH);
item.setText("Button Two");
new ToolItem(toolBar, SWT.SEPARATOR);
item = new ToolItem(toolBar, SWT.CHECK);
item.setText("Check One");
item = new ToolItem(toolBar, SWT.CHECK);
item.setText("Check Two");
new ToolItem(toolBar, SWT.SEPARATOR);
```

```
item = new ToolItem(toolBar, SWT.RADIO);
item.setText("Radio One");
item = new ToolItem(toolBar, SWT.RADIO);
item.setText("Radio Two");
new ToolItem(toolBar, SWT.SEPARATOR);
item = new ToolItem(toolBar, SWT.DROP_DOWN);
item.setText("Dropdown One");
item = new ToolItem(toolBar, SWT.DROP_DOWN);
item.setText("Dropdown Two");
```

The toolbar produced by this code appears in Figure 8-6; click the buttons to demonstrate the statelessness of the push buttons and the statefulness of the check and radio buttons (see Figure 8-7).

Figure 8-6. A simple toolbar

Figure 8-7. A simple toolbar with some buttons pressed

The ToolItem class offers methods to control its behavior, listed in Table 8-8.

Table 8-8. ToolItem Methods

Method	Description
void addSelectionListener (SelectionListener listener)	Adds a listener that gets notified when this item is selected.
Rectangle getBounds()	Returns the containing Rectangle for this item, relative to the parent toolbar.
Control getControl()	Returns the control associated with this item; valid only when this item is a separator.
Image getDisabledImage()	Returns the image to display when this item is disabled, or null if no disabled image has been set.
boolean getEnabled()	Returns true if this item is enabled, or false if it's disabled.
Image getHotImage()	Returns the image to display when this item is "hot" (selected); applies to check and radio buttons only. Returns null if no hot image has been set.
Image getImage()	Returns the image to display for this item, or null if no image has been set. Defined in superclass Item.

Table 8-8. ToolItem *Methods (continued)*

Method	Description
Toolbar getParent()	Returns the parent toolbar.
boolean getSelection()	Returns true if this item is selected, or false if it isn't selected.
String getText()	Returns this item's text, or null if no text has been set. Defined in superclass Item.
String getToolTipText()	Returns this item's tool tip text, or null if no tool tip text has been set.
int getWidth()	Returns the width, in pixels, of this item.
boolean isEnabled()	Returns true if this item and its ancestors are enabled, or false if they aren't.
void removeSelectionListener (SelectionListener listener)	Removes the listener from the notification list.
void setControl(Control control)	Sets the control for this item; valid only for separators.
void setDisabledImage(Image image)	Sets the image to display when this item is disabled.
void setEnabled(boolean enabled)	If enabled is true, enables this item; if enabled is false, disables this item.
void setHotImage(Image image)	Sets the image to display when this item is "hot" (selected); applies to check and radio buttons only. Pass null for no "hot" image.
void setImage(Image image)	Sets the image to display for this item. Defined in superclass Item.
void setSelection(boolean selected)	If selected is true, selects this item; if selected is false, deselects this item.
void setText(String text)	Sets the text to display for this item. Defined in superclass Item.
void setToolTipText(String toolTipText)	Sets the tool tip text for this item.
void setWidth(int width)	Sets this item's width in pixels.

Traditionally, toolbars contain a set of push buttons that display an image and no text, and perform some action when pushed. They also display some text (inside a tool tip) when the mouse hovers over them, describing what they do when pushed. The tool tip is provided in case the image doesn't adequately communicate the button's function. For some reason, Web browsers foisted upon the world the notion that buttons in a toolbar should carry both images and text, redundantly declaring their functions and usurping valuable screen space. Though the practice of putting both text and image on a toolbar button seems absurd, SWT nonetheless allows you to do this. However, we recommend that you stick with images that unambiguously indicate the function of the toolbar button, and leave the text for tool tips.

To create a toolbar button with image, text, and tool tip, use code that looks like this:

```
ToolItem item = new ToolItem(toolBar, SWT.PUSH);
item.setText("Button One");
item.setImage(myImage);
item.setToolTipText("This is button one");
```

The preceding code creates a "push button" toolbar item that displays the image contained in myImage above the text "Button One." Hovering the mouse pointer over the button causes a tool tip to appear displaying the text "This is button one."

Creating Radio Groups

Radio buttons allow only one option from the group to be selected, and allow any number of options in the group. To create more than one group of radio buttons in the same toolbar, separate each group using a separator. The following code creates two radio button groups, each with three options:

```
ToolItem item = new ToolItem(toolBar, SWT.RADIO);
item.setText("One");
item = new ToolItem(toolBar, SWT.RADIO);
item.setText("Two");
item = new ToolItem(toolBar, SWT.RADIO);
item.setText("Three");
new ToolItem(toolBar, SWT.SEPARATOR); // Signals end of group
item = new ToolItem(toolBar, SWT.RADIO);
item.setText("One");
item = new ToolItem(toolBar, SWT.RADIO);
item.setText("Two");
item = new ToolItem(toolBar, SWT.RADIO);
item.setText("Three");
```

Each radio group is independent of the other, and each group allows only one button within it to be selected, as shown in Figure 8-8.

Figure 8-8. Two radio groups

Working with Dropdowns

The otherwise straightforward SWT API might have lulled you into thinking that dropdown tool items would provide methods for adding strings to the dropdown list and for getting the selected item from the list. This thinking certainly sounds reasonable; the Combo class, which is also a dropdown, provides these methods and more. A dropdown tool item looks similar to a Combo object, as Figure 8-9 demonstrates.

Figure 8-9. A Combo *and a dropdown*

Though they share functionality, appearance, and a button with a downward-pointing arrow (or other indicator, depending on the underlying window manager), ToolItem dropdowns and Combos don't offer the same API. Whereas a Combo maintains a list of selectable items, a dropdown tool item possesses no such list. It's just a button made up to look like a Combo, almost like an imposter. To offer the dropdown list and selection functionality, you must implement them yourself.

However, a dropdown tool item isn't just a Combo with an abbreviated API. You can click it like a "push" button, which is something you can't do to a Combo. A good use for this widget, then, is to provide several actions from one button. Users can click the down arrow to select the action that the button will perform, and click the button itself to perform the action.

To provide Combo-like functionality to a dropdown tool item, create an event listener, derived from SelectionAdapter, for the item that displays and manages a menu to mimic a Combo's dropdown menu. Store the parent dropdown item in a member variable, as you need it in various places in the code. The constructor for your event handler receives the parent item, which you use to get the parent Shell and create the Menu object that implements the dropdown list:

```
public DropdownSelectionListener(ToolItem dropdown) {
  this.dropdown = dropdown;
  menu = new Menu(dropdown.getParent().getShell());
}
```

The appropriately named add() method adds an item to the dropdown list. It adds the item to the menu, and adds an event handler so that if the item is selected, the parent dropdown's text changes to the text of the selected menu item:

```
public void add(String item) {
  MenuItem menuItem = new MenuItem(menu, SWT.NONE);
  menuItem.setText(item);
  menuItem.addSelectionListener(new SelectionAdapter() {
    public void widgetSelected(SelectionEvent event) {
      MenuItem selected = (MenuItem) event.widget;
      dropdown.setText(selected.getText());
    }
  });
}
```

The widgetSelected() method responds appropriately when the dropdown is selected. If the user clicks the dropdown arrow, the menu displays. If the user clicks the dropdown itself, the appropriate action executes. In the present implementation, a message box pops up that tells the user what has been selected.

```
public void widgetSelected(SelectionEvent event) {
  // If they clicked the arrow, show the list
  if (event.detail == SWT.ARROW) {
    // Determine where to put the dropdown list
    ToolItem item = (ToolItem) event.widget;
    Rectangle rect = item.getBounds();
    Point pt = item.getParent().toDisplay(new Point(rect.x, rect.y));
    menu.setLocation(pt.x, pt.y + rect.height);
    menu.setVisible(true);
  } else {
    // They pushed the button; take appropriate action
    MessageBox msgBox =
      new MessageBox(dropdown.getParent().getShell(), SWT.OK);
    msgBox.setMessage(dropdown.getText() + " Pressed");
    msgBox.open();
  }
}
```

Creating Feature-Rich Toolbars

The ToolBarComplex application in Listing 8-3 combines the various tool item types to create a functioning toolbar.

Listing 8-3. ToolBarComplex.java

```java
package examples.ch8;

import java.io.*;

import org.eclipse.swt.SWT;
import org.eclipse.swt.events.*;
import org.eclipse.swt.graphics.Image;
import org.eclipse.swt.layout.*;
import org.eclipse.swt.widgets.*;

/**
 * This class creates a complex toolbar. It has two regular push buttons, two
 * "toggle" push buttons, two "radio" push buttons, and two dropdowns.
 */
public class ToolBarComplex {
  private static final String IMAGE_PATH = "images"
      + System.getProperty("file.separator");

  // Images to use on our tool items
  private Image circle, grayCircle;
  private Image square, graySquare;
  private Image star, grayStar;
  private Image triangle, grayTriangle;
```

```
// Labels to display tool item statuses
private Label checkOneStatus;
private Label checkTwoStatus;
private Label radioStatus;
private Label dropdownOneStatus;
private Label dropdownTwoStatus;

/**
 * Runs the application
 */
public void run() {
  Display display = new Display();
  Shell shell = new Shell(display);
  shell.setText("Toolbar with Images");
  createImages(shell);
  createContents(shell);
  shell.open();
  while (!shell.isDisposed()) {
    if (!display.readAndDispatch()) {
      display.sleep();
    }
  }
  disposeImages();
  display.dispose();
}

/**
 * Creates the images
 *
 * @param shell the parent shell
 */
private void createImages(Shell shell) {
  try {
    circle = new Image(shell.getDisplay(), new FileInputStream(IMAGE_PATH
        + "circle.gif"));
    grayCircle = new Image(shell.getDisplay(), new FileInputStream(IMAGE_PATH
        + "grayCircle.gif"));
    square = new Image(shell.getDisplay(), new FileInputStream(IMAGE_PATH
        + "square.gif"));
    graySquare = new Image(shell.getDisplay(), new FileInputStream(IMAGE_PATH
        + "graySquare.gif"));
    star = new Image(shell.getDisplay(), new FileInputStream(IMAGE_PATH
        + "star.gif"));
    grayStar = new Image(shell.getDisplay(), new FileInputStream(IMAGE_PATH
        + "grayStar.gif"));
    triangle = new Image(shell.getDisplay(), new FileInputStream(IMAGE_PATH
        + "triangle.gif"));
    grayTriangle = new Image(shell.getDisplay(), new FileInputStream(IMAGE_PATH
        + "grayTriangle.gif"));
```

```
      } catch (IOException e) {
        // Images not found; handle gracefully
      }
    }

    /**
     * Disposes the images
     */
    private void disposeImages() {
      if (circle != null)
        circle.dispose();
      if (grayCircle != null)
        grayCircle.dispose();
      if (square != null)
        square.dispose();
      if (graySquare != null)
        graySquare.dispose();
      if (star != null)
        star.dispose();
      if (grayStar != null)
        grayStar.dispose();
      if (triangle != null)
        triangle.dispose();
      if (grayTriangle != null)
        grayTriangle.dispose();
    }

    /**
     * Creates the window contents
     *
     * @param shell the parent shell
     */
    private void createContents(Shell shell) {
      shell.setLayout(new RowLayout(SWT.VERTICAL));
      createToolbar(shell);

      // Create the labels to display the statuses of
      // the "check" and "radio" buttons
      Composite composite = new Composite(shell, SWT.NONE);
      composite.setLayout(new GridLayout(2, true));

      new Label(composite, SWT.RIGHT).setText("Check One Status:");
      checkOneStatus = new Label(composite, SWT.LEFT);
      checkOneStatus.setText("Off");

      new Label(composite, SWT.RIGHT).setText("Check Two Status:");
      checkTwoStatus = new Label(composite, SWT.LEFT);
      checkTwoStatus.setText("Off");
```

```
  new Label(composite, SWT.RIGHT).setText("Radio Status:");
  radioStatus = new Label(composite, SWT.LEFT);
  radioStatus.setText("None");
}

/**
 * Creates the toolbar
 *
 * @param shell the parent shell
 */
private void createToolbar(final Shell shell) {
  ToolBar toolBar = new ToolBar(shell, SWT.HORIZONTAL);

  // Create push buttons
  ToolItem item = createToolItem(toolBar, SWT.PUSH, "Button One", circle, null,
      "This is button one");
  item.addSelectionListener(new SelectionAdapter() {
    public void widgetSelected(SelectionEvent event) {
      showMessage(shell, "Button One Pressed");
    }
  });

  item = createToolItem(toolBar, SWT.PUSH, "Button Two", square, null,
      "This is button two");
  item.addSelectionListener(new SelectionAdapter() {
    public void widgetSelected(SelectionEvent event) {
      showMessage(shell, "Button Two Pressed");
    }
  });

  ToolItem myItem = new ToolItem(toolBar, SWT.SEPARATOR);

  // Create "check" buttons
  item = createToolItem(toolBar, SWT.CHECK, "Check One", grayStar, star,
      "This is check one");
  item.addSelectionListener(new SelectionAdapter() {
    public void widgetSelected(SelectionEvent event) {
      ToolItem item = (ToolItem) event.widget;
      checkOneStatus.setText(item.getSelection() ? "On" : "Off");
    }
  });

  item = createToolItem(toolBar, SWT.CHECK, "Check Two", grayTriangle,
      triangle, "This is check two");
  item.addSelectionListener(new SelectionAdapter() {
    public void widgetSelected(SelectionEvent event) {
      ToolItem item = (ToolItem) event.widget;
      checkTwoStatus.setText(item.getSelection() ? "On" : "Off");
```

```
      }
    });

    new ToolItem(toolBar, SWT.SEPARATOR);

    // Create "radio" buttons
    item = createToolItem(toolBar, SWT.RADIO, "Radio One", grayCircle, circle,
        "This is radio one");
    item.addSelectionListener(new SelectionAdapter() {
      public void widgetSelected(SelectionEvent event) {
        radioStatus.setText("One");
      }
    });

    item = createToolItem(toolBar, SWT.RADIO, "Radio Two", graySquare, square,
        "This is radio two");
    item.addSelectionListener(new SelectionAdapter() {
      public void widgetSelected(SelectionEvent event) {
        radioStatus.setText("Two");
      }
    });

    new ToolItem(toolBar, SWT.SEPARATOR);

    // Create dropdowns
    item = createToolItem(toolBar, SWT.DROP_DOWN, "Dropdown One", star, null,
        "This is dropdown one");
    DropdownSelectionListener listenerOne = new DropdownSelectionListener(item);
    listenerOne.add("Option One for One");
    listenerOne.add("Option Two for One");
    listenerOne.add("Option Three for One");
    item.addSelectionListener(listenerOne);

    item = createToolItem(toolBar, SWT.DROP_DOWN, "Dropdown Two", triangle, null,
        "This is dropdown two");
    DropdownSelectionListener listenerTwo = new DropdownSelectionListener(item);
    listenerTwo.add("Option One for Two");
    listenerTwo.add("Option Two for Two");
    listenerTwo.add("Option Three for Two");
    item.addSelectionListener(listenerTwo);
  }

  /**
   * Helper function to create tool item
   *
   * @param parent the parent toolbar
   * @param type the type of tool item to create
   * @param text the text to display on the tool item
```

```
 * @param image the image to display on the tool item
 * @param hotImage the hot image to display on the tool item
 * @param toolTipText the tool tip text for the tool item
 * @return ToolItem
 */
private ToolItem createToolItem(ToolBar parent, int type, String text,
    Image image, Image hotImage, String toolTipText) {
  ToolItem item = new ToolItem(parent, type);
  item.setText(text);
  item.setImage(image);
  item.setHotImage(hotImage);
  item.setToolTipText(toolTipText);
  return item;
}


/**
 * Helper method to display a message box. We use it to display a message when
 * a "push" button or "dropdown" button is pushed.
 *
 * @param shell the parent shell for the message box
 * @param message the message to display
 */
public static void showMessage(Shell shell, String message) {
  MessageBox msgBox = new MessageBox(shell, SWT.OK);
  msgBox.setMessage(message);
  msgBox.open();
}


/**
 * The application entry point
 *
 * @param args the command line arguments
 */
public static void main(String[] args) {
  new ToolBarComplex().run();
}
}
```

This program uses the same images from the tab section earlier in this chapter, adding some grayscale images so that the "hot" images stand out. Again, these are all in the downloaded code, and are used from the same location that they were in the tab example.

To cut down on the amount of code, ToolBarComplex uses a helper method to create the toolbar items, called createToolItem(). This method creates the toolbar item and sets its text, image, hot image, and tool tip text. The program doesn't use any disabled images, but you could easily modify the createToolItem() method to accept and set a disabled image as well.

For the dropdowns to function, create a listener patterned after the one in the previous section, as shown in Listing 8-4.

Listing 8-4. DropdownSelectionListener.java

```java
package examples.ch8;

import org.eclipse.swt.*;
import org.eclipse.swt.events.*;
import org.eclipse.swt.graphics.*;
import org.eclipse.swt.widgets.*;

/**
 * This class provides the "drop down" functionality for our dropdown tool items.
 */
public class DropdownSelectionListener extends SelectionAdapter {
  private ToolItem dropdown;
  private Menu menu;

  /**
   * Constructs a DropdownSelectionListener
   *
   * @param dropdown the dropdown this listener belongs to
   */
  public DropdownSelectionListener(ToolItem dropdown) {
    this.dropdown = dropdown;
    menu = new Menu(dropdown.getParent().getShell());
  }

  /**
   * Adds an item to the dropdown list
   *
   * @param item the item to add
   */
  public void add(String item) {
    MenuItem menuItem = new MenuItem(menu, SWT.NONE);
    menuItem.setText(item);
    menuItem.addSelectionListener(new SelectionAdapter() {
      public void widgetSelected(SelectionEvent event) {
        MenuItem selected = (MenuItem) event.widget;
        dropdown.setText(selected.getText());
      }
    });
  }

  /**
```

```
 * Called when either the button itself or the dropdown arrow is clicked
 *
 * @param event the event that trigged this call
 */
public void widgetSelected(SelectionEvent event) {
  // If they clicked the arrow, we show the list
  if (event.detail == SWT.ARROW) {
    // Determine where to put the dropdown list
    ToolItem item = (ToolItem) event.widget;
    Rectangle rect = item.getBounds();
    Point pt = item.getParent().toDisplay(new Point(rect.x, rect.y));
    menu.setLocation(pt.x, pt.y + rect.height);
    menu.setVisible(true);
  } else {
    // They pushed the button; take appropriate action
    ToolBarComplex.showMessage(dropdown.getParent().getShell(), dropdown
        .getText()
        + " Pressed");
  }
}
}
}
```

Compiling and running this program produces the window shown in Figure 8-10. Figure 8-11 shows the window with some buttons pressed and a dropdown menu visible.

Figure 8-10. The feature-rich toolbar

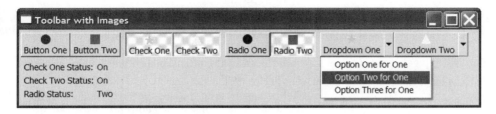

Figure 8-11. The feature-rich toolbar in action

Coolbars

During the one-upmanship of the browser wars of the 1990s, when new versions of Internet Explorer and Netscape Navigator seemed to appear weekly and everyone talked about "Internet Time," Microsoft introduced the coolbar. It first appeared in Internet Explorer 3.0 and carried the name "rebar," but even pasty programmers know that rebar mundanely reinforces concrete, so the name was hastily changed to something more hip.[3] Coolbars contain other controls—toolbars, combo boxes, edit fields, and so forth—and can be moved around inside the containing window. You recognize a coolbar by its distinctive "gripper": a vertical line or lines at the left edge of the coolbar that allows resizing, as seen in Figure 8-12.

Figure 8-12. A coolbar with its gripper

Creating Coolbars

SWT uses two classes to implement coolbars: CoolBar, which contains the items, and CoolItem, which displays a gripper and the associated control. These two classes are to coolbars what ToolBar and ToolItem are to toolbars, and shouldn't be subclassed.

Create a coolbar by constructing a CoolBar object, then constructing CoolItem objects and adding controls to them. CoolBar offers a single constructor:

```
public CoolBar(Composite parent, int style)
```

Because no styles are appropriate, you should pass SWT.NONE for style. Table 8-9 lists the CoolBar methods.

Table 8-9. CoolBar *Methods*

Method	Description
CoolItem getItem(int index)	Returns the item currently displayed at the specified zero-based index.
int getItemCount()	Returns the number of items that this CoolBar contains.
int[] getItemOrder()	Returns an array of integers that reflect the currently displayed order of the items.
CoolItem[] getItems()	Returns an array containing the items in their currently displayed order.
Point[] getItemSizes()	Returns an array containing the Points that describe the sizes of the items in their currently displayed order.
boolean getLocked()	Returns whether this CoolBar is locked (immovable).

---

3. http://msdn.microsoft.com/library/default.asp?url=/library/en-us/dnwui/html/msdn_rebar.asp

Table 8-9. CoolBar *Methods (continued)*

Method	Description
int[] getWrapIndices()	Returns an array of integers that reflect the currently displayed order of the items that have wrapped to a second row.
int indexOf(CoolItem item)	Returns the zero-based index of the specified item as it's currently displayed.
void setItemLayout(int[] itemOrder, int[] wrapIndices, Point[] sizes)	Convenience method to set order, wrap, and sizes in one method call.
void setLocked(boolean locked)	Sets whether this CoolBar is locked (immovable).
void setWrapIndices(int[] wrapIndices)	Sets the indices of the items that will wrap to the next row.

Like an empty toolbar, an empty coolbar offers little. The next section discusses how to add items to a coolbar.

Plugging in CoolItems

CoolBars contain CoolItems, which contain other controls. To add a CoolItem to a CoolBar, construct the CoolItem and pass the CoolBar as the first argument to the constructor. CoolItem offers two constructors, listed in Table 8-10.

Table 8-10. CoolItem *Constructors*

Constructor	Description
CoolItem(CoolBar parent, int style)	Constructs a CoolItem at the next logical index.
CoolItem(CoolBar parent, int style, int index)	Constructs a CoolItem, using index for the index.

Passing SWT.NONE for style creates a standard cool item. Alternatively, you can pass SWT.DROP_DOWN, which displays a button with a chevron on the cool item if it's sized too small to display its contents. However, the button doesn't do anything, so you would have to write code to make it functional.

Table 8-11 lists CoolItem's methods.

Table 8-11. CoolItem *Methods*

Method	Description
void addSelectionListener (SelectionListener listener)	Adds a listener that's notified when this CoolItem is selected.
Point computeSize(int wHint, int hHint)	Returns the preferred size of this CoolItem.
Rectangle getBounds()	Returns the bounding rectangle for this CoolItem, relative to its parent.

Table 8-11. `CoolItem` *Methods (continued)*

Method	Description
`Control getControl()`	Returns the control associated with this `CoolItem`, or null if no control has been set.
`Display getDisplay()`	Returns the `Display` associated with this `CoolItem`.
`Point getMinimumSize()`	Returns the `Point` describing this `CoolItem`'s minimum size.
`CoolBar getParent()`	Returns this `CoolItem`'s parent.
`Point getPreferredSize()`	Returns the `Point` describing this `CoolItem`'s preferred size.
`Point getSize()`	Returns the `Point` describing this `CoolItem`'s current size.
`void removeSelectionListener (SelectionListener listener)`	Removes the listener from this `CoolItem`'s notification list.
`void setControl(Control control)`	Sets the control for this `CoolItem`.
`void setMinimumSize(int width, int height)`	Sets the minimum size for this `CoolItem`.
`void setMinimumSize(Point size)`	Sets the minimum size for this `CoolItem`.
`void setPreferredSize(int width, int height)`	Sets the preferred or ideal size for this `CoolItem` to the specified width and height.
`void setPreferredSize(Point size)`	Sets the preferred or ideal size for this `CoolItem` to the specified size.
`void setSize(int width, int height)`	Sets the actual size for this `CoolItem` to the specified width and height.
`void setSize(Point size)`	Sets the actual size for this `CoolItem` to the specified size.

Create a simple `CoolBar` containing one button like this:

```
CoolBar coolbar = new CoolBar(shell, SWT.NONE);
CoolItem item = new CoolItem(coolbar, SWT.NONE);
Button button = new Button(coolbar, SWT.PUSH);
button.setText("Cool One");
item.setControl(button);
// Compute the size by first computing the control's default size
Point pt = button.computeSize(SWT.DEFAULT, SWT.DEFAULT);
// Now we take into account the size of the cool item
pt = item.computeSize(pt.x, pt.y);
// Now we set the size
item.setSize(pt);
```

Each `CoolItem` contains exactly one control, which can be a composite containing multiple controls. Notice that you must size the `CoolItem` yourself, or it won't be sized properly. Compute the size by first getting the default size for the control. Then, get the size for the item by passing in the size of its control. Finally, set the computed size back into the item. The preceding code creates a coolbar that looks like Figure 8-13.

Figure 8-13. A coolbar containing one button

A cool item often contains a toolbar, but can contain any number and type of controls. Add a control to a cool item by calling the cool item's setControl() method, passing the control. To add multiple controls, create a composite, add the controls to the composite, and pass the composite to the cool item's setControl() method.

Currently, setting a Combo as the control in a CoolItem doesn't work properly in Windows; the list won't drop down. To skirt the issue, create a composite whose only control is a Combo, and set the composite into the CoolItem.

The CoolBarTest program in Listing 8-5 creates a coolbar with three items, one containing a toolbar, one containing a standard dropdown (using the trick from the previous paragraph so that it works properly in Windows), and one containing two buttons stacked vertically. The item containing the toolbar uses the SWT.DROP_DOWN style, so a chevron displays if the item is displayed too small to display the full toolbar. The program uses an event handler to detect when the user clicks the chevron button, and responds to the click by restoring the item to its full size.

Listing 8-5. CoolBarTest.java

```java
package examples.ch8;

import java.io.*;

import org.eclipse.swt.events.*;
import org.eclipse.swt.graphics.*;
import org.eclipse.swt.layout.*;
import org.eclipse.swt.widgets.*;
import org.eclipse.swt.SWT;

public class CoolBarTest {
    private static final String IMAGE_PATH = "images"
        + System.getProperty("file.separator");

    private Image circle;
    private Image square;
    private Image star;
    private Image triangle;

    /**
     * Runs the application
     */
```

```
public void run() {
  Display display = new Display();
  Shell shell = new Shell(display);
  shell.setText("CoolBar Test");
  createImages(shell);
  createContents(shell);
  shell.open();
  while (!shell.isDisposed()) {
    if (!display.readAndDispatch()) {
      display.sleep();
    }
  }
  disposeImages();
  display.dispose();
}

/**
 * Creates the window contents
 *
 * @param shell the parent shell
 */
private void createContents(Shell shell) {
  shell.setLayout(new GridLayout(1, false));
  CoolBar coolbar = createCoolBar(shell);
  coolbar.setLayoutData(new GridData(GridData.FILL_HORIZONTAL));
}

/**
 * Creates the CoolBar
 *
 * @param shell the parent shell
 * @return CoolBar
 */
private CoolBar createCoolBar(Shell shell) {
  CoolBar coolbar = new CoolBar(shell, SWT.NONE);

  // Create toolbar coolitem
  final CoolItem item = new CoolItem(coolbar, SWT.DROP_DOWN);
  item.setControl(createToolBar(coolbar));
  calcSize(item);

  // Add a listener to handle clicks on the chevron button
  item.addSelectionListener(new SelectionAdapter() {
    public void widgetSelected(SelectionEvent event) {
      calcSize(item);
    }
  });
```

```
    // Create combo coolitem
    CoolItem item2 = new CoolItem(coolbar, SWT.NONE);
    item2.setControl(createCombo(coolbar));
    calcSize(item2);

    // Create a dropdown coolitem
    item2 = new CoolItem(coolbar, SWT.NONE);
    item2.setControl(createStackedButtons(coolbar));
    calcSize(item2);

    return coolbar;
  }

  /**
   * Creates the ToolBar
   *
   * @param composite the parent composite
   * @return Control
   */
  private Control createToolBar(Composite composite) {
    ToolBar toolBar = new ToolBar(composite, SWT.NONE);
    ToolItem item = new ToolItem(toolBar, SWT.PUSH);
    item.setImage(circle);
    item = new ToolItem(toolBar, SWT.PUSH);
    item.setImage(square);
    item = new ToolItem(toolBar, SWT.PUSH);
    item.setImage(star);
    item = new ToolItem(toolBar, SWT.PUSH);
    item.setImage(triangle);
    return toolBar;
  }

  /**
   * Creates the Combo
   *
   * @param composite the parent composite
   * @return Control
   */
  private Control createCombo(Composite composite) {
    // A bug with Windows causes the Combo not to drop
    // down if you add it directly to the CoolBar.
    // To work around this, create a Composite, add the
    // Combo to it, and add the Composite to the CoolBar.
    // This should work both on Windows and on all other
    // platforms.
    Composite c = new Composite(composite, SWT.NONE);
    c.setLayout(new FillLayout());
```

```
    Combo combo = new Combo(c, SWT.DROP_DOWN);
    combo.add("Option One");
    combo.add("Option Two");
    combo.add("Option Three");
    return c;
}

/**
 * Creates two stacked buttons
 *
 * @param composite the parent composite
 * @return Control
 */
private Control createStackedButtons(Composite composite) {
    Composite c = new Composite(composite, SWT.NONE);
    c.setLayout(new GridLayout(1, false));
    new Button(c, SWT.PUSH).setText("Button One");
    new Button(c, SWT.PUSH).setText("Button Two");
    return c;
}

/**
 * Helper method to calculate the size of the cool item
 *
 * @param item the cool item
 */
private void calcSize(CoolItem item) {
    Control control = item.getControl();
    Point pt = control.computeSize(SWT.DEFAULT, SWT.DEFAULT);
    pt = item.computeSize(pt.x, pt.y);
    item.setSize(pt);
}

/**
 * Creates the images
 *
 * @param shell the parent shell
 */
private void createImages(Shell shell) {
    try {
        circle = new Image(shell.getDisplay(), new FileInputStream(IMAGE_PATH
            + "circle.gif"));
        square = new Image(shell.getDisplay(), new FileInputStream(IMAGE_PATH
            + "square.gif"));
        star = new Image(shell.getDisplay(), new FileInputStream(IMAGE_PATH
            + "star.gif"));
        triangle = new Image(shell.getDisplay(), new FileInputStream(IMAGE_PATH
            + "triangle.gif"));
```

```
    } catch (IOException e) {
      // Images not found; handle gracefully
    }
  }

  /**
   * Disposes the images
   */
  private void disposeImages() {
    if (circle != null)
      circle.dispose();
    if (square != null)
      square.dispose();
    if (star != null)
      star.dispose();
    if (triangle != null)
      triangle.dispose();
  }

  /**
   * The entry point for the application
   *
   * @param args the command line arguments
   */
  public static void main(String[] args) {
    new CoolBarTest().run();
  }
}
```

Figure 8-14 shows the program's window with the three items all in a row. Remember that you can move cool items around; try moving them around both within the same row and to other rows. Figure 8-15 shows the items after rearranging.

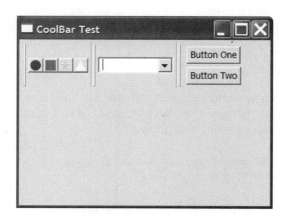

Figure 8-14. Three cool items

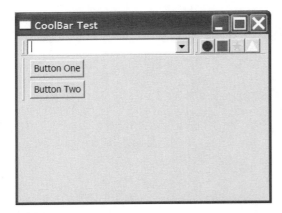

Figure 8-15. Three cool items rearranged

Try dragging the various cool items over each other, partially obscuring their contents. Notice that the cool item containing the toolbar displays a chevron when it's partially covered, as seen in Figure 8-16, while the other cool items don't. Click the chevron button to restore the toolbar's cool item to its original size.

Figure 8-16. A cool item with the SWT.DROP_DOWN *style*

Sashes

Sashes, also called splitters, relinquish control of the allocation of screen space to the user. They divide a window, but let the user decide where the division occurs. They can be dragged from side to side or up and down, and offer a flexible way to display two groups of information in a limited space. Perhaps the most familiar use of sashes is in Windows Explorer, which has a list of drives and directories on the left of a vertical sash, and a list of files and subdirectories on the right. Users can drag the dividing sash left or right, depending on where they prefer the space to be allocated.

Creating Sashes

Sashes can be horizontal or vertical; the type is determined at construction time, and cannot be changed. The default is vertical. Passing SWT.HORIZONTAL or SWT.VERTICAL to the constructor determines the type, as the following code shows:

```
Sash horizontalSash = new Sash(shell, SWT.HORIZONTAL); // Horizontal sash
Sash verticalSash = new Sash(shell, SWT.VERTICAL); // Vertical sash
```

The Sash class provides a limited API that is nonetheless important to ensure proper sash behavior. Table 8-12 lists the methods that Sash provides.

Table 8-12. Sash *Methods*

Method	Description
void addSelectionListener (SelectionListener listener)	Adds a listener that's notified when this Sash is selected.
Point computeSize(int wHint, int hHint, boolean changed)	Computes the size for this Sash.
void removeSelectionListener (SelectionListener listener)	Removes the listener from this Sash's notification list.

When a sash is created, the parent composite determines its size and location according to the parent's layout. For example, if you create a sash in a composite that's using a FillLayout, the sash will assume the same size and shape as the other controls in the layout. The SashExampleOne application in Listing 8-6 shows a sash in a FillLayout.

Listing 8-6. SashExampleOne.java

```java
package examples.ch8;

import org.eclipse.swt.*;
import org.eclipse.swt.layout.*;
import org.eclipse.swt.widgets.*;

/**
 * This class demonstrates a Sash
 */
public class SashExampleOne {
  /**
   * Runs the application
   */
  public void run() {
    Display display = new Display();
    Shell shell = new Shell(display);
    shell.setText("Sash One");
    createContents(shell);
    shell.pack();
    shell.open();
    while (!shell.isDisposed()) {
      if (!display.readAndDispatch()) {
        display.sleep();
      }
    }
    display.dispose();
  }

  /**
   * Creates the contents of the main window
```

```
 *
 * @param composite the parent composite
 */
public void createContents(Composite composite) {
  composite.setLayout(new FillLayout());
  new Text(composite, SWT.BORDER);
  new Sash(composite, SWT.VERTICAL);
  new Text(composite, SWT.BORDER);
}

/**
 * Application entry point
 *
 * @param args the command line arguments
 */
public static void main(String[] args) {
  new SashExampleOne().run();
}
}
```

This application creates two text fields, separated by a sash, in a FillLayout. The window it displays looks like Figure 8-17. The gap between the text fields is the sash, and you can drag it left or right (though it won't stay where you drag it).

Figure 8-17. A sash between two text fields

However, because a sash is just a divider, you likely don't want one to usurp the same amount of space as your other controls. In fact, you most likely want the sash to be a thin stripe, with the controls on either side attached. As the sash moves, you want the adjacent edges of the controls on either side of the sash to move as well. Use a FormLayout and its FormData and FormAttachment helper classes to implement this behavior.

Switching the preceding code to use a FormLayout makes the createContents() method look like this:

```
public void createContents(Composite composite) {
  composite.setLayout(new FormLayout());

  // Create the sash first, so the other controls
  // can be attached to it.
```

```
    Sash sash = new Sash(composite, SWT.VERTICAL);
    FormData data = new FormData();
    data.top = new FormAttachment(0, 0); // Attach to top
    data.bottom = new FormAttachment(100, 0); // Attach to bottom
    data.left = new FormAttachment(50, 0); // Attach halfway across
    sash.setLayoutData(data);

    // Create the first text box and attach its right edge
    // to the sash
    Text one = new Text(composite, SWT.BORDER);
    data = new FormData();
    data.top = new FormAttachment(0, 0);
    data.bottom = new FormAttachment(100, 0);
    data.left = new FormAttachment(0, 0);
    data.right = new FormAttachment(sash, 0);
    one.setLayoutData(data);

    // Create the second text box and attach its left edge
    // to the sash
    Text two = new Text(composite, SWT.BORDER);
    data = new FormData();
    data.top = new FormAttachment(0, 0);
    data.bottom = new FormAttachment(100, 0);
    data.left = new FormAttachment(sash, 0);
    data.right = new FormAttachment(100, 0);
    two.setLayoutData(data);
}
```

Review Chapter 4, if necessary, to understand the parameters you're passing to the various FormAttachment objects.

The application now looks as it should, as shown in Figure 8-18. The sash is now the correct width.

Figure 8-18. The sash revisited

Dragging the sash left or right displays an outline of where the sash should go when you release the mouse button, as seen in Figure 8-19. However, releasing the mouse button doesn't cause the sash to relocate; the sash stubbornly remains at its initial location, ignoring your dragging action. The next section explains how to make the sash obey the requested move.

Figure 8-19. Dragging the sash

Making a Sash Stick

The default behavior of the sash allows dragging, but you must write code to make the sash stay where the users drag it. Fortunately, this code is simple. You implement an event handler to adjust the FormAttachment object associated with the sash's movable direction. For a vertical sash, adjust the left FormAttachment; for a horizontal sash, adjust the top FormAttachment.

Add this code to createContents():

```
sash.addSelectionListener(new SelectionAdapter() {
  public void widgetSelected(SelectionEvent event) {
    // Reattach to the left edge, and use the x value of the event to
    // determine the offset from the left
    ((FormData) sash.getLayoutData()).left = new FormAttachment(0, event.x);

    // Until the parent window does a layout, the sash will not be redrawn in
    // its new location. So, force a layout.
    sash.getParent().layout();
  }
});
```

You also must make the sash variable final, so that you can use it in the event handler:

```
final Sash sash = new Sash(composite, SWT.VERTICAL);
```

You must also import the SWT events package:

```
import org.eclipse.swt.events.*;
```

Now the sash will stay where you move it (see Figure 8-20).

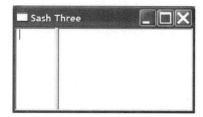

Figure 8-20. A sash that sticks

Tables

Presenting columnar data without the aid of tables would prove difficult at best. Tables, sometimes called grids, excel at organizing data in a format popularized by spreadsheet programs. SWT tables can display either text or graphics in each table cell, support single-line, clickable headers (often used to allow the user to sort the data in the column), and can either show or hide their grid lines. They also can contain other widgets inside their cells (discussed in the next chapter). They use three classes—Table, TableColumn, and TableItem—that correspond to the table, its columns, and its rows, respectively. None of these classes should be subclassed.

Creating Tables

The Table class offers a lone constructor, which takes a parent and a style:

```
public Table(Composite parent, int style)
```

Table 8-13 lists its style constants. You can combine styles using the bitwise OR operator.

Table 8-13. Table Styles

Style	Description
SWT.SINGLE	Only one table row may be selected at a time. This is the default.
SWT.MULTI	Multiple table rows may be selected, usually by holding down a key on the keyboard (typically the Ctrl key) while clicking the table row.
SWT.CHECK	Places a checkbox at the beginning of each table row. Note that the checked state of the checkbox is independent from the selected state of the table row.
SWT.FULL_SELECTION	Highlights the entire row, rather than just the first column of the row, when the row is selected. The default is to highlight only the first column.
SWT.HIDE_SELECTION	Removes the highlight from the selected row (if any) when the window containing the table isn't the foreground window. The default is to keep the row highlighted whether or not the parent window is the foreground window.
SWT.VIRTUAL	Creates a virtual table. A virtual table doesn't contain all its rows at once, but only those that are currently visible. See the VirtualTable example in the source code for this chapter for more information.

Figure 8-21 shows a table created with the SWT.SINGLE and SWT.CHECK styles, as created by this code:

```
Table table = new Table(parent, SWT.SINGLE | SWT.CHECK);
```

Figure 8-22 shows a table created with the SWT.MULTI and SWT.FULL_SELECTION styles, as created by this code:

```
Table table = new Table(parent, SWT.MULTI | SWT.FULL_SELECTION);
```

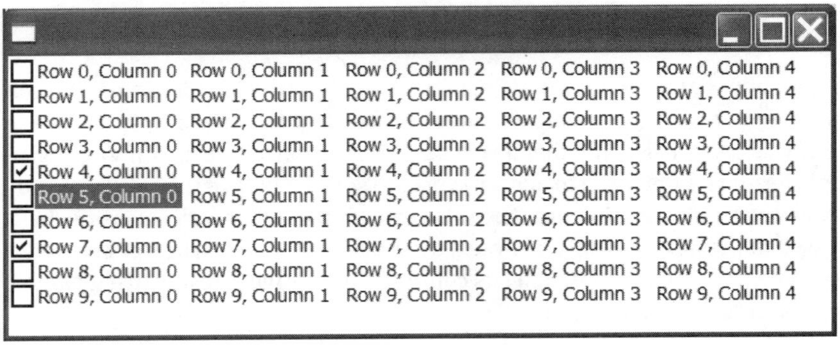

Figure 8-21. A single-selection, checkbox table

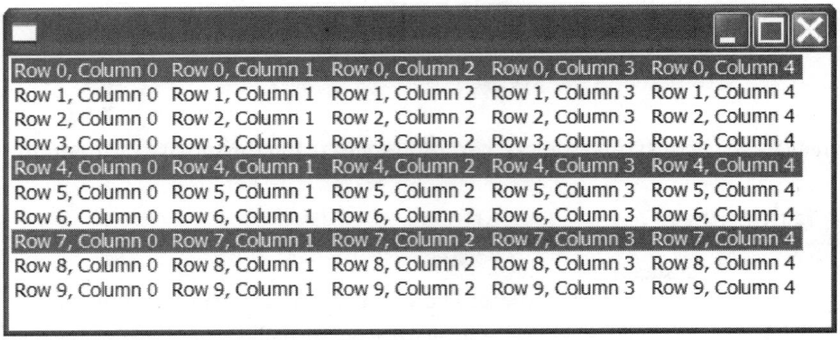

Figure 8-22. A multi- and full-selection table

A rich control such as Table merits a rich API, and Table certainly offers that. Most of Table's public methods deal with selecting and deselecting items in the table, but other methods allow you to show or hide headers or grid lines, or set or retrieve display properties such as the font. Table 8-14 lists Table's methods.

Table 8-14. Table *Methods*

Method	Description
void addSelectionListener (SelectionListener listener)	Adds a listener that's notified when this table is selected.
void deselect(int index)	Deselects the item at the specified zero-based index.
void deselect(int[] indices)	Deselects the items at the specified zero-based indices. Valid for multiselection tables.
void deselect(int start, int end)	Deselects the range of items specified by start and end, inclusive. Valid for multiselection tables.
void deselectAll()	Deselects all items.
TableColumn getColumn(int index)	Returns the column at the specified zero-based index.
int getColumnCount()	Returns the number of columns in the table.
TableColumn[] getColumns()	Returns all the columns in the table.
int getGridLineWidth()	Returns the width, in pixels, of the grid lines used to separate table cells.
int getHeaderHeight()	Returns the height, in pixels, of the header.
boolean getHeaderVisible()	Returns true if the header is visible, false if it isn't.
TableItem getItem(int index)	Returns the item at the specified zero-based index.
TableItem getItem(Point point)	Returns the item at the specified point, or null if no item exists at the point.
int getItemCount()	Returns the number of items in the table.
int getItemHeight()	Returns the height in pixels of a single item in the table.
TableItem[] getItems()	Returns all the items in the table.
boolean getLinesVisible()	Returns true if the grid lines separating the table cells are visible, false if they aren't.
TableItem[] getSelection()	Returns all the selected items.
int getSelectionCount()	Returns the number of selected items.
int getSelectionIndex()	Returns the zero-based index of the selected item, or -1 if no items are selected. In the case of multiselect tables with multiple items selected, returns the index of the first selected item only.
int[] getSelectionIndices()	Returns the zero-based indices of all selected items, or an empty array if no items are selected. Valid for multiselect tables.
int getTopIndex()	Returns the zero-based index of the item currently displayed at the top of the table.
int indexOf(TableColumn column)	Returns the zero-based index of the specified column.
int indexOf(TableItem item)	Returns the zero-based index of the specified item.
boolean isSelected(int index)	Returns true if the item at the specified zero-based index is selected, or false if it isn't.
void remove(int index)	Removes the item at the specified zero-based index. Throws an IllegalArgumentException if no item exists at the index.

Table 8-14. Table *Methods (continued)*

Method	Description
void remove(int[] indices)	Removes the items at the specified zero-based indices. Throws an IllegalArgumentException if any of the items don't exist.
void remove(int start, int end)	Removes all items in the range specified by start and end, inclusive. Throws an IllegalArgumentException if any of the items don't exist.
void removeAll()	Removes all items in the table.
void removeSelectionListener (SelectionListener listener)	Removes the listener from the notification list.
void select(int index)	Selects the item at the specified zero-based index.
void select(int[] indices)	Selects the items at the specified zero-based indices. Valid for multiselect tables.
void select(int start, int end)	Selects the items in the range specified by start and end, inclusive. Valid for multiselect tables.
void selectAll()	Selects all the items in the table.
void setFont(Font font)	Sets the font used to display text in the table. Passing null causes the default font to be used.
void setHeaderVisible(boolean show)	If show is true, displays the header. If show is false, doesn't display the header. The table defaults to not showing the header.
void setLinesVisible(boolean show)	If show is true, displays the grid lines separating the table cells. If show is false, doesn't display the grid lines. The table defaults to not showing the grid lines.
void setRedraw(boolean redraw)	If redraw is false, subsequent drawing operations will be ignored. Warning: leaving this set at false causes your table never to be redrawn. Use this before inserting items into the table to prevent flashing and multiple repaints, but be sure to set this back to true.
void setSelection(int index)	Selects the item at the specified zero-based index.
void setSelection(int[] indices)	Selects the items at the specified zero-based indices.
void setSelection(int start, int end)	Selects the range of items specified by start and end, inclusive.
void setSelection(TableItem[] items)	Selects the specified items.
void setTopIndex(int index)	Moves the item indicated by the specified zero-based index to the top (or as close to the top as scrolling allows) of the displayed table.
void showItem(TableItem item)	Moves the specified item into view, scrolling the table if necessary.
void showSelection()	Shows the selected item or items.
void showColumn(TableColumn column)	Moves the specified column into view, scrolling the table horizontally if necessary.

Adding Columns

The TableColumn class represents a column in the table. You create a column with a parent table, a style, and optionally an index. If you don't specify an index, the column assumes the next available zero-based index. Here are TableColumn's constructors:

```
public TableColumn(Table parent, int style)
public TableColumn(Table parent, int style, int index)
```

The supported styles all specify the alignment for the column's contents: SWT.LEFT for left alignment, SWT.CENTER for center alignment, and SWT.RIGHT for right alignment. You should specify only one of these; specifying more than one results in undefined behavior. You can change alignment after construction using the setAlignment() method. Alignment defaults to left and affects all rows in the column.

Columns in the table can display headers. Each header can have a single line of text (embedding carriage returns or linefeeds in the text causes the ASCII representation of the character to be displayed; see Figure 8-23). The parent table controls whether headers are displayed through its setHeadersVisible() method.

Line One♪◙Line Two?

Figure 8-23. An attempt to show two lines of text in a column header

Columns in the table can be clicked or resized. However, nothing happens when the column header is clicked, so if you want the column to sort when the header is clicked, you must write an event handler.

Table 8-15 lists TableColumn's methods.

Table 8-15. TableColumn *Methods*

Method	Description
void addControlListener (ControlListener listener)	Adds a listener that's notified when the column is resized or moved.
void addSelectionListener (SelectionListener listener)	Adds a listener that's notified when the column header is selected.
int getAlignment()	Returns the alignment for this column, which is SWT.LEFT, SWT.CENTER, or SWT.RIGHT.
Image getImage()	Returns the image displayed in this column's header.
Table getParent()	Returns the parent table for this column.
boolean getResizable()	Returns true if this column can be resized, false if it can't.
String getText()	Returns the text displayed in this column's header.
int getWidth()	Returns the width, in pixels, of this column.
void pack()	Resizes this column to the minimum width that will still fit all its contents (not including the header's contents).

Table 8-15. `TableColumn` *Methods (continued)*

Method	Description
void removeControlListener (ControlListener listener)	Removes the listener from the notification list.
void removeSelectionListener (SelectionListener listener)	Removes the listener from the notification list.
void setAlignment(int alignment)	Sets the alignment for this column, which should be one of SWT.LEFT, SWT.CENTER, or SWT.RIGHT.
void setImage(Image image)	Sets the image to display in this column's header. Pass null for no image.
void setResizable(boolean resizable)	Sets whether this column can be resized.
void setText(String string)	Sets the text to display in this column's header.
void setWidth(int width)	Sets the width, in pixels, for this column.

Adding Rows

The `TableItem` class represents rows in the table. The parent of a `TableItem`, as with a `TableColumn`, is the containing `Table`. Therefore, here are its constructors:

```
TableItem(Table parent, int style)
TableItem(Table parent, int style, int index)
```

Using the second constructor inserts the row at the specified zero-based index, and shifts existing rows downward. Passing an index out of range throws an `IllegalArgumentException`. For example, if no rows currently exist in the table, try writing this code:

```
new TableItem(table, SWT.NONE, 1);
```

The preceding code results in this exception:

```
java.lang.IllegalArgumentException: Index out of bounds
```

No styles apply for `TableItem`, so you should always pass `SWT.NONE`. SWT ignores any other value.

You can change both the background color and the foreground color for a `TableItem`, either on a row-wide or an individual-cell basis. Cells can display text, images, or both. If you specify both, the image will display to the left of the text. Rows in the table can also sport a checkbox, displayed to the left of the row. Table 8-16 lists the API that makes these possible.

Table 8-16. `TableItem` *Methods*

Method	Description
`Color getBackground()`	Returns the background color (for the entire row) for this table item.
`Color getBackground(int index)`	Returns the background color for this table item for the column at the specified zero-based index.
`Rectangle getBounds(int index)`	Returns the size and location for this table item for the column at the specified zero-based index.
`boolean getChecked()`	Returns `true` if the checkbox for this table item is checked, `false` if it's not checked.
`Color getForeground()`	Returns the foreground color (for the entire row) for this table item.
`Color getForeground(int index)`	Returns the foreground color for this table item for the column at the specified zero-based index.
`boolean getGrayed()`	If this table item has a checkbox, returns `true` if the table item is grayed (indeterminate), `false` if it's not grayed.
`Image getImage()`	Returns the image for this table item (for the entire row).
`Image getImage(int index)`	Returns the image for this table item for the column at the specified zero-based index.
`Rectangle getImageBounds(int index)`	Returns the size and location for the image for this table item for the column at the specified zero-based index.
`int getImageIndent()`	Returns the image indent (the padding to the left of the image), in increments of the image's width.
`Table getParent()`	Returns this table item's parent.
`String getText(int index)`	Returns the text for the column at the specified zero-based index, or an empty string (not `null`) if no text has been set.
`void setBackground(Color color)`	Sets the background color for this table item for the entire row.
`void setBackground(int index, Color color)`	Sets the background color for this table item for the column at the specified zero-based index.
`void setChecked(boolean checked)`	If this table item has a checkbox, sets its checked status.
`void setForeground(Color color)`	Sets the foreground color for this table item for the entire row.
`void setForeground(int index, Color color)`	Sets the foreground color for this table item for the column at the specified zero-based index.
`void setGrayed(boolean grayed)`	If this table item has a checkbox, sets its grayed (indeterminate) status.
`void setImage(Image image)`	Sets the image for this table item for the first column.
`void setImage(Image[] images)`	Sets the images for this table item for multiple columns. Each image in the array is set into the column at the corresponding zero-based index.

Table 8-16. `TableItem` *Methods (continued)*

Method	Description
void setImage(int index, Image image)	Sets the image for this table item for the column at the specified zero-based index.
void setImageIndent(int indent)	Sets the image indent (the padding to use to the left of the image) in increments of the image's width.
void setText(int index, String string)	Sets the text for this row item for the column at the specified zero-based index. Passing null for string throws an IllegalArgumentException.
void setText(String string)	Sets the text for this row item for the first column. Passing null for string throws an IllegalArgumentException.
void setText(String[] strings)	Sets the text for this table item for multiple columns. Each string in the array is set into the column at the corresponding zero-based index. Passing null for any of the String objects in the array throws an IllegalArgumentException.

One invaluable application for software developers, one that begs for a table, is a simple ASCII table that displays ASCII characters and their decimal, hexadecimal, octal, and binary representations. Displaying ASCII tables using Java is a little tricky, because Java stores all characters as Unicode. Unicode is sprinkled with control characters, but as long as you confine yourself to the first 128 characters in the ASCII set, you should have no issues.

The AsciiTable application in Listing 8-7 uses a table to display the first 128 characters in the ASCII set, along with their decimal, hexadecimal, octal, and binary representations. It also displays the names of the first 32 characters. It uses the table's headers to label the columns, and puts each display value in its own cell. For fun, it uses various background colors for the rows, demonstrating how easy changing colors in rows is.

Listing 8-7. `AsciiTable.java`

```
package examples.ch8;

import org.eclipse.swt.*;
import org.eclipse.swt.graphics.Font;
import org.eclipse.swt.graphics.Color;
import org.eclipse.swt.layout.*;
import org.eclipse.swt.widgets.*;

/**
 * Displays ASCII Codes
 */
public class AsciiTable {
  // The number of characters to show.
  private static final int MAX_CHARS = 128;
```

```java
// Names for each of the columns
private static final String[] COLUMN_NAMES = { "Char", "Dec", "Hex", "Oct",
    "Bin", "Name"};

// The names of the first 32 characters
private static final String[] CHAR_NAMES = { "NUL", "SOH", "STX", "ETX", "EOT",
    "ENQ", "ACK", "BEL", "BS", "TAB", "LF", "VT", "FF", "CR", "SO", "SI",
    "DLE", "DC1", "DC2", "DC3", "DC4", "NAK", "SYN", "ETB", "CAN", "EM", "SUB",
    "ESC", "FS", "GS", "RS", "US", "Space"};

// The font to use for displaying characters
private Font font;

// The background colors to use for the rows
private Color[] colors = new Color[MAX_CHARS];

/**
 * Runs the application
 */
public void run() {
  Display display = new Display();
  Shell shell = new Shell(display);
  shell.setText("ASCII Codes");
  createContents(shell);
  shell.pack();
  shell.open();
  while (!shell.isDisposed()) {
    if (!display.readAndDispatch()) {
      display.sleep();
    }
  }
  // Call dispose to dispose any resources
  // we have created
  dispose();
  display.dispose();
}

/**
 * Disposes the resources created
 */
private void dispose() {
  // We created this font; we must dispose it
  if (font != null) {
    font.dispose();
  }

  // We created the colors; we must dispose them
  for (int i = 0, n = colors.length; i < n; i++) {
```

```
      if (colors[i] != null) {
        colors[i].dispose();
      }
    }
  }

  /**
   * Creates the font
   */
  private void createFont() {
    // Create a font that will display the range
    // of characters. "Terminal" works well in
    // Windows
    font = new Font(Display.getCurrent(), "Terminal", 10, SWT.NORMAL);
  }

  /**
   * Creates the columns for the table
   *
   * @param table the table
   * @return TableColumn[]
   */
  private TableColumn[] createColumns(Table table) {
    TableColumn[] columns = new TableColumn[COLUMN_NAMES.length];
    for (int i = 0, n = columns.length; i < n; i++) {
      // Create the TableColumn with right alignment
      columns[i] = new TableColumn(table, SWT.RIGHT);

      // This text will appear in the column header
      columns[i].setText(COLUMN_NAMES[i]);
    }
    return columns;
  }

  /**
   * Creates the window's contents (the table)
   *
   * @param composite the parent composite
   */
  private void createContents(Composite composite) {
    composite.setLayout(new FillLayout());

    // The system font will not display the lower 32
    // characters, so create one that will
    createFont();

    // Create a table with visible headers
    // and lines, and set the font that we
    // created
```

```java
    Table table = new Table(composite, SWT.SINGLE | SWT.FULL_SELECTION);
    table.setHeaderVisible(true);
    table.setLinesVisible(true);
    table.setRedraw(false);
    table.setFont(font);

    // Create the columns
    TableColumn[] columns = createColumns(table);

    for (int i = 0; i < MAX_CHARS; i++) {
      // Create a background color for this row
      colors[i] = new Color(table.getDisplay(), 255 - i, 127 + i, i);

      // Create the row in the table by creating
      // a TableItem and setting text for each
      // column
      int c = 0;
      TableItem item = new TableItem(table, SWT.NONE);
      item.setText(c++, String.valueOf((char) i));
      item.setText(c++, String.valueOf(i));
      item.setText(c++, Integer.toHexString(i).toUpperCase());
      item.setText(c++, Integer.toOctalString(i));
      item.setText(c++, Integer.toBinaryString(i));
      item.setText(c++, i < CHAR_NAMES.length ? CHAR_NAMES[i] : "");
      item.setBackground(colors[i]);
    }

    // Now that we've set the text into the columns,
    // we call pack() on each one to size it to the
    // contents
    for (int i = 0, n = columns.length; i < n; i++) {
      columns[i].pack();
    }

    // Set redraw back to true so that the table
    // will paint appropriately
    table.setRedraw(true);
  }

  /**
   * The application entry point
   *
   * @param args the command line arguments
   */
  public static void main(String[] args) {
    new AsciiTable().run();
  }
}
```

Run the application to see the ASCII table shown in Figure 8-24.

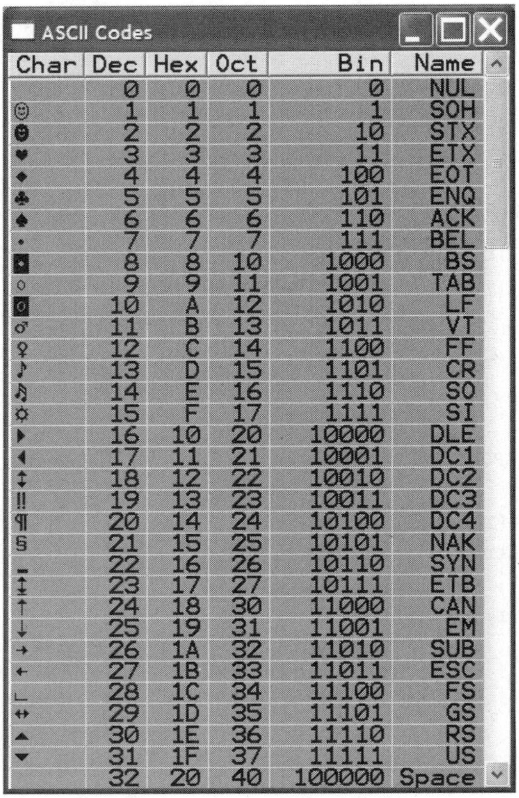

Char	Dec	Hex	Oct	Bin	Name
	0	0	0	0	NUL
☺	1	1	1	1	SOH
☻	2	2	2	10	STX
♥	3	3	3	11	ETX
♦	4	4	4	100	EOT
♣	5	5	5	101	ENQ
♠	6	6	6	110	ACK
•	7	7	7	111	BEL
◘	8	8	10	1000	BS
○	9	9	11	1001	TAB
◙	10	A	12	1010	LF
♂	11	B	13	1011	VT
♀	12	C	14	1100	FF
♪	13	D	15	1101	CR
♫	14	E	16	1110	SO
☼	15	F	17	1111	SI
►	16	10	20	10000	DLE
◄	17	11	21	10001	DC1
↕	18	12	22	10010	DC2
‼	19	13	23	10011	DC3
¶	20	14	24	10100	DC4
§	21	15	25	10101	NAK
▬	22	16	26	10110	SYN
↨	23	17	27	10111	ETB
↑	24	18	30	11000	CAN
↓	25	19	31	11001	EM
→	26	1A	32	11010	SUB
←	27	1B	33	11011	ESC
∟	28	1C	34	11100	FS
↔	29	1D	35	11101	GS
▲	30	1E	36	11110	RS
▼	31	1F	37	11111	US
	32	20	40	100000	Space

Figure 8-24. The AsciiTable application

Sorting Tables

Users expect that clicking table headers will sort the rows by that column, alternating between ascending and descending order. SWT's `Table` doesn't do that automatically, but sorting is trivial to implement. To implement sorting, you do the following:

1. Add a listener to detect when the column header is clicked.
2. Retain the current sort information (which column the table is currently sorted by, and which direction it's sorted—ascending or descending).
3. Sort the data within the table and redisplay.

The PlayerTable application illustrates sorting. It displays baseball players' names and lifetime batting averages. You can sort the table by first name, last name, or batting average. Download the code to see this application; this section highlights the classes and their functions.

The Player class holds the player information: first name, last name, and batting average. It offers standard getters and setters for those fields. The application stores the Player objects in a java.util.List, and relies on Collections.sort(list, comparator) to do the sorting.

The PlayerComparator class performs the comparisons. Its implementation of compare(Object obj1, Object obj2) sorts on the specified column and in the specified direction, so it contains state variables and setters for column and direction. It could also provide a getter for the direction, so that reversing the direction would entail the following:

1. Getting the current direction from the comparator

2. Calculating the value for the reversed direction

3. Setting the new direction back into the comparator

Because this seems more complicated than it should be, the PlayerComparator class instead has a convenience method that simply reverses the direction.

Finally, the PlayerTable class launches the application, creates and stores a list of players, and also creates an instance of PlayerComparator to use in the event handlers. The application creates a table, adds three columns (first name, last name, and batting average), and adds listeners to each column that are triggered when the column's header is clicked. This listener does the following:

1. Sets the column for sorting into the comparator

2. Reverses the direction for the sort

3. Calls the fillTable() helper method, which empties the table, sorts the players, and reinserts them into the table

The code for each listener looks something like this:

```
columns[0].addSelectionListener(new SelectionAdapter() {
  public void widgetSelected(SelectionEvent event) {
    comparator.setColumn(PlayerComparator.FIRST_NAME);
    comparator.reverseDirection();
    fillTable(table);
  }
});
```

Each time the user clicks a table header, the listener sets the comparator's column member to the clicked column. It then reverses the direction for the sort, and refills the table with the sorted data.

Compile and run the application. You should see a window like the one in Figure 8-25. Click the column headers to sort the players; Figure 8-26 shows the players sorted by batting average.

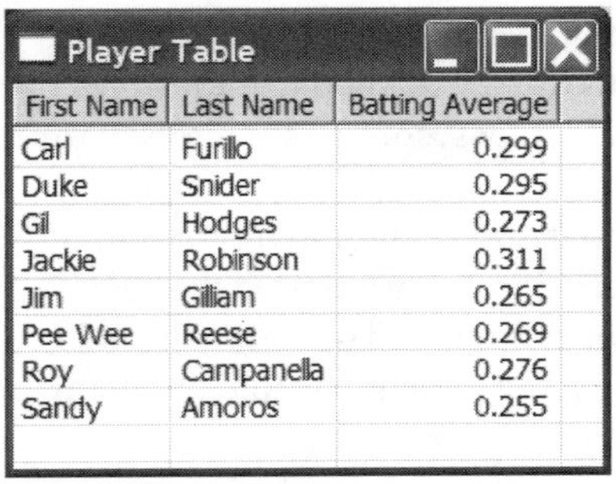

First Name	Last Name	Batting Average
Carl	Furillo	0.299
Duke	Snider	0.295
Gil	Hodges	0.273
Jackie	Robinson	0.311
Jim	Gilliam	0.265
Pee Wee	Reese	0.269
Roy	Campanella	0.276
Sandy	Amoros	0.255

Figure 8-25. The players

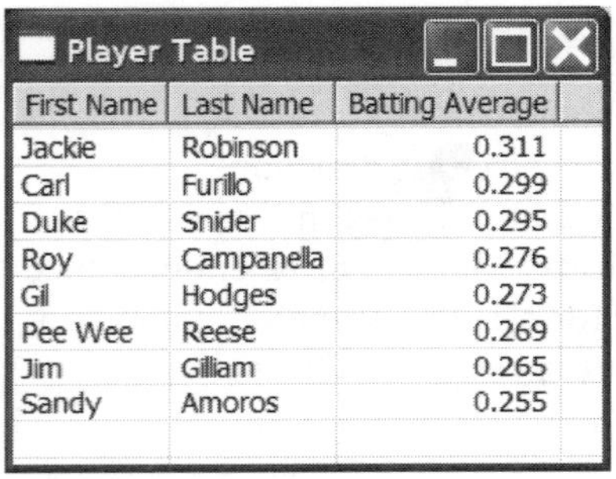

First Name	Last Name	Batting Average
Jackie	Robinson	0.311
Carl	Furillo	0.299
Duke	Snider	0.295
Roy	Campanella	0.276
Gil	Hodges	0.273
Pee Wee	Reese	0.269
Jim	Gilliam	0.265
Sandy	Amoros	0.255

Figure 8-26. The players sorted by batting average

If you're a Swing developer, you're probably smirking about how tedious it was to sort the table: drop the data, reorder it, and reinsert it. Programming with SWT means programming at the widget level, with data (model), view, and the means to manipulate that view (controller) inseparably intertwined. Separating data, view, and controller in an MVC pattern, as Swing's table does, makes sorting more straightforward. However, remember that although SWT exposes only the widget interface, JFace provides an MVC layer on top of SWT that makes table sorting in JFace as simple as in Swing. Chapter 14 covers tables, along with how to sort them, in JFace.

Putting Widgets in the Cells

Sometimes you'll use tables purely for displaying data, but other times you'll want to provide means for editing that data. Tables in SWT support widgets in cells, so you can allow users to edit table data within the table. The `TableEditor` class, part of the `org.eclipse.swt.custom` package, provides this functionality. Chapter 9 covers the `org.eclipse.swt.custom` package, including putting widgets in table cells.

Trees

Trees present hierarchical data. Like tables, trees contain items. However, instead of being arranged in columns and rows, items in trees can contain other items, creating parent-child relationships between them. Users can hide or show the children of each item in the tree—a process called contraction and expansion, respectively. The selective display ability of trees allows them to use their allotted space economically to present large amounts of data.

Creating Trees

SWT uses two classes, Tree and TreeItem, to implement tree controls. Neither of these should be subclassed. You create a tree by instantiating a Tree object, passing the parent and the desired style, as shown by this constructor:

```
public Tree(Composite parent, int style)
```

Trees can allow either a single selection or multiple selections. They also can have a checkbox displayed to the left of each item in the tree. These attributes are controlled by the style constants passed to the constructor, shown in Table 8-17. You can combine style constants using the bitwise OR operator. However, you should specify only one of SWT.SINGLE and SWT.MULTI.

Table 8-17. Tree *Styles*

Style	Description
SWT.SINGLE	Allows only one item in the tree to be selected at a time. This is the default.
SWT.MULTI	Allows multiple items in the tree to be selected at the same time, usually by holding down a key on the keyboard (typically the Ctrl key) while clicking each tree node.
SWT.CHECK	Displays a checkbox to the left of each of the root items in the tree.

Table 8-18 lists Tree's methods.

Table 8-18. Tree *Methods*

Method	Description
void addSelectionListener (SelectionListener listener)	Adds a listener that's notified when the tree's selection changes.
void addTreeListener (TreeListener listener)	Adds a listener that's notified when any part of the tree is expanded or collapsed.
void deselectAll()	Deselects any selected items in the tree.
TreeItem getItem(Point point)	Returns the item that contains the specified point, or null if the point isn't contained by any item.

Table 8-18. Tree *Methods (continued)*

Method	Description
int getItemCount()	Returns the number of items in the tree.
int getItemHeight()	Returns the height, in pixels, of a single item in the tree.
TreeItem[] getItems()	Returns the items in the tree.
TreeItem getParentItem()	Returns the parent item in the tree.
TreeItem[] getSelection()	Returns the selected items in the tree.
int getSelectionCount()	Returns the number of items selected in the tree.
TreeItem getTopItem()	Returns the item currently displayed at the top of the tree.
void removeAll()	Removes all items from the tree.
void removeSelection Listener(SelectionListener listener)	Removes the specified listener from the notification list.
void removeTreeListener (TreeListener listener)	Removes the specified listener from the notification list.
void selectAll()	Selects all the items in the tree.
void setInsertMark (TreeItem item, boolean before)	Shows the insertion point where a new item would be inserted into the tree. If before is true, shows the mark above the specified item; otherwise, shows the mark below the item.
void setRedraw(boolean redraw)	If redraw is false, suspends further drawing of the tree. Otherwise, resumes drawing the tree anytime the tree needs to be redrawn.
void setSelection (TreeItem[] items)	Selects the specified items in the tree.
void setTopItem (TreeItem item)	Moves the item to the top (or as close to the top as scrolling will allow) of the displayed portion of the tree.
void showItem(TreeItem item)	Displays the specified item in the tree, scrolling the view of the tree if necessary.
void showSelection()	Displays the selected item in the tree, scrolling the view of the tree if necessary.

Adding Nodes

Nodes in a tree, also called leaves and branches (stretching the metaphor beyond its usefulness), are implemented by the TreeItem class. Nodes can be at the root of the tree, or they can be children of another node. You determine the parent of a node at construction time, and it cannot be changed. For root nodes, pass the Tree itself as the parent; for child nodes, pass the parent TreeItem. Table 8-19 lists the TreeItem constructors.

Table 8-19. TreeItem *Constructors*

Constructor	Description
public TreeItem(Tree parent, int style)	Creates a root tree item with the specified style.
public TreeItem(Tree parent, int style, int index)	Creates a root tree item with the specified style and at the specified zero-based index.
public TreeItem(TreeItem parentItem, int style)	Creates a tree item that is a child to parentItem, with the specified style.
public TreeItem(TreeItem parentItem, int style, int index)	Creates a tree item that is a child to parentItem, with the specified style and at the specified zero-based index, relative to parentItem.

The nodes in a tree can display images and text. Each node can display a background color, and can have a checkbox at its left (for trees created with the SWT.CHECK style). Table 8-20 lists the methods for TreeItem.

Table 8-20. TreeItem *Methods*

Method	Description
Color getBackground()	Returns the background color for this item.
Rectangle getBounds()	Returns the bounding Rectangle for this item, relative to the parent tree.
boolean getChecked()	Returns true if the checkbox for this item is checked, false if it isn't checked. Used for items in tables created with the SWT.CHECK style.
boolean getExpanded()	Returns true if the item is expanded, false if it isn't expanded.
Color getForeground()	Returns the foreground color for this item.
boolean getGrayed()	Returns true if the checkbox for this item is in the indeterminate state, false if it isn't in the indeterminate state. Used for items in tables created with the SWT.CHECK style.
Image getImage()	Gets the image for this item.
int getItemCount()	Returns the number of items that are children of this item.
TreeItem[] getItems()	Returns the items that are children of this item.
Tree getParent()	Returns the parent tree of this item.
TreeItem getParentItem()	Returns the parent item of this tree, or null if this item is at the root of the tree.
String getText()	Returns the text for this item. Defined in superclass Item.
void setBackground (Color color)	Sets the background color for this item.
void setChecked (boolean checked)	If checked is true, places a check in the checkbox for this item. Otherwise, removes the check from the checkbox for this item. Used for items in trees created with the SWT.CHECK style.
void setExpanded (boolean expanded)	If expanded is true, expands the item. Otherwise, collapses the item.

Table 8-20. TreeItem *Methods (continued)*

Method	Description
void setForeground (Color color)	Sets the foreground color for this item.
void setGrayed (boolean grayed)	If grayed is true, sets the checkbox for this item in the indeterminate state. Otherwise, removes it from indeterminate state.
void setImage(Image image)	Sets the image for this item.
void setText(String text)	Sets the text for this item.

The TreeExample application in Listing 8-8 creates three trees: a single-selection tree, a multiselection tree, and a checkbox tree. You can expand and contract the nodes in the trees, select them, and check and uncheck their checkboxes.

Listing 8-8. TreeExample.java

```
package examples.ch8;

import org.eclipse.swt.*;
import org.eclipse.swt.layout.*;
import org.eclipse.swt.widgets.*;

/**
 * Displays a single-selection tree, a multiselection tree, and a checkbox tree
 */
public class TreeExample {
  /**
   * Runs the application
   */
  public void run() {
    Display display = new Display();
    Shell shell = new Shell(display);
    shell.setText("TreeExample");
    createContents(shell);
    shell.open();
    while (!shell.isDisposed()) {
      if (!display.readAndDispatch()) {
        display.sleep();
      }
    }
    display.dispose();
  }

  private void createContents(Composite composite) {
    // Set the single-selection tree in the upper left,
    // the multiselection tree in the upper right,
```

```
    // and the checkbox tree across the bottom.
    // To do this, create a 1x2 grid, and in the top
    // cell, a 2x1 grid.
    composite.setLayout(new GridLayout(1, true));
    Composite top = new Composite(composite, SWT.NONE);
    GridData data = new GridData(GridData.FILL_BOTH);
    top.setLayoutData(data);

    top.setLayout(new GridLayout(2, true));
    Tree single = new Tree(top, SWT.SINGLE | SWT.BORDER);
    data = new GridData(GridData.FILL_BOTH);
    single.setLayoutData(data);
    fillTree(single);

    Tree multi = new Tree(top, SWT.MULTI | SWT.BORDER);
    data = new GridData(GridData.FILL_BOTH);
    multi.setLayoutData(data);
    fillTree(multi);

    Tree check = new Tree(composite, SWT.CHECK | SWT.BORDER);
    data = new GridData(GridData.FILL_BOTH);
    check.setLayoutData(data);
    fillTree(check);
}

/**
 * Helper method to fill a tree with data
 *
 * @param tree the tree to fill
 */
private void fillTree(Tree tree) {
    // Turn off drawing to avoid flicker
    tree.setRedraw(false);

    // Create five root items
    for (int i = 0; i < 5; i++) {
        TreeItem item = new TreeItem(tree, SWT.NONE);
        item.setText("Root Item " + i);

        // Create three children below the root
        for (int j = 0; j < 3; j++) {
            TreeItem child = new TreeItem(item, SWT.NONE);
            child.setText("Child Item " + i + " - " + j);

            // Create three grandchildren under the child
            for (int k = 0; k < 3; k++) {
                TreeItem grandChild = new TreeItem(child, SWT.NONE);
```

```
        grandChild.setText("Grandchild Item " + i + " - " + j + " - " + k);
      }
    }
  }
  // Turn drawing back on!
  tree.setRedraw(true);
}

/**
 * The entry point for the application
 *
 * @param args the command line arguments
 */
public static void main(String[] args) {
  new TreeExample().run();
}
}
```

Compile and run the program to see the main window, shown in Figure 8-27. Figure 8-28 shows the tree after some manipulation.

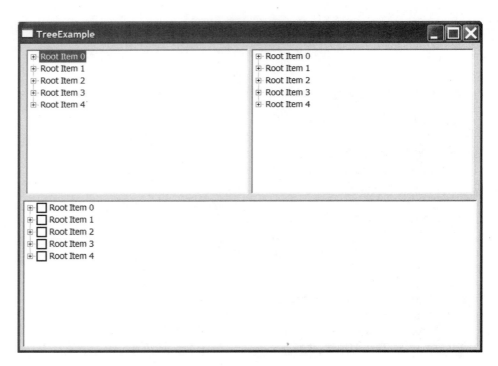

Figure 8-27. A single-selection tree, a multiselection tree, and a checkbox tree

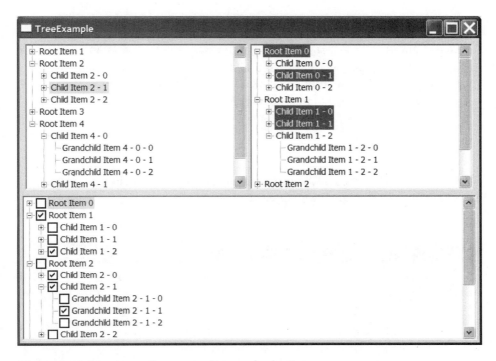

Figure 8-28. The trees after expanding and selecting

Combining Advanced Controls

Using several advanced controls in concert demonstrates their power. The code you can download contains an XML viewer program (called, imaginatively, XmlView) that uses a tree to navigate the hierarchy of the XML, and a table to display the attributes of the selected tree node. A sash separates the tree and table, so you can reallocate the division of space between them. You can open multiple XML files simultaneously, and each file displays in its own tab. The program offers both a menu and a toolbar to open and close files.

The program uses a toolkit called JDOM to read and parse the XML files. See the sidebar "What Is JDOM?" for more information on JDOM. To build and run the application, you need JDOM, available for download from http://www.jdom.org/, in your classpath.

What Is JDOM?

JDOM (which doesn't stand for anything) is an open-source toolkit for reading and writing XML data. Written in and designed especially for Java, it meshes well with existing Java constructs, APIs, and classes. Though the library officially claims beta status (the current version is JDOM Beta 10 Release Candidate #1), it nonetheless is sufficiently robust for prime-time use.

Reading and writing XML data has typically meant using the Document Object Model (DOM), which stretches the capabilities of all but the elite. In response to the complexities, Jason Hunter and Brett McLaughlin launched the JDOM Project "to build a complete, Java-based solution for accessing, manipulating, and outputting XML data from Java code" (from the JDOM Web site).

Read more about the JDOM Project at `http://www.jdom.org/`.

When you first run the XmlView application, the window looks like Figure 8-29. Figure 8-30 shows the program with three open files.

Figure 8-29. The XmlView application

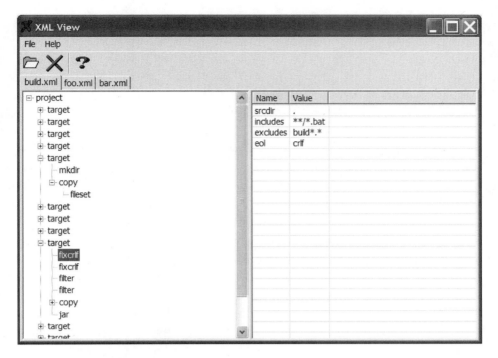

Figure 8-30. The XmlView application with three open files

Summary

By using SWT's advanced controls, you expand the domain of problems you can solve with your applications. The controls aren't difficult to program, and add professionalism to your programs. Leveraging your users' familiarity with these controls eases their learning curve with your applications.

The next chapter discusses SWT's custom controls, which enhance some of the controls discussed in this chapter and some from Chapter 5. As promised, it also explains how to place controls inside cells in a table.

CHAPTER 9

The Custom
Controls

CHAPTER 5 DETAILS the basic widgets offered by SWT, and Chapter 8 explores advanced widgets suitable for most tasks. The Eclipse developers, however, aimed for a best-of-breed IDE and thus had interface requirements that neither the basic nor the advanced widgets could handle. To answer their requirements, they created the org.eclipse.swt.custom package, which contains new controls to add functionality, makes enhancements to existing controls, and contains new controls to work with existing controls. This chapter examines the following:

- BusyIndicator

- CCombo

- CLabel

- CTabFolder

- TableTree

- Control editors

- TableCursor

- PopupList

- SashForm

- ScrolledComposite

- ViewForm

Using these controls adds a professional touch to your applications, improving the user experience and adding polish.

Introducing BusyIndicator

Ideally, your applications will perform all operations instantaneously, responding immediately to every user input and never making your users wait. Sometimes, however, your
applications can't avoid performing tasks that take time, and they can't respond to user
input until they're done. In these situations, informing users you're temporarily paying
them no attention usually only makes your inattentiveness forgivable. The busy cursor,
implemented by SWT's BusyIndicator class, provides this simple feedback, saying, "Don't
worry—I'm busy, but I'll be right back."

Using a BusyIndicator

To use most SWT classes, you instantiate an object of the desired type, passing it a parent and a style. Although you can create a BusyIndicator object, you can't pass it any
parameters. What's more, you can't do much with it—it has no public methods beyond
those offered by java.lang.Object. It has no member variables, either, and preserves
no state. In other words, don't bother creating a BusyIndicator.

   Instead, use BusyIndicator's only method, which is static:

```
void showWhile(Display display, Runnable runnable)
```

The display parameter represents the display on which the busy cursor should display.
If you pass null for this parameter, the current thread's display is used; if the current
thread has no display, no busy cursor displays, but the specified operation still executes. The runnable parameter contains the thread that executes your long-running
operation and can't be null. When this method executes, it shows the busy cursor,
spawns the specified thread, and blocks until the thread completes. When the thread
completes, the busy cursor reverts to the normal cursor, and execution of the calling
thread resumes.

Showing the Busy Cursor

The BusyIndicatorTest program displays a window with a single button (see Listing 9-1).
Click the button to display the busy cursor and launch a thread that sleeps for three seconds. When the thread completes, you see the cursor return to normal.

Listing 9-1. BusyIndicatorTest.java

```
package examples.ch9;

import org.eclipse.swt.*;
import org.eclipse.swt.custom.*;
import org.eclipse.swt.events.*;
import org.eclipse.swt.layout.*;
import org.eclipse.swt.widgets.*;
```

```java
/**
 * This program demonstrates BusyIndicator
 */
public class BusyIndicatorTest {
  // The amount of time to sleep (in ms)
  private static final int SLEEP_TIME = 3000;

  // Labels for the button
  private static final String RUN = "Press to Run";
  private static final String IS_RUNNING = "Running...";

  /**
   * Runs the application
   */
  private void run() {
    Display display = new Display();
    Shell shell = new Shell(display);
    shell.setText("BusyIndicator Test");
    createContents(shell);
    shell.pack();
    shell.open();
    while (!shell.isDisposed()) {
      if (!display.readAndDispatch()) {
        display.sleep();
      }
    }
    display.dispose();
  }

  /**
   * Create the window's contents
   *
   * @param shell the parent shell
   */
  private void createContents(Shell shell) {
    shell.setLayout(new FillLayout());
    final Button button = new Button(shell, SWT.PUSH);
    button.setText(RUN);
    button.addSelectionListener(new SelectionAdapter() {
      public void widgetSelected(SelectionEvent event) {
        // Change the button's text
        button.setText(IS_RUNNING);

        // Show the busy indicator
        BusyIndicator.showWhile(button.getDisplay(),
          new SleepThread(SLEEP_TIME));
```

```
        // Thread has completed; reset the button's text
        button.setText(RUN);
      }
    });
  }

  /**
   * Application's entry point
   *
   * @param args the command line arguments
   */
  public static void main(String[] args) {
    new BusyIndicatorTest().run();
  }
}

/**
 * This class is a thread that sleeps the specified number of milliseconds
 */

class SleepThread extends Thread {
  private long ms;

  /**
   * SleepThread constructor
   *
   * @param ms the number of milliseconds to sleep
   */
  public SleepThread(long ms) {
    this.ms = ms;
  }

  /**
   * Runs the thread
   */
  public void run() {
    try {
      sleep(ms);
    } catch (InterruptedException e) {}
  }
}
```

Figure 9-1 shows the program's window, and Figure 9-2 shows the window while the long-running thread executes. Notice the hourglass cursor, which tells you that the program is busy.

Figure 9-1. The BusyIndicatorTest application

Figure 9-2. The BusyIndicatorTest application while busy

Introducing CCombo

Chapter 5 covers the Combo widget, which implements a dropdown or combo box. You'll rarely stray from Combo for your dropdown needs. The custom package, however, adds an additional dropdown widget called CCombo. Table 9-1 compares Combo and CCombo, but essentially the CCombo widget exists for use in table cells. Combo widgets don't assume the proper height inside table cells, but CCombo widgets do.[1] Figure 9-3 shows a Combo and a CCombo in a table—the Combo overlaps the lower edge of its table cell, but the CCombo fits within its table cell.

The Combo widget wraps a native combo box widget, which generally doesn't offer enough control to size it properly in a table cell. A CCombo, on the other hand, aggregates a Text, a List, and a Button. The Text always displays, and it shows the currently selected item. The Button shows at the right edge of the Text, and it displays the expected downward arrow. Together, they fill the table cell without overlapping. When users click the button, the List containing all the options displays below the Text.

Table 9-1. Combo vs. CCombo

Description	Combo	CCombo
Can be set to read-only	Yes	Yes
Can be drawn with or without a border	Yes	Yes
Can be drawn with a flat button	No	Yes
Can be set to always display the list	Yes	No
Fits the height of a table cell	No	Yes

Figure 9-3. A Combo and a CCombo in a table

1. http://dev.eclipse.org/newslists/news.eclipse.platform.swt/msg01832.html. (This link requires a password to access.)

Creating a CCombo

Create a CCombo by passing a parent and a style to the constructor:

```
public CCombo(Composite parent, int style)
```

Table 9-2 lists the styles that apply to CCombo. You can combine style constants using the bitwise OR operator. Figure 9-4 shows the effects of the styles.

Table 9-2. CCombo *Styles*

Style	Description
SWT.BORDER	Draws a border around the combo box.
SWT.FLAT	Draws the arrow button with a flat look. The default is a three-dimensional look.
SWT.READ_ONLY	Creates a combo that doesn't allow users to type in the text box; they can only select an option from the list.

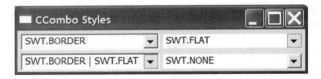

Figure 9-4. Some CCombo *styles*

Using a CCombo

You use a CCombo much as you do a Combo: You create one, add items to it, and retrieve the selected values. With minor exceptions, the methods that CCombo offers mirror those offered by Combo. Table 9-3 describes CCombo's methods.

Table 9-3. CCombo *Methods*

Method	Description
void add(String string)	Adds an item to the list.
void add(String string, int index)	Adds an item to the list at the specified zero-based index.
void addModifyListener (ModifyListener listener)	Adds a listener that's notified when the text in the text box is changed by typing.
void addSelectionListener (SelectionListener listener)	Adds a listener that's notified when the selection changes.
void clearSelection()	Clears any selection.
Point computeSize(int wHint, int hHint, boolean changed)	Computes this CCombo's size using the specified hints.
void deselect(int index)	Deselects the item at the specified zero-based index.

Table 9-3. CCombo *Methods (continued)*

Method	Description
void deselectAll()	Deselects all items.
Control[] getChildren()	Though you'd expect this method to return all the children of this combo (the Text, List, and Button), it currently returns only an empty array.
boolean getEditable()	Returns true if the CCombo is editable. Otherwise, returns false.
String getItem(int index)	Returns the item at the specified zero-based index.
int getItemCount()	Returns the number of items in this CCombo.
int getItemHeight()	Returns the height in pixels of a single item in the list.
String[] getItems()	Returns all the items in the list.
Point getSelection()	Returns a point describing the location of the selected text in the Text portion of this CCombo. The x value contains the starting point of the selection, and the y value contains the ending part.
int getSelectionIndex()	Returns the zero-based index of the selected item or -1 if no items are selected.
String getText()	Returns the text in the Text portion of this CCombo.
int getTextHeight()	Returns the height, in pixels, of the Text portion of this CCombo.
int getTextLimit()	Returns the maximum number of characters the Text portion of this CCombo can hold.
int indexOf(String string)	Returns the zero-based index of the first item in the list that matches string.
int indexOf(String string, int start)	Returns the zero-based index of the first item at or after start that matches string.
boolean isFocusControl()	Returns true if this CCombo has the focus and false if it doesn't.
void redraw()	Marks this CCombo to be redrawn.
void redraw(int x, int y, int width, int height, boolean all)	Marks the portion of this CCombo specified by the arguments to be redrawn.
void remove(int index)	Removes the item at the specified zero-based index.
void remove(int start, int end)	Removes the items between the zero-based indices specified by start and end inclusive.
void remove(String string)	Removes the first item matching the text specified by string.
void removeAll()	Removes all the items.
void removeModifyListener (ModifyListener listener)	Removes the specified listener from the notification list.
void removeSelectionListener (SelectionListener listener)	Removes the specified listener from the notification list.
void select(int index)	Selects the item at the specified zero-based index.
void setBackground(Color color)	Sets the background to the specified color.

Table 9-3. CCombo *Methods (continued)*

Method	Description
void setEditable(boolean editable)	If editable is true, makes this CCombo editable. Otherwise, makes it uneditable.
boolean setFocus()	Sets the keyboard focus to this CCombo.
void setFont(Font font)	Sets the font to the specified font.
void setForeground(Color color)	Sets the foreground to the specified color.
void setItem(int index, String string)	Sets the text of the item at the specified zero-based index to string. If index specifies an item that doesn't exist, throws an IllegalArgumentException.
void setItems(String[] items)	Replaces any existing items with the items specified by items.
void setSelection(Point selection)	Sets the selected characters in the Text portion of this CCombo. The x value contains the beginning of the selection, while the y value contains the end.
void setText(String string)	Sets the displayed text to string.
void setTextLimit(int limit)	Sets the maximum number of characters that the Text portion of this CCombo will allow.
void setToolTipText(String string)	Sets the tool tip text to string.
void setVisible(boolean visible)	If visible is true, shows this CCombo. If visible is false, hides it.

Use CCombo whenever you need its sizing flexibility, such as inside table cells. Otherwise, you'll probably use Combo. The "Using TableEditor" section in this chapter demonstrates CCombo usage.

Introducing CLabel

Labels, covered in Chapter 5, display either text or an image. They communicate directly to users, and their Spartan nature lends them well to many usages. You'll use labels extensively throughout your applications. Sometimes, however, you'll want much more from your labels. How about text *and* an image? Why choose? And why must you settle for monochrome backgrounds? Enter CLabel, which saunters forth as a debutante at the ball to Label's pedestrianism, providing glitz and glamour to Label's drabness.

Creating a CLabel

Calling CLabel's only constructor produces a CLabel:

```
CLabel(Composite parent, int style)
```

Table 9-4 describes the valid values for style. You can combine an alignment constant, such as SWT.CENTER, with a shadow constant, such as SWT.SHADOW_OUT, using the bitwise

OR operator. Combining more than one alignment constant or more than one shadow constant, however, produces undefined results.

Table 9-4. CLabel *Styles*

Style	Description
SWT.LEFT	Creates a left-aligned CLabel
SWT.CENTER	Creates a center-aligned CLabel
SWT.RIGHT	Creates a right-aligned CLabel
SWT.SHADOW_IN	Creates a CLabel that appears recessed into the screen
SWT.SHADOW_OUT	Creates a CLabel that appears to extrude from the screen
SWT.SHADOW_NONE	Creates a CLabel with no shadow

The CLabelTest program, shown in Listing 9-2, creates three CLabels using various style combinations. Figure 9-5 shows the program's main window.

Listing 9-2. CLabelTest.java

```java
package examples.ch9;

import org.eclipse.swt.SWT;
import org.eclipse.swt.custom.CLabel;
import org.eclipse.swt.layout.*;
import org.eclipse.swt.widgets.*;

/**
 * This class demonstrates CLabel
 */
public class CLabelTest {
  /**
   * Runs the application
   */
  public void run() {
    Display display = new Display();
    Shell shell = new Shell(display);
    shell.setText("CLabel Test");
    createContents(shell);
    shell.open();
    while (!shell.isDisposed()) {
      if (!display.readAndDispatch()) {
        display.sleep();
      }
    }
    display.dispose();
  }
```

```
/**
 * Creates the main window's contents
 *
 * @param parent the main window
 */
private void createContents(Composite parent) {
  parent.setLayout(new GridLayout(1, false));

  // Create the CLabels
  CLabel left = new CLabel(parent, SWT.LEFT | SWT.SHADOW_IN);
  left.setText("Left and Shadow In");
  left.setLayoutData(new GridData(GridData.FILL_HORIZONTAL));
  CLabel center = new CLabel(parent, SWT.CENTER | SWT.SHADOW_OUT);
  center.setText("Center and Shadow Out");
  center.setLayoutData(new GridData(GridData.FILL_HORIZONTAL));
  CLabel right = new CLabel(parent, SWT.RIGHT | SWT.SHADOW_NONE);
  right.setText("Right and Shadow None");
  right.setLayoutData(new GridData(GridData.FILL_HORIZONTAL));
}

/**
 * The application entry point
 *
 * @param args the command line arguments
 */
public static void main(String[] args) {
  new CLabelTest().run();
}
}
```

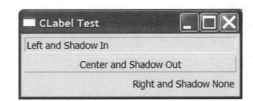

Figure 9-5. CLabel *styles*

Label vs. CLabel

CLabel presents a much prettier face than Label; not all of CLabel's enhancements are cosmetic, however. CLabel responds better to limited space than Label, as demonstrated in the "CLabels in Limited Space" section later in this chapter. Table 9-5 compares Label and CLabel.

Table 9-5. Label *vs.* CLabel

Description	Label	CLabel
Alignment (left, right, and center)	Yes	Yes
Shadow (in, out, and none)	Yes	Yes
Wrap	Yes	No
Text	Yes	Yes
Image	Yes	Yes
Text and image	No	Yes
Tool tip	Yes	Yes
Background color	Yes	Yes
Background color gradient	No	Yes
Background image	No	Yes
Font	Yes	Yes
Automatically shorten text	No	Yes

If you're just displaying some text, such as to label a text field or to display an error message, you'll likely just use Label. Any time you want to spice up your label with background images or color gradients, want to display both an image and a label together, or want automatic space handling for limited space, use CLabel.

Configuring CLabel

Greater power brings greater responsibility—or so says conventional wisdom. CLabel exposes a fuller API than Label, to accommodate its greater power. Table 9-6 describes CLabel's methods. Most of these methods are easy to understand, except for the setBackground() method that takes an array of Color objects and an array of ints. This section explains that method.

Table 9-6. CLabel *Methods*

Method	Description
Point computeSize(int wHint, int hHint, boolean changed)	Computes the preferred size of this CLabel.
int getAlignment()	Returns the alignment of this CLabel (SWT.LEFT, SWT.CENTER, or SWT.RIGHT).
Image getImage()	Returns this CLabel's image or null if no image has been set.
String getText()	Returns this CLabel's text or null if no text has been set.
String getToolTipText()	Returns this CLabel's tool tip text or null if no tool tip text has been set.
void setAlignment(int alignment)	Sets the alignment of this CLabel (SWT.LEFT, SWT.CENTER, or SWT.RIGHT).
void setBackground(Color color)	Sets the background color for this CLabel.

Table 9-6. CLabel *Methods (continued)*

Method	Description
void setBackground(Color[] colors, int[] percents)	Sets the background gradient colors for this CLabel.
void setBackground(Image image)	Sets the background image for this CLabel.
void setFont(Font font)	Sets the font for this CLabel. Pass null to use the default font.
void setImage(Image image)	Sets the image for this CLabel.
void setText(String text)	Sets the text for this CLabel.
void setToolTipText(String text)	Sets the tool tip text for this CLabel.

To draw a gradient background in a CLabel, call the setBackground() method that takes an array of Color objects and an array of ints. The Colors can be any number of colors, and they can be system colors or colors you create. You can also include null in the array, and the original background color will be substituted.

The ints must all lie within the range 0–100, inclusive. They must be in ascending order; each member in the array must be greater than or equal to the previous member. Finally, the int array must have exactly one fewer member than the Color array. Failing to meet these criteria results in an exception.

Each int in the array specifies a stopping point, as a percentage, for a gradient drawn with the corresponding color in the Color array and the subsequent color. For example, if you write code like this:

```
cLabel.setBackground(new Color[] { red, green, blue }, new int[] { 25, 50 });
```

a red/green gradient is drawn from the left edge of the CLabel to the point 25% of the CLabel's total width. From there, a green/blue gradient is drawn to the point 50% of the CLabel's total width. The balance of the background isn't redrawn. Because the ints represent stopping points, to have a gradient span the entire CLabel you must pass 100 as the final entry in the array. Currently, having your gradient stop short of 100% causes display problems (the background shows behind the window), as Figure 9-6 shows.

Figure 9-6. A gradient that stops short of 100%

The CLabelGradient program demonstrates background gradients (see Listing 9-3). It creates two CLabels and sets them to show gradients in their backgrounds. The first CLabel uses the red/green/blue example shown in Figure 9-6. The second CLabel draws a gradient from white to gray to dark gray to black.

Listing 9-3. `CLabelGradient.java`

```java
package examples.ch9;

import org.eclipse.swt.SWT;
import org.eclipse.swt.custom.CLabel;
import org.eclipse.swt.graphics.Color;
import org.eclipse.swt.layout.*;
import org.eclipse.swt.widgets.*;

/**
 * This class demonstrates CLabel gradients
 */
public class CLabelGradient {
  /**
   * Runs the application
   */
  public void run() {
    Display display = new Display();
    Shell shell = new Shell(display);
    shell.setText("CLabel Gradient");
    createContents(shell);
    shell.open();
    while (!shell.isDisposed()) {
      if (!display.readAndDispatch()) {
        display.sleep();
      }
    }
    display.dispose();
  }

  /**
   * Creates the main window's contents
   *
   * @param parent the main window
   */
  private void createContents(Composite parent) {
    parent.setLayout(new GridLayout(1, false));

    // Create the CLabels
    CLabel one = new CLabel(parent, SWT.LEFT);
    one.setText("First Gradient Example");
    one.setLayoutData(new GridData(GridData.FILL_HORIZONTAL));
    one.setBackground(parent.getDisplay().getSystemColor(SWT.COLOR_GRAY));
```

```
            // Set the background gradient
            one.setBackground(new Color[] {
                parent.getDisplay().getSystemColor(SWT.COLOR_RED),
                parent.getDisplay().getSystemColor(SWT.COLOR_GREEN),
                parent.getDisplay().getSystemColor(SWT.COLOR_BLUE)},
                new int[] { 25, 50});

            CLabel two = new CLabel(parent, SWT.LEFT);
            two.setText("Second Gradient Example");
            two.setLayoutData(new GridData(GridData.FILL_HORIZONTAL));

            // Set the background gradient
            two.setBackground(new Color[] {
                parent.getDisplay().getSystemColor(SWT.COLOR_WHITE),
                parent.getDisplay().getSystemColor(SWT.COLOR_GRAY),
                parent.getDisplay().getSystemColor(SWT.COLOR_DARK_GRAY),
                parent.getDisplay().getSystemColor(SWT.COLOR_BLACK)}, new int[] { 33, 67,
                100});
        }

        /**
         * The application entry point
         *
         * @param args the command line arguments
         */
        public static void main(String[] args) {
          new CLabelGradient().run();
        }
    }
```

This program produces the window shown in Figure 9-7. Note the display problems with the first CLabel, whose gradient stops at 50%.

Figure 9-7. CLabel *gradients*

CLabels in Limited Space

When space shrinks and a CLabel can't fit into what's been allotted, it adopts the following strategy:

- It eliminates any indent when left-aligned.

- It hides any image and its requisite gap.

- It shortens the text by replacing the center portion of the text with an ellipsis (...).

- It shortens the text by removing the center portion.

This functionality requires no effort on your part—it just automatically happens with CLabel. Cynics might grouse that you can't prevent it, either, but if you don't like this default behavior, subclass CLabel and provide your own implementation for the shortening method:

```
protected String shortenText(GC gc, String t, int width)
```

The CLabelShort program displays a CLabel with both an image and some text (see Listing 9-4). Resizing the window shows how CLabel responds to a reduction in space, as shown in Figures 9-8, 9-9, and 9-10.

Listing 9-4. CLabelShort.java

```
package examples.ch9;

import org.eclipse.swt.SWT;
import org.eclipse.swt.custom.CLabel;
import org.eclipse.swt.graphics.Image;
import org.eclipse.swt.layout.FillLayout;
import org.eclipse.swt.widgets.*;

/**
 * This class demonstrates CLabel
 */
public class CLabelShort {
  private Image lookImage;

  /**
   * Runs the application
   */
  public void run() {
    Display display = new Display();
    Shell shell = new Shell(display);
    shell.setText("CLabel Short");
```

```
    // Load the image
    lookImage = new Image(display, this.getClass().getResourceAsStream(
        "/images/look.gif"));

    createContents(shell);
    shell.pack();
    shell.open();
    while (!shell.isDisposed()) {
      if (!display.readAndDispatch()) {
        display.sleep();
      }
    }

    // Dispose the image
    if (lookImage != null) lookImage.dispose();

    display.dispose();
  }

  /**
   * Creates the main window's contents
   *
   * @param parent the main window
   */
  private void createContents(Composite parent) {
    parent.setLayout(new FillLayout());

    // Create the CLabel
    CLabel label = new CLabel(parent, SWT.LEFT);
    label.setText("This is a CLabel with a lot of long-winded text");
    label.setImage(lookImage);
  }

  /**
   * The application entry point
   *
   * @param args the command line arguments
   */
  public static void main(String[] args) {
    new CLabelShort().run();
  }
}
```

Figure 9-8. The full-sized CLabel

Figure 9-9. The CLabel *after the image disappears*

Figure 9-10. The CLabel *with an ellipsis*

Introducing CTabFolder

Tabs, covered in Chapter 8, separate controls into pages using a notebook metaphor. A selectable tab adorns each page, allowing users to quickly select any page of controls by clicking the tab. Each tab can display text, an image, or both. SWT uses two classes, TabFolder and TabItem, to implement tabs. Review Chapter 8 for more information on tabs.

The custom packages CTabFolder and CTabItem add flexibility to the standard tabs. Table 9-7 compares TabFolder/TabItem to CTabFolder/CTabItem. Most of the changes enhance aesthetics, but these new tab classes also allow for a close button to show at the top right.

CAUTION *In the late stages of Eclipse 3.0 development, the Eclipse team has focused much attention on* CTabFolder *and* CTabItem. *Consequently, warnings fill the associated Javadoc documentation about anticipated changes to the API. While this section faithfully reports current information at the time of its writing, you should review the Javadoc for the most complete and accurate information.*

Table 9-7. TabFolder/TabItem *vs.* CTabFolder/CTabItem

Description	TabFolder/ TabItem	CTabFolder/ CTabItem
Tab position	On top or on bottom	On top or on bottom
Supports text	Yes	Yes
Supports tool tips	Yes	Yes
Supports images	Yes	Yes

Table 9-7. TabFolder/TabItem *vs.* CTabFolder/CTabItem *(continued)*

Description	TabFolder/ TabItem	CTabFolder/ CTabItem
Supports disabled images	No	Yes
Supports flat look	No	Yes
Supports customizable margins	No	Yes
Supports a control in the top-right corner	No	Yes
Supports a gradient background	No	Yes
Supports an image background	No	Yes

Creating a CTabFolder

Create a CTabFolder by passing a parent and a style to the constructor:

```
CTabFolder(Composite parent, int style)
```

Table 9-8 describes the style constants.

Table 9-8. CTabFolder *Style Constants*

Style	Description
SWT.TOP	Displays the children tabs along the top edge of this CTabFolder.
SWT.BOTTOM	Displays the children tabs along the bottom edge of this CTabFolder.
SWT.FLAT	If borders are visible, displays the children tabs with a flat look. If SWT.FLAT isn't specified and borders are visible, displays the children tabs with a three-dimensional look. Also, displays any scrolling controls with a flat look.
SWT.CLOSE	Adds a close button to each child tab of this CTabFolder.

You can combine SWT.FLAT with either SWT.TOP or SWT.BOTTOM using the bitwise OR operator, but you shouldn't combine SWT.TOP and SWT.BOTTOM. Figure 9-11 shows top, flat tabs, and Figure 9-12 shows bottom, three-dimensional tabs.

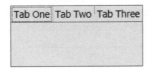

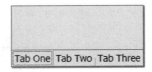

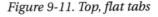

Figure 9-11. Top, flat tabs   *Figure 9-12. Bottom, three-dimensional tabs*

Configuring CTabFolder

CTabFolder offers several fields to modify its appearance. Some of these are static, so changing their values affects all CTabFolder instances running within the Java Virtual Machine (JVM). Table 9-9 describes the fields.

Table 9-9. `CTabFolder` *Fields*

Field	Description
`static RGB borderInsideRGB`	Red, green, blue (RGB) value used to create the color of the inside line of the drop shadow border. Affects all `CTabFolder` instances.
`static RGB borderMiddleRGB`	RGB value used to create the color of the middle line of the drop shadow border. Affects all `CTabFolder` instances.
`static RGB borderOutsideRGB`	RGB value used to create the color of the outside line of the drop shadow border. Affects all `CTabFolder` instances.
`int marginHeight`	Height, in pixels, of the margin used on the top and bottom of each tab's form.
`int marginWidth`	Width, in pixels, of the margin used on the left and right of each tab's form.
`int MIN_TAB_WIDTH`	The minimum width, in multiples of the tab's height, to which each tab will be compressed before scrolling arrows will be displayed for navigation. Note that this field, though capitalized, *isn't* final.

Of more interest are the methods that `CTabFolder` offers. Table 9-10 describes these methods.

Table 9-10. `CTabFolder` *Methods*

Method	Description
`void addCTabFolderListener (CTabFolderListener listener)`	Adds a listener that's notified when a child tab is closed. Also adds a close button to each tab in this `CTabFolder`.
`void addSelectionListener (SelectionListener listener)`	Adds a listener that's notified when a child tab is selected.
`Point computeSize(int wHint, int hHint, boolean changed)`	Computes this `CTabFolder`'s preferred size.
`Rectangle computeTrim(int x, int y, int width, int height)`	Computes the size of the overall `CTabFolder` required to house the client area specified by the arguments.
`Rectangle getClientArea()`	Returns a `Rectangle` describing the client area of this `CTabFolder`.
`CTabItem getItem(int index)`	Returns the tab at the specified zero-based index.
`CTabItem getItem(Point point)`	Returns the tab at the specified point, or `null` if no item exists at the specified point.
`int getItemCount()`	Returns the number of tabs in this `CTabFolder`.
`CTabItem[] getItems()`	Returns the tabs in this `CTabFolder`.
`CTabItem getSelection()`	Returns the selected tab, or `null` if no tabs are selected.
`int getSelectionIndex()`	Returns the zero-based index of the selected tab, or `-1` if no tabs are selected.
`int getTabHeight()`	Returns the height, in pixels, of the children tabs.
`Control getTopRight()`	Returns the control in the top-right corner of this `CTabFolder`.

Table 9-10. CTabFolder *Methods (continued)*

Method	Description
int indexOf(CTabItem)	Returns the zero-based index of the specified item, or -1 if the item doesn't exist in this CTabFolder.
void removeCTabFolderListener (CTabFolderListener listener)	Removes the specified listener from the notification list.
void removeSelectionListener (SelectionListener listener)	Removes the specified listener from the notification list.
void setBackground(Color color)	Sets the background color of all the tabs and their forms.
void setBorderVisible (boolean show)	If show is true, displays a border around this CTabFolder.
void setFont(Font font)	Sets the font to use for the tabs.
void setInsertMark(CTabItem item, boolean after)	Shows a marker beside the specified tab; shows the marker before the tab if after is false, and after the tab if after is true.
void setInsertMark(int index, boolean after)	Shows a marker beside the tab corresponding to the specified zero-based index; shows the marker before the tab if after is false, and shows it after the tab if after is true.
void setSelection(CTabItem item)	Selects the specified tab.
void setSelection(int index)	Selects the tab corresponding to the specified zero-based index.
void setSelectionBackground (Color[] colors, int[] percents)	Draws a gradient background using the specified colors on the selected tab. The percents array holds percentages between 0–100 indicating where the next color in the colors array should begin. percents must hold one fewer item than colors, or an InvalidArgumentException is thrown.
void setSelectionBackground (Image image)	Displays the specified image in the background of the selected tab.
void setSelectionForeground (Color color)	Sets the specified color to use for the foreground of the selected tab.
void setTabHeight(int height)	Sets the height, in pixels, for the tabs.
void setTopRight(Control control)	Sets the control to display in the top-right portion of this CTabFolder.
void showItem(CTabItem item)	Shows the specified tab.
void showSelection()	Shows the selected tab, scrolling left or right as necessary.

 CAUTION *The Javadoc documentation for* setInsertMark() *claims that passing* -1 *for index, or* null *for item, will erase the mark. This doesn't work—the mark doesn't go away. This has been reported and is bug #32846. To work around this, call* setInsertMark(), *passing either* -1 *or* null, *and then call* CTabFolder.redraw().

Adding CTabItems

Like TabFolder, CTabFolder holds little interest without any tabs. To add tabs to a CTabFolder, construct CTabItem instances by calling one of its two constructors, passing the CTabFolder for the parent. Because no styles apply, pass SWT.NONE for the style. Optionally, you can pass an index to specify the zero-based order of the tab. The constructors are as follows:

```
public CTabItem(CTabFolder parent, int style)
public CTabItem(CTabFolder parent, int style, int index)
```

Configuring CTabItem

Each tab in a CTabFolder can display text, an image, and a tool tip. Additionally, it can display an alternate image when disabled. Like TabFolder, its window contents are set by calling the setControl() method. Table 9-11 describes CTabItem's methods.

Table 9-11. CTabItem *Methods*

Method	Description
void dispose()	Closes this tab, disposing its resources and its children's resources
Rectangle getBounds()	Returns a Rectangle describing this tab's size and location relative to its parent
Control getControl()	Returns the control associated with this tab
Image getDisabledImage()	Returns the image displayed when this tab is disabled
Image getImage()	Returns the image displayed on this tab
CTabFolder getParent()	Returns the parent of this tab
String getText()	Returns the text displayed on this tab
String getToolTipText()	Returns the tool tip text for this tab
void setControl(Control control)	Sets the control associated with this tab
void setDisabledImage(Image image)	Sets the image to display when this tab is disabled
void setImage(Image image)	Sets the image to display on this tab
void setText(String string)	Sets the text to display on this tab
void setToolTipText(String string)	Sets the tool tip text for this tab

Closing a CTabItem

Chapter 8's Extensible Markup Language (XML) viewer application provides both a menu option and a toolbar button to close a tab and its associated file. Though functional, the implementation could confuse some users because the close mechanisms have no visible tie to the tabs. Putting a close button directly on the tab would clearly demonstrate how to close a tab, and CTabFolder allows you to do just that.

To add a close button to each tab, pass the SWT.CLOSE style to the CTabFolder con-structor. Alternatively, you can add a CTabFolderListener to the CTabFolder (though this method is deprecated):

```
tabFolder.addCTabFolderListener(new CTabFolderAdapter() {
  public void itemClosed(CTabFolderEvent event) {
  }
}
```

That's it—that's all you have to do. Your application will display a close button on each tab when the user moves the mouse over the tab, and clicking the button will close the tab. Figure 9-13 shows a set of tabs, with the first tab displaying a close button.

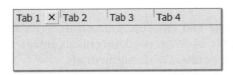

Figure 9-13. Tab 1 has the close button displayed.

Although the previous itemClosed() method has no implementation, and none is required to get the working close button on each tab, you can certainly add some code. Because itemClosed() is called before the tab closes, you can use this method to ask for confirmation before closing the tab. That code might look something like this:

```
tabFolder.addCTabFolderListener(new CTabFolderAdapter() {
  public void itemClosed(CTabFolderEvent event) {
    MessageBox mb = new MessageBox(shell, SWT.ICON_QUESTION | SWT.YES | SWT.NO);
    mb.setMessage("Are you sure you want to close the tab?");
    if (SWT.NO == mb.open())
    {
      event.doIt = false; // Cancel the event processing, so tab stays open
    }
  }
}
```

Setting the Insert Mark

CTabFolder sports an optional insertion mark—a vertical line between tabs, used to indicate where a new tab would be inserted into the "notebook." You specify where to display the insert mark by calling one of these two setInsertMark() methods:

```
public void setInsertMark(CTabItem item, boolean after)
public void setInsertMark(int index, boolean after)
```

The first parameter specifies by which tab to show the insert mark. You pass either the tab itself or its zero-based index. The second parameter indicates whether to show the insert mark before or after the tab. Pass `false` to show the insert mark before the tab, or pass `true` to show it after the tab.

Displaying a Gradient Background

You can configure the selected tab to display a gradient background using `CTabFolder`'s `setSelectionBackground()` method. It takes two parameters: an array of colors and an array of integers. The array of colors must have exactly one more item than the array of integers. The array of integers must be in ascending order and must include only numbers from the range 0–100, inclusive.

The colors array contains the colors you want to use in the gradient. You can create the colors yourself, remembering to dispose them when you're through with them, or you can use system colors. If you use system colors, make sure you don't dispose them.

Each integer in the integer array specifies a percentage of the total tab's width at which the gradient should switch to the next set of colors. The gradients work just like those in `CLabel`. Refer to the "Configuring CLabel" section for more information about gradients.

Seeing CTabFolder

The ShowCTabFolder program demonstrates `CTabFolder` (see Listing 9-5). It displays a button to add new tabs, and it displays a button to move the insert mark left and right for where new tabs will be added. New tabs display the location of the insert mark when they were added. Figure 9-14 shows the main window without any added tabs.

The selected tab displays a gradient background. Click a tab's close button to close it. Move the insert mark left and right before clicking Add Tab to add the new tab to a different location within the `CTabFolder`. Figure 9-15 shows the program with various tabs added.

Listing 9-5. ShowCTabFolder.`java`

```
package examples.ch9;

import org.eclipse.swt.*;
import org.eclipse.swt.custom.*;
import org.eclipse.swt.events.*;
import org.eclipse.swt.graphics.*;
import org.eclipse.swt.layout.*;
import org.eclipse.swt.widgets.*;

/**
 * This class demonstrates CTabFolder
 */
public class ShowCTabFolder {
```

```java
// Because CTabFolder doesn't have a getInsertMark() method,
// store the value so you can keep track of it
private int insertMark = -1;
private CTabFolder tabFolder;

/**
 * Runs the application
 */
public void run() {
  Display display = new Display();
  Shell shell = new Shell(display);
  shell.setText("Show CTabFolder");
  createContents(shell);
  shell.open();
  while (!shell.isDisposed()) {
    if (!display.readAndDispatch()) {
      display.sleep();
    }
  }
  display.dispose();
}

/**
 * Creates the window's contents
 *
 * @param shell the parent shell
 */
private void createContents(Shell shell) {
  shell.setLayout(new GridLayout(1, true));

  // Create the buttons to create tabs
  Composite composite = new Composite(shell, SWT.NONE);
  composite.setLayoutData(new GridData(GridData.FILL_HORIZONTAL));
  composite.setLayout(new RowLayout());
  createButtons(composite);

  // Create the tabs
  tabFolder = new CTabFolder(shell, SWT.TOP);
  tabFolder.setBorderVisible(true);
  tabFolder.setLayoutData(new GridData(GridData.FILL_BOTH));
  Display display = shell.getDisplay();

  // Set up a gradient background for the selected tab
  tabFolder.setSelectionBackground(new Color[] {
      display.getSystemColor(SWT.COLOR_WIDGET_DARK_SHADOW),
      display.getSystemColor(SWT.COLOR_WIDGET_NORMAL_SHADOW),
      display.getSystemColor(SWT.COLOR_WIDGET_LIGHT_SHADOW)}, new int[] { 50,
      100});
```

```java
      // Add a listener to get the close button on each tab
      tabFolder.addCTabFolderListener(new CTabFolderAdapter() {
        public void itemClosed(CTabFolderEvent event) {}
      });
   }

   /**
    * Creates the buttons for moving the insert mark and adding a tab
    *
    * @param composite the parent composite
    */
   private void createButtons(Composite composite) {
      // Move mark left
      Button button = new Button(composite, SWT.PUSH);
      button.setText("<<");
      button.addSelectionListener(new SelectionAdapter() {
        public void widgetSelected(SelectionEvent event) {
          if (insertMark > -1) {
            --insertMark;
            resetInsertMark();
          }
        }
      });

      // Move mark right
      button = new Button(composite, SWT.PUSH);
      button.setText(">>");
      button.addSelectionListener(new SelectionAdapter() {
        public void widgetSelected(SelectionEvent event) {
          if (insertMark < tabFolder.getItemCount() - 1) {
            ++insertMark;
            resetInsertMark();
          }
        }
      });

      // Add a tab
      button = new Button(composite, SWT.PUSH);
      button.setText("Add Tab");
      button.addSelectionListener(new SelectionAdapter() {
        public void widgetSelected(SelectionEvent event) {
          new CTabItem(tabFolder, SWT.NONE, insertMark + 1).setText("Tab ("
              + (insertMark + 1) + ")");
        }
      });
   }
```

```java
/**
 * Moves the insert mark to the new location
 */
private void resetInsertMark() {
  tabFolder.setInsertMark(insertMark, true);

  // Workaround for bug #32846
  if (insertMark == -1) {
    tabFolder.redraw();
  }
}

/**
 * The application entry point
 *
 * @param args the command line arguments
 */
public static void main(String[] args) {
  new ShowCTabFolder().run();
}
}
```

Figure 9-14. The ShowCTabFolder program

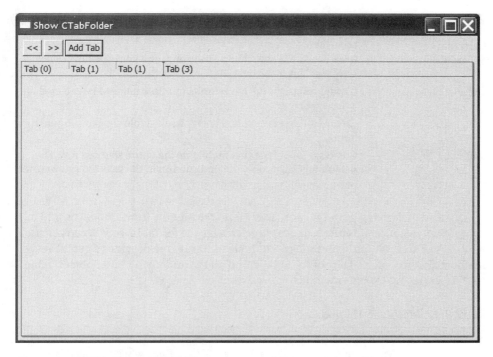

Figure 9-15. The ShowCTabFolder program with some tabs added

Introducing TableTree

Chapter 8 discusses both tables and trees, and the XmlView sample application shows the power of using them side by side. Recognizing the synergies created by juxtaposing tables and trees, SWT's creators hatched the TableTree: a blend of a tree and a table. It has columns like a table, but each row can have children like a tree. The synergies created by the combination of the two widgets offer great power. Use this widget for hierarchical columnar data.

Creating a TableTree

TableTree has a single constructor:

```
TableTree(Composite parent, int style)
```

The style parameter controls whether users can select multiple items from the table at a time and also how the selection is displayed (first column only or the entire row). It also can specify whether to display a checkbox by each row. You can combine various styles using the bitwise OR operator, though the styles for single selection vs. multiple selection are mutually exclusive. Table 9-12 describes the style constants.

Table 9-12. TableTree *Style Constants*

Constant	Description
SWT.SINGLE	Creates a TableTree that permits only one item at a time to be selected. This is the default.
SWT.MULTI	Creates a TableTree that permits multiple items to be selected at a time.
SWT.CHECK	Creates a TableTree that displays a selectable checkbox by each item.
SWT.FULL_SELECTION	Creates a TableTree that highlights the entire selected row. The default highlights only the first column in the selected row or rows.

Instead of deriving from Table or Tree, TableTree inherits from Composite, and it contains an instance of Table. It doesn't provide a façade for Table, so you can't create a TableTree and call Table methods on it. Instead, TableTree provides a getTable() method, and you can call any of Table's method on the underlying Table object. Table 9-13 describes TableTree's methods.

Table 9-13. TableTree *Methods*

Method	Description
void addSelectionListener (SelectionListener listener)	Adds a listener that's notified when the selection changes.
void addTreeListener (TreeListener listener)	Adds a listener that's notified when the tree is expanded or collapsed.
Point computeSize(int wHint, int hHint, boolean changed)	Computes the preferred size for the TableTree.
Rectangle computeTrim(int x, int y, int width, int height)	Computes the bounding rectangle for the TableTree from the client area specified by the parameters.
void deselectAll()	Deselects all items in the TableTree.
Color getBackground()	Returns the background color used by this TableTree.
Rectangle getClientArea()	Returns the bounding rectangle for the client area only of this TableTree.
boolean getEnabled()	Returns true if this TableTree is enabled or false if it's disabled.
Font getFont()	Returns the font used by this TableTree.
Color getForeground()	Returns the foreground color used by this TableTree.
TableTreeItem getItem(Point point)	Returns the item that contains the point specified by point, or null if no item contains the specified point.
int getItemCount()	Returns the number of items this TableTree contains.
int getItemHeight()	Returns the height in pixels of one item in this TableTree.
TableTreeItem[] getItems()	Returns the items this TableTree contains.
TableTreeItem[] getSelection()	Returns the selected items in this TableTree.
int getSelectionCount()	Returns the number of items selected in this TableTree.

Table 9-13. `TableTree` *Methods (continued)*

Method	Description
int getStyle()	Returns this TableTree's style.
Table getTable()	Returns the underlying Table.
String getToolTipText()	Returns the tool tip text for this TableTree.
int indexOf(TableTreeItem item)	Returns the zero-based index of the item specified by item, or -1 if item doesn't exist in this TableTree.
void removeAll()	Removes all the items from this TableTree.
void removeSelectionListener (SelectionListener listener)	Removes the listener from the notification list.
void removeTreeListener (TreeListener listener)	Removes the listener from the notification list.
void selectAll()	Selects all the items in this TableTree.
void setBackground(Color color)	Sets the background color used by this TableTree.
void setEnabled(boolean enabled)	If enabled is true, enables this TableTree. If enabled is false, disables it.
void setFont(Font font)	Sets the font used by this TableTree.
void setForeground(Color color)	Sets the foreground color used by this TableTree.
void setMenu(Menu menu)	Sets the pop-up menu used by this TableTree.
void setSelection (TableTreeItem[] items)	Selects the items specified by items.
void setToolTipText(String text)	Sets the tool tip text for this TableTree.
void showItem(TableTreeItem item)	Shows the item specified by item, scrolling the table if necessary.
void showSelection()	Shows the selected item, scrolling the table if necessary.

Adding Items to a TableTree

SWT uses the `TableTreeItem` class to represent items in a `TableTree`. It offers four constructors, described in Table 9-14. No styles apply to `TableTree` items, so use `SWT.NONE`. A `TableTree` item's parent can be a `TableTree`, in which case it's a root item in the `TableTree`, or it can be another `TableTree` item.

Table 9-14. `TableTreeItem` *Constructors*

Constructor	Description
TableTreeItem(TableTree parent, int style)	Constructs a root item with the specified style
TableTreeItem(TableTree parent, int style, int index)	Constructs a root item at the specified zero-based index with the specified style
TableTreeItem(TableTreeItem parent, int style)	Constructs a child item with the specified style
TableTreeItem(TableTreeItem parent, int style, int index)	Constructs a child item at the specified zero-based index with the specified style

Once you've constructed a TableTreeItem, you can call its methods to customize its behavior. Table 9-15 describes TableTreeItem's methods.

Table 9-15. TableTreeItem *Methods*

Method	Description
void dispose()	Removes this item from the table.
Color getBackground()	Returns this item's background color.
Rectangle getBounds(int index)	Returns this item's bounding rectangle.
boolean getChecked()	Returns true if this item's checkbox is checked, or false if it's not checked. Valid when parent table's style includes SWT.CHECK.
boolean getExpanded()	Returns true if this item's contents are currently expanded, or false otherwise.
Color getForeground()	Returns this item's foreground color.
boolean getGrayed()	Returns true if this item's checkbox is grayed, or false if it's not grayed. Valid when parent table's style includes SWT.CHECK.
Image getImage()	Returns the image associated with this item.
Image getImage(int index)	Returns the image associated with this image at the zero-based column specified by index.
int getItemCount()	Returns the number of children this item has.
TableTreeItem[] getItems()	Returns the items that are children of this item.
TableTree getParent()	Returns this item's parent TableTree.
TableTreeItem getParentItem()	Returns this item's parent item. Returns null if this is a root item.
String getText()	Returns this item's text.
String getText(int index)	Return this item's text for the specified zero-based column.
int indexOf(TableTreeItem item)	Returns the zero-based index of the specified item, or null if specified item doesn't exist in the TableTree.
void setBackground(Color color)	Sets the background color for this item.
void setChecked(boolean checked)	If checked is true, checks this item. Otherwise, clears the checkbox. Valid when parent table's style includes SWT.CHECK.
void setExpanded(boolean expanded)	If expanded is true, expands this item. Otherwise, contracts this item.
void setForeground(Color color)	Sets the foreground color for this item.
void setGrayed(boolean grayed)	If grayed is true, grays this item's checkbox. Otherwise, clears the checkbox. Valid when parent table's style includes SWT.CHECK.
void setImage(Image image)	Sets the image for this item.
void setImage(int index, Image image)	Sets the image for this item for the specified zero-based column.
void setText(String text)	Sets the text for this item.
void setText(int index, String text)	Sets the text for this item for the specified zero-based column.

TableTree differs most significantly from Table in that each row in the table can have children. If a row has a child or children, it displays a plus sign to its left. Click the plus to expand the tree. Each row, whether parent or child, can display data in each column. Also, you can programmatically expand an item's children by calling setExpanded(true). You create a parent-child relationship by passing the parent to the child's constructor, like so:

```
TableTreeItem parent = new TableTreeItem(tableTree, SWT.NONE);
parent.setText(0, "Parent column 1");
parent.setText(1, "Parent column 2");

// Create the child
TableTreeItem child = new TableTreeItem(parent, SWT.NONE);
child.setText(0, "Child column 1");
child.setText(1, "Child column 2");

// Expand the parent
parent.setExpanded(true);
```

Adding Columns to a TableTree

SWT contains no TableTreeColumn class for adding columns to a TableTree, and you can't pass a TableTree to a TableColumn's constructor. How, then, can you add columns to a TableTree? Remember that TableTree has a getTable() method that returns the underlying Table object. You'll use this method to set table-specific data on your TableTrees. For example, to add a column to a TableTree, use code like this:

```
TableColumn column = new TableColumn(tableTree.getTable(), SWT.LEFT);
```

To turn on the headers and grid lines in your TableTree, use getTable() again:

```
tableTree.getTable().setHeaderVisible(true);
tableTree.getTable().setLinesVisible(true);
```

You can also assign a Table reference to the underlying table, and use that wherever you want to call methods on the table:

```
Table table = tableTree.getTable();
table.setLinesVisible(false);
```

Using TableTree

The TableTreeTest program creates a TableTree with three columns, three root items, and three child items for each root item (see Listing 9-6). It displays data in each column for each item, whether parent or child. Figure 9-16 shows the program's window.

Listing 9-6. `TableTreeTest.java`

```java
package examples.ch9;

import org.eclipse.swt.SWT;
import org.eclipse.swt.custom.*;
import org.eclipse.swt.layout.*;
import org.eclipse.swt.widgets.*;

/**
 * This class demonstrates TableTree
 */
public class TableTreeTest {
  // The number of rows and columns
  private static final int NUM = 3;

  /**
   * Runs the application
   */
  public void run() {
    Display display = new Display();
    Shell shell = new Shell(display);
    shell.setText("TableTree Test");
    createContents(shell);
    shell.pack();
    shell.open();
    while (!shell.isDisposed()) {
      if (!display.readAndDispatch()) {
        display.sleep();
      }
    }
    display.dispose();
  }

  /**
   * Creates the main window's contents
   *
   * @param shell the main window
   */
  private void createContents(final Shell shell) {
    shell.setLayout(new FillLayout());

    // Create the TableTree and set some attributes on the underlying table
    TableTree tableTree = new TableTree(shell, SWT.NONE);
    Table table = tableTree.getTable();
    table.setHeaderVisible(true);
    table.setLinesVisible(false);
```

```java
    // Create the columns, passing the underlying table
    for (int i = 0; i < NUM; i++) {
      new TableColumn(table, SWT.LEFT).setText("Column " + (i + 1));
    }

    // Create the data
    for (int i = 0; i < NUM; i++) {
      // Create a parent item and add data to the columns
      TableTreeItem parent = new TableTreeItem(tableTree, SWT.NONE);
      parent.setText(0, "Parent " + (i + 1));
      parent.setText(1, "Data");
      parent.setText(2, "More data");

      // Add children items
      for (int j = 0; j < NUM; j++) {
        // Create a child item and add data to the columns
        TableTreeItem child = new TableTreeItem(parent, SWT.NONE);
        child.setText(0, "Child " + (j + 1));
        child.setText(1, "Some child data");
        child.setText(2, "More child data");
      }
      // Expand the parent item
      parent.setExpanded(true);
    }

    // Pack the columns
    TableColumn[] columns = table.getColumns();
    for (int i = 0, n = columns.length; i < n; i++) {
      columns[i].pack();
    }
  }

  /**
   * The application entry point
   *
   * @param args the command line arguments
   */
  public static void main(String[] args) {
    new TableTreeTest().run();
  }
}
```

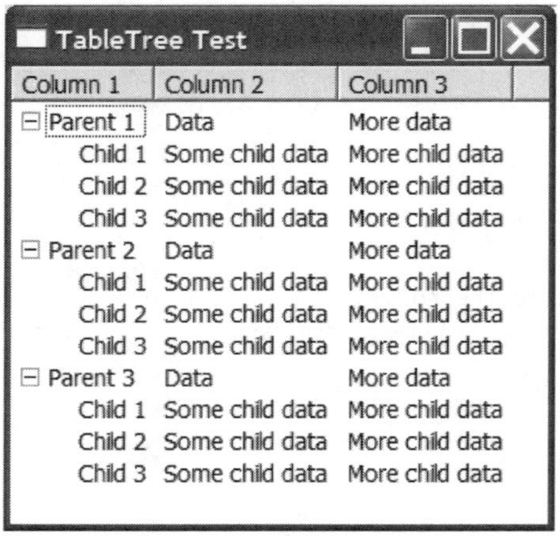

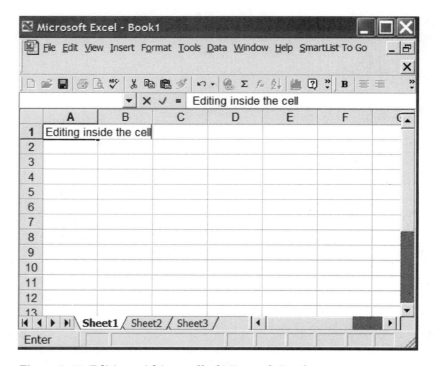

Figure 9-16. A `TableTree` control

Introducing Control Editors

Early spreadsheet programs used the grid to display data only—all editing occurred on a data-entry line above the grid. The data editor always appeared in a separate location from the data display. Like a vestigial tail, today's spreadsheet programs still display the edit line above the grid, but they also allow editing within the appropriate cell in the grid, as Figure 9-17 shows.

Figure 9-17. Editing within a cell of Microsoft Excel

Control editors allow users to edit data where the data lies. They appear on top of, and move and size with, the associated control. They can completely cover the associated control, or you can anchor them to a certain side or sides and fill them either vertically or horizontally. Use them to edit cells in a table and to edit nodes in a tree, or use them as buttons to launch a dialog box for editing a property.

SWT provides a base class, ControlEditor, that offers basic control-editing abilities: You can create a control editor, attach it to a control, and specify how it should move and resize as the parent control moves and resizes. SWT also offers three derived classes: TableEditor, TreeEditor, and TableTreeEditor. This chapter examines all four classes and shows how to use them.

Using ControlEditor

You can associate a ControlEditor with any Composite, which you pass to ControlEditor's only constructor, like this:

```
ControlEditor(Composite parent)
```

You control the editor's behavior—sizing and moving—with respect to its parent by setting the fields described in Table 9-16.

Table 9-16. ControlEditor *Fields*

Field	Description
boolean grabHorizontal	If set to true, causes this editor to assume the entire width of its parent. The default is false.
boolean grabVertical	If set to true, causes this editor to assume the entire height of its parent. The default is false.
int minimumHeight	Specifies the minimum height, in pixels, for this editor.
int minimumWidth	Specifies the minimum width, in pixels, for this editor.
int horizontalAlignment	Specifies the horizontal alignment for this editor, relative to its parent. Use SWT.LEFT for left alignment, SWT.RIGHT for right alignment, or SWT.CENTER for center alignment. SWT.CENTER is the default and is used if an invalid value is specified.
int verticalAlignment	Specifies the vertical alignment for this editor, relative to its parent. Use SWT.TOP for top alignment, SWT.BOTTOM for bottom alignment, or SWT.CENTER for center alignment. SWT.CENTER is the default and is used if an invalid value is specified.

For example, to create a ControlEditor that's anchored to the upper-left corner of its parent, you code the following:

```
ControlEditor editor = new ControlEditor(parent);
editor.horizontalAlignment = SWT.LEFT;
editor.verticalAlignment = SWT.TOP;
```

ControlEditor's methods, described in Table 9-17, allow you to get and set the control associated with the editor, as well as force a redraw and dispose of the editor. The control you associate with the editor must have the same parent composite as the editor, or the results are undefined. Because they both have the same parent, they're governed by the same layout, if any.

 CAUTION *A control editor and its associated control should both have the same parent.*

Table 9-17. ControlEditor *Methods*

Method	Description
void dispose()	Disposes this editor and disassociates it from its parent.
Control getEditor()	Returns the control associated with this ControlEditor.
void layout()	Forces the associated control to compute its size and position and redraw itself.
void setEditor(Control editor)	Sets the control associated with this ControlEditor, which must have the same parent as the ControlEditor.

The ControlEditorTest program, as shown in Listing 9-7, fills a window with a color and creates a control editor associated with the window (which is a Shell object). It sets a Text object as the control associated with the editor; type the name of the color to change the color displayed in the window.

Listing 9-7. ControlEditorTest.java

```java
package examples.ch9;

import java.util.*;

import org.eclipse.swt.SWT;
import org.eclipse.swt.custom.*;
import org.eclipse.swt.events.*;
import org.eclipse.swt.graphics.*;
import org.eclipse.swt.widgets.*;

/**
 * This class demonstrates ControlEditor
 */
public class ControlEditorTest {
```

```java
// Create a map to hold all the supported colors
private static final Map COLORS = new HashMap();
static {
  COLORS.put("red", new RGB(255, 0, 0));
  COLORS.put("green", new RGB(0, 255, 0));
  COLORS.put("blue", new RGB(0, 0, 255));
  COLORS.put("yellow", new RGB(255, 255, 0));
  COLORS.put("black", new RGB(0, 0, 0));
  COLORS.put("white", new RGB(255, 255, 255));
}

private Color color;

/**
 * Runs the application
 */
public void run() {
  Display display = new Display();
  Shell shell = new Shell(display);
  shell.setText("Control Editor");
  createContents(shell);
  shell.pack();
  shell.open();
  while (!shell.isDisposed()) {
    if (!display.readAndDispatch()) {
      display.sleep();
    }
  }
  if (color != null) color.dispose();
  display.dispose();
}

/**
 * Creates the main window's contents
 *
 * @param shell the main window
 */
private void createContents(final Shell shell) {
  color = new Color(shell.getDisplay(), 255, 0, 0);

  // Create a composite that will be the parent of the editor
  final Composite composite = new Composite(shell, SWT.NONE);
  composite.setBackground(color);
  composite.setBounds(0, 0, 300, 100);

  // Create the editor
  ControlEditor editor = new ControlEditor(composite);
```

```
// Create the control associated with the editor
final Text text = new Text(composite, SWT.BORDER);
text.addModifyListener(new ModifyListener() {
  public void modifyText(ModifyEvent event) {
    RGB rgb = (RGB) COLORS.get(text.getText());
    if (rgb != null) {
      if (color != null) color.dispose();
      color = new Color(shell.getDisplay(), rgb);
      composite.setBackground(color);
    }
  }
});

// Place the editor in the top middle of the parent composite
editor.horizontalAlignment = SWT.CENTER;
editor.verticalAlignment = SWT.TOP;
Point size = text.computeSize(SWT.DEFAULT, SWT.DEFAULT);
editor.minimumWidth = size.x;
editor.minimumHeight = size.y;
editor.setEditor(text);
}

/**
 * The application entry point
 *
 * @param args the command line arguments
 */
public static void main(String[] args) {
  new ControlEditorTest().run();
}
}
```

The program produces the window shown in Figure 9-18. Type the name of a supported color inside the editor's Text control, and the composite's color changes, as Figure 9-19 demonstrates.

Figure 9-18. A Text *control associated with an editor*

Figure 9-19. The changed color

The ControlEditorTestTwo program takes a different approach to changing the color (see Listing 9-8). Instead of being wholly self-contained, it displays a button as its editor control. When clicked, the button launches the standard color dialog box. For a change of pace, it aligns the button along the entire bottom edge of the parent composite.

Listing 9-8. `ControlEditorTestTwo.java`

```java
package examples.ch9;

import org.eclipse.swt.SWT;
import org.eclipse.swt.custom.*;
import org.eclipse.swt.events.*;
import org.eclipse.swt.graphics.*;
import org.eclipse.swt.widgets.*;

/**
 * This class demonstrates ControlEditor
 */
public class ControlEditorTestTwo {
  private Color color;

  /**
   * Runs the application
   */
  public void run() {
    Display display = new Display();
    Shell shell = new Shell(display);
    shell.setText("Control Editor Two");
    createContents(shell);
    shell.pack();
    shell.open();
    while (!shell.isDisposed()) {
      if (!display.readAndDispatch()) {
        display.sleep();
      }
    }
```

```
      if (color != null) color.dispose();
      display.dispose();
   }

   /**
    * Creates the main window's contents
    *
    * @param shell the main window
    */
   private void createContents(final Shell shell) {
      color = new Color(shell.getDisplay(), 255, 0, 0);

      // Create a composite that will be the parent of the editor
      final Composite composite = new Composite(shell, SWT.NONE);
      composite.setBackground(color);
      composite.setBounds(0, 0, 300, 100);

      // Create the editor
      ControlEditor editor = new ControlEditor(composite);

      // Create the control associated with the editor
      Button button = new Button(composite, SWT.PUSH);
      button.setText("Change Color...");
      button.addSelectionListener(new SelectionAdapter() {
         public void widgetSelected(SelectionEvent event) {
            ColorDialog dialog = new ColorDialog(shell);
            if (color != null) dialog.setRGB(color.getRGB());
            RGB rgb = dialog.open();
            if (rgb != null) {
               if (color != null) color.dispose();
               color = new Color(shell.getDisplay(), rgb);
               composite.setBackground(color);
            }
         }
      });

      // Place the editor along the bottom of the parent composite
      editor.grabHorizontal = true;
      editor.verticalAlignment = SWT.BOTTOM;
      Point size = button.computeSize(SWT.DEFAULT, SWT.DEFAULT);
      editor.minimumHeight = size.y;
      editor.setEditor(button);
   }

   /**
    * The application entry point
```

```
 *
 * @param args the command line arguments
 */
public static void main(String[] args) {
  new ControlEditorTestTwo().run();
}
}
```

Figure 9-20 shows this program's main window, and Figure 9-21 shows it after using the dialog box to change the color to white.

Figure 9-20. A button associated with an editor

Figure 9-21. The changed color

Using `TableEditor`

As in the aforementioned example of spreadsheets, `TableEditor` allows users to edit the data inside a table cell. Like `ControlEditor`, `TableEditor` can use a wholly self-contained control, such as `Text` or `CCombo`, or can use a button to launch a dialog box for editing the data. This section examines both approaches.

A `TableEditor`'s parent must be a `Table`, which is passed in `TableEditor`'s only constructor, as shown here:

```
public TableEditor(Table parent)
```

Because `TableEditor` derives from `ControlEditor`, it inherits the fields used to control its size and position and adds no new ones. It does add a few new methods, described in Table 9-18.

Table 9-18. `TableEditor` *Methods*

Method	Description
int getColumn()	Returns the zero-based index of the column this editor occupies
TableItem getItem()	Returns the item this editor is using
void setColumn(int column)	Sets the zero-based index of the column this editor should occupy
void setEditor(Control editor, TableItem item, int column)	Sets the control, item, and column for this editor
void setItem(TableItem item)	Sets the item for this editor

Though a TableEditor has a Table for a parent, it also has an associated row (TableItem) and column. In other words, a TableEditor actually belongs to a cell in the parent Table. Use the setters for row and column to set the cell, like this:

```
TableEditor editor = new TableEditor(myTable);
editor.setEditor(myControl);
editor.setItem(myItem);
editor.setColumn(myColumn);
```

You can also use TableEditor's new setEditor() method that takes three parameters—an editor, an item, and a column—to set everything in one call, like this:

```
TableEditor editor = new TableEditor(myTable);
editor.setEditor(myControl, myItem, myColumn);
```

Exchanging Data

You might expect the association between editor and cell to run so deep that values typed into the editor would pass seamlessly into the cell, and from the cell into the editor, with no intervention on your part. No such luck—you must write code to pass the text back and forth. You'll usually set the text from the cell into your editor's control when you create the control, and you'll set the text from the control back into the cell any time it's modified. Here's some code to exchange data between a cell and a Text control:

```
// User has selected a cell in the table
// Create the Text object for the editor
final Text text = new Text(table, SWT.NONE);

// Transfer any text from the cell to the Text control and select it
text.setText(item.getText(column));
text.selectAll();
text.setFocus();

// Set the Text control into the editor
editor.setEditor(text, item, column);
```

```
// Add a handler to transfer the text back to the cell
// any time it's modified
text.addModifyListener(new ModifyListener() {
  public void modifyText(ModifyEvent event) {
    item.setText(column, text.getText());
  }
});
```

Placing the Editor

If you're always editing the same column in a table, determining which cell to place the control for the editor in is straightforward. Add a selection listener to the table, overriding the widgetSelected() method. The event object received in that method contains the selected row, so you can place the editor with code like this:

```
table.addSelectionListener(new SelectionAdapter() {
  public void widgetSelected(SelectionEvent event) {
    // Figure out which row was selected
    TableItem item = (TableItem) event.item;
    if (item != null) {
      // Create the Text object for your editor
      Text text = new Text(table, SWT.NONE);
      editor.setEditor(text, item, 2); // Always edit the third column
    }
  }
});
```

Determining the column selected, however, is trickier. Tables have methods for determining the selected row, but none for the selected column. The SelectionEvent object contains x and y data members; if you can use those to determine where the user clicked the mouse, you could iterate through the columns to see where the point lies. Unfortunately, for SelectionEvent, both x and y are always zero. Those values are always in MouseEvent, however, so if you use a mouse listener instead of a selection listener, you can determine both row and column with little fuss. That code might look something like this:

```
table.addMouseListener(new MouseAdapter() {
  public void mouseDown(MouseEvent event) {
    // Determine where the mouse was clicked
    Point pt = new Point(event.x, event.y);

    // Get the row
    TableItem item = table.getItem(pt);
    if (item != null) {
      // Iterate through the columns to determine which column was clicked
      int column = -1;
      for (int i = 0, n = table.getColumnCount(); i < n; i++) {
```

```
          Rectangle rect = item.getBounds(i);
          if (rect.contains(pt)) {
            // This column contains the clicked point
            column = i;
            break;
          }
        }
        if (column > -1) {
          // Create control, set into editor, etc.
        }
      }
    }
  });
```

Cleaning Up

Creating a new control to associate with the editor each time the user clicks a cell is fine, but you've got to clean up after yourself. You usually dispose any associated control in your event handler, before you create a new control and associate it with the editor. That code looks like this:

```
table.addMouseListener(new MouseAdapter() {
  public void mouseDown(MouseEvent event) {
    // Dispose any existing control from the editor
    Control control = editor.getEditor();
    if (control != null)
      control.dispose();
    // The rest of the code . . .
  }
});
```

In some situations, you know when the user is through editing. For example, if the editing control is a CCombo, users have completed an editing session when they select an item from the dropdown. You can end the editing session then, like this:

```
CCombo combo = new CCombo(table, SWT.READ_ONLY);

// Add data, set into editor, etc.

combo.addSelectionListener(new SelectionAdapter() {
  public void widgetSelected(SelectionEvent event) {
    item.setText(column, combo.getText());
    combo.dispose(); // End the editing session
  }
});
```

Using a Button

Though Text and CCombo seem the obvious choices for TableEditor controls, you can
also use a button that launches a dialog box. To make the button fit within the cell, be
sure to use the height of the table's items for the button's height. Then, set the button's
sizes into the editor. The code to do that looks like this:

```
// Create the button and set its height
Button button = new Button(table, SWT.PUSH);
button.setText("Font...");
button.computeSize(SWT.DEFAULT, table.getItemHeight());

// Create the editor and set the button as its control
TableEditor editor = new TableEditor(table);
editor.grabHorizontal = true;
editor.minimumWidth = button.getSize().x;
editor.minimumHeight = button.getSize().y;
editor.setEditor(button, item, column);

// Set the handler to open the dialog box when the button is clicked, etc.
```

Putting It Together

The TextTableEditor program creates a table with five rows and five columns (see Listing 9-9). The first column contains buttons, one for each row, for changing the foreground color of the row. The second column contains CCombo objects for selecting data
from a dropdown. You can edit the rest of the cells in the table in place—just click the
desired cell in the table and start typing. Click outside the cell to stop editing.

Listing 9-9. TextTableEditor.java

```
package examples.ch9;

import org.eclipse.swt.SWT;
import org.eclipse.swt.custom.*;
import org.eclipse.swt.events.*;
import org.eclipse.swt.graphics.*;
import org.eclipse.swt.layout.*;
import org.eclipse.swt.widgets.*;

/**
 * This class demonstrates TableEditor.
 */
public class TextTableEditor {
  // Number of rows and columns
  private static final int NUM = 5;
```

```java
    // Colors for each row
    private Color[] colors = new Color[NUM];

    // Options for each dropdown
    private String[] options = { "Option 1", "Option 2", "Option 3"};

    /**
     * Runs the application
     */
    public void run() {
      Display display = new Display();
      Shell shell = new Shell(display);
      shell.setText("Text Table Editor");
      createContents(shell);
      shell.pack();
      shell.open();
      while (!shell.isDisposed()) {
        if (!display.readAndDispatch()) {
          display.sleep();
        }
      }
      // Dispose any created colors
      for (int i = 0; i < NUM; i++) {
        if (colors[i] != null) colors[i].dispose();
      }
      display.dispose();
    }

    /**
     * Creates the main window's contents
     *
     * @param shell the main window
     */
    private void createContents(final Shell shell) {
      shell.setLayout(new FillLayout());

      // Create the table
      final Table table = new Table(shell, SWT.SINGLE | SWT.FULL_SELECTION
          | SWT.HIDE_SELECTION);
      table.setHeaderVisible(true);
      table.setLinesVisible(true);

      // Create five columns
      for (int i = 0; i < NUM; i++) {
        TableColumn column = new TableColumn(table, SWT.CENTER);
        column.setText("Column " + (i + 1));
        column.pack();
      }
```

```
// Create five table editors for color
TableEditor[] colorEditors = new TableEditor[NUM];

// Create five buttons for changing color
Button[] colorButtons = new Button[NUM];

// Create five rows and the editors for those rows. The first column has the
// color change buttons. The second column has dropdowns. The final three
// have text fields.
for (int i = 0; i < NUM; i++) {
  // Create the row
  final TableItem item = new TableItem(table, SWT.NONE);

  // Create the editor and button
  colorEditors[i] = new TableEditor(table);
  colorButtons[i] = new Button(table, SWT.PUSH);

  // Set attributes of the button
  colorButtons[i].setText("Color...");
  colorButtons[i].computeSize(SWT.DEFAULT, table.getItemHeight());

  // Set attributes of the editor
  colorEditors[i].grabHorizontal = true;
  colorEditors[i].minimumHeight = colorButtons[i].getSize().y;
  colorEditors[i].minimumWidth = colorButtons[i].getSize().x;

  // Set the editor for the first column in the row
  colorEditors[i].setEditor(colorButtons[i], item, 0);

  // Create a handler for the button
  final int index = i;
  colorButtons[i].addSelectionListener(new SelectionAdapter() {
    public void widgetSelected(SelectionEvent event) {
      ColorDialog dialog = new ColorDialog(shell);
      if (colors[index] != null) dialog.setRGB(colors[index].getRGB());
      RGB rgb = dialog.open();
      if (rgb != null) {
        if (colors[index] != null) colors[index].dispose();
        colors[index] = new Color(shell.getDisplay(), rgb);
        item.setForeground(colors[index]);
      }
    }
  });
}

// Create an editor object to use for text editing
final TableEditor editor = new TableEditor(table);
editor.horizontalAlignment = SWT.LEFT;
editor.grabHorizontal = true;
```

```
// Use a mouse listener, not a selection listener, because you're interested
// in the selected column as well as row
table.addMouseListener(new MouseAdapter() {
  public void mouseDown(MouseEvent event) {
    // Dispose any existing editor
    Control old = editor.getEditor();
    if (old != null) old.dispose();

    // Determine where the mouse was clicked
    Point pt = new Point(event.x, event.y);

    // Determine which row was selected
    final TableItem item = table.getItem(pt);
    if (item != null) {
      // Determine which column was selected
      int column = -1;
      for (int i = 0, n = table.getColumnCount(); i < n; i++) {
        Rectangle rect = item.getBounds(i);
        if (rect.contains(pt)) {
          // This is the selected column
          column = i;
          break;
        }
      }

      // Column 2 holds dropdowns
      if (column == 1) {
        // Create the dropdown and add data to it
        final CCombo combo = new CCombo(table, SWT.READ_ONLY);
        for (int i = 0, n = options.length; i < n; i++) {
          combo.add(options[i]);
        }

        // Select the previously selected item from the cell
        combo.select(combo.indexOf(item.getText(column)));

        // Compute the width for the editor
        // Also, compute the column width, so that the dropdown fits
        editor.minimumWidth = combo.computeSize(SWT.DEFAULT, SWT.DEFAULT).x;
        table.getColumn(column).setWidth(editor.minimumWidth);

        // Set the focus on the dropdown and set into the editor
        combo.setFocus();
        editor.setEditor(combo, item, column);

        // Add a listener to set the selected item back into the cell
        final int col = column;
```

```
        combo.addSelectionListener(new SelectionAdapter() {
          public void widgetSelected(SelectionEvent event) {
            item.setText(col, combo.getText());

            // They selected an item; end the editing session
            combo.dispose();
          }
        });
      } else if (column > 1) {
        // Create the Text object for your editor
        final Text text = new Text(table, SWT.NONE);
        text.setForeground(item.getForeground());

        // Transfer any text from the cell to the Text control,
        // set the color to match this row, select the text,
        // and set focus to the control
        text.setText(item.getText(column));
        text.setForeground(item.getForeground());
        text.selectAll();
        text.setFocus();

        // Recalculate the minimum width for the editor
        editor.minimumWidth = text.getBounds().width;

        // Set the control into the editor
        editor.setEditor(text, item, column);

        // Add a handler to transfer the text back to the cell
        // any time it's modified
        final int col = column;
        text.addModifyListener(new ModifyListener() {
          public void modifyText(ModifyEvent event) {
            // Set the text of the editor's control back into the cell
            item.setText(col, text.getText());
          }
        });
      }
    }
  }
});
}

/**
 * The application entry point
 *
 * @param args the command line arguments
 */
```

```
    public static void main(String[] args) {
      new TextTableEditor().run();
    }
}
```

The application's main window looks like Figure 9-22. Figure 9-23 shows the application with some colors changed, some options selected, and some text typed into a few cells.

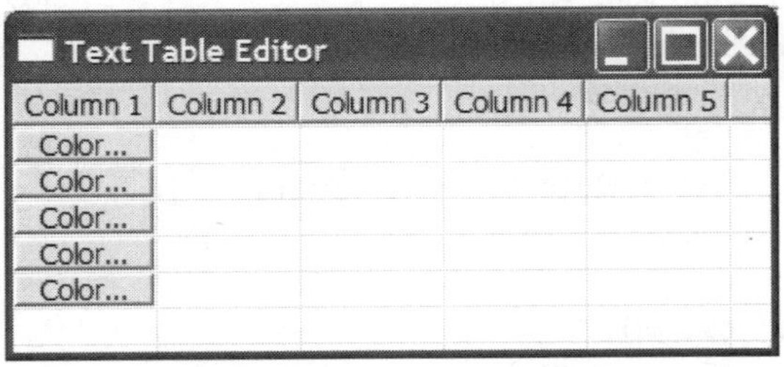

Figure 9-22. The TextTableEditor program

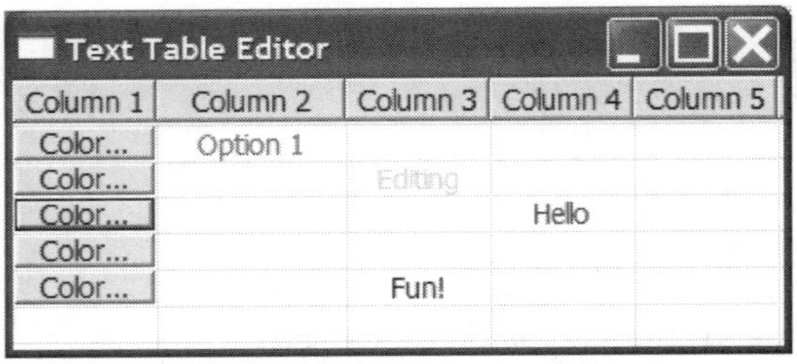

Figure 9-23. The TextTableEditor program with some cells edited

Using TableTreeEditor

Learning to use a TableEditor flattens the learning curve for a TableTreeEditor—they're virtually the same. You use TableEditor for Tables and TableTreeEditor for TableTrees, and everything else you know about TableEditor applies to TableTreeEditor.

Create a TableTreeEditor by calling its only constructor:

```
public TableTreeEditor(TableTree tableTree)
```

TableTreeEditor inherits all the same fields as methods that TableEditor does, because it also derives from ControlEditor. It adds the methods described in Table 9-19.

Table 9-19. TableTreeEditor *Methods*

Method	Description
void dispose()	Disposes this editor
int getColumn()	Returns the zero-based index of the column this editor occupies
TableTreeItem getItem()	Returns the item this editor is using
void setColumn(int column)	Sets the zero-based index of the column this editor should occupy
void setEditor(Control editor, TableTreeItem item, int column)	Sets the control, item, and column for this editor
void setItem(TableTreeItem item)	Sets the item for this editor

You'll notice that the API for TableTreeEditor matches the API for TableEditor, except that it uses TableTreeItem in place of TreeItem for all items. Otherwise, you can use TableTreeEditor just as you use TableEditor.

Using TreeEditor

A TreeEditor allows users to edit the text associated with a tree's nodes. It's derived from ControlEditor, and it inherits all the methods and data members from ControlEditor. Its parent is always a Tree, which is passed in the constructor:

```
public TreeEditor(Tree parent)
```

It adds no data members and adds the methods described in Table 9-20.

Table 9-20. TreeEditor *Methods*

Method	Description
void dispose()	Disposes this editor
TreeItem getItem()	Returns the item associated with this TreeEditor
void setEditor(Control editor, TreeItem item)	Sets the control and item for this editor
void setItem(TreeItem item)	Sets the item for this editor

You'll most often use a TreeEditor to allow in-place editing of item text in the tree. You can also associate the editor with a button to launch a dialog box for editing tree nodes. You create the editor and control just like you do with the other editor classes. Here's some sample code:

```
TreeEditor editor = new TreeEditor(tree);
editor.horizontalAlignment = SWT.LEFT;
editor.grabHorizontal = true;

Text text = new Text(tree, SWT.NONE);
editor.setEditor(text, treeItem);
```

The TextTreeEditor program implements a TreeEditor that uses a Text control for its editing (see Listing 9-10). It mimics the following standard Windows keystrokes for editing data in place:

- Press F2 to edit the selected item.

- While editing, press Enter to accept the changes and stop editing.

- While editing, press Escape to throw away the changes and stop editing.

You can also click outside the item being edited to save the changes and stop editing.

Listing 9-10. TextTreeEditor.java

```java
package examples.ch9;

import org.eclipse.swt.SWT;
import org.eclipse.swt.custom.*;
import org.eclipse.swt.events.*;
import org.eclipse.swt.layout.*;
import org.eclipse.swt.widgets.*;

/**
 * This class demonstrates TreeEditor
 */
public class TextTreeEditor {
  // Constant for how many items to create at each level
  private static final int NUM = 3;

  /**
   * Runs the application
   */
  public void run() {
    Display display = new Display();
    Shell shell = new Shell(display);
    shell.setText("Text Tree Editor");
    createContents(shell);
    shell.open();
    while (!shell.isDisposed()) {
      if (!display.readAndDispatch()) {
        display.sleep();
      }
    }
    display.dispose();
  }
```

```
/**
 * Creates the contents of the main window
 *
 * @param shell the main window
 */
public void createContents(Shell shell) {
  shell.setLayout(new FillLayout());

  // Create the tree
  final Tree tree = new Tree(shell, SWT.SINGLE);

  // Fill the tree with data
  for (int i = 0; i < NUM; i++) {
    TreeItem iItem = new TreeItem(tree, SWT.NONE);
    iItem.setText("Item " + (i + 1));
    for (int j = 0; j < NUM; j++) {
      TreeItem jItem = new TreeItem(iItem, SWT.NONE);
      jItem.setText("Sub Item " + (j + 1));
      for (int k = 0; k < NUM; k++) {
        new TreeItem(jItem, SWT.NONE).setText("Sub Sub Item " + (k + 1));
      }
      jItem.setExpanded(true);
    }
    iItem.setExpanded(true);
  }

  // Create the editor and set its attributes
  final TreeEditor editor = new TreeEditor(tree);
  editor.horizontalAlignment = SWT.LEFT;
  editor.grabHorizontal = true;

  // Add a key listener to the tree that listens for F2.
  // If F2 is pressed, you do the editing
  tree.addKeyListener(new KeyAdapter() {
    public void keyPressed(KeyEvent event) {
      // Make sure one and only one item is selected when F2 is pressed
      if (event.keyCode == SWT.F2 && tree.getSelectionCount() == 1) {
        // Determine the item to edit
        final TreeItem item = tree.getSelection()[0];

        // Create a text field to do the editing
        final Text text = new Text(tree, SWT.NONE);
        text.setText(item.getText());
        text.selectAll();
        text.setFocus();
```

```
                    // If the text field loses focus, set its text into the tree
                    // and end the editing session
                    text.addFocusListener(new FocusAdapter() {
                      public void focusLost(FocusEvent event) {
                        item.setText(text.getText());
                        text.dispose();
                      }
                    });

                    // If they hit Enter, set the text into the tree and end the editing
                    // session. If they hit Escape, ignore the text and end the editing
                    // session
                    text.addKeyListener(new KeyAdapter() {
                      public void keyPressed(KeyEvent event) {
                        switch (event.keyCode) {
                        case SWT.CR:
                          // Enter hit--set the text into the tree and drop through
                          item.setText(text.getText());
                        case SWT.ESC:
                          // End editing session
                          text.dispose();
                          break;
                        }
                      }
                    });

                    // Set the text field into the editor
                    editor.setEditor(text, item);
                  }
                }
              });
            }

  /**
   * The application entry point
   *
   * @param args the command line arguments
   */
  public static void main(String[] args) {
    new TextTreeEditor().run();
  }
}
```

In the createContents() method, the code creates a TreeEditor and sets its data. It adds a key listener to listen for an F2 key press. When F2 is pressed, it first makes sure that only one item in the tree is selected, and then it begins the editing session. It creates a Text for the editor's control and adds two listeners to it: one to detect loss of focus and one to detect key presses. On loss of focus, it saves the text into the tree and ends the editing by calling `text.dispose()`. In the key listener, if Enter is pressed, it saves the text into the tree. If Escape is pressed, it ignores the text. For either of those two keys, it ends the editing session by calling `text.dispose()`.

Figure 9-24 shows the running application. Figure 9-25 shows the running application with an active editing session.

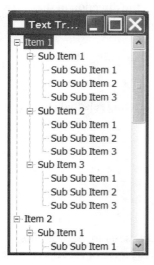

Figure 9-24. The TextTreeEditor program

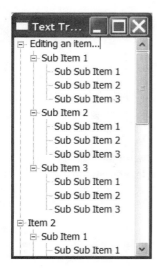

Figure 9-25. The TextTreeEditor program with the first node being edited

Introducing TableCursor

Despite its name, TableCursor has nothing to do with databases. Instead, it provides a means to navigate around a table widget using the keyboard. In addition to highlighting a row in the table, it selects a single cell in the table, as Figure 9-26 shows. To navigate, use the following keys:

- Arrows, which move the selection one row or column in the direction of the arrow

- Home, which moves the selection to the first row of the currently selected column

- End, which moves the selection to the last row of the currently selected column

- Page Up, which moves the selection up a page

- Page Down, which moves the selection down a page

- Enter, which generates a Default Selection event

You'll typically react to the Enter key by initiating an editing session. Because the parent of the editor is a TableCursor, not a Table, use ControlEditor, not TableEditor.

Figure 9-26. A TableCursor *with the middle cell selected*

Creating a TableCursor

TableCursor has a single constructor:

```
public TableCursor(Table parent, int style)
```

The parent is always a Table, and the style can be either SWT.NONE or SWT.BORDER. Figure 9-26 (earlier) shows a TableCursor with the SWT.NONE style, and Figure 9-27 shows one with the SWT.BORDER style.

Figure 9-27. A TableCursor *with the border style*

While calling the TableCursor constructor creates a TableCursor and associates it with a Table, the TableCursor is necessarily event driven. The next section discusses the event handling you'll use to make TableCursor useful.

Using a TableCursor

A TableCursor with no event handlers displays a selection box around the currently selected cell. Pressing the navigation keys listed previously moves the selection accordingly. It doesn't, however, change the selected row in the table. It also doesn't provide any editing capabilities. It's just a box, roaming around the screen on demand.

Table 9-21 describes TableCursor's methods. You'll want to add a selection listener so your TableCursor can respond to user requests as expected. Listing 9-11 shows a sample selection listener.

Listing 9-11. A Selection Listener

```java
cursor.addSelectionListener(new SelectionAdapter() {
  // This is called as the user navigates around the table
  public void widgetSelected(SelectionEvent event) {
    // Select the row in the table where the TableCursor is
    table.setSelection(new TableItem[] { cursor.getRow() });
  }

  // This is called when the user hits Enter
  public void widgetDefaultSelected(SelectionEvent event) {
    // Begin an editing session
    // Notice that the parent of the Text is the TableCursor, not the Table
    final Text text = new Text(cursor, SWT.NONE);

    // Copy the text from the cell to the Text
    text.setText(cursor.getRow().getText(cursor.getColumn()));
    text.setFocus();

    // Add a handler to detect key presses
    text.addKeyListener(new KeyAdapter() {
      public void keyPressed(KeyEvent event) {
        // End the editing and save the text if the user presses Enter
        // End the editing and throw away the text if the user presses Escape
        switch (event.keyCode)
        {
        case SWT.CR:
          cursor.getRow().setText(cursor.getColumn(), text.getText());
        case SWT.ESC:
          text.dispose();
          break;
        }
      }
    });
    editor.setEditor(text);
  }
});
```

Table 9-21. TableCursor *Methods*

Method	Description
void addSelectionListener (SelectionListener listener)	Adds a listener to the notification list that's notified when this TableCursor is selected.
int getColumn()	Returns the zero-based index of the currently selected column.
TableItem getRow()	Returns the currently selected row.
void setSelection(int row, int column)	Selects the cell at the zero-based row and column.
void setSelection(TableItem row, int column)	Selects the cell at the row and zero-based column.
void setVisible(boolean visible)	If visible is true, shows this TableCursor. Otherwise, hides this TableCursor.

The TableCursorTest program creates a table with five rows and columns (see Listing 9-12). It also creates a TableCursor to navigate through the table, adding the selection listener code listed previously to provide editing.

Listing 9-12. TableCursorTest.java

```
package examples.ch9;

import org.eclipse.swt.SWT;
import org.eclipse.swt.custom.*;
import org.eclipse.swt.events.*;
import org.eclipse.swt.layout.*;
import org.eclipse.swt.widgets.*;

/**
 * This class demonstrates TableCursor
 */
public class TableCursorTest {
  // The number of rows and columns
  private static final int NUM = 5;

  /**
   * Runs the program
   */
  public void run() {
    Display display = new Display();
    Shell shell = new Shell(display);
    shell.setText("Table Cursor Test");
    createContents(shell);
    shell.pack();
    shell.open();
```

```
    while (!shell.isDisposed()) {
      if (!display.readAndDispatch()) {
        display.sleep();
      }
    }
    display.dispose();
  }

  /**
   * Creates the main window's contents
   *
   * @param shell the main window
   */
  private void createContents(Shell shell) {
    shell.setLayout(new FillLayout());

    // Create the table
    final Table table = new Table(shell, SWT.SINGLE | SWT.FULL_SELECTION);
    table.setHeaderVisible(true);
    table.setLinesVisible(true);

    // Create the columns
    for (int i = 0; i < NUM; i++) {
      TableColumn column = new TableColumn(table, SWT.CENTER);
      column.setText("Column " + (i + 1));
      column.pack();
    }

    // Create the rows
    for (int i = 0; i < NUM; i++) {
      new TableItem(table, SWT.NONE);
    }

    // Create the TableCursor
    final TableCursor cursor = new TableCursor(table, SWT.NONE);

    // Create the editor
    // Use a ControlEditor, not a TableEditor, because the cursor is the parent
    final ControlEditor editor = new ControlEditor(cursor);
    editor.grabHorizontal = true;
    editor.grabVertical = true;

    // Add the event handling
    cursor.addSelectionListener(new SelectionAdapter() {
      // This is called as the user navigates around the table
      public void widgetSelected(SelectionEvent event) {
```

```
            // Select the row in the table where the TableCursor is
            table.setSelection(new TableItem[] { cursor.getRow()});
          }

        // This is called when the user hits Enter
        public void widgetDefaultSelected(SelectionEvent event) {
          // Begin an editing session
          // Notice that the parent of the Text is the TableCursor, not the Table
          final Text text = new Text(cursor, SWT.NONE);
          text.setFocus();

          // Copy the text from the cell to the Text control
          text.setText(cursor.getRow().getText(cursor.getColumn()));
          text.setFocus();

          // Add a handler to detect key presses
          text.addKeyListener(new KeyAdapter() {
            public void keyPressed(KeyEvent event) {
              // End the editing and save the text if the user presses Enter
              // End the editing and throw away the text if the user presses Escape
              switch (event.keyCode) {
              case SWT.CR:
                cursor.getRow().setText(cursor.getColumn(), text.getText());
              case SWT.ESC:
                text.dispose();
                break;
              }
            }
          });
          editor.setEditor(text);
        }
      });
    }

  /**
   * The application entry point
   *
   * @param args the command line arguments
   */
  public static void main(String[] args) {
    new TableCursorTest().run();
  }
}
```

Figure 9-28 shows the program's main window with the TableCursor showing, and Figure 9-29 shows the program with several cells edited.

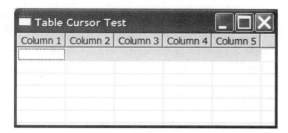

Figure 9-28. The TableCursorTest program

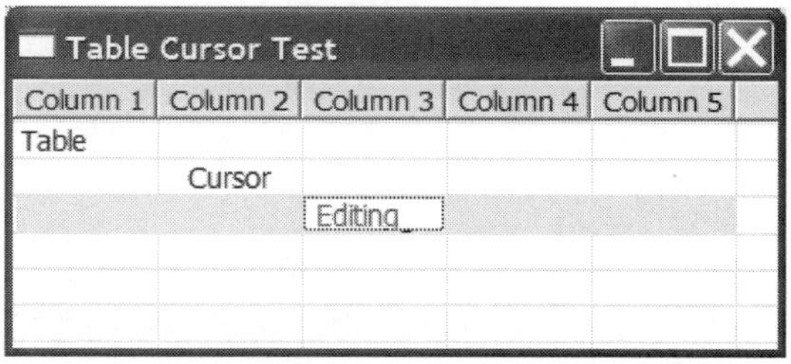

Figure 9-29. The TableCursorTest program with some cells edited

Introducing PopupList

The custom package offers another control, PopupList, that functions much like a Combo or CCombo. It displays a list of items, allows the user to select an item, and disappears. Where it displays the list and how many items it shows, however, depends on the available screen room.

Creating a PopupList

PopupList offers two constructors:

```
public PopupList(Shell shell);
public PopupList(Shell shell, int style);
```

Because no styles apply, however, you'll likely use the single-argument constructor. Note that the parent is a Shell, not a Composite. You then show the popup list by calling the open() method. Table 9-22 describes PopupList's methods.

Table 9-22. `PopupList` *Methods*

Method	Description
Font getFont()	Returns the font associated with this PopupList
String[] getItems()	Returns the items in the list
int getMinimumWidth()	Returns the minimum width for the list in pixels
String open(Rectangle rectangle)	Opens the list, using the specified Rectangle to determine size and placement, and returns the selected item (or null if none selected)
void select(String string)	Selects the first item in the list that starts with the specified string
void setFont(Font font)	Sets the font for this PopupList
void setItems(String[] strings)	Sets the items for this list
void setMinimumWidth(int width)	Sets the minimum width, in pixels, for this PopupList

Using PopupList

You usually create and launch a `PopupList` in response to some event. You might, for example, launch the list when a button is clicked. To accomplish this, create a selection listener for the button that looks something like this:

```
Button button = new Button(shell, SWT.PUSH);
button.addSelectionListener(new SelectionAdapter() {
  public void widgetSelected(SelectionEvent event) {
    PopupList list = new PopupList(shell);
    list.setItems(new String[] { "one", "two", "three" });
    String selected = list.open(shell.getBounds());
  }
});
```

Because `PopupList` offers no `add()` method to add a single string or set of strings, you must call `setItems()`, passing an array of strings, to set the options available in the list.

The PopupListTest program shows a button that launches a `PopupList` when clicked (see Listing 9-13). It uses the shell's bounds to determine where to place the list and prints the selected item to the console.

Listing 9-13. `PopupListTest.java`

```
package examples.ch9;

import org.eclipse.swt.SWT;
import org.eclipse.swt.custom.*;
import org.eclipse.swt.events.*;
import org.eclipse.swt.layout.*;
import org.eclipse.swt.widgets.*;
```

```java
/**
 * This class demonstrates PopupList
 */
public class PopupListTest {
  // These are the options that display in the list
  private static final String[] OPTIONS = { "Apple", "Banana", "Cherry",
      "Doughnut", "Eggplant", "Filbert", "Greens", "Hummus", "Ice Cream", "Jam"};

  /**
   * Runs the application
   */
  public void run() {
    Display display = new Display();
    Shell shell = new Shell(display);
    shell.setText("PopupList Test");
    createContents(shell);
    shell.pack();
    shell.open();
    while (!shell.isDisposed()) {
      if (!display.readAndDispatch()) {
        display.sleep();
      }
    }
    display.dispose();
  }

  /**
   * Creates the main window's contents
   *
   * @param shell the main window
   */
  private void createContents(final Shell shell) {
    shell.setLayout(new RowLayout());

    // Create a button to launch the list
    Button button = new Button(shell, SWT.PUSH);
    button.setText("Push Me");
    button.addSelectionListener(new SelectionAdapter() {
      public void widgetSelected(SelectionEvent event) {
        // Create a list
        PopupList list = new PopupList(shell);

        // Add the items to the list
        list.setItems(OPTIONS);

        // Open the list and get the selected item
        String selected = list.open(shell.getBounds());
```

```
            // Print the item to the console
            System.out.println(selected);
        }
    });
  }

  /**
   * The application entry point
   *
   * @param args the command line arguments
   */
  public static void main(String[] args) {
    new PopupListTest().run();
  }
}
```

Figure 9-30 shows the program with the list below the window. Figure 9-31 shows the program after its main window has been moved to the bottom of the screen—the list has moved above the window.

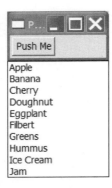

Figure 9-30. A PopupList *below the main window*

Figure 9-31. A PopupList *above the main window*

Introducing SashForm

You learned about sashes—draggable splitters dividing two controls—in Chapter 8. SashForm wraps the setup of a sash, removing the tedium from creating and using sashes. To recap, you create a sash by following these steps:

1. Instantiating a Sash object

2. Creating a FormData object for the sash with the appropriate attachments

3. Creating the controls for either side of the sash

4. Creating FormData objects for the controls and attaching them to the sash

5. Creating an event handler to make the sash stick when it's dragged

Aside from deciding whether to make the sash horizontal or vertical, and determining which controls to place on the sides of the sash, you won't change much code in your sash setup routines—and it's a lot of code each time. SashForm takes care of this burden for you—to use SashForm, you do the following:

1. Instantiate a SashForm.

2. Create the controls for each side.

You'll find this a considerable improvement.

Creating a SashForm

You instantiate a SashForm by calling its only constructor:

```
SashForm(Composite parent, int style)
```

Like sashes, SashForms can be either horizontal or vertical. You specify the desired orientation with the style you pass to the constructor—either SWT.HORIZONTAL or SWT.VERTICAL, for horizontal or vertical orientation, respectively. This orientation, however, refers to the controls, not the sash. A horizontal orientation places the controls horizontally, divided by a vertical sash. A vertical orientation places the controls vertically, with a horizontal sash. Figure 9-32 shows a horizontal SashForm, and Figure 9-33 shows a vertical SashForm.

Figure 9-32. A SashForm *with the* SWT.HORIZONTAL *style*

Figure 9-33. A SashForm *with the* SWT.VERTICAL *style*

To create a horizontal SashForm, use code like this:

```
SashForm sashForm = new SashForm(parent, SWT.HORIZONTAL);
new Button(sashForm, SWT.PUSH).setText("Left");
new Button(sashForm, SWT.PUSH).setText("Right");
```

These three lines of code create two buttons, side by side, separated by a vertical sash that sticks when you move it. You don't have to attach the buttons to the sash; SashForm takes care of that detail for you.

To see SashForm yourself, compile and run the SashFormTest program shown in Listing 9-14.

Listing 9-14. SashFormTest.java

```java
package examples.ch9;

import org.eclipse.swt.SWT;
import org.eclipse.swt.custom.SashForm;
import org.eclipse.swt.layout.FillLayout;
import org.eclipse.swt.widgets.*;

/**
 * This class demonstrates SashForm
 */
public class SashFormTest {
  /**
   * Runs the application
   */
  public void run() {
    Display display = new Display();
    Shell shell = new Shell(display);
    shell.setText("SashForm Test");
    createContents(shell);
    shell.open();
    while (!shell.isDisposed()) {
      if (!display.readAndDispatch()) {
        display.sleep();
      }
    }
    display.dispose();
  }

  /**
   * Creates the main window's contents
   *
   * @param parent the parent window
   */
  private void createContents(Composite parent) {
    // Fill the parent window with the buttons and sash
    parent.setLayout(new FillLayout());

    // Create the SashForm and the buttons
    SashForm sashForm = new SashForm(parent, SWT.HORIZONTAL);
    new Button(sashForm, SWT.PUSH).setText("Left");
    new Button(sashForm, SWT.PUSH).setText("Right");
  }
```

```
/**
 * The application entry point
 *
 * @param args the command line arguments
 */
public static void main(String[] args) {
  new SashFormTest().run();
}
}
```

Configuring a SashForm

Although you can create a sticky sash and its two controls with three lines of code, you're stuck with two equally sized controls and a sash with a fixed orientation. Your requirements, however, might dictate a little more flexibility. You might want to change the sash's width, or even create more than one sash. You might want the user to be able to change the sash's orientation during run time. Perhaps you want one control to claim all of the space allocated to the sashing area. Maybe you want to change the colors or weights for the controls. Though SashForm does allow you to get off the ground quickly with minimum fuss, it also provides methods to customize its stock behavior. Table 9-23 describes these methods.

Table 9-23. SashForm *Methods*

Method	Description
Point computeSize(int wHint, int hHint, boolean changed)	Computes the preferred size of this SashForm.
Control getMaxmimizedControl()	Returns the control that's currently maximized or null if no control is maximized.
int getOrientation()	Returns SWT.HORIZONTAL for horizontally aligned SashForms or SWT.VERTICAL for vertically aligned SashForms.
int[] getWeights()	Returns the relative weights for the controls in this SashForm.
void layout(boolean changed)	Forces the SashForm to recalculate the sizes and positions of its sashes and controls and to redraw itself.
void setBackground(Color color)	Sets the background color for this SashForm.
void setForeground(Color color)	Sets the foreground color for this SashForm.
void setLayout(Layout layout)	Currently does nothing.
void setMaximizedControl(Control control)	Sets the control to maximize in this SashForm, restoring any previously maximized control. Passing null restores all controls.
void setOrientation(int orientation)	Sets the orientation for this SashForm. Valid values are SWT.HORIZONTAL and SWT.VERTICAL.
void setWeights(int[] weights)	Sets the relative weights for the controls in this SashForm.

Additionally, SashForm has a public member, int SASH_WIDTH, which controls the width in pixels of all sashes in this SashForm. You get and set the value of this member directly, like this:

```
sashForm.SASH_WIDTH = 5;
```

The SashFormAdvanced program demonstrates some of SashForm's capabilities (see Listing 9-15). It creates three buttons in a SashForm and uses green, extra-wide sashes to divide them. It sets the relative weights for the three buttons, so they're not all the same size. Clicking one of the buttons maximizes that button; clicking it again restores it. The program also provides two extra buttons: one labeled *Switch Orientation* and one labeled *Restore Weights*. Clicking the Switch Orientation button will toggle the SashForm between horizontal and vertical orientations. Clicking the Restore Weights button will restore the original relative weights for the SashForm's buttons (you'll see the effects only if you've dragged the sashes to new locations).

Listing 9-15. SashFormAdvanced.java

```
package examples.ch9;

import org.eclipse.swt.SWT;
import org.eclipse.swt.custom.SashForm;
import org.eclipse.swt.events.*;
import org.eclipse.swt.layout.*;
import org.eclipse.swt.widgets.*;

/**
 * This class demonstrates SashForm
 */
public class SashFormAdvanced {
  /**
   * Runs the application
   */
  public void run() {
    Display display = new Display();
    Shell shell = new Shell(display);
    shell.setText("SashForm Advanced");
    createContents(shell);
    shell.open();
    while (!shell.isDisposed()) {
      if (!display.readAndDispatch()) {
        display.sleep();
      }
    }
    display.dispose();
  }
```

```java
/**
 * Creates the main window's contents
 *
 * @param parent the parent window
 */
private void createContents(Composite parent) {
  // The layout will have a row of buttons, and
  // then a SashForm below it.
  parent.setLayout(new GridLayout(1, false));

  // Create the row of buttons
  Composite buttonBar = new Composite(parent, SWT.NONE);
  buttonBar.setLayout(new RowLayout());
  Button flip = new Button(buttonBar, SWT.PUSH);
  flip.setText("Switch Orientation");
  Button weights = new Button(buttonBar, SWT.PUSH);
  weights.setText("Restore Weights");

  // Create the SashForm
  Composite sash = new Composite(parent, SWT.NONE);
  sash.setLayout(new FillLayout());
  sash.setLayoutData(new GridData(GridData.FILL_BOTH));
  final SashForm sashForm = new SashForm(sash, SWT.HORIZONTAL);

  // Change the width of the sashes
  sashForm.SASH_WIDTH = 20;

  // Change the color used to paint the sashes
  sashForm.setBackground(parent.getDisplay().getSystemColor(SWT.COLOR_GREEN));

  // Create the buttons and their event handlers
  final Button one = new Button(sashForm, SWT.PUSH);
  one.setText("One");
  one.addSelectionListener(new SelectionAdapter() {
    public void widgetSelected(SelectionEvent event) {
      maximizeHelper(one, sashForm);
    }
  });

  final Button two = new Button(sashForm, SWT.PUSH);
  two.setText("Two");
  two.addSelectionListener(new SelectionAdapter() {
    public void widgetSelected(SelectionEvent event) {
      maximizeHelper(two, sashForm);
    }
  });
```

```
    final Button three = new Button(sashForm, SWT.PUSH);
    three.setText("Three");
    three.addSelectionListener(new SelectionAdapter() {
      public void widgetSelected(SelectionEvent event) {
        maximizeHelper(three, sashForm);
      }
    });

    // Set the relative weights for the buttons
    sashForm.setWeights(new int[] { 1, 2, 3});

    // Add the Switch Orientation functionality
    flip.addSelectionListener(new SelectionAdapter() {
      public void widgetSelected(SelectionEvent event) {
        switch (sashForm.getOrientation()) {
        case SWT.HORIZONTAL:
          sashForm.setOrientation(SWT.VERTICAL);
          break;
        case SWT.VERTICAL:
          sashForm.setOrientation(SWT.HORIZONTAL);
          break;
        }
      }
    });

    // Add the Restore Weights functionality
    weights.addSelectionListener(new SelectionAdapter() {
      public void widgetSelected(SelectionEvent event) {
        sashForm.setWeights(new int[] { 1, 2, 3});
      }
    });
  }

  /**
   * Helper method for our maximize behavior. If the passed control is already
   * maximized, restore it. Otherwise, maximize it.
   *
   * @param control the control to maximize or restore
   * @param sashForm the parent SashForm
   */
  private void maximizeHelper(Control control, SashForm sashForm) {
    // See if the control is already maximized
    if (control == sashForm.getMaximizedControl()) {
      // Already maximized; restore it
      sashForm.setMaximizedControl(null);
    } else {
```

```
      // Not yet maximized, so maximize it
      sashForm.setMaximizedControl(control);
    }
  }

  /**
   * The application entry point
   *
   * @param args the command line arguments
   */
  public static void main(String[] args) {
    new SashFormAdvanced().run();
  }
}
```

Figure 9-34 shows the program's main window, Figure 9-35 shows the program after the orientation has been switched, and Figure 9-36 shows one of the buttons maximized.

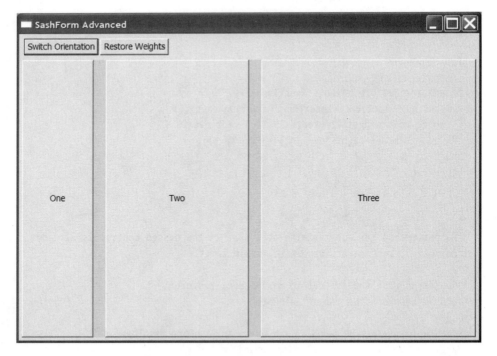

Figure 9-34. The SashFormAdvanced program

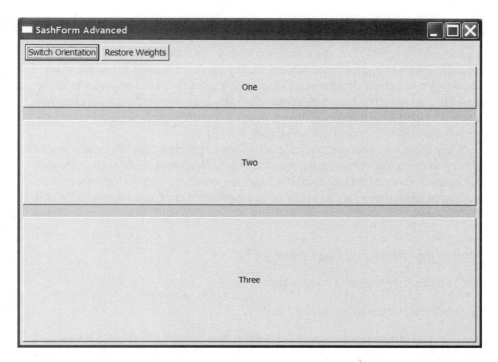

Figure 9-35. The SashFormAdvanced program with the orientation switched

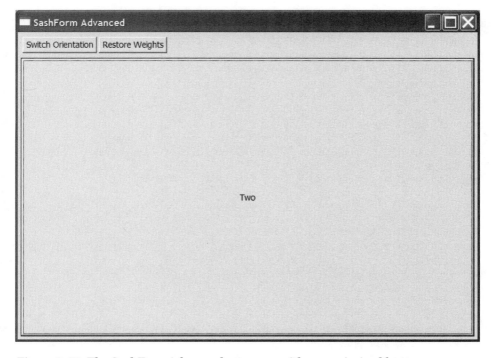

Figure 9-36. The SashFormAdvanced program with a maximized button

Introducing ScrolledComposite

Until now, all the controls in the example code have fit inside the application window. Sometimes, however, your controls won't fit, and you'll want users to be able to scroll left and right or up and down to see them, as if panning over your application using a smaller view port. The ScrollableComposite class is a concrete Composite class with scrollbars. Use it anywhere you'd use a Composite but want users to be able to scroll through the Composite's contents when they don't fit.

A key difference between Composites and ScrolledComposites lies in how you add children to them. With Composites, you simply pass the Composite to each of the children's constructors. ScrolledComposite, however, scrolls through a single control, so you can specify either a single control or another Composite that contains all the children controls.

Creating a ScrolledComposite

ScrolledComposite has one constructor:

```
ScrolledComposite(Composite parent, int style)
```

where style is SWT.H_SCROLL to enable horizontal scrolling, SWT.V_SCROLL to enable vertical scrolling, or SWT.H_SCROLL | SWT.V_SCROLL to enable both. Figure 9-37 shows a ScrolledComposite with the style SWT.H_SCROLL | SWT.V_SCROLL.

Figure 9-37. A ScrolledComposite

Sizing a ScrolledComposite

You take one of the following two approaches to size the scrollable area of a ScrolledComposite:

- You can set the size of the child control, and the ScrolledComposite will show scrollbars whenever the child control can't be fully displayed.

- You can set the minimum size of the child control, and the ScrolledComposite will resize the control to fill the ScrolledComposite's area, down to the pre-scribed minimum size. Scrollbars will display when the child control can't be fully displayed.

The next two sections examine these two approaches, respectively.

Setting the Child Control's Size

When you set the size of the child control, the child control never shrinks or expands. The ScrolledComposite's scrollbars display whenever its child control can't completely fit within it. You implement this approach with code like this:

```
// Create the ScrolledComposite to scroll horizontally and vertically
ScrolledComposite sc = new ScrolledComposite(parent, SWT.H_SCROLL
  | SWT.V_SCROLL);

// Create a child composite to hold the controls
Composite child = new Composite(sc, SWT.NONE);
child.setLayout(new FillLayout());

// Create the buttons
new Button(child, SWT.PUSH).setText("One");
new Button(child, SWT.PUSH).setText("Two");

// Set the absolute size of the child
child.setSize(400, 400);

// Set the child as the scrolled content of the ScrolledComposite
sc.setContent(child);
```

This code produces the window shown in Figure 9-38. Figure 9-39 shows the same window after resizing smaller than the child control's specified size.

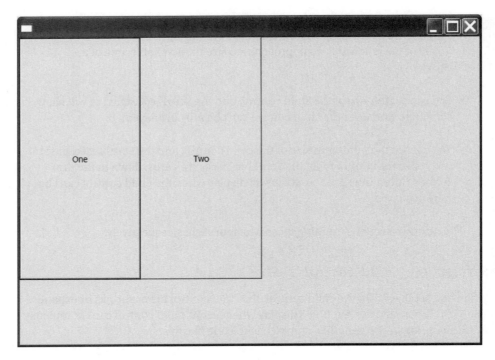

Figure 9-38. A ScrolledComposite *with a sized child control*

Figure 9-39. The resized ScrolledComposite

Setting the Child Control's Minimum Size

Sometimes you want controls to fill a given area, expanding or contracting as necessary, and you want to set a limit on how far the controls will contract. To implement this, you set the minimum size for the child control, either by calling setMinSize() to set both the minimum width and minimum height in one method call or by calling both setMinWidth() and setMinHeight() to set the minimum width and the minimum height, respectively. You also must specify the axes along which the child control will expand. Call setExpandHorizontal(true) to expand horizontally, and call setExpandHorizontal(true) to expand vertically.

Listing 9-16 shows some example code.

Listing 9-16. Setting Minimum Size for a Child Control

```
// Create the ScrolledComposite to scroll horizontally and vertically
ScrolledComposite sc = new ScrolledComposite(parent, SWT.H_SCROLL
  | SWT.V_SCROLL);

// Create a child composite to hold the controls
Composite child = new Composite(sc, SWT.NONE);
child.setLayout(new FillLayout());

// Create the buttons
new Button(child, SWT.PUSH).setText("One");
new Button(child, SWT.PUSH).setText("Two");

// Set the child as the scrolled content of the ScrolledComposite
sc.setContent(child);

// Set the minimum size
sc.setMinSize(400, 400);

// Expand both horizontally and vertically
sc.setExpandHorizontal(true);
sc.setExpandVertical(true);
```

This code produces the window shown in Figure 9-40. Note how the buttons now fill the window. Figure 9-41 shows the same window after resizing, and Figure 9-42 shows it after resizing smaller than the child control's specified minimum size.

Figure 9-40. A ScrolledComposite *with an expanding child control*

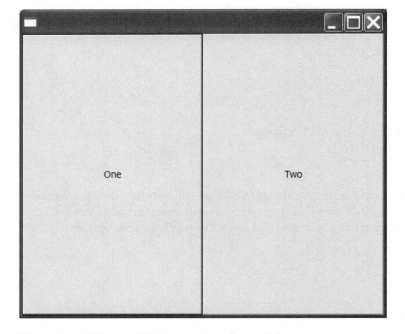

Figure 9-41. The ScrolledComposite *after resizing*

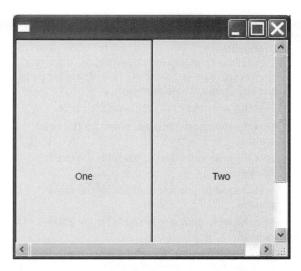

Figure 9-42. The ScrolledComposite *after resizing smaller than the minimum size*

Configuring a ScrolledComposite

You've seen some of ScrolledComposite's methods, but it offers a few more, described in Table 9-24.

Table 9-24. ScrolledComposite *Methods*

Method	Description
Point computeSize(int wHint, int hHint, boolean changed)	Computes the preferred size of this ScrolledComposite.
boolean getAlwaysShowScrollBars()	Returns true if the scrollbars are set to always show, or false if they aren't.
Control getContent()	Returns the child control for this ScrolledComposite.
Point getOrigin()	Returns the point in the child control that's currently displayed in the upper left of this ScrolledComposite.
void layout(boolean changed)	Forces this ScrolledComposite to recalculate the size of its child control and redraw itself.
void setAlwaysShowScrollBars (boolean show)	If show is true, sets the scrollbars to always display. If show is false, sets the scrollbars to display only when necessary.
void setContent(Control content)	Sets the child control for this ScrolledComposite.
void setExpandHorizontal(boolean expand)	If expand is true, expands the child control along the horizontal axis. If expand is false, doesn't expand the child control along the horizontal axis.

Table 9-24. `ScrolledComposite` *Methods (continued)*

Method	Description
`void setExpandVertical(boolean expand)`	If expand is `true`, expands the child control along the vertical axis. If expand is `false`, doesn't expand the child control along the vertical axis.
`void setLayout(Layout layout)`	Sets the layout for this `ScrolledComposite`.
`void setMinHeight(int height)`	Sets the minimum height in pixels for the child control.
`void setMinSize(int width, int height)`	Sets the minimum size in pixels for the child control.
`void setMinSize(Point size)`	Sets the minimum size in pixels for the child control.
`void setMinWidth(int width)`	Sets the minimum size in pixels for the child control.
`void setOrigin(int x, int y)`	Scrolls the child control until the point specified by `x, y` displays in the upper left of this `ScrolledComposite`.
`void setOrigin(Point origin)`	Scrolls the child control until the point specified by `origin` displays in the upper left of this `ScrolledComposite`.

Introducing `ViewForm`

The Eclipse developers created `ViewForm` to institute a standard mechanism to display the many views that Eclipse offers. There's no reason to let them hog all the fun, however—you can use `ViewForm` as a shortcut for creating views in your applications as well.

`ViewForm` creates three controls in a row across the top of a `Composite`, with a content area below the controls. See Figure 9-43 for an example of a `ViewForm`, taken from Eclipse. The first control contains the image in the upper left and the text *Outline*. The second control contains the toolbar buttons to the right of the text *Outline*, up to, but not including, the close button in the upper right. The third control is the close button in the upper right. Everything else is the content area.

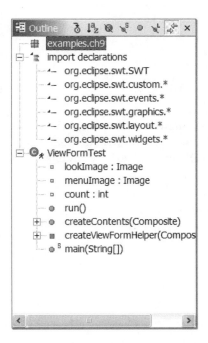

Figure 9-43. An example ViewForm

The second of the three controls can wrap to a second line, as shown in Figure 9-44. It will automatically wrap when the size of the ViewForm can't accommodate all three controls. You can force this behavior to occur, regardless of size, as you'll see in the next section.

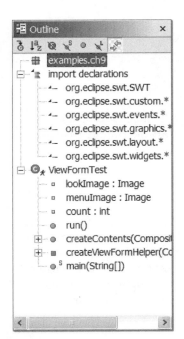

Figure 9-44. An example ViewForm, *with the second control wrapped*

Creating a ViewForm

You create a ViewForm by calling its only constructor:

```
ViewForm(Composite parent, int style)
```

The applicable styles for ViewForm are SWT.BORDER, which draws a visible border and a drop shadow around the ViewForm, and SWT.FLAT, which eliminates the drop shadow. SWT.FLAT must be combined with SWT.BORDER (using the bitwise OR operator) to have any effect.

This code creates the ViewForm shown in Figure 9-45:

```
ViewForm viewForm = new ViewForm(parent, SWT.BORDER);
```

Figure 9-45. A plain ViewForm

You can discern a drop shadow around its edges, but not much else of interest. Without the three top controls or the content area, a ViewForm offers little. The next section discusses how to get more from your ViewForms.

Configuring a ViewForm

The three controls lined across the top of a ViewForm are called the *top-left* control, the *top-center* control, and the *top-right* control. The control for the content area is called the *content* control. Although ViewForm offers a setLayout() method, it ignores the layout passed and lays out these controls according to its preset rules. However, the top-center control wraps to its own line below the top-left and top-right controls either if there's not enough space to display it on the same line or if you call the following:

```
viewForm.setTopCenterSeparate(true);
```

You can change which controls you set into the ViewForm. You can also change the colors used to paint the drop shadows, as well as the margins surrounding the controls. You can hide or display the border at run time, and you can change the font used for the three top controls with a single method call. Some behaviors are controlled by public member variables, and some are controlled by methods. Table 9-25 describes ViewForm's public member variables, and Table 9-26 describes ViewForm's methods.

Table 9-25. ViewForm *Member Variables*

Member	Description
static RGB borderInsideRGB	RGB describing the color used to paint the innermost line of the drop shadow. Note that it's static and thus will affect all instances of ViewForm.
static RGB borderMiddleRGB	RGB describing the color used to paint the middle line of the drop shadow. Note that it's static and thus will affect all instances of ViewForm.
static RGB borderOutsideRGB	RGB describing the color used to paint the outermost line of the drop shadow. Note that it's static and thus will affect all instances of ViewForm.
int marginHeight	The height of the margin, in pixels, along the top and bottom edges of this ViewForm.
int marginWidth	The width of the margin, in pixels, along the left and right edges of this ViewForm.

Table 9-26. ViewForm *Methods*

Method	Description
Point computeSize(int wHint, int hHint, boolean changed)	Computes the preferred size of the ViewForm.
Rectangle computeTrim(int x, int y, int width, int height)	Computes the bounding rectangle necessary to produce the client area specified.
Rectangle getClientArea()	Returns the bounding rectangle of the client area only.
Control getContent()	Returns the content control.
Control getTopCenter()	Returns the top-center control.
Control getTopLeft()	Returns the top-left control.
Control getTopRight()	Returns the top-right control.
void layout(boolean changed)	Forces the ViewForm to recalculate the sizes and positions of its controls and to redraw itself.
void setBorderVisible(boolean show)	If show is true, displays the border. If show is false, hides the border.
void setContent(Control content)	Sets the content control.
void setFont(Font font)	Sets the font for the three top controls.
void setLayout(Layout layout)	Currently does nothing.
void setTopCenter(Control control)	Sets the top center control.

Table 9-26. `ViewForm` *Methods (continued)*

Method	Description
void setTopCenterSeparate(boolean separate)	If separate is true, forces the top-center control to its own row below the other two top controls. If separate is false, and the top row has enough room to accommodate the top-center control, the top-center control displays in the same row as the other two top controls.
void setTopLeft(Control control)	Sets the top left control.
void setTopRight(Control control)	Sets the top right control.

NOTE *You shouldn't subclass* `ViewForm`.

The Look program, shown in Figure 9-46, implements an extremely low-budget text editor. Each time you click the New Document button, Look creates a new `ViewForm`. The top-left control of each `ViewForm` displays an attractive Look icon and the text *Document xx*, where *xx* is the number of the document. The top-center control shows a downward-pointing arrow; click the arrow to display a menu with a single option, Clear, that clears the text in the content control. The top-right control is a close button that closes the `ViewForm`. Finally, the content control is a multiline text box. Feel free to use Look as your full-time programming editor—just remember to cut and paste the code you write into a program that will actually save it, or you'll lose all your work.

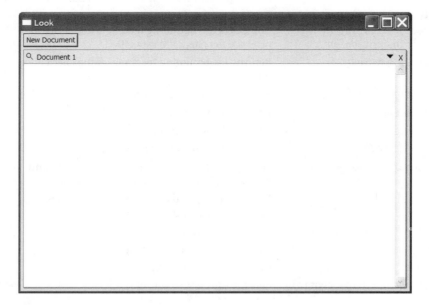

Figure 9-46. The Look program

Listing 9-17 shows the source code for Look.

Listing 9-17. Look.java

```java
package examples.ch9;

import org.eclipse.swt.SWT;
import org.eclipse.swt.custom.*;
import org.eclipse.swt.events.*;
import org.eclipse.swt.graphics.*;
import org.eclipse.swt.layout.*;
import org.eclipse.swt.widgets.*;

/**
 * This class demonstrates ViewForm
 */
public class Look {
  // Images used in the ViewForm
  private Image lookImage;
  private Image menuImage;

  // Counter for titles of ViewForms
  private int count = 0;

  /**
   * Runs the application
   */
  public void run() {
    Display display = new Display();
    Shell shell = new Shell(display);
    shell.setText("Look");

    // Load the images
    lookImage = new Image(display, this.getClass().getResourceAsStream(
        "/images/look.gif"));
    menuImage = new Image(display, this.getClass().getResourceAsStream(
        "/images/down.gif"));

    createContents(shell);
    shell.open();
    while (!shell.isDisposed()) {
      if (!display.readAndDispatch()) {
        display.sleep();
      }
    }
```

```
        // You created the images, so you must dispose
        if (lookImage != null) lookImage.dispose();
        if (menuImage != null) menuImage.dispose();
        display.dispose();
    }

    /**
     * Creates the main window's contents
     *
     * @param parent the main window
     */
    public void createContents(Composite parent) {
        parent.setLayout(new GridLayout(1, false));

        // Clicking the New Document button will create a new ViewForm
        Button button = new Button(parent, SWT.PUSH);
        button.setText("New Document");

        // Create the composite that holds the ViewForms
        final Composite composite = new Composite(parent, SWT.NONE);
        composite.setLayoutData(new GridData(GridData.FILL_BOTH));
        composite.setLayout(new FillLayout());

        // Add the event handler to create the ViewForms
        button.addSelectionListener(new SelectionAdapter() {
            public void widgetSelected(SelectionEvent event) {
                createViewFormHelper(composite, "Document " + (++count));
                composite.layout();
            }
        });
    }

    /**
     * Helper function for creating the ViewForms
     *
     * @param parent the parent Composite
     * @param text the title text
     */
    private void createViewFormHelper(final Composite parent, String text) {
        // Create the ViewForm
        final ViewForm vf = new ViewForm(parent, SWT.BORDER);

        // Create the CLabel for the top left, which will have an image and text
        CLabel label = new CLabel(vf, SWT.NONE);
        label.setText(text);
        label.setImage(lookImage);
        label.setAlignment(SWT.LEFT);
        vf.setTopLeft(label);
```

```java
// Create the downward-pointing arrow to display the menu
// and set it as the top center
final ToolBar tbMenu = new ToolBar(vf, SWT.FLAT);
final ToolItem itemMenu = new ToolItem(tbMenu, SWT.PUSH);
itemMenu.setImage(menuImage);
vf.setTopCenter(tbMenu);

// Create the close button and set it as the top right
ToolBar tbClose = new ToolBar(vf, SWT.FLAT);
ToolItem itemClose = new ToolItem(tbClose, SWT.PUSH);
itemClose.setText("X");
itemClose.addSelectionListener(new SelectionAdapter() {
  public void widgetSelected(SelectionEvent event) {
    vf.dispose();
    parent.layout();
  }
});
vf.setTopRight(tbClose);

// Create the content--a multiline text box
final Text textArea = new Text(vf, SWT.MULTI | SWT.WRAP | SWT.V_SCROLL);
vf.setContent(textArea);

// Create the menu to display when the down arrow is pressed
final Menu menu = new Menu(tbMenu);
MenuItem clear = new MenuItem(menu, SWT.NONE);
clear.setText("Clear");
clear.addSelectionListener(new SelectionAdapter() {
  public void widgetSelected(SelectionEvent event) {
    textArea.setText("");
  }
});

// Add the handler to display the menu
itemMenu.addSelectionListener(new SelectionAdapter() {
  public void widgetSelected(SelectionEvent event) {
    // Place the menu right below the toolbar button
    Rectangle rect = itemMenu.getBounds();
    menu.setLocation(tbMenu.toDisplay(rect.x, rect.y + rect.height));
    menu.setVisible(true);
  }
});
}

/**
 * The application entry point
 *
 * @param args the command line arguments
 */
```

```
public static void main(String[] args) {
    new Look().run();
}
}
```

Figure 9-47 shows Look with three open "documents," each containing the source code of the Look program.

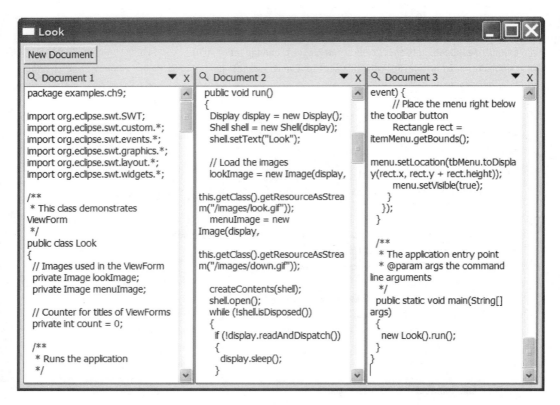

Figure 9-47. The Look program with three ViewForms

Creating a Usable Example

You can combine widgets from the custom package with widgets from other packages to create usable applications. The source code for this chapter includes an application called *Password* that securely stores passwords. Though it doesn't compare in features to other commercial or open-source solutions, it provides a lightweight solution for secure password storage and a base for developing better applications.

The Password application uses a TableTree to display passwords by category. Each password entry contains a name, user ID, and password. You could, for example, create a category called *Web Sites* and then create an entry named *Slashdot* with your Slashdot user ID and password. It stores all the password information in files, and it displays each open file in its own tab using CTabFolder. Each file has a master password. The master password itself is never stored. Instead, the Password application stores a hash for the master password, making it virtually impossible to crack. It uses this master password to encrypt or decrypt the other entries, using password-based encryption. Beyond those bare essentials, encryption lies outside the scope of this book.

Figure 9-48 shows the application's main window. Figure 9-49 shows the password entry dialog box, and Figure 9-50 shows the main window with a few items entered.

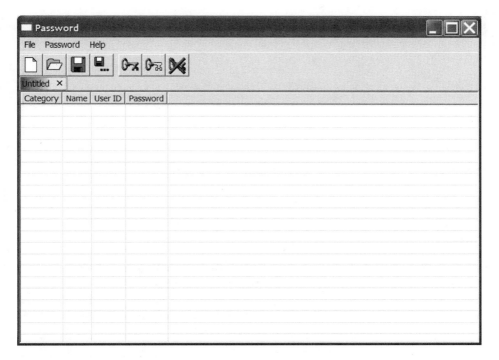

Figure 9-48. The Password application

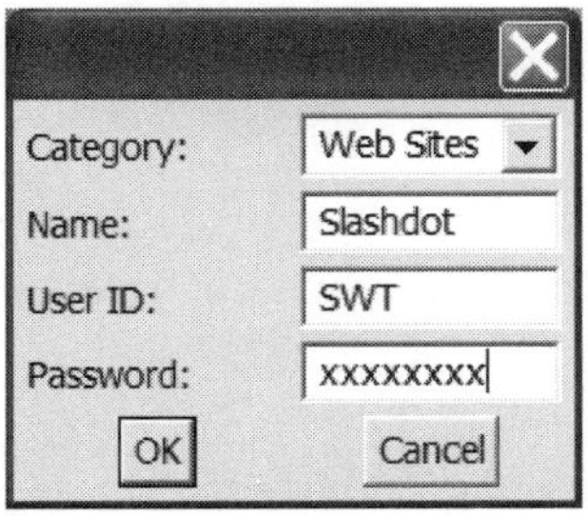

Figure 9-49. The Password Entry dialog box

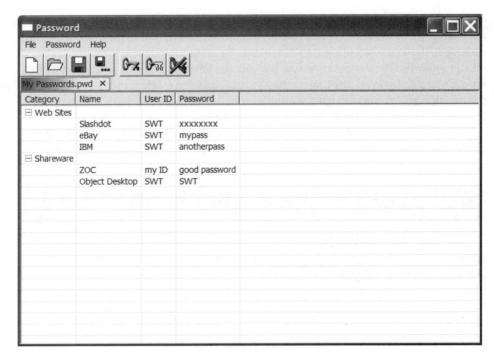

Figure 9-50. The Password application with some passwords entered

Summary

The same custom controls that separate the Eclipse IDE from average programs can differentiate your applications from the rest. Used judiciously, the custom controls improve both the appearance and usability of your applications. Don't ignore their power or utility, and you'll produce professional-looking and professional-responding programs without having to create mountains of code.

CHAPTER 10

Graphics

GUIs RELY ON GRAPHICS. They present data and offer interaction through graphical widgets. Although SWT offers graphical widgets for most types of display and interaction, you might want to draw some things that SWT won't natively draw. In these situations, use SWT's graphics capabilities to unleash the Picasso within you.

The GC class (short for graphical context) forms the core of SWT's graphics engine. GC offers all the methods required for drawing shapes, text, and images. You can draw on Controls, Devices, or other Images. Generally, drawing lifecycles consists of the following:

1. Creating or obtaining a GC to draw on the desired target

2. Drawing

3. If you created the GC, disposing the GC

In code, the drawing lifecycle looks like this:

```
GC gc = new GC(display);
gc.drawRectangle(...);
gc.drawText(...);
gc.drawImage(...);
gc.dispose();
```

You generally put drawing code in a paint handler, like this:

```
shell.addPaintListener(new PaintListener() {
  public void paintControl(PaintEvent event) {
    // Create GC, draw, and dispose
  }
});
```

Because the PaintEvent passed to the paintControl() method contains a valid GC instance, you can avoid creating a GC and just use the one from the event. If you do this, you shouldn't dispose that GC. That code looks like this:

```
shell.addPaintListener(new PaintListener() {
  public void paintControl(PaintEvent event) {
    event.gc.drawRectangle();
  }
});
```

To create a GC, call the constructor, passing a Drawable (a Control, a Device, or an Image) and optionally a style. You can pass either SWT.LEFT_TO_RIGHT or SWT.RIGHT_TO_LEFT for the style, demonstrating bidirectional support. This chapter examines GC's drawing methods.

Drawing Shapes

Although you can draw on any component with an associated GC, SWT offers the Canvas class specifically for drawing arbitrary graphics. Canvases, like shells, are composites, which means that they can contain other widgets. Create canvases by specifying their parent composite and style.

As a canvas is a control, it inherits the setForeground() and getForeground() methods. Setting this value controls the color with which graphics and text are drawn. In the same vein, Canvas offers you the setFont() method, controlling the font used to render text. You draw on a Canvas by getting a reference to its GC, as in Listing 10-1.

Listing 10-1. CanvasExample.java

```java
package examples.ch10;

import org.eclipse.swt.SWT;
import org.eclipse.swt.events.*;
import org.eclipse.swt.graphics.*;
import org.eclipse.swt.layout.*;
import org.eclipse.swt.widgets.*;

/**
 * This class demonstrates a Canvas
 */
public class CanvasExample {
  /**
   * Runs the application
   */
  public void run() {
    Display display = new Display();
    Shell shell = new Shell(display);
    shell.setText("Canvas Example");
    createContents(shell);
    shell.open();
    while (!shell.isDisposed()) {
      if (!display.readAndDispatch()) {
        display.sleep();
      }
    }
    display.dispose();
  }
```

```
/**
 * Creates the main window's contents
 *
 * @param shell the main window
 */
private void createContents(Shell shell) {
  shell.setLayout(new FillLayout());

  // Create a canvas
  Canvas canvas = new Canvas(shell, SWT.NONE);

  // Create a button on the canvas
  Button button = new Button(canvas, SWT.PUSH);
  button.setBounds(10, 10, 300, 40);
  button.setText("You can place widgets on a canvas");

  // Create a paint handler for the canvas
  canvas.addPaintListener(new PaintListener() {
    public void paintControl(PaintEvent e) {
      // Do some drawing
      Rectangle rect = ((Canvas) e.widget).getBounds();
      e.gc.setForeground(e.display.getSystemColor(SWT.COLOR_RED));
      e.gc.drawFocus(5, 5, rect.width - 10, rect.height - 10);
      e.gc.drawText("You can draw text directly on a canvas", 60, 60);
    }
  });
}

/**
 * The application entry point
 *
 * @param args the command line arguments
 */
public static void main(String[] args) {
  new CanvasExample().run();
}
}
```

This example, shown in Figure 10-1, uses a Canvas as the parent of a Button, and uses a layout to control the button's size and placement. It implements a PaintListener for the canvas, which gets notified whenever a GUI component needs to be repainted. This implementation uses the associated GC to draw a rectangle and some text. The version of drawRectangle() it calls takes four integers: the x and y locations of the upper-left corner of the rectangle to draw, relative to the upper-left corner of the canvas, and the width and height of the rectangle. You can instead pass a Rectangle instance to drawRectangle(). Because this code uses the GC from the event, it doesn't dispose it.

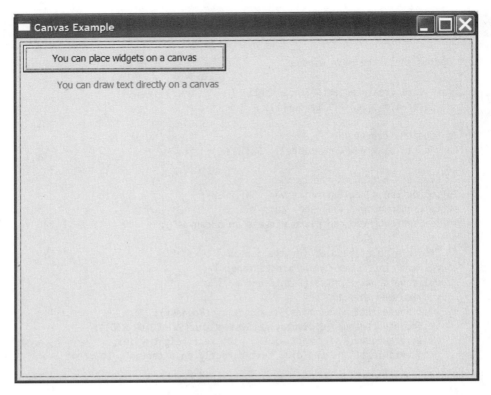

Figure 10-1. Putting a widget, some text, and some graphics on a Canvas

You can create "filled" rectangles using the fillRectangle() methods. These methods create a solid rectangle based on the background color of their parent component. In general, you draw outlined shapes using methods that begin with "draw" and solid shapes using methods that begin with "fill." Here's an example of code that draws a "filled" rectangle, shown in Figure 10-2:

```
private class CanvasExamplePaintListener implements PaintListener {
  public void paintControl(PaintEvent e) {
    e.gc.setBackground(e.display.getSystemColor(SWT.COLOR_RED));
    e.gc.fillRectangle(30, 40, 400, 200);
  }
}
```

Figure 10-2. A "filled" rectangle

Drawing Points and Lines

GC offers the drawLine() method for drawing explicit lines. drawLine() takes four integers that define two Cartesian points, relative to the upper-left corner of the component. For instance, to divide a canvas into four equal sections (see Figure 10-3), use the code in Listing 10-2.

Listing 10-2. Painting a line

```
public void paintControl(PaintEvent e) {
    Canvas canvas = (Canvas) e.widget;
    int maxX = canvas.getSize().x;
    int maxY = canvas.getSize().y;

    int halfX = (int) maxX/2;
    int halfY = (int) maxY/2;

    e.gc.setForeground(e.display.getSystemColor(SWT.COLOR_BLUE));
    e.gc.setLineWidth(10);
    e.gc.drawLine(halfX, 0, halfX, maxY);
    e.gc.drawLine(0, halfY, maxX, halfY);
}
```

Figure 10-3. Drawing lines

You can also draws sets of connecting lines with GC's drawPolyline() method. You pass an integer array containing concatenated (x,y) pairs, which are connected via a series of drawn lines. Changing the PaintListener implementation to that shown in Listing 10-3 renders the display shown in Figure 10-4.

Listing 10-3. Polyline

```
private class CanvasExamplePaintListener implements PaintListener {
  public void paintControl(PaintEvent e) {
    e.gc.setLineWidth(4);
    int[] points = { 0, 0, 100, 0, 0, 100, 100, 100, 0, 200};
    e.gc.drawPolyline(points);
  }
}
```

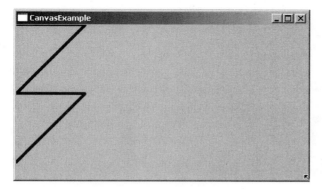

Figure 10-4. Drawing multiple lines

Use the drawPoint() method to plot points. Listing 10-4 draws a horizontal line to represent the x axis of the standard Cartesian diagram. Next, it draws a standard sine wave, which is somewhat complex because it's based on angles in radians. To move this complexity out of the graphics rendering code, the PointExample program uses a private method that takes the x value (the location as the curve moves from left to right across the canvas) and calculates the appropriate y value. Figure 10-5 shows the sine wave.

Listing 10-4. PointExample.java

```java
package examples.ch10;

import org.eclipse.swt.SWT;
import org.eclipse.swt.events.*;
import org.eclipse.swt.layout.FillLayout;
import org.eclipse.swt.widgets.*;

/**
 * This class demonstrates drawing points. It draws a sine wave.
 */
public class PointExample {
  /**
   * Runs the application
   */
  public void run() {
    Display display = new Display();
    Shell shell = new Shell(display);
    shell.setText("Point Example");
    createContents(shell);
    shell.open();
    while (!shell.isDisposed()) {
      if (!display.readAndDispatch()) {
        display.sleep();
      }
    }
    display.dispose();
```

```
    }

    /**
     * Creates the main window's contents
     *
     * @param shell the main window
     */
    private void createContents(Shell shell) {
      shell.setLayout(new FillLayout());

      // Create the canvas for drawing on
      Canvas canvas = new Canvas(shell, SWT.NONE);

      // Add the paint handler to draw the sine wave
      canvas.addPaintListener(new PointExamplePaintListener());

      // Use a white background
      canvas.setBackground(shell.getDisplay().getSystemColor(SWT.COLOR_WHITE));
    }

    /**
     * This class draws a sine wave using points
     */
    private class PointExamplePaintListener implements PaintListener {
      public void paintControl(PaintEvent e) {
        // Get the canvas and its dimensions
        Canvas canvas = (Canvas) e.widget;
        int maxX = canvas.getSize().x;
        int maxY = canvas.getSize().y;

        // Calculate the middle
        int halfX = (int) maxX / 2;
        int halfY = (int) maxY / 2;

        // Set the line color and draw a horizontal axis
        e.gc.setForeground(e.display.getSystemColor(SWT.COLOR_BLACK));
        e.gc.drawLine(0, halfY, maxX, halfY);

        // Draw the sine wave
        for (int i = 0; i < maxX; i++) {
          e.gc.drawPoint(i, getNormalizedSine(i, halfY, maxX));
        }
      }

    /**
     * Calculates the sine value
     *
     * @param x the value along the x-axis
     * @param halfY the value of the y-axis
     * @param maxX the width of the x-axis
     * @return int
     */
    int getNormalizedSine(int x, int halfY, int maxX) {
```

```
        double piDouble = 2 * Math.PI;
        double factor = piDouble / maxX;
        return (int) (Math.sin(x * factor) * halfY + halfY);
    }
}

/**
 * The application entry point
 *
 * @param args the command line arguments
 */
public static void main(String[] args) {
    new PointExample().run();
}
}
```

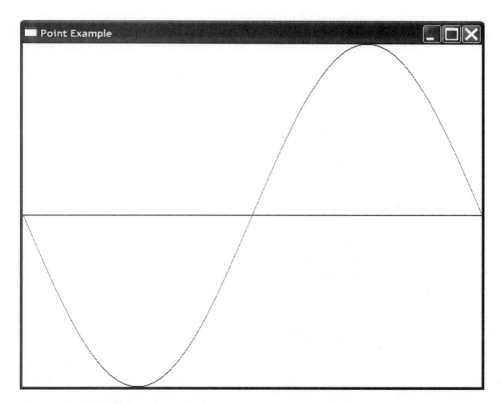

Figure 10-5. Plotting the sine function

Drawing a Round Rectangle

You can draw a rectangle with rounded corners with GC's drawRoundRectangle() method, which looks like this:

```
drawRoundRectangle(int x, int y, int width, int height, int arcWidth,
  int arcHeight)
```

The last two parameters specify the number of pixels from the corner to begin the rounding: arcWidth for the top and bottom sides and arcHeight for the left and right sides of the rectangle. The example in Listing 10-5 draws a rectangle, then allows you to input the arcWidth and arcHeight parameters to see the rounded drawing in action. Figure 10-6 shows this program's output.

Listing 10-5. RoundRectangleExample.java

```java
package examples.ch10;

import org.eclipse.swt.SWT;
import org.eclipse.swt.events.*;
import org.eclipse.swt.layout.*;
import org.eclipse.swt.widgets.*;

public class RoundRectangleExample {
  private Text txtArcWidth = null;
  private Text txtArcHeight = null;

  /**
   * Runs the application
   */
  public void run() {
    Display display = new Display();
    Shell shell = new Shell(display);
    shell.setText("RoundRectangle Example");
    createContents(shell);
    shell.open();
    while (!shell.isDisposed()) {
      if (!display.readAndDispatch()) {
        display.sleep();
      }
    }
    display.dispose();
  }

  /**
   * Creates the main window's contents
   *
   * @param shell the main window
   */
  private void createContents(Shell shell) {
    shell.setLayout(new FillLayout(SWT.VERTICAL));
```

```
    // Create the composite that holds the input fields
    Composite widgetComposite = new Composite(shell, SWT.NONE);
    widgetComposite.setLayout(new GridLayout(2, false));

    // Create the input fields
    new Label(widgetComposite, SWT.NONE).setText("Arc Width:");
    txtArcWidth = new Text(widgetComposite, SWT.BORDER);

    new Label(widgetComposite, SWT.NONE).setText("Arc Height");
    txtArcHeight = new Text(widgetComposite, SWT.BORDER);

    // Create the button that launches the redraw
    Button button = new Button(widgetComposite, SWT.PUSH);
    button.setText("Redraw");
    shell.setDefaultButton(button);

    // Create the canvas to draw the round rectangle on
    final Canvas drawingCanvas = new Canvas(shell, SWT.NONE);
    drawingCanvas.addPaintListener(new RoundRectangleExamplePaintListener());

    // Add a handler to redraw the round rectangle when pressed
    button.addSelectionListener(new SelectionAdapter() {
      public void widgetSelected(SelectionEvent e) {
        drawingCanvas.redraw();
      }
    });
  }

  /**
   * This class gets the user input and draws the requested round rectangle
   */
  private class RoundRectangleExamplePaintListener implements PaintListener {
    public void paintControl(PaintEvent e) {
      // Get the canvas for drawing and its width and height
      Canvas canvas = (Canvas) e.widget;
      int x = canvas.getBounds().width;
      int y = canvas.getBounds().height;

      // Determine user input, defaulting everything to zero.
      // Any blank fields are converted to zero
      int arcWidth = 0;
      int arcHeight = 0;
      try {
        arcWidth = txtArcWidth.getText().length() == 0 ? 0 : Integer
            .parseInt(txtArcWidth.getText());
        arcHeight = txtArcWidth.getText().length() == 0 ? 0 : Integer
            .parseInt(txtArcHeight.getText());
      } catch (NumberFormatException ex) {
        // Any problems, set them both to zero
        arcWidth = 0;
        arcHeight = 0;
      }
```

```
        // Set the line width
        e.gc.setLineWidth(4);

        // Draw the round rectangle
        e.gc.drawRoundRectangle(10, 10, x - 20, y - 20, arcWidth, arcHeight);
    }
}

/**
 * The application entry point
 *
 * @param args the command line arguments
 */
public static void main(String[] args) {
    new RoundRectangleExample().run();
}
}
```

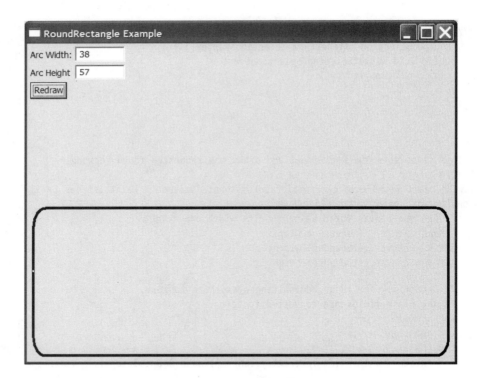

Figure 10-6. Demonstrating a rounded rectangle

Drawing a Focus Rectangle

In addition to the rectangles mentioned earlier, you can also draw a focus rectangle, if the underlying system supports it. A focus rectangle outlines a component when the component has the application focus. On most Windows platforms, this appears as a light dotted rectangle. You create focus rectangles with GC's drawFocus() method, which looks like this:

```
void drawFocus(int x, int y, int width, int height)
```

It functions just like its rectangular cousin.

If your underlying system doesn't support focus rectangles, the system draws a rectangle using the current characteristics of the GC (line width, foreground color, and so on).

Figure 10-7 shows a focus rectangle.

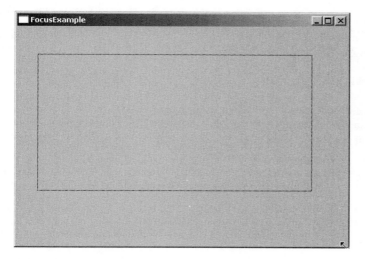

Figure 10-7. A focus rectangle

Drawing Ovals

To draw an oval, specify the x and y coordinates of the upper-left corner, along with the height and width of the oval's bounding rectangle. Specifying the same value for the width and the height renders a circle. Like rectangles, ovals can also be filled; use fillOval() instead of drawOval(). The OvalExample program in Listing 10-6 demonstrates drawing ovals, as Figure 10-8 shows.

Listing 10-6. OvalExample.java

```java
package examples.ch10;

import org.eclipse.swt.SWT;
import org.eclipse.swt.events.*;
import org.eclipse.swt.layout.*;
import org.eclipse.swt.widgets.*;

/**
 * This class demonstrates drawing ovals
 */
public class OvalExample {
  private Text txtWidth = null;
  private Text txtHeight = null;

  /**
   * Runs the application
   */
  public void run() {
    Display display = new Display();
    Shell shell = new Shell(display);
    shell.setText("Oval Example");
    createContents(shell);
    shell.open();
    while (!shell.isDisposed()) {
      if (!display.readAndDispatch()) {
        display.sleep();
      }
    }
    display.dispose();
  }

  /**
   * Creates the main window's contents
   *
   * @param shell the main window
   */
  private void createContents(Shell shell) {
    shell.setLayout(new FillLayout(SWT.VERTICAL));

    // Create the composite that holds the input fields
    Composite widgetComposite = new Composite(shell, SWT.NONE);
    widgetComposite.setLayout(new GridLayout(2, false));

    // Create the input fields
    new Label(widgetComposite, SWT.NONE).setText("Width:");
    txtWidth = new Text(widgetComposite, SWT.BORDER);

    new Label(widgetComposite, SWT.NONE).setText("Height");
    txtHeight = new Text(widgetComposite, SWT.BORDER);
```

```
    // Create the button that launches the redraw
    Button button = new Button(widgetComposite, SWT.PUSH);
    button.setText("Redraw");
    shell.setDefaultButton(button);

    // Create the canvas to draw the oval on
    final Canvas drawingCanvas = new Canvas(shell, SWT.NONE);
    drawingCanvas.addPaintListener(new OvalExamplePaintListener());

    // Add a handler to redraw the oval when pressed
    button.addSelectionListener(new SelectionAdapter() {
      public void widgetSelected(SelectionEvent e) {
        drawingCanvas.redraw();
      }
    });
}

/**
 * This class gets the user input and draws the requested oval
 */
private class OvalExamplePaintListener implements PaintListener {
  public void paintControl(PaintEvent e) {
    // Get the canvas for drawing and its width and height
    Canvas canvas = (Canvas) e.widget;
    int x = canvas.getBounds().width;
    int y = canvas.getBounds().height;

    // Determine user input, defaulting everything to zero.
    // Any blank fields are converted to zero
    int width = 0;
    int height = 0;
    try {
      width = txtWidth.getText().length() == 0 ? 0 : Integer.parseInt(txtWidth
          .getText());
      height = txtHeight.getText().length() == 0 ? 0 : Integer
          .parseInt(txtHeight.getText());
    } catch (NumberFormatException ex) {
      // Any problems, set them both to zero
      width = 0;
      height = 0;
    }

    // Set the drawing width for the oval
    e.gc.setLineWidth(4);

    // Draw the requested oval
    e.gc.drawOval((x - width) / 2, (y - height) / 2, width, height);
  }
}

/**
 * The application entry point
```

```
    *
    * @param args the command line arguments
    */
   public static void main(String[] args) {
     new OvalExample().run();
   }
}
```

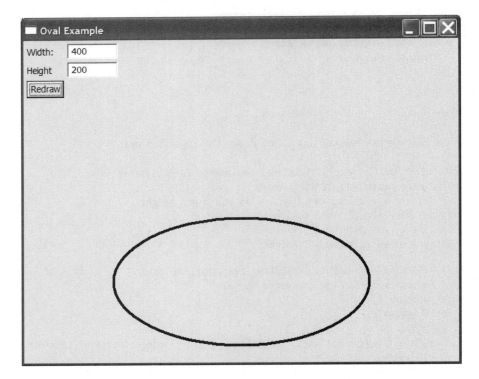

Figure 10-8. An oval

Drawing Arcs

Think of arcs as subsections or parts of ovals. To draw an arc, you specify the same parameters as drawing ovals, with the addition of two parameters: the beginning point and length of the arc. The beginning point is an angle between zero and 360 degrees. In this model, zero degrees indicates the same position as 3:00 on a clock dial. The length of the arc is also expressed in degrees. Positive values draw the arc counterclockwise the number of indicated degrees, while negative values draw the arc clockwise. Specifying 360 for the angle draws a complete oval.

Like the other shapes in this chapter, arcs can be filled. Filled arcs appear roughly like pie chart sections. Endpoints of the arc are connected to the point that would be the center of the associated oval. The ArcExample program in Listing 10-7 shows how to draw arcs (see Figure 10-9).

Listing 10-7. ArcExample.java

```java
package examples.ch10;

import org.eclipse.swt.SWT;
import org.eclipse.swt.events.*;
import org.eclipse.swt.layout.*;
import org.eclipse.swt.widgets.*;

/**
 * This class demonstrates drawing an Arc
 */
public class ArcExample {
  private Text txtWidth = null;
  private Text txtHeight = null;
  private Text txtBeginAngle = null;
  private Text txtAngle = null;

  /**
   * Runs the application
   */
  public void run() {
    Display display = new Display();
    Shell shell = new Shell(display);
    shell.setText("Arc Example");
    createContents(shell);
    shell.open();

    while (!shell.isDisposed()) {
      if (!display.readAndDispatch()) {
        display.sleep();
      }
    }
    display.dispose();
  }

  /**
   * Creates the main window's contents
   *
   * @param shell the main window
   */
  private void createContents(Shell shell) {
    shell.setLayout(new FillLayout(SWT.VERTICAL));

    // Create the composite that holds the input fields
    Composite widgetComposite = new Composite(shell, SWT.NONE);
    widgetComposite.setLayout(new GridLayout(2, false));

    // Create the input fields
    new Label(widgetComposite, SWT.NONE).setText("Width:");
    txtWidth = new Text(widgetComposite, SWT.BORDER);
```

```
      new Label(widgetComposite, SWT.NONE).setText("Height");
      txtHeight = new Text(widgetComposite, SWT.BORDER);

      new Label(widgetComposite, SWT.NONE).setText("Begin Angle:");
      txtBeginAngle = new Text(widgetComposite, SWT.BORDER);

      new Label(widgetComposite, SWT.NONE).setText("Angle:");
      txtAngle = new Text(widgetComposite, SWT.BORDER);

      // Create the button that launches the redraw
      Button button = new Button(widgetComposite, SWT.PUSH);
      button.setText("Redraw");
      shell.setDefaultButton(button);

      // Create the canvas to draw the arc on
      final Canvas drawingCanvas = new Canvas(shell, SWT.NONE);
      drawingCanvas.addPaintListener(new ArcExamplePaintListener());

      // Add a handler to redraw the arc when pressed
      button.addSelectionListener(new SelectionAdapter() {
        public void widgetSelected(SelectionEvent e) {
          drawingCanvas.redraw();
        }
      });
    }

    /**
     * This class gets the user input and draws the requested arc
     */
    private class ArcExamplePaintListener implements PaintListener {
      public void paintControl(PaintEvent e) {
        // Get the canvas for drawing and its dimensions
        Canvas canvas = (Canvas) e.widget;
        int x = canvas.getBounds().width;
        int y = canvas.getBounds().height;

        // Determine user input, defaulting everything to zero.
        // Any blank fields are converted to zero
        int width = 0;
        int height = 0;
        int begin = 0;
        int angle = 0;

        try {
          width = txtWidth.getText().length() == 0 ? 0 : Integer.parseInt(txtWidth
              .getText());
          height = txtHeight.getText().length() == 0 ? 0 : Integer
              .parseInt(txtHeight.getText());
          begin = txtBeginAngle.getText().length() == 0 ? 0 : Integer
              .parseInt(txtBeginAngle.getText());
          angle = txtAngle.getText().length() == 0 ? 0 : Integer.parseInt(txtAngle
              .getText());
        } catch (NumberFormatException ex) {
```

```
        // Any problems, reset them all to zero
        width = 0;
        height = 0;
        begin = 0;
        angle = 0;
      }
      // Set the drawing color to black
      e.gc.setBackground(e.display.getSystemColor(SWT.COLOR_BLACK));

      // Draw the arc, centered on the canvas
      e.gc.fillArc((x - width) / 2, (y - height) / 2, width, height, begin,
        angle);
    }
  }

  /**
   * The application entry point
   *
   * @param args the command line arguments
   */
  public static void main(String[] args) {
    new ArcExample().run();
  }
}
```

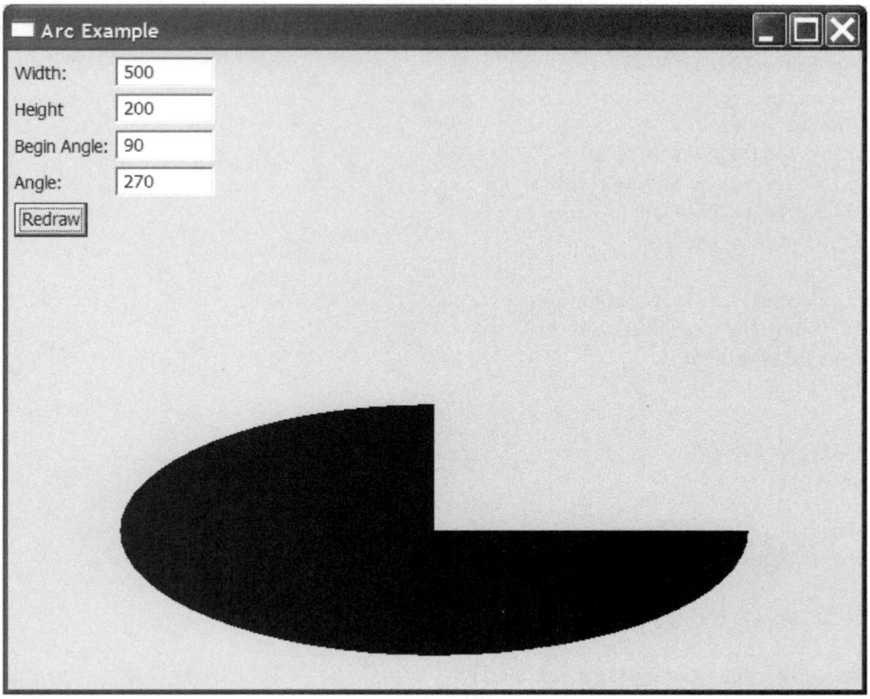

Figure 10-9. Drawing filled arcs

Drawing Polygons

You can draw polygons with an arbitrary number of sides and vertices with the drawPolygon() method, which takes an array of ints. Like the drawPolyline() method discussed earlier, drawPolygon() draws a number of lines connecting the (x,y) pairs defined in the array points. However, unlike drawPolyline(), drawPolygon() connects the last point in the array to the first point in the array to create a closed shape. GC also offers a fillPolygon() method that draws a filled polygon. The PolygonExample program in Listing 10-8 demonstrates polygons, as shown in Figure 10-10.

Listing 10-8. PolygonExample.java

```java
package examples.ch10;

import org.eclipse.swt.SWT;
import org.eclipse.swt.events.*;
import org.eclipse.swt.layout.*;
import org.eclipse.swt.widgets.*;

/**
 * This class demonstrates drawing polygons
 */
public class PolygonExample {
  private Text txtWidth = null;
  private Text txtHeight = null;

  /**
   * Runs the application
   */
  public void run() {
    Display display = new Display();
    Shell shell = new Shell(display);
    shell.setText("Polygon Example");
    createContents(shell);
    shell.open();
    while (!shell.isDisposed()) {
      if (!display.readAndDispatch()) {
        display.sleep();
      }
    }
    display.dispose();
  }

  /**
   * Creates the main window's contents
   *
   * @param shell the main window
   */
  private void createContents(Shell shell) {
    shell.setLayout(new FillLayout(SWT.VERTICAL));
```

```
    // Create the canvas to draw the polygons on
    Canvas drawingCanvas = new Canvas(shell, SWT.NONE);
    drawingCanvas.addPaintListener(new PolygonExamplePaintListener());
  }

  /**
   * This class gets the user input and draws the requested oval
   */
  private class PolygonExamplePaintListener implements PaintListener {
    public void paintControl(PaintEvent e) {
      // Get the canvas for drawing and its dimensions
      Canvas canvas = (Canvas) e.widget;
      int x = canvas.getBounds().width;
      int y = canvas.getBounds().height;

      // Set the drawing color
      e.gc.setBackground(e.display.getSystemColor(SWT.COLOR_BLACK));

      // Create the points for drawing a triangle in the upper left
      int[] upper_left = { 0, 0, 200, 0, 0, 200};

      // Create the points for drawing a triangle in the lower right
      int[] lower_right = { x, y, x, y - 200, x - 200, y};

      // Draw the triangles
      e.gc.fillPolygon(upper_left);
      e.gc.fillPolygon(lower_right);
    }
  }

  /**
   * The application entry point
   *
   * @param args the command line arguments
   */
  public static void main(String[] args) {
    new PolygonExample().run();
  }
}
```

Figure 10-10. Arbitrary polygons

Drawing Text

In addition to shapes, SWT can draw text on the screen. You can change the font, size, color, style, and even orientation of the text. You can display the text on a single line, or wrap the text to the next line automatically. This section explains how to use SWT's text-drawing facilities.

Displaying Text

GC provides five methods, listed in Table 10-1, for drawing text. drawString() is a cinch to use, and drawText() isn't much harder. The drawText() family of methods differs from the drawString() family in its handling of newlines and tabs; unless explicitly instructed not to, drawText() processes newlines and tabs as these elements intend. In other words, newlines shunt subsequent characters to the next line, and tabs leave noticeable gaps between words. The drawString() family, on the other hand, displays newlines and tabs as nonprintable characters, retaining all text on a single line.

Table 10-1. GC's Text Drawing Methods

Method	Description
void drawString(String string, int x, int y)	Draws the specified string with its origin at the point specified by (x, y), displaying newlines and tabs as nonprintable characters.
void drawString(String string, int x, int y, boolean isTransparent)	Draws the specified string with its origin at the point specified by (x, y), displaying newlines and tabs as nonprintable characters. If isTransparent is true, GC will use a transparent background, allowing the original background to show through. Otherwise, GC will use an opaque background.
void drawText(String text, int x, int y)	Draws the specified string with its origin at the point specified by (x, y), processing newlines and expanding tabs.
void drawText(String text, int x, int y, boolean isTransparent)	Draws the specified string with its origin at the point specified by (x, y), processing newlines and expanding tabs. If isTransparent is true, GC will use a transparent background, allowing the original background to show through. Otherwise, GC uses an opaque background.
void drawText(String text, int x, int y, int flags)	Draws the specified string with its origin at the point specified by (x, y), processing newlines and expanding tabs. Uses the rules specified by flags (see Table 10-2 for more information).

The last method listed in Table 10-1 indicates an int parameter called flags. This parameter contains zero or more constants, combined using the bitwise OR operator, that affect the way drawText() draws the passed string. Table 10-2 lists the applicable constants.

Table 10-2. drawText() Flags

Constant	Description
SWT.DRAW_DELIMITER	Processes newlines by drawing subsequent characters on the next line.
SWT.DRAW_TAB	Processes tabs by displaying a gap between surrounding characters.
SWT.DRAW_MNEMONIC	Draws an underline beneath the mnemonic character—the character preceded by an ampersand (&). Use this when drawing menus.
SWT.DRAW_TRANSPARENT	Uses a transparent background when drawing the string.

To draw the text "Hello, World," use code that looks like this:

```
gc.drawString("Hello, World", 5, 5);
```

The following code draws "Hello, World" with the "W" in "World" underlined, and with a transparent background:

```
gc.drawText("Hello, &World", 5, 5, SWT.DRAW_MNEMONIC |
   SWT.DRAW_TRANSPARENT);
```

The DrawText program in Listing 10-9 draws text using each of the five text drawing methods. It displays a background image to demonstrate the difference between using a transparent background or an opaque background. Figure 10-11 shows the program's window.

Listing 10-9. DrawText.java

```
package examples.ch10;

import org.eclipse.swt.SWT;
import org.eclipse.swt.events.*;
import org.eclipse.swt.graphics.*;
import org.eclipse.swt.widgets.*;

/**
 * This class demonstrates how to draw text
 */
public class DrawText {
  // The string to draw
  private static final String HELLO = "Hello,\n&World!\tFrom SWT";

  /**
   * Runs the application
   */
  public void run() {
    Display display = new Display();
    final Shell shell = new Shell(display);

    // Load an image to use as the background
    final Image image = new Image(display, this.getClass().getResourceAsStream(
        "/images/square.gif"));

    shell.addPaintListener(new PaintListener() {
      public void paintControl(PaintEvent event) {
        // Stretch the image to fill the window
        Rectangle rect = shell.getClientArea();
        event.gc.drawImage(image, 0, 0, image.getImageData().width, image
            .getImageData().height, 0, 0, rect.width, rect.height);

        // This will draw the string on one line, with nonprinting characters
        // for \n and \t, with an ampersand, and with an opaque background
        event.gc.drawString(HELLO, 5, 0);

        // This will draw the string on one line, with nonprinting characters
        // for \n and \t, with an ampersand, and with a transparent background
        event.gc.drawString(HELLO, 5, 40, true);
```

```
      // This will draw the string on two lines, with a tab between World! and
      // From, with an ampersand, and with an opaque background
      event.gc.drawText(HELLO, 5, 80);

      // This will draw the string on two lines, with a tab between World! and
      // From, with an ampersand, and with a transparent background
      event.gc.drawText(HELLO, 5, 120, true);

      // This will draw the string on two lines, with a tab between World! and
      // From, with the W underlined, and with a transparent background
      event.gc.drawText(HELLO, 5, 160, SWT.DRAW_MNEMONIC | SWT.DRAW_DELIMITER
          | SWT.DRAW_TAB | SWT.DRAW_TRANSPARENT);
    }
  });
  shell.setText("Draw Text");
  shell.open();
  while (!shell.isDisposed()) {
    if (!display.readAndDispatch()) {
      display.sleep();
    }
  }
  image.dispose();
  display.dispose();
}

/**
 * The application entry point
 *
 * @param args the command line arguments
 */
public static void main(String[] args) {
  new DrawText().run();
}
}
```

Figure 10-11. Drawing text using drawString() *and* drawText()

Changing Fonts

Unless you tell GC otherwise, it draws all text in the default font (the one returned by Display.getSystemFont()). To change the font, call GC's setFont() method, passing the desired font. As with any font you create, you're responsible for disposing the font when you're done with it. You can create the font inside your paint handler, draw your text, and dispose the font. This has the advantage of minimizing the scope of your font. However, it incurs the expense of creating and disposing the font each time your application paints. Alternatively, you can create the font for the lifetime of the application, disposing it when your application closes.

If you choose to create and dispose the font each time through your paint handler, your code will look something like this:

```
GC gc = new GC(shell);
Font font = new Font(shell.getDisplay(), "Helvetica", 18, SWT.NORMAL);
gc.drawText("My Text", 0, 0);
font.dispose();
```

The DrawHelveticaText program in Listing 10-10 takes the other approach: it creates the font once and disposes it when the application closes.

Listing 10-10. DrawHelveticaText.java

```
package examples.ch10;

import org.eclipse.swt.SWT;
import org.eclipse.swt.events.*;
import org.eclipse.swt.graphics.*;
import org.eclipse.swt.widgets.*;

/**
 * This class demonstrates how to draw text
 */
public class DrawHelveticaText {
  public void run() {
    Display display = new Display();
    final Shell shell = new Shell(display);

    // Create the font
    final Font font = new Font(display, "Helvetica", 18, SWT.NORMAL);

    shell.addPaintListener(new PaintListener() {
      public void paintControl(PaintEvent event) {
        // Set the font
        event.gc.setFont(font);

        // Draw the text
        event.gc.drawText("My Text", 0, 0);
      }
    });
```

```
    shell.setText("Draw Helvetica Text");
    shell.open();
    while (!shell.isDisposed()) {
      if (!display.readAndDispatch()) {
        display.sleep();
      }
    }
    font.dispose();
    display.dispose();
  }

  public static void main(String[] args) {
    new DrawHelveticaText().run();
  }
}
```

Figure 10-12 shows the program's window. Note the larger font used by drawText().

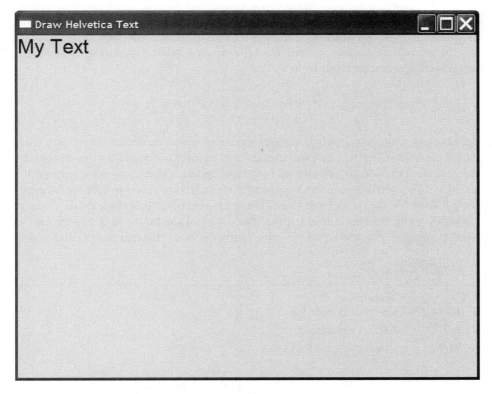

Figure 10-12. Drawing with a different font

Creating Fonts

In the previous section, you created and used a different font for drawing text. Fonts, which are represented by Font objects, are constructed like any other Java class. Font offers three constructors, listed in Table 10-3.

Table 10-3. Font Constructors

Constructor	Description
public Font(Device device, FontData fd)	Creates a font using the specified device and font data.
public Font(Device device, FontData[] fds)	Creates a font using the specified device and array of font data.
public Font(Device device, String name, int height, int style)	Creates a font using the specified device, name, height (in points), and style. Style constants are SWT.NORMAL, SWT.BOLD, and SWT.ITALIC.

In this chapter, the Device object you pass is always the target Display object. When printing (covered in Chapter 12), you'll pass the appropriate Printer object. SWT must know the medium onto which it will render the font to create it properly.

The DrawHelveticaText program from the previous section creates its font using the third constructor with this code:

```
Font font = new Font(display, "Helvetica", 18, SWT.NORMAL);
```

The first parameter, display, specifies the target rendering device (the screen). The second parameter, "Helvetica", specifies the font name. SWT does a best-guess match with the name you specify, falling back to the system font if you pass something bewildering. If the underlying platform supports font foundries, you can specify the foundry name along with the name in the form "foundry-fontName" (see the sidebar "Font Foundries"). The third parameter, 18, specifies the point size for the font. Finally, the fourth parameter, SWT.NORMAL, specifies the font style. Table 10-4 lists the possible styles.

Table 10-4. Font Styles

Style	Description
SWT.NORMAL	Creates a normal font
SWT.BOLD	Creates a bold font
SWT.ITALIC	Creates an italic font

You can combine style constants using the bitwise OR operator.

Font Foundries

Font foundries originally described buildings or works in which metal typefaces were cast. In today's digital age, the term "font foundries" has been extended to mean companies that create digital fonts—for example, Adobe. SWT respects font foundries on platforms that support them, so that Adobe's Courier font carries the name "adobe-courier."

Using either of the other constructors requires understanding a new class, FontData. Fortunately, FontData is little more than a data structure containing the same fields passed to that third constructor: font name, height, and style. You can construct a FontData object using those fields, changing the code to this:

```
Font font = new Font(display, new FontData("Helvetica", 18, SWT.NORMAL));
```

Table 10-5 lists FontData's constructors, and Table 10-6 lists FontData's methods, which are getters and setters for the data members. Because a FontData instance merely represents data, you should never dispose it.

Table 10-5. FontData *Constructors*

Constructor	Description
public FontData()	Creates an empty FontData.
public FontData(String string)	Creates a FontData from the specified string. The string must be in the format generated by FontData's toString() method, which contains data about the font delimited by pipe characters. For example, the string to create the font used in the DrawHelveticaText program on Windows is 1|Helvetica|18|0|WINDOWS|1|-30|0|0| 0|0|0|0|0|1|0|0|0|0|Helvetica.
public FontData(String name, int height, int style)	Creates a FontData from the specified parameters. See the discussion of the Font(String name, int height, int style) constructor for more information.

Table 10-6. FontData *Methods*

Method	Description
`public int getHeight()`	Returns the height in points
`public String getLocale()`	Returns the locale
`public String getName()`	Returns the name
`public int getStyle()`	Returns the style
`public void setHeight(int height)`	Sets the height in points
`public void setLocale(String locale)`	Sets the locale
`public void setName()`	Sets the name
`public void setStyle(int style)`	Sets the style, using the style constants listed in Table 10-4
`public String toString()`	Returns a string suitable to use to create a new font

The second constructor for Font listed in Table 10-3 takes an array of FontData objects instead of a single FontData object. Most platforms require only one FontData instance to create any font, but the X Window System can require more than one. SWT 2.1 added this constructor to accommodate the X Window System. Platforms that don't require multiple FontData instances, like Windows, use only the first entry in the array.

Besides its constructors and its dispose() method (which you should always call on fonts you create when you're done with them), Font offers a few interesting methods. Table 10-7 lists Font's methods.

Table 10-7. Font *Methods*

Method	Description
`void dispose()`	Disposes the resources associated with this font.
`boolean equals(Object obj)`	Returns true if this font represents the same font specified by obj, or false if it doesn't.
`FontData[] getFontData()`	Returns an array of FontData objects containing the data underlying this font. Most platforms return an array with only one entry.
`boolean isDisposed()`	Returns true if this font has been disposed, or false if it hasn't.
`String toString()`	Returns a string representation of this font suitable for constructing another font.

Getting Font Characteristics

The FontData object underlying a Font instance specifies the font's name, height (in points), and style. This data represents the font in a vacuum—it reveals nothing about how much space the font occupies. Until the font is melded with a device, either a Display or a Printer, it has no size characteristics. The font must know its rendering target before it knows its size.

Once you select a font into a GC using setFont(), it assumes physical characteristics pertaining to that GC's device. You can retrieve those characteristics, also known as the font's metrics, by calling GC's getFontMetrics() method. As expected, getFontMetrics() returns the metrics for the GC's current font, when rendered on the GC's device. The metrics are returned in a FontMetrics object, which is read only. Its only constructor is package private, and it has no setters. However, creating or altering a FontMetrics instance would make no sense, because it reports how a given font renders on a specific device.

You retrieve the metrics from a FontMetrics object using the methods listed in Table 10-8. Understanding the data returned by FontMetrics' getter methods requires knowledge of font-specific terms, listed in Table 10-9 and displayed in Figure 10-13.

Table 10-8. FontMetrics *Methods*

Method	Description
int getAscent()	Returns the ascent in pixels
int getAverageCharWidth()	Returns the width of an average character in pixels
int getDescent()	Returns the descent in pixels
int getHeight()	Returns the height in pixels
int getLeading()	Returns the leading area in pixels

Table 10-9. Font Terminology

Term	Meaning
baseline	The imaginary line the font sits on
ascent	The number of pixels that characters reach above the baseline to the top of typical lowercase characters
descent	The number of pixels that characters reach below the baseline
height	The total height of characters in pixels, equal to the ascent plus the descent plus the leading area
leading area	The number of pixels above the top of typical lowercase characters

Figure 10-13. Leading area, ascent, descent, and height demonstrated

For example, to determine the height of the "b," the "o," and the "y" from Figure 10-13, as well as the total height occupied by "boy," use code such as this:

```
FontMetrics fm = gc.getFontMetrics();
int bHeight = fm.getLeading() + fm.getAscent();
int oHeight = fm.getAscent();
int yHeight = fm.getAscent() + fm.getDescent();
int totalHeight = fm.getHeight(); // Equals fm.getLeading() + fm.getAscent()
                                  // + fm.getDescent();
```

Although `FontMetrics` returns the width of an average character, wouldn't it be important to know the exact width of a given string? You could get the width of an average character and multiply by the number of characters, but if your string was "iiiiiii" or "wwwwwww," you'd be off by a large margin. The width and the height that a string occupies when drawn with a specific font on a specific device is called its extent. `FontMetrics` offers no method to get the extent of a string, but `GC` does. In fact, it offers three, listed in Table 10-10.

Table 10-10. `GC` Methods to Determine Width of a String

Method	Description
Point stringExtent(String string)	Returns the extent of the specified string, without processing newlines or expanding tabs.
Point textExtent(String string)	Returns the extent of the specified string. Processes newlines and expands tabs.
Point textExtent(String string, int flags)	Returns the extent of the specified string, using the flags specified in `flags`. These flags are the same as the flags passed to `drawText()`, and are listed in Table 10-2.

To retrieve the extent of the string "iiiiiii," for example, call this:

```
Point point = gc.stringExtent("iiiiiii");
```

The Extents program fills the window with the uplifting message "Go Celtics!" It provides a dropdown (using a `ControlEditor`) to change the size of the font. When you change the value in the dropdown, the font changes size to match the selected value and redraws the screen. It uses both `GC.getStringExtent()` and `GC.getFontMetrics()` to determine where to draw the strings. Listing 10-11 contains the source.

Listing 10-11. `Extents.java`

```
package examples.ch10;

import org.eclipse.swt.SWT;
import org.eclipse.swt.custom.*;
import org.eclipse.swt.events.*;
```

```java
import org.eclipse.swt.graphics.*;
import org.eclipse.swt.widgets.*;

/**
 * This class demonstrates FontMetrics and extents
 */
public class Extents {
  // The string to display
  private static final String STRING = "Go Celtics!";

  // The size options for the combo
  private static final String[] SIZES = { "8", "10", "12", "14", "16", "18"};

  // The font used to draw the string
  private Font font;

  /**
   * Runs the application
   */
  public void run() {
    Display display = new Display();
    Shell shell = new Shell(display);
    shell.setText("Extents");
    createContents(shell);
    shell.open();
    while (!shell.isDisposed()) {
      if (!display.readAndDispatch()) {
        display.sleep();
      }
    }
    if (font != null) font.dispose();
    display.dispose();
  }

  /**
   * Creates the main window's contents
   *
   * @param shell the main window
   */
  private void createContents(final Shell shell) {
    // Create a canvas to draw on
    final Canvas canvas = new Canvas(shell, SWT.NONE);

    // Add a listener to the shell to resize the canvas to fill the window
    // any time the window is resized
    shell.addControlListener(new ControlAdapter() {
      public void controlResized(ControlEvent event) {
        canvas.setBounds(shell.getClientArea());
      }
    });
```

```
        // Add a listener to the canvas. This is where we draw the text.
        canvas.addPaintListener(new PaintListener() {
          public void paintControl(PaintEvent event) {
            // Set the font into the gc
            event.gc.setFont(font);

            // Calculate the width (nad height) of the string
            Point pt = event.gc.stringExtent(STRING);

            // Figure out how big our drawing area is
            Rectangle rect = canvas.getBounds();

            // Calculate the height of the font. We could have used pt.y,
            // but this demonstrates FontMetrics
            int height = event.gc.getFontMetrics().getHeight();

            // Outside loop goes from the top of the window to the bottom.
            // Since the (x, y) passed to drawString represents the upper left
            // corner, subtract the height of the font from the height of the
            // drawing area, so we don't have any partial drawing.
            for (int i = 0, n = rect.height - height; i < n; i += height) {
              // Inside loop goes from the left to the right, stopping far enough
              // from the right to ensure no partial string drawing.
              for (int j = 0, m = rect.width - pt.x; j < m; j += pt.x) {
                // Draw the string
                event.gc.drawString(STRING, j, i);
              }
            }
          }
        });

        // Create an editor to house the dropdown
        ControlEditor editor = new ControlEditor(canvas);

        // Create the combo and fill it
        final Combo combo = new Combo(canvas, SWT.READ_ONLY);
        for (int i = 0, n = SIZES.length; i < n; i++) {
          combo.add(SIZES[i]);
        }

        // Set up the editor
        editor.horizontalAlignment = SWT.CENTER;
        editor.verticalAlignment = SWT.TOP;
        Point size = combo.computeSize(SWT.DEFAULT, SWT.DEFAULT);
        editor.minimumWidth = size.x;
        editor.minimumHeight = size.y;
        editor.setEditor(combo);

        // Add a listener to the combo, so that when the selection changes,
        // we change the font and redraw the canvas
        combo.addSelectionListener(new SelectionAdapter() {
```

```
    public void widgetSelected(SelectionEvent event) {
        if (font != null) font.dispose();
        font = new Font(shell.getDisplay(), "Helvetica", new Integer(combo
            .getText()).intValue(), SWT.BOLD);
        canvas.redraw();
    }
});

// Select the first item in the combo
combo.select(0);
}

/**
 * The application entry point
 *
 * @param args the command line arguments
 */
public static void main(String[] args) {
    new Extents().run();
}
}
```

Figure 10-14 shows the program's main window. Figure 10-15 shows the window after changing the dropdown's value to 18.

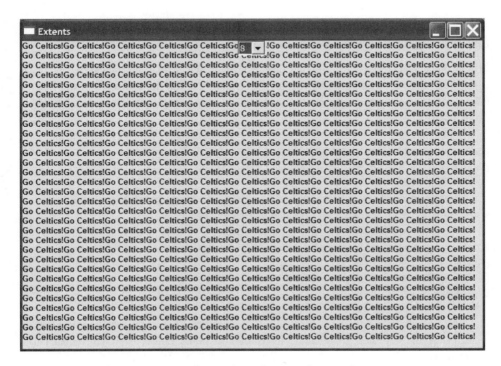

Figure 10-14. Using extents to determine where to draw strings

Figure 10-15. Using extents with a larger font

Changing Colors

The fonts thus far have been only in black, but an entire array of colors awaits. As Chapter 7 explains, fonts themselves have no color. Instead, the font's container has a foreground color, which it uses to draw the font. For example, to draw some text in blue, use this code:

```
gc.setForeground(display.getSystemColor(SWT.COLOR_BLUE));
gc.drawText("I'm in blue!");
```

The foreground color affects only subsequent drawing operations, so to follow some blue text with some green text, use code such as this:

```
gc.setForeground(display.getSystemColor(SWT.COLOR_BLUE));
gc.drawText("I'm in blue!");
gc.setForeground(display.getSystemColor(SWT.COLOR_GREEN));
gc.drawText("I'm in green!");
```

The ColorFont program in Listing 10-12 uses various colors to display some text in a column. It uses GC.setForeground() to change the color. Figure 10-16 shows the running program.

Listing 10-12. ColorFont.java

```java
package examples.ch10;

import org.eclipse.swt.SWT;
import org.eclipse.swt.events.*;
import org.eclipse.swt.widgets.*;

/**
 * This class demonstrates how to draw text in colors
 */
public class ColorFont {
  // The color indices to use for the text
  private static final int[] COLOR_INDICES = { SWT.COLOR_BLUE, SWT.COLOR_GREEN,
      SWT.COLOR_RED, SWT.COLOR_GRAY};

  /**
   * Runs the application
   */
  public void run() {
    Display display = new Display();
    final Shell shell = new Shell(display);

    // Handler to do the drawing
    shell.addPaintListener(new PaintListener() {
      public void paintControl(PaintEvent event) {
        // Loop through the colors, moving down the screen each iteration
        for (int i = 0, n = COLOR_INDICES.length, y = 0, height = event.gc
            .getFontMetrics().getHeight(); i < n; i++, y += height) {
          event.gc.setForeground(shell.getDisplay().getSystemColor(
              COLOR_INDICES[i]));
          event.gc.drawText("Hooray for Color!", 0, y);
        }
      }
    });
    shell.setText("Color Font");
    shell.open();
    while (!shell.isDisposed()) {
      if (!display.readAndDispatch()) {
        display.sleep();
      }
    }
    display.dispose();
  }

  /**
   * The application entry point
   *
   * @param args the command line arguments
   */
  public static void main(String[] args) {
    new ColorFont().run();
  }
}
```

Figure 10-16. Drawing fonts in colors

Drawing Vertical Text

Because GC has no drawVerticalText() method, and the drawText() method that accepts flags ignores SWT.VERTICAL, you might think yourself stuck with horizontal text. Although SWT doesn't directly support vertical text, you can still draw vertical text by following these steps:

1. Draw the text to an offscreen image.

2. Rotate the offscreen image.

3. Draw the rotated image to the screen.

To draw the text to an offscreen image, calculate the dimensions of the text and create an Image instance that's the same size as the text, like this:

```
FontMetrics fm = gc.getFontMetrics();
Point pt = gc.textExtent(string);
Image stringImage = new Image(display, pt.x, pt.y);
```

Next, create a GC associated with this image, and set the original GC's attributes into it, so that it uses the same colors and font:

```
GC stringGc = new GC(stringImage);
stringGc.setForeground(gc.getForeground());
stringGc.setBackground(gc.getBackground());
stringGc.setFont(gc.getFont());
```

Draw the string onto the new GC, which isn't associated with anything on the screen, so nothing displays (yet):

```
stringGc.drawText(string, 0, 0);
```

Make sure to pass zeroes for x and y; these values are relative to the new GC, not the original GC. Finally, rotate the image, draw it to the original GC, and clean up.

The GraphicsUtils class in Listing 10-13 holds two methods: drawVerticalText() and drawVerticalImage(). drawVerticalText() uses drawVerticalImage() to do the rotation and drawing to the original GC. Both methods take as parameters the x and y coordinates for the top left corner of the drawing rectangle, the GC to ultimately draw on, and a style constant (SWT.UP or SWT.DOWN) for whether to rotate +90 degrees or –90 degrees.

drawVerticalImage() rotates the image by iterating through its pixels and swapping the x coordinate for the y coordinate, and vice versa, using rules that depend on whether it's rotating the image up or down.

Listing 10-13. GraphicsUtils.java

```
package examples.ch10;

import org.eclipse.swt.*;
import org.eclipse.swt.graphics.*;
import org.eclipse.swt.widgets.Display;

/**
 * This class contains utility methods for drawing graphics
 */
public class GraphicsUtils {
  /**
   * Draws text vertically (rotates plus or minus 90 degrees). Uses the current
   * font, color, and background.
   * <dl>
   * <dt><b>Styles: </b></dt>
   * <dd>UP, DOWN</dd>
   * </dl>
   *
   * @param string the text to draw
   * @param x the x coordinate of the top left corner of the drawing rectangle
   * @param y the y coordinate of the top left corner of the drawing rectangle
   * @param gc the GC on which to draw the text
   * @param style the style (SWT.UP or SWT.DOWN)
   *
   *          <p>
   *          Note: Only one of the style UP or DOWN may be specified.
   *          </p>
   */
  public static void drawVerticalText(String string, int x, int y, GC gc,
      int style) {
    // Get the current display
    Display display = Display.getCurrent();
    if (display == null) SWT.error(SWT.ERROR_THREAD_INVALID_ACCESS);

    // Determine string's dimensions
    FontMetrics fm = gc.getFontMetrics();
    Point pt = gc.textExtent(string);

    // Create an image the same size as the string
    Image stringImage = new Image(display, pt.x, pt.y);

    // Create a GC so we can draw the image
    GC stringGc = new GC(stringImage);

    // Set attributes from the original GC to the new GC
    stringGc.setForeground(gc.getForeground());
```

```
    stringGc.setBackground(gc.getBackground());
    stringGc.setFont(gc.getFont());

    // Draw the text onto the image
    stringGc.drawText(string, 0, 0);

    // Draw the image vertically onto the original GC
    drawVerticalImage(stringImage, x, y, gc, style);

    // Dispose the new GC
    stringGc.dispose();

    // Dispose the image
    stringImage.dispose();
}

/**
 * Draws an image vertically (rotates plus or minus 90 degrees)
 * <dl>
 * <dt><b>Styles: </b></dt>
 * <dd>UP, DOWN</dd>
 * </dl>
 *
 * @param image the image to draw
 * @param x the x coordinate of the top left corner of the drawing rectangle
 * @param y the y coordinate of the top left corner of the drawing rectangle
 * @param gc the GC on which to draw the image
 * @param style the style (SWT.UP or SWT.DOWN)
 *           <p>
 *           Note: Only one of the style UP or DOWN may be specified.
 *           </p>
 */
public static void drawVerticalImage(Image image, int x, int y, GC gc, int
    style) {
    // Get the current display
    Display display = Display.getCurrent();
    if (display == null) SWT.error(SWT.ERROR_THREAD_INVALID_ACCESS);

    // Use the image's data to create a rotated image's data
    ImageData sd = image.getImageData();
    ImageData dd = new ImageData(sd.height, sd.width, sd.depth, sd.palette);

    // Determine which way to rotate, depending on up or down
    boolean up = (style & SWT.UP) == SWT.UP;

    // Run through the horizontal pixels
    for (int sx = 0; sx < sd.width; sx++) {
        // Run through the vertical pixels
        for (int sy = 0; sy < sd.height; sy++) {
            // Determine where to move pixel to in destination image data
            int dx = up ? sy : sd.height - sy - 1;
            int dy = up ? sd.width - sx - 1 : sx;
```

```
        // Swap the x, y source data to y, x in the destination
        dd.setPixel(dx, dy, sd.getPixel(sx, sy));
    }
  }

  // Create the vertical image
  Image vertical = new Image(display, dd);

  // Draw the vertical image onto the original GC
  gc.drawImage(vertical, x, y);

  // Dispose the vertical image
  vertical.dispose();
}

/**
 * Creates an image containing the specified text, rotated either plus or minus
 * 90 degrees.
 * <dl>
 * <dt><b>Styles: </b></dt>
 * <dd>UP, DOWN</dd>
 * </dl>
 *
 * @param text the text to rotate
 * @param font the font to use
 * @param foreground the color for the text
 * @param background the background color
 * @param style direction to rotate (up or down)
 * @return Image
 *         <p>
 *         Note: Only one of the style UP or DOWN may be specified.
 *         </p>
 */
public static Image createRotatedText(String text, Font font, Color foreground,
    Color background, int style) {
  // Get the current display
  Display display = Display.getCurrent();
  if (display == null) SWT.error(SWT.ERROR_THREAD_INVALID_ACCESS);

  // Create a GC to calculate font's dimensions
  GC gc = new GC(display);
  gc.setFont(font);

  // Determine string's dimensions
  FontMetrics fm = gc.getFontMetrics();
  Point pt = gc.textExtent(text);

  // Dispose that gc
  gc.dispose();

  // Create an image the same size as the string
  Image stringImage = new Image(display, pt.x, pt.y);
```

```
      // Create a gc for the image
      gc = new GC(stringImage);
      gc.setFont(font);
      gc.setForeground(foreground);
      gc.setBackground(background);

      // Draw the text onto the image
      gc.drawText(text, 0, 0);

      // Draw the image vertically onto the original GC
      Image image = createRotatedImage(stringImage, style);

      // Dispose the new GC
      gc.dispose();

      // Dispose the horizontal image
      stringImage.dispose();

      // Return the rotated image
      return image;
    }

    /**
     * Creates a rotated image (plus or minus 90 degrees)
     * <dl>
     * <dt><b>Styles: </b></dt>
     * <dd>UP, DOWN</dd>
     * </dl>
     *
     * @param image the image to rotate
     * @param style direction to rotate (up or down)
     * @return Image
     *           <p>
     *           Note: Only one of the style UP or DOWN may be specified.
     *           </p>
     */
    public static Image createRotatedImage(Image image, int style) {
      // Get the current display
      Display display = Display.getCurrent();
      if (display == null) SWT.error(SWT.ERROR_THREAD_INVALID_ACCESS);

      // Use the image's data to create a rotated image's data
      ImageData sd = image.getImageData();
      ImageData dd = new ImageData(sd.height, sd.width, sd.depth, sd.palette);

      // Determine which way to rotate, depending on up or down
      boolean up = (style & SWT.UP) == SWT.UP;

      // Run through the horizontal pixels
      for (int sx = 0; sx < sd.width; sx++) {
```

```
      // Run through the vertical pixels
      for (int sy = 0; sy < sd.height; sy++) {
        // Determine where to move pixel to in destination image data
        int dx = up ? sy : sd.height - sy - 1;
        int dy = up ? sd.width - sx - 1 : sx;

        // Swap the x, y source data to y, x in the destination
        dd.setPixel(dx, dy, sd.getPixel(sx, sy));
      }
    }

    // Create the vertical image
    return new Image(display, dd);
  }
}
```

To illustrate the code, the VerticalText program (see Listing 10-14) draws "Hello" going up in the upper-left corner of the window, and "Good Bye" going down in the lower right. Drawing "Hello" in the upper left is easy:

```
GraphicsUtils.drawVerticalText("Hello", 0, 0, gc, SWT.UP);
```

Drawing "Good Bye" in the lower right is a bit trickier, because you must determine where the top left corner of the vertical text should be. To calculate the top left corner of the text, get the extent of the text, and then use its width to calculate the height portion of the offset from the extreme lower-right corner, and use the extent's height to calculate the width portion. That code looks like this:

```
Point pt = gc.textExtent(goodBye);
Rectangle rect = shell.getClientArea();
GraphicsUtils.drawVerticalText(goodBye, rect.width - pt.y,
  rect.height - pt.x, gc, SWT.DOWN);
```

Listing 10-14. VerticalText.java

```
package examples.ch10;

import org.eclipse.swt.SWT;
import org.eclipse.swt.events.*;
import org.eclipse.swt.graphics.*;
import org.eclipse.swt.widgets.*;

/**
 * This class demonstrates how to draw vertical text
 */
public class VerticalText {
  /**
   * Runs the application
   */
```

```
        public void run() {
          Display display = new Display();
          final Shell shell = new Shell(display);
          final Font font = new Font(display, "Arial", 36, SWT.ITALIC);

          shell.addPaintListener(new PaintListener() {
            public void paintControl(PaintEvent event) {
              // Set the font
              event.gc.setFont(font);

              // Draw some text up in the upper left
              GraphicsUtils.drawVerticalText("Hello", 0, 0, event.gc, SWT.UP);

              // Draw some text down in the lower right
              // Note how we calculate the origin
              String goodBye = "Good Bye";
              Point pt = event.gc.textExtent(goodBye);
              Rectangle rect = shell.getClientArea();
              GraphicsUtils.drawVerticalText(goodBye, rect.width - pt.y, rect.height
                  - pt.x, event.gc, SWT.DOWN);
            }
          });
          shell.setText("Vertical Text");
          shell.open();
          while (!shell.isDisposed()) {
            if (!display.readAndDispatch()) {
              display.sleep();
            }
          }
          font.dispose();
          display.dispose();
        }

        /**
         * The application entry point
         *
         * @param args the command line arguments
         */
        public static void main(String[] args) {
          new VerticalText().run();
        }
      }
```

Figure 10-17 shows this program.

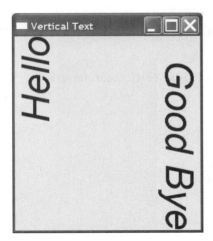

Figure 10-17. Vertical text

The drawVerticalText() method boasts an interface similar to drawText(), and completely hides the implementation fact that it converts the text to an image before rotating and drawing. You can blithely call it and remain completely ignorant of the image layer. However, after the euphoria of the great interface passes, the performance overhead of this implementation settles in. Every time the application paints the text, it must go through the overhead of creating the image, rotating it, and drawing it to the screen. Hmm. Although some applications can afford the cycles, others will bog down. Perhaps another go would be helpful.

Two new methods, createRotatedText() and createRotatedImage(), each of which returns an Image, seem the best solution. Users of these methods pass either text or an image, depending on which of the two methods they call, and receive an image back. Both methods begin with create to remind users that they're responsible for disposing the image. Listing 10-15 contains the code for these methods, which you should add to GraphicsUtils.java.

Listing 10-15. Additional methods for GraphicsUtils.java

```
/**
 * Creates an image containing the specified text, rotated either
 * plus or minus 90 degrees.
 * <dl>
 * <dt><b>Styles:</b></dt>
 * <dd>UP, DOWN</dd>
 * </dl>
 * @param text the text to rotate
 * @param font the font to use
 * @param foreground the color for the text
 * @param background the background color
 * @param style direction to rotate (up or down)
 * @return Image
```

```
   * <p>
   * Note: Only one of the style UP or DOWN may be specified.
   * </p>
   */
  public static Image createRotatedText(String text, Font font, Color foreground,
    Color background, int style)
  {
    // Get the current display
    Display display = Display.getCurrent();
    if (display == null)
      SWT.error(SWT.ERROR_THREAD_INVALID_ACCESS);
    // Create a GC to calculate font's dimensions
    GC gc = new GC(display);
    gc.setFont(font);

    // Determine string's dimensions
    FontMetrics fm = gc.getFontMetrics();
    Point pt = gc.textExtent(text);

    // Dispose that gc
    gc.dispose();

    // Create an image the same size as the string
    Image stringImage = new Image(display, pt.x, pt.y);

    // Create a gc for the image
    gc = new GC(stringImage);
    gc.setFont(font);
    gc.setForeground(foreground);
    gc.setBackground(background);

    // Draw the text onto the image
    gc.drawText(text, 0, 0);

    // Draw the image vertically onto the original GC
    Image image = createRotatedImage(stringImage, style);

    // Dispose the new GC
    gc.dispose();

    // Dispose the horizontal image
    stringImage.dispose();

    // Return the rotated image
    return image;
  }

  /**
   * Creates a rotated image (plus or minus 90 degrees)
   * <dl>
   * <dt><b>Styles:</b></dt>
```

```
 * <dd>UP, DOWN</dd>
 * </dl>
 * @param image the image to rotate
 * @param style direction to rotate (up or down)
 * @return Image
 * <p>
 * Note: Only one of the style UP or DOWN may be specified.
 * </p>
 */
public static Image createRotatedImage(Image image, int style)
{
  // Get the current display
  Display display = Display.getCurrent();
  if (display == null)
    SWT.error(SWT.ERROR_THREAD_INVALID_ACCESS);

  // Use the image's data to create a rotated image's data
  ImageData sd = image.getImageData();
  ImageData dd = new ImageData(sd.height, sd.width, sd.depth, sd.palette);

  // Determine which way to rotate, depending on up or down
  boolean up = (style & SWT.UP) == SWT.UP;

  // Run through the horizontal pixels
  for (int sx = 0; sx < sd.width; sx++)
  {
    // Run through the vertical pixels
    for (int sy = 0; sy < sd.height; sy++)
    {
      // Determine where to move pixel to in destination image data
      int dx = up ? sy : sd.height - sy - 1;
      int dy = up ? sd.width - sx - 1 : sx;

      // Swap the x, y source data to y, x in the destination
      dd.setPixel(dx, dy, sd.getPixel(sx, sy));
    }
  }

  // Create the vertical image
  return new Image(display, dd);
}
```

To use these two methods, create your rotated text once, like this:

```
Image image = GraphicsUtils.createRotatedText("My text", font, foreground,
  background, SWT.UP);
```

Then draw the new image in your drawing handler. Finally, call dispose() on the image when you're through with it.

The VerticalTextSpanish program in Listing 10-16 uses createRotatedText() to duplicate the VerticalText program, translating to Spanish.

Listing 10-16. VerticalTextSpanish.java

```java
package examples.ch10;

import org.eclipse.swt.SWT;
import org.eclipse.swt.events.*;
import org.eclipse.swt.graphics.*;
import org.eclipse.swt.widgets.*;

/**
 * This class demonstrates how to draw vertical text
 */
public class VerticalTextSpanish {
  /**
   * Runs the application
   */
  public void run() {
    Display display = new Display();
    final Shell shell = new Shell(display);
    final Font font = new Font(display, "Arial", 36, SWT.ITALIC);

    // Create "Hello" image
    final Image hello = GraphicsUtils.createRotatedText("Hola", font, shell
        .getForeground(), shell.getBackground(), SWT.UP);

    // Create "Good Bye" image
    final Image goodBye = GraphicsUtils.createRotatedText("Chao Pescado", font,
        shell.getForeground(), shell.getBackground(), SWT.DOWN);

    shell.addPaintListener(new PaintListener() {
      public void paintControl(PaintEvent event) {
        // Set the font
        event.gc.setFont(font);

        // Draw hello in the upper left
        event.gc.drawImage(hello, 0, 0);

        // Draw good bye in the lower right
        // Note how we calculate the origin
        Rectangle rcImage = goodBye.getBounds();
        Rectangle rect = shell.getClientArea();
        event.gc.drawImage(goodBye, rect.width - rcImage.width, rect.height
            - rcImage.height);
      }
    });
    shell.setText("Vertical Text Spanish");
    shell.open();
    while (!shell.isDisposed()) {
```

```
      if (!display.readAndDispatch()) {
        display.sleep();
      }
    }
    goodBye.dispose();
    hello.dispose();
    font.dispose();
    display.dispose();
  }

  /**
   * The application entry point
   *
   * @param args the command line arguments
   */
  public static void main(String[] args) {
    new VerticalTextSpanish().run();
  }
}
```

Figure 10-18 shows this program's main window.

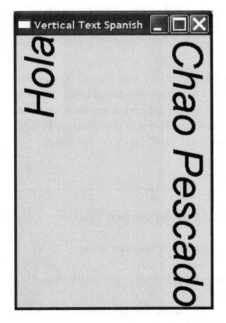

Figure 10-18. Vertical text in Spanish

Drawing Images

You've learned that you can use SWT to generate graphics on the fly by drawing shapes and text. SWT can also display graphic images from files. It supports the following graphic file formats:

- Graphics Interchange Format (GIF), including animated GIFs

- Portable Network Graphics (PNG)

- Joint Photographic Experts Group (JPEG)

- Tagged Image File Format (TIFF)

- Windows Icon (ICO)

- Windows Bitmap (BMP)

- Windows Bitmap with run-length encoding (RLE)

SWT uses the Image class to represent images. Although you'll usually load formatted images from files, you can also use the Image class to create images in memory. However, whether you load them from files or create them in memory, you must dispose all Images that you create.

Creating Images

You'll usually load an image file from disk when you create an Image object. Image offers four constructors for creating an Image object from an image file. Sometimes, as with the rotated text example, you'll create an empty Image object and draw on it. You can also create an Image from an ImageData structure, discussed later in this chapter. Finally, you can create an Image from another Image. Table 10-11 lists Image's constructors.

Table 10-11. Image *Constructors*

Constructor	Description
Image(Device device, String filename)	Creates an image from the specified file name
Image(Device device, InputStream stream)	Creates an image from the specified stream
Image(Device device, int width, int height)	Creates an empty image of the specified width and height (in pixels)
Image(Device device, Rectangle bounds)	Creates an empty image of the specified size
Image(Device device, ImageData data)	Creates an image from the specified ImageData
Image(Device device, ImageData source, ImageData mask)	Creates an image by combining the specified ImageData objects
Image(Device device, Image source, int flag)	Creates an image from the specified image, using the value specified by flag

The Device you pass is the device on which the image will be rendered, usually the primary Display instance. The next three sections examine the various constructors.

Creating an Image from a File

When your image sits in a file on a disk, and you want to display the image just as it sits, you can create it by passing its file name to the constructor. For example, to load the file whose path is c:\temp\swt.png, use this code:

```
Image image = new Image(display, "c:\\temp\\swt.png");
```

Another way to load an image from a file is to create an input stream from it and pass the input stream to the constructor, like this:

```
Image image = new Image(display, new FileInputStream("c:\\temp\\swt.png"));
```

You can also use the constructor that takes an input stream in conjunction with the Class.getResourceAsStream() method, which returns an InputStream instance, like this:

```
Image image = new Image(display, MyClass.getResourceAsStream("/temp/swt.png"));
```

Creating an Empty Image

Suppose you have a complicated visual that depends on some values entered at run time. You could render the image each time your window paints, but that might cause performance issues. However, if the values are entered only once, you'll end up reworking the same complications each time. In situations such as this, you can create an image, draw it once, and then save the image. Only the saved image is repainted.

To create an empty image, pass the desired size to the constructor. You can specify the size as a width and a height, or you can pass a Rectangle. The two ways would look like this:

```
Image image1 = new Image(display, 300, 200);
Image image2 = new Image(display, myRect);
```

Because an Image is a Drawable, you can pass it to a GC to draw on it, like this:

```
GC gc = new GC(image);
```

You can then call GC's drawing methods to draw on the image.

Creating an Image from an ImageData

To understand how to create an image from an ImageData instance, you must first understand what an ImageData is. ImageData encapsulates the body of metadata describing an Image. This data is device independent (that is, the data doesn't depend on the target rendering device, be it a screen or a printer). ImageData's constructors, listed in Table 10-12, allow you to either create an ImageData from a file, or to create one using predetermined data.

Table 10-12. ImageData *Constructors*

Constructor	Description
ImageData(InputStream stream)	Creates an ImageData from an image passed as a stream.
ImageData(String filename)	Creates an ImageData from the image specified by filename.
ImageData(int width, int height, int depth, PaletteData palette)	Creates an ImageData with the specified width, height, color depth, and palette.
ImageData(int width, int height, int depth, PaletteData palette, int scanlinePad, byte[] data)	Creates an ImageData with the specified width, height, color depth, palette, scanline pad, and data. data holds the image's pixel data.

The last two constructors introduce two new concepts: palettes and scanline pads. Palettes represent the colors in an image, and are represented in SWT by PaletteData objects. A scanline is a row in the image, and the scanline pad is the amount of padding on each scanline.

ImageData has numerous fields, listed in Table 10-13, that contain data about the image. These fields are all public, so you can access them directly. Table 10-14 contains constants used by ImageData's disposalMethod field, to specify how to dispose the image, and Table 10-15 lists constants used by ImageData's type field, for specifying the type or format of the image.

Table 10-13. ImageData *Fields*

Field	Description
int alpha	The alpha value used by every pixel in the image. Alpha values are used to describe transparency.
byte[] alphaData	The alpha data for the entire image.
int bytesPerLine	The number of bytes per scanline (row) in the image.
byte[] data	The pixel data for the entire image.
int delayTime	The number of milliseconds to delay before showing the next frame of the animation. This field corresponds to an animated GIF's Delay Time field.
int depth	The color depth, in bits per pixel, of the image.
int disposalMethod	A constant specifying how to dispose the current image before displaying the next. See Table 10-14 for possible values and descriptions. This field corresponds to an animated GIF's Disposal Method field.
int height	The image's height, in pixels.
byte[] maskData	The mask data for an icon.
int maskPad	The mask pad value for an icon.
PaletteData palette	The image's palette.

Table 10-13. ImageData *Fields (continued)*

Field	Description
int scanlinePad	The scanline pad.
int transparentPixel	The value of transparent pixels; all pixels with this value are drawn transparent.
int type	A constant specifying this image's format. See Table 10-15 for possible values.
int width	The image's width, in pixels.
int x	The x coordinate of the image's top left corner. This field corresponds to an animated GIF's Image Left Position field.
int y	The y coordinate of the image's top left corner. This field corresponds to an animated GIF's Image Top Position field.

Table 10-14. Disposal Method Constants

Constant	Description
SWT.DM_UNSPECIFIED	Unspecified disposal method
SWT.DM_FILL_NONE	Don't dispose; leave current image in place
SWT.DM_FILL_BACKGROUND	Fill the image with the background color
SWT.DM_FILL_PREVIOUS	Restore the previous image

Table 10-15. Type Constants

Constant	Description
SWT.IMAGE_UNDEFINED	Unknown image type
SWT.IMAGE_BMP	BMP
SWT.IMAGE_BMP_RLE	RLE
SWT.IMAGE_GIF	GIF
SWT.IMAGE_ICO	ICO
SWT.IMAGE_JPEG	JPEG
SWT.IMAGE_TIFF	TIFF
SWT.IMAGE_PNG	PNG

ImageData's fields contain most of what you need to know about the corresponding image: they contain data pertaining to the entire image. However, to get or set data corresponding to individual pixels within the image, you must use ImageData's methods, listed in Table 10-16.

Table 10-16. ImageData *Methods*

Method	Description
Object clone()	A safe cloning operation that returns a duplicate of this ImageData.
int getAlpha(int x, int y)	Returns the alpha value for the pixel specified by (x, y).
void getAlphas(int x, int y, int getWidth, byte[] alphas, int startIndex)	Returns the number of alpha values specified by getWidth, from the pixel specified by (x, y). Returns the values in the alphas array, starting at the index specified by startIndex.
int getPixel(int x, int y)	Returns the pixel value for the pixel specified by (x, y).
void getPixels(int x, int y, int getWidth, byte[] pixels, int startIndex)	Returns the number of pixel values specified by getWidth, from the pixel specified by (x, y). Returns the values in the pixels array, starting at the index specified by startIndex.
void getPixels(int x, int y, int getWidth, int[] pixels, int startIndex)	Identical to the previous method, but returns the data in an array of ints instead of an array of bytes.
RGB[] getRGBs()	Returns the image's indexed color table as an array of RGB objects.
ImageData getTransparencyMask()	Returns the transparency mask for the image, or null if the image has no transparency mask.
ImageData scaledTo(int width, int height)	Returns an ImageData that contains the data for the image scaled to width and height.
void setAlpha(int x, int y, int alpha)	Sets the alpha value for the pixel specified by (x, y).
void setAlphas(int x, int y, int putWidth, byte[] alphas, int startIndex)	Sets the number of alpha values specified by putWidth, starting at the pixel specified by (x, y). The values are passed in the alphas array, starting at the index specified by startIndex.
void setPixel(int x, int y, int pixelValue)	Sets the pixel value for the pixel specified by (x, y).
void setPixels(int x, int y, int putWidth, byte[] pixels, int startIndex)	Sets the number of pixels specified by putWidth, starting at the pixel specified by (x, y). The values are passed in the pixels array, starting at the index specified by startIndex.
void setPixels(int x, int y, int putWidth, int[] pixels, int startIndex)	Identical to the previous method, except that the pixel data is specified in an array of ints instead of an array of bytes.

You can get an ImageData instance from an existing Image by calling the getImageData() method, like this:

```
ImageData data = myImage.getImageData();
```

You can use this ImageData as is to create a new image, or you can manipulate it by changing its fields' values or calling its setter methods, and then create an image. You can also create an ImageData object using one of its constructors listed earlier. Once you have an ImageData object, you create an image by passing it to one of the constructors that accepts an ImageData. For example, you create an image from a single ImageData like this:

```
Image image = new Image(display, data);
```

If you have two ImageData objects, one containing the data for the image and one containing the data for the image's mask, you create the image like this:

```
Image image = new Image(display, sourceData, maskData);
```

Creating an Image from Another Image

To create an image that duplicates another image, or that has a disabled or a grayscale look, use the constructor that takes an Image and a flag:

```
Image image = new Image(display, otherImage, flag);
```

Table 10-17 lists the possible values for flag.

Table 10-17. flag *Constants*

Constant	Description
SWT.IMAGE_COPY	Create an exact copy of the image
SWT.IMAGE_DISABLE	Create an image that has a disabled look
SWT.IMAGE_GRAY	Create an image that has the grayscale look

The ShowImageFlags program in Listing 10-17 demonstrates the effects of the flag values. It loads an image, then creates three more images from it. The first passes SWT.IMAGE_COPY, the second passes SWT.IMAGE_DISABLE, and the third passes SWT.IMAGE_GRAY. Figure 10-19 shows the program's main window.

Listing 10-17. ShowImageFlags.java

```
package examples.ch10;

import org.eclipse.swt.*;
import org.eclipse.swt.graphics.*;
import org.eclipse.swt.layout.*;
import org.eclipse.swt.widgets.*;
```

```
/**
 * This class demonstrates the effects of the flags on the constructor:
 *
 * <code>Image(Device device, Image srcImage, int flag)</code>
 */
public class ShowImageFlags {
  // Members to hold the images
  private Image image;
  private Image copy;
  private Image disable;
  private Image gray;

  /**
   * Runs the program
   */
  public void run() {
    Display display = new Display();
    Shell shell = new Shell(display);
    shell.setText("Show Image Flags");

    // Load the image
    image = new Image(display, this.getClass().getResourceAsStream(
        "/images/swt.png"));

    // Create the duplicate image
    copy = new Image(display, image, SWT.IMAGE_COPY);

    // Create the disabled image
    disable = new Image(display, image, SWT.IMAGE_DISABLE);

    // Create the gray image
    gray = new Image(display, image, SWT.IMAGE_GRAY);

    createContents(shell);
    shell.pack();
    shell.open();
    while (!shell.isDisposed()) {
      if (!display.readAndDispatch()) {
        display.sleep();
      }
    }

    // Dispose the images
    image.dispose();
    copy.dispose();
    disable.dispose();
    gray.dispose();

    display.dispose();
  }
```

```
/**
 * Creates the main window's contents
 *
 * @param shell the main window
 */
private void createContents(Shell shell) {
  shell.setLayout(new FillLayout());

  // Create labels to hold each image
  new Label(shell, SWT.NONE).setImage(image);
  new Label(shell, SWT.NONE).setImage(copy);
  new Label(shell, SWT.NONE).setImage(disable);
  new Label(shell, SWT.NONE).setImage(gray);
}

/**
 * The application entry point
 *
 * @param args the command line arguments
 */
public static void main(String[] args) {
  new ShowImageFlags().run();
}
}
```

Figure 10-19. Images created using different flags

Drawing Images

Once you have an image, whether you've loaded it from disk or created it in memory, you can draw it to the screen by calling one of GC's drawImage() methods, listed in Table 10-18. You can also set the image into any of SWT's widgets that display an image, as the ShowImageFlags program does with Labels.

Table 10-18. GC's drawImage() *Methods*

Method	Description
void drawImage(Image image, int x, int y)	Draws the image with its top left corner at the point specified by (x, y)
void drawImage(Image image, int srcX, int srcY, int srcWidth, int srcHeight, int destX, int destY, int destWidth, int destHeight)	Draws the image or part of the image, starting from the point (srcX, srcY), with the width and height specified by srcWidth and srcHeight, respectively, at the point specified by (destX, destY), with the width and height specified by destWidth and destHeight, respectively

The first drawImage() method adds no complications: take the image and draw it at the specified location. However, the second drawImage() method complicates things a bit: you specify which part of the image to draw, and where to draw it to. SWT shrinks or stretches the image (or the portion of the image) to fit the specified area. The Draw-Images program in Listing 10-18 shows both drawImage() methods. In the upper-left corner of the window, it draws the image. In the lower-right corner, it draws half the image, taken out of the middle of the image, but doubles its size. This displays two same-sized images, one a close-up of the other.

Listing 10-18. DrawImages.java

```
package examples.ch10;

import org.eclipse.swt.events.*;
import org.eclipse.swt.graphics.*;
import org.eclipse.swt.widgets.*;

/**
 * This class demonstrates how to draw images
 */
public class DrawImages {
  public void run() {
    Display display = new Display();
    final Shell shell = new Shell(display);

    // Load an image
    final Image image = new Image(display, this.getClass().getResourceAsStream(
        "/images/swt.png"));
    System.out.println(image.getImageData().scanlinePad);
    image.getImageData().scanlinePad = 40;
    System.out.println(image.getImageData().scanlinePad);

    shell.addPaintListener(new PaintListener() {
      public void paintControl(PaintEvent event) {
        // Draw the untainted image
        event.gc.drawImage(image, 0, 0);
```

```
        // Determine how big the drawing area is
        Rectangle rect = shell.getClientArea();

        // Get information about the image
        ImageData data = image.getImageData();

        // Calculate drawing values
        int srcX = data.width / 4;
        int srcY = data.height / 4;
        int srcWidth = data.width / 2;
        int srcHeight = data.height / 2;
        int destWidth = 2 * srcWidth;
        int destHeight = 2 * srcHeight;

        // Draw the image
        event.gc.drawImage(image, srcX, srcY, srcWidth, srcHeight, rect.width
            - destWidth, rect.height - destHeight, destWidth, destHeight);
      }
    });
    shell.setText("Draw Images");
    shell.open();
    while (!shell.isDisposed()) {
      if (!display.readAndDispatch()) {
        display.sleep();
      }
    }
    image.dispose();
    display.dispose();
  }

  /**
   * The application entry point
   *
   * @param args the command line arguments
   */
  public static void main(String[] args) {
    new DrawImages().run();
  }
}
```

Figure 10-20 shows the program's main window.

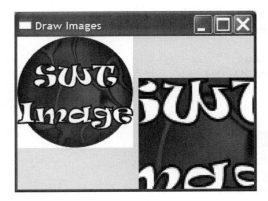

Figure 10-20. An image and a zoomed image

Double Buffering

Game developers and animators must deal with flickering, when a moving image flashes, and tearing, when a moving image seems to shift in one direction partway through the image, causing it to no longer line up properly. Either annoyance causes the animation not to display properly, ruining the entire effect.

To combat flickering and tearing, animators invented double buffering. When you double buffer, you perform all your drawing operations on an invisible canvas. When you're completely through drawing, you then draw that canvas onto the screen. In SWT, you implement this by creating an Image, creating a GC for that image, drawing on the GC, and then drawing that Image to the screen. The drawVerticalText() method in this chapter uses this approach.

The Animator program in Listing 10-19 doesn't use double buffering, and can result in flickering and tearing. AnimatorDoubleBuffer, which draws the same animation, uses double buffering, and thus avoids flickering and tearing.

Listing 10-19. Animator.java

```java
package examples.ch10;

import org.eclipse.swt.SWT;
import org.eclipse.swt.events.*;
import org.eclipse.swt.graphics.*;
import org.eclipse.swt.layout.*;
import org.eclipse.swt.widgets.*;

/**
 * This class demonstrates animation.
 */
public class Animator {
    // The width (and height) of the image
    private static final int IMAGE_WIDTH = 100;
```

```java
// The timer interval in milliseconds
private static final int TIMER_INTERVAL = 10;

// The location of the "ball"
private int x = 0;
private int y = 0;

// The direction the "ball" is moving
private int directionX = 1;
private int directionY = 1;

// We draw everything on this canvas
private Canvas canvas;

/**
 * Runs the application
 */
public void run() {
  final Display display = new Display();
  Shell shell = new Shell(display);
  shell.setText("Animator");
  createContents(shell);
  shell.open();

  // Set up the timer for the animation
  Runnable runnable = new Runnable() {
    public void run() {
      animate();
      display.timerExec(TIMER_INTERVAL, this);
    }
  };

  // Launch the timer
  display.timerExec(TIMER_INTERVAL, runnable);

  while (!shell.isDisposed()) {
    if (!display.readAndDispatch()) {
      display.sleep();
    }
  }

  // Kill the timer
  display.timerExec(-1, runnable);
  display.dispose();
}

/**
 * Creates the main window's contents
 *
 * @param shell the main window
 */
private void createContents(final Shell shell) {
  shell.setLayout(new FillLayout());
```

```java
    // Create the canvas for drawing
    canvas = new Canvas(shell, SWT.NO_BACKGROUND);
    canvas.addPaintListener(new PaintListener() {
      public void paintControl(PaintEvent event) {
        // Draw the background
        event.gc.fillRectangle(canvas.getBounds());

        // Set the color of the ball
        event.gc.setBackground(shell.getDisplay().getSystemColor(SWT.COLOR_RED));

        // Draw the ball
        event.gc.fillOval(x, y, IMAGE_WIDTH, IMAGE_WIDTH);
      }
    });
}

/**
 * Animates the next frame
 */
public void animate() {
  // Determine the ball's location
  x += directionX;
  y += directionY;

  // Determine out of bounds
  Rectangle rect = canvas.getClientArea();
  if (x < 0) {
    x = 0;
    directionX = 1;
  } else if (x > rect.width - IMAGE_WIDTH) {
    x = rect.width - IMAGE_WIDTH;
    directionX = -1;
  }
  if (y < 0) {
    y = 0;
    directionY = 1;
  } else if (y > rect.height - IMAGE_WIDTH) {
    y = rect.height - IMAGE_WIDTH;
    directionY = -1;
  }

  // Force a redraw
  canvas.redraw();
}

/**
 * The application entry point
 *
 * @param args the command line arguments
 */
public static void main(String[] args) {
```

```
      new Animator().run();
   }
}
```

The code for the two programs is nearly identical, except for the paint handlers. The paint handler in Animator draws everything to the screen: it first erases the background, then draws the ball in the proper position. The paint handler in AnimatorDoubleBuffer also first erases the background, then draws the ball in the proper position. The difference is that it does all its drawing off screen to an Image. Only after all the drawing is complete does it draw the completed image to the screen. If you run these two programs, you'll see flickering in Animator and no flickering in AnimatorDoubleBuffer. This is AnimatorDoubleBuffer's paint handler:

```
canvas.addPaintListener(new PaintListener() {
  public void paintControl(PaintEvent event) {
    // Create the image to fill the canvas
    Image image = new Image(shell.getDisplay(), canvas.getBounds());

    // Set up the offscreen gc
    GC gcImage = new GC(image);

    // Draw the background
    gcImage.setBackground(event.gc.getBackground());
    gcImage.fillRectangle(image.getBounds());

    // Set the color of the ball
    gcImage.setBackground(shell.getDisplay().getSystemColor(SWT.COLOR_RED));

    // Draw the ball
    gcImage.fillOval(x, y, IMAGE_WIDTH, IMAGE_WIDTH);

    // Draw the offscreen buffer to the screen
    event.gc.drawImage(image, 0, 0);

    // Clean up
    image.dispose();
    gcImage.dispose();
  }
});
```

Understanding Device

The graphics package contains a class, Device, that represents a physical device. It's an abstract class, and has two concrete subclasses: Display and Printer. Chapter 12, which discusses printing, examines the Printer class. The present chapter focuses on drawing graphics on the screen, which is what the Display class represents. Sometimes you'll want to know some attributes of the current screen you're drawing on. Turn to the Device class to retrieve that data. Device also offers a few other interesting methods, such as the one to get a color from the underlying system without having to create and manage one yourself (getSystemColor()). Table 10-19 lists Device's methods.

Table 10-19. Device *Methods*

Method	Description
void dispose()	Disposes this device, freeing any resources.
Rectangle getBounds()	Returns the bounding rectangle for this device.
Rectangle getClientArea()	Returns the bounding rectangle for the drawing area of this device.
int getDepth()	Returns the bit depth of this device.
DeviceData getDeviceData()	Returns the DeviceData instance associated with this device.
Point getDPI()	Returns this device's dots per inch (DPI). The x data member of the returned point contains the horizontal DPI, and the y data member contains the vertical DPI.
FontData[] getFontList(String faceName, boolean scalable)	Returns an array of FontData objects that match the specified faceName and scalable.
Color getSystemColor(int id)	Returns the color specified by id. Note that because you didn't create the returned color, you shouldn't dispose it.
Font getSystemFont()	Returns the system font.
boolean getWarnings()	Returns true if printing warnings to the console has been turned on.
boolean isDisposed()	Returns true if this device has been disposed, or false if it hasn't.
void setWarnings(boolean warnings)	If warnings is true, turns on printing warnings to the console. Note that not all platforms support printing warnings to the console.

Run the ShowDevice program (see Listing 10-20) to discover your current display's capabilities. This program lists the display's boundaries, client area, color depth, DPI, and whether or not it supports printing warnings to the console.

Listing 10-20. ShowDevice.java

```java
package examples.ch10;

import org.eclipse.swt.SWT;
import org.eclipse.swt.graphics.*;
import org.eclipse.swt.layout.*;
import org.eclipse.swt.widgets.*;

/**
 * This class displays information about the display device.
 */
public class ShowDevice {
```

```
/**
 * Runs the application
 */
public void run() {
  Display display = new Display();
  Shell shell = new Shell(display);
  shell.setText("Display Device");
  createContents(shell);
  shell.pack();
  shell.open();
  while (!shell.isDisposed()) {
    if (!display.readAndDispatch()) {
      display.sleep();
    }
  }
  display.dispose();
}

/**
 * Creates the main window's contents
 *
 * @param shell the main window
 */
private void createContents(Shell shell) {
  shell.setLayout(new FillLayout());

  // Create a text box to hold the data
  Text text = new Text(shell, SWT.MULTI | SWT.H_SCROLL | SWT.V_SCROLL);

  // Get the display device
  Device device = shell.getDisplay();

  // Put its data into a buffer
  StringBuffer buf = new StringBuffer();
  buf.append("getBounds(): ").append(device.getBounds()).append("\n");
  buf.append("getClientArea(): ").append(device.getClientArea()).append("\n");
  buf.append("getDepth(): ").append(device.getDepth()).append("\n");
  buf.append("getDPI(): ").append(device.getDPI()).append("\n");

  // By setting warnings to true and then getting warnings, we know if the
  // current platform supports it
  device.setWarnings(true);
  buf.append("Warnings supported: ").append(device.getWarnings()).append("\n");

  // Put the collected information into the text box
  text.setText(buf.toString());
}
```

```
/**
 * The application entry point
 *
 * @param args the command line arguments
 */
public static void main(String[] args) {
  new ShowDevice().run();
}
}
```

Figure 10-21 shows this program running under Windows XP. You can see that the computer it's running on has a screen resolution of 1024×768, that it's using 16 bits per color and 120 DPI, and that it doesn't support printing warnings to the console.

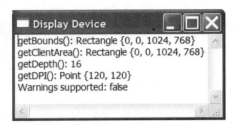

Figure 10-21. The display's attributes

Summary

SWT offers a rich array of drawing tools you can use any time you want to escape the bounds of the existing GUI widgets. You can draw various shapes: squares, rectangles, circles, ovals, lines, arcs, and other polygons. You can draw text in different sizes and fonts. You can draw all of these in different colors. You can draw images, whether loaded from files or created in memory. You can manipulate images when you draw them. You can draw animations, with or without flickers.

The heart of GUIs is graphics, and SWT equips you to draw whatever graphics you can imagine.

CHAPTER 11

Displaying and Editing Text

BENEATH ALL THE fancy widgets and advanced UI, Eclipse is, at its heart, a text editor. Naturally, then, a main focus of SWT is its ability to display and edit text. SWT's Styled-Text widget displays text in different colors, styles, sizes, and fonts, though it's limited to one size and font per StyledText widget. StyledText is geared toward editing source code, but you can use it for many other applications. It offers a full-featured text editor, complete with clipboard functionality and printing.

You have two approaches when using a StyledText widget: you can program directly to its API, or you can provide listeners for the StyledText widget to call. You can accomplish the same results using either method, but you shouldn't mix the two. This chapter first examines programming to the API, and then explores providing listeners.

Using the StyledText API

Plopping a StyledText into your application gives you a text editor that likely performs almost every task you expect. You can do things such as type text into it, move the caret around inside it using the arrow keys, page up and down through what you've typed, select text, cut or copy text to the clipboard, and paste text from the clipboard. However, to harness the range of its power, and do things such as print its contents, display its content using color syntax highlighting, control word wrapping, set tabs, restrict keystrokes, or attach actions to keystrokes, you must dig deeper and write code. Controlling the power of StyledText requires an extensive API, as Table 11-1 shows. However, the API isn't nearly as daunting as it seems at first blush, and soon you'll be able to port vi to SWT.

Table 11-1. The StyledText API

Method	Description
void addBidiSegmentListener (BidiSegmentListener listener)	Adds a bidirectional segment listener to the notification list.
void addExtendedModifyListener (ExtendedModifyListener listener)	Adds a listener to the notification list that's notified when text is modified. The event passed to the modifyText() method of this listener contains more information than the one passed to a ModifyListener's modifyText() method.
void addLineBackgroundListener (LineBackgroundListener listener)	Adds a listener to the notification list that's notified when a line is about to be drawn, in order to determine the line's background color. Use this method with the listener/callback approach.

Table 11-1. The `StyledText` *API (continued)*

Method	Description
`void addLineStyleListener` `(LineStyleListener listener)`	Adds a listener to the notification list that's notified when a line is about to be drawn, in order to determine the line's style. Use this method with the listener/callback approach.
`void addModifyListener` `(ModifyListener listener)`	Adds a listener to the notification list that's notified when text is modified.
`void addSelectionListener` `(SelectionListener listener)`	Adds a listener to the notification list that's notified when this `StyledText` is selected.
`void addVerifyKeyListener` `(VerifyKeyListener listener)`	Adds a listener to the notification list that's notified when a key is pressed.
`void addVerifyListener` `(VerifyListener listener)`	Adds a listener to the notification list that's notified when the text in this `StyledText` is about to change.
`void append(String text)`	Appends the text in `text` to the end of the text in this `StyledText`.
`Point computeSize(int wHint,` `int hHint, boolean changed)`	Computes the preferred size of this `StyledText`.
`void copy()`	Copies the selected text to the clipboard.
`void cut()`	Cuts the selected text to the clipboard.
`Color getBackground()`	Returns the background color for this `StyledText`.
`int getCaretOffset()`	Returns the zero-based position of the caret relative to the start of the text.
`int getCharCount()`	Returns the number of characters in this `StyledText`.
`StyledTextContent getContent()`	Returns the `StyledTextContent` associated with this `StyledText`, or `null` if no `StyledTextContent` is associated with this `StyledText`.
`boolean getDoubleClickEnabled()`	Returns `true` if this `StyledText` has been set to respond to double clicks with the mouse. Otherwise, returns `false`.
`boolean getEditable()`	Returns `true` if the text in this `StyledText` can be edited. Otherwise, returns `false`.
`Color getForeground()`	Returns the color this `StyledText` uses to draw text.
`int getHorizontalIndex()`	Returns the zero-based character position of the horizontal scroll relative to the start of the line.
`int getHorizontalPixel()`	Returns the zero-based pixel position of the horizontal scroll relative to the start of the line.
`int getKeyBinding(int key)`	Returns the binding associated with the key press specified by `key`.
`int getLineAtOffset(int offset)`	Returns the zero-based index of the line containing the zero-based offset specified by `offset`.
`Color getLineBackground(int index)`	Returns the background color of the line at the zero-based index specified by `index`.
`int getLineCount()`	Returns the number of lines of text in this `StyledText`.
`String getLineDelimiter()`	Returns the delimiter used at the end of lines.
`int getLineHeight()`	Returns the height of a line, in pixels.
`Point getLocationAtOffset(int offset)`	Returns the upper-left corner of the character at the zero-based offset specified by `offset`.

Table 11-1. The StyledText *API (continued)*

Method	Description
int getOffsetAtLine(int lineIndex)	Returns the zero-based offset into the text of the first character in the line specified by lineIndex.
int getOffsetAtLocation(Point point)	Returns the zero-based offset into the text of the character at the location specified by point.
int getOrientation()	Returns the orientation for this StyledText (either SWT.LEFT_TO_RIGHT or SWT.RIGHT_TO_LEFT).
Point getSelection()	Returns the current selection. The returned Point's x member contains the offset of the first selected character, and the y member contains the offset after the last selected character.
Color getSelectionBackground()	Returns the color used for the background of the selection.
int getSelectionCount()	Returns the number of selected characters.
Color getSelectionForeground()	Returns the color used for the selected text.
Point getSelectionRange()	Returns the selection as the offset of the first selected character, contained in the returned Point's x member, and the length of the selection, contained in the y member.
String getSelectedText()	Returns the selected text.
int getStyle()	Returns the style for this StyledText.
StyleRange getStyleRangeAtOffset (int offset)	Returns the style range at the zero-based offset.
StyleRange[] getStyleRanges()	Returns the style ranges for this StyledText.
StyleRange[] getStyleRanges (int start, int length)	Returns the style ranges starting at the zero-based index specified by start and continuing for length characters.
int getTabs()	Returns the number of characters used for tabs.
String getText()	Returns a copy of the text in this StyledText.
String getText(int start, int end)	Returns a copy of the text in this StyledText starting at the offset specified by start and ending at the offset specified by end.
int getTextLimit()	Returns the maximum number of characters this StyledText will hold.
String getTextRange(int start, int length)	Returns a copy of the text in this StyledText starting at the offset specified by start and continuing for length characters.
int getTopIndex()	Returns the zero-based index of the line currently shown at the top of this StyledText.
int getTopPixel()	Returns the pixel position of the line currently shown at the top of this StyledText.
boolean getWordWrap()	Returns true if word wrap for this StyledText is turned on. Otherwise, returns false.
void insert(String string)	Inserts the text specified by string at the selection point, replacing any selected text.
void invokeAction(int action)	Invokes an action. See Table 11-4 for possible actions.
void paste()	Pastes the text from the clipboard into this StyledText at the current caret position.
void print()	Prints this StyledText's text to the default printer.

Table 11-1. The StyledText *API (continued)*

Method	Description
Runnable print(Printer printer)	Returns a runnable that you can run to print this StyledText's text to the specified printer.
Runnable print(Printer printer, StyledTextPrintOptions options)	Returns a runnable that you can run to print this StyledText's text, using the specified options, to the specified printer.
void redraw()	Marks this StyledText to be redrawn.
void redraw(int x, int y, int width, int height, boolean all)	Marks the area of this StyledText specified by x, y, width, and height to be redrawn. If all is true, also marks the intersecting area of any of this StyledText's children to be redrawn.
void redrawRange(int start, int length, boolean clearBackground)	Redraws the range of characters staring at the zero-based offset specified by start and continuing for length characters. If clearBackground is true, clears the background before redrawing. Otherwise, doesn't clear the background.
void removeBidiSegmentListener (BidiSegmentListener listener)	Removes the specified listener from the notification list.
void removeExtendedModifyListener (ExtendedModifyListener listener)	Removes the specified listener from the notification list.
void removeLineBackgroundListener (LineBackgroundListener listener)	Removes the specified listener from the notification list.
void removeLineStyleListener (LineStyleListener listener)	Removes the specified listener from the notification list.
void removeModifyListener (ModifyListener listener)	Removes the specified listener from the notification list.
void removeSelectionListener (SelectionListener listener)	Removes the specified listener from the notification list.
void removeVerifyKeyListener (VerifyKeyListener listener)	Removes the specified listener from the notification list.
void removeVerifyListener (VerifyListener listener)	Removes the specified listener from the notification list.
void replaceStyleRanges(int start, int length, StyleRange[] ranges)	Replaces the style ranges from the zero-based offset specified by start and continuing length characters with the style ranges specified by ranges.
void replaceTextRange(int start, int length, String text)	Replaces the text from the zero-based offset specified by start and continuing length characters with the text specified by text.
void selectAll()	Selects all the text in this StyledText.
void setBackground(Color color)	Sets the background color for this StyledText.
void setCaret(Caret caret)	Sets the caret for this StyledText.
void setCaretOffset(int offset)	Sets the caret's zero-based offset.
void setContent(StyledTextContent content)	Sets the content for this StyledText.
void setCursor(Cursor cursor)	Sets the cursor for this StyledText.

Table 11-1. The StyledText *API (continued)*

Method	Description
void setDoubleClickEnabled (boolean enable)	If enable is true, enables double-click mouse behavior (selects an entire word) for this StyledText. Otherwise, disables it.
void setEditable(boolean editable)	If editable is true, allows the text of this StyledText to be edited. Otherwise, disallows editing.
void setFont(Font font)	Sets the font for this StyledText.
void setForeground(Color color)	Sets the color to use for drawing text in this StyledText.
void setHorizontalIndex(int offset)	Sets the horizontal scroll to the specified zero-based offset from the start of the line.
void setHorizontalPixel(int pixel)	Sets the horizontal scroll to the specified pixel relative to the start of the line.
void setKeyBinding(int key, int action)	Sets the key binding for the key specified by key to the action specified by action.
void setLineBackground(int startLine, int lineCount, Color color)	Sets the background color for the specified lines, starting at the line at the zero-based index specified by startLine and continuing for lineCount lines.
void setOrientation(int orientation)	Sets this StyledText's orientation. orientation should be either SWT.LEFT_TO_RIGHT or SWT.RIGHT_TO_LEFT.
void setSelection(int start)	Sets the selection to the character at the zero-based index specified by start, and scrolls the selection into view.
void setSelection(int start, int end)	Sets the selection beginning at the character at the zero-based index specified by start and ending at the character at the zero-based index specified by end, and scrolls the selection into view.
void setSelection(Point point)	Sets the selection beginning at the character at the zero-based index specified by point.x and ending at the character at the zero-based index specified by point.y, and scrolls the selection into view.
void setSelectionBackground(Color color)	Sets the background color for the selection.
void setSelectionForeground(Color color)	Sets the text color for the selection.
void setSelectionRange(int start, int length)	Sets the selection beginning at the character at the zero-based index specified by start and continuing length characters.
void setStyleRange(StyleRange range)	Adds the style specified by range.
void setStyleRanges(StyleRange[] ranges)	Replaces all style ranges for this StyledText with the style ranges specified by ranges.
void setTabs(int tabs)	Sets the number of characters to use for tabs in this StyledText.
void setText(String text)	Sets the text for this StyledText.
void setTextLimit(int limit)	Sets the maximum number of characters for this StyledText.
void setTopIndex(int index)	Scrolls the text in this StyledText so that the zero-based line specified by index displays at the top.

Table 11-1. The StyledText *API (continued)*

Method	Description
void setTopPixel(int pixel)	Scrolls the text in this StyledText so that the pixel specified by pixel displays at the top.
void setWordWrap(boolean wrap)	If wrap is true, turns on wrapping for this StyledText. Otherwise, turns off wrapping.
void showSelection()	Scrolls the selection into view.

Creating a StyledText Widget

The StyledText constructor adheres to SWT's parent/style pattern:

```
StyledText(Composite parent, int style)
```

Table 11-2 lists the possible constants for style, which you can combine using the bit-wise OR operator.

Table 11-2. StyledText *Styles*

Constant	Description
SWT.BORDER	Draws a border around the StyledText.
SWT.SINGLE	Creates a single-line StyledText.
SWT.MULTI	Creates a multiline StyledText. This is the default.
SWT.H_SCROLL	Enables horizontal scrolling.
SWT.V_SCROLL	Enables vertical scrolling.
SWT.WRAP	Turns on word wrapping, trumping the horizontal scrolling style.
SWT.READ_ONLY	Makes the StyledText read-only.
SWT.FULL_SELECTION	Causes redrawing operations to redraw the full line instead of only the invalidated portion.

For example, to create a StyledText that scrolls vertically, wraps text, and displays a border, use this code:

```
StyledText text = new StyledText(parent, SWT.V_SCROLL | SWT.WRAP | SWT.BORDER);
```

Using the Clipboard

Using the clipboard with StyledText is almost embarrassingly easy. To cut from, copy from, or paste to a SyledText, call cut(), copy(), or paste(), respectively. For example, to cut the selected text from StyledText st1 and put it on the clipboard, and then paste it into the current caret position of StyledText st2, use this code:

```
st1.cut();
st2.paste();
```

That's all there is to it. StyledText already supports the platform's keystrokes for cutting, copying, and pasting, so you don't even have to call these methods to get clipboard functionality in your application. If you want to allow clipboard operations from a menu or toolbar handler, though, call these methods.

Using Word Wrap

When the caret reaches the right margin and the user continues to type, two things can happen: the additional text can continue on the same line, or it can wrap to the next line. Word processors usually wrap to the next line, while programmers' text editors usually continue on the same line. Wrapping to the next line is called word wrap, and is off by default in StyledText. You can turn word wrap on at construction time by passing the SWT.WRAP style bit.

You can retrieve word wrap settings at run time by calling getWordWrap(), which returns true if word wrap is on or false if it isn't. You can change word wrap settings at run time as well, using the setWordWrap() method. You pass true to turn on word wrap, or false to turn it off. For example, you can toggle word wrap settings like this:

```
styledText.setWordWrap(!styledText.getWordWrap());
```

Getting Statistics

Many word processors and text editors display running counts of data concerning the current text being edited. For example, the word processor we're using to type this displays the current page number of the present document, the total number of pages, the current column, and the current line. Additionally, we can see the number of words, characters, paragraphs, and lines in the present document.

StyledText records a few statistics about the text it holds as well, which you can retrieve using the API. For example, you can get the zero-based offset into the StyledText's text of the current caret position by calling getCaretOffset(). The following code prints the caret's offset, the total number of lines of text, the total number of characters, and the current (one-based) line:

```
System.out.println("Caret Offset: " + styledText.getCaretOffset());
System.out.println("Total Lines of Text: " + styledText.getLineCount());
System.out.println("Total Characters: " + styledText.getCharCount());
System.out.println("Current Line: " +
  (styledText.getLineAtOffset(styledText.getCaretOffset()) + 1));
```

Printing

Chapter 12 covers printing, printers, and the print dialog, but printing the contents of a StyledText requires little understanding of printing. At its simplest, you can print a StyledText's contents like this:

```
styledText.print();
```

This prints the contents to the default printer, in the same thread as the calling program. For long documents or slow printing subsystems, this will tie up your GUI. You can print to the default printer in a separate thread, thus maintaining a responsive GUI, like this:

```
styledText.print(myPrinter).run();
```

Calling new Printer() returns the default printer, but you can pass any Printer object. However, you must dispose any Printer object that you create. Chapter 12 covers how to enumerate the available printers. Finally, you can set various options on the print job by passing a StyledTextPrintOptions object in addition to the printer. Styled-TextPrintOptions adds no new methods, but maintains all options as public data members, listed in Table 11-3.

Table 11-3. StyledTextPrintOptions *Members*

Member	Description
String footer	The footer to display on each page. The footer is formatted in three sections: left, center, and right, separated by StyledTextPrintOptions.SEPARATOR characters.
String header	The header to display on each page. It's formatted the same as the footer.
String jobName	The name for the print job.
boolean printLineBackground	If true, prints the line background color.
boolean printTextBackground	If true, prints the text background color.
boolean printTextFontStyle	If true, prints the text styles (bold or italic).
boolean printTextForeground	If true, prints the text foreground color.
static String SEPARATOR	The string used to separate the left, center, and right sections of the header and footer.
static String PAGE_TAG	The constant used in header and footer to indicate that the page number should be printed.

For example, to print the name of the file on top of each page, the page number at the bottom of each page, the word "Confidential" in the lower-right corner, and the text in the appropriate colors and styles, use code such as this:

```
StyledTextPrintOptions options = new StyledTextPrintOptions();
options.header = StyledTextPrintOptions.SEPARATOR + filename +
  StyledTextPrintOptions.SEPARATOR;
options.footer = StyledTextPrintOptions.SEPARATOR +
  StyledTextPrintOptions.PAGE_TAG + StyledTextPrintOptions.SEPARATOR +
  "Confidential";
options.printLineBackground = true;
options.printTextbackground = true;
options.printTextFontStyle = true;
options.printTextForeground = true;
st.print(new Printer(), options).run();
```

Getting and Setting Key Bindings

Programmers settle into certain key bindings, and chafe when the editor they're using doesn't support them. Whether they use GNU Emacs, vi, Brief, or Common User Access (CUA) key bindings, developers grow comfortable with certain keys performing certain actions. StyledText defaults to several common CUA key bindings, so you should immediately find yourself in familiar surroundings when editing text in a StyledText widget.

StyledText can associate one key and modifier combination with one action. The ST class contains the possible actions that keys can bind to. Table 11-4 lists the actions.

Table 11-4. Key Binding Actions from the ST *Class*

Constant	Description
static int COLUMN_NEXT	Moves the caret to the next column.
static int COLUMN_PREVIOUS	Moves the caret to the previous column.
static int COPY	Copies the currently selected text to the clipboard.
static int CUT	Cuts the currently selected text to the clipboard.
static int DELETE_NEXT	Deletes the next character.
static int DELETE_PREVIOUS	Deletes the previous character.
static int DELETE_WORD_NEXT	Deletes the next word.
static int DELETE_WORD_PREVIOUS	Deletes the previous word.
static int LINE_DOWN	Moves the caret down one line.
static int LINE_END	Moves the caret to the end of the current line.
static int LINE_START	Moves the caret to the start of the current line.
static int LINE_UP	Moves the caret up one line.
static int PAGE_DOWN	Moves the caret down one page.
static int PAGE_UP	Moves the caret up one page.
static int PASTE	Pastes the text from the clipboard to the current caret position.
static int SELECT_COLUMN_NEXT	Selects the character in the next column and moves the caret to the next column.
static int SELECT_COLUMN_PREVIOUS	Selects the character in the previous column and moves the caret to the previous column.
static int SELECT_LINE_DOWN	Moves the caret down one line, selecting the text between the previous caret position and the new caret position.
static int SELECT_LINE_END	Moves the caret to the end of the current line, selecting the text between the previous caret position and the new caret position.
static int SELECT_LINE_START	Moves the caret to the start of the current line, selecting the text between the previous caret position and the new caret position.
static int SELECT_LINE_UP	Moves the caret up one line, selecting the text between the previous caret position and the new caret position.

Table 11-4. Key Binding Actions from the ST *Class*

Constant	Description
static int SELECT_PAGE_DOWN	Moves the caret down one page, selecting the text between the previous caret position and the new caret position.
static int SELECT_PAGE_UP	Moves the caret up one page, selecting the text between the previous caret position and the new caret position.
static int SELECT_TEXT_END	Moves the caret to the end of the text, selecting the text between the previous caret position and the new caret position.
static int SELECT_TEXT_START	Moves the caret to the start of the text, selecting the text between the previous caret position and the new caret position.
static int SELECT_WINDOW_END	Moves the caret to the end of the text currently displayed in the window, selecting the text between the previous caret position and the new caret position.
static int SELECT_WINDOW_START	Moves the caret to the start of the text currently displayed in the window, selecting the text between the previous caret position and the new caret position.
static int SELECT_WORD_NEXT	Moves the caret to the next word, selecting the text between the previous caret position and the new caret position.
static int SELECT_WORD_PREVIOUS	Moves the caret to the previous word, selecting the text between the previous caret position and the new caret position.
static int TEXT_END	Moves the caret to the end of the text.
static int TEXT_START	Moves the caret to the start of the text.
static int TOGGLE_OVERWRITE	Toggles the insert/overwrite flag.
static int WINDOW_END	Moves the caret to the end of the text currently displayed in the window.
static int WINDOW_START	Moves the caret to the start of the text currently displayed in the window.
static int WORD_NEXT	Moves the caret to the next word.
static int WORD_PREVIOUS	Moves the caret to the previous word.

To get the action a key is bound to, call getKeyBinding(), passing the key you want to get the binding for. The key you pass can be a character or a key constant from the SWT class. You can also use the bitwise OR operator to pass modifier keys as well (Shift, Ctrl, and so on). For example, to get the action bound to Alt+E, use this code:

```
int altEAction = styledText.getKeyBinding('e' | SWT.ALT);
```

To get the action for Shift+Left, use this code:

```
int shiftLeftAction = styledText.getKeyBinding(SWT.ARROW_LEFT | SWT.SHIFT);
```

Passing a modifier constant isn't necessary, as this code shows:

```
int zAction = styledText.getKeyBinding('z');
```

To set a key binding, call setKeyBinding() and pass both the key and the action. The possible values for the key are the same as for getKeyBinding(): characters or key constants from SWT, optionally bitwise ORed with modifier key constants. The possible values for the action are the constants from the ST class. For example, to bind the insert/overwrite toggle action to Alt+I, use this code:

```
styledText.setKeyBinding('i' | SWT.ALT, ST.TOGGLE_OVERWRITE);
```

To clear any key bindings, pass SWT.NULL for the action. For example, to remove the preceding insert/overwrite toggle, use this code:

```
styledText.setKeyBinding('i' | SWT.ALT, SWT.NULL);
```

Changing Miscellaneous Settings

You can get and set the number of columns used to display tabs using getTabs() and setTabs(), respectively. StyledText defaults to a tab width of four columns. For example, you can set the tab width to two, like this:

```
styledText.setTabs(2);
```

You can make a StyledText read-only, useful for viewing files without allowing editing, or preventing users from making changes to files that they don't have permission to save. To make the StyledText read only, you can pass the SWT.READ_ONLY style to the constructor, or you can call setEditable(false). Calling setEditable(true) turns on editing capabilities.

You can limit the number of characters that the StyledText accepts by calling setTextLimit(), passing the maximum number of characters to accept. For example, to limit a StyledText to 100 characters, use this code:

```
styledText.setTextLimit(100);
```

Handling Events

When users type, delete from, cut from, or paste to a StyledText, four events fire: key verification, verification, modification, and extended modification. Before the StyledText allows the changes to itself, it first processes the key verification and the verification. These handlers, VerifyKeyListeners and VerifyListeners, can allow, veto, or alter the requested text change. After the change has happened, ModifyListeners and ExtendedModifyListeners react to the changes.

Filtering Change

Sometimes reacting to a change that has already occurred doesn't suffice for your application needs. In some situations, you want to step in before the change occurs and either veto it, modify the change, or let it pass through. StyledText notifies two sets of handlers before allowing changes to its contents: VerifyKeyListeners and VerifyListeners.

When the user presses a key, all registered VerifyKeyListeners are notified. You add a VerifyKeyListener by calling addVerifyKeyListener(). It has a single method:

```
public void verifyKey(VerifyEvent event)
```

Note that the passed event isn't VerifyKeyEvent, which doesn't exist, but the recycled VerifyEvent that VerifyListeners also use. We examine VerifyEvent's fields when we discuss VerifyListeners. No VerifyEvent fields are filled when VerifyKeyListeners are called.

 CAUTION *No* VerifyEvent-*specific fields contain appropriate data in* VerifyKeyListeners.

VerifyEvent derives from KeyEvent, which contains pertinent fields for VerifyKeyListeners. Table 11-5 lists the fields.

Table 11-5. KeyEvent *Fields*

Field	Description
char character	The character that the typed key represents. Changing this value has no effect on event processing.
boolean doit	A flag that specifies whether this event should be processed. Setting doit to false cancels event processing for this event.
int keyCode	The code of the typed key, as defined in the SWT class. Changing this value has no effect on event processing.
int stateMask	The state of the keyboard modifier keys when this event was generated. Possible values are combinations of SWT.ALT, SWT.COMMAND, SWT.CONTROL, SWT.CTRL, SWT.MOD1, SWT.MOD2, SWT.MOD3, SWT.MOD4, and SWT.SHIFT.

KeyEvent, in turn, derives from TypedEvent, but you'll likely not reference any of TypedEvent's fields in your VerifyKeyEvent handlers.

To illustrate VerifyKeyListeners, suppose you're developing a hex editor. You want to allow users to type 0–9, a–f, and A–F only. You also want to allow basic editing keys (arrows, Backspace, Delete, and Enter). Your handler might look like this:

```
st.addVerifyKeyListener(new VerifyKeyListener() {
  public void verifyKey(VerifyEvent event) {
    // Assume this is an invalid key
    event.doit = false;
```

```
    // Allow 0 - 9
    if (Character.isDigit(event.character))
      event.doit = true;

    // Allow a - f
    else if (event.character >= 'a' && event.character <= 'f')
      event.doit = true;

    // Allow A - F
    else if (event.character >= 'A' && event.character <= 'F')
      event.doit = true;

    // Allow backspace and delete
    else if (event.character == '\u0008' || event.character == '\u007F')
      event.doit = true;

    // Allow arrow keys
    else if (event.keyCode == SWT.ARROW_UP || event.keyCode == SWT.ARROW_DOWN
      || event.keyCode == SWT.ARROW_LEFT || event.keyCode == SWT.ARROW_RIGHT)
      event.doit = true;

    // Allow return
    else if (event.character == '\r')
      event.doit = true;
  }
});
```

After all VerifyKeyListeners are notified, any VerifyListeners are then notified. Again, this happens before the change is effected, so you still have veto power. VerifyListener defines one method that you must implement:

```
public void verifyText(VerifyEvent e)
```

In contrast to VerifyEvents passed to VerifyKeyListeners, the VerifyEvent objects passed to VerifyListeners contain relevant data. Table 11-6 lists VerifyEvent's fields.

Table 11-6. VerifyEvent *Fields*

Field	Description
int start	The zero-based offset of the start of the range of the text to be changed. Changing this value has no effect on event processing.
int end	The zero-based offset of the end of the range of the text to be changed. Changing this value has no effect on event processing.
String text	The text that will be inserted. Changing this value changes the text to be inserted.

Each time users type a key, SWT fires a VerifyEvent and triggers all VerifyListeners. The fields in VerifyEvent contain data related to that key press. For example, if the current caret position is at offset 714 and the user types **B**, VerifyEvent's data will be as follows:

```
event.start = 714
event.end = 714
event.text = "B"
```

When users paste text of more than one character into a StyledText, text contains more than one character—it contains the full text to paste. For example, if the clipboard contains the text "home runs," and the current caret position is at offset 755, if the user elects to paste from the clipboard then VerifyEvent's data will be as follows:

```
event.start = 755
event.end = 755
event.text = "home runs"
```

When text is selected in the StyledText and the user either types a character or pastes text from the clipboard, start and end don't equal. If the user has three characters selected starting at offset 60, and then types **R**, VerifyEvent's data will contain this code:

```
event.start = 60
event.end = 63
event.text = "R"
```

Deleting text fires a VerifyEvent filled with the proper data as well. Remember that start refers to the starting offset in the affected range, not the starting position of the caret. This means that start is always less than or equal to end, even if the caret moves backwards (as in the case of Backspace). For example, if the caret is at offset 70, and the user presses the Backspace key, VerifyEvent will contain this code:

```
event.start = 69
event.end = 70
event.text = ""
```

You can modify the data in VerifyEvent to change the effect of user's keystrokes. For example, you might have a vendetta against cut-and-paste programmers, and decide to insert belittling remarks anytime a user pastes text. When text contains more than one character, you go for the jugular like this:

```
styledText.addVerifyListener(new VerifyListener() {
  public void verifyText(VerifyEvent event) {
    if (event.text.length() > 1)
    {
      event.text = "Stop pasting, you buffoon!";
    }
  }
});
```

You can also veto the event by setting its doit member to false. For example, if you were penning a lipogram and decided to stretch your linguistic abilities and exclude the letter "E," you might put in a handler that prevents the letter "E," uppercase or lowercase, from being either typed or pasted:

```
styledText.addVerifyListener(new VerifyListener() {
  public void verifyText(VerifyEvent event) {
    // If the text contains E or e, throw it all away
    if (event.text.indexOf('e') > -1 ||
        event.text.indexOf('E') > -1) {
      event.text = "";
    }
  }
});
```

Reacting to Change

As a text editor, StyledText encourages editing. Users type, delete, cut, paste, and perpetually alter the contents of a StyledText. When they do, listeners are notified so you can react to the changes. All ModifyListeners are notified first, and then all ExtendedModifyListeners. These notifications occur after the text has already changed inside the StyledText.

You call addModifyListener() to register a ModifyListener, which must implement the modifyText() method, like this:

```
public void modifyText(ModifyEvent event) {}
```

ModifyEvent contains no information about the specific change; it just tells you that something happened. For example, suppose that your application displays a running count of the number of characters in the StyledText. Your handler might look like this:

```
styledText.addModifyListener(new ModifyListener() {
  public void modifyText(ModifyEvent event) {
    charCountLabel.setText("Character Count: " + styledText.getCharCount());
  }
});
```

Call addExtendedModifyListener() to add an ExtendedModifyListener. Your ExtendedModifyListener implementation also must implement modifyText(), like this:

```
public void modifyText(ExtendedModifyEvent event) {}
```

In contrast to ModifyEvent, ExtendedModifyEvent contains change-specific information. In other words, you're not merely notified that a change has occurred. Instead, you're told what the change was. Table 11-7 lists ExtendedModifyEvent's fields.

Table 11-7. `ExtendedModifyEvent` *Fields*

Field	Description
`int start`	The zero-based offset, relative to the start of the `StyledText`, of the first position of the changed text.
`int length`	The length of the changed text, in characters.
`String replacedText`	The text that was replaced by this change.

If you're using `StyleRanges` to color and style sections of the text, you might use an `ExtendedModifyListener` to color and style the new text appropriately. The fields `start` and `length` tell you where the new text is, and you can query the surrounding text to determine how to color or style it.

Another use for an `ExtendedModifyListener` is to capture the change information for undo purposes. For example, you might allow users to undo the latest change they make in a `StyledText`. In your `ExtendedModifyListener` you store the change information in member variables so you can reapply it if the user chooses to undo. The code for the listener might look something like this:

```
styledText.addExtendedModifyListener(new ExtendedModifyListener() {
  public void modifyText(ExtendedModifyEvent event) {
    start = event.start;
    length = event.length;
    replacedText = event.replacedText;
  }
});
```

Your undo method looks something like this:

```
public void undo()
{
  styledText.replaceTextRange(start, length, replacedText);
}
```

You call your undo method from a menu selection or keystroke.

Using StyleRanges

Older programmers remember the magical feeling when they saw syntax coloring for the first time. They fired up some new editor, started coding, and suddenly keywords changed to one color and font style, comments to another, and punctuation to still another. It seemed like wizardry. Code was instantly easier to understand, a quick glance at the code told you things that before required scrutiny, and syntax errors such as unclosed strings or comments glared tellingly, affording quick fixes. Syntax coloring represents perhaps the biggest advance in editors since the jump from line editors to screen editors.

Of course, Luddites scoffed at the colors and styles, calling the concept a frivolous toy and saying it made their source files look like a jellybean jar. They steadfastly refused to adopt syntax coloring, clinging fiercely to monochromatic editing. They've since all become managers.

StyledText incorporates syntax coloring and styling, though it's a bit of work to implement. It uses instances of the StyleRange class to track the colors and styles. Each StyleRange controls a portion of the StyledText's text, storing the starting offset of the controlled portion, the length (in characters) of the portion, and the foreground color, background color, and font style to use. StyleRange stores this data in public fields, listed in Table 11-8.

Table 11-8. StyleRange *Fields*

Field	Description
Color background	The background color, or null to for the default background color.
int fontStyle	The font style (SWT.NORMAL, SWT.BOLD, SWT.ITALIC, or SWT.BOLD | SWT.ITALIC).
Color foreground	The foreground color, or null for the default foreground color.
int length	The length, in number of characters.
int start	The starting offset.

You create a StyleRange by calling one of its constructors, listed in Table 11-9. The following code creates two identical StyleRange objects:

```
// Use the empty constructor and set the fields
StyleRange sr1 = new StyleRange();
sr1.start = 7;
sr1.length = 14;
sr1.foreground = display.getSystemColor(SWT.COLOR_GREEN);
sr1.background = display.getSystemColor(SWT.COLOR_WHITE);
sr1.fontStyle = SWT.BOLD;

// Use the constructor that accepts the fields
StyleRange sr2 = new StyleRange(7, 14, display.getSystemColor(SWT.COLOR_GREEN),
  display.getSystemColor(SWT.COLOR_WHITE), SWT.BOLD);
```

Table 11-9. StyleRange *Constructors*

Constructor	Description
StyleRange()	Creates an empty StyleRange.
StyleRange(int start, int length, Color foreground, Color background)	Creates a StyleRange with the specified start, length, foreground color, and background color.
StyleRange(int start, int length, Color foreground, Color background, int fontStyle)	Creates a StyleRange with the specified start, length, foreground color, background color, and font style.

StyleRange offers a few methods, listed in Table 11-10. One useful method, similarTo(), compares the display data for two StyleRange objects for equality: the foreground color, the background color, and the font style. It ignores which portion of the text the StyleRanges correspond to (their start and length fields).

Table 11-10. StyleRange *Methods*

Method	Description
Object clone()	Creates a new StyleRange with the same field values as this StyleRange.
boolean equals(Object object)	Returns true if this StyleRange equals the one specified by object. Otherwise, returns false.
boolean isUnstyled()	Returns true if this StyleRange doesn't contain font style information. Otherwise, returns false.
boolean similarTo(StyleRange range)	Returns true if this StyleRange is similar to the one specified by range; that is, if they have the same foreground color, background color, and font style. Otherwise, returns false.
String toString()	Returns a string representation of this StyleRange.

Because a StyleRange specifies not only how to display certain text, but also which text the display values correspond to, you can't reuse StyleRange instances. Each range of text that should have display characteristics different from the defaults must have its own StyleRange instance.

As listed in Table 11-1, StyledText offers the following methods to set StyleRanges:

```
void setStyleRange(StyleRange range)
void setStyleRanges(StyleRange[] ranges)
void replaceStyleRanges(int start, int length, StyleRange[] ranges)
```

You retrieve StyleRange data using these StyledText methods, also listed in Table 11-1:

```
StyleRange getStyleRangeAtOffset(int offset)
StyleRange[] getStyleRanges()
StyleRange[] getStyleRanges(int start, int length)
```

However, you'll find that using the API to set StyleRanges (and thereby to incorporate dynamic syntax coloring and highlighting) is stodgy, limiting, and more prone to coding errors. You'll likely prefer to use LineStyleListeners, which this chapter discusses. Nevertheless, the StyledText API regarding StyleRanges follows.

Set a single StyleRange into a StyledText like this:

```
styledText.setStyleRange(myStyleRange);
```

This sets the properties for the text in the range specified by myStyleRange, trumping any previous StyleRange whose range overlaps the specified range. It doesn't affect text outside the specified range. For example, the following code prints "Go" in orange and "Gators" in blue (the space remains orange, but you can't see it anyway):

```
// Set the text
styledText.setText("Go Gators");

// Turn all of the text orange, with the default background color
styledText.setStyleRange(new StyleRange(0, 9, orange, null));
```

```
// Turn "Gators" blue
styledText.setStyleRange(new StyleRange(3, 6, blue, null));
```

Figure 11-1 shows this code in action. A few interesting things to note: the colors used must be valid (not disposed) for the life of the StyleRanges. Also, the offsets and lengths of the StyleRanges must be valid. That is, they must be within the range of existing text—when created, or when an exception is thrown. However, as text is modified, added, or deleted, the offsets and lengths need not remain valid. Any added text, even within the "Go Gators," doesn't pick up the colors, nor does it disrupt the existing colors. Figure 11-2 shows this same program with the text "Florida" inserted. "Florida" displays in black, the default color.

Figure 11-1. Two StyleRange*s*

Figure 11-2. Two StyleRange*s with text inserted*

This example uses the setStyleRange() method to set each StyleRange individually. It could have aggregated the StyleRanges into an array, and called setStyleRanges(), which replaces all the StyleRanges in the StyledText with the new ones. Passing the StyleRanges at once reduces the amount of flashing as the StyledText repaints.

However, the results are undefined if the ranges in the array overlap, as they do in this example. To rectify this, change the range of the "Go" style to include only the desired characters. The code looks like this:

```
// Create the array to hold the StyleRanges
StyleRange[] ranges = new StyleRange[2];

// Create the first StyleRange, making sure not to overlap. Include the space.
ranges[0] = new StyleRange(0, 3, orange, null);

// Create the second StyleRange
ranges[1] = new StyleRange(3, 6, blue, null);

// Replace all the StyleRanges for the StyledText
styledText.setStyleRanges(ranges);
```

The program renders the same output, and reacts the same to text additions and deletions. It's slightly more efficient as well, because it repaints the StyledText only once, instead of repainting twice. However, this code directs the entire StyledText to repaint, instead of just the affected area. In this case the affected area is the entire text, so the point is moot. However, other cases might reflect an affected area that represents only a portion of the entire text, so repainting the entire StyledText would be inefficient. To avoid this inefficiency, use the replaceStyleRanges() method, which specifies which portion of the StyledText to repaint. Modifying the example code to use replaceStyleRanges() results in this:

```
// Create the array to hold the StyleRanges
StyleRange[] ranges = new StyleRange[2];

// Create the first StyleRange, making sure not to overlap. Include the space.
ranges[0] = new StyleRange(0, 3, orange, null);

// Create the second StyleRange
ranges[1] = new StyleRange(3, 6, blue, null);

// Replace only the StyleRanges in the affected area
styledText.replaceStyleRanges(0, 9, ranges);
```

Listing 11-1 contains the complete source for the program, including all three StyleRange-setting methods. Uncomment the different sections to prove that the results are the same, however you set the ranges.

Listing 11-1. StyleRangeTest.java

```
package examples.ch11;

import org.eclipse.swt.SWT;
import org.eclipse.swt.custom.*;
import org.eclipse.swt.graphics.Color;
import org.eclipse.swt.layout.*;
import org.eclipse.swt.widgets.*;

/**
 * This class demonstrates StyleRanges
 */
public class StyleRangeTest {
  private Color orange;
  private Color blue;

  /**
   * Runs the application
   */
  public void run() {
    Display display = new Display();
    Shell shell = new Shell(display);
```

```
  // Create colors for style ranges
  orange = new Color(display, 255, 127, 0);
  blue = display.getSystemColor(SWT.COLOR_BLUE);

  createContents(shell);
  shell.open();
  while (!shell.isDisposed()) {
    if (!display.readAndDispatch()) {
      display.sleep();
    }
  }

  // We created orange, but not blue
  orange.dispose();

  display.dispose();
}

/**
 * Creates the main window contents
 *
 * @param shell the main window
 */
private void createContents(Shell shell) {
  shell.setLayout(new FillLayout());

  // Create the StyledText
  StyledText styledText = new StyledText(shell, SWT.BORDER);

  // Set the text
  styledText.setText("Go Gators");

  /*
   * The multiple setStyleRange() method // Turn all of the text orange, with
   * the default background color styledText.setStyleRange(new StyleRange(0, 9,
   * orange, null));
   *   // Turn "Gators" blue styledText.setStyleRange(new StyleRange(3, 6, blue,
   * null));
   */

  /*
   * The setStyleRanges() method // Create the array to hold the StyleRanges
   * StyleRange[] ranges = new StyleRange[2];
   *   // Create the first StyleRange, making sure not to overlap. Include the
   * space. ranges[0] = new StyleRange(0, 3, orange, null);
   *   // Create the second StyleRange ranges[1] = new StyleRange(3, 6, blue,
   * null);
   *   // Replace all the StyleRanges for the StyledText
   * styledText.setStyleRanges(ranges);
   */
```

```
    /* The replaceStyleRanges() method */
    // Create the array to hold the StyleRanges
    StyleRange[] ranges = new StyleRange[2];

    // Create the first StyleRange, making sure not to overlap. Include the
    // space.
    ranges[0] = new StyleRange(0, 3, orange, null);

    // Create the second StyleRange
    ranges[1] = new StyleRange(3, 6, blue, null);

    // Replace only the StyleRanges in the affected area
    styledText.replaceStyleRanges(0, 9, ranges);
  }

  /**
   * The application entry point
   *
   * @param args the command line arguments
   */
  public static void main(String[] args) {
    new StyleRangeTest().run();
  }
}
```

This code sets the StyleRanges statically. To use the API to implement dynamic syntax coloring, add an event handler to detect the change, analyze the affected text, and set any appropriate StyleRange. The SyntaxTest program detects any punctuation (whether typed or pasted) and turns it red and bold. To detect the punctuation, it uses an ExtendedModifyListener that looks like this:

```
// Add the syntax coloring handler
styledText.addExtendedModifyListener(new ExtendedModifyListener() {
  public void modifyText(ExtendedModifyEvent event) {
    // Determine the ending offset
    int end = event.start + event.length - 1;

    // If they typed something, get it
    if (event.start <= end)
    {
      // Get the text
      String text = styledText.getText(event.start, end);

      // Create a collection to hold the StyleRanges
      java.util.List ranges = new java.util.ArrayList();

      // Turn any punctuation red
      for (int i = 0, n = text.length(); i < n; i++)
      {
        if (PUNCTUATION.indexOf(text.charAt(i)) > -1)
        {
```

```
            ranges.add(new StyleRange(event.start + i, 1, red, null, SWT.BOLD));
        }
    }

    // If we have any ranges to set, set them
    if (!ranges.isEmpty())
    {
        styledText.replaceStyleRanges(event.start, event.length,
            (StyleRange[]) ranges.toArray(new StyleRange[0]));
    }
    }
    }
}
});
```

This handler first determines if the modification was an addition or a deletion. It ignores deletions. For additions, it gets the affected text from the StyledText, and then examines it, character by character, for punctuation. For any punctuation characters, it creates a StyleRange. After examining all the affected text, it calls replaceStyleRanges() to set all the created StyleRange objects into the StyledText. Figure 11-3 shows the SyntaxTest program with its code pasted into itself. Listing 11-2 shows the entire source code for the program.

Listing 11-2. SyntaxTest.java

```
package examples.ch11;

import org.eclipse.swt.SWT;
import org.eclipse.swt.custom.*;
import org.eclipse.swt.graphics.Color;
import org.eclipse.swt.layout.*;
import org.eclipse.swt.widgets.*;

/**
 * This class implements syntax coloring using the StyledText API
 */
public class SyntaxTest {
    // Punctuation
    private static final String PUNCTUATION = "(){};!&|.+-*/";

    // Color for the StyleRanges
    private Color red;

    /**
     * Runs the application
     */
    public void run() {
        Display display = new Display();
        Shell shell = new Shell(display);

        // Get color for style ranges
        red = display.getSystemColor(SWT.COLOR_RED);
```

```
    createContents(shell);
    shell.open();
    while (!shell.isDisposed()) {
      if (!display.readAndDispatch()) {
        display.sleep();
      }
    }

    // No need to dispose red

    display.dispose();
  }

  /**
   * Creates the main window contents
   *
   * @param shell the main window
   */
  private void createContents(Shell shell) {
    shell.setLayout(new FillLayout());

    // Create the StyledText
    final StyledText styledText = new StyledText(shell, SWT.BORDER);

    // Add the syntax coloring handler
    styledText.addExtendedModifyListener(new ExtendedModifyListener() {
      public void modifyText(ExtendedModifyEvent event) {
        // Determine the ending offset
        int end = event.start + event.length - 1;

        // If they typed something, get it
        if (event.start <= end) {
          // Get the text
          String text = styledText.getText(event.start, end);

          // Create a collection to hold the StyleRanges
          java.util.List ranges = new java.util.ArrayList();

          // Turn any punctuation red
          for (int i = 0, n = text.length(); i < n; i++) {
            if (PUNCTUATION.indexOf(text.charAt(i)) > -1) {
              ranges.add(new StyleRange(event.start + i, 1, red, null,
                SWT.BOLD));
            }
          }

          // If we have any ranges to set, set them
          if (!ranges.isEmpty()) {
            styledText.replaceStyleRanges(event.start, event.length,
                (StyleRange[]) ranges.toArray(new StyleRange[0]));
          }
```

```
      }
    }
  });
  }

  /**
   * The application entry point
   *
   * @param args the command line arguments
   */
  public static void main(String[] args) {
    new SyntaxTest().run();
  }
}
```

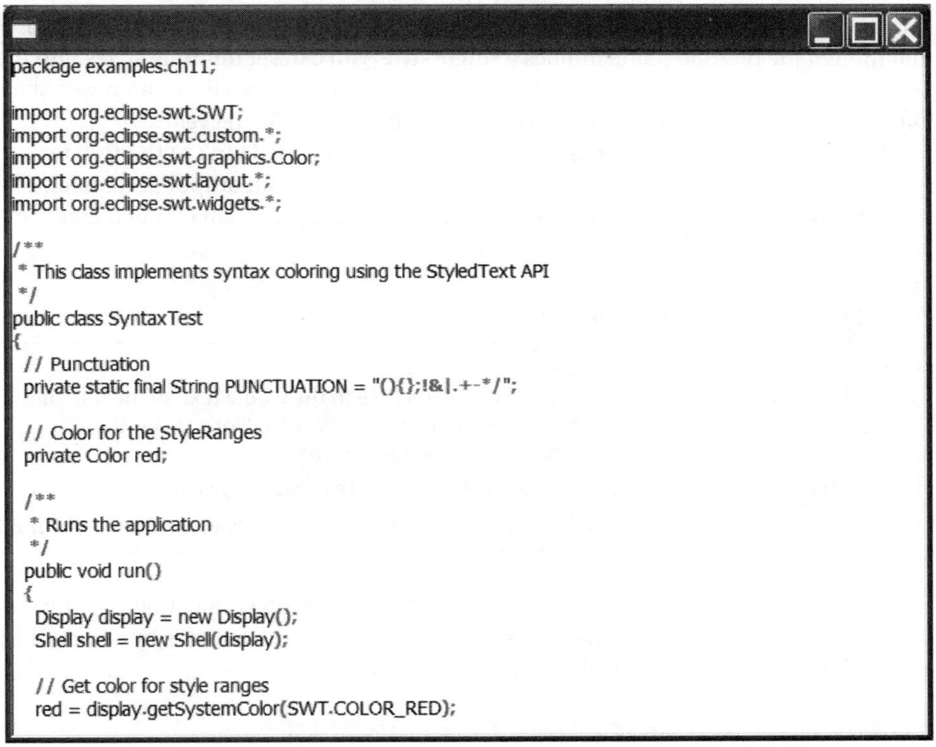

```
package examples.ch11;

import org.eclipse.swt.SWT;
import org.eclipse.swt.custom.*;
import org.eclipse.swt.graphics.Color;
import org.eclipse.swt.layout.*;
import org.eclipse.swt.widgets.*;

/**
 * This class implements syntax coloring using the StyledText API
 */
public class SyntaxTest
{
  // Punctuation
  private static final String PUNCTUATION = "(){};!&|.+-*/";

  // Color for the StyleRanges
  private Color red;

  /**
   * Runs the application
   */
  public void run()
  {
    Display display = new Display();
    Shell shell = new Shell(display);

    // Get color for style ranges
    red = display.getSystemColor(SWT.COLOR_RED);
```

Figure 11-3. Dynamic syntax coloring and styling

Dynamically coloring and styling the punctuation requires a fair amount of work, but it represents the most trivial case: examining single characters. Dynamically coloring and styling whole words becomes more difficult. You must analyze characters surrounding the change to determine if any words were created or deleted, and set or remove StyledRanges accordingly. The pain quickly outweighs the return it brings. The next section bypasses this pain by shunning the API and using a LineStyleListener instead.

Using a LineStyleListener

In contrast to the StyledText API, which requires you to treat the text as a whole and drive the coloring and styling process, LineStyleListeners examine single lines at a time. Further, they don't worry about when and which lines require coloring and styling—the StyledText invokes the LineStyleListener as necessary.

To add a LineStyleListener to a StyledText, use the addLineStyleListener() method. LineStyleListener defines a single method:

```
void lineGetStyle(LineStyleEvent event)
```

Note that, despite the "Get" in the method name, the method returns void. Note, too, that though the method name implies a single style, you can set multiple styles into the line. This method is called when the StyledText is about to draw a line, and needs style information. You return the style information inside the LineStyleEvent.

LineStyleEvent contains the fields listed in Table 11-11. Think of the first two, lineOffset and lineText, as input parameters, and styles as an output parameter. You create StyleRange objects based on the offset and text passed in lineOffset and lineText, respectively, and return them in styles.

Table 11-11. LineStyleEvent *Fields*

Field	Description
int lineOffset	The zero-based offset, relative to the whole text, of the line the StyledText needs style information for. Note: this is the character offset, not the line number.
String lineText	The text of the line the StyledText needs style information for.
StyleRange[] styles	The array that holds the StyleRange objects you create for the line.

The StyleRanges you create include an offset, as described earlier, that's relative to the start of the entire text, not the start of the line. You can calculate this by adding the offset relative to the start of the line to lineOffset, like this:

```
int styleRangeOffset = offsetIntoLine + event.lineOffset;
```

Creating a LineStyleListener

To create a LineStyleListener that sets all "e" characters to red, first create the Styled-Text that uses the LineStyleListener:

```
StyledText styledText = new StyledText(shell, SWT.BORDER | SWT.H_SCROLL
    | SWT.V_SCROLL);
```

Next, add the LineStyleListener to it. Its code scans through the text passed to it, searching for "e" characters. When it finds an "e," it creates a StyleRange for it. An optimization it creates is that, upon finding an "e," it searches for any successive "e" characters and creates one StyleRange for each run of successive "e" characters. The code looks like this:

```
styledText.addLineStyleListener(new LineStyleListener() {
  public void lineGetStyle(LineStyleEvent event) {
    // Create a collection to hold the StyleRanges
    java.util.List styles = new java.util.ArrayList();

    // Iterate through the text
    for (int i = 0, n = event.lineText.length(); i < n; i++)
    {
      // Check for 'e'
      if (event.lineText.charAt(i) == 'e')
      {
        // Found an 'e'; combine all subsequent e's into the same StyleRange
        int start = i;
        for ( ; i < n && event.lineText.charAt(i) == 'e'; i++);

        // Create the StyleRange and add it to the collection
        styles.add(new StyleRange(event.lineOffset + start,
          i - start, red, null));
      }
    }
    // Set the styles for the line
    event.styles = (StyleRange[]) styles.toArray(new StyleRange[0]);
  }
});
```

The most complex part of this code is the search for successive "e" characters, and the subsequent calculations for the length of the created StyleRange. Deleting this optimization and creating new StyleRange objects for each "e" results in a tighter loop:

```
// Iterate through the text
for (int i = 0, n = event.lineText.length(); i < n; i++)
{
  // Check for 'e'
  if (event.lineText.charAt(i) == 'e')
  {
    // Create the StyleRange and add it to the collection
    styles.add(new StyleRange(event.lineOffset + i, 1, red, null));
  }
}
```

The RedEListener program (see Listing 11-3) uses this listener to make all "e" characters red. Figure 11-4 shows the program's window.

Listing 11-3. `RedEListener.java`

```java
package examples.ch11;

import org.eclipse.swt.SWT;
import org.eclipse.swt.custom.*;
import org.eclipse.swt.graphics.Color;
import org.eclipse.swt.layout.*;
import org.eclipse.swt.widgets.*;

/**
 * This class turns 'e' characters red using a LineStyleListener
 */
public class RedEListener {
  // Color for the StyleRanges
  private Color red;

  /**
   * Runs the application
   */
  public void run() {
    Display display = new Display();
    Shell shell = new Shell(display);

    // Get color for style ranges
    red = display.getSystemColor(SWT.COLOR_RED);

    createContents(shell);
    shell.open();
    while (!shell.isDisposed()) {
      if (!display.readAndDispatch()) {
        display.sleep();
      }
    }
    display.dispose();
  }

  /**
   * Creates the main window contents
   *
   * @param shell the main window
   */
  private void createContents(Shell shell) {
    shell.setLayout(new FillLayout());
```

```
    // Create the StyledText
    final StyledText styledText = new StyledText(shell, SWT.BORDER | SWT.H_SCROLL
        | SWT.V_SCROLL);

    // Add the syntax coloring handler
    styledText.addLineStyleListener(new LineStyleListener() {
      public void lineGetStyle(LineStyleEvent event) {
        // Create a collection to hold the StyleRanges
        java.util.List styles = new java.util.ArrayList();

        // Iterate through the text
        for (int i = 0, n = event.lineText.length(); i < n; i++) {
          // Check for 'e'
          if (event.lineText.charAt(i) == 'e') {
            // Found an 'e'; combine all subsequent e's into the same StyleRange
            int start = i;
            for (; i < n && event.lineText.charAt(i) == 'e'; i++);

            // Create the StyleRange and add it to the collection
            styles.add(new StyleRange(event.lineOffset + start, i - start, red,
                null));
          }
        }
        // Set the styles for the line
        event.styles = (StyleRange[]) styles.toArray(new StyleRange[0]);
      }
    });
  }

  /**
   * The application entry point
   *
   * @param args the command line arguments
   */
  public static void main(String[] args) {
    new RedEListener().run();
  }
}
```

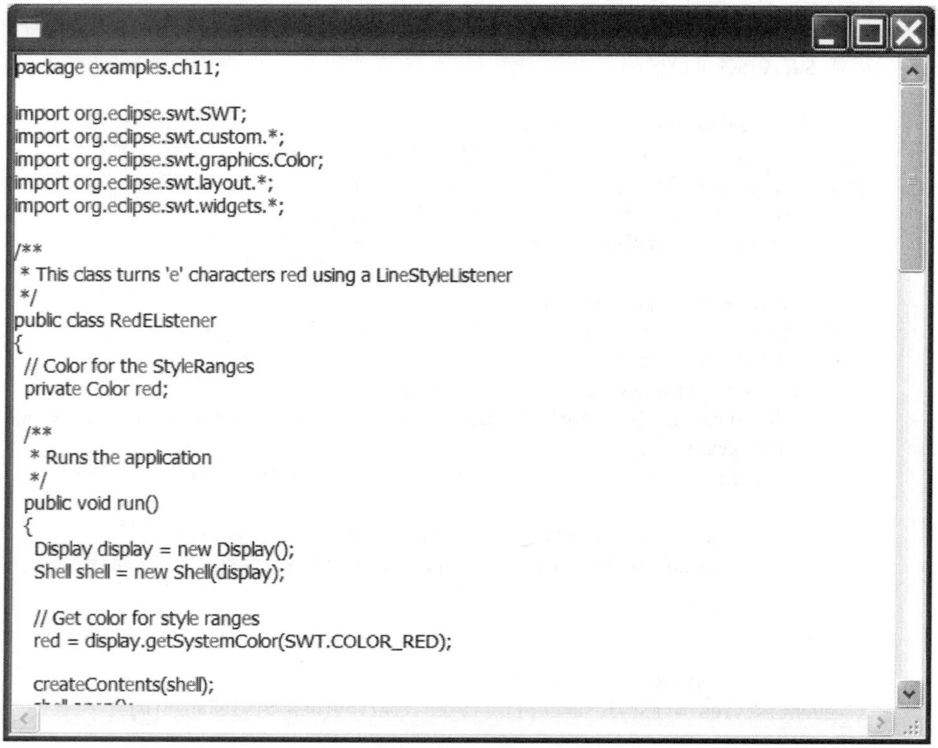

Figure 11-4. Using a LineStyleListener *to turn all the "e" characters red*

Not much work at all, though for admittedly not many results. Red "e" text editors have never garnered much of a following. However, this code provides a solid foundation for doing more with dynamic syntax coloring and styling.

Crossing Lines

LineStyleListener receives only one line at a time, which is usually sufficient for applying StyleRanges. However, many languages, including Java, support comments that span more than one line. Because LineStyleListener doesn't support parsing multiple lines or applying styles across lines, you must determine whether a line is inside or outside a comment yourself. In addition, you might need to manage redrawing, because you might make a line a comment that the StyledText wasn't planning to redraw.

StyledText offers three methods for redrawing its contents. The easiest to use, void redraw(), redraws the entire contents of the StyledText. It's also the most inefficient, because it redraws text that might not need redrawing. To restrict what's redrawn, use one of the other two redrawing methods:

- void redraw(int x, int y, int width, int height, boolean all)

- void redrawRange(int start, int length, boolean clearBackground)

See Table 11-1 for more information on these methods.

The MultiLineComment program displays a StyledText that supports multiline comments, beginning with /* and ending with */. It uses the MultiLineCommentListener class to do the following:

- Recalculate the comment offsets

- Provide the StyleRange information

MultiLineComment, shown in Listing 11-4, registers an instance of MultiLineCommentListener (see Listing 11-5) as its LineStyleListener, like this:

```
final MultiLineCommentListener lineStyleListener =
  new MultiLineCommentListener();
styledText.addLineStyleListener(lineStyleListener);
```

It also registers an ExtendedModifyListener that uses the created instance of MultiLineCommentListener to recalculate the comment offsets. It then redraws all the text. The code looks like this:

```
styledText.addExtendedModifyListener(new ExtendedModifyListener() {
  public void modifyText(ExtendedModifyEvent event) {
    // Recalculate the comments
    lineStyleListener.refreshMultilineComments(styledText.getText());

    // Redraw the text
    styledText.redraw();
  }
});
```

MultiLineCommentListener provides the lineGetStyle() method, which iterates through the collection of comments to determine if the current line is part of a comment. The offsets for each comment are stored in a two-element array: offsets[0] stores the starting offset and offsets[1] stores the ending offset. To determine whether any part of the current line falls within the comment, the code tests that

- the starting offset is before the end of the current line, and

- the ending offset is after the start of the current line.

The code for the test looks like this:

```
if (offsets[0] <= event.lineOffset + length && offsets[1] >= event.lineOffset)
```

If the code determines that the current line contains comments, or is part of a larger comment, it creates the appropriate StyleRanges and adds them to the collection.

Listing 11-4. MultiLineComment.java

```java
package examples.ch11;

import org.eclipse.swt.*;
import org.eclipse.swt.custom.*;
import org.eclipse.swt.layout.*;
import org.eclipse.swt.widgets.*;

/**
 * This program demonstrates multiline comments. It uses MultiLineCommentListener
 * to do the syntax coloring
 */
public class MultiLineComment {
  /**
   * Runs the application
   */
  public void run() {
    Display display = new Display();
    Shell shell = new Shell(display);
    shell.setText("Multiline Comments");
    createContents(shell);
    shell.open();
    while (!shell.isDisposed()) {
      if (!display.readAndDispatch()) {
        display.sleep();
      }
    }
    display.dispose();
  }

  /**
   * Creates the main window contents
   *
   * @param shell the main window
   */
  private void createContents(Shell shell) {
    shell.setLayout(new FillLayout());
    final StyledText styledText = new StyledText(shell, SWT.BORDER | SWT.H_SCROLL
        | SWT.V_SCROLL);

    // Add the line style listener
    final MultiLineCommentListener lineStyleListener =
      new MultiLineCommentListener();
    styledText.addLineStyleListener(lineStyleListener);

    // Add the modification listener
    styledText.addExtendedModifyListener(new ExtendedModifyListener() {
      public void modifyText(ExtendedModifyEvent event) {
        // Recalculate the comments
        lineStyleListener.refreshMultilineComments(styledText.getText());
```

```
            // Redraw the text
            styledText.redraw();
         }
      });
   }

   /**
    * The application entry point
    *
    * @param args the command line arguments
    */
   public static void main(String[] args) {
      new MultiLineComment().run();
   }
}
```

Listing 11-5. MultiLineCommentListener.java

```
package examples.ch11;

import java.util.*;

import org.eclipse.swt.SWT;
import org.eclipse.swt.custom.*;
import org.eclipse.swt.graphics.Color;
import org.eclipse.swt.widgets.Display;

/**
 * This class supports multiline comments. It turns comments green.
 */
public class MultiLineCommentListener implements LineStyleListener {
   // Markers for multiline comments
   private static final String COMMENT_START = "/*";
   private static final String COMMENT_END = "*/";

   // Color for comments
   private static final Color COMMENT_COLOR = Display.getCurrent().getSystemColor(
        SWT.COLOR_DARK_GREEN);

   // Offsets for all multiline comments
   List commentOffsets;

   /**
    * MultilineCommentListener constructor
    */
   public MultiLineCommentListener() {
      commentOffsets = new LinkedList();
   }

   /**
    * Refreshes the offsets for all multiline comments in the parent StyledText.
```

```
 * The parent StyledText should call this whenever its text is modified. Note
 * that this code doesn't ignore comment markers inside strings.
 *
 * @param text the text from the StyledText
 */
public void refreshMultilineComments(String text) {
  // Clear any stored offsets
  commentOffsets.clear();

  // Go through all the instances of COMMENT_START
  for (int pos = text.indexOf(COMMENT_START); pos > -1; pos = text.indexOf(
      COMMENT_START, pos)) {
    // offsets[0] holds the COMMENT_START offset
    // and COMMENT_END holds the ending offset
    int[] offsets = new int[2];
    offsets[0] = pos;

    // Find the corresponding end comment.
    pos = text.indexOf(COMMENT_END, pos);

    // If no corresponding end comment, use the end of the text
    offsets[1] = pos == -1 ? text.length() - 1 :
      pos + COMMENT_END.length() - 1;
    pos = offsets[1];

    // Add the offsets to the collection
    commentOffsets.add(offsets);
  }
}

/**
 * Called by StyledText to get the styles for a line
 *
 * @param event the event
 */
public void lineGetStyle(LineStyleEvent event) {
  // Create a collection to hold the StyleRanges
  List styles = new ArrayList();

  // Store the length for convenience
  int length = event.lineText.length();

  for (int i = 0, n = commentOffsets.size(); i < n; i++) {
    int[] offsets = (int[]) commentOffsets.get(i);

    // If starting offset is past current line--quit
    if (offsets[0] > event.lineOffset + length) break;

    // Check if we're inside a multiline comment
    if (offsets[0] <= event.lineOffset + length
```

```
            && offsets[1] >= event.lineOffset) {
        // Calculate starting offset for StyleRange
        int start = Math.max(offsets[0], event.lineOffset);

        // Calculate length for style range
        int len = Math.min(offsets[1], event.lineOffset + length) - start + 1;

        // Add the style range
        styles.add(new StyleRange(start, len, COMMENT_COLOR, null));
      }
    }

    // Copy all the ranges into the event
    event.styles = (StyleRange[]) styles.toArray(new StyleRange[0]);
  }
}
```

Figure 11-5 shows the MultiLineComment program displaying part of its code. Figure 11-6 shows the same display, but with a comment added.

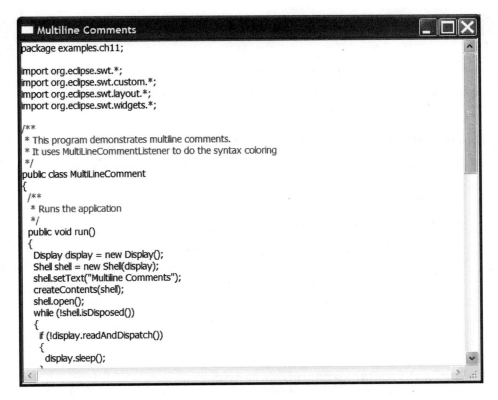

Figure 11-5. The MultiLineComment *program*

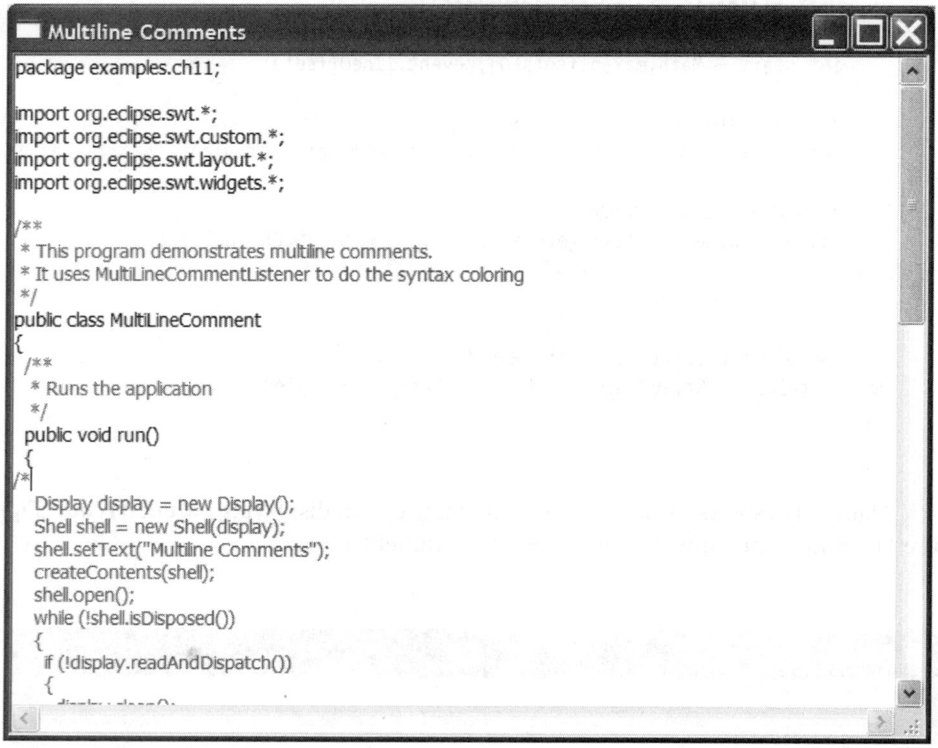

Figure 11-6. The `MultiLineComment` *program with a comment added*

Understanding the Repercussions

When you use a `LineStyleListener`, you shouldn't use the following API calls:

- `getStyleRangeAtOffset(int offset)`

- `StyleRange[] getStyleRanges()`

- `void replaceStyleRanges(int start, int length, StyleRange[] ranges)`

- `void setStyleRange(StyleRange range)`

- `void setStyleRanges(StyleRange[] ranges)`

Mixing these API calls with a `LineStyleListener` is unsupported.

Using a LineBackgroundListener

Although you can set background colors using `StyleRanges`, you can also use `StyledText.setLineBackground()`, detailed in Table 11-1. For example, the following code turns the background blue for the first six lines of the `StyledText`:

```
styledText.setLineBackground(0, 6, blue);
```

Just as you can use either the API or a listener to set StyleRanges, you can use either the API or a listener to set background colors. The listener you use for background colors, called LineBackgroundListener, defines a single method:

```
void lineGetBackground(LineBackgroundEvent event)
```

Background colors set via setLineBackground() or a LineBackgroundListener, in contrast to those in StyleRanges, color the line for the width of the StyledText. Background colors in StyleRanges color the line for the width of the text only.

If you use a LineBackgroundListener, you shouldn't use getLineBackground() or setLineBackground(). Mixing these API calls with a listener is unsupported.

Understanding LineBackgroundEvent

As with LineStyleListener's lineGetStyle(), lineGetBackground() returns its data inside the event. LineBackgroundEvent has two input fields and one output field, listed in Table 11-12.

Table 11-12. LineBackgroundEvent *Fields*

Field	Description
int lineOffset	The zero-based offset, relative to the whole text, of the line the StyledText needs background color information for. Note: this is the character offset, not the line number.
String lineText	The text of the line the StyledText needs background color information for.
Color lineBackground	The field that holds the color you set. The StyledText uses this field to set the background color for the line.

Creating a LineBackgroundListener

To create a LineBackgroundListener, create a new class that defines the lineGetBackground() method, and call addLineBackgroundListener() to add it to your StyledText. For example, the following code adds a listener that turns all lines that contain the text "SWT" red:

```
styledText.addLineBackgroundListener(new LineBackgroundListener() {
  public void lineGetBackground(LineBackgroundEvent event) {
    if (event.lineText.indexOf("SWT") > -1)
    {
      event.lineBackground = red;
    }
  }
});
```

The LineBackgroundListenerTest program in Listing 11-6 uses this listener to turn lines red. Here's the complete code:

Listing 11-6. LineBackgroundListenerTest.java

```java
package examples.ch11;

import org.eclipse.swt.SWT;
import org.eclipse.swt.custom.*;
import org.eclipse.swt.graphics.*;
import org.eclipse.swt.layout.*;
import org.eclipse.swt.widgets.*;

/**
 * This class demonstrates LineBackgroundListeners
 */
public class LineBackgroundListenerTest {
  // The color to use for backgrounds
  Color red;

  /**
   * Runs the application
   */
  public void run() {
    Display display = new Display();
    red = display.getSystemColor(SWT.COLOR_RED);
    Shell shell = new Shell(display);
    createContents(shell);
    shell.open();
    while (!shell.isDisposed()) {
      if (!display.readAndDispatch()) {
        display.sleep();
      }
    }
    display.dispose();
  }

  /**
   * Creates the main window's contents
   *
   * @param shell the main window
   */
  private void createContents(Shell shell) {
    shell.setLayout(new FillLayout());
    StyledText styledText = new StyledText(shell, SWT.BORDER);

    // Add the line background listener
    styledText.addLineBackgroundListener(new LineBackgroundListener() {
      public void lineGetBackground(LineBackgroundEvent event) {
        if (event.lineText.indexOf("SWT") > -1) {
```

```
        event.lineBackground = red;
      }
    }
  });

}

/**
 * The application entry point
 *
 * @param args the command line arguments
 */
public static void main(String[] args) {
  new LineBackgroundListenerTest().run();
}
}
```

Figure 11-7 shows this program's main window with some text typed, including lines that contain "SWT."

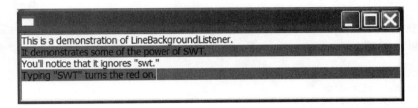

Figure 11-7. A LineBackgroundListener

Adding Complexity

You can push a little farther into StyledText to create highly functional text editors. The Poor Man's Programmer's Editor (PmpEditor) demonstrates some of the more advanced capabilities of StyledText. It supports common clipboard operations. It supports printing. It adds two custom key bindings: Ctrl+K deletes the next word, and Ctrl+$ moves the caret to the end of the current line. It supports word wrap. It supports multilevel undo. It maintains and reports statistics about the current file in a status bar at the bottom of the window.

It also supports syntax highlighting for any file extension via properties files. Properties files for Java source files and MS-DOS batch files are included (java.properties and bat.properties). You may create your own properties files for different extensions. The properties file for a file extension must have the same name as the extension, followed by .properties. The file name for .java files, for example, is java.properties. The format is as follows:

```
comment=(the marker for single line comments)
multilinecommentstart=(the marker for starting a multiline comment)
multilinecommentend=(the marker for ending a multiline comment)
keywords=(a space-delimited list of keywords)
punctuation=(all punctuation characters, concatenated together)
```

You'll find that the syntax highlighting trips occasionally. For example, type **_break**
in a .java file, and you'll see that "break" appears as a keyword. The highlighting works
pretty well for most purposes, but has purposely been kept relatively simple.

This program doesn't compete with real editors such as Visual SlickEdit, CodeWright,
vi, GNU Emacs, jEdit, or even the editor embedded in the Eclipse IDE. It's not guaranteed
to make your programming life easier, and you'll probably never use it as your primary
source code editor. Read through its code, though, for a deeper understanding of how to
use StyledText in your programs.

The PmpEditor class in Listing 11-7 provides the main program, creating the view
and controlling user interaction.

Listing 11-7. PmpEditor.java

```
package examples.ch11;

import java.io.IOException;
import java.util.Stack;

import org.eclipse.swt.SWT;
import org.eclipse.swt.custom.*;
import org.eclipse.swt.events.*;
import org.eclipse.swt.graphics.*;
import org.eclipse.swt.layout.*;
import org.eclipse.swt.printing.*;
import org.eclipse.swt.widgets.*;

/**
 * This program demonstrates StyledText
 */
public class PmpEditor {
  // The number of operations that can be undone
  private static final int UNDO_LIMIT = 500;

  // Contains a reference to this application
  private static PmpEditor app;

  // Contains a reference to the main window
  private Shell shell;

  // Displays the file
  private StyledText st;

  // The full path of the current file
  private String filename;
```

```java
// The font for the StyledText
private Font font;

// The label to display statistics
private Label status;

// The print options and printer
private StyledTextPrintOptions options;
private Printer printer;

// The stack used to store the undo information
private Stack changes;

// Flag to set before performaing an undo, so the undo
// operation doesn't get stored with the rest of the undo
// information
private boolean ignoreUndo = false;

// Syntax data for the current extension
private SyntaxData sd;

// Line style listener
private PmpeLineStyleListener lineStyleListener;

/**
 * Gets the reference to this application
 *
 * @return HexEditor
 */
public static PmpEditor getApp() {
  return app;
}

/**
 * Constructs a PmpEditor
 */
public PmpEditor() {
  app = this;
  changes = new Stack();

  // Set up the printing options
  options = new StyledTextPrintOptions();
  options.footer = StyledTextPrintOptions.SEPARATOR
      + StyledTextPrintOptions.PAGE_TAG + StyledTextPrintOptions.SEPARATOR
      + "Confidential";
}

/**
 * Runs the application
 */
public void run() {
  Display display = new Display();
  shell = new Shell(display);
```

```java
  // Choose a monospaced font
  font = new Font(display, "Terminal", 12, SWT.NONE);

  createContents(shell);
  shell.open();
  while (!shell.isDisposed()) {
    if (!display.readAndDispatch()) {
      display.sleep();
    }
  }
  font.dispose();
  display.dispose();
  if (printer != null)
    printer.dispose();
}

/**
 * Creates the main window's contents
 *
 * @param shell the main window
 */
private void createContents(Shell shell) {
  // Set the layout and the menu bar
  shell.setLayout(new FormLayout());
  shell.setMenuBar(new PmpEditorMenu(shell).getMenu());

  // Create the status bar
  status = new Label(shell, SWT.BORDER);
  FormData data = new FormData();
  data.left = new FormAttachment(0, 0);
  data.right = new FormAttachment(100, 0);
  data.bottom = new FormAttachment(100, 0);
  data.height = status.computeSize(SWT.DEFAULT, SWT.DEFAULT).y;
  status.setLayoutData(data);

  // Create the styled text
  st = new StyledText(shell, SWT.BORDER | SWT.H_SCROLL | SWT.V_SCROLL);
  data = new FormData();
  data.left = new FormAttachment(0);
  data.right = new FormAttachment(100);
  data.top = new FormAttachment(0);
  data.bottom = new FormAttachment(status);
  st.setLayoutData(data);

  // Set the font
  st.setFont(font);

  // Add Brief delete next word
  // Use SWT.MOD1 instead of SWT.CTRL for portability
  st.setKeyBinding('k' | SWT.MOD1, ST.DELETE_NEXT);

  // Add vi end of line (kind of)
  // Use SWT.MOD1 instead of SWT.CTRL for portability
  // Use SWT.MOD2 instead of SWT.SHIFT for portability
```

```
    // Shift+4 is $
    st.setKeyBinding('4' | SWT.MOD1 | SWT.MOD2, ST.LINE_END);

    // Handle key presses
    st.addKeyListener(new KeyAdapter() {
      public void keyPressed(KeyEvent event) {
        // Update the status bar
        updateStatus();
      }
    });

    // Handle text modifications
    st.addModifyListener(new ModifyListener() {
      public void modifyText(ModifyEvent event) {
        // Update the status bar
        updateStatus();

        // Update the comments
        if (lineStyleListener != null) {
          lineStyleListener.refreshMultilineComments(st.getText());
          st.redraw();
        }
      }
    });

    // Store undo information
    st.addExtendedModifyListener(new ExtendedModifyListener() {
      public void modifyText(ExtendedModifyEvent event) {
        if (!ignoreUndo) {
          // Push this change onto the changes stack
          changes.push(new TextChange(event.start, event.length,
              event.replacedText));
          if (changes.size() > UNDO_LIMIT) changes.remove(0);
        }
      }
    });

    // Update the title bar and the status bar
    updateTitle();
    updateStatus();
  }

/**
 * Opens a file
 */
public void openFile() {
  FileDialog dlg = new FileDialog(shell);
  String temp = dlg.open();
  if (temp != null) {
    try {
      // Get the file's contents
      String text = PmpeIoManager.getFile(temp);
```

```
            // File loaded, so save the file name
            filename = temp;

            // Update the syntax properties to use
            updateSyntaxData();

            // Put the new file's data in the StyledText
            st.setText(text);

            // Update the title bar
            updateTitle();

            // Delete any undo information
            changes.clear();
        } catch (IOException e) {
          showError(e.getMessage());
        }
      }
    }
  }

  /**
   * Saves a file
   */
  public void saveFile() {
    if (filename == null) {
      saveFileAs();
    } else {
      try {
        // Save the file and update the title bar based on the new file name
        PmpeIoManager.saveFile(filename, st.getText().getBytes());
        updateTitle();
      } catch (IOException e) {
        showError(e.getMessage());
      }
    }
  }

  /**
   * Saves a file under a different name
   */
  public void saveFileAs() {
    SafeSaveDialog dlg = new SafeSaveDialog(shell);
    if (filename != null) {
      dlg.setFileName(filename);
    }
    String temp = dlg.open();
    if (temp != null) {
      filename = temp;

      // The extension may have changed; update the syntax data accordingly
      updateSyntaxData();
      saveFile();
    }
  }
```

```
/**
 * Prints the document to the default printer
 */
public void print() {
  if (printer == null)
    printer = new Printer();
  options.header = StyledTextPrintOptions.SEPARATOR + filename
      + StyledTextPrintOptions.SEPARATOR;
  st.print(printer, options).run();
}

/**
 * Cuts the current selection to the clipboard
 */
public void cut() {
  st.cut();
}

/**
 * Copies the current selection to the clipboard
 */
public void copy() {
  st.copy();
}

/**
 * Pastes the clipboard's contents
 */
public void paste() {
  st.paste();
}

/**
 * Selects all the text
 */
public void selectAll() {
  st.selectAll();
}

/**
 * Undoes the last change
 */
public void undo() {
  // Make sure undo stack isn't empty
  if (!changes.empty()) {
    // Get the last change
    TextChange change = (TextChange) changes.pop();

    // Set the flag. Otherwise, the replaceTextRange call will get placed
    // on the undo stack
    ignoreUndo = true;
```

```
        // Replace the changed text
        st.replaceTextRange(change.getStart(), change.getLength(), change
            .getReplacedText());

        // Move the caret
        st.setCaretOffset(change.getStart());

        // Scroll the screen
        st.setTopIndex(st.getLineAtOffset(change.getStart()));
        ignoreUndo = false;
    }
}

/**
 * Toggles word wrap
 */
public void toggleWordWrap() {
    st.setWordWrap(!st.getWordWrap());
}

/**
 * Gets the current word wrap settings
 *
 * @return boolean
 */
public boolean getWordWrap() {
    return st.getWordWrap();
}

/**
 * Shows an about box
 */
public void about() {
    MessageBox mb = new MessageBox(shell, SWT.ICON_INFORMATION | SWT.OK);
    mb.setMessage("Poor Man's Programming Editor");
    mb.open();
}

/**
 * Updates the title bar
 */
private void updateTitle() {
    String fn = filename == null ? "Untitled" : filename;
    shell.setText(fn + " -- PmPe");
}

/**
 * Updates the status bar
 */
private void updateStatus() {
    // Show the offset into the file, the total number of characters in the file,
    // the current line number (1-based) and the total number of lines
    StringBuffer buf = new StringBuffer();
```

```
      buf.append("Offset: ");
      buf.append(st.getCaretOffset());
      buf.append("\tChars: ");
      buf.append(st.getCharCount());
      buf.append("\tLine: ");
      buf.append(st.getLineAtOffset(st.getCaretOffset()) + 1);
      buf.append(" of ");
      buf.append(st.getLineCount());
      status.setText(buf.toString());
  }

  /**
   * Updates the syntax data based on the filename's extension
   */
  private void updateSyntaxData() {
    // Determine the extension of the current file
    String extension = "";
    if (filename != null) {
      int pos = filename.lastIndexOf(".");
      if (pos > -1 && pos < filename.length() - 2) {
        extension = filename.substring(pos + 1);
      }
    }

    // Get the syntax data for the extension
    sd = SyntaxManager.getSyntaxData(extension);

    // Reset the line style listener
    if (lineStyleListener != null) {
      st.removeLineStyleListener(lineStyleListener);
    }
    lineStyleListener = new PmpeLineStyleListener(sd);
    st.addLineStyleListener(lineStyleListener);

    // Redraw the contents to reflect the new syntax data
    st.redraw();
  }

  /**
   * Shows an error message
   *
   * @param error the text to show
   */
  private void showError(String error) {
    MessageBox mb = new MessageBox(shell, SWT.ICON_ERROR | SWT.OK);
    mb.setMessage(error);
    mb.open();
  }

  /**
   * The application entry point
   *
   * @param args the command line arguments
```

```
    */
  public static void main(String[] args) {
    new PmpEditor().run();
  }
}
```

The PmpEditorMenu class in Listing 11-8 provides the main menu for the application. It creates all the menu options and the selection listeners for those options. All the listeners call into methods in PmpEditor.

Listing 11-8. PmpEditorMenu.java

```java
package examples.ch11;

import org.eclipse.swt.*;
import org.eclipse.swt.events.*;
import org.eclipse.swt.widgets.*;

/**
 * This class contains the menu for the Poor Man's Programming Editor application
 */
public class PmpEditorMenu {
  // The underlying menu this class wraps
  Menu menu = null;

  /**
   * Constructs a PmpEditorMenu
   *
   * @param shell the parent shell
   */
  public PmpEditorMenu(final Shell shell) {
    // Create the menu
    menu = new Menu(shell, SWT.BAR);

    // Create the File top-level menu
    MenuItem item = new MenuItem(menu, SWT.CASCADE);
    item.setText("File");
    Menu dropMenu = new Menu(shell, SWT.DROP_DOWN);
    item.setMenu(dropMenu);

    // Create File->Open
    item = new MenuItem(dropMenu, SWT.NULL);
    item.setText("Open...\tCtrl+O");
    item.setAccelerator(SWT.CTRL + 'O');
    item.addSelectionListener(new SelectionAdapter() {
      public void widgetSelected(SelectionEvent event) {
        PmpEditor.getApp().openFile();
      }
    });

    // Create File->Save
    item = new MenuItem(dropMenu, SWT.NULL);
```

```
item.setText("Save\tCtrl+S");
item.setAccelerator(SWT.CTRL + 'S');
item.addSelectionListener(new SelectionAdapter() {
  public void widgetSelected(SelectionEvent event) {
    PmpEditor.getApp().saveFile();
  }
});

// Create File->Save As
item = new MenuItem(dropMenu, SWT.NULL);
item.setText("Save As...");
item.addSelectionListener(new SelectionAdapter() {
  public void widgetSelected(SelectionEvent event) {
    PmpEditor.getApp().saveFileAs();
  }
});

new MenuItem(dropMenu, SWT.SEPARATOR);

// Create File->Print
item = new MenuItem(dropMenu, SWT.NULL);
item.setText("Print\tCtrl+P");
item.setAccelerator(SWT.CTRL + 'P');
item.addSelectionListener(new SelectionAdapter() {
  public void widgetSelected(SelectionEvent event) {
    PmpEditor.getApp().print();
  }
});

new MenuItem(dropMenu, SWT.SEPARATOR);

// Create File->Exit
item = new MenuItem(dropMenu, SWT.NULL);
item.setText("Exit\tAlt+F4");
item.addSelectionListener(new SelectionAdapter() {
  public void widgetSelected(SelectionEvent event) {
    shell.close();
  }
});

// Create Edit
item = new MenuItem(menu, SWT.CASCADE);
item.setText("Edit");
dropMenu = new Menu(shell, SWT.DROP_DOWN);
item.setMenu(dropMenu);

// Create Edit->Cut
item = new MenuItem(dropMenu, SWT.NULL);
item.setText("Cut\tCtrl+X");
item.setAccelerator(SWT.CTRL + 'X');
item.addSelectionListener(new SelectionAdapter() {
```

```java
  public void widgetSelected(SelectionEvent event) {
    PmpEditor.getApp().cut();
  }
});

// Create Edit->Copy
item = new MenuItem(dropMenu, SWT.NULL);
item.setText("Copy\tCtrl+C");
item.setAccelerator(SWT.CTRL + 'C');
item.addSelectionListener(new SelectionAdapter() {
  public void widgetSelected(SelectionEvent event) {
    PmpEditor.getApp().copy();
  }
});

// Create Edit->Paste
item = new MenuItem(dropMenu, SWT.NULL);
item.setText("Paste\tCtrl+V");
item.setAccelerator(SWT.CTRL + 'V');
item.addSelectionListener(new SelectionAdapter() {
  public void widgetSelected(SelectionEvent event) {
    PmpEditor.getApp().paste();
  }
});

new MenuItem(dropMenu, SWT.SEPARATOR);

// Create Select All
item = new MenuItem(dropMenu, SWT.NULL);
item.setText("Select All\tCtrl+A");
item.setAccelerator(SWT.CTRL + 'A');
item.addSelectionListener(new SelectionAdapter() {
  public void widgetSelected(SelectionEvent event) {
    PmpEditor.getApp().selectAll();
  }
});

new MenuItem(dropMenu, SWT.SEPARATOR);

// Create Undo
item = new MenuItem(dropMenu, SWT.NULL);
item.setText("Undo\tCtrl+Z");
item.setAccelerator(SWT.CTRL + 'Z');
item.addSelectionListener(new SelectionAdapter() {
  public void widgetSelected(SelectionEvent event) {
    PmpEditor.getApp().undo();
  }
});

new MenuItem(dropMenu, SWT.SEPARATOR);
```

```
    // Create Word Wrap
    final MenuItem wwItem = new MenuItem(dropMenu, SWT.CHECK);
    wwItem.setText("Word Wrap\tCtrl+W");
    wwItem.setAccelerator(SWT.CTRL + 'W');
    wwItem.addSelectionListener(new SelectionAdapter() {
      public void widgetSelected(SelectionEvent event) {
        PmpEditor.getApp().toggleWordWrap();
      }
    });
    wwItem.addArmListener(new ArmListener() {
      public void widgetArmed(ArmEvent event) {
        wwItem.setSelection(PmpEditor.getApp().getWordWrap());
      }
    });

    // Create Help
    item = new MenuItem(menu, SWT.CASCADE);
    item.setText("Help");
    dropMenu = new Menu(shell, SWT.DROP_DOWN);
    item.setMenu(dropMenu);

    // Create Help->About
    item = new MenuItem(dropMenu, SWT.NULL);
    item.setText("About\tCtrl+A");
    item.setAccelerator(SWT.CTRL + 'A');
    item.addSelectionListener(new SelectionAdapter() {
      public void widgetSelected(SelectionEvent event) {
        PmpEditor.getApp().about();
      }
    });
  }

  /**
   * Gets the underlying menu
   *
   * @return Menu
   */
  public Menu getMenu() {
    return menu;
  }
}
```

The PmpeIoManager class in Listing 11-9 loads and saves files for editing.

Listing 11-9. PmpeIoManager.java

```
package examples.ch11;

import java.io.*;
```

```java
/**
 * This class handles loading and saving files
 */
public class PmpeIoManager {
  /**
   * Gets a file (loads it) from the filesystem
   *
   * @param filename the full path of the file
   * @return String
   * @throws IOException if file cannot be loaded
   */
  public static String getFile(String filename) throws IOException {
    InputStream in = new BufferedInputStream(new FileInputStream(filename));
    StringBuffer buf = new StringBuffer();
    int c;
    while ((c = in.read()) != -1) {
      buf.append((char) c);
    }
    return buf.toString();
  }

  /**
   * Saves a file
   *
   * @param filename the full path of the file to save
   * @param data the data to save
   * @throws IOException if file cannot be saved
   */
  public static void saveFile(String filename, byte[] data) throws IOException {
    File outputFile = new File(filename);
    FileOutputStream out = new FileOutputStream(outputFile);
    out.write(data);
    out.close();
  }
}
```

Listing 11-10 shows the TextChange class, which contains each discrete change in the editor. The editor uses this information to perform undo operations.

Listing 11-10. TextChange.java

```java
package examples.ch11;

/**
 * This class contains a single change, used for Undo processing
 */
public class TextChange {
  // The starting offset of the change
  private int start;
```

```java
    // The length of the change
    private int length;

    // The replaced text
    String replacedText;

    /**
     * Constructs a TextChange
     *
     * @param start the starting offset of the change
     * @param length the length of the change
     * @param replacedText the text that was replaced
     */
    public TextChange(int start, int length, String replacedText) {
      this.start = start;
      this.length = length;
      this.replacedText = replacedText;
    }

    /**
     * Returns the start
     *
     * @return int
     */
    public int getStart() {
      return start;
    }

    /**
     * Returns the length
     *
     * @return int
     */
    public int getLength() {
      return length;
    }

    /**
     * Returns the replacedText
     *
     * @return String
     */
    public String getReplacedText() {
      return replacedText;
    }
}
```

The SyntaxData class (see Listing 11-11) contains extension-specific information for syntax coloring and styling. Each loaded file extension has its own instance of SyntaxData (or null if no properties file exists for that extension).

Listing 11-11. SyntaxData.java

```java
package examples.ch11;

import java.util.*;

/**
 * This class contains information for syntax coloring and styling for an
 * extension
 */
public class SyntaxData {
  private String extension;
  private Collection keywords;
  private String punctuation;
  private String comment;
  private String multiLineCommentStart;
  private String multiLineCommentEnd;

  /**
   * Constructs a SyntaxData
   *
   * @param extension the extension
   */
  public SyntaxData(String extension) {
    this.extension = extension;
  }

  /**
   * Gets the extension
   *
   * @return String
   */
  public String getExtension() {
    return extension;
  }

  /**
   * Gets the comment
   *
   * @return String
   */
  public String getComment() {
    return comment;
  }

  /**
   * Sets the comment
   *
   * @param comment The comment to set.
   */
  public void setComment(String comment) {
    this.comment = comment;
  }
```

```java
/**
 * Gets the keywords
 *
 * @return Collection
 */
public Collection getKeywords() {
  return keywords;
}

/**
 * Sets the keywords
 *
 * @param keywords The keywords to set.
 */
public void setKeywords(Collection keywords) {
  this.keywords = keywords;
}

/**
 * Gets the multiline comment end
 *
 * @return String
 */
public String getMultiLineCommentEnd() {
  return multiLineCommentEnd;
}

/**
 * Sets the multiline comment end
 *
 * @param multiLineCommentEnd The multiLineCommentEnd to set.
 */
public void setMultiLineCommentEnd(String multiLineCommentEnd) {
  this.multiLineCommentEnd = multiLineCommentEnd;
}

/**
 * Gets the multiline comment start
 *
 * @return String
 */
public String getMultiLineCommentStart() {
  return multiLineCommentStart;
}

/**
 * Sets the multiline comment start
 *
 * @param multiLineCommentStart The multiLineCommentStart to set.
 */
public void setMultiLineCommentStart(String multiLineCommentStart) {
  this.multiLineCommentStart = multiLineCommentStart;
}
```

```
/**
 * Gets the punctuation
 *
 * @return String
 */
public String getPunctuation() {
  return punctuation;
}

/**
 * Sets the punctuation
 *
 * @param punctuation The punctuation to set.
 */
public void setPunctuation(String punctuation) {
  this.punctuation = punctuation;
}
}
```

The SyntaxManager class in Listing 11-12 loads the syntax properties files and converts them into SyntaxData instances. It caches each file it loads to avoid having to reload properties files. If no properties file exists for an extension, it doesn't create a SyntaxData instance and no syntax coloring or styling is performed on the file.

Listing 11-12. SyntaxManager.java

```
package examples.ch11;

import java.util.*;

/**
 * This class manages the syntax coloring and styling data
 */
public class SyntaxManager {
  // Lazy cache of SyntaxData objects
  private static Map data = new Hashtable();

  /**
   * Gets the syntax data for an extension
   */
  public static synchronized SyntaxData getSyntaxData(String extension) {
    // Check in cache
    SyntaxData sd = (SyntaxData) data.get(extension);
    if (sd == null) {
      // Not in cache; load it and put in cache
      sd = loadSyntaxData(extension);
      if (sd != null) data.put(sd.getExtension(), sd);
    }
    return sd;
  }
```

```
/**
 * Loads the syntax data for an extension
 *
 * @param extension the extension to load
 * @return SyntaxData
 */
private static SyntaxData loadSyntaxData(String extension) {
  SyntaxData sd = null;
  try {
    ResourceBundle rb = ResourceBundle.getBundle("examples.ch11." + extension);
    sd = new SyntaxData(extension);
    sd.setComment(rb.getString("comment"));
    sd.setMultiLineCommentStart(rb.getString("multilinecommentstart"));
    sd.setMultiLineCommentEnd(rb.getString("multilinecommentend"));

    // Load the keywords
    Collection keywords = new ArrayList();
    for (StringTokenizer st = new StringTokenizer(rb.getString("keywords"),
      " "); st.hasMoreTokens();) {
      keywords.add(st.nextToken());
    }
    sd.setKeywords(keywords);

    // Load the punctuation
    sd.setPunctuation(rb.getString("punctuation"));
  } catch (MissingResourceException e) {
    // Ignore
  }
  return sd;
}
}
```

Finally, the `PmpeLineStyleListener` class in Listing 11-13 implements the syntax coloring and styling for the editor.

Listing 11-13. `PmpeLineStyleListener.java`

```
package examples.ch11;

import java.util.*;

import org.eclipse.swt.SWT;
import org.eclipse.swt.custom.*;
import org.eclipse.swt.graphics.Color;
import org.eclipse.swt.widgets.Display;

/**
 * This class performs the syntax highlighting and styling for Pmpe
 */
public class PmpeLineStyleListener implements LineStyleListener {
  // Colors
```

```
private static final Color COMMENT_COLOR = Display.getCurrent().getSystemColor(
    SWT.COLOR_DARK_GREEN);
private static final Color COMMENT_BACKGROUND = Display.getCurrent()
    .getSystemColor(SWT.COLOR_GRAY);
private static final Color PUNCTUATION_COLOR = Display.getCurrent()
    .getSystemColor(SWT.COLOR_DARK_CYAN);
private static final Color KEYWORD_COLOR = Display.getCurrent().getSystemColor(
    SWT.COLOR_DARK_MAGENTA);

// Holds the syntax data
private SyntaxData syntaxData;

// Holds the offsets for all multiline comments
List commentOffsets;

/**
 * PmpeLineStyleListener constructor
 *
 * @param syntaxData the syntax data to use
 */
public PmpeLineStyleListener(SyntaxData syntaxData) {
  this.syntaxData = syntaxData;
  commentOffsets = new LinkedList();
}

/**
 * Refreshes the offsets for all multiline comments in the parent StyledText.
 * The parent StyledText should call this whenever its text is modified. Note
 * that this code doesn't ignore comment markers inside strings.
 *
 * @param text the text from the StyledText
 */
public void refreshMultilineComments(String text) {
  // Clear any stored offsets
  commentOffsets.clear();

  if (syntaxData != null) {
    // Go through all the instances of COMMENT_START
    for (int pos = text.indexOf(syntaxData.getMultiLineCommentStart());
      pos > -1; pos = text.indexOf(syntaxData.getMultiLineCommentStart(), pos))
    {
      // offsets[0] holds the COMMENT_START offset
      // and COMMENT_END holds the ending offset
      int[] offsets = new int[2];
      offsets[0] = pos;

      // Find the corresponding end comment.
      pos = text.indexOf(syntaxData.getMultiLineCommentEnd(), pos);

      // If no corresponding end comment, use the end of the text
      offsets[1] = pos == -1 ? text.length() - 1 : pos
          + syntaxData.getMultiLineCommentEnd().length() - 1;
      pos = offsets[1];
```

```
        // Add the offsets to the collection
        commentOffsets.add(offsets);
      }
    }
}

/**
 * Checks to see if the specified section of text begins inside a multiline
 * comment. Returns the index of the closing comment, or the end of the line if
 * the whole line is inside the comment. Returns -1 if the line doesn't begin
 * inside a comment.
 *
 * @param start the starting offset of the text
 * @param length the length of the text
 * @return int
 */
private int getBeginsInsideComment(int start, int length) {
    // Assume section doesn't being inside a comment
    int index = -1;

    // Go through the multiline comment ranges
    for (int i = 0, n = commentOffsets.size(); i < n; i++) {
        int[] offsets = (int[]) commentOffsets.get(i);

        // If starting offset is past range, quit
        if (offsets[0] > start + length) break;

        // Check to see if section begins inside a comment
        if (offsets[0] <= start && offsets[1] >= start) {
            // It does; determine if the closing comment marker is inside
            // this section
            index = offsets[1] > start + length ? start + length : offsets[1]
                + syntaxData.getMultiLineCommentEnd().length() - 1;
        }
    }
    return index;
}

/**
 * Called by StyledText to get styles for a line
 */
public void lineGetStyle(LineStyleEvent event) {
    // Only do styles if syntax data has been loaded
    if (syntaxData != null) {
        // Create collection to hold the StyleRanges
        List styles = new ArrayList();

        int start = 0;
        int length = event.lineText.length();

        // Check if line begins inside a multiline comment
        int mlIndex = getBeginsInsideComment(event.lineOffset, event.lineText
            .length());
        if (mlIndex > -1) {
```

```
      // Line begins inside multiline comment; create the range
      styles.add(new StyleRange(event.lineOffset, mlIndex - event.lineOffset,
          COMMENT_COLOR, COMMENT_BACKGROUND));
      start = mlIndex;
    }
    // Do punctuation, single-line comments, and keywords
    while (start < length) {
      // Check for multiline comments that begin inside this line
      if (event.lineText.indexOf(syntaxData.getMultiLineCommentStart(), start)
        == start) {
        // Determine where comment ends
        int endComment = event.lineText.indexOf(syntaxData
            .getMultiLineCommentEnd(), start);

        // If comment doesn't end on this line, extend range to end of line
        if (endComment == -1)
          endComment = length;
        else
          endComment += syntaxData.getMultiLineCommentEnd().length();
        styles.add(new StyleRange(event.lineOffset + start, endComment - start,
            COMMENT_COLOR, COMMENT_BACKGROUND));

        // Move marker
        start = endComment;
      }
      // Check for single line comments
      else if (event.lineText.indexOf(syntaxData.getComment(), start) == start)
      {
        // Comment rest of line
        styles.add(new StyleRange(event.lineOffset + start, length - start,
            COMMENT_COLOR, COMMENT_BACKGROUND));

        // Move marker
        start = length;
      }
      // Check for punctuation
      else if (syntaxData.getPunctuation()
          .indexOf(event.lineText.charAt(start)) > -1) {
        // Add range for punctuation
        styles.add(new StyleRange(event.lineOffset + start, 1,
            PUNCTUATION_COLOR, null));
        ++start;
      } else if (Character.isLetter(event.lineText.charAt(start))) {
        // Get the next word
        StringBuffer buf = new StringBuffer();
        int i = start;

        // Call any consecutive letters a word
        for (; i < length && Character.isLetter(event.lineText.charAt(i)); i++)
        {
          buf.append(event.lineText.charAt(i));
        }
```

```
          // See if the word is a keyword
          if (syntaxData.getKeywords().contains(buf.toString())) {
            // It's a keyword; create the StyleRange
            styles.add(new StyleRange(event.lineOffset + start, i - start,
                KEYWORD_COLOR, null, SWT.BOLD));
          }
          // Move the marker to the last char (the one that wasn't a letter)
          // so it can be retested in the next iteration through the loop
          start = i;
        } else
          // It's nothing we're interested in; advance the marker
          ++start;
      }

      // Copy the StyleRanges back into the event
      event.styles = (StyleRange[]) styles.toArray(new StyleRange[0]);
    }
  }
}
```

Figure 11-8 shows The Poor Man's Programming Editor's main window, containing the source code for PmpeLineStyleListener.java.

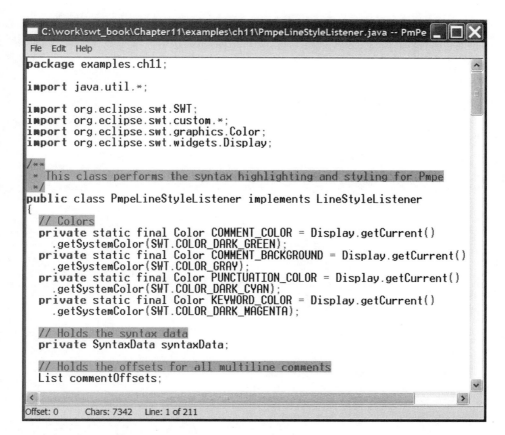

Figure 11-8. The Poor Man's Programming Editor

Summary

You can add powerful text editing to your application simply by adding a StyledText widget. You get clipboard operations, word wrap, custom key binding, and a host of other features for free or almost free. However, adding colors and styles increases your workload significantly. Using listeners eases the burden, but expect to do some work to convert StyledText into a competitive source code editor with dynamic syntax coloring and styling.

CHAPTER 12

Advanced
Topics

SMALL TOUCHES can make the difference between applications that get used and applications that get uninstalled. For example, an e-mail client might have a polished interface, perform efficiently, and offer powerful search capabilities. However, if users can't organize their e-mails by dragging them and dropping them onto storage folders, or can't print out their e-mails or address books, they might turn to a different e-mail client. This chapter examines advanced topics that might supply the necessary touch for your applications.

Dragging and Dropping

Drag and Drop (DND) allows users to exchange data among graphical components. The components can belong to the same application or different applications. Although the semantics and implementation of DND might vary drastically from system to system, SWT's creators have succeeded in abstracting these differences and creating a robust and straightforward DND framework. Take advantage of DND to provide users the interoperability they've come to expect from applications.

A DND operation involves dragging something from a component and dropping it on another component. The component you drag from is called the drag source, and the component you drop on is called the drop target, also known as a source and sink, respectively. This terminology applies universally to all components in the windowing system, not just those in SWT or Java applications. SWT supports DND operations between any windowing system components.

Drag Source

SWT uses the DragSource class to represent drag sources. It offers a single constructor:

```
DragSource(Control control, int style)
```

It converts the specified control into a drag source, so you can drag from it. Table 12-1 lists the valid styles for the style parameter, which you can combine using the bitwise OR operator. Table 12-2 lists DragSource's methods.

Table 12-1. DragSource *Styles*

Style	Description
DND.DROP_NONE	No drag or drop supported
DND.DROP_COPY	Copies the dragged data to the drop target
DND.DROP_MOVE	Moves the dragged data to the drop target
DND.DROP_LINK	Creates a link from the dragged data to the drop target

Table 12-2. DragSource *Methods*

Method	Description
void addDragListener (DragSourceListener listener)	Adds the specified listener to the list of listeners notified before, during, and after a DND operation
Control getControl()	Returns the control wrapped by this DragSource
Transfer[] getTransfer()	Returns the list of data types supported by this DragSource
void removeDragListener (DragSourceListener listener)	Removes the specified listener from the notification list
void setTransfer(Transfer[] transferAgents)	Sets the data types this DragSource supports

This brief API reveals two crucial parts of drag operations: Transfer objects and DragSourceListeners. Transfer objects, used for drop operations as well, convert data from its Java representation to the underlying platform's data representation, and vice versa. You can write your own Transfer classes, but you'll usually use one of SWT's concrete Transfer classes—usually FileTransfer, to drag and drop files, or TextTransfer, to drag and drop text. The array of Transfer objects you pass to setTransfer() describes the types of data you can drag from the drag source. These Transfer objects follow the singleton pattern, so use their static getInstance() methods to get instances to pass to setTransfer(). For example, to create a drag source that you can drag either text or files from, use code such as this:

```
DragSource ds = new DragSource(control, DND.DROP_COPY);
ds.setTransfer(new Transfer[] { FileTransfer.getInstance(),
  TextTransfer.getInstance() });
```

The other crucial drag component, DragSourceListener, dictates how your drag sources react to drag operations. You can add multiple drag source listeners to a drag source. Table 12-3 lists DragSourceListener's methods. You can implement the interface directly, or extend from SWT's DragSourceAdapter class to avoid writing implementations of methods for which you don't need any behavior.

Table 12-3. DragSourceListener *Methods*

Method	Description
void dragStart(DragSourceEvent event)	Called when a drag operation begins. You can cancel the drag by setting event.doIt to false.
void dragSetData(DragSourceEvent event)	Called when a drag operation requests the data, usually when the data has been dropped. You should set event.data to the data dragged, so the drop target can do something with it.
void dragFinished(DragSourceEvent event)	Called when a drag operation ends. Performs any final activity for your application, such as deleting the source data of a move.

 CAUTION   *When you implement any of the functions in* DragSourceListener *or its peer* DropTargetListener, *you must handle all exceptions within the function. Due to low-level differences in implementations, the library traps exceptions and this is your only opportunity to handle them gracefully.*

Drop Target

To implement drop targets, SWT uses the DropTarget class. Its semantics mirror those of DragSource, and its lone constructor looks like this:

DropTarget(Control control, int style)

In parallel with DragSource, DropTarget converts the specified control into a drop target. Refer to Table 12-1 to see the available constants for style. Table 12-4 lists DropTarget's methods.

Table 12-4. DropTarget *Methods*

Method	Description
void addDropListener (DropTargetListener listener)	Adds the specified listener to the list of listeners notified before, during, and after a drop operation
Control getControl()	Returns the control wrapped by this DropTarget
Transfer[] getTransfer()	Returns the list of data types supported by this DropTarget
void removeDropListener (DropTargetListener listener)	Removes the specified listener from the notification list
void setTransfer(Transfer[] transferAgents)	Sets the data types this DropTarget supports

Use the same `Transfer` objects discussed in conjunction with `DragSource` for `DropTarget`, passing the ones you wish to support to `setTransfer()`. For example, to create a drop target that supports having files or text dropped on it, use code such as this:

```
DropTarget dt = new DropTarget(control, DND.DROP_COPY);
dt.setTransfer(new Transfer[] { FileTransfer.getInstance(),
  TextTransfer.getInstance() });
```

As with drag sources, a listener dictates how your drop target reacts to drop operations. You can add multiple drop listeners to a single drop target. You can implement `DropTargetListener` directly, or start from the `DropTargetAdapter` class, which provides empty implementations of all `DropTargetListener` methods. Table 12-5 lists `DropTargetListener`'s methods.

Table 12-5. `DropTargetListener` *Methods*

Method	Description
void dragEnter(DropTargetEvent event)	Called when the cursor drags data into the bounds of your drop target
void dragLeave(DropTargetEvent event)	Called when the cursor leaves the bounds of your drop target
void dragOperationChanged (DropTargetEvent event)	Called when the user changes the DND operation, usually by changing the pressed modifier keys
void dragOver(DropTargetEvent event)	Called as the cursor drags data within the bounds of your drop target
void drop(DropTargetEvent event)	Called when data has been dropped on your drop target
void dropAccept(DropTargetEvent event)	Called when the drop operation is about to happen. You can veto the drop by setting event.detail to DND.DROP_NONE

Witnessing a Drop

Many applications offer, in addition to the File ➤ Open menu, the ability to open files by dragging and dropping the files onto the applications' main windows. This section adds that ability to Chapter 11's Poor Man's Programming Editor. You can drag files from any file manager that supports dragging and drop them on PmpEditor's main window. All necessary modifications occur in the `PmpEditor.java` file.

To begin, import the DND library:

```
import org.eclipse.swt.dnd.*;
```

Next, create the drop target. Use the application's existing `StyledText` control, which virtually fills the main application window, as the drop target. You also must create the transfer types and a DropTargetListener implementation and add them to the drop target. The following code creates the drop target, the transfer types, and the listener as an anonymous inner class, derived from DropTargetAdapter. Add this code to the end of the createContents() method:

```
// Create the drag and drop types
Transfer[] types = new Transfer[] { FileTransfer.getInstance()};

// Create the drop target
DropTarget target = new DropTarget(st, DND.DROP_MOVE | DND.DROP_COPY
  | DND.DROP_DEFAULT);
target.setTransfer(types);
target.addDropListener(new DropTargetAdapter() {
  /**
   * Called when the cursor enters
   */
  public void dragEnter(DropTargetEvent event) {
    // Allow a copy
    if (event.detail == DND.DROP_DEFAULT) {
      event.detail = (event.operations & DND.DROP_COPY) != 0 ? DND.DROP_COPY
        : DND.DROP_NONE;
    }
  }

  /**
   * Called when the cursor drags over the target
   */
  public void dragOver(DropTargetEvent event) {
    // Give feedback
    event.feedback = DND.FEEDBACK_SELECT | DND.FEEDBACK_SCROLL;
  }

  /**
   * Called when user drops the files
   */
  public void drop(DropTargetEvent event) {
    // See if it's a file
    if (FileTransfer.getInstance().isSupportedType(event.currentDataType)) {
      String[] files = (String[]) event.data;
      // Since we support only one file, open the first one
      if (files.length > 0) openFile(files[0]);
    }
  }
});
```

Finally, you must provide an openFile() method that accepts a file name, so it can open a dropped file. Change the existing openFile() implementation to accept a String, and add the following code to test whether to open a file selection dialog box.

```
public void openFile(String temp) {
  if (temp == null) {
    FileDialog dlg = new FileDialog(shell);
    temp = dlg.open();
  }

  if (temp != null) {
    // The rest of the existing code goes here
```

Add a no-parameter openFile() method for File ➤ Open that calls the other openFile():

```
public void openFile() {
  openFile(null);
}
```

Figure 12-1 shows the program with a file dragged onto it. Note the plus sign adjoining the cursor.

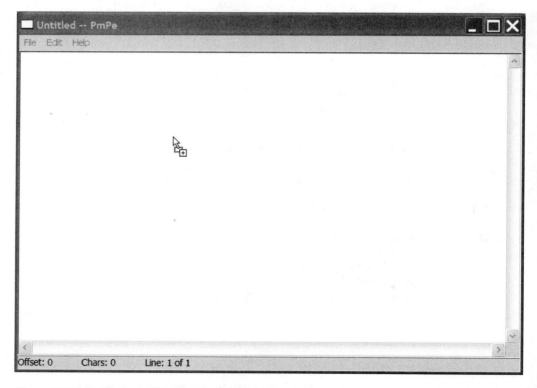

Figure 12-1. Dragging a file onto PmpEditor

Dragging Data

The SnippetBoard program demonstrates dragging data. It creates a table and seeds it with a few code snippets. You can drag the snippets and drop them onto the same table. You can also drag snippets from SnippetBoard and drop them on any program that accepts dragged text. Finally, you can drag text from any program that allows it and drop the text onto SnippetBoard, to add the text to the table. Listing 12-1 contains the program's code.

Listing 12-1. SnippetBoard.java

```java
package examples.ch12;

import org.eclipse.swt.*;
import org.eclipse.swt.dnd.*;
import org.eclipse.swt.layout.*;
import org.eclipse.swt.widgets.*;

/**
 * This program illustrates dragging
 */
public class SnippetBoard {
  /**
   * Runs the application
   */
  public void run() {
    Display display = new Display();
    Shell shell = new Shell(display);
    createContents(shell);
    shell.open();

    while (!shell.isDisposed()) {
      if (!display.readAndDispatch()) {
        display.sleep();
      }
    }

    display.dispose();
  }

  private void createContents(Shell shell) {
    shell.setLayout(new FillLayout());

    Table table = new Table(shell, SWT.BORDER | SWT.H_SCROLL | SWT.V_SCROLL);

    // Create the types
    Transfer[] types = new Transfer[] { TextTransfer.getInstance()};

    // Create the drag source
    DragSource source = new DragSource(table, DND.DROP_MOVE | DND.DROP_COPY);
    source.setTransfer(types);
    source.addDragListener(new DragSourceAdapter() {
      public void dragSetData(DragSourceEvent event) {
        // Get the selected items in the drag source
        DragSource ds = (DragSource) event.widget;
```

```
      Table table = (Table) ds.getControl();
      TableItem[] selection = table.getSelection();

      // Create a buffer to hold the selected items and fill it
      StringBuffer buff = new StringBuffer();
      for (int i = 0, n = selection.length; i < n; i++) {
        buff.append(selection[i].getText());
      }

      // Put the data into the event
      event.data = buff.toString();
    }
  });

  // Create the drop target
  DropTarget target = new DropTarget(table,
    DND.DROP_MOVE | DND.DROP_COPY | DND.DROP_DEFAULT);
  target.setTransfer(types);
  target.addDropListener(new DropTargetAdapter() {
    public void dragEnter(DropTargetEvent event) {
      if (event.detail == DND.DROP_DEFAULT) {
        event.detail = (event.operations & DND.DROP_COPY) != 0 ? DND.DROP_COPY
          : DND.DROP_NONE;
      }

      // Allow dropping text only
      for (int i = 0, n = event.dataTypes.length; i < n; i++) {
        if (TextTransfer.getInstance().isSupportedType(event.dataTypes[i])) {
          event.currentDataType = event.dataTypes[i];
        }
      }
    }

    public void dragOver(DropTargetEvent event) {
      // Provide visual feedback
      event.feedback = DND.FEEDBACK_SELECT | DND.FEEDBACK_SCROLL;
    }

    public void drop(DropTargetEvent event) {
      // If any text was dropped . . .
      if (TextTransfer.getInstance().isSupportedType(event.currentDataType)) {
        // Get the dropped data
        DropTarget target = (DropTarget) event.widget;
        Table table = (Table) target.getControl();
        String data = (String) event.data;

        // Create a new item in the table to hold the dropped data
        TableItem item = new TableItem(table, SWT.NONE);
        item.setText(new String[] { data});
        table.redraw();
      }
    }
  });
```

```
    TableColumn column = new TableColumn(table, SWT.NONE);

    // Seed the table
    TableItem item = new TableItem(table, SWT.NONE);
    item.setText(new String[] { "private static final int"});
    item = new TableItem(table, SWT.NONE);
    item.setText(new String[] { "String"});
    item = new TableItem(table, SWT.BORDER);
    item.setText(new String[] { "private static void main(String[] args) {"});

    column.pack();
  }

  /**
   * The application entry point
   * @param args the command line arguments
   */
  public static void main(String[] args) {
    new SnippetBoard().run();
  }
}
```

Figure 12-2 shows SnippetBoard in action.

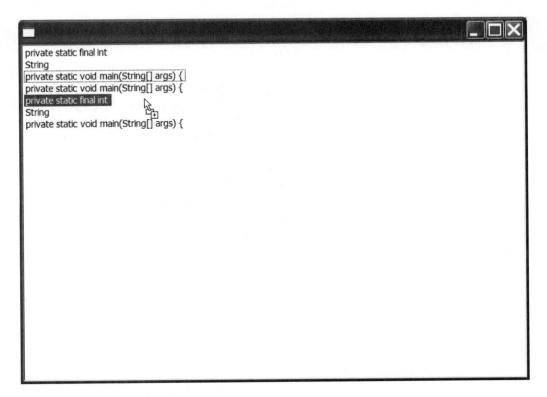

Figure 12-2. SnippetBoard

Printing

Despite prognostications of paperless offices, application users generally expect the option of printing their data onto paper. SWT's StyledText widget directly supports printing its contents, but if your data doesn't sit inside a StyledText widget, you must delve into SWT's printing API. Three classes, all found in the org.eclipse.swt.printing package, make up this API: Printer, PrinterData, and PrintDialog.

Printer descends from Device. As such, you can create a graphical context from it and draw on the graphical context. You can draw text, images, or both, using the standard drawing methods explained in Chapter 10. You create a Printer object using either its empty constructor, or the one that takes a PrinterData object. As with the other Device class you've used, Display, you must dispose Printer objects you create. However, Printer's needs diverge from Display's because you're drawing on a physical, more permanent surface. Table 12-6 lists the API developed to meet those needs.

Table 12-6. Printer Methods

Method	Description
void cancelJob()	Cancels a print job.
Rectangle computeTrim(int x, int y, int width, int height)	Returns the total page size in pixels for this Printer, including both printable and nonprintable areas.
void endJob()	Ends the current print job.
void endPage()	Ends the current page.
Rectangle getBounds()	Returns the page size in pixels for this Printer.
Rectangle getClientArea()	Returns the size of the printable area on the page, in pixels, for this Printer.
static PrinterData getDefaultPrinterData()	Returns the information that describes the default printer, or null if no printers are available.
Point getDPI()	Returns the horizontal and vertical DPI of this Printer. The returned Point's x value contains the horizontal DPI, and its y value contains the vertical DPI.
PrinterData getPrinterData()	Returns the data that describes this Printer and print job.
static PrinterData[] getPrinterList()	Returns an array of PrinterData objects that represent all the Printer devices available on the system.
boolean startJob(String jobName)	Starts a print job with the specified job name. Returns true if the job starts successfully. Otherwise, returns false.
boolean startPage()	Starts a new page. Returns true if the page starts successfully. Otherwise, returns false.

The standard pattern for printing involves the following steps:

1. Create a Printer object.

2. Start a print job.

3. Create a GC.

4. Start a page.

5. Draw on the page.

6. End the page.

7. Repeat steps 4–6 as necessary.

8. End the print job.

9. Clean up.

For example, the following code draws some text on a Printer (or, in other words, prints some text onto a piece of paper), and then cleans up after itself:

```
Printer printer = new Printer();
if (printer.startJob("Printing . . .")) {
  GC gc = new GC(printer);
  if (printer.startPage()) {
    gc.drawText("Hello, World!", 20, 20);
    printer.endPage();
  }
  gc.dispose();
}
printer.dispose();
```

Each time you create a print job, you create an instance of a PrinterData object to describe the print job. The PrinterData object encapsulates information pertaining to the printer on which this print job runs: the number of pages to print, the selected pages to print, and so on. Table 12-7 lists PrinterData's members.

Table 12-7. PrinterData *Members*

Member	Description
boolean collate	If true, collates printed pages. Otherwise, doesn't collate.
int copyCount	The number of copies to print.
String driver	The name of the printer driver.
int endPage	When scope is PAGE_RANGE, the number of the last page in the print range.
String fileName	When printToFile is true, the file name to print to.
String name	The name of the printer.
boolean printToFile	If true, prints the document to a file. Otherwise, prints to a printer.
int scope	The scope or range of pages to print. See Table 12-8 for supported values.
int startPage	When scope is PAGE_RANGE, the number of the first page in the page range.

PrinterData's scope member describes the range of pages to print, whether it's all pages, a range of pages denoted by startPage and endPage, or just the selected portion of the document. Table 12-8 lists the valid values for scope.

Table 12-8. PrinterData *Scope Constants*

Constant	Description
static int ALL_PAGES	Sets print scope to all pages in the document
static int PAGE_RANGE	Sets print scope to the range beginning with startPage and ending with endPage
static int SELECTION	Sets print scope to the selected portion of the document

You can create a PrinterData object directly, making assumptions about what values the user would like concerning which printer to use, which pages to print, and so forth. Usually, however, you'll use SWT's PrintDialog class, which displays the standard print dialog and allows users to make their own print selections. Figure 12-3 shows PrintDialog on Windows XP.

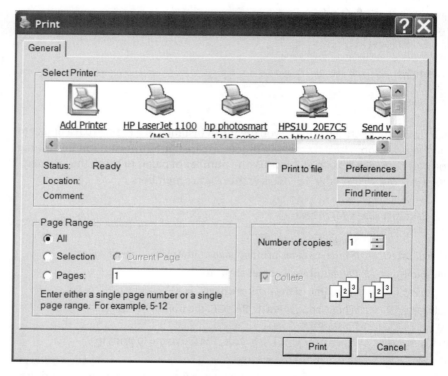

Figure 12-3. The PrintDialog *class*

You use PrintDialog in the same way that you use other dialog classes: instantiate, call open(), and use the return value from open(). PrintDialog.open() returns a PrinterData object, so a typical usage looks like this:

```
PrintDialog dlg = new PrintDialog(shell);
PrinterData printerData = dlg.open();
if (printerData != null) {
  Printer printer = new Printer(printerData);
  // Use printer . . .
  printer.dispose();
}
```

You might want to select some options programmatically before displaying the dialog. For example, you might detect that the user has selected some text in your application, so you guess that the desired scope is PrinterData.SELECTION. To set and get options, use PrintDialog's API, listed in Table 12-9.

Table 12-9. PrintDialog *Methods*

Method	Description
int getEndPage()	Returns the selected end page.
boolean getPrintToFile()	Returns true if the user selected to print to a file. Otherwise, returns false.
int getScope()	Returns the selected scope. See Table 12-8 for valid values.
int getStartPage()	Returns the selected start page.
PrinterData open()	Opens the dialog and returns the selected options as a PrinterData object.
void setEndPage(int endPage)	Sets the end page.
void setPrintToFile(boolean printToFile)	Sets the print to file setting.
void setScope(int scope)	Sets the scope. See Table 12-8 for valid values.
void setStartPage(int startPage)	Sets the start page.

Determining Where to Print

The more permanent nature of ink on paper, as opposed to pixels on a screen, elevates the importance of proper placement of your drawing. You don't get "do overs" with paper. Also, different printers have different capabilities, including where they can print. You can't just pass arbitrary (x, y) values to your drawing calls that work on your machine— you must determine, at run time, how to draw to the selected printer, and adjust your drawing accordingly.

To determine the entire printable area of the page for the selected printer, call Printer's getClientArea() method, which returns a Rectangle object that contains the printable area's boundaries. Sometimes users will want to print to the entire printable surface of each piece of paper, but often they'll want to specify different margins. Because you specify drawing locations using pixels, you might try to force users to specify margins in pixels. However, not only will you confuse and confound your users, but also, not all pixels are the same size. Different printers render the same pixel-based margins in different sizes, depending on the printers' capabilities. Users expect to specify margins using units of measurements that remain consistent no matter the printer: inches or centimeters. How do you translate pixels to inches or centimeters?

The Printer class has a method—getDPI()—that neatly performs these translations. Because getDPI() returns a Point whose x value contains the number of dots, or pixels, per inch that the printer prints horizontally in an inch, and whose y value contains the vertical counterpart, you can use the returned Point to determine your margins precisely. For example, to get half-inch margins, divide each dimension of the returned Point in half to get the number of pixels of spacing to add. If you need centimeters instead of inches, multiply each inch value by 2.54 to get the number of centimeters.

You might naively add your margins to the values returned by getClientArea(), but this spaces margins from the printable area of the page, not from the edges of the paper. Users expect margins to space from the edges of the paper, so you must do a little extra work. Specifically, you must call Printer.computeTrim() to get the entire area of the paper, and add your margins to that. For example, the following code places one-inch margins on the page:

```
Point dpi = printer.getDPI(); // Get the DPI
Rectangle rect = printer.getClientArea(); // Get the printable area
Rectangle trim = printer.computeTrim(0, 0, 0, 0); // Get the whole page
int left = trim.x + dpi.x; // Set left margin one inch from left side of paper
int top = trim.y + dpi.y; // Set top margin
int right = (rect.width + trim.x + trim.width) - dpi.x; // 1st three values give
    // you the right side of the page
int bottom = (rect.height + trim.y + trim.height) - dpi.y; // Set bottom margin
```

You then use left, top, right, and bottom as the boundaries that govern where you draw on the page.

Printing Text

Use GC.drawString() or GC.drawText() to print text. If all your lines of text fit neatly on the page, both horizontally and vertically, you'll find printing text straightforward and simple. Generally, however, your text won't always fit so neatly, and you'll have to reformat the text, wrapping to the next line, to produce the expected result.

The TextPrinterExample program in Listing 12-2 demonstrates how to wrap text on word boundaries to fit the target printer and page. It displays a file selection dialog, prompting you to select a file to print. It then displays a printer dialog, requesting the target printer. It then prints the file.

Note that the program displays no main window, so it prints the document in the same thread as the main program. In typical programs, you'll usually spawn your printing code in a separate thread, so you don't tie up the UI.

Listing 12-2. TextPrinterExample.java

```java
package examples.ch12;

import org.eclipse.swt.*;
import org.eclipse.swt.graphics.*;
import org.eclipse.swt.printing.*;
import org.eclipse.swt.widgets.*;

import java.io.*;

/**
 * This class demonstrates printing text
 */
public class TextPrinterExample {
  /**
   * Runs the application
   */
  public void run() {
    Display display = new Display();
    Shell shell = new Shell(display);

    // Get the file to print
    FileDialog fileChooser = new FileDialog(shell, SWT.OPEN);
    String fileName = fileChooser.open();
    if (fileName != null) {
      // Have user select a printer
      PrintDialog dialog = new PrintDialog(shell);
      PrinterData printerData = dialog.open();
      if (printerData != null) {
        // Create the printer
        Printer printer = new Printer(printerData);

        try {
          // Print the contents of the file
          new WrappingPrinter(printer, fileName,
            getFileContents(fileName)).print();
        } catch (Exception e) {
          MessageBox mb = new MessageBox(shell, SWT.ICON_ERROR | SWT.OK);
          mb.setMessage(e.getMessage());
          mb.open();
        }

        // Dispose the printer
        printer.dispose();
      }
    }
    display.dispose();
  }
```

```
    /**
     * Read in the file and return its contents
     * @param fileName
     * @return
     * @throws FileNotFoundException
     * @throws IOException
     */
    private String getFileContents(String fileName)
    throws FileNotFoundException, IOException {
      StringBuffer contents = new StringBuffer();
      BufferedReader reader = null;
      try {
        // Read in the file
        reader = new BufferedReader(new FileReader(fileName));
        while (reader.ready()) {
          contents.append(reader.readLine());
          contents.append("\n"); // Throw away LF chars, and just replace CR
        }
      } finally {
        if (reader != null) try {
          reader.close();
        } catch (IOException e) {}
      }
      return contents.toString();
    }

    /**
     * The application entry point
     *
     * @param args the command line arguments
     */
    public static void main(String[] args) {
      new TextPrinterExample().run();
    }
}

/**
 * This class performs the printing, wrapping text as necessary
 */
class WrappingPrinter {
  private Printer printer; // The printer
  private String fileName; // The name of the file to print
  private String contents; // The contents of the file to print
  private GC gc; // The GC to print on
  private int xPos, yPos; // The current x and y locations for print
  private Rectangle bounds; // The boundaries for the print
  private StringBuffer buf; // Holds a word at a time
  private int lineHeight; // The height of a line of text

  /**
   * WrappingPrinter constructor
   * @param printer the printer
```

```
 * @param fileName the fileName
 * @param contents the contents
 */
WrappingPrinter(Printer printer, String fileName, String contents) {
  this.printer = printer;
  this.fileName = fileName;
  this.contents = contents;
}

/**
 * Prints the file
 */
void print() {
  // Start the print job
  if (printer.startJob(fileName)) {
    // Determine print area, with margins
    bounds = computePrintArea(printer);
    xPos = bounds.x;
    yPos = bounds.y;

    // Create the GC
    gc = new GC(printer);

    // Determine line height
    lineHeight = gc.getFontMetrics().getHeight();

    // Determine tab width--use three spaces for tabs
    int tabWidth = gc.stringExtent("   ").x;

    // Print the text
    printer.startPage();
    buf = new StringBuffer();
    char c;
    for (int i = 0, n = contents.length(); i < n; i++) {
      // Get the next character
      c = contents.charAt(i);

      // Check for newline
      if (c == '\n') {
        printBuffer();
        printNewline();
      }
      // Check for tab
      else if (c == '\t') {
        xPos += tabWidth;
      }
      else {
        buf.append(c);
        // Check for space
        if (Character.isWhitespace(c)) {
          printBuffer();
        }
```

```
        }
      }
      printer.endPage();
      printer.endJob();
      gc.dispose();
    }
  }

  /**
   * Prints the contents of the buffer
   */
  void printBuffer() {
    // Get the width of the rendered buffer
    int width = gc.stringExtent(buf.toString()).x;

    // Determine if it fits
    if (xPos + width > bounds.x + bounds.width) {
      // Doesn't fit--wrap
      printNewline();
    }

    // Print the buffer
    gc.drawString(buf.toString(), xPos, yPos, false);
    xPos += width;
    buf.setLength(0);
  }

  /**
   * Prints a newline
   */
  void printNewline() {
    // Reset x and y locations to next line
    xPos = bounds.x;
    yPos += lineHeight;

    // Have we gone to the next page?
    if (yPos > bounds.y + bounds.height) {
      yPos = bounds.y;
      printer.endPage();
      printer.startPage();
    }
  }

  /**
   * Computes the print area, including margins
   * @param printer the printer
   * @return Rectangle
   */
  Rectangle computePrintArea(Printer printer) {
    // Get the printable area
    Rectangle rect = printer.getClientArea();
```

```
    // Compute the trim
    Rectangle trim = printer.computeTrim(0, 0, 0, 0);

    // Get the printer's DPI
    Point dpi = printer.getDPI();

    // Calculate the printable area, using 1 inch margins
    int left = trim.x + dpi.x;
    if (left < rect.x) left = rect.x;
    int right = (rect.width + trim.x + trim.width) - dpi.x;
    if (right > rect.width) right = rect.width;

    int top = trim.y + dpi.y;
    if (top < rect.y) top = rect.y;
    int bottom = (rect.height + trim.y + trim.height) - dpi.y;
    if (bottom > rect.height) bottom = rect.height;

    return new Rectangle(left, top, right - left, bottom - top);
  }
}
```

Printing Graphics

To print graphics, you must address the same physical paper constraints that you do with text. You calculate the margins the same way, of course, but you likely scale any images according to the printer's DPI to fit the page. After calculating the scale factor, you pass it to the drawing methods that accept scale factors.

The ImagePrinterExample program in Listing 12-3 prints the contents of an image file, scaling it to fit the page. It first presents a file selection dialog, allowing you to select an image. It then presents a printer selection dialog so you can select the desired printer. It then prints the image.

Listing 12-3. ImagePrinterExample.java

```java
package examples.ch12;

import org.eclipse.swt.*;
import org.eclipse.swt.graphics.*;
import org.eclipse.swt.printing.*;
import org.eclipse.swt.widgets.*;

/**
 * This class demonstrates printing images
 */
public class ImagePrinterExample {
  /**
   * The application entry point
   * @param args the command line arguments
   */
```

```java
public static void main(String[] args) {
  Display display = new Display();
  Shell shell = new Shell(display, SWT.NONE);

  try {
    // Prompt the user for an image file
    FileDialog fileChooser = new FileDialog(shell, SWT.OPEN);
    String fileName = fileChooser.open();

    if (fileName == null) { return; }

    // Load the image
    ImageLoader loader = new ImageLoader();
    ImageData[] imageData = loader.load(fileName);

    if (imageData.length > 0) {
      // Show the Choose Printer dialog
      PrintDialog dialog = new PrintDialog(shell, SWT.NULL);
      PrinterData printerData = dialog.open();

      if (printerData != null) {
        // Create the printer object
        Printer printer = new Printer(printerData);

        // Calculate the scale factor between the screen resolution and printer
        // resolution in order to size the image correctly for the printer
        Point screenDPI = display.getDPI();
        Point printerDPI = printer.getDPI();
        int scaleFactor = printerDPI.x / screenDPI.x;

        // Determine the bounds of the entire area of the printer
        Rectangle trim = printer.computeTrim(0, 0, 0, 0);

        // Start the print job
        if (printer.startJob(fileName)) {
          if (printer.startPage()) {
            GC gc = new GC(printer);
            Image printerImage = new Image(printer, imageData[0]);

            // Draw the image
            gc.drawImage(printerImage, 0, 0, imageData[0].width,
              imageData[0].height, -trim.x, -trim.y,
              scaleFactor * imageData[0].width,
              scaleFactor * imageData[0].height);

            // Clean up
            printerImage.dispose();
            gc.dispose();
            printer.endPage();
          }
        }
```

```
            // End the job and dispose the printer
            printer.endJob();
            printer.dispose();
         }
      }
   } catch (Exception e) {
      MessageBox messageBox = new MessageBox(shell, SWT.ICON_ERROR);
      messageBox.setMessage("Error printing test image");
      messageBox.open();
   }
 }
}
```

Web Browsing

Delivering dynamic content to your applications through the Internet can differentiate them from the heap of me-too programs. SWT offers a Web-browsing component—one that supports both Hypertext Transfer Protocol (HTTP) and Hypertext Transfer Protocol Secure (HTTPS), as well as JavaScript—that you can embed in your applications, along with an API for controlling that component. Although published, the browser API is still in flux, and might change up to the release of SWT 3.0.

 CAUTION *The Web browser API might change. The present chapter accurately reflects the API at the time of this writing.*

Only the following platforms support the Web browser component:

- Windows (requires Internet Explorer 5.0 or greater)

- Linux GTK (requires Mozilla 1.5 GTK2)

- Linux Motif (requires Mozilla 1.5 GTK2)

- Mac OS X (requires Safari)

- Photon

- QNX

Getting the Web browser component to work under Linux presents some challenges; see the sidebar "Using the SWT Browser Under Linux" for more details.

Using the SWT Browser Under Linux

Whereas running SWT's Web browsing component under Windows requires only that Internet Explorer 5.0 or later be installed, running under Linux can prove daunting. The SWT FAQ found at http://dev.eclipse.org/viewcvs/index.cgi/%7Echeckout%7E/platform-swt-home/faq.html#mozillaredhat states the following:

Q: Which version of Mozilla do I need to install to run the SWT Browser on Linux GTK or Linux Motif (RedHat 9 users)?

A: You need the Mozilla version 1.5 GTK2 RPMs for RedHat9. These RPMs can be downloaded from the Mozilla ftp site.

- Uninstall any prior Mozilla version

- Install Mozilla into the default folder set by the RPM (/usr/lib/mozilla-1.5). If you install Mozilla into a non default folder, you will need to set the LD_LIBRARY_PATH to your custom mozilla folder before executing an application using the SWT Browser widget.

- Run Mozilla once. Verify the application opens HTML documents correctly. Check the version number (1.5) in the Mozilla About dialog. Verify you now have the following Mozilla configuration file: /etc/gre.conf. You can now use the SWT Browser widget.

Q: Which version of Mozilla do I need to install to run the SWT Browser on Linux GTK or Linux Motif (non RedHat 9 users)?

A: You need the Mozilla version 1.5 GTK2.

- Check if your Linux distribution provides Mozilla 1.5 GTK2. Install this build if it is available. Otherwise you need to download the Mozilla 1.5 source code from the Mozilla website and follow their build instructions. In this case you need to configure the Mozilla makefile to build a Mozilla GTK2 non debug build.

- Uninstall any prior Mozilla version

- You must ensure the Mozilla 1.5 GTK2 build is installed under the /usr/lib/mozilla-1.5 folder. If you install Mozilla into a different folder, you will need to set the LD_LIBRARY_PATH to your custom mozilla folder before executing an application using the SWT Browser widget.

- Run Mozilla once. Verify the application runs correctly and check the version number (1.5) in the Mozilla About dialog. Verify you now have the following configuration file /etc/gre.conf. You can now use the SWT Browser widget.

Follow these instructions before attempting to use SWT's Web browsing component in your applications. Understand as well that your target audience must also install Mozilla 1.5 GTK2.

The `org.eclipse.swt.browser.Browser` class represents the Web browser component, and shouldn't be subclassed. It offers a single constructor:

```
Browser(Composite parent, int style)
```

You can pass `SWT.BORDER` for style to create a border around the browser, or `SWT.NONE` for no border. And no, you can't currently use Mozilla on Windows, however much the mix of open source and closed source might rankle.

A Web browser, left to itself, remains conspicuously blank and uninspiring. It depends on Web pages to provide content. Browser's method for opening a Web page, setUrl(), takes a Uniform Resource Locator (URL) as a parameter. It returns a boolean for success or failure, but it measures as success only that the URL-opening mechanism worked. Hitting an unreachable or nonexistent URL, one that returns a 404 to the browser, still returns true.

 CAUTION   *Although* setUrl() *returns success or failure, it doesn't indicate if a page was successfully received.*

The ShowSlashdot program in Listing 12-4 creates a Web browser component and opens the Slashdot home page. One wonders if the popularity of this book might cause the Slashdot site to be Slashdotted . . . probably not.

Listing 12-4. ShowSlashdot.java

```java
package examples.ch12;

import org.eclipse.swt.SWT;
import org.eclipse.swt.browser.*;
import org.eclipse.swt.layout.*;
import org.eclipse.swt.widgets.*;

/**
 * This class uses a web browser to display Slashdot's home page
 */
public class ShowSlashdot {
  /**
   * Runs the application
   */
  public void run() {
    Display display = new Display();
    Shell shell = new Shell(display);
    shell.setText("Slashdot");
    createContents(shell);
    shell.open();
    while (!shell.isDisposed()) {
      if (!display.readAndDispatch()) {
        display.sleep();
      }
    }
    display.dispose();
  }
```

```
/**
 * Creates the main window's contents
 *
 * @param shell the main window
 */
private void createContents(Shell shell) {
  shell.setLayout(new FillLayout());

  // Create a web browser
  Browser browser = new Browser(shell, SWT.NONE);

  // Navigate to Slashdot
  browser.setUrl("http://slashdot.org");
}

/**
 * The application entry point
 *
 * @param args the command line arguments
 */
public static void main(String[] args) {
  new ShowSlashdot().run();
}
}
```

The browser code for opening and displaying Slashdot's home page totals two lines:

```
Browser browser = new Browser(shell, SWT.NONE);
browser.setUrl("http://slashdot.org");
```

Figure 12-4 shows this program displaying early morning headlines from January 13, 2004. Because this application doesn't create an address bar, you can't type a different URL to navigate to. However, notice that the browser functions fully; you can log in, click links, and fill out forms.

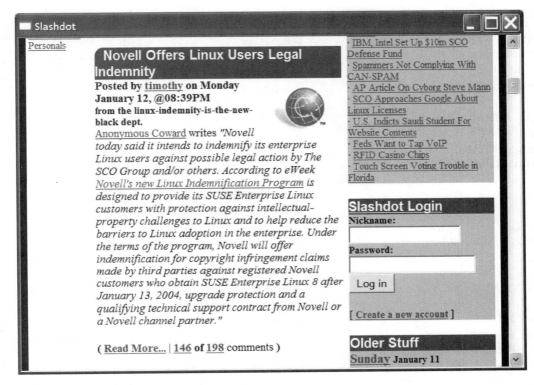

Figure 12-4. A Web browser displaying Slashdot's home page

Controlling the Browser

From their early Mosaic incarnation, Web browsers have offered forward and back navigation. To counter the possibility of network issues, they've offered the ability to stop the loading of a page. They've also supported refreshing the current page. SWT's Web browser offers these methods and more, listed in Table 12-10. The section titled "Responding to Events" provides more information about the events and listeners in Browser's API.

Table 12-10. Browser *Methods*

Method	Description
void addCloseWindowListener (CloseWindowListener listener)	Adds a listener to the notification list that's notified when the parent window should be closed.
void addLocationListener (LocationListener listener)	Adds a listener to the notification list that's notified when the current location is about to change or has changed.
void addOpenWindowListener (OpenWindowListener listener)	Adds a listener to the notification list that's notified when a new window should be created.
void addProgressListener (ProgressListener listener)	Adds a listener to the notification list that's notified when progress is made on loading the current document, and also when loading is complete.

Table 12-10. Browser *Methods (continued)*

Method	Description
`boolean isBackEnabled()`	Returns true if the browser can go back in its history. Otherwise, returns false.
`boolean isForwardEnabled()`	Returns true if the browser can go forward in its history. Otherwise, returns false.
`void addStatusTextListener (StatusTextListener listener)`	Adds a listener to the notification list that's notified when the status text changes.
`void addVisibilityWindowListener (VisibilityWindowListener listener)`	Adds a listener to the notification list that's notified when this browser receives a request to show or hide itself.
`boolean back()`	Takes the browser back one page in its history. Returns true for a successful operation, or false for an unsuccessful operation.
`boolean forward()`	Takes the browser forward one page in its history. Returns true for a successful operation, or false for an unsuccessful operation.
`String getUrl()`	Returns this browser's current URL, or an empty string if it has no current URL.
`void refresh()`	Refreshes the current page.
`void removeCloseWindowListener (CloseWindowListener listener)`	Removes the specified listener from the notification list.
`void removeLocationListener (LocationListener listener)`	Removes the specified listener from the notification list.
`void removeOpenWindowListener (OpenWindowListener listener)`	Removes the specified listener from the notification list.
`void removeProgressListener (ProgressListener listener)`	Removes the specified listener from the notification list.
`void removeStatusTextListener (StatusTextListener listener)`	Removes the specified listener from the notification list.
`void removeVisibilityWindowListener (VisibilityWindowListener listener)`	Removes the specified listener from the notification list.
`boolean setText(String html)`	Renders the HTML code specified by html. Returns true for a successful operation, or false for an unsuccessful operation.
`boolean setUrl(String url)`	Loads the URL specified by url. Returns true for a successful operation, or false for an unsuccessful operation.
`void stop()`	Stops loading the current page. Note that you don't have to write multithreading code to use this method.

The SimpleBrowser program in Listing 12-5 displays an address bar, so users can type a target URL, along with a Go button to trigger loading. It also sports Back, Forward, Refresh, and Stop buttons. You probably won't be tempted to use SimpleBrowser as your full-time Web browser, but you could.

Listing 12-5. SimpleBrowser.java

```java
package examples.ch12;

import org.eclipse.swt.SWT;
import org.eclipse.swt.browser.*;
import org.eclipse.swt.events.*;
import org.eclipse.swt.layout.*;
import org.eclipse.swt.widgets.*;

/**
 * This class implements a web browser
 */
public class SimpleBrowser {
  /**
   * Runs the application
   */
  public void run() {
    Display display = new Display();
    Shell shell = new Shell(display);
    shell.setText("Simple Browser");
    createContents(shell);
    shell.open();
    while (!shell.isDisposed()) {
      if (!display.readAndDispatch()) {
        display.sleep();
      }
    }
    display.dispose();
  }

  /**
   * Creates the main window's contents
   *
   * @param shell the main window
   */
  private void createContents(Shell shell) {
    shell.setLayout(new FormLayout());

    // Create the composite to hold the buttons and text field
    Composite controls = new Composite(shell, SWT.NONE);
    FormData data = new FormData();
    data.top = new FormAttachment(0, 0);
    data.left = new FormAttachment(0, 0);
    data.right = new FormAttachment(100, 0);
    controls.setLayoutData(data);

    // Create the web browser
    final Browser browser = new Browser(shell, SWT.NONE);
    data = new FormData();
    data.top = new FormAttachment(controls);
    data.bottom = new FormAttachment(100, 0);
    data.left = new FormAttachment(0, 0);
```

```
  data.right = new FormAttachment(100, 0);
  browser.setLayoutData(data);

  // Create the controls and wire them to the browser
  controls.setLayout(new GridLayout(6, false));

  // Create the back button
  Button button = new Button(controls, SWT.PUSH);
  button.setText("Back");
  button.addSelectionListener(new SelectionAdapter() {
    public void widgetSelected(SelectionEvent event) {
      browser.back();
    }
  });

  // Create the forward button
  button = new Button(controls, SWT.PUSH);
  button.setText("Forward");
  button.addSelectionListener(new SelectionAdapter() {
    public void widgetSelected(SelectionEvent event) {
      browser.forward();
    }
  });

  // Create the refresh button
  button = new Button(controls, SWT.PUSH);
  button.setText("Refresh");
  button.addSelectionListener(new SelectionAdapter() {
    public void widgetSelected(SelectionEvent event) {
      browser.refresh();
    }
  });

  // Create the stop button
  button = new Button(controls, SWT.PUSH);
  button.setText("Stop");
  button.addSelectionListener(new SelectionAdapter() {
    public void widgetSelected(SelectionEvent event) {
      browser.stop();
    }
  });

  // Create the address entry field and set focus to it
  final Text url = new Text(controls, SWT.BORDER);
  url.setLayoutData(new GridData(GridData.FILL_HORIZONTAL));
  url.setFocus();

  // Create the go button
  button = new Button(controls, SWT.PUSH);
  button.setText("Go");
  button.addSelectionListener(new SelectionAdapter() {
    public void widgetSelected(SelectionEvent event) {
      browser.setUrl(url.getText());
```

```
        }
    });

    // Allow users to hit enter to go to the typed URL
    shell.setDefaultButton(button);
}

/**
 * The application entry point
 *
 * @param args the command line arguments
 */
public static void main(String[] args) {
    new SimpleBrowser().run();
}
}
```

Figure 12-5 shows the SimpleBrowser program displaying Apress's Web site.

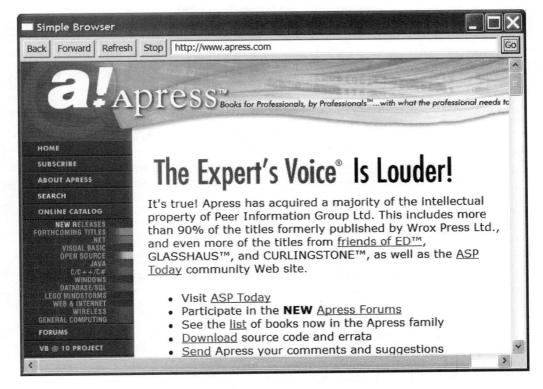

Figure 12-5. The SimpleBrowser program

Responding to Events

You might have noticed the unidirectional nature of SimpleBrowser's address field. Typing a URL into it and clicking the Go button loads that URL. However, clicking a link within that page loads the new URL, but doesn't update the address field with the new URL. To detect when users click links, as well as to detect various other events, you must add event handling to your `Browser` objects. `Browser` supports the following listeners:

- `CloseWindowListener`

- `LocationListener`

- `OpenWindowListener`

- `ProgressListener`

- `StatusTextListener`

- `VisibilityWindowListener`

Users have come to expect functionality such as animated progress loaders and status-bar messages from their browsers. You must handle events to have any hope of competing with Internet Explorer, Mozilla, Netscape, Opera, Konqueror, Safari, Galeon, et al.

Handling CloseWindowListener

Most applications can be closed using platform-specific actions, usually by clicking a standard close button on the title bar of the application's main window, or selecting File ➤ Exit from the application's main menu. However, HTML and JavaScript present an interesting twist: together, they can close a browser window. For example, the following HTML link closes the browser window:

```
<a href="javascript:window.close()">Close this Window</a>
```

When the browser closes, you'll usually want to close the browser's parent window, or the browser's parent tab if you've created a tabbed interface for your browser application. To receive notification when the browser closes, add an event handler that implements the `CloseWindowListener` interface. It declares a single method:

```
public void close(WindowEvent event)
```

In addition to the members inherited from `TypedEvent`, the `WindowEvent` object that `close()` receives has three fields:

- `Browser browser`

- `Point location`

- `Point size`

However, these members are all `null` when `CloseWindowListeners` are notified. The member you'll likely work with in your `close()` method is one inherited from `TypedEvent`: `widget`, which references the browser that's closing. You can get the `widget`'s parent shell and close it, as the following example does:

```
public class SampleCloseWindowListener implements CloseWindowListener {
 // Called when the browser closes
 public void close(WindowEvent event) {
  // Get the browser that's closing
  Browser browser = (Browser) event.widget;

  // Get the browser's parent shell
  Shell shell = browser.getShell();

  // Close the parent shell
  shell.close();
 }
}
```

Using *LocationListener*

The "Location" in `LocationListener` refers to URLs. Specifically, it refers to the URL the browser is loading. The `LocationListener` interface defines two methods:

- `void changed(LocationEvent event)`

- `void changing(LocationEvent event)`

`changed()` is called after the displayed location changes, while `changing()` is called when a location change has been requested, but the location hasn't yet changed. SWT includes a `LocationAdapter` class that implements the `LocationListener` interface, so you can subclass `LocationAdapter` and override only one of the methods if you wish.

`LocationEvent` has two fields:

- `boolean cancel`

- `String location`

You can set `cancel` to `true` in your `changing()` method to cancel loading the requested URL. `location` contains the requested URL; changing this value has no effect. A sample `LocationListener` might block attempts to go to pornographic sites (those with "xxx" in the URL), and log all loaded URLs. Its code might look like this:

```
public class SampleLocationListener implements Listener {
 // This method is called after the location has changed
 public void changed(LocationEvent event) {
  // Log the URL to stdout
  System.out.println(event.location);
 }
```

```
// This method is called before the location has changed
public void changing(LocationEvent event) {
 // Don't load pornographic sites
 // Do they all have "xxx" in the URL?
 if (event.location.indexOf("xxx") != -1) {
  event.cancel = true;
 }
 }
}
```

Using *OpenWindowListener*

Browser conventions allow spawning new browser windows. Things that can trigger a new browser window include the following:

- The user right-clicks a link and selects Open in New Window from the context menu (note that you must build this functionality yourself).

- The user holds down Shift while clicking a link.

- The user clicks a link that has a named target for which no browser currently exists.

When the user performs an action within the browser that spawns a new browser window, any OpenWindowListeners are first notified. OpenWindowListener declares one method:

```
public void open(WindowEvent event)
```

As with CloseWindowListener, the three WindowEvent fields (browser, location, and field) are null when passed to open(), and the widget field inherited from TypedEvent contains a reference to the current browser.

Using *ProgressListener*

From the spinning "e" to the shining "N" to the progress bar, and everything in between, browsers have responded to network latency by keeping something moving while waiting for pages to load. Animated feedback does much to mollify impatient users. You can use ProgressListener implementations to receive progress events while URLs load. ProgressListener declares two methods:

- void changed(ProgressEvent event)

- void completed(ProgressEvent event)

As loading of a URL progresses, changed() is called. When the URL finishes loading, complete() is called. SWT includes a class called ProgressAdapter that implements both methods, so you can extend ProgressAdapter and override only one of the methods, if you wish. ProgressEvent contains two fields:

- int current

- int total

When changed() is called, current contains an int representing the current progress of the load, while total contains an int representing the total to load. These numbers are more arbitrary than accurate, but give some indication of what's going on. When completed() is called, neither field contains meaningful data.

```
public class SampleProgressListener implements ProgressListener {
  // This method is called when progress is made
  public void changed(ProgressEvent event) {
    System.out.println(event.current + " of " + event.total + " loaded");
  }

  // This method is called when the page finishes loading
  public void completed(ProgressEvent event) {
    System.out.println("Loaded!");
  }
}
```

Using StatusTextListener

Most browsers feature a status bar along the bottom of the browser window that reports information to the user. For instance, hover over a link in your default browser to see the target URL for that link displayed in the status bar. However, SWT's Browser class has no status bar, so you must manage status messages yourself. SWT does provide StatusTextListener to assist you in status reporting. It declares a single method:

```
void changed(StatusTextEvent event)
```

changed() is called when the status text has changed. StatusTextEvent contains a single field, text, that contains the new status text. The following example StatusTextListener implementation prints each status text change to stdout:

```
public class SampleStatusTextListener implements StatusTextListener {
  public void changed(StatusTextEvent event) {
    System.out.println(event.text);
  }
}
```

Using VisibilityWindowListener

You can detect when the browser is about to be hidden, or redisplayed after being hidden, using a VisibilityWindowListener. It defines two methods:

- void hide(WindowEvent event)

- void show(WindowEvent event)

hide() is called when the browser is about to be hidden, and show() is called when the browser is about to be redisplayed. Implement these methods to react to these events.

Advancing the Browser

Adding event handling to a browser increases its usability dramatically. The Advanced-Browser program in Listing 12-6 leverages event handling to do the following:

- Keep the address text field in sync with the displayed URL.

- Display status messages in a status bar.

- Display progress information as a percentage.

- Close the parent shell when the browser closes.

Listing 12-6. AdvancedBrowser.java

```java
package examples.ch12;

import org.eclipse.swt.SWT;
import org.eclipse.swt.browser.*;
import org.eclipse.swt.events.*;
import org.eclipse.swt.layout.*;
import org.eclipse.swt.widgets.*;

/**
 * This class implements a web browser
 */
public class AdvancedBrowser {
  // The "at rest" text of the throbber
  private static final String AT_REST = "Ready";

  /**
   * Runs the application
   *
   * @param location the initial location to display
   */
  public void run(String location) {
    Display display = new Display();
    Shell shell = new Shell(display);
    shell.setText("Advanced Browser");
    createContents(shell, location);
    shell.open();
    while (!shell.isDisposed()) {
      if (!display.readAndDispatch()) {
        display.sleep();
      }
    }
    display.dispose();
  }
```

```java
/**
 * Creates the main window's contents
 *
 * @param shell the main window
 * @param location the initial location
 */
public void createContents(Shell shell, String location) {
  shell.setLayout(new FormLayout());

  // Create the composite to hold the buttons and text field
  Composite controls = new Composite(shell, SWT.NONE);
  FormData data = new FormData();
  data.top = new FormAttachment(0, 0);
  data.left = new FormAttachment(0, 0);
  data.right = new FormAttachment(100, 0);
  controls.setLayoutData(data);

  // Create the status bar
  Label status = new Label(shell, SWT.NONE);
  data = new FormData();
  data.left = new FormAttachment(0, 0);
  data.right = new FormAttachment(100, 0);
  data.bottom = new FormAttachment(100, 0);
  status.setLayoutData(data);

  // Create the web browser
  final Browser browser = new Browser(shell, SWT.BORDER);
  data = new FormData();
  data.top = new FormAttachment(controls);
  data.bottom = new FormAttachment(status);
  data.left = new FormAttachment(0, 0);
  data.right = new FormAttachment(100, 0);
  browser.setLayoutData(data);

  // Create the controls and wire them to the browser
  controls.setLayout(new GridLayout(7, false));

  // Create the back button
  Button button = new Button(controls, SWT.PUSH);
  button.setText("Back");
  button.addSelectionListener(new SelectionAdapter() {
    public void widgetSelected(SelectionEvent event) {
      browser.back();
    }
  });

  // Create the forward button
  button = new Button(controls, SWT.PUSH);
  button.setText("Forward");
  button.addSelectionListener(new SelectionAdapter() {
    public void widgetSelected(SelectionEvent event) {
      browser.forward();
    }
  });
```

```
    // Create the refresh button
    button = new Button(controls, SWT.PUSH);
    button.setText("Refresh");
    button.addSelectionListener(new SelectionAdapter() {
      public void widgetSelected(SelectionEvent event) {
        browser.refresh();
      }
    });

    // Create the stop button
    button = new Button(controls, SWT.PUSH);
    button.setText("Stop");
    button.addSelectionListener(new SelectionAdapter() {
      public void widgetSelected(SelectionEvent event) {
        browser.stop();
      }
    });

    // Create the address entry field and set focus to it
    final Text url = new Text(controls, SWT.BORDER);
    url.setLayoutData(new GridData(GridData.FILL_HORIZONTAL));
    url.setFocus();

    // Create the go button
    button = new Button(controls, SWT.PUSH);
    button.setText("Go");
    button.addSelectionListener(new SelectionAdapter() {
      public void widgetSelected(SelectionEvent event) {
        browser.setUrl(url.getText());
      }
    });

    // Create the animated "throbber"
    Label throbber = new Label(controls, SWT.NONE);
    throbber.setText(AT_REST);

    // Allow users to hit enter to go to the typed URL
    shell.setDefaultButton(button);

    // Add event handlers
    browser.addCloseWindowListener(new AdvancedCloseWindowListener());
    browser.addLocationListener(new AdvancedLocationListener(url));
    browser.addProgressListener(new AdvancedProgressListener(throbber));
    browser.addStatusTextListener(new AdvancedStatusTextListener(status));

    // Go to the initial URL
    if (location != null) {
      browser.setUrl(location);
    }
  }

  /**
   * This class implements a CloseWindowListener for AdvancedBrowser
   */
```

```
class AdvancedCloseWindowListener implements CloseWindowListener {
  /**
   * Called when the parent window should be closed
   */
  public void close(WindowEvent event) {
    // Close the parent window
    ((Browser) event.widget).getShell().close();
  }
}

/**
 * This class implements a LocationListener for AdvancedBrowser
 */
class AdvancedLocationListener implements LocationListener {
  // The address text box to update
  private Text location;

  /**
   * Constructs an AdvancedLocationListener
   *
   * @param text the address text box to update
   */
  public AdvancedLocationListener(Text text) {
    // Store the address box for updates
    location = text;
  }

  /**
   * Called before the location changes
   *
   * @param event the event
   */
  public void changing(LocationEvent event) {
    // Show the location that's loading
    location.setText("Loading " + event.location + "...");
  }

  /**
   * Called after the location changes
   *
   * @param event the event
   */
  public void changed(LocationEvent event) {
    // Show the loaded location
    location.setText(event.location);
  }
}

/**
 * This class implements a ProgressListener for AdvancedBrowser
 */
class AdvancedProgressListener implements ProgressListener {
  // The label on which to report progress
  private Label progress;
```

```java
/**
 * Constructs an AdvancedProgressListener
 *
 * @param label the label on which to report progress
 */
public AdvancedProgressListener(Label label) {
  // Store the label on which to report updates
  progress = label;
}

/**
 * Called when progress is made
 *
 * @param event the event
 */
public void changed(ProgressEvent event) {
  // Avoid divide-by-zero
  if (event.total != 0) {
    // Calculate a percentage and display it
    int percent = (int) (event.current / event.total);
    progress.setText(percent + "%");
  } else {
    // Since we can't calculate a percent, show confusion :-)
    progress.setText("???");
  }
}

/**
 * Called when load is complete
 *
 * @param event the event
 */
public void completed(ProgressEvent event) {
  // Reset to the "at rest" message
  progress.setText(AT_REST);
}
}

/**
 * This class implements a StatusTextListener for AdvancedBrowser
 */
class AdvancedStatusTextListener implements StatusTextListener {
  // The label on which to report status
  private Label status;

  /**
   * Constructs an AdvancedStatusTextListener
   *
   * @param label the label on which to report status
   */
  public AdvancedStatusTextListener(Label label) {
    // Store the label on which to report status
    status = label;
  }
```

```
  /**
   * Called when the status changes
   *
   * @param event the event
   */
  public void changed(StatusTextEvent event) {
    // Report the status
    status.setText(event.text);
  }
}

/**
 * The application entry point
 *
 * @param args the command line arguments
 */
public static void main(String[] args) {
  new AdvancedBrowser().run(args.length == 0 ? null : args[0]);
}
}
```

Figure 12-6 shows the AdvancedBrowser program displaying eBay's home page.

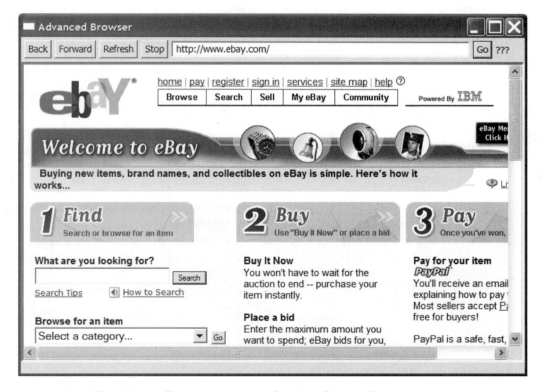

Figure 12-6. The AdvancedBrowser program showing the eBay home page

Digging into Programs

You can launch other programs from within your applications using java.lang.Runtime's exec() family of methods. You don't need any help from SWT to accomplish this. For example, the following snippet launches Notepad:

```
Runtime.getRuntime().exec("notepad.exe");
```

Suppose, however, that you have the name of a data file, and you want to run the appropriate program for that data file, loading the data file into the program. exec() won't help you in that situation. SWT comes to the rescue in the form of the Program class, which represents programs and their associated extensions. That it works with extensions tips off its Windows centricity, but it also works, albeit with varying results, on other platforms. For example, problems with the K Desktop Environment (KDE) render Program virtually useless when run under that desktop environment, while running Program under Gnome works fine.

In addition to launching files, Program can list the known programs on your system, the known file extensions, and the program associated with a specific file extension. Table 12-11 lists Program's methods.

Table 12-11. Program *Methods*

Method	Description
boolean equals(Object obj)	Returns true if this Program represents the same program that obj represents.
boolean execute(String fileName)	Executes the program represented by this Program, passing fileName as an argument. Returns true if the program successfully launches. Otherwise, returns false.
static Program findProgram (String extension)	Returns the program that handles the specified extension.
static String[] getExtensions()	Returns all the registered extensions on the system.
ImageData getImageData()	Returns the image data associated with this Program.
String getName()	Gets a name for the program. This isn't the executable name, but rather the name by which the program is known by the system. On Windows, it's the name in the Registry.
static Program[] getPrograms()	Returns all the registered programs on the system.
static boolean launch(String filename)	Launches the file specified by filename using the default program for that file extension.
String toString()	Returns a user-friendly string representing this Program.

For example, to launch an HTML file in the default browser, use code such as this:

```
Program.launch("index.html");
```

This code automatically looks up which program to use. You can do the lookup yourself using the findProgram() method to get the Program object that represents the default browser. Then, you call execute(), like this:

```
Program program = Program.findProgram(".html");
program.execute("index.html");
```

The ShowPrograms program in Listing 12-7 exercises Program's capabilities. It displays, in a combo, all the extensions on your system. Selecting an extension from the combo displays the program associated with that extension. In addition, Show-Progams displays all the programs known to your system in a list box. Double-click a program in the list to launch the program. You can specify the data file for the program to open by typing the full path to the file in the Data File text box. This uses the execute() method to launch the program. Alternatively, you can click the button labeled "Use Program.launch() instead of Program.execute()" to launch the program and data file using the launch() method.

Listing 12-7. ShowPrograms.java

```java
package examples.ch12;

import org.eclipse.swt.SWT;
import org.eclipse.swt.events.*;
import org.eclipse.swt.layout.*;
import org.eclipse.swt.program.Program;
import org.eclipse.swt.widgets.*;

/**
 * This class shows the extensions on the system and their associated programs.
 */
public class ShowPrograms {
  /**
   * Runs the application
   */
  public void run() {
    Display display = new Display();
    Shell shell = new Shell(display);
    shell.setText("Show Programs");
    createContents(shell);
    shell.open();
    while (!shell.isDisposed()) {
      if (!display.readAndDispatch()) {
        display.sleep();
      }
    }
```

```
      display.dispose();
    }

    /**
     * Creates the main window's contents
     *
     * @param shell the main window
     */
    private void createContents(Shell shell) {
      shell.setLayout(new GridLayout(2, false));

      // Create the label and combo for the extensions
      new Label(shell, SWT.NONE).setText("Extension:");
      Combo extensionsCombo = new Combo(shell, SWT.BORDER | SWT.READ_ONLY);
      extensionsCombo.setLayoutData(new GridData(GridData.FILL_HORIZONTAL));

      // Create the labels
      new Label(shell, SWT.NONE).setText("Program:");
      final Label programName = new Label(shell, SWT.NONE);
      programName.setLayoutData(new GridData(GridData.FILL_HORIZONTAL));

      // Fill the combo with the extensions on the system
      String[] extensions = Program.getExtensions();
      for (int i = 0, n = extensions.length; i < n; i++) {
        extensionsCombo.add(extensions[i]);
      }

      // Add a handler to get the selected extension, look up the associated
      // program, and display the program's name
      extensionsCombo.addSelectionListener(new SelectionAdapter() {
        public void widgetSelected(SelectionEvent event) {
          Combo combo = (Combo) event.widget;

          // Get the program for the extension
          Program program = Program.findProgram(combo.getText());

          // Display the program's name
          programName.setText(program == null ? "(None)" : program.getName());
        }
      });

      // Create a list box to show all the programs on the system
      List allPrograms = new List(shell, SWT.SINGLE | SWT.BORDER | SWT.H_SCROLL
          | SWT.V_SCROLL);
      GridData data = new GridData(GridData.FILL_BOTH);
      data.horizontalSpan = 2;
      allPrograms.setLayoutData(data);

      // Put all the known programs into the list box
      Program[] programs = Program.getPrograms();
```

```
    for (int i = 0, n = programs.length; i < n; i++) {
      String name = programs[i].getName();
      allPrograms.add(name);
      allPrograms.setData(name, programs[i]);
    }

    // Add a field for a data file
    new Label(shell, SWT.NONE).setText("Data File:");
    final Text dataFile = new Text(shell, SWT.BORDER);
    dataFile.setLayoutData(new GridData(GridData.FILL_HORIZONTAL));

    // Double-clicking a program in the list launches the program
    allPrograms.addMouseListener(new MouseAdapter() {
      public void mouseDoubleClick(MouseEvent event) {
        List list = (List) event.widget;
        if (list.getSelectionCount() > 0) {
          String programName = list.getSelection()[0];
          Program program = (Program) list.getData(programName);
          program.execute(dataFile.getText());
        }
      }
    });

    // Let them use launch instead of execute
    Button launch = new Button(shell, SWT.PUSH);
    data = new GridData(GridData.FILL_HORIZONTAL);
    data.horizontalSpan = 2;
    launch.setLayoutData(data);
    launch.setText("Use Program.launch() instead of Program.execute()");
    launch.addSelectionListener(new SelectionAdapter() {
      public void widgetSelected(SelectionEvent event) {
        // Use launch
        Program.launch(dataFile.getText());
      }
    });
  }

  /**
   * The application entry point
   *
   * @param args the command line arguments
   */
  public static void main(String[] args) {
    new ShowPrograms().run();
  }
}
```

Figure 12-7 shows the program running on a Windows XP box with several applications installed. You can see that we're WinCustomize and Paint Shop Pro fans.

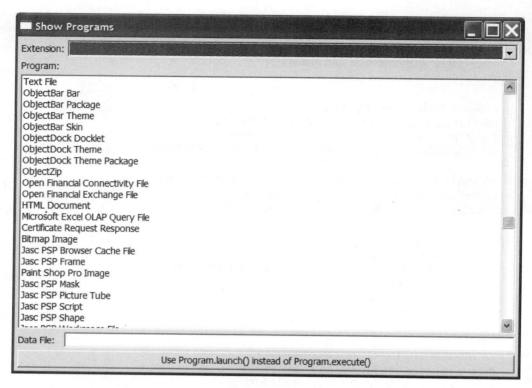

Figure 12-7. The ShowPrograms program

Summary

You might not include all the topics covered in this chapter in all your applications. You might not include any of them in any of your programs. However, skipping this chapter's solutions where users expect them shortchanges your applications and decimates the audience willing to use them. The advanced topics covered in this chapter can make the difference between the latest rage and the latest shelfware.

Part III

Using JFace

CHAPTER 13

Your First JFace Application

PICASSO, IN HIS abstract art, painted only the essential elements of his subject matter. Business proposals and other writings often carry abstracts, or summarizations, of their contents. In this vein, object-oriented programming preaches abstraction: the elimination of the extraneous and the retention of only necessary. For example, if you're developing management software for veterinarians, you'll create a Dog class (derived from a Pet class) that contains pertinent data about dogs. This Dog class represents an abstraction of real-life dogs, in that it doesn't model a dog exactly; it only models the aspects of dogs necessary for the software. For example, you wouldn't include a chew(Shoe shoe) method or a lickEmbarrassingly() method because your software has no need to model these dog actions. Distilling an object to the minimum representation required reduces complexity, accelerates development, and slashes defects.

JFace layers an abstraction on top of SWT. In SWT, you typically create widgets, add data to them, and call methods on them. JFace steps back from the nitty-gritty of working directly with widgets, wrapping them in layers to make the widgets simpler to use. It hides many implementation details and reduces the number of lines of code you must write to accomplish your objectives.

Unlike SWT, JFace has no ready-made distribution apart from Eclipse, which means that you must install Eclipse to obtain JFace. JFace doesn't require that you retain Eclipse on your hard drive, so feel free to copy the JFace JAR files to another directory and remove Eclipse if you'd like. The JFace JAR files all reside beneath the eclipse/plugins directory, spread across various JAR files:

- jface.jar in org.eclipse.jface_3.0.0

- runtime.jar in org.eclipse.core.runtime_3.0.0

- osgi.jar in org.eclipse.osgi_3.0.0

- jfacetext.jar in org.eclipse.jface.text_3.0.0

- text.jar in org.eclipse.text_3.0.0

You can copy these files wherever you'd like, and you must distribute them (or at least the ones you use) with your JFace applications. You won't necessarily use all of these in each of your applications, so you can distribute only the ones your application relies on.

Greeting the World with JFace

The HelloWorld program greets the world anew, but this time using JFace. Because JFace adds some Java libraries (but no native libraries—remember that it builds on SWT), you'll need a new Ant file (see Listing 13-1) to build and run the program.

Listing 13-1. build.xml

```xml
<project name="GenericJFaceApplication" default="run" basedir=".">
  <description>
    Generic JFace Application build and execution file
  </description>

  <property name="main.class"  value=""/>
  <property name="src"         location="."/>
  <property name="build"       location="."/>

  <!-- Update location to match your eclipse home directory  -->
  <property name="ecl.home"    location="c:\eclipse"/>

  <!-- Update value to match your windowing system (win32, gtk, motif, etc.) -->
  <property name="win.sys"     value="win32"/>

  <!-- Update value to match your os (win32, linux, etc.) -->
  <property name="os.sys"      value="win32"/>

  <!-- Update value to match your architecture -->
  <property name="arch"        value="x86"/>

  <!-- Update value to match your SWT version -->
  <property name="swt.ver"     value="3.0.0"/>

  <!-- Do not edit below this line -->
  <property name="swt.subdir"
location="${ecl.home}/plugins/org.eclipse.swt.${win.sys}_${swt.ver}"/>
  <property name="swt.jar.lib" location="${swt.subdir}/ws/${win.sys}"/>
  <property name="swt.jni.lib" location="${swt.subdir}/os/${os.sys}/${arch}"/>
  <property name="runtime.jar.lib"
    location="${ecl.home}/plugins/org.eclipse.core.runtime_${swt.ver}"/>
  <property name="jface.jar.lib"
    location="${ecl.home}/plugins/org.eclipse.jface_${swt.ver}"/>
  <property name="osgi.jar.lib"
    location="${ecl.home}/plugins/org.eclipse.osgi_${swt.ver}"/>
  <property name="jfacetext.jar.lib"
    location="${ecl.home}/plugins/org.eclipse.jface.text_${swt.ver}"/>
  <property name="text.jar.lib"
    location="${ecl.home}/plugins/org.eclipse.text_${swt.ver}"/>

  <path id="project.class.path">
    <pathelement path="${build}"/>
```

```
        <fileset dir="${swt.jar.lib}">
            <include name="**/*.jar"/>
        </fileset>
        <fileset dir="${runtime.jar.lib}">
            <include name="**/*.jar"/>
        </fileset>
        <fileset dir="${jface.jar.lib}">
            <include name="**/*.jar"/>
        </fileset>
        <fileset dir="${osgi.jar.lib}">
            <include name="**/*.jar"/>
        </fileset>
        <fileset dir="${jfacetext.jar.lib}">
            <include name="**/*.jar"/>
        </fileset>
        <fileset dir="${text.jar.lib}">
            <include name="**/*.jar"/>
        </fileset>
    </path>

    <target name="compile">
        <javac srcdir="${src}" destdir="${build}">
            <classpath refid="project.class.path"/>
        </javac>
    </target>

    <target name="run" depends="compile">
        <java classname="${main.class}" fork="true" failonerror="true">
            <jvmarg value="-Djava.library.path=${swt.jni.lib}"/>
            <classpath refid="project.class.path"/>
        </java>
    </target>
</project>
```

As you can see, this build.xml file adds some JFace JAR files to the classpath. Make sure to update this file with your operating system, windowing system, and so on, following the comments in the file. If you're using Eclipse, you can add these JAR files to the Java Build Path section of the project's properties page.

Listing 13-2 contains the source code for HelloWorld.

Listing 13-2. HelloWorld.java

```
package examples.ch13;

import org.eclipse.jface.window.ApplicationWindow;
import org.eclipse.swt.SWT;
import org.eclipse.swt.widgets.*;

/**
 * Your first JFace application
 */
```

```java
public class HelloWorld extends ApplicationWindow {
  /**
   * HelloWorld constructor
   */
  public HelloWorld() {
    super(null);
  }

  /**
   * Runs the application
   */
  public void run() {
    // Don't return from open() until window closes
    setBlockOnOpen(true);

    // Open the main window
    open();

    // Dispose the display
    Display.getCurrent().dispose();
  }

  /**
   * Creates the main window's contents
   *
   * @param parent the main window
   * @return Control
   */
  protected Control createContents(Composite parent) {
    // Create a Hello, World label
    Label label = new Label(parent, SWT.CENTER);
    label.setText("Hello, World");
    return label;
  }

  /**
   * The application entry point
   *
   * @param args the command line arguments
   */
  public static void main(String[] args) {
    new HelloWorld().run();
  }
}
```

You compile and run HelloWorld just as you did with the SWT programs:

```
ant -Dmain.class=examples.ch13.HelloWorld
```

Issue this command from a prompt to see the window shown in Figure 13-1.

Figure 13-1. Hello, World from JFace

One of the first things to notice is that the HelloWorld class subclasses something called ApplicationWindow, which is JFace's abstraction of Shell. SWT makes you feel guilty any time you type **extends** into your code editor, because so many of its classes (including Shell) carry warnings that they're not designed to be subclassed. Don't worry— subclassing ApplicationWindow is not only legit, it's encouraged.

Next, you can't find the typical SWT event loop:

```
Display display = new Display();
Shell shell = new Shell();
// Create shell's contents
shell.open();
while (!shell.isDisposed()) {
  if (!display.readAndDispatch()) {
    display.sleep();
  }
}
display.dispose();
```

In its place, you find the much briefer code:

```
setBlockOnOpen(true);
open();
Display.getCurrent().dispose();
```

The first method call, setBlockOnOpen(), sets a flag that, if true, tells the next method call, open(), to enter an event loop remarkably similar to the familiar SWT event loop. Passing true to setBlockOnOpen() causes open() not to return until the window is closed. The euphoria of the elegance of JFace fades slightly, however, as you stare at the third method call: Display.getCurrent().dispose(). You still must dispose your creations. However, it's a small price to pay for the simplicity of using JFace.

The HelloWorld program doesn't specifically set a layout either, defaulting to an internal class called ApplicationWindowLayout that should suffice for all your needs. It also never explicitly calls its createContents() method, relying on the JFace framework to do that. The code is sleeker, exposing far fewer details than the SWT examples in this book.

Understanding the Relationship Between SWT and JFace

Lest you begin to feel that you've wasted your time learning SWT, that once you embrace JFace you'll never see SWT again, rest assured that SWT does more than simply peek its head through the JFace layer from time to time. Not only do abstractions leak, but also they never cover everything. You'll get plenty of mileage from your SWT knowledge, even as you immerse yourself in JFace.

Because JFace uses SWT, and because it builds on top of SWT, it requires both the SWT JAR files and the SWT native libraries. In other words, your JFace applications require everything your SWT applications do, plus the JFace JAR files that they use.

Your JFace applications will sometimes be sprinkled, and sometimes smothered, with calls directly to SWT. Use the JFace abstractions when both available and applicable, and rely on SWT as a fallback position to meet your programs' requirements.

Understanding the ApplicationWindow Class

The HelloWorld program in this chapter subclasses JFace's ApplicationWindow class. The ApplicationWindow class represents, as its name suggests, a window in an application. It has a parent Shell, which is passed to the constructor:

```
ApplicationWindow(Shell parentShell)
```

If parentShell is null, the ApplicationWindow represents a top-level window. Otherwise, it's a child of parentShell. It contains support for a menu bar, a toolbar, a coolbar, and a status line.

When you construct an ApplicationWindow, little beyond its construction occurs. The work begins when you call its open() method, and most of the interesting stuff happens only when the parent Shell is null. In these cases, the parent Shell is created. Then, configureShell() is called. The ApplicationWindow implementation of configureShell() does the following:

- Sets the default image

- Sets a GridLayout

- If a menu bar has been set, creates the menu bar

- Changes the layout to an ApplicationWindowLayout

- If a toolbar has been set, creates the toolbar

- If a coolbar has been set, creates the coolbar

- If a status line has been set, creates the status line

You can override configureShell() to change the default behavior.

Next, the ApplicationWindow is resized, if necessary, so it's not larger than the display. It's then opened and, if set to block—that is, setBlockOnOpen(true) has been called—enters the event loop, where it stays until it's closed.

To use ApplicationWindow in your programs, you'll usually create a subclass of ApplicationWindow that contains your application-specific code. Many of ApplicationWindow's methods, as well as those of its parent class, Window, are protected. Some you'll call from your derived class, and some you'll override. For example, to add a menu bar to your ApplicationWindow-derived class, you call the protected method addMenuBar() before the parent Shell has been created—usually in your constructor. This method calls the protected method createMenuManager(), which you'll override to create the proper menu for your window. Chapter 16 contains more information on creating menu bars, toolbars, coolbars, and status lines.

A Word on WindowManagers

JFace includes a class called WindowManager, which isn't a drop-in for IceWM, sawfish, or Enlightenment. It doesn't control the appearance of windows. It doesn't manage user interaction with windows. Instead, it simply groups windows, so you can iterate through them or close them as a group. Instances of WindowManager own both windows and, optionally, other instances of WindowManager. WindowManager offers two constructors, listed in Table 13-1.

Table 13-1. WindowManager *constructors*

Constructor	Description
WindowManager()	Creates a root window manager (that is, one without a parent)
WindowManager(WindowManager parent)	Creates a window manager that's a child of parent

Most of WindowManager's methods act only on itself, but the close() method cascades to all child WindowManagers. Table 13-2 lists WindowManager's methods.

Table 13-2. WindowManager *methods*

Method	Description
void add(Window window)	Adds the window specified by window to this WindowManager.
boolean close()	Closes all windows belonging to this WindowManager, as well as windows belonging to any child WindowManagers. If any window fails to close, stops trying to close windows and returns false. Otherwise, returns true.
int getWindowCount()	Returns the number of windows belonging to this WindowManager.
Window[] getWindows()	Returns an array containing all child windows of this WindowManager.
void remove(Window window)	Removes the window specified by window from this WindowManager.

To use a WindowManager, construct one, add your windows to it, and call methods on it as appropriate. The following code creates a WindowManager, adds three windows to it, and then closes them all, printing a diagnostic message if the windows fail to close:

```
WindowManager wm = new WindowManager();
wm.add(windowOne);
wm.add(windowTwo);
if (!wm.close())
  System.err.println("Windows failed to close");
```

Summary

Though you've barely peeled back the cover on JFace, you've already seen some of its benefits. By abstracting some of the details of SWT, JFace allows you to shift your focus from how your application works to what you want your application to do. The power of the abstraction eases application development, and represents a mainstay of object-oriented programming.

Using JFace requires distributing more libraries with your applications. Don't chafe at that, however, as you'll reap the benefits of using tested code. This should speed your development cycles and reduce your bug counts.

CHAPTER 14

Creating
Viewers

PRESENTING HIERARCHICAL, ordered, or tabular data in SWT-based applications, using SWT's Tree, List, or Table classes, is simple. Create the Tree, List, or Table, add the data, and voila: you have a polished view of your data.

However, stuffing data into widgets harbors a dark side: the view owns the data, in defiance of the proven MVC architecture. No matter how you retrieve the data, you meekly hand it over to the widget, where it lies tightly coupled to its presentation. You might opt to maintain the data outside the widget as well, taking care to synchronize changes between the two sets of data, but you'll eventually surrender and allow the widgets to hold your data hostage.

JFace addresses the tight coupling between Tables, Trees, and data, introducing an abstraction layer that acts as a liaison between the widgets and the data. Instead of shoveling data into the Table or Tree you've created, you provide the widget interfaces to call that determine how to display the data. You maintain your data outside the widgets, and achieve the proper decoupling between model and view.

Tree Viewers

Chapter 8 describes SWT's Tree widget, which displays hierarchical data. The Tree widget allows users to expand and collapse its nodes to display or hide child nodes. As a programmer, you create the Tree widget, add nodes to it, manage nodes to ascertain that you add children to the correct parents, and in essence duplicate your data structure in the Tree widget's display.

JFace wraps SWT's Tree widget with a class called TreeViewer. To use a TreeViewer, you construct one. You tell it how to determine its content (using a class that implements the ITreeContentProvider interface). You tell it how to determine how to display the content (using a class that implements the ILabelProvider interface). Finally, you pass it the root node (or nodes) of your data. Using the content and label providers you've specified, TreeViewer assumes the remaining tasks of displaying your hierarchical data.

Creating a TreeViewer

Create a TreeViewer by calling one of its three constructors, listed in Table 14-1. For example, the following code creates a TreeViewer as a child of shell:

```
TreeViewer treeViewer = new TreeViewer(shell);
```

The constructors that don't take an existing Tree control create one for you. You can also create a TreeViewer to wrap an existing Tree control, like this:

```
Tree tree = new Tree(shell, SWT.SINGLE);
TreeViewer treeViewer = new TreeViewer(tree);
```

Creating a TreeViewer from an existing Tree control ostensibly has the advantage of giving you a reference to the Tree control underlying the TreeViewer, but as you'll see, any TreeViewer readily coughs up a reference to the Tree control it wraps.

Table 14-1. TreeViewer *Constructors*

Constructor	Description
TreeViewer(Composite parent)	Creates a TreeViewer as a child of parent
TreeViewer(Composite parent, int style)	Creates a TreeViewer with the specified style as a child of parent
TreeViewer(Tree tree)	Creates a TreeViewer that wraps the tree control specified by tree

Using a TreeViewer

Although your requirements can dictate a more complicated usage of TreeViewer, the general way to use a TreeViewer—a way that fits most situations—involves the following steps:

1. Creating a TreeViewer

2. Creating a content provider class and setting it on the TreeViewer using setContentProvider()

3. Creating a label provider class and setting it on the TreeViewer using setLabelProvider()

4. Setting the root input for the tree using setInput()

The content provider class, which must implement the ITreeContentProvider interface, returns the content for the tree. The TreeViewer passes it a parent node, and the content provider returns its child nodes. The label provider class, which must implement the ILabelProvider interface, returns the labels for the nodes in the tree. The TreeViewer passes it a node, and the label provider returns the label to display. Both the content provider and the label provider can do a little more than that, as this chapter describes, but at their essence, this is what they do.

To launch the tree, you pass it the root node (or nodes) of your hierarchical data. Using your content and label provider classes, the TreeViewer takes over to provide a fully navigable tree.

Creating a Content Provider

The content provider provides the content, or data, for the tree. The tree viewer can request the children for a parent node. It can request the parent for a child node. It can also ask what to do if the underlying data changes. Your content provider responds to all these requests, and must define the methods from ITreeContentProvider and its superclasses listed in Table 14-2.

Table 14-2. ITreeContentProvider *(and Inherited) Methods*

Method	Description
void dispose()	Called when the TreeViewer is being disposed. In this method, dispose anything you've created that needs to be disposed.
Object[] getChildren(Object parentElement)	Called when the TreeViewer wants the children for a parent element. In this method, return the child elements of the specified parent element.
Object[] getElements(Object inputElement)	Called when the TreeViewer wants the root element or elements of the tree. In this method, return the root element or elements of the tree.
Object getParent(Object element)	Called when the TreeViewer wants the parent for a child element. In this method, return the parent element of the specified child element.
boolean hasChildren(Object element)	Called when the TreeViewer wants to know whether the specified element has children. In this method, return true if the specified element has at least one child. Otherwise, return false.
void inputChanged(Viewer viewer, Object oldInput, Object newInput)	Called when the root underlying data is switched to other root data. In this method, perform any action appropriate for a data change.

For example, suppose you have a class called Node that represents a node in a hierarchical data structure. It has a method called getChildren() that returns a List of its child nodes. It has a method called getParent() that returns its parent node. To use Node with a TreeViewer, you set the root node as the TreeViewer's input. The code might look like this:

```
TreeViewer treeViewer = new TreeViewer(shell);
treeViewer.setContentProvider(new MyTreeContentProvider());
treeViewer.setLabelProvider(new MyLabelContentProvider());
Node rootNode = new Node();
treeViewer.setInput(rootNode);
```

The content provider class you create might look like this:

```
public class MyTreeContentProvider implements ITreeContentProvider {
  public void dispose() {
    // Nothing to dispose
  }
```

```java
public Object[] getChildren(Object parentElement) {
  return ((Node) parentElement()).getChildren().toArray();
}

public Object[] getElements(Object inputElement) {
  // inputElement is already the root node, so return it in the expected format
  return new Object[] { inputElement };
}

public Object getParent(Object element) {
  return ((Node) element).getParent();
}

public boolean hasChildren(Object element) {
  // If the size of the list of children is > 0, return true.
  // Otherwise, return false.
  return ((Node) element).getChildren().size() > 0;
}

public void inputChanged(Viewer viewer, Object oldInput, Object newInput) {
  // The root node has changed; load the new data
  newInput.loadData();
}
}
```

The names of the methods you define from ITreeContentProvider make clear their usage and what you should do in them. For example, the purpose of the hasChildren() method is obviously to return whether or not the specified element has children. The one exception is the inputChanged() method; it's obviously called when the root input changes, but what should you do there? The preceding example uses this method to load a root node's data. However, a more common usage is when the viewer listens for changes on the data model, so that it can automatically update when the underlying data changes. In these cases, you use this method to unregister the viewer as a listener on the old model, and register it as a listener on the new model. That code might look like this:

```java
public void inputChanged(Viewer viewer, Object oldInput, Object newInput) {
  // Unregister the viewer as a listener of the old model
  if (oldInput != null) {
    ((MyHierarchicalModel) oldInput).removeChangeListener(viewer);
  }
  ((MyHierarchicalModel) newInput).addChangeListener(viewer);
}
```

However, no matter how much content you add to your TreeViewer, until you tell the TreeViewer what to display, all you see is an empty box. You must have a label provider to be able to see your tree's content.

Creating a Label Provider

The label provider provides both the text and images, if desired, for the nodes in the tree. Your label provider must implement the ILabelProvider interface, whose methods are listed in Table 14-3.

Table 14-3. ILabelProvider *(and Inherited) Methods*

Method	Description
void addListener(ILabelProvider Listener listener)	Called when a listener is added to this label provider. In this method, add the listener to a list that you maintain.
void dispose()	Called when the TreeViewer is being disposed. In this method, dispose anything you've created that needs to be disposed.
Image getImage(Object element)	Called when the TreeViewer wants the image to display for a specific element. In this method, return the proper image for the specified element, or null for no image.
String getText(Object element)	Called when the TreeViewer wants the label to display for a specific element. In this method, return the proper text for the specified element.
boolean isLabelProperty(Object element, String property)	Called when the TreeViewer wants to determine if a change to the specified property on the specified element would affect the label. In this method, return true if changing the specified property would affect the label for the specified element, or false if it wouldn't.
void removeListener(ILabel ProviderListener listener)	Called when a listener is removed from this label provider. In this method, remove the listener from a list that you maintain.

To complete the preceding Node example, you create a class that implements ILabelProvider. You decide to call Node's getName() method to get the text to display for a node. You also decide to show a filled circle for nodes with children, and an empty circle for nodes without children. The class might look like this:

```
public class MyLabelProvider implements ILabelProvider {
  // The list to hold the listeners
  private java.util.List listeners;

  // The images
  private Image filledCircle;
  private Image emptyCircle;

  public MyLabelProvider() {
    // Create the listener list
    listeners  = new java.util.ArrayList();
```

```
    // Create the images
    try {
      filledCircle = new Image(null, new FileInputStream("filledCircle.png"));
      emptyCircle = new Image(null, new FileInputStream("emptyCircle.png"));
    }
    catch (FileNotFoundException e) { // Swallow it }
  }

  public void addListener(ILabelProviderListener listener) {
    // Add the listener
    listeners.add(listener);
  }

  public void dispose() {
    // Dispose the images
    if (filledCircle != null)
      filledCircle.dispose();
    if (emptyCircle != null)
      emptyCircle.dispose();
  }

  public Image getImage(Object element) {
    // Return filled circle if it has children, or empty circle if it doesn't
    return ((Node) element).getChildren().size() > 0 ? filledCircle :
      emptyCircle;
  }

  public String getText(Object element) {
    // Return the node's name
    return ((Node) element).getName();
  }

  public boolean isLabelProperty(Object element, String property) {
    // Only if the property is the name is the label affected
    return "name".equals(property);
  }

  public void removeListener(ILabelProviderListener listener) {
    // Remove the listener
    listeners.remove(listener);
  }
}
```

Notice that this class maintains a list of listeners, adding and removing as instructed, but never does anything with them. If this class had some state that could be changed, and if changing that state would affect how the labels were computed, you'd notify the listeners of the state change. That code might look something like this:

```
public void changeSomeState(Object someState) {
  this.someState = someState;
  LabelProviderChangedEvent = new LabelProviderChangedEvent(this);
```

```
for (int i = 0, n = listeners.size(); i < n; i++) {
  ILabelProviderListener listener = (ILabelProviderListener) listeners.get(i);
  listener.labelProviderChanged(event);
}
}
```

The TreeViewer adds itself to the label provider as a listener, so when you notify it of the change, it calls back to the label provider for the labels.

Seeing a TreeViewer in Action

The ever-present hierarchical data example for computer users is the file system, which consists of directories that contain both files and other directories. The FileTree example program uses a TreeViewer to allow users to navigate through the file system on their computers. It displays directories, subdirectories, and files. It displays a folder icon next to directories, and a piece-of-paper icon next to files. It also allows users to change how the files are displayed by toggling the checkbox next to "Preserve case." When the box is checked, the display mirrors the case of the files on the file system. When unchecked, it displays everything in uppercase.

The FileTree class contains the main() method and creates the TreeViewer (see Listing 14-1). In its createContents() method, it creates the TreeViewer and sets both its content provider and its label provider. Listing 14-2 contains the content provider class, FileTreeContentProvider, and Listing 14-3 contains the label provider class, FileTreeLabelProvider.

Listing 14-1. FileTree.java

```
package examples.ch14;

import org.eclipse.jface.viewers.TreeViewer;
import org.eclipse.jface.window.ApplicationWindow;
import org.eclipse.swt.SWT;
import org.eclipse.swt.events.*;
import org.eclipse.swt.layout.*;
import org.eclipse.swt.widgets.*;

/**
 * This class demonstrates TreeViewer. It shows the drives, directories, and files
 * on the system.
 */
public class FileTree extends ApplicationWindow {
  /**
   * FileTree constructor
   */
  public FileTree() {
    super(null);
  }
```

```
/**
 * Runs the application
 */
public void run() {
  // Don't return from open() until window closes
  setBlockOnOpen(true);

  // Open the main window
  open();

  // Dispose the display
  Display.getCurrent().dispose();
}

/**
 * Configures the shell
 *
 * @param shell the shell
 */
protected void configureShell(Shell shell) {
  super.configureShell(shell);

  // Set the title bar text and the size
  shell.setText("File Tree");
  shell.setSize(400, 400);
}

/**
 * Creates the main window's contents
 *
 * @param parent the main window
 * @return Control
 */
protected Control createContents(Composite parent) {
  Composite composite = new Composite(parent, SWT.NONE);
  composite.setLayout(new GridLayout(1, false));

  // Add a checkbox to toggle whether the labels preserve case
  Button preserveCase = new Button(composite, SWT.CHECK);
  preserveCase.setText("&Preserve case");

  // Create the tree viewer to display the file tree
  final TreeViewer tv = new TreeViewer(composite);
  tv.getTree().setLayoutData(new GridData(GridData.FILL_BOTH));
  tv.setContentProvider(new FileTreeContentProvider());
  tv.setLabelProvider(new FileTreeLabelProvider());
  tv.setInput("root"); // pass a non-null that will be ignored

  // When user checks the checkbox, toggle the preserve case attribute
  // of the label provider
  preserveCase.addSelectionListener(new SelectionAdapter() {
    public void widgetSelected(SelectionEvent event) {
```

```
      boolean preserveCase = ((Button) event.widget).getSelection();
      FileTreeLabelProvider ftlp = (FileTreeLabelProvider) tv
          .getLabelProvider();
      ftlp.setPreserveCase(preserveCase);
    }
  });
  return composite;
}


/**
 * The application entry point
 *
 * @param args the command line arguments
 */
public static void main(String[] args) {
  new FileTree().run();
}
}
```

Listing 14-2. FileTreeContentProvider.java

```
package examples.ch14;

import java.io.*;

import org.eclipse.jface.viewers.ITreeContentProvider;
import org.eclipse.jface.viewers.Viewer;

/**
 * This class provides the content for the tree in FileTree
 */
public class FileTreeContentProvider implements ITreeContentProvider {
  /**
   * Gets the children of the specified object
   *
   * @param arg0 the parent object
   * @return Object[]
   */
  public Object[] getChildren(Object arg0) {
    // Return the files and subdirectories in this directory
    return ((File) arg0).listFiles();
  }

  /**
   * Gets the parent of the specified object
   *
   * @param arg0 the object
   * @return Object
   */
  public Object getParent(Object arg0) {
```

```
      // Return this file's parent file
      return ((File) arg0).getParentFile();
    }

    /**
     * Returns whether the passed object has children
     *
     * @param arg0 the parent object
     * @return boolean
     */
    public boolean hasChildren(Object arg0) {
      // Get the children
      Object[] obj = getChildren(arg0);

      // Return whether the parent has children
      return obj == null ? false : obj.length > 0;
    }

    /**
     * Gets the root element(s) of the tree
     *
     * @param arg0 the input data
     * @return Object[]
     */
    public Object[] getElements(Object arg0) {
      // These are the root elements of the tree
      // We don't care what arg0 is, because we just want all
      // the root nodes in the file system
      return File.listRoots();
    }

    /**
     * Disposes any created resources
     */
    public void dispose() {
    // Nothing to dispose
    }

    /**
     * Called when the input changes
     *
     * @param arg0 the viewer
     * @param arg1 the old input
     * @param arg2 the new input
     */
    public void inputChanged(Viewer arg0, Object arg1, Object arg2) {
    // Nothing to change
    }
  }
```

Listing 14-3. `FileTreeLabelProvider.java`

```java
package examples.ch14;

import java.io.*;
import java.util.*;

import org.eclipse.jface.viewers.ILabelProvider;
import org.eclipse.jface.viewers.ILabelProviderListener;
import org.eclipse.jface.viewers.LabelProviderChangedEvent;
import org.eclipse.swt.graphics.Image;

/**
 * This class provides the labels for the file tree
 */
public class FileTreeLabelProvider implements ILabelProvider {
  // The listeners
  private List listeners;

  // Images for tree nodes
  private Image file;
  private Image dir;

  // Label provider state: preserve case of file names/directories
  boolean preserveCase;

  /**
   * Constructs a FileTreeLabelProvider
   */
  public FileTreeLabelProvider() {
    // Create the list to hold the listeners
    listeners = new ArrayList();

    // Create the images
    try {
      file = new Image(null, new FileInputStream("images/file.gif"));
      dir = new Image(null, new FileInputStream("images/directory.gif"));
    } catch (FileNotFoundException e) {
      // Swallow it; we'll do without images
    }
  }

  /**
   * Sets the preserve case attribute
   *
   * @param preserveCase the preserve case attribute
   */
  public void setPreserveCase(boolean preserveCase) {
    this.preserveCase = preserveCase;
```

```java
    // Since this attribute affects how the labels are computed,
    // notify all the listeners of the change.
    LabelProviderChangedEvent event = new LabelProviderChangedEvent(this);
    for (int i = 0, n = listeners.size(); i < n; i++) {
      ILabelProviderListener ilpl = (ILabelProviderListener) listeners.get(i);
      ilpl.labelProviderChanged(event);
    }
  }

  /**
   * Gets the image to display for a node in the tree
   *
   * @param arg0 the node
   * @return Image
   */
  public Image getImage(Object arg0) {
    // If the node represents a directory, return the directory image.
    // Otherwise, return the file image.
    return ((File) arg0).isDirectory() ? dir : file;
  }

  /**
   * Gets the text to display for a node in the tree
   *
   * @param arg0 the node
   * @return String
   */
  public String getText(Object arg0) {
    // Get the name of the file
    String text = ((File) arg0).getName();

    // If name is blank, get the path
    if (text.length() == 0) {
      text = ((File) arg0).getPath();
    }

    // Check the case settings before returning the text
    return preserveCase ? text : text.toUpperCase();
  }

  /**
   * Adds a listener to this label provider
   *
   * @param arg0 the listener
   */
  public void addListener(ILabelProviderListener arg0) {
    listeners.add(arg0);
  }
```

```
/**
 * Called when this LabelProvider is being disposed
 */
public void dispose() {
  // Dispose the images
  if (dir != null) dir.dispose();
  if (file != null) file.dispose();
}

/**
 * Returns whether changes to the specified property on the specified element
 * would affect the label for the element
 *
 * @param arg0 the element
 * @param arg1 the property
 * @return boolean
 */
public boolean isLabelProperty(Object arg0, String arg1) {
  return false;
}

/**
 * Removes the listener
 *
 * @param arg0 the listener to remove
 */
public void removeListener(ILabelProviderListener arg0) {
  listeners.remove(arg0);
}
}
```

If you want icons displayed next to your folders and directories, you must create or download them. The graphics should be in the images directory, and should be called file.gif and directory.gif. Run the application using Ant:

```
ant -Dmain.class=examples.ch14.FileTree
```

Figure 14-1 shows the program with "Preserve case" unchecked. Check "Preserve case" to see Figure 14-2.

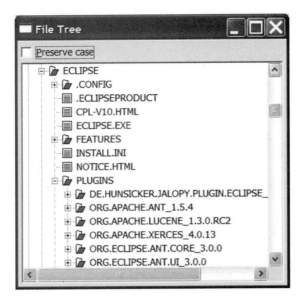

Figure 14-1. The FileTree program

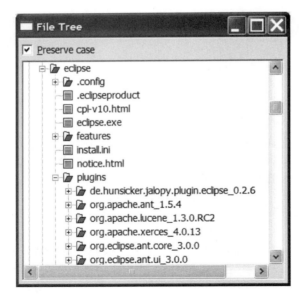

Figure 14-2. The FileTree program with "Preserve case" checked

Climbing Higher into TreeViewers

Much of the work associated with using a TreeViewer doesn't involve methods you call on TreeViewer, but instead relies on the provider classes you create. However, TreeViewer offers an extensive API, spread through both itself and its superclasses.

Analyzing `TreeViewer`'s public methods quickly plunges you into a morass of super-classes brimming with inherited methods. Climb high enough into `TreeViewer`'s inheritance tree, however, and you reach viewer classes common to `ListViewer` and `TableViewer` as well. Therefore, you can leverage your understanding across viewers. Table 14-4 lists `TreeViewer`'s public methods.

Table 14-4. `TreeViewer` *Methods*

Method	Description
`Control getControl()`	Returns a reference to this `TreeViewer`'s underlying `Tree` control.
`IBaseLabelProvider getLabelProvider()`	Returns the label provider for this `TreeViewer`.
`Tree getTree()`	Returns a reference to this `TreeViewer`'s underlying `Tree` control.
`void setLabelProvider (IBaseLabelProvider labelProvider)`	Sets the label provider for this `TreeViewer`. `labelProvider` must be an `ILabelProvider` instance.

`TreeViewer` derives from `AbstractTreeViewer`, which piles on a host of methods. Table 14-5 lists `AbstractTreeViewer`'s methods.

Table 14-5. `AbstractTreeViewer` *Methods*

Method	Description
`void add(Object parentElement, Object childElement)`	Adds the element specified by `childElement` to the tree as a child of the element specified by `parentElement`.
`void add(Object parentElement, Object[] childElements)`	Adds the elements specified by `childElements` to the tree as children of the element specified by `parentElement`.
`void addTreeListener(ITreeViewListener listener)`	Adds a listener that's notified when the tree is expanded or collapsed.
`void collapseAll()`	Collapses all the nodes in the tree.
`void collapseToLevel(Object element, int level)`	Collapses the tree from the root specified by `element` to the level specified by `level`.
`void expandAll()`	Expands all the nodes in the tree.
`void expandToLevel(int level)`	Expands the nodes in the tree from the root to the level specified by `level`.
`void expandToLevel(Object element, int level)`	Expands the nodes in the tree from the root specified by `element` to the level specified by `level`.
`int getAutoExpandLevel()`	Returns the level to which the nodes in the tree are automatically expanded.
`Object[] getExpandedElements()`	Returns the nodes that are expanded.
`boolean getExpandedState(Object element)`	Returns `true` if the node specified by `element` is expanded. Otherwise, returns `false`.
`Object[] getVisibleExpandedElements()`	Returns the visible nodes that are expanded.

Table 14-5. `AbstractTreeViewer` *Methods (continued)*

Method	Description
boolean isExpandable(Object element)	Returns true if the node specified by element can be expanded. Otherwise, returns false.
void remove(Object element)	Removes the element specified by element from the tree.
void remove(Object[] elements)	Removes the elements specified by elements from the tree.
void removeTreeListener(ITreeViewListener listener)	Removes the specified listener from the notification list.
void reveal(Object element)	Makes the element specified by element visible, scrolling if necessary.
Item scrollDown(int x, int y)	Scrolls the tree down one item from the point specified by (x, y).
Item scrollUp(int x, int y)	Scrolls the tree up one item from the point specified by (x, y).
void setAutoExpandLevel(int level)	Sets the level to which the nodes in the tree are automatically expanded.
void setContentProvider(IContentProvider provider)	Sets the content provider for this TreeViewer. provider must be an ITreeContentProvider instance.
void setExpandedElements(Object[] elements)	Sets the expanded elements in the tree to the elements specified by elements.
void setExpandedState(Object element, boolean expanded)	If expanded is true, expands the element specified by element. Otherwise, collapses it.

AbstractTreeViewer derives from StructuredViewer, which is the common ancestor for TreeViewer, ListViewer, and TableViewer. Its methods, then, apply to all types of viewers. Table 14-6 lists StructuredViewer's methods.

Table 14-6. `StructuredViewer` *Methods*

Method	Description
void addDoubleClickListener (IDoubleClickListener listener)	Adds a listener that's notified when the user double-clicks the mouse.
void addDragSupport(int operations, Transfer[] transferTypes, DragSourceListener listener)	Adds support for dragging an item or items out of this TreeViewer.
void addDropSupport(int operations, Transfer[] transferTypes, DropTargetListener listener)	Adds support for dropping an item or items into this TreeViewer.
void addFilter(ViewerFilter filter)	Adds the filter specified by filter to this TreeViewer and refilters the items.
void addOpenListener(IOpenListener listener)	Adds a listener that's notified when the user opens a selection.
void addPostSelectionChangedListener (ISelectionChangedListener listener)	Adds a listener that's notified when a selection changes via the mouse.

Table 14-6. StructuredViewer *Methods (continued)*

Method	Description
IElementComparer getComparer()	Returns the comparer used for comparing elements in this TreeViewer.
ViewerFilter[] getFilters()	Returns all the filters associated with this TreeViewer.
ISelection getSelection()	Returns this TreeViewer's selection.
ViewerSorter getSorter()	Returns this TreeViewer's sorter.
void refresh()	Refreshes this TreeViewer from the underlying data.
void refresh(boolean updateLabels)	Refreshes this TreeViewer from the underlying data. If updateLabels is true, updates the labels for all elements. If updateLabels is false, updates labels only for new elements.
void refresh(Object element)	Refreshes this TreeViewer from the underlying data, starting with the specified element.
void refresh(Object element, boolean updateLabels)	Refreshes this TreeViewer from the underlying data, starting with the specified element. If updateLabels is true, updates the labels for all elements. If updateLabels is false, updates labels only for new elements.
void removeDoubleClickListener (IDoubleClickListener listener)	Removes the specified listener from the notification list.
void removeFilter(ViewerFilter filter)	Removes the specified filter.
void removeOpenListener(IOpenListener listener)	Removes the specified listener from the notification list.
void removePostSelectionChangedListener (ISelectionChangedListener listener)	Removes the specified listener from the notification list.
void resetFilters()	Removes all filters.
void setComparer(IElementComparer comparer)	Sets the comparer used to compare elements.
void setContentProvider(IContentProvider provider)	Sets the content provider, which must be an IStructuredContentProvider instance.
void setInput(Object input)	Sets the input data.
void setSelection(ISelection selection, boolean reveal)	Sets the selection to the specified selection. If reveal is true, scrolls the viewer as necessary to display the selection.
void setSorter(ViewerSorter sorter)	Sets the sorter used to sort the elements.
void setHashlookup(boolean enable)	If enable is true, sets this viewer to use an internal hash table to map elements with widget items. You must call this before setInput().
void update(Object[] elements, String[] properties)	Updates the display of the specified elements, using the specified properties.
void update(Object element, String[] properties)	Updates the display of the specified element, using the specified properties.

StructuredViewer inherits ContentViewer. Table 14-7 lists ContentViewer's methods.

Table 14-7. ContentViewer *Methods*

Method	Description
IContentProvider getContentProvider()	Returns the content provider for this viewer
Object getInput()	Returns the input data for this viewer
IBaseLabelProvider getLabelProvider()	Returns the label provider for this viewer
void setContentProvider (IContentProvider contentProvider)	Sets the content provider for this viewer
void setInput(Object input)	Sets the input data for this viewer
void setLabelProvider (IBaseLabelProvider labelProvider)	Sets the label provider for this viewer

Finally, StructuredViewer derives from Viewer. Table 14-8 lists Viewer's methods.

Table 14-8. Viewer *Methods*

Method	Description
void addHelpListener(HelpListener listener)	Adds a listener to the notification list that's notified when help is requested.
void addSelectionChangedListener (ISelectionChangedListener listener)	Adds a listener to the notification list that's notified when the selection changes.
Object getData(String key)	Returns the data for the specified key that's associated with this viewer.
void removeHelpListener(HelpListener listener)	Removes the specified listener from the notification list.
void removeSelectionChangedListener (ISelectionChangedListener listener)	Removes the specified listener from the notification list.
Item scrollDown(int x, int y)	Scrolls down by one item from the item at the point specified by (x, y). Returns the new Item, or null if no new item was scrolled to.
Item scrollUp(int x, int y)	Scrolls up by one item from the item at the point specified by (x, y). Returns the new Item, or null if no new item was scrolled to.
void setData(String key, Object data)	Sets the data for the specified key into the viewer.
void setSelection(ISelection selection)	Sets the selection in this viewer.

If you're using an editor or IDE that automatically displays method completions, you might become overwhelmed by the panoply of methods offered by TreeViewer and the other viewer classes.

Using a CheckboxTreeViewer

JFace offers an extension to TreeViewer that adds a checkbox to each node in the tree. Aptly named CheckboxTreeViewer, it adds methods for managing the checkboxes. You create a CheckboxTreeViewer in the same way you create a TreeViewer, calling one of the three constructors that take the same parameters and behave the same as the TreeViewer constructors. Table 14-9 lists CheckboxTreeViewer's methods.

Table 14-9. CheckboxTreeViewer *Methods*

Method	Description
void addCheckStateListener (ICheckStateListener listener)	Adds a listener to the notification list that's notified when the checked state of any checkbox changes.
boolean getChecked(Object element)	Returns true if the specified element is checked. Otherwise, returns false.
Object[] getCheckedElements()	Returns all the checked elements in the tree.
boolean getGrayed(Object element)	Returns true if the specified element is grayed (indeterminate). Otherwise, returns false.
Object[] getGrayedElements()	Returns all the grayed (indeterminate) elements in the tree.
void removeCheckStateListener (ICheckStateListener listener)	Removes the listener from the notification list.
boolean setChecked(Object element, boolean state)	If state is true, sets the specified element to checked. Otherwise, sets the specified element to unchecked. Returns true if setting the checked state was successful. Otherwise, returns false.
void setCheckedElements(Object[] elements)	Sets the specified elements in the tree to checked, and sets any other elements in the tree to unchecked.
boolean setGrayChecked(Object element, boolean state)	If state is true, sets the specified element to grayed and checked. Otherwise, sets the specified element to ungrayed and unchecked. Returns true if setting the grayed and checked state was successful. Otherwise, returns false.
boolean setGrayed(Object element, boolean state)	If state is true, sets the specified element to grayed. Otherwise, sets the specified element to ungrayed. Returns true if setting the grayed state was successful. Otherwise, returns false.
void setGrayedElements(Object[] elements)	Sets the specified elements in the tree to grayed, and sets any other elements in the tree to ungrayed.
boolean setParentsGrayed(Object element, boolean state)	If state is true, sets the specified element and all its ancestors to grayed. Otherwise, sets the specified element and all its ancestors to ungrayed. Returns true if setting the grayed state was successful. Otherwise, returns false.
boolean setSubtreeChecked(Object element, boolean state)	If state is true, sets the specified element and all its children to checked. Otherwise, sets the specified element and all its children to unchecked. Returns true if setting the checked state was successful. Otherwise, returns false.

The CheckFileTree program revisits the FileTree program, adding checkboxes to each node in the tree. Checking a file or directory causes all its child files and directories to be checked as well. Unchecking has no such effect. Any file whose checkbox is checked displays the length of the file beside the filename.

The CheckFileTree program leverages the FileTree program, subclassing FileTree and reusing its content and label provider classes (see Listing 14-4).

Listing 14-4. `CheckFileTree.java`

```java
package examples.ch14;

import org.eclipse.jface.viewers.*;
import org.eclipse.swt.SWT;
import org.eclipse.swt.events.*;
import org.eclipse.swt.layout.*;
import org.eclipse.swt.widgets.*;

/**
 * This class demonstrates the CheckboxTreeViewer
 */
public class CheckFileTree extends FileTree {
  /**
   * Configures the shell
   *
   * @param shell the shell
   */
  protected void configureShell(Shell shell) {
    super.configureShell(shell);
    shell.setText("Check File Tree");
  }

  /**
   * Creates the main window's contents
   *
   * @param parent the main window
   * @return Control
   */
  protected Control createContents(Composite parent) {
    Composite composite = new Composite(parent, SWT.NONE);
    composite.setLayout(new GridLayout(1, false));

    // Add a checkbox to toggle whether the labels preserve case
    Button preserveCase = new Button(composite, SWT.CHECK);
    preserveCase.setText("&Preserve case");

    // Create the tree viewer to display the file tree
    final CheckboxTreeViewer tv = new CheckboxTreeViewer(composite);
    tv.getTree().setLayoutData(new GridData(GridData.FILL_BOTH));
    tv.setContentProvider(new FileTreeContentProvider());
    tv.setLabelProvider(new FileTreeLabelProvider());
    tv.setInput("root"); // pass a non-null that will be ignored
```

```
    // When user checks the checkbox, toggle the preserve case attribute
    // of the label provider
    preserveCase.addSelectionListener(new SelectionAdapter() {
      public void widgetSelected(SelectionEvent event) {
        boolean preserveCase = ((Button) event.widget).getSelection();
        FileTreeLabelProvider ftlp = (FileTreeLabelProvider) tv
            .getLabelProvider();
        ftlp.setPreserveCase(preserveCase);
      }
    });

    // When user checks a checkbox in the tree, check all its children
    tv.addCheckStateListener(new ICheckStateListener() {
      public void checkStateChanged(CheckStateChangedEvent event) {
        // If the item is checked . . .
        if (event.getChecked()) {
          // . . . check all its children
          tv.setSubtreeChecked(event.getElement(), true);
        }
      }
    });
    return composite;
  }

  /**
   * The application entry point
   *
   * @param args the command line arguments
   */
  public static void main(String[] args) {
    new CheckFileTree().run();
  }
}
```

Besides creating a CheckboxTreeViewer instead of a TreeViewer, the biggest difference in this class is the addition of a listener for when checkboxes are checked or unchecked. Review the preceding checkStateChanged() implementation.

Compiling and running the program shows the big difference: checkboxes by each node, as Figure 14-3 demonstrates. Check a checkbox to see that all its child checkboxes are checked as well. Take care, however—if you check the root checkbox, you might have to wait awhile for all the children to become checked.

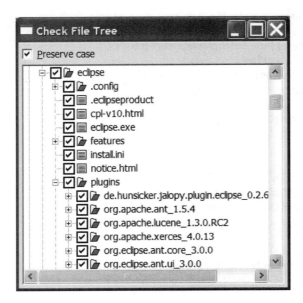

Figure 14-3. The CheckFileTree program

List Viewers

The List widget in SWT wraps a list box. You can add and remove items from a list. You can allow users to select only one item at a time, or to select many items simultaneously. Working directly with the widget, however, requires more detailed data management than you'll probably care for. JFace provides the ListViewer class to allow you to use an MVC approach to using lists.

Creating a ListViewer

ListViewer's constructors, listed in Table 14-10, will look familiar, as they mimic those for TreeViewer. The two constructors that don't take a List control as a parameter create one, as a ListViewer always wraps a List control.

Table 14-10. ListViewer Constructors

Constructor	Description
ListViewer(Composite parent)	Creates a ListViewer as a child of parent
ListViewer(Composite parent, int style)	Creates a ListViewer with the specified style as a child of parent
ListViewer(List list)	Creates a ListViewer that wraps the list control specified by list

To create a ListViewer, call one of its constructors. For example, the following code creates a composite and fills it with a ListViewer:

```
Composite composite = new Composite(shell, SWT.NONE);
composite.setLayout(new FillLayout());
ListViewer listViewer = new ListViewer(composite);
```

Using a ListViewer

You use a ListViewer the same way you use the other viewer classes:

1. Create a ListViewer.

2. Add a content provider.

3. Add a label provider.

4. Set the input.

For example, the following code demonstrates the pattern for creating and using a ListViewer:

```
ListViewer listViewer = new ListViewer(parent);
listViewer.setContentProvider(new MyContentProvider());
listViewer.setLabelProvider(new MyLabelProvider());
listViewer.setInput(myData);
```

The content provider must implement the IStructuredContentProvider interface, requiring definitions for a subset of the methods required in the ITreeContentProvider interface. Table 14-11 lists the three required methods for IStructuredContentProvider. The label provider must implement the same ILabelProvider interface that a TreeViewer's label provider requires.

Table 14-11. IStructuredContentProvider *(and Inherited) Methods*

Method	Description
void dispose()	Called when the ListViewer is being disposed. In this method, dispose anything you've created that needs to be disposed.
Object[] getElements(Object inputElement)	Called when the ListViewer wants the rows for the list. In this method, return the rows of data for the list.
void inputChanged(Viewer viewer, Object oldInput, Object newInput)	Called when the underlying data is switched to other data. In this method, perform any action appropriate for a data change.

Sometimes you'll want to access the List control that underpins the ListViewer. For example, you might want to retrieve the number of items in the ListViewer. Because ListViewer has no direct means of reporting its count of items, you must call the getItemCount() method on the List. ListViewer offers two methods for returning the List control that it wraps: getControl() (which returns the List as a Control) and getList() (which returns it as a List). This code prints to the console the number of items in a ListViewer:

```
System.out.println(listViewer.getList().getItemCount());
```

Table 14-12 details `ListViewer`'s API. Because `ListViewer` derives from `StructuredViewer`, refer to Table 14-6 to follow its inherited methods.

Table 14-12. `ListViewer` *Methods*

Method	Description
void add(Object element)	Adds the specified element to the list.
void add(Object[] elements)	Adds the specified elements to the list.
Control getControl()	Returns a reference to this `ListViewer`'s `List` control.
Object getElementAt(int index)	Returns the element at the specified zero-based index in the list.
IBaseLabelProvider getLabelProvider()	Returns this `ListViewer`'s label provider.
List getList()	Returns a reference to this `ListViewer`'s `List` control.
void remove(Object element)	Removes the specified element from the list.
void remove(Object[] elements)	Removes the specified elements from the list.
void reveal(Object element)	Shows the specified element, scrolling the list as necessary.
void setLabelProvider(IBaseLabel Provider labelProvider)	Sets the label provider for this `ListViewer`. `labelProvider` must be an `ILabelProvider` instance.

Filtering Data

All viewers (at least, all viewers derived from `StructuredViewer`, which includes the viewers in this chapter) can selectively display data using filters. To apply a filter to the viewer, you first create a subclass of `ViewerFilter` and implement its `select()` method, which is abstract. Its signature looks like this:

```
boolean select(Viewer viewer, Object parentElement, Object element)
```

The `viewer` parameter contains a reference to the viewer this filter acts on. The `parentElement` parameter refers to the parent of the element in question, while the `element` parameter refers to the element that might or might not be filtered out of the viewer. Filtering an element doesn't remove it from the underlying data, but only suppresses it from the view.

Your implementation of the `select()` method should return `true` if the viewer should display the element, or `false` if it shouldn't. For example, the following `MyFilter` class hides any element whose `toString()` method returns a string that exceeds 15 characters:

```
public class MyFilter extends ViewerFilter {
  public boolean select(Viewer viewer, Object parentElement, Object element) {
```

```
    // Hide anything longer than 15 characters.
    // Note that this will throw a NullPointerException
    // if toString() returns null.
    return element.toString().length() <= 15;
  }
}
```

Your filters can also use the `viewer` and `parentElement` parameters to determine what value to return from `select()`.

You can apply multiple filters to a viewer. Call the `addFilter()` method, defined in `StructuredViewer`, to apply a filter, like this:

```
listViewer.addFilter(new MyFilter());
```

The viewer reacts immediately to the newly added filter, filtering all its data anew using it and any other applied filters. You can use the `removeFilter()` method to remove a filter, which also triggers the viewer to filter and redisplay its data. To use it, pass the filter you want to remove, like this:

```
listViewer.removeFilter(myFilter);
```

You must have a reference to the filter object you want to remove. You can also remove all filters with a single call to `resetFilters()`:

```
listViewer.resetFilters();
```

Seeing ListViewer in Action

The FoodList application uses a `ListViewer` to display a list of food. It contains both healthy and junk food. (To determine healthy vs. junk, we relied on years of our mothers' training; we apologize for any offense our arbitrary choices might give.) The application displays a checkbox, marked "Show only healthy," for filtering the data. Checking the checkbox applies a filter to the data, hiding all the junk food.

You can find the code for the FoodList program in the Downloads section of the Apress Web site at http://www.apress.com. The `Food` class represents each food item, and stores the food's name and whether or not it's healthy. The `GroceryList` class represents the data model for the program. It creates ten food items—half healthy, half junk. The `ListViewer` uses an instance of this class as its input data. `FoodContentProvider` institutes the content provider for the program, and returns the list of `Food` objects associated with the viewer's `GroceryList` instance. `FoodLabelProvider` provides the labels for the list, using `Food.getName()`.

The `HealthyFilter` class provides the filter that's applied when the user checks the "Show only healthy" checkbox (see Listing 14-5). Its `select()` method returns the value of `Food.getHealthy()` to determine whether a food should display.

Listing 14-5. HealthyFilter.java

```java
package examples.ch14;

import org.eclipse.jface.viewers.Viewer;
import org.eclipse.jface.viewers.ViewerFilter;

/**
 * This class filters only healthy items from the grocery list
 */
public class HealthyFilter extends ViewerFilter {
  /**
   * Returns whether the specified element passes this filter
   *
   * @param arg0 the viewer
   * @param arg1 the parent element
   * @param arg2 the element
   * @return boolean
   */
  public boolean select(Viewer arg0, Object arg1, Object arg2) {
    return ((Food) arg2).isHealthy();
  }
}
```

Finally, the FoodList class launches the program, creates the window and controls (including the ListViewer), and responds to user input. It applies or removes the "healthy filter" as appropriate. To accomplish this, it creates a member instance of HealthyFilter:

```java
private HealthyFilter filter = new HealthyFilter();
```

Then, it creates a checkbox to let users toggle the filter, and responds to user input by either adding or removing the filter, like this:

```java
// Add a checkbox to toggle filter
Button filterHealthy = new Button(composite, SWT.CHECK);
filterHealthy.setText("&Show only healthy");

// When user checks the checkbox, toggle the filter
filterHealthy.addSelectionListener(new SelectionAdapter() {
  public void widgetSelected(SelectionEvent event) {
    if (((Button) event.widget).getSelection())
      lv.addFilter(filter);
    else
      lv.removeFilter(filter);
  }
});
```

Figure 14-4 shows FoodList's main window, and Figure 14-5 shows the window with the healthy filter applied.

Figure 14-4. The food list

Figure 14-5. The food list with the healthy filter applied

Table Viewers

SWT's Table widget, discussed in Chapter 8, displays data in columns and rows. You create a Table, then create TableItem objects to place data into the table. You manage the rows, manage the columns, sort the data as necessary, and find yourself steeped in data management.

JFace's TableViewer takes the pain out of tables. As with the other viewers, you create the TableViewer, set the content provider, set the label provider, and set the input. Table 14-13 lists TableViewer's three constructors. The two that don't take a Table as a parameter create a Table for the TableViewer to wrap.

Table 14-13. `TableViewer` *Constructors*

Constructor	Description
`TableViewer(Composite parent)`	Creates a `TableViewer` as a child of parent
`TableViewer(Composite parent, int style)`	Creates a `TableViewer` with the specified style as a child of parent
`TableViewer(Table table)`	Creates a `TableViewer` that wraps the table control specified by `table`

Using a TableViewer

As with the other viewers, you create a content provider class to add content to the table, and a label provider class to tell the table viewer how to display that content. You also must set the input data. The code might look like this:

```
TableViewer tableViewer = new TableViewer(parent);
tableViewer.setContentProvider(new MyContentProvider());
tableViewer.setLabelProvider(new MyLabelProvider());
tableViewer.setInput(myData);
```

As with `ListViewer`, the content provider must implement the `IStructuredContentProvider` interface, which requires definitions for the three methods listed in Table 14-14.

Table 14-14. `IStructuredContentProvider` *(and Inherited) Methods*

Method	Description
`void dispose()`	Called when the `TableViewer` is being disposed. In this method, dispose anything you've created that needs to be disposed.
`Object[] getElements(Object inputElement)`	Called when the `TableViewer` wants the rows for the table. In this method, return the rows of data for the table.
`void inputChanged(Viewer viewer, Object oldInput, Object newInput)`	Called when the underlying data is switched to other data. In this method, perform any action appropriate for a data change.

For example, suppose an `ArrayList` called `myList` contains your data. Each item in `myList` contains an object called `Widget`, which possesses a name, a color, and a price. Each `Widget` also contains an image of itself. Your content provider might look like this:

```
public class MyContentProvider implements IStructuredContentProvider {
  public void dispose() {
    // Nothing to dispose
  }
```

```
public Object[] getElements(Object inputElement) {
  // inputElement, the input data, is myList
  return ((List) myList).toArray();
}

public void inputChanged(Viewer viewer, Object oldInput, Object newInput) {
  // Nothing to do
}
}
```

The getElements() method returns all the Widgets in an array. Each item in the array becomes a row in the table. However, without the label provider, nothing displays in the table. To achieve visibility, you must create the label provider.

The label provider must implement the ITableLabelProvider interface, requiring definitions for the six methods listed in Table 14-15.

Table 14-15. ITableLabelProvider *(and Inherited) Methods*

Method	Description
void addListener(ILabelProvider Listener listener)	Called when a listener is added to this label provider. In this method, add the listener to a list that you maintain.
void dispose()	Called when the TableViewer is being disposed. In this method, dispose anything you've created that needs to be disposed.
Image getColumnImage(Object element, int columnIndex)	Called when the TableViewer wants the image to display for a specific element, for the specified column. In this method, return the proper image for the specified element and column, or null for no image.
String getColumnText(Object element, int columnIndex)	Called when the TableViewer wants the label to display for a specific element, for the specified column. In this method, return the proper text for the specified element and column.
boolean isLabelProperty(Object element, String property)	Called when the TableViewer wants to determine if a change to the specified property on the specified element would affect the label. In this method, return true if changing the specified property would affect the label for the specified element, or false if it wouldn't.
void removeListener(ILabelProvider Listener listener)	Called when a listener is removed from this label provider. In this method, remove the listener from a list that you maintain.

For the Widget example, your label provider might look like this:

```
public class MyLabelProvider implements ITableLabelProvider {
  // Holds the listeners
  List listeners = new ArrayList();
```

```
  public void addListener(ILabelProviderListener listener) {
    // Add the listener
    listeners.add(listener);
  }

  public void dispose() {
    // Nothing to dispose--the widgets own their own images,
    // so THEY must dispose them
  }

  public Image getColumnImage(Object element, int columnIndex) {
    // Show the image by the name
    if (columnIndex == NAME_COLUMN)
      return ((Widget) element).getImage();
    return null;
  }

  public String getColumnText(Object element, int columnIndex) {
    Widget w = (Widget) element;
    switch(columnIndex) {
    case NAME_COLUMN:
      return w.getName();
    case COLOR_COLUMN:
      return w.getColor();
    case PRICE_COLUMN:
      return w.getPrice();
    }
    // Should never get here
    return "";
  }

  public boolean isLabelProperty(Object element, String property) {
    return false;
  }

  public void removeListener(ILabelProviderListener listener) {
    listeners.remove(listener);
  }
}
```

You must define the column constants (NAME_COLUMN, COLOR_COLUMN, and PRICE_COLUMN) somewhere. They correspond to the columns in the table. Note that you must create the table column on the table that the TableViewer wraps. That code might look like this:

```
// Get the underlying table
Table table = tableViewer.getTable();
new TableColumn(table, SWT.LEFT).setText("Name");
new TableColumn(table, SWT.LEFT).setText("Color");
new TableColumn(table, SWT.LEFT).setText("Price");
```

You might never need to call more of TableViewer's API, but that API lurks patiently, awaiting your needs. Many of the methods deal with editing table data, which this chapter covers. Table 14-16 lists TableViewer's methods.

Table 14-16. TableViewer *Methods*

Method	Description
void add(Object element)	Adds the specified element to the table.
void add(Object[] elements)	Adds the specified elements to the table.
void cancelEditing()	Cancels the current editing session.
void editElement(Object element, int column)	Starts an editing session on the cell specified by element and column.
CellEditor[] getCellEditors()	Returns this TableViewer's cell editors.
ICellModifier getCellModifier()	Returns this TableViewer's cell modifier.
Object[] getColumnProperties()	Returns the column properties for this TableViewer.
Control getControl()	Returns the Table control that this TableViewer wraps.
Object getElementAt(int index)	Returns the element at the specified zero-based row in the table.
IBaseLabelProvider getLabelProvider()	Returns the label provider for this TableViewer.
Table getTable()	Returns the Table control that this TableViewer wraps.
void insert(Object element, int position)	Inserts the specified element into the table, at the zero-based row specified by position.
boolean isCellEditorActive()	Returns true if a cell editor is active. Otherwise, returns false.
void remove(Object element)	Removes the specified element from the table.
void remove(Object[] elements)	Removes the specified elements from the table.
void reveal(Object element)	Scrolls the specified element into view.
void setCellEditors(CellEditor[] cellEditors)	Sets the cell editors for this TableViewer.
void setCellModifier(ICellModifier cellModifier)	Sets the cell modifier for this TableViewer.
void setColumnProperties(String[] columnProperties)	Sets the column properties for this TableViewer.
void setLabelProvider(IBaseLabel Provider labelProvider)	Sets the label provider for this TableViewer, which must be either an instance of ITableLabelProvider or ILabelProvider.

TableViewer derives from StructuredViewer, so refer to Table 14-6 to follow the rest of its API.

Seeing a TableViewer in Action

The PlayerTable program uses a TableViewer to display the names and statistics of the players from three of the greatest teams in NBA history: the 1985-86 Boston Celtics, the 1987-88 Los Angeles Lakers, and the 1995-96 Chicago Bulls. You can find the code in the downloaded files.

The Player class represents each player, storing his name, points per game, rebounds per game, and assists per game. It also stores a reference to the team the player belongs to, and adds a method to determine whether the player led his team in a specified category. The Team class contains the collection of players that belong to it, as well as the team name and the year. It also contains a method for determining whether a player led his team in the given category; Player's ledTeam() method calls this method. The PlayerConst class contains constants for the application. Specifically, it contains constants for the column indices in the table. The PlayerTableModel class creates and manages the teams and players. The application uses this class to retrieve the specified team as the current data for the table.

The PlayerContentProvider class provides the content for the table. When passed a team, it returns all the players for that team. The PlayerLabelProvider class provides both the labels and the images for the table. If a player led his team in a category, the table displays an image next to that category. For example, because Michael Jordan led his team in scoring average, the table displays a graphic next to his points value. No image displays when the player didn't lead his team. You'll need to create the image to display, or copy it from the downloaded files.

The PlayerViewerSorter class, shown in Listing 14-6, provides sorting for the table. Click a column header to sort the data ascending; click the header again to sort descending. It extends the ViewerSorter class, and uses StructuredViewer's setSorter() method to set the sorter into the table. The TableViewer calls the sorter's compare() method to determine sort order. PlayerViewerSorter retains the index of the sorted column and the direction of the sort, so that it can determine which direction to sort the data. If the sort column is different from the last sorted column, it sorts the data in ascending order. If the sort column is the same column, it toggles the sort direction between ascending and descending order.

Listing 14-6. PlayerViewerSorter.java

```java
package examples.ch14;

import org.eclipse.jface.viewers.*;

/**
 * This class implements the sorting for the Player Table
 */
public class PlayerViewerSorter extends ViewerSorter {
  private static final int ASCENDING = 0;
  private static final int DESCENDING = 1;

  private int column;
  private int direction;
```

```
/**
 * Does the sort. If it's a different column from the previous sort, do an
 * ascending sort. If it's the same column as the last sort, toggle the sort
 * direction.
 *
 * @param column
 */
public void doSort(int column) {
  if (column == this.column) {
    // Same column as last sort; toggle the direction
    direction = 1 - direction;
  } else {
    // New column; do an ascending sort
    this.column = column;
    direction = ASCENDING;
  }
}

/**
 * Compares the object for sorting
 */
public int compare(Viewer viewer, Object e1, Object e2) {
  int rc = 0;
  Player p1 = (Player) e1;
  Player p2 = (Player) e2;

  // Determine which column and do the appropriate sort
  switch (column) {
  case PlayerConst.COLUMN_FIRST_NAME:
    rc = collator.compare(p1.getFirstName(), p2.getFirstName());
    break;
  case PlayerConst.COLUMN_LAST_NAME:
    rc = collator.compare(p1.getLastName(), p2.getLastName());
    break;
  case PlayerConst.COLUMN_POINTS:
    rc = p1.getPoints() > p2.getPoints() ? 1 : -1;
    break;
  case PlayerConst.COLUMN_REBOUNDS:
    rc = p1.getRebounds() > p2.getRebounds() ? 1 : -1;
    break;
  case PlayerConst.COLUMN_ASSISTS:
    rc = p1.getAssists() > p2.getAssists() ? 1 : -1;
    break;
  }

  // If descending order, flip the direction
  if (direction == DESCENDING) rc = -rc;

  return rc;
}
}
```

Finally, the PlayerTable class runs the program. It creates the main window, including the TableViewer, and provides the controller. It creates a dropdown to allow users to select which of the three teams to display. It responds to clicks on the column headers to change the sorting. To implement the sorting, it creates a PlayerViewerSorter instance and passes it to the TableViewer's setSorter() method. Then, as it adds each column, it adds a handler to respond to clicks on that column's header. In the handler, it retrieves the sorter from the TableViewer and calls its doSort() method, passing the column that was clicked. That part of the code looks like this:

```
tv.setSorter(new PlayerViewerSorter());

// Add the first name column
TableColumn tc = new TableColumn(table, SWT.LEFT);
tc.setText("First Name");
tc.addSelectionListener(new SelectionAdapter() {
  public void widgetSelected(SelectionEvent event) {
    ((PlayerViewerSorter) tv.getSorter())
      .doSort(PlayerConst.COLUMN_FIRST_NAME);
    tv.refresh();
  }
});

// Add the last name column
tc = new TableColumn(table, SWT.LEFT);
tc.setText("Last Name");
tc.addSelectionListener(new SelectionAdapter() {
  public void widgetSelected(SelectionEvent event) {
    ((PlayerViewerSorter) tv.getSorter())
      .doSort(PlayerConst.COLUMN_LAST_NAME);
    tv.refresh();
  }
});

// Add the points column
tc = new TableColumn(table, SWT.RIGHT);
tc.setText("Points");
tc.addSelectionListener(new SelectionAdapter() {
  public void widgetSelected(SelectionEvent event) {
    ((PlayerViewerSorter) tv.getSorter())
      .doSort(PlayerConst.COLUMN_POINTS);
    tv.refresh();
  }
});

// Add the rebounds column
tc = new TableColumn(table, SWT.RIGHT);
tc.setText("Rebounds");
tc.addSelectionListener(new SelectionAdapter() {
  public void widgetSelected(SelectionEvent event) {
```

```
    ((PlayerViewerSorter) tv.getSorter())
      .doSort(PlayerConst.COLUMN_REBOUNDS);
    tv.refresh();
  }
});

// Add the assists column
tc = new TableColumn(table, SWT.RIGHT);
tc.setText("Assists");
tc.addSelectionListener(new SelectionAdapter() {
  public void widgetSelected(SelectionEvent event) {
    ((PlayerViewerSorter) tv.getSorter())
      .doSort(PlayerConst.COLUMN_ASSISTS);
    tv.refresh();
  }
});
```

Compile and run the application to see the window shown in Figure 14-6; notice that Larry Bird led his team in all three categories. Figure 14-7 shows the Chicago Bulls, sorted by points per game. No surprise on whose name stands at the top of the list.

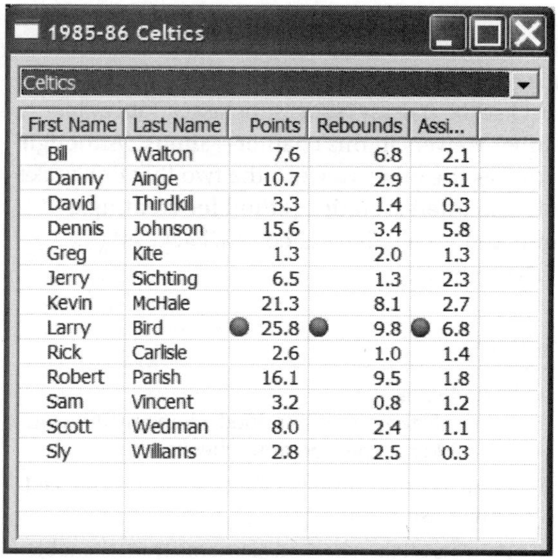

First Name	Last Name	Points	Rebounds	Assi...
Bill	Walton	7.6	6.8	2.1
Danny	Ainge	10.7	2.9	5.1
David	Thirdkill	3.3	1.4	0.3
Dennis	Johnson	15.6	3.4	5.8
Greg	Kite	1.3	2.0	1.3
Jerry	Sichting	6.5	1.3	2.3
Kevin	McHale	21.3	8.1	2.7
Larry	Bird	● 25.8	● 9.8	● 6.8
Rick	Carlisle	2.6	1.0	1.4
Robert	Parish	16.1	9.5	1.8
Sam	Vincent	3.2	0.8	1.2
Scott	Wedman	8.0	2.4	1.1
Sly	Williams	2.8	2.5	0.3

Window title: 1985-86 Celtics — Dropdown: Celtics

Figure 14-6. The 1985–86 Boston Celtics

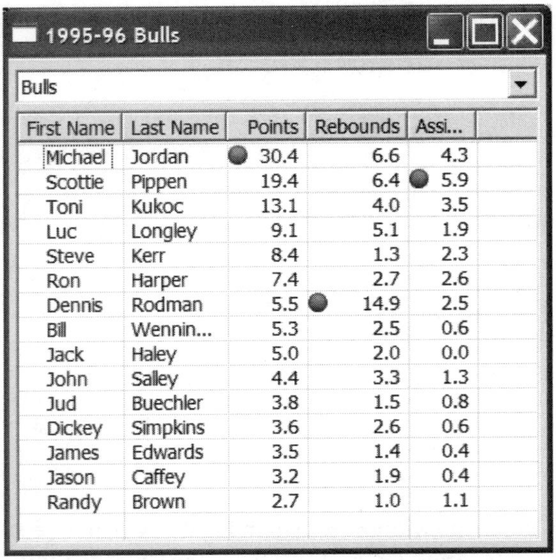

Figure 14-7. The 1995–96 Chicago Bulls

CheckboxTableViewer

Not to be outdone by TreeViewer and CheckboxTreeViewer, TableViewer also offers a version with checkboxes. This class, CheckboxTableViewer, subclasses TableViewer, and follows the same pattern as the other viewers in this chapter—almost. Although it does offer the same three constructors as the other viewers, the two that don't take the control to wrap are deprecated. It also offers a static method for creating a CheckboxTableViewer with one column and no header, called newCheckList(). Table 14-17 lists CheckboxTableViewer's methods.

Table 14-17. CheckboxTableViewer *Methods*

Method	Description
void addCheckStateListener (ICheckStateListener listener)	Adds a listener that's notified when any items in the table are checked or unchecked.
boolean getChecked(Object element)	Returns true if the specified element is checked. Otherwise, returns false.
Object[] getCheckedElements()	Returns all the checked elements from the table.
boolean getGrayed(Object element)	Returns true if the specified element is grayed. Otherwise, returns false.
Object[] getGrayedElements()	Returns all the grayed elements from the table.
void removeCheckStateListener (ICheckStateListener listener)	Removes the specified listener from the notification list.
void setAllChecked(boolean state)	If state is true, sets all the elements in the table to checked. Otherwise, sets all the elements in the table to unchecked.

Table 14-17. `CheckboxTableViewer` *Methods (continued)*

Method	Description
void setAllGrayed(boolean state)	If state is true, sets all the elements in the table to grayed. Otherwise, sets all the elements in the table to ungrayed.
boolean setChecked(Object element, boolean state)	If state is true, sets the specified element to checked. Otherwise, sets the specified element to unchecked. Returns true if setting the checked state was successful. Otherwise, returns false.
void setCheckedElements(Object[] elements)	Sets the specified elements in the table to checked, and sets any other elements in the table to unchecked.
boolean setGrayed(Object element, boolean state)	If state is true, sets the specified element to grayed. Otherwise, sets the specified element to ungrayed. Returns true if setting the grayed state was successful. Otherwise, returns false.
void setGrayedElements(Object[] elements)	Sets the specified elements in the table to grayed, and sets any other elements in the table to ungrayed.

The BackupFiles program shows a typical usage of `CheckboxTableViewer`: it uses `CheckboxTableViewer.newCheckList()` to create a single column table, with no header, that lists all the files in a directory. It allows you to enter the directory for which to list files, and it allows you to enter a destination directory. Check the files you want to copy to the destination directory, and then click the copy button to copy the files. Though only a neophyte sysadmin would use BackupFiles as a backup solution, it ably demonstrates `CheckboxTableViewer`.

The program, which you can find in the downloaded files, comprises three files: the content provider, the label provider, and the main program. The content provider, `BackupFilesContentProvider`, implements `IStructuredContentProvider`, and returns all the files (but not directories or subdirectories) for the input directory. The label provider, `BackupFilesLabelProvider`, implements `ILabelProvider`. It could, instead, implement `ITableLabelProvider`. However, the BackupFiles program displays only one column in the table, so `ILabelProvider` adequately fills the need. It returns the file name, sans path, for each file. The `BackupFiles` class launches the program, creates the user interface (including the `CheckboxTableViewer` and its content and label providers), and responds to user input. Here's the code it uses to create the `CheckboxTableViewer` and set its providers:

```
// Create the CheckboxTableViewer to display the files in the source dir
final CheckboxTableViewer ctv =
  CheckboxTableViewer.newCheckList(composite, SWT.BORDER);
ctv.getTable().setLayoutData(new GridData(GridData.FILL_BOTH));
ctv.setContentProvider(new BackupFilesContentProvider());
ctv.setLabelProvider(new BackupFilesLabelProvider());
```

Compile and run the program. Figure 14-8 shows the program with a source and a destination directory set.

Figure 14-8. The BackupFiles program

TableTreeViewer

Another viewer that looks like a table, TableTreeViewer, combines a table and a tree. Based on SWT's TableTree control described in Chapter 9, it follows the same viewer pattern as the other viewers in this chapter:

1. Create the TableTreeViewer.

2. Set the content provider.

3. Set the label provider.

4. Set the input data.

It offers the standard three viewer constructors, listed in Table 14-18, and the methods listed in Table 14-19. It derives, not from TreeViewer, but from AbstractTreeViewer, which is the parent of TreeViewer. It's technically a TreeViewer, but has columns like a table. It's included here after the discussion of both TreeViewer and TableViewer to leverage their explanations.

Table 14-18. TableTreeViewer *Constructors*

Constructor	Description
TableTreeViewer(Composite parent)	Creates a TableTreeViewer as a child of parent
TableTreeViewer(Composite parent, int style)	Creates a TableTreeViewer with the specified style as a child of parent
TableTreeViewer(TableTree tableTree)	Creates a TableTreeViewer that wraps the TableTree control specified by tableTree

Table 14-19. `TableTreeViewer` *Methods*

Method	Description
void cancelEditing()	Cancels the current editing session.
void editElement(Object element, int column)	Starts an editing session with the cell specified by element and column.
CellEditor[] getCellEditors()	Returns all the cell editors for this TableTreeViewer.
ICellModifier getCellModifier()	Returns the cell modifier for this TableTreeViewer.
Object[] getColumnProperties()	Returns the column properties for this TableTreeViewer.
Control getControl()	Returns the TableTree that this TableTreeViewer wraps.
Object getElementAt(int index)	Returns the element at the specified zero-based index.
IBaseLabelProvider getLabelProvider()	Returns the label provider for this TableTreeViewer.
TableTree getTableTree()	Returns the TableTree that this TableTreeViewer wraps.
boolean isCellEditorActive()	Returns true if an editing session is active. Otherwise, returns false.
void setCellEditors(CellEditor[] cellEditors)	Sets the cell editors for this TableTreeViewer.
void setCellModifier (ICellModifier cellModifier)	Sets the cell modifier for this TableTreeViewer.
void setColumnProperties(String[] columnProperties)	Sets the column properties for this TableTreeViewer.
void setLabelProvider(IBase LabelProvider labelProvider)	Sets the label provider for this TableTreeViewer. labelProvider must be an instance of either ITableLabelProvider or ILabelProvider.

The PlayerTableTree program, which you can find in the downloaded files, displays the same data as the PlayerTable program, but in a TableTreeViewer instead of a TableViewer. Instead of listing the three teams in a combo box, requiring users to select one team at a time, it displays the teams as root nodes in the tree. Expand the nodes to see the players in that team.

The content provider for a TableTreeViewer must implement the ITreeContentProvider interface. The PlayerTreeContentProvider class must handle both Team and Player objects as nodes. It returns the teams from the model as the root elements.

You can almost use the same label provider that you used with the PlayerTable program, except that it can't handle Team objects, spewing out strange and misleading messages saying that the application hasn't yet been initialized. To correct this, create a new label provider class that extends the PlayerLabelProvider class. Call it PlayerTreeLabelProvider. When it receives requests, it passes any requests for Player objects to PlayerLabelProvider, and handles requests for Team objects. Its getColumnImage() and getColumnText() implementations look like this:

```
/**
 * Gets the image for the specified column
 * @param arg0 the player or team
 * @param arg1 the column
 * @return Image
 */
public Image getColumnImage(Object arg0, int arg1) {
  // Teams have no image
  if (arg0 instanceof Player)
    return super.getColumnImage(arg0, arg1);
  return null;
}

/**
 * Gets the text for the specified column
 * @param arg0 the player or team
 * @param arg1 the column
 * @return String
 */
public String getColumnText(Object arg0, int arg1) {
  if (arg0 instanceof Player)
      return super.getColumnText(arg0, arg1);
  Team team = (Team) arg0;
  return arg1 == 0 ? team.getYear() + " " + team.getName() : "";
}
```

The PlayerTableTree class creates the user interface, including the TableTreeViewer. It creates an instance of PlayerTableModel and uses it as the input for the TableTreeViewer. It creates the content and label providers and launches the application. The part of the code that creates and sets up the TableTreeViewer looks like this:

```
// Create the table viewer to display the players
ttv = new TableTreeViewer(parent);
ttv.getTableTree().setLayoutData(new GridData(GridData.FILL_BOTH));

// Set the content and label providers
ttv.setContentProvider(new PlayerTreeContentProvider());
ttv.setLabelProvider(new PlayerTreeLabelProvider());
ttv.setInput(new PlayerTableModel());

// Set up the table
Table table = ttv.getTableTree().getTable();
new TableColumn(table, SWT.LEFT).setText("First Name");
new TableColumn(table, SWT.LEFT).setText("Last Name");
new TableColumn(table, SWT.RIGHT).setText("Points");
new TableColumn(table, SWT.RIGHT).setText("Rebounds");
new TableColumn(table, SWT.RIGHT).setText("Assists");

// Expand everything
ttv.expandAll();
```

```
// Pack the columns
for (int i = 0, n = table.getColumnCount(); i < n; i++) {
  table.getColumn(i).pack();
}

// Turn on the header and the lines
table.setHeaderVisible(true);
table.setLinesVisible(true);
```

Compiling and running the application produces the window seen in Figure 14-9.

First Name	Last Name	Points	Rebounds	Assists
Team Tree				
⊟ 1985-86 Celtics				
Larry	Bird	● 25.8	● 9.8	● 6.8
Kevin	McHale	21.3	8.1	2.7
Robert	Parish	16.1	9.5	1.8
Dennis	Johnson	15.6	3.4	5.8
Danny	Ainge	10.7	2.9	5.1
Scott	Wedman	8.0	2.4	1.1
Bill	Walton	7.6	6.8	2.1
Jerry	Sichting	6.5	1.3	2.3
David	Thirdkill	3.3	1.4	0.3
Sam	Vincent	3.2	0.8	1.2
Sly	Williams	2.8	2.5	0.3
Rick	Carlisle	2.6	1.0	1.4
Greg	Kite	1.3	2.0	1.3
⊟ 1995-96 Bulls				
Michael	Jordan	● 30.4	6.6	4.3
Scottie	Pippen	19.4	6.4	● 5.9
Toni	Kukoc	13.1	4.0	3.5
Luc	Longley	9.1	5.1	1.9
Steve	Kerr	8.4	1.3	2.3
Ron	Harper	7.4	2.7	2.6
Dennis	Rodman	5.5	● 14.9	2.5
Bill	Wennington	5.3	2.5	0.6
Jack	Haley	5.0	2.0	0.0
John	Salley	4.4	3.3	1.3
Jud	Buechler	3.8	1.5	0.8
Dickey	Simpkins	3.6	2.6	0.6
James	Edwards	3.5	1.4 ·	0.4
Jason	Caffey	3.2	1.9	0.4
Randy	Brown	2.7	1.0	1.1
⊟ 1987-1988 Lakers				
Magic	Johnson	● 23.9	6.3	● 12.2
James	Worthy	19.4	5.7	2.8
Kareem	Abdul-Jabbar	17.5	6.7	2.6
Byron	Scott	17.0	3.5	3.4
A.C.	Green	10.8	● 7.8	1.1
Michael	Cooper	10.5	3.1	4.5

Figure 14-9. A TableTreeViewer

Cell Editors

Users expect to be able to edit data in a table. To this point in the chapter, all the tables have presented read-only data. Editing data in place does add complexity, but JFace eases that burden significantly by using cell editors.

The `CellEditor` class stands as the base for all the cell editor classes. It's an abstract class, so you can't create a `CellEditor` instance. Instead, you create one of its concrete subclasses:

- `TextCellEditor`

- `CheckboxCellEditor`

- `ComboBoxCellEditor`

- `ColorCellEditor`

`ColorCellEditor` derives from a subclass of `CellEditor` called `DialogCellEditor`. You can create your own cell editors that rely on dialogs by subclassing `DialogCellEditor`.

`CellEditor` exposes a number of methods, listed in Table 14-20. Fortunately, the other cell editors expose no new methods, except for `ComboBoxCellEditor`. It exposes a method to set the items for the combo and a method to get the items from the combo:

- `void setItems(String[] items)` to set the items

- `String[] getItems()` to get the items

Table 14-20. `CellEditor` *Methods*

Method	Description
void activate()	Activates this cell editor.
void addListener(ICellEditor Listener listener)	Adds a listener that's notified when the user changes the cell editor's value, attempts to apply a change to the cell, or cancels editing.
void addPropertyChangeListener (IPropertyChangeListener listener)	Adds a listener that's notified when a property changes.
void create(Composite parent)	Creates the underlying control for this cell editor.
void deactivate()	Deactivates this cell editor.
void dispose()	Disposes this cell editor.
Control getControl()	Returns the underlying control for this cell editor.
String getErrorMessage()	Returns the current error message for this cell editor.
CellEditor.layoutData getLayoutData()	Returns the layout data for this cell editor.
int getStyle()	Returns the style values for this cell editor.
ICellEditorValidator getValidator()	Returns the validator for this cell editor.

Table 14-20. `CellEditor` *Methods (continued)*

Method	Description
`Object getValue()`	Returns the value of this cell editor.
`boolean isActivated()`	Returns true if this cell editor is activated. Otherwise, returns false.
`boolean isCopyEnabled()`	Returns true if this cell editor can copy to the clipboard. Otherwise, returns false.
`boolean isCutEnabled()`	Returns true if this cell editor can cut to the clipboard. Otherwise, returns false.
`boolean isDeleteEnabled()`	Returns true if this cell editor can perform a delete. Otherwise, returns false.
`boolean isDirty()`	Returns true if the value in this cell editor has changed and not been saved. Otherwise, returns false.
`boolean isFindEnabled()`	Returns true if this cell editor can perform a find. Otherwise, returns false.
`boolean isPasteEnabled()`	Returns true if this cell editor can paste from the clipboard. Otherwise, returns false.
`boolean isRedoEnabled()`	Returns true if this cell editor can redo the last action. Otherwise, returns false.
`boolean isSelectAllEnabled()`	Returns true if this cell editor can select all its contents. Otherwise, returns false.
`boolean isUndoEnabled()`	Returns true if this cell editor can undo the last action. Otherwise, returns false.
`boolean isValueValid()`	Returns true if this cell editor has a valid value. Otherwise, returns false.
`void performCopy()`	Copies this cell editor's value to the clipboard.
`void performCut()`	Cuts this cell editor's value to the clipboard.
`void performDelete()`	Performs a delete.
`void performFind()`	Performs a find.
`void performPaste()`	Pastes the value from the clipboard into this cell editor.
`void performRedo()`	Redoes the last action on this cell editor.
`void performSelectAll()`	Selects all the contents of this cell editor.
`void performUndo()`	Undoes the last action on this cell editor.
`void removeListener(ICellEditor Listener listener)`	Removes the specified listener from the notification list.
`void removePropertyChange Listener(IPropertyChangeListener listener)`	Removes the specified listener from the notification list.
`void setFocus()`	Sets the focus to this cell editor's control.
`void setStyle(int style)`	Sets the style values for this cell editor.
`void setValidator(ICellEditor Validator validator)`	Sets the validator for this cell editor.
`void setValue(Object value)`	Sets this cell editor's value.

Using Cell Editors

Cell editors use column properties in conjunction with an `ICellModifier` class to transfer data between the editor controls and the data model. The editing process uses the column property name, instead of a column index, to denote the column being modified. The `ICellModifier` interface declares the methods listed in Table 14-21.

Table 14-21. `ICellModifier` *Methods*

Method	Description
`boolean canModify(Object element, String property)`	Called to determine whether to allow modifications to the specified property on the specified element. Return `true` to allow modification, or `false` to disallow it.
`Object getValue(Object element, String property)`	Called to get the value of the specified property from the specified element, to put into the cell editor. Return the element's value for the specified property.
`void modify(Object element, String property, Object value)`	Called to transfer the value, specified by `value`, for the property specified by `property`, from the cell editor to the element. Copy the value to the appropriate location in the element. Note that this doesn't automatically refresh the view.

Suppose, for example, that you have a `TableViewer` that displays your entire vehicle inventory—both make and model—using instances of the `Car` class shown here:

```
public class Car {
   public String make;
   public String model;
}
```

You'll set up column properties on your `TableViewer` that look like this:

```
tableViewer.setColumnProperties(new String[] { "make", "model" });
```

These properties are passed to your `ICellModifier` implementation, which might look like this:

```
public class MyCellModifier implements ICellModifier {
   public boolean canModify(Object element, String property) {
      // Allow editing of everything
      return true;
   }
```

```
public Object getValue(Object element, String property) {
  Car car = (Car) element;
  if ("make".equals(property))
    return element.make;
  if ("model".equals(property))
    return element.model;
  // Shouldn't get here
  return null;
}

public void modify(Object element, String property, Object value) {
  // element can be passed as an Item
  if (element instanceof Item)
    element = ((Item) element).getData();

  Car car = (Car) element;
  if ("make".equals(property))
    car.make = (String) value;
  else if ("model".equals(property))
    car.model = (String) value;
  }
}
```

You set your `ICellModifier` class as the cell modifier for your `TableViewer` like this:

```
tableViewer.setCellModifier(new MyCellModifier());
```

Finally, you set your cell editors using `TableViewer.setCellEditors()`, which takes an array of `CellEditor` objects. The array indices correspond to the column indices, so leave slots in your array blank for any columns for which you don't want editing. For your car inventory program, your editor setup might look like this:

```
CellEditor[] editors = new CellEditor[2];
editors[0] = new TextCellEditor(tableViewer.getTable());
editors[1] = new TextCellEditor(tableViewer.getTable());
tableViewer.setCellEditors(editors);
```

Now you can edit your vehicles by typing directly into the `TableViewer`.

Seeing Cell Editors in Action

The PersonEditor program lists people in a `TableViewer`. It shows their names, whether or not they're male, their age range, and also allows you to change their shirt color. It uses a `TextCellEditor` to edit their names, a `CheckboxCellEditor` to edit whether they're male, a `ComboBoxCellEditor` to edit their age ranges, and a `ColorCellEditor` to edit their shirt colors. Listing 14-7 shows the code to hold a `Person`.

Listing 14-7. Person.java

```
package examples.ch14;

import org.eclipse.swt.graphics.RGB;

/**
 * This class represents a person
 */
public class Person {
  private String name;
  private boolean male;
  private Integer ageRange;
  private RGB shirtColor;

  /**
   * @return Returns the ageRange.
   */
  public Integer getAgeRange() {
    return ageRange;
  }

  /**
   * @param ageRange The ageRange to set.
   */
  public void setAgeRange(Integer ageRange) {
    this.ageRange = ageRange;
  }

  /**
   * @return Returns the male.
   */
  public boolean isMale() {
    return male;
  }

  /**
   * @param male The male to set.
   */
  public void setMale(boolean male) {
    this.male = male;
  }

  /**
   * @return Returns the name.
   */
  public String getName() {
    return name;
  }
```

```java
/**
 * @param name The name to set.
 */
public void setName(String name) {
  this.name = name;
}

/**
 * @return Returns the shirtColor.
 */
public RGB getShirtColor() {
  return shirtColor;
}

/**
 * @param shirtColor The shirtColor to set.
 */
public void setShirtColor(RGB shirtColor) {
  this.shirtColor = shirtColor;
}
}
```

Notice that Person stores its age range as an Integer. The value of a ComboBoxCellEditor is a zero-based index into its available options, stored as an Integer. Person uses the Integer to avoid having to map the index back to the value; you might find that in your applications you'll want to store the value instead. If so, you must perform the mapping, because ComboBoxCellEditor refuses anything but an Integer.

Because the PersonEditor program uses a TableViewer to display the people, you must create both a content provider and a label provider, shown in Listing 14-8 and Listing 14-9, respectively.

Listing 14-8. PersonContentProvider.java

```java
package examples.ch14;

import java.util.List;

import org.eclipse.jface.viewers.IStructuredContentProvider;
import org.eclipse.jface.viewers.Viewer;

/**
 * This class provides the content for the person table
 */
public class PersonContentProvider implements IStructuredContentProvider {
  /**
   * Returns the Person objects
   */
  public Object[] getElements(Object inputElement) {
    return ((List) inputElement).toArray();
  }
```

```
/**
 * Disposes any created resources
 */
public void dispose() {
// Do nothing
}

/**
 * Called when the input changes
 */
public void inputChanged(Viewer viewer, Object oldInput, Object newInput) {
// Ignore
}
}
```

Listing 14-9. `PersonLabelProvider.java`

```
package examples.ch14;

import org.eclipse.jface.viewers.ILabelProviderListener;
import org.eclipse.jface.viewers.ITableLabelProvider;
import org.eclipse.swt.graphics.Image;

/**
 * This class provides the labels for the person table
 */
public class PersonLabelProvider implements ITableLabelProvider {
  /**
   * Returns the image
   *
   * @param element the element
   * @param columnIndex the column index
   * @return Image
   */
  public Image getColumnImage(Object element, int columnIndex) {
    return null;
  }

  /**
   * Returns the column text
   *
   * @param element the element
   * @param columnIndex the column index
   * @return String
   */
  public String getColumnText(Object element, int columnIndex) {
    Person person = (Person) element;
    switch (columnIndex) {
    case 0:
      return person.getName();
```

```
    case 1:
      return Boolean.toString(person.isMale());
    case 2:
      return AgeRange.INSTANCES[person.getAgeRange().intValue()];
    case 3:
      return person.getShirtColor().toString();
    }
    return null;
}

/**
 * Adds a listener
 *
 * @param listener the listener
 */
public void addListener(ILabelProviderListener listener) {
// Ignore it
}

/**
 * Disposes any created resources
 */
public void dispose() {
// Nothing to dispose
}

/**
 * Returns whether altering this property on this element will affect the label
 *
 * @param element the element
 * @param property the property
 * @return boolean
 */
public boolean isLabelProperty(Object element, String property) {
    return false;
}

/**
 * Removes a listener
 *
 * @param listener the listener
 */
public void removeListener(ILabelProviderListener listener) {
// Ignore
}
}
```

The PersonCellModifier class, shown in Listing 14-10, implements the ICellModifier interface. It requires a reference to the parent viewer, so that it can force the viewer to refresh after any modifications.

Listing 14-10. `PersonCellModifier.java`

```java
package examples.ch14;

import org.eclipse.jface.viewers.*;
import org.eclipse.swt.graphics.RGB;
import org.eclipse.swt.widgets.Item;

/**
 * This class represents the cell modifier for the PersonEditor program
 */
public class PersonCellModifier implements ICellModifier {
  private Viewer viewer;

  public PersonCellModifier(Viewer viewer) {
    this.viewer = viewer;
  }

  /**
   * Returns whether the property can be modified
   *
   * @param element the element
   * @param property the property
   * @return boolean
   */
  public boolean canModify(Object element, String property) {
    // Allow editing of all values
    return true;
  }

  /**
   * Returns the value for the property
   *
   * @param element the element
   * @param property the property
   * @return Object
   */
  public Object getValue(Object element, String property) {
    Person p = (Person) element;
    if (PersonEditor.NAME.equals(property))
      return p.getName();
    else if (PersonEditor.MALE.equals(property))
      return Boolean.valueOf(p.isMale());
    else if (PersonEditor.AGE.equals(property))
      return p.getAgeRange();
    else if (PersonEditor.SHIRT_COLOR.equals(property))
      return p.getShirtColor();
    else
      return null;
  }
```

```
    /**
     * Modifies the element
     *
     * @param element the element
     * @param property the property
     * @param value the value
     */
    public void modify(Object element, String property, Object value) {
      if (element instanceof Item) element = ((Item) element).getData();

      Person p = (Person) element;
      if (PersonEditor.NAME.equals(property))
        p.setName((String) value);
      else if (PersonEditor.MALE.equals(property))
        p.setMale(((Boolean) value).booleanValue());
      else if (PersonEditor.AGE.equals(property))
        p.setAgeRange((Integer) value);
      else if (PersonEditor.SHIRT_COLOR.equals(property))
          p.setShirtColor((RGB) value);

      // Force the viewer to refresh
      viewer.refresh();
    }
}
```

The PersonEditor class launches the program, creates the interface, and sets up the column properties, the cell modifier, and the cell editors (see Listing 14-11).

Listing 14-11. PersonEditor.java

```
package examples.ch14;

import java.util.*;

import org.eclipse.jface.window.ApplicationWindow;
import org.eclipse.jface.viewers.*;
import org.eclipse.swt.SWT;
import org.eclipse.swt.events.*;
import org.eclipse.swt.graphics.*;
import org.eclipse.swt.layout.*;
import org.eclipse.swt.widgets.*;

/**
 * This class demonstrates CellEditors. It allows you to create and edit Person
 * objects.
 */
public class PersonEditor extends ApplicationWindow {
  // Table column names/properties
  public static final String NAME = "Name";
  public static final String MALE = "Male?";
```

```java
    public static final String AGE = "Age Range";
    public static final String SHIRT_COLOR = "Shirt Color";

    public static final String[] PROPS = { NAME, MALE, AGE, SHIRT_COLOR};

    // The data model
    private java.util.List people;

    /**
     * Constructs a PersonEditor
     */
    public PersonEditor() {
      super(null);
      people = new ArrayList();
    }

    /**
     * Runs the application
     */
    public void run() {
      // Don't return from open() until window closes
      setBlockOnOpen(true);

      // Open the main window
      open();

      // Dispose the display
      Display.getCurrent().dispose();
    }

    /**
     * Configures the shell
     *
     * @param shell the shell
     */
    protected void configureShell(Shell shell) {
      super.configureShell(shell);
      shell.setText("Person Editor");
      shell.setSize(400, 400);
    }

    /**
     * Creates the main window's contents
     *
     * @param parent the main window
     * @return Control
     */
    protected Control createContents(Composite parent) {
      Composite composite = new Composite(parent, SWT.NONE);
      composite.setLayout(new GridLayout(1, false));
```

```java
// Add a button to create the new person
Button newPerson = new Button(composite, SWT.PUSH);
newPerson.setText("Create New Person");

// Add the TableViewer
final TableViewer tv = new TableViewer(composite, SWT.FULL_SELECTION);
tv.setContentProvider(new PersonContentProvider());
tv.setLabelProvider(new PersonLabelProvider());
tv.setInput(people);

// Set up the table
Table table = tv.getTable();
table.setLayoutData(new GridData(GridData.FILL_BOTH));

new TableColumn(table, SWT.CENTER).setText(NAME);
new TableColumn(table, SWT.CENTER).setText(MALE);
new TableColumn(table, SWT.CENTER).setText(AGE);
new TableColumn(table, SWT.CENTER).setText(SHIRT_COLOR);

for (int i = 0, n = table.getColumnCount(); i < n; i++) {
  table.getColumn(i).pack();
}

table.setHeaderVisible(true);
table.setLinesVisible(true);

// Add a new person when the user clicks button
newPerson.addSelectionListener(new SelectionAdapter() {
  public void widgetSelected(SelectionEvent event) {
    Person p = new Person();
    p.setName("Name");
    p.setMale(true);
    p.setAgeRange(Integer.valueOf("0"));
    p.setShirtColor(new RGB(255, 0, 0));
    people.add(p);
    tv.refresh();
  }
});

// Create the cell editors
CellEditor[] editors = new CellEditor[4];
editors[0] = new TextCellEditor(table);
editors[1] = new CheckboxCellEditor(table);
editors[2] = new ComboBoxCellEditor(table, AgeRange.INSTANCES,
  SWT.READ_ONLY);
editors[3] = new ColorCellEditor(table);

// Set the editors, cell modifier, and column properties
tv.setColumnProperties(PROPS);
tv.setCellModifier(new PersonCellModifier(tv));
tv.setCellEditors(editors);
```

```
      return composite;
   }

   /**
    * The application entry point
    *
    * @param args the command line arguments
    */
   public static void main(String[] args) {
     new PersonEditor().run();
   }
}
```

Compile and run the program to see an empty table, as Figure 14-10 shows. Click the Create New Person button to create a new person in the table, as seen in Figure 14-11. You can then edit the person by clicking the appropriate cell and performing the appropriate edits. Figure 14-12 shows the program with some edits occurring.

Figure 14-10. The PersonEditor program

Figure 14-11. The PersonEditor program with one unedited person

Figure 14-12. The PersonEditor program with an edited person

Summary

Complex data, such as hierarchical or tabular data, can be difficult to manage—especially if widgets force you to manage it twice (once in your data storage, once in the widget). Even lists of data can be painful to work with when view and data inextricably merge, as they do when you work directly with widgets. Turn to JFace to remove this data management pain, using its MVC layer atop SWT's Tree, List, and Table widgets. JFace's viewers make dealing with views of complex data simple.

CHAPTER 15

JFace
Dialogs

SWT OFFERS A SLEW of dialogs, as Chapter 7 details. These dialogs cover color selection, font selection, directory selection, file selection, printer selection, and message display. They're a cinch to use: instantiate, call open(), and check the return value. No abstraction layer could make them easier to use than they already are. Yet JFace offers dialog classes. Why?

Closer inspection reveals that JFace's dialogs overlap SWT's only slightly. JFace doesn't contain the array of selection dialogs that SWT does. Instead, JFace offers dialogs to display error messages, accept input, and other helpful utility functions. Sure, you could build all JFace's dialogs yourself using SWT's dialog classes, but JFace's versions not only are already built, but have undergone extensive testing. However, they're designed to fill specific Eclipse needs, so you might find them inappropriate for your requirements. Use as appropriate, but don't shrink from falling back on SWT's dialog classes when they're better suited for what you're trying to accomplish.

This chapter covers the following JFace dialogs:

- ErrorDialog, for displaying errors

- InputDialog, for receiving input

- MessageDialog, for displaying messages

- ProgressMonitorDialog, for displaying progress during lengthy operations

- TitleAreaDialog, for building your own dialogs with a title, image, and message

- IconAndMessageDialog, for building your own dialogs with an icon and message

The org.eclipse.jface.dialogs package contains these classes.

Showing Errors

Up to this point, the examples in this book have cobbled together various error dialogs to give feedback to users. JFace offers a dialog for displaying errors. However, it betrays its Eclipse roots with its reliance on a non-null instance of IStatus, which is relatively unwieldy to set up. This error mechanism, though handy for use in Eclipse plug-ins, might prove more trouble than it's worth in desktop applications.

Creating a Status

The IStatus interface declares the methods listed in Table 15-1. JFace includes two classes that implement IStatus: Status and MultiStatus. As their names suggest, Status represents a single status (or error), while MultiStatus represents multiple statuses (or errors). Although IStatus, Status, and MultiStatus all refer to plug-in specifics (such as a plug-in-specific code or a plug-in identifier), you can shamelessly fake these values without repercussions.

Table 15-1. IStatus *Methods*

Method	Description
IStatus[] getChildren()	Returns the children of this IStatus for MultiStatuses, or an empty array for Statuses.
int getCode()	Returns the plug-in-specific code.
Throwable getException()	Returns the exception.
String getMessage()	Returns the message.
String getPlugin()	Returns the plug-in identifier.
int getSeverity()	Returns the severity code (see Table 15-2).
boolean isMultiStatus()	Returns true if this is a MultiStatus. Otherwise, returns false.
boolean isOK()	Returns true if this IStatus represents an OK state.
boolean matches(int severityMask)	Returns true if the severity code of this IStatus matches the specified severity mask.

Each IStatus instance requires a severity code. IStatus declares a set of constants for these severity codes, listed in Table 15-2.

Table 15-2. IStatus *Severity Codes*

Code	Description
int IStatus.CANCEL	Indicates that this status represents a cancellation
int IStatus.ERROR	Indicates that this status represents an error
int IStatus.INFO	Indicates that this status represents information
int IStatus.OK	Indicates that this status represents an OK state
int IStatus.WARNING	Indicates that this status represents a warning

To create a Status, call its only constructor:

```
Status(int severity, String pluginId, int code, String message,
  Throwable exception);
```

You can pass null for exception, but you're on the hook for the other values. severity should be one of the IStatus severity codes. You can pass whatever values you wish for the other parameters. The following code creates an error status:

```
Status status = new Status(IStatus.ERROR, "My Plug-in", 100, "An error happened",
  null);
```

Displaying the Error

With the IStatus instance created, you're ready to display an error. ErrorDialog offers a static method to do all the work for you: openError(). To display the error dialog, you call the following:

```
ErrorDialog.openError(shell, dialogTitle, message, status);
```

This code creates the dialog, displays it, and blocks until the user dismisses it. You'll notice that you pass two messages: one directly, and one in the Status object. The one you pass directly displays first; the one in the Status object displays below the text "Reason," as Figure 15-1 shows.

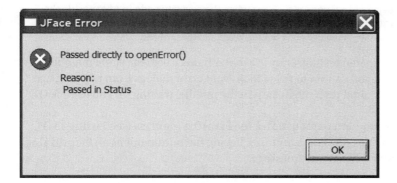

Figure 15-1. An ErrorDialog

You can, instead, construct an ErrorDialog and call its open() method. The constructor takes the same parameters as the openError() method, with the addition of an int representing a display mask. This display mask should contain one or more severity codes drawn from the IStatus constants, using the bitwise OR operator to chain multiples together. If the severity code in the passed Status object matches the display mask, the dialog displays. Otherwise, it doesn't. For example, the following code displays an error dialog:

```
Status status = new Status(IStatus.ERROR, "Will display", 0, "Error", null);
ErrorDialog dlg = new ErrorDialog(shell, "Title", "Message", status,
  IStatus.ERROR);
dlg.open();
```

However, the following code displays no dialog.

```
Status status = new Status(IStatus.ERROR, "Won't display", 0, "Error", null);
ErrorDialog dlg = new ErrorDialog(shell, "Title", "Message", status,
  IStatus.INFO);
dlg.open();
```

Table 15-3 lists `ErrorDialog`'s methods.

Table 15-3. `ErrorDialog` *Methods*

Method	Description
`boolean close()`	Closes this dialog and returns true
`int open()`	Opens the dialog, blocks until it's dismissed, and returns 0
`static int openError(Shell parent, String dialogTitle, String message, IStatus status)`	Creates a dialog, opens it, blocks until it's dismissed, and returns 0
`static int openError(Shell parent, String dialogTitle, String message, IStatus status, int displayMask)`	Creates a dialog, opens it if the display mask matches the severity code in `status`, blocks until it's dismissed, and returns 0

To facilitate automated testing, `ErrorDialog` contains a boolean static member—`AUTOMATED_MODE`—that you can set to `false` to prevent error dialogs from popping up. Otherwise, your automated tests might stop in the middle, waiting for you to click OK on an error message.

The ShowError program demonstrates the `ErrorDialog` class (see Listing 15-1). It displays a multiline text box and a button. Clicking the button opens an `ErrorDialog`, using the text in the text box for the message.

Listing 15-1. `ShowError.java`

```java
package examples.ch15;

import org.eclipse.core.runtime.*;
import org.eclipse.jface.dialogs.ErrorDialog;
import org.eclipse.jface.window.ApplicationWindow;
import org.eclipse.swt.SWT;
import org.eclipse.swt.events.*;
import org.eclipse.swt.layout.*;
import org.eclipse.swt.widgets.*;

/**
 * This class demonstrates JFace's ErrorDialog class
 */
public class ShowError extends ApplicationWindow {
  /**
   * ShowError constructor
   */
  public ShowError() {
    super(null);
  }
```

```
/**
 * Runs the application
 */
public void run() {
  // Don't return from open() until window closes
  setBlockOnOpen(true);

  // Open the main window
  open();

  // Dispose the display
  Display.getCurrent().dispose();
}

/**
 * Configures the shell
 *
 * @param shell the shell
 */
protected void configureShell(Shell shell) {
  super.configureShell(shell);

  // Set the title bar text and the size
  shell.setText("Show Error");
  shell.setSize(400, 400);
}

/**
 * Creates the main window's contents
 *
 * @param parent the main window
 * @return Control
 */
protected Control createContents(Composite parent) {
  Composite composite = new Composite(parent, SWT.NONE);
  composite.setLayout(new GridLayout(1, false));

  // Create a big text box to accept error text
  final Text text = new Text(composite, SWT.MULTI | SWT.BORDER | SWT.V_SCROLL);
  text.setLayoutData(new GridData(GridData.FILL_BOTH));

  // Create the button to launch the error dialog
  Button show = new Button(composite, SWT.PUSH);
  show.setText("Show Error");
  show.addSelectionListener(new SelectionAdapter() {
    public void widgetSelected(SelectionEvent event) {
      // Create the required Status object
      Status status = new Status(IStatus.ERROR, "My Plug-in ID", 0,
          "Status Error Message", null);
```

```
      // Display the dialog
      ErrorDialog.openError(Display.getCurrent().getActiveShell(),
          "JFace Error", text.getText(), status);
    }
  });

  return composite;
}

/**
 * The application entry point
 *
 * @param args the command line arguments
 */
public static void main(String[] args) {
  new ShowError().run();
}
}
```

Figure 15-2 shows the program with some error text swiped from the Project Gutenberg site (http://www.gutenberg.net/). Figure 15-3 shows the ErrorDialog resulting from that error text.

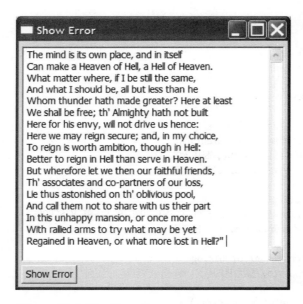

Figure 15-2. The ShowError program

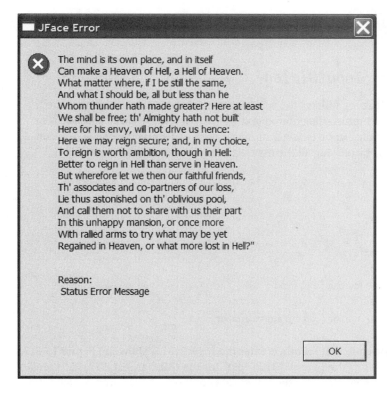

Figure 15-3. An ErrorDialog

Receiving Input

In contrast to ErrorDialog, InputDialog breaks free from any Eclipse underpinnings. You'll find it generally useful any time you want a line of text from the user. The dialog displays text in the title bar, a message, a Text field for input, and OK and Cancel buttons. You control the text in the title bar, the message, and the initial value for the input. Figure 15-4 displays a sample InputDialog.

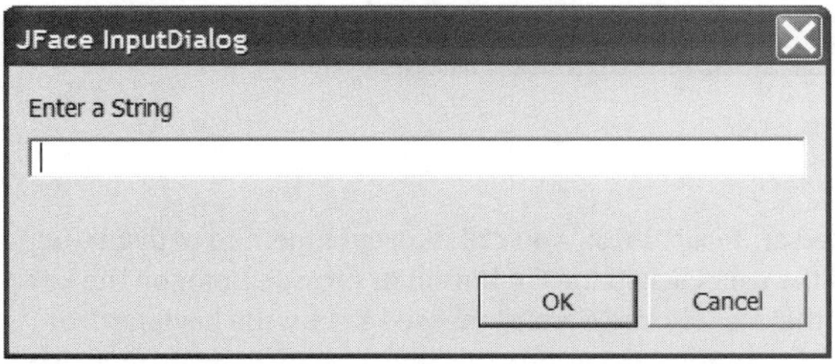

Figure 15-4. An InputDialog

Optionally, you can validate the text the user types. You can also subclass InputDialog to customize it to fit your needs.

Displaying an InputDialog

Displaying an InputDialog follows the typical pattern for dialogs, except that the open() method doesn't return the entered text. Instead, it returns either Window.OK or Window.CANCEL, depending upon which button was used to dismiss the dialog. You construct an InputDialog by passing all the necessary information to the constructor:

- The parent Shell

- The title bar text

- The message text

- The initial value for the Text field

- The validator to use, or null for no validator

For example, the code that follows creates the InputDialog shown in Figure 15-5. It uses the active Shell as the parent, "Title Text" for the title bar text, "This is a message" for the message text, blank for the initial value of the Text field, and no validator.

```
InputDialog dlg = new InputDialog(Display.getCurrent().getActiveShell(),
  "Title Text", "This is a message", "", null);
```

Figure 15-5. Another InputDialog

Once you've constructed an InputDialog, you call its open() method to display it. open() returns Window.OK if the user clicked the OK button or pressed Enter on the keyboard, or Window.CANCEL if the user clicked Cancel, pressed Esc on the keyboard, or clicked the window's close button. You can capture this return value to determine how the user dismissed the dialog.

Pranksters might consider crossing up users by reversing their reactions to OK and Cancel. However, JFace foils miscreant behavior: it preserves the typed value only when users click OK (or hit Enter). In other words, unless you subclass InputDialog and capture the typed value even if users cancel the dialog, you have no access to what the users typed unless they click OK.

To extract the text that a user typed in the InputDialog, call InputDialog.getValue(). It returns a String containing the text if the user clicked OK, or null if the user cancelled the dialog. The following code displays the dialog constructed earlier. It prints the typed text when the user clicks OK, or "User cancelled" when the user clicks Cancel.

```
int rc = dlg.open();
if (rc == Window.OK)
  System.out.println(dlg.getValue());
else
  System.out.println("User cancelled");
```

Validating Input

Once users click OK and you retrieve the input, you can validate that input however you'd like, accepting or rejecting it based on some relevant criteria. Perhaps you were expecting a ZIP code, and users typed the first seven words of the Gettysburg Address. You'd probably want to reject the input, display an error message, and display the InputDialog again. Though you're free to go the rounds with your users in this fashion, JFace offers a better alternative: in-place validating. Using a validator, you can validate the input as it's typed. In fact, until you approve the input, the user can't even click OK. The user can't give you bad input.

To use a validator, create a validator class that implements the IInputValidator interface. It declares one method:

```
String isValid(String newText)
```

InputDialog calls your implementation of the isValid() method every time the text in the input field changes, passing the complete text from the input field in the newText parameter. You return null if the text is copacetic, or an error message describing the problem if not. InputDialog unobtrusively displays any error message below the input field. Figure 15-6 shows an example; the error message in this case is "No way."

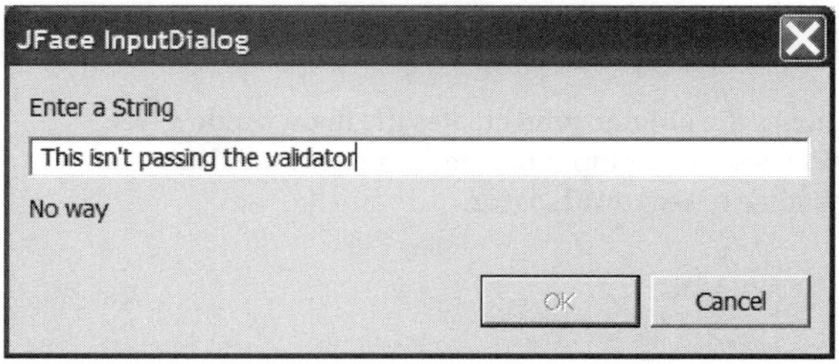

Figure 15-6. An InputDialog *with an error message*

To use your validator class, pass it as the ultimate parameter to the InputDialog constructor.

The GetInput program displays a Label and a Button. Click the button to display an InputDialog. Type text into the input field and click OK, and the text you typed displays in the Label in the main window.

The InputDialog uses a validator that enforces input that's between five and eight characters. The message in the dialog describes these parameters, and the error message gives appropriate feedback: if the input text is too short, it displays an error message that says, "Too short." If the input text is too long, the dialog displays an error message that says, "Too long." Listing 15-2 shows the validator class that affects this behavior, LengthValidator.

Listing 15-2. LengthValidator.java

```
package examples.ch15;

import org.eclipse.jface.dialogs.IInputValidator;

/**
 * This class validates a String. It makes sure that the String is between 5 and
 * 8 characters
 */
public class LengthValidator implements IInputValidator {
  /**
   * Validates the String. Returns null for no error, or an error message
   *
   * @param newText the String to validate
   * @return String
   */
  public String isValid(String newText) {
    int len = newText.length();

    // Determine if input is too short or too long
    if (len < 5) return "Too short";
    if (len > 8) return "Too long";

    // Input must be OK
    return null;
  }
}
```

The GetInput class launches the program and creates the main window (see Listing 15-3). When the user clicks the Get Input button, it creates and displays an InputDialog that uses an instance of LengthValidator.

Listing 15-3. `GetInput.java`

```java
package examples.ch15;

import org.eclipse.jface.dialogs.InputDialog;
import org.eclipse.jface.window.*;
import org.eclipse.swt.SWT;
import org.eclipse.swt.events.*;
import org.eclipse.swt.layout.*;
import org.eclipse.swt.widgets.*;

/**
 * This class demonstrates JFace's InputDialog class
 */
public class GetInput extends ApplicationWindow {
  /**
   * GetInput constructor
   */
  public GetInput() {
    super(null);
  }

  /**
   * Runs the application
   */
  public void run() {
    // Don't return from open() until window closes
    setBlockOnOpen(true);

    // Open the main window
    open();

    // Dispose the display
    Display.getCurrent().dispose();
  }

  /**
   * Configures the shell
   *
   * @param shell the shell
   */
  protected void configureShell(Shell shell) {
    super.configureShell(shell);

    // Set the title bar text
    shell.setText("Get Input");
  }
```

```
/**
 * Creates the main window's contents
 *
 * @param parent the main window
 * @return Control
 */
protected Control createContents(Composite parent) {
  Composite composite = new Composite(parent, SWT.NONE);
  composite.setLayout(new GridLayout(1, false));

  // Create a label to display what the user typed in
  final Label label = new Label(composite, SWT.NONE);
  label.setText("This will display the user input from InputDialog");

  // Create the button to launch the error dialog
  Button show = new Button(composite, SWT.PUSH);
  show.setText("Get Input");
  show.addSelectionListener(new SelectionAdapter() {
    public void widgetSelected(SelectionEvent event) {
      InputDialog dlg = new InputDialog(Display.getCurrent().getActiveShell(),
          "", "Enter 5-8 characters", label.getText(), new LengthValidator());
      if (dlg.open() == Window.OK) {
        // User clicked OK; update the label with the input
        label.setText(dlg.getValue());
      }
    }
  });

  parent.pack();
  return composite;
}

/**
 * The application entry point
 *
 * @param args the command line arguments
 */
public static void main(String[] args) {
  new GetInput().run();
}
}
```

Figure 15-7 shows this program's main window. Figure 15-8 shows the InputDialog when too few characters have been entered.

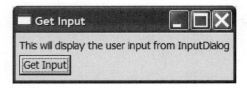

Figure 15-7. The GetInput program

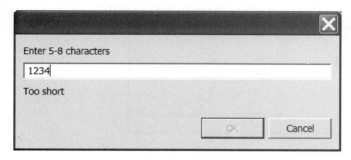

Figure 15-8. The InputDialog *with an error message*

Sending Messages

SWT's MessageBox class presents a message dialog to the user. Easy and compact to use, it's difficult to improve on. You just construct a MessageBox , passing the style values you want; call open(); and check the return value to detect the user's response. For example, you can display an error message such as this:

```
MessageBox mb = new MessageBox(shell, SWT.ICON_ERROR | SWT.OK);
mb.setText("Error");
mb.setMessage("An error occurred");
mb.open();
```

Simple. Concise. How do you improve on four lines of code?

JFace's MessageDialog manages to improve on SWT's MessageBox by shrinking the four lines to one:

```
MessageDialog.openError(shell, "Error", "An error occurred");
```

Not only is it more concise, it leaves no dialog reference in scope once the user dismisses the dialog. However, the resulting dialog looks a little different. Figure 15-9 shows the SWT version, and Figure 15-10 shows the JFace version.

Figure 15-9. An SWT MessageBox

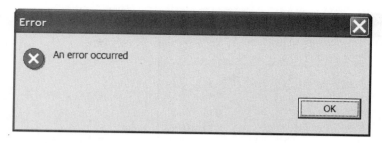

Figure 15-10. A JFace MessageDialog

You can construct a MessageDialog using its only constructor, and then call open(). However, once you see the constructor's signature, you likely won't consider using MessageDialog this way. The constructor is as follows:

```
MessageDialog(Shell parentShell, String dialogTitle, Image dialogTitleImage,
    String dialogMessage, int dialogImageType, String[] dialogButtonLabels,
    int defaultIndex)
```

The construct/open approach entails too much work. Instead, MessageDialog exposes five static methods, each for a different type of dialog, that you can succinctly call to create and display the dialog. Table 15-4 lists the methods.

Table 15-4. MessageDialog *Static Methods*

Method	Description
static boolean openConfirm(Shell parent, String title, String message)	Displays a confirmation dialog with an OK and a Cancel button. Returns true if OK is clicked, or false if Cancel is clicked.
static void openError(Shell parent, String title, String message)	Displays an error dialog with an OK button.
static void openInformation(Shell parent, String title, String message)	Displays an information dialog with an OK button.
static boolean openQuestion(Shell parent, String title, String message)	Displays a question dialog with a Yes and a No button. Returns true if Yes is clicked, or false if No is clicked.
static void openWarning(Shell parent, String title, String message)	Displays a warning dialog with an OK button.

The SendMessage program allows you to explore how these five methods work (see Listing 15-4). It displays a multiline text box and five buttons: one for each type of dialog. The application uses whatever text you type in the text box as the message parameter. Type some text and click a button to see the corresponding dialog. Below the buttons, a Label displays the return value of the last displayed dialog.

Listing 15-4. `SendMessage.java`

```java
package examples.ch15;

import org.eclipse.jface.dialogs.MessageDialog;
import org.eclipse.jface.window.ApplicationWindow;
import org.eclipse.swt.SWT;
import org.eclipse.swt.events.*;
import org.eclipse.swt.layout.*;
import org.eclipse.swt.widgets.*;

/**
 * This class demonstrates JFace's MessageDialog class
 */
public class SendMessage extends ApplicationWindow {
  /**
   * SendMessage constructor
   */
  public SendMessage() {
    super(null);
  }

  /**
   * Runs the application
   */
  public void run() {
    // Don't return from open() until window closes
    setBlockOnOpen(true);

    // Open the main window
    open();

    // Dispose the display
    Display.getCurrent().dispose();
  }

  /**
   * Configures the shell
   *
   * @param shell the shell
   */
  protected void configureShell(Shell shell) {
    super.configureShell(shell);

    // Set the title bar text and the size
    shell.setText("Send Message");
    shell.setSize(500, 400);
  }
```

```java
/**
 * Creates the main window's contents
 *
 * @param parent the main window
 * @return Control
 */
protected Control createContents(Composite parent) {
    Composite composite = new Composite(parent, SWT.NONE);
    composite.setLayout(new GridLayout(5, true));

    // Create a big text box for the message text
    final Text text = new Text(composite, SWT.MULTI | SWT.BORDER | SWT.V_SCROLL);
    GridData data = new GridData(GridData.FILL_BOTH);
    data.horizontalSpan = 5;
    text.setLayoutData(data);

    // Create the Confirm button
    Button confirm = new Button(composite, SWT.PUSH);
    confirm.setText("Confirm");
    confirm.setLayoutData(new GridData(GridData.FILL_HORIZONTAL));

    // Create the Error button
    Button error = new Button(composite, SWT.PUSH);
    error.setText("Error");
    error.setLayoutData(new GridData(GridData.FILL_HORIZONTAL));

    // Create the Information button
    Button information = new Button(composite, SWT.PUSH);
    information.setText("Information");
    information.setLayoutData(new GridData(GridData.FILL_HORIZONTAL));

    // Create the Question button
    Button question = new Button(composite, SWT.PUSH);
    question.setText("Question");
    question.setLayoutData(new GridData(GridData.FILL_HORIZONTAL));

    // Create the Warning button
    Button warning = new Button(composite, SWT.PUSH);
    warning.setText("Warning");
    warning.setLayoutData(new GridData(GridData.FILL_HORIZONTAL));

    // Create the label to display the return value
    final Label label = new Label(composite, SWT.NONE);
    data = new GridData(GridData.FILL_HORIZONTAL);
    data.horizontalSpan = 5;
    label.setLayoutData(data);

    // Save ourselves some typing
    final Shell shell = parent.getShell();

    // Display a Confirmation dialog
    confirm.addSelectionListener(new SelectionAdapter() {
```

```
        public void widgetSelected(SelectionEvent event) {
          boolean b = MessageDialog.openConfirm(shell, "Confirm", text.getText());
          label.setText("Returned " + Boolean.toString(b));
        }
    });

    // Display an Error dialog
    error.addSelectionListener(new SelectionAdapter() {
      public void widgetSelected(SelectionEvent event) {
        MessageDialog.openError(shell, "Error", text.getText());
        label.setText("Returned void");
      }
    });

    // Display an Information dialog
    information.addSelectionListener(new SelectionAdapter() {
      public void widgetSelected(SelectionEvent event) {
        MessageDialog.openInformation(shell, "Information", text.getText());
        label.setText("Returned void");
      }
    });

    // Display a Question dialog
    question.addSelectionListener(new SelectionAdapter() {
      public void widgetSelected(SelectionEvent event) {
        boolean b = MessageDialog.openQuestion(shell, "Question",
          text.getText());
        label.setText("Returned " + Boolean.toString(b));
      }
    });

    // Display a Warning dialog
    warning.addSelectionListener(new SelectionAdapter() {
      public void widgetSelected(SelectionEvent event) {
        MessageDialog.openWarning(shell, "Warning", text.getText());
        label.setText("Returned void");
      }
    });

    return composite;
  }

  /**
   * The application entry point
   *
   * @param args the command line arguments
   */
  public static void main(String[] args) {
    new SendMessage().run();
  }
}
```

Figure 15-11 shows the application's main window. Figure 15-12 shows a confirmation dialog, Figure 15-13 shows an error dialog, Figure 15-14 shows an information dialog, Figure 15-15 shows a question dialog, and Figure 15-16 shows a warning dialog.

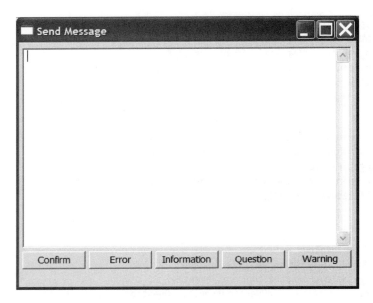

Figure 15-11. The SendMessage program

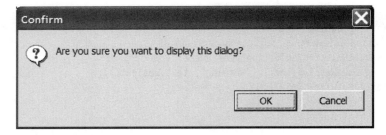

Figure 15-12. A confirmation dialog

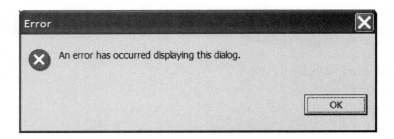

Figure 15-13. An error dialog

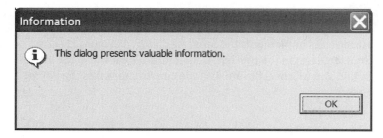

Figure 15-14. An information dialog

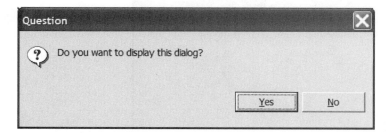

Figure 15-15. A question dialog

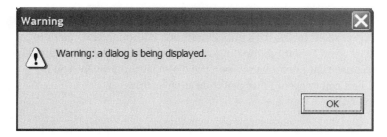

Figure 15-16. A warning dialog

Showing Progress

Moore's Law ensures that computers continually get faster, meaning that fewer and fewer operations take long enough that users notice the slightest hiccup in application responsiveness. However, the demands we throw at computers seem to at least keep pace with, if not outgain, the speed increases. Add the latency inherent to the increased levels of network reliance in the latest applications, and you create many situations in which applications must perform lengthy operations.

Although users, it seems, become more and more impatient with programs that make them wait, they're usually mollified by visual feedback that keeps them abreast of the progress of any lengthy operations. Incorporating such feedback in your applications using JFace's ProgressMonitorDialog places little burden on you, and in business parlance represents a terrific return on investment (ROI).

Understanding ProgressMonitorDialog

The ProgressMonitorDialog class implements the progress dialog. As Figure 15-17 shows, it displays customizable text in the title bar, a customizable message, the information icon, a progress bar, and a Cancel button. Its lone constructor takes the parent Shell as its only parameter:

```
ProgressMonitorDialog(Shell parent)
```

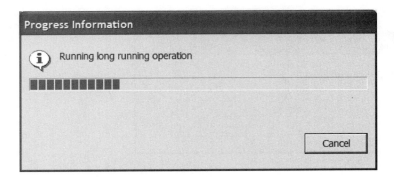

Figure 15-17. A ProgressMonitorDialog

Table 15-5 lists ProgressMonitorDialog's public methods. Although you can construct a dialog and call its open() method, the long-running operation doesn't begin until you call run(). Because run() defaults to open the dialog automatically, you'll typically bypass an explicit call to open() and use code such as this:

```
new ProgressMonitorDialog(shell).run(true, true, runnable);
```

Table 15-5. ProgressMonitorDialog *Methods*

Method	Description
boolean close()	Closes the dialog, only if no runnables are running.
boolean getOpenOnRun()	Returns true if the dialog will open before running the long-running operation. Otherwise, returns false.
IProgressMonitor getProgressMonitor()	Returns the progress monitor for this ProgressMonitorDialog.
int open()	Opens this ProgressMonitorDialog.
void run(boolean fork, boolean cancelable, IRunnableWithProgress runnable)	Runs the long-running operation. If the dialog is set to open on run, displays the dialog. If fork is true, runs the long-running operation in a separate thread. Otherwise, runs it in the same thread. If cancelable is true, enables the Cancel button on the dialog. Otherwise, disables the Cancel button.

Table 15-5. `ProgressMonitorDialog` *Methods (continued)*

Method	Description
`void setCancelable(boolean cancelable)`	If cancelable is true, enables the Cancel button on the dialog. Otherwise, disables the Cancel button.
`void setOpenOnRun(boolean openOnRun)`	If openOnRun is true, sets the dialog to open automatically when run() is called. Otherwise, sets the dialog not to open when run() is called.

Creating the Slow Operation

`ProgressMonitorDialog`'s `run()` method takes a reference to an `IRunnableWithProgress` instance. The `IRunnableWithProgress` interface defines one method:

```
void run(IProgressMonitor monitor)
```

You should perform your long-running operation in this method. This method throws two exceptions: `InvocationTargetException` and `InterruptedException`. If you need to throw another type of exception from your implementation's `run()` method, you should wrap it in an `InvocationTargetException`.

　　Your `IRunnableWithProgress.run()` implementation should call methods on the passed `IProgressMonitor` instance to update the dialog. Table 15-6 lists the methods that `IProgressMonitor` declares.

Table 15-6. `IProgressMonitor` *Methods*

Method	Description
`void beginTask(String name, int totalWork)`	Indicates that the work of the long-running operation is beginning. The dialog displays the text specified by name as the message. The progress bar uses totalWork as its 100% value. If you pass IProgressMonitor.UNKNOWN for totalWork, the progress will animate repeatedly.
`void done()`	Indicates that the long-running operation is done.
`boolean isCanceled()`	Returns true if the user clicked the Cancel button. Otherwise, returns false.
`void setCanceled(boolean canceled)`	If canceled is true, sets the dialog to cancelled. Otherwise, sets it to not cancelled.
`void setTaskName(String name)`	Sets the name of the task (the message).
`void subTask(String name)`	Displays the text specified by name below the progress bar.
`void worked(int worked)`	Increments the progress bar by the number of units specified by worked, as a percentage of the totalWork passed to beginTask().

A typical run() implementation calls beginTask(), starts the long-running operations, updates the progress bar periodically by calling worked(), checks periodically whether the user has clicked Cancel, and throws an InterruptedException if so. It looks something like this:

```
public void run(IProgressMonitor monitor)
throws InvocationTargetException, InterruptedException {
  // Begin the task
  monitor.beginTask("Running", 100);

  // Enter loop, check for either task completion or Cancel pressed
  for (int i = 0; i < 100 && !monitor.isCanceled(); i += 5) {
    // Perform some of the work

    . . .

    // Increment the progress bar
    monitor.worked(5);
  }

  // Set task to done
  monitor.done();

  // If user clicked cancel, throw an exception
  if (monitor.isCanceled())
    throw new InterruptedException("User canceled");
}
```

Seeing It Work

The ShowProgress program displays a window with a checkbox marked Indeterminate and a button, as Figure 15-18 shows. Click the button to launch a ProgressMonitorDialog, which simulates a long-running operation and updates the progress bar accordingly. If you check the Indeterminate checkbox before launching the dialog, the progress bar animates repeatedly. When the long-running operation reaches the halfway point, it begins a subtask called "Doing second half." If the user clicks Cancel, the long-running operation stops and an information dialog displays.

Figure 15-18. The ShowProgress program

The LongRunningOperation class represents the long-running operation, implementing the IRunnableWithProgress interface (see Listing 15-5).

Listing 15-5. LongRunningOperation.java

```java
package examples.ch15;

import java.lang.reflect.InvocationTargetException;

import org.eclipse.core.runtime.IProgressMonitor;
import org.eclipse.jface.operation.IRunnableWithProgress;

/**
 * This class represents a long-running operation
 */
public class LongRunningOperation implements IRunnableWithProgress {
  // The total sleep time
  private static final int TOTAL_TIME = 10000;

  // The increment sleep time
  private static final int INCREMENT = 500;

  private boolean indeterminate;

  /**
   * LongRunningOperation constructor
   *
   * @param indeterminate whether the animation is unknown
   */
  public LongRunningOperation(boolean indeterminate) {
    this.indeterminate = indeterminate;
  }

  /**
   * Runs the long running operation
   *
   * @param monitor the progress monitor
   */
  public void run(IProgressMonitor monitor) throws InvocationTargetException,
      InterruptedException {
    monitor.beginTask("Running long running operation",
        indeterminate ? IProgressMonitor.UNKNOWN : TOTAL_TIME);
    for (int total = 0; total < TOTAL_TIME && !monitor.isCanceled();
      total += INCREMENT) {
      Thread.sleep(INCREMENT);
      monitor.worked(INCREMENT);
      if (total == TOTAL_TIME / 2) monitor.subTask("Doing second half");
    }
    monitor.done();
    if (monitor.isCanceled())
      throw new InterruptedException("The long running operation was cancelled");
  }
}
```

The ShowProgress class launches the program, creates the main window, and responds to clicks of its Show Progress button by showing the progress dialog (see Listing 15-6).

Listing 15-6. ShowProgress.java

```java
package examples.ch15;

import java.lang.reflect.InvocationTargetException;

import org.eclipse.jface.dialogs.*;
import org.eclipse.jface.window.ApplicationWindow;
import org.eclipse.swt.SWT;
import org.eclipse.swt.events.*;
import org.eclipse.swt.layout.*;
import org.eclipse.swt.widgets.*;

/**
 * This class demonstrates JFace's ProgressMonitorDialog class
 */
public class ShowProgress extends ApplicationWindow {
  /**
   * ShowProgress constructor
   */
  public ShowProgress() {
    super(null);
  }

  /**
   * Runs the application
   */
  public void run() {
    // Don't return from open() until window closes
    setBlockOnOpen(true);

    // Open the main window
    open();

    // Dispose the display
    Display.getCurrent().dispose();
  }

  /**
   * Configures the shell
   *
   * @param shell the shell
   */
  protected void configureShell(Shell shell) {
    super.configureShell(shell);

    // Set the title bar text
    shell.setText("Show Progress");
  }
```

```java
/**
 * Creates the main window's contents
 *
 * @param parent the main window
 * @return Control
 */
protected Control createContents(Composite parent) {
  Composite composite = new Composite(parent, SWT.NONE);
  composite.setLayout(new GridLayout(1, true));

  // Create the indeterminate checkbox
  final Button indeterminate = new Button(composite, SWT.CHECK);
  indeterminate.setText("Indeterminate");

  // Create the ShowProgress button
  Button showProgress = new Button(composite, SWT.NONE);
  showProgress.setText("Show Progress");

  final Shell shell = parent.getShell();

  // Display the ProgressMonitorDialog
  showProgress.addSelectionListener(new SelectionAdapter() {
    public void widgetSelected(SelectionEvent event) {
      try {
        new ProgressMonitorDialog(shell).run(true, true,
            new LongRunningOperation(indeterminate.getSelection()));
      } catch (InvocationTargetException e) {
        MessageDialog.openError(shell, "Error", e.getMessage());
      } catch (InterruptedException e) {
        MessageDialog.openInformation(shell, "Cancelled", e.getMessage());
      }
    }
  });

  parent.pack();
  return composite;
}

/**
 * The application entry point
 *
 * @param args the command line arguments
 */
public static void main(String[] args) {
  new ShowProgress().run();
}
}
```

Figure 15-19 shows the progress dialog during its second half.

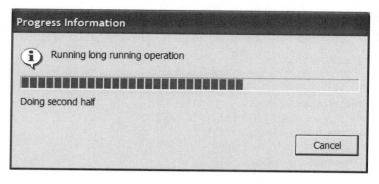

Figure 15-19. A progress dialog with a subtask

Building Your Own Dialogs

The gamut of dialogs offered by both SWT and JFace, however extensive, can never anticipate or meet every dialog need developers might have. When faced with dialog requirements that no existing dialog can answer, you must create your own. You may begin from scratch, or you can take advantage of JFace's extensible dialog classes to give yourself a head start. This section describes how to customize TitleAreaDialog and IconAndMessageDialog.

Building on TitleAreaDialog

The TitleAreaDialog class displays a dialog with a title, an image, a message with an optional icon, an OK button, and a Cancel button. Figure 15-20 shows a vanilla TitleAreaDialog without anything (title, message, and so on) set.

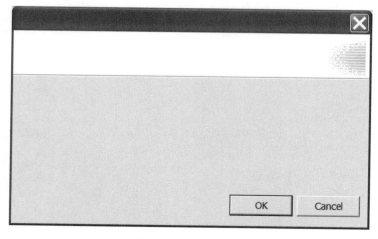

Figure 15-20. A plain TitleAreaDialog

The `TitleAreaDialog` class exposes an attractive API, as Table 15-7 displays. The methods seem so inviting that they might tempt you to write code such as this:

```
TitleAreaDialog dlg = new TitleAreaDialog(shell);
dlg.setMessage("This is the message for my Title Area Dialog"); // WRONG!
dlg.open();
```

This code, strangely, throws a `NullPointerException`, even though you haven't passed any `null` parameters. Investigation reveals that what you might expect—that `TitleAreaDialog` would store the `String` you pass for the message until it's ready to display it—doesn't match what actually happens. Instead, `TitleAreaDialog` attempts to set the message directly into the control that displays it. However, the control isn't created until after the dialog is opened, which happens when you call `dlg.open()`. Before creation, it points to `null`, and stands guilty as the culprit for the `NullPointerException`.

Table 15-7. `TitleAreaDialog` *Methods*

Method	Description
void setErrorMessage(String newErrorMessage)	Sets the error message.
void setMessage(String newMessage)	Sets the message.
void setMessage(String newMessage, int type)	Sets the message and the message type. Table 15-8 lists the message types.
void setTitle(String newTitle)	Sets the title.
void setTitleAreaColor(RGB color)	Sets the color of the title area.
void setTitleImage(Image newTitleImage)	Sets the image to display.

Table 15-8. Message Types

Constant	Description
IMessageProvider.NONE	Displays no icon by the message
IMessageProvider.ERROR	Displays an error icon by the message
IMessageProvider.INFORMATION	Displays an information icon by the message
IMessageProvider.WARNING	Displays a warning icon by the message

To solve this puzzler, subclass `TitleAreaDialog` and override its `createContents()` method. Its signature looks like this:

```
protected Control createContents(Composite parent)
```

After calling the superclass's `createContents()` (which creates the necessary controls), call `setMessage()`, `setTitleImage()`, or any of the other methods. Your `createContents()` implementation might look like this:

```
protected Control createContents(Composite parent) {
  Control contents = super.createContents(parent);
  setMessage("This is a TitleAreaDialog-derived dialog");
  setTitle("My Dialog");
  return contents;
}
```

That code produces the dialog shown in Figure 15-21.

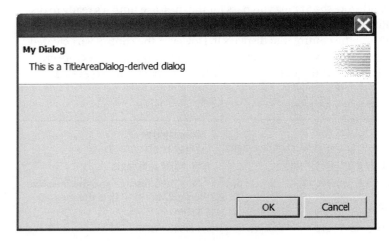

Figure 15-21. A TitleAreaDialog-*derived dialog*

Customizing TitleAreaDialog Further

You'll notice that the layout for TitleAreaDialog breaks cleanly into three sections:

- The white area that contains the title, message, and image

- An empty gray area, directly below the white "title" area

- The strip along the bottom that contains the OK and Cancel buttons

The createContents() method calls three separate methods to create these three sections: createTitleArea(), createDialogArea(), and createButtonBar(), respectively. createTitleArea() is private, so you're stuck with that implementation. However, createDialogArea() and createButtonBar() are both protected, so you're free to override their implementations.

Changing the Gray Area

To add content to the expansive gray area above the buttons, override the createDialogArea() method in your TitleAreaDialog-derived class. Typically, you'll call the superclass's implementation, storing the returned `Control` as a `Composite` and passing it to the additional controls you create. Your implementation might look like this:

```
protected Control createDialogArea(Composite parent) {
  Composite composite = (Composite) super.createDialogArea(parent);
  new Label(composite, SWT.NONE).setText("Here's a label to blot the canvas");
  new Label(composite, SWT.NONE).setText("Do you like it?");
  new Button(composite, SWT.RADIO).setText("Yes");
  new Button(composite, SWT.RADIO).setText("No");
  return composite;
}
```

Figure 15-22 shows the derived dialog after adding the `createDialogArea()` override.

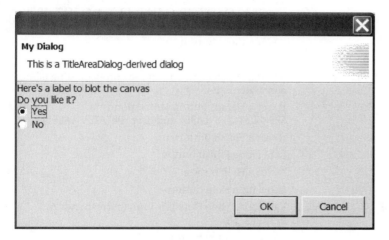

Figure 15-22. Adding to the dialog area

Changing the Buttons

Before you plunge headlong into overriding `createButtonBar()`, pause a moment. You're probably content with the button bar as it stands; you probably just want to change which buttons it displays. If so, forget about overriding `createButtonBar()`, and turn instead to `createButtonsForButtonBar()`, which `createButtonBar()` calls to create the actual buttons. In your implementation, call `createButton()` for each button you want created. Its signature looks like this:

```
protected Button createButton(Composite parent, int id, String label,
  boolean defaultButton)
```

Keep track of the value you pass in id—the dialog's `open()` method returns the id value for the button the user clicks to dismiss the dialog. `label` supplies the text for the button. Pass `true` for `defaultButton` to indicate which button should be triggered if the user presses Enter on the keyboard.

You can create your own IDs and labels, but you can also use some standard values from IDialogConstants. Table 15-9 lists the relevant values.

Table 15-9. IDialogConstants *Values for Button IDs and Labels*

Constant	Description
static int ABORT_ID	ID for an Abort button.
static String ABORT_LABEL	Label for an Abort button.
static int BACK_ID	ID for a Back button.
static String BACK_LABEL	Label for a Back button.
static int CANCEL_ID	ID for a Cancel button.
static String CANCEL_LABEL	Label for a Cancel button.
static int CLIENT_ID	Constant that marks the beginning of ID constants you should use when extending the dialogs and adding new buttons. The IDs for your new buttons should be CLIENT_ID, CLIENT_ID + 1, CLIENT_ID + 2, and so on.
static int CLOSE_ID	ID for a Close button.
static String CLOSE_LABEL	Label for a Close button.
static int DESELECT_ALL_ID	ID for a Deselect All button (no corresponding label constant exists).
static int DETAILS_ID	ID for a Details button (corresponds to SHOW_DETAILS_LABEL and HIDE_DETAILS_LABEL).
static int FINISH_ID	ID for a Finish button.
static String FINISH_LABEL	Label for a Finish button.
static int HELP_ID	ID for a Help button.
static String HELP_LABEL	Label for a Help button.
static String HIDE_DETAILS_LABEL	Label for a Hide Details button (corresponds to DETAILS_ID).
static int IGNORE_ID	ID for an Ignore button.
static String IGNORE_LABEL	Label for an Ignore button.
static int NEXT_ID	ID for a Next button.
static String NEXT_LABEL	Label for a Next button.
static int NO_ID	ID for a No button.
static String NO_LABEL	Label for a No button.
static int NO_TO_ALL_ID	ID for a No to All button.
static String NO_TO_ALL_LABEL	Label for a No to All button.
static int OK_ID	ID for an OK button.
static String OK_LABEL	Label for an OK button.
static int OPEN_ID	ID for an Open button.
static String OPEN_LABEL	Label for an Open button.
static int PROCEED_ID	ID for a Proceed button.
static String PROCEED_LABEL	Label for a Proceed button.
static int RETRY_ID	ID for a Retry button.
static String RETRY_LABEL	Label for a Retry button.
static int ABORT_ID	ID for an Abort button.

Table 15-9. IDialogConstants *Values for Button IDs and Labels (continued)*

Constant	Description
static int SELECT_ALL_ID	ID for a Select All button (no corresponding label constant exists).
static int SELECT_TYPES_ID	ID for a Select Types button (no corresponding label constant exists).
static String SHOW_DETAILS_LABEL	Label for a Show Details button (corresponds to DETAILS_ID).
static int SKIP_ID	ID for a Skip button.
static String SKIP_LABEL	Label for a Skip button.
static int STOP_ID	ID for a Stop button.
static String STOP_LABEL	Label for a Stop button.
static int YES_ID	ID for a Yes button.
static String YES_LABEL	Label for a Yes button.
static int YES_TO_ALL_ID	ID for a Yes to All button.
static String YES_TO_ALL_LABEL	Label for a Yes to All button.

For example, suppose you want three buttons to appear in the button area of your dialog: Yes, No, and Cancel. Your createButtonsForButtonBar() implementation looks something like this:

```
protected void createButtonsForButtonBar(Composite parent) {
  createButton(parent, IDialogConstants.YES_ID, IDialogConstants.YES_LABEL,
    true);
  createButton(parent, IDialogConstants.NO_ID, IDialogConstants.NO_LABEL, false);
  createButton(parent, IDialogConstants.CANCEL_ID, IDialogConstants.CANCEL_LABEL,
    false);
}
```

Adding this code to the TitleAreaDialog-derived class from earlier produces the dialog shown in Figure 15-23.

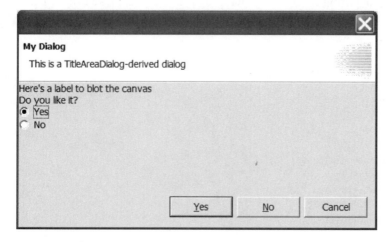

Figure 15-23. Changing the buttons

Handling Buttons

Clicking Yes or No in the dialog shown in Figure 15-23 doesn't dismiss the dialog; only clicking Cancel does. In fact, of all the buttons available, only the OK and Cancel buttons do anything. The rest dutifully depress and spring back, but nothing else happens. To detect and handle button clicks, you must override the buttonPressed() method, which has the following signature:

```
protected void buttonPressed(int buttonId)
```

When you call createButton() to create your button, it wires an event handler to call buttonPressed(), passing the ID you pass to createButton(), whenever the button is clicked. Your implementation should probably detect the range of buttons you offer, set the appropriate return code, and close the dialog. For example, to handle the three buttons from earlier, your buttonPressed() implementation might look like this:

```
protected void buttonPressed(int buttonId) {
    // Do the same for all the buttons--use the ID as the return code
    // and close the dialog
    setReturnCode(buttonId);
    close();
}
```

You can detect which button the user clicked by examining buttonId, and then take different actions based on the ID. However, if your dialog has any buttons other than OK and Cancel, you should always override buttonPressed(). Otherwise, users won't understand why you're ignoring their responses to your dialog.

Seeing TitleAreaDialog in Action

The ShowMyTitleAreaDialog program displays a dialog that's designed to function as an About box for some great JFace application. It uses a TitleAreaDialog-derived class, MyTitleAreaDialog (see Listing 15-7), which changes the image, displays a title and an informational message, creates a table in the gray area, and changes the buttons to a single OK button.

Listing 15-7. MyTitleAreaDialog.java

```
package examples.ch15;

import java.io.*;

import org.eclipse.jface.dialogs.*;
import org.eclipse.swt.SWT;
import org.eclipse.swt.graphics.*;
import org.eclipse.swt.layout.*;
import org.eclipse.swt.widgets.*;
```

```java
/**
 * This class shows an about box, based on TitleAreaDialog
 */
public class MyTitleAreaDialog extends TitleAreaDialog {
  // The image to display
  private Image image;

  /**
   * MyTitleAreaDialog constructor
   *
   * @param shell the parent shell
   */
  public MyTitleAreaDialog(Shell shell) {
    super(shell);

    // Create the image
    try {
      image = new Image(null, new FileInputStream("images/jface.gif"));
    } catch (FileNotFoundException e) {
      // Ignore
    }
  }

  /**
   * Closes the dialog box Override so we can dispose the image we created
   */
  public boolean close() {
    if (image != null) image.dispose();
    return super.close();
  }

  /**
   * Creates the dialog's contents
   *
   * @param parent the parent composite
   * @return Control
   */
  protected Control createContents(Composite parent) {
    Control contents = super.createContents(parent);

    // Set the title
    setTitle("About This Application");

    // Set the message
    setMessage("This is a JFace dialog", IMessageProvider.INFORMATION);

    // Set the image
    if (image != null) setTitleImage(image);

    return contents;
  }
```

```
/**
 * Creates the gray area
 *
 * @param parent the parent composite
 * @return Control
 */
protected Control createDialogArea(Composite parent) {
  Composite composite = (Composite) super.createDialogArea(parent);

  // Create a table
  Table table = new Table(composite, SWT.FULL_SELECTION | SWT.BORDER);
  table.setLayoutData(new GridData(GridData.FILL_BOTH));

  // Create two columns and show headers
  TableColumn one = new TableColumn(table, SWT.LEFT);
  one.setText("Real Name");

  TableColumn two = new TableColumn(table, SWT.LEFT);
  two.setText("Preferred Name");

  table.setHeaderVisible(true);

  // Add some data
  TableItem item = new TableItem(table, SWT.NONE);
  item.setText(0, "Robert Harris");
  item.setText(1, "Bobby");

  item = new TableItem(table, SWT.NONE);
  item.setText(0, "Robert Warner");
  item.setText(1, "Rob");

  item = new TableItem(table, SWT.NONE);
  item.setText(0, "Gabor Liptak");
  item.setText(1, "Gabor");

  one.pack();
  two.pack();

  return composite;
}

/**
 * Creates the buttons for the button bar
 *
 * @param parent the parent composite
 */
protected void createButtonsForButtonBar(Composite parent) {
  createButton(parent, IDialogConstants.OK_ID, IDialogConstants.OK_LABEL, true);
}
}
```

The ShowMyTitleAreaDialog class launches the program and displays a button labeled Show (see Listing 15-8). Click the button to display the dialog.

Listing 15-8. ShowMyTitleAreaDialog.java

```java
package examples.ch15;

import org.eclipse.jface.window.ApplicationWindow;
import org.eclipse.swt.SWT;
import org.eclipse.swt.events.*;
import org.eclipse.swt.layout.*;
import org.eclipse.swt.widgets.*;

/**
 * This class demonstrates JFace's TitleAreaDialog class
 */
public class ShowMyTitleAreaDialog extends ApplicationWindow {
  /**
   * ShowCustomDialog constructor
   */
  public ShowMyTitleAreaDialog() {
    super(null);
  }

  /**
   * Runs the application
   */
  public void run() {
    // Don't return from open() until window closes
    setBlockOnOpen(true);

    // Open the main window
    open();

    // Dispose the display
    Display.getCurrent().dispose();
  }

  /**
   * Creates the main window's contents
   *
   * @param parent the main window
   * @return Control
   */
  protected Control createContents(Composite parent) {
    Composite composite = new Composite(parent, SWT.NONE);
    composite.setLayout(new GridLayout(1, true));

    // Create the button
    Button show = new Button(composite, SWT.NONE);
    show.setText("Show");

    final Shell shell = parent.getShell();
```

```
    // Display the TitleAreaDialog
    show.addSelectionListener(new SelectionAdapter() {
      public void widgetSelected(SelectionEvent event) {
        // Create and show the dialog
        MyTitleAreaDialog dlg = new MyTitleAreaDialog(shell);
        dlg.open();
      }
    });

    parent.pack();
    return composite;
  }

  /**
   * The application entry point
   *
   * @param args the command line arguments
   */
  public static void main(String[] args) {
    new ShowMyTitleAreaDialog().run();
  }
}
```

Figure 15-24 shows the application's main window. Figure 15-25 shows the new dialog box.

Figure 15-24. The program to show the dialog box

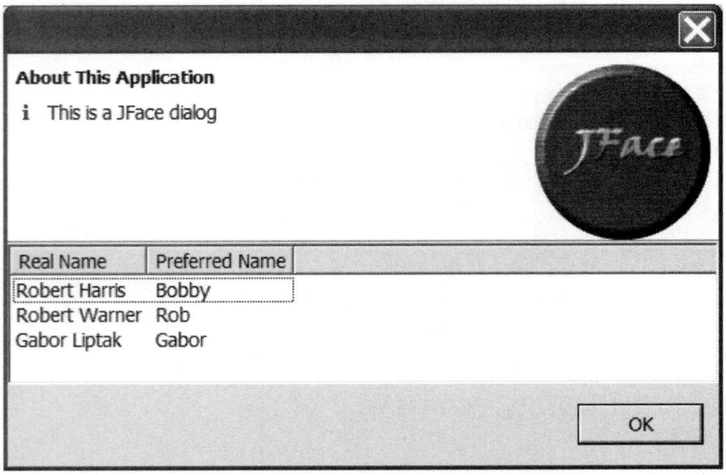

Real Name	Preferred Name	
Robert Harris	Bobby	
Robert Warner	Rob	
Gabor Liptak	Gabor	

About This Application

i   This is a JFace dialog

OK

Figure 15-25. The dialog box

Building on IconAndMessageDialog

Because IconAndMessageDialog derives from the same superclass, Dialog, that TitleAreaDialog does, much of the same information applies. However, IconAndMessageDialog offers no new public methods. Also, although you can override createContents(), you're probably better off overriding createDialogArea(). Its signature looks like this:

```
protected Control createDialogArea(Composite parent)
```

In that method, you should first call createMessageArea() to set up the icon and the message. Then, create whatever controls you wish. To set up the icon to display, define the getImage() method, which looks like this:

```
protected Image getImage()
```

To set up the message to display, set the message data member, which is a String.

To set up which buttons to display, override createButtonsForButtonBar(), as before. Again, if you display buttons other than OK and Cancel, override buttonPressed() to respond to button clicks.

To illustrate IconAndMessageDialog, create the dialog you've always wanted to create, but never had the courage to: the DumbMessageDialog class for all the dumb users you tolerate (see Listing 15-9). It displays a stylized "loser" icon and a patronizing, customizable message. It displays three buttons: Yes, No, and I Dunno. Only the last button dismisses the dialog; the first two insult the user without closing the dialog.

Listing 15-9. DumbMessageDialog.java

```java
package examples.ch15;

import java.io.*;

import org.eclipse.jface.dialogs.*;
import org.eclipse.swt.SWT;
import org.eclipse.swt.graphics.Image;
import org.eclipse.swt.layout.*;
import org.eclipse.swt.widgets.*;

/**
 * This class demonstrates the IconAndMessageDialog class
 */
public class DumbMessageDialog extends IconAndMessageDialog {
  public static final int I_DUNNO_ID = IDialogConstants.CLIENT_ID;
  public static final String I_DUNNO_LABEL = "I Dunno";

  // The image
  private Image image;
```

```
// The label for the "hidden" message
private Label label;

/**
 * DumbMessageDialog constructor
 *
 * @param parent the parent shell
 */
public DumbMessageDialog(Shell parent) {
  super(parent);

  // Create the image
  try {
    image = new Image(parent.getDisplay(), new FileInputStream(
        "images/loser.gif"));
  } catch (FileNotFoundException e) {}

  // Set the default message
  message = "Are you sure you want to do something that dumb?";
}

/**
 * Sets the message
 *
 * @param message the message
 */
public void setMessage(String message) {
  this.message = message;
}

/**
 * Closes the dialog
 *
 * @return boolean
 */
public boolean close() {
  if (image != null) image.dispose();
  return super.close();
}

/**
 * Creates the dialog area
 *
 * @param parent the parent composite
 * @return Control
 */
protected Control createDialogArea(Composite parent) {
  createMessageArea(parent);

  // Create a composite to hold the label
  Composite composite = new Composite(parent, SWT.NONE);
  GridData data = new GridData(GridData.FILL_BOTH);
```

```
    data.horizontalSpan = 2;
    composite.setLayoutData(data);
    composite.setLayout(new FillLayout());

    // Create the label for the "hidden" message
    label = new Label(composite, SWT.LEFT);

    return composite;
  }

  /**
   * Creates the buttons
   *
   * @param parent the parent composite
   */
  protected void createButtonsForButtonBar(Composite parent) {
    createButton(parent, IDialogConstants.YES_ID, IDialogConstants.YES_LABEL,
        true);
    createButton(parent, IDialogConstants.NO_ID, IDialogConstants.NO_LABEL,
        false);
    createButton(parent, I_DUNNO_ID, I_DUNNO_LABEL, false);
  }

  /**
   * Handles a button press
   *
   * @param buttonId the ID of the pressed button
   */
  protected void buttonPressed(int buttonId) {
    // If they press I Dunno, close the dialog
    if (buttonId == I_DUNNO_ID) {
      setReturnCode(buttonId);
      close();
    } else {
      // Otherwise, have some fun
      label.setText("Yeah, right. You know nothing.");
    }
  }

  /**
   * Gets the image to use
   */
  protected Image getImage() {
    return image;
  }
}
```

The DumbUser class launches the program and displays the one-button application from before (see Listing 15-10). When you click the button, it displays a DumbUserDialog.

Listing 15-10. `DumbUser.java`

```java
package examples.ch15;

import org.eclipse.jface.window.ApplicationWindow;
import org.eclipse.swt.SWT;
import org.eclipse.swt.events.*;
import org.eclipse.swt.layout.*;
import org.eclipse.swt.widgets.*;

/**
 * This class demonstrates JFace's IconAndMessageDialog class
 */
public class DumbUser extends ApplicationWindow {
  /**
   * DumbUser constructor
   */
  public DumbUser() {
    super(null);
  }

  /**
   * Runs the application
   */
  public void run() {
    // Don't return from open() until window closes
    setBlockOnOpen(true);

    // Open the main window
    open();

    // Dispose the display
    Display.getCurrent().dispose();
  }

  /**
   * Creates the main window's contents
   *
   * @param parent the main window
   * @return Control
   */
  protected Control createContents(Composite parent) {
    Composite composite = new Composite(parent, SWT.NONE);
    composite.setLayout(new GridLayout(1, true));

    // Create the button
    Button show = new Button(composite, SWT.NONE);
    show.setText("Show");

    final Shell shell = parent.getShell();
```

```
      // Display the dialog
      show.addSelectionListener(new SelectionAdapter() {
        public void widgetSelected(SelectionEvent event) {
          // Create and show the dialog
          DumbMessageDialog dlg = new DumbMessageDialog(shell);
          dlg.open();
        }
      });

      parent.pack();
      return composite;
  }

  /**
   * The application entry point
   *
   * @param args the command line arguments
   */
  public static void main(String[] args) {
    new DumbUser().run();
  }
}
```

Figure 15-26 displays the DumbUserDialog.

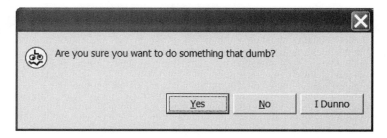

Figure 15-26. Getting revenge on dumb users

Summary

In your applications, you'll probably continue to use many of SWT's dialogs. For example, JFace has no replacement file or font selection dialog. However, the dialogs that JFace does offer are quick and simple to use, and you might find yourself turning to them again and again in your applications.

When creating your own dialogs, remember to consider one of JFace's dialogs as a launching point. When you subclass TitleAreaDialog or IconAndMessageDialog, you get useful framework code such as button handling for free. Using a JFace dialog as the superclass for your dialog speeds development and debugging time.

User Interaction

No MAN IS AN ISLAND, and no application lives long without interacting with users. The previous chapter explained how applications communicate to users through dialogs. The other half of the communication equation involves users communicating to applications. Users communicate to applications when they select commands on the applications' menus or click buttons in the applications' toolbars or coolbars. This chapter describes how to encourage and receive such communications from users within your JFace applications.

Understanding Actions

Applications usually give users several means to accomplish the same thing. For example, to print the current document in Microsoft Word, you can select File ➤ Print from the main menu, click the printer button in the toolbar, or press Ctrl-P on the keyboard. Each action triggers different sections of code within the program, but each should ultimately converge on the same code to perform the task.

To achieve code reuse pertaining to user actions, JFace introduces the concept of *actions*. A JFace action responds to a user action, whether the user has selected an item in a menu, clicked a button in a toolbar, or pressed a key or keys on the keyboard. In response to the user action, the JFace action does something, whether it's printing a document, opening a file, displaying a dialog, or whatever you can dream up. Different user actions that should all accomplish the same thing should all call the same JFace action, ensuring that the application responds appropriately and consistently.

Creating an Action

To create an action for your application, subclass the Action class found in the org.eclipse.jface.action package. This abstract class provides all the plumbing necessary for performing an action. In fact, you could create and use an empty action class, like this:

```
public class EmptyAction extends Action {
}
```

However, this action class flouts the convention that action classes *do* something. Besides, not only doesn't this action class do anything, it doesn't even report its name.

For example, if used in a menu, it would appear completely blank, as Figure 16-1 shows.

Figure 16-1. An empty action

To make a useful action, you should at least give your action the ability to describe itself to its users, so that if used in a menu, for example, it would display something. To accomplish this, provide a constructor in your class that calls one of Action's constructors (which are all protected), listed in Table 16-1.

Table 16-1. Action *Constructors*

Constructor	Description
Action()	Creates an empty action
Action(String text)	Creates an action with the specified text
Action(String text, ImageDescriptor image)	Creates an action with the specified text and image
Action(String text, int style)	Creates an action with the specified text and style

The empty constructor doesn't improve things, but the constructor that takes a String looks promising:

```
public class DescriptiveAction extends Action {
  super("I have a name!");
}
```

Now when you add this action to a menu, it identifies itself, as Figure 16-2 shows. Don't worry about how to add an action to a menu right now; the next section covers how to do that.

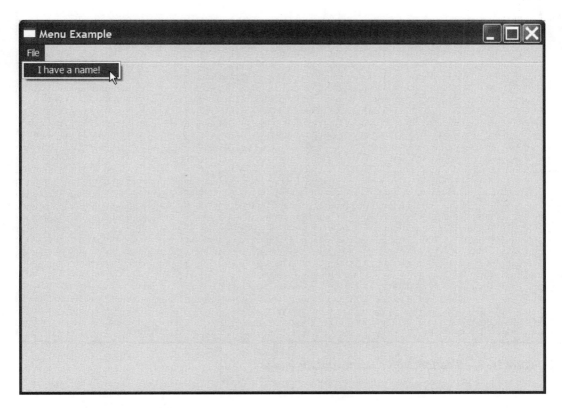

Figure 16-2. An action with a name

The constructor that accepts an ImageDescriptor allows action classes more self-expression: they can carry an associated image. Chapter 19 covers the ImageDescriptor class, found in the org.eclipse.jface.resource package. For now, all you need to know is that an ImageDescriptor knows how to create an image, and you can create one by calling ImageDescriptor.createFromFile(Class location, String filename). Dress up the preceding DescriptiveAction class by adding an image, like this:

```
public class DescriptiveAction extends Action {
  super("I have a name!",
    ImageDescriptor.createFromFile(DescriptiveAction.class, "image.gif");
}
```

Figure 16-3 shows this version of DescriptiveAction in a menu. Notice the arrow to the left of the text.

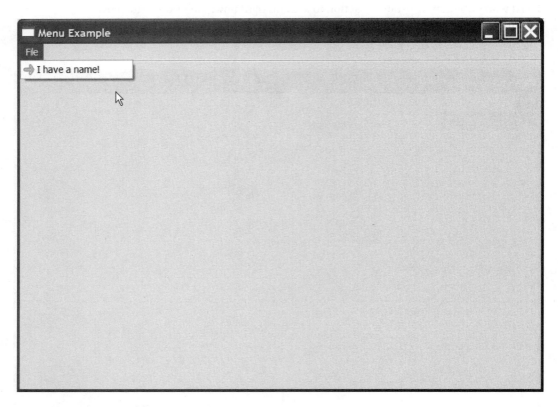

Figure 16-3. An action with a name and an image

The final constructor takes a String and a style. The style constants, listed in Table 16-2, are mutually exclusive, and shape how the action both displays and functions. For example, if you pass IAction.AS_CHECK_BOX for the style, you get an action that toggles on and off. When displayed in a menu, it shows a check mark to the left of the text when on, and nothing when off. Change the preceding action to this:

```
public class DescriptiveAction extends Action {
  super("I have a name!", IAction.AS_CHECK_BOX);
}
```

This produces the menu item shown in Figure 16-4. Notice the check mark to the left of the text, indicating that the action is on.

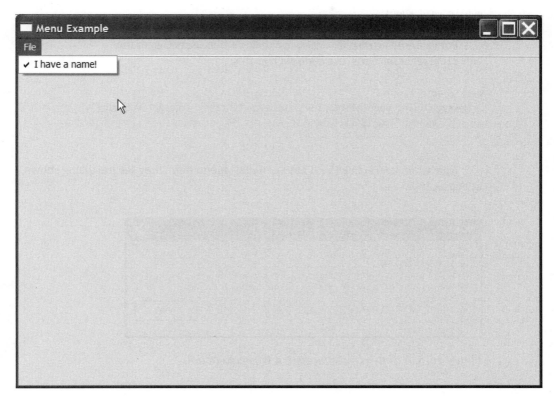

Figure 16-4. A checkbox action

Table 16-2. Action *Style Constants*

Style	Description
IAction.AS_PUSH_BUTTON	Creates a push button action
IAction.AS_CHECK_BOX	Creates a checkbox or toggle button action
IAction.AS_DROP_DOWN_MENU	Creates a dropdown menu action
IAction.AS_RADIO_BUTTON	Creates a radio button action
IAction.AS_UNSPECIFIED	Creates an unspecified action

Acting on Actions

The DescriptiveAction class dutifully identifies itself, but it still doesn't *do* anything. You can't justify creating or using a no-op action. When someone clicks the action in a menu or a toolbar, it should respond appropriately. To detect when a user triggers an action, override the run() method, which IAction declares. Its signature looks like this:

```
public void run()
```

For example, to display a message dialog when users trigger the DescriptiveAction class, use code such as this:

```
public void run() {
  MessageDialog.openInformation(Display.getCurrent().getActiveShell(),
    "Click!", "You clicked me!");
}
```

Now when users click the "I have a name!" menu item, they see the dialog shown in Figure 16-5.

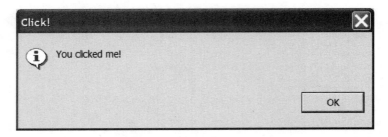

Figure 16-5. A dialog in response to a triggered action

Configuring Actions

As you'd expect, the Action class provides methods to get and set its attributes. Some of the attributes are specific to setting up Eclipse plug-ins, and aren't covered in this book. It also provides some utility methods for translating key codes to their String representations, and vice versa. JFace uses these methods internally for determining accelerators. Table 16-3 lists Action's API, along with IAction's methods, and identifies the plug-in-specific attributes.

Table 16-3. Action *Methods*

Method	Description
void addPropertyChangeListener (IPropertyChangeListener listener)	Adds a listener that's notified when a property changes.
static String convertAccelerator (int keyCode)	Returns the string representation of the key accelerator specified by keyCode.
static int convertAccelerator (String acceleratorText)	Returns the key code for the key accelerator specified by acceleratorText.
static int findKeyCode(String token)	Returns the key code for the key specified by token.

Table 16-3. Action *Methods (continued)*

Method	Description
static String findKeyString(int keyCode)	Returns the string representation of a key for the specified key code.
static int findModifier(String token)	Returns the code for the modifier key specified by token.
static String findModifierString (int keyCode)	Returns the string representation of the modifier key specified by keyCode.
int getAccelerator()	Returns the key code for this action's accelerator.
String getActionDefinitionId()	Returns the action definition ID, which is specific to Eclipse plug-ins.
String getDescription()	Returns the description, which is specific to Eclipse plug-ins.
ImageDescriptor getDisabledImage Descriptor()	Returns the ImageDescriptor for the image to display for this action when it's disabled.
HelpListener getHelpListener()	Returns the help listener.
ImageDescriptor getHoverImage Descriptor()	Returns the ImageDescriptor for the image to display for this action when the mouse pointer hovers over it.
String getId()	Returns this action's unique ID, which is specific to Eclipse plug-ins.
ImageDescriptor getImageDescriptor()	Returns the ImageDescriptor for the image to display for this action.
IMenuCreator getMenuCreator()	Returns the menu creator for creating any popup menus for this action.
int getStyle()	Returns the style.
String getText()	Returns the text.
String getToolTipText()	Returns the tool tip text.
boolean isChecked()	Returns true if this action is checked. Otherwise, returns false.
boolean isEnabled()	Returns true if this action is enabled. Otherwise, returns false.
static String removeAccelerator Text(String text)	Returns just the text contained in text, parsing out and removing the accelerator definition.
void removePropertyChangeListener (IPropertyChangeListener listener)	Removes the specified listener from the notification list.
void run()	Called when the user triggers this action. Override to perform an action.
void runWithEvent(Event event)	Called when the user triggers this action. Override to perform an action when you want the event object. However, the documentation says this method is experimental and is subject to change.
void setAccelerator(int keyCode)	Sets the accelerator key code.
void setActionDefinitionId (String id)	Sets the action definition ID, which is specific to Eclipse plug-ins.
void setChecked(boolean checked)	Sets the checked status.

Table 16-3. Action *Methods (continued)*

Method	Description
void setDescription(String text)	Sets the description, which is specific to Eclipse plug-ins.
void setDisabledImageDescriptor (ImageDescriptor descriptor)	Sets the ImageDescriptor for the image to display for this action when it's disabled.
void setEnabled(boolean enabled)	If enabled is true, enables this action. Otherwise, disables it.
void setHelpListener(HelpListener listener)	Sets the help listener.
void setHoverImageDescriptor (ImageDescriptor descriptor)	Sets the ImageDescriptor for the image to display for this action when the mouse pointer hovers over it.
void setId(String id)	Sets the ID, which is specific to Eclipse plug-ins.
void setImageDescriptor (ImageDescriptor descriptor)	Sets the ImageDescriptor for the image to display for this action.
void setMenuCreator(IMenuCreator creator)	Sets the menu creator for creating any popup menu for this action.
void setText(String text)	Sets the text.
void setToolTipText(String toolTipText)	Sets the tool tip text.

The preceding constructors allow you to set the Action's text, its text and ImageDescriptor, or its text and style. Except for the style, you can set all these attributes, plus several others, after construction. For example, the following code creates an action class with some text, an image, and a tool tip:

```
public class AnotherAction extends Action {
  public AnotherAction() {
    super();
    setText("Another Action");
    setImageDescriptor(ImageDescriptor.createFromFile(AnotherAction.class,
      "AnotherAction.gif"));
    setToolTipText("Runs another action");
  }
}
```

You specify a mnemonic for an action by including an ampersand in the text, like this:

```
setText("&Another Action");
```

The mnemonic (in this case, "A") displays with an underline, and users can press the Alt key in conjunction with the mnemonic to activate the action.

You can also specify an accelerator to trigger an action. For example, you can allow the user to trigger the action from anywhere in the application by pressing Ctrl-A (which isn't case-sensitive). To set the accelerator, pass the key code to the setAccelerator() method:

```
setAccelerator(SWT.CTRL + 'A');
```

To be more platform-agnostic, use the Mod key constant instead of the Control key constant:

```
setAccelerator(SWT.MOD1 + 'A');
```

To communicate accelerators to users, so they can take advantage of them, items in menus that have accelerators traditionally display them in the menu. Adding an accelerator to an action takes care of this for you, automatically displaying the accelerator in the menu item (see Figure 16-6).

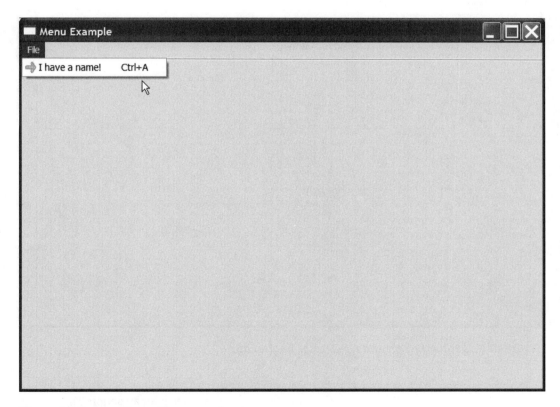

Figure 16-6. An action with an accelerator

The convention of displaying the accelerator key by the menu label has become so ingrained in application development that JFace offers a quick way to set both the text and the accelerator in one call. You pass the text in the following format to either the constructor or the setText() method:

```
<Text>@<Accelerator>
```

For example, you could set up the "Another Action" action like this:

```
setText("&Another Action@Ctrl+A");
```

Figure 16-7 shows this action and accelerator in a menu.

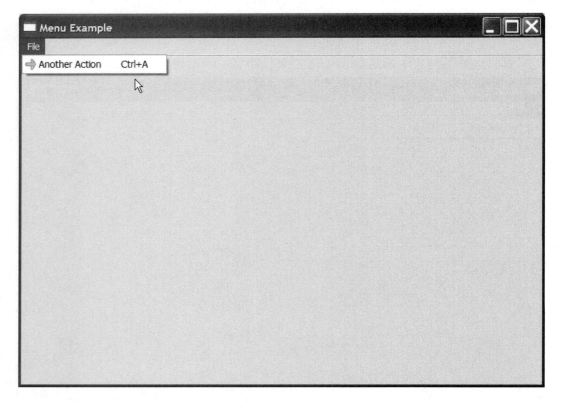

Figure 16-7. Setting the text and accelerator in one call

Call the setToolTipText() method to set the tool tip text for an action. The tool tip displays when the mouse hovers over the action. This works for actions added to tool-bars or coolbars. For example, the following code adds tool tip text for the action:

```
setToolTipText("Runs another action");
```

Figure 16-8 displays a window with a toolbar that contains the "Another Action" action; note the button displaying an arrow. As the mouse pointer hovers over the button, the tool tip displays.

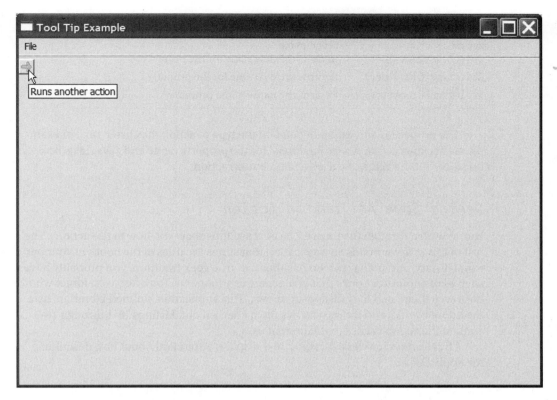

Figure 16-8. An action with a tool tip

Receiving Notice of Changes

One of Action's methods, addPropertyChangeListener(), notifies you when a property changes via the action. For example, suppose that you've created a checkbox action class, like this:

```
public class MyCheckboxAction extends Action {
  public MyCheckboxAction() {
    super("My Checkbox", IAction.AS_CHECK_BOX);
  }
}
```

When you create an instance of this action, you can also add a property change listener to it that detects when you've changed the action to checked or unchecked. The IPropertyChangeListener interface declares one method:

```
public void PropertyChange(PropertyChangeEvent event)
```

The PropertyChangeEvent that this method receives contains the property that changes, the old value for the property, and the new value for the property. You retrieve those values using the methods listed in Table 16-4.

Table 16-4. `PropertyChangeEvent` *Methods*

Method	Description
`Object getNewValue()`	Returns the new value for the property
`Object getOldValue()`	Returns the old value for the property
`String getProperty()`	Returns the name of the property

The properties and values depend on the type of action they listen on. For example, a checkbox action passes "checked" for the property name and `java.lang.Boolean` instances for the values. So does a radio button action.

Seeing Some Actions in Action

You've waded through the theory. The next sections show you how to use actions. The rest of this chapter builds an application that stores the titles of the books in your personal library, and manages who has them. In true geek tradition, you probably have shelves of computer books that you generously loan out. Too often, you forget who borrowed them, and they disappear forever. This application, dubbed Librarian, lists the books by title, and shows who has them checked out. Listings 16-1 through 16-9 contain the action classes that Librarian uses.

The `AboutAction` class in Listing 16-1 displays a standard About box, describing the application.

Listing 16-1. `AboutAction.java`

```
package examples.ch16;

import org.eclipse.jface.action.Action;
import org.eclipse.jface.dialogs.MessageDialog;
import org.eclipse.jface.resource.ImageDescriptor;

/**
 * This action class shows an About box
 */
public class AboutAction extends Action {
  /**
   * AboutAction constructor
   */
  public AboutAction() {
    super("&About@Ctrl+A", ImageDescriptor.createFromFile(AboutAction.class,
        "/images/about.gif"));
    setDisabledImageDescriptor(ImageDescriptor.createFromFile(AboutAction.class,
        "/images/disabledAbout.gif"));
    setToolTipText("About");
  }

  /**
   * Shows an about box
   */
```

```
  public void run() {
    MessageDialog.openInformation(Librarian.getApp().getShell(), "About",
        "Librarian--to manage your books");
  }
}
```

The AddBookAction class in Listing 16-2 adds a book to the current library. It uses a static method on the Librarian class called getApp() that returns a reference to the currently running Librarian program. You'll notice calls to Librarian.getApp() sprinkled throughout these action classes. The ExitAction class in Listing 16-3 exits the application. The NewAction class creates a new library file (see Listing 16-4). Listing 16-5, the OpenAction class, opens a file to display and edit. The RemoveBookAction class in Listing 16-6 removes the currently selected book from both the view and the library. The SaveAction class saves the current file (see Listing 16-7). The SaveAsAction class in Listing 16-8 saves the current file, but first prompts for where to save it. It uses the SafeSaveDialog class from earlier chapters. Finally, the ShowBookCountAction class in Listing 16-9 toggles whether or not to show the number of books currently in the library. It's a checkbox action, and will have a property listener added to it to detect when it's triggered.

Listing 16-2. AddBookAction.java

```java
package examples.ch16;

import org.eclipse.jface.action.Action;
import org.eclipse.jface.resource.ImageDescriptor;

/**
 * This action class adds a book
 */
public class AddBookAction extends Action {
  /**
   * AddBookAction constructor
   */
  public AddBookAction() {
    super("&Add Book@Ctrl+B", ImageDescriptor.createFromFile(AddBookAction.class,
        "/images/addBook.gif"));
    setDisabledImageDescriptor(ImageDescriptor.createFromFile(
        AddBookAction.class, "/images/disabledAddBook.gif"));
    setToolTipText("Add");
  }

  /**
   * Adds a book to the current library
   */
  public void run() {
    Librarian.getApp().addBook();
  }
}
```

Listing 16-3. ExitAction.java

```java
package examples.ch16;

import org.eclipse.jface.action.Action;

/**
 * This action class exits the application
 */
public class ExitAction extends Action {
  /**
   * ExitAction constructor
   */
  public ExitAction() {
    super("E&xit@Alt+F4");
    setToolTipText("Exit");
  }

  /**
   * Exits the application
   */
  public void run() {
    Librarian.getApp().close();
  }
}
```

Listing 16-4. NewAction.java

```java
package examples.ch16;

import org.eclipse.jface.action.Action;
import org.eclipse.jface.resource.ImageDescriptor;

/**
 * This action class responds to requests for a new file
 */
public class NewAction extends Action {
  /**
   * NewAction constructor
   */
  public NewAction() {
    super("&New@Ctrl+N", ImageDescriptor.createFromFile(NewAction.class,
        "/images/new.gif"));
    setDisabledImageDescriptor(ImageDescriptor.createFromFile(NewAction.class,
        "/images/disabledNew.gif"));
    setToolTipText("New");
  }
```

```
  /**
   * Creates a new file
   */
  public void run() {
    Librarian.getApp().newFile();
  }
}
```

Listing 16-5. OpenAction.java

```
package examples.ch16;

import org.eclipse.jface.action.*;
import org.eclipse.jface.resource.ImageDescriptor;
import org.eclipse.swt.SWT;
import org.eclipse.swt.widgets.FileDialog;

/**
 * This action class responds to requests to open a file
 */
public class OpenAction extends Action {
  /**
   * OpenAction constructor
   */
  public OpenAction() {
    super("&Open...@Ctrl+O", ImageDescriptor.createFromFile(OpenAction.class,
        "/images/open.gif"));
    setDisabledImageDescriptor(ImageDescriptor.createFromFile(OpenAction.class,
        "/images/disabledOpen.gif"));
    setToolTipText("Open");
  }

  /**
   * Opens an existing file
   */
  public void run() {
    // Use the file dialog
    FileDialog dlg = new FileDialog(Librarian.getApp().getShell(), SWT.OPEN);
    String fileName = dlg.open();
    if (fileName != null) {
      Librarian.getApp().openFile(fileName);
    }
  }
}
```

Listing 16-6. RemoveBookAction.java

```java
package examples.ch16;

import org.eclipse.jface.action.Action;
import org.eclipse.jface.dialogs.*;
import org.eclipse.jface.resource.ImageDescriptor;

/**
 * This action class deletes a book
 */
public class RemoveBookAction extends Action {
  /**
   * RemoveBookAction constructor
   */
  public RemoveBookAction() {
    super("&Remove Book@Ctrl+X", ImageDescriptor.createFromFile(
        RemoveBookAction.class, "/images/removeBook.gif"));
    setDisabledImageDescriptor(ImageDescriptor.createFromFile(
        RemoveBookAction.class, "/images/disabledRemoveBook.gif"));
    setToolTipText("Remove");
  }

  /**
   * Removes the selected book after confirming
   */
  public void run() {
    if (MessageDialog.openConfirm(Librarian.getApp().getShell(), "Are you sure?",
        "Are you sure you want to remove the selected book?")) {
      Librarian.getApp().removeSelectedBook();
    }
  }
}
```

Listing 16-7. SaveAction.java

```java
package examples.ch16;

import org.eclipse.jface.action.Action;
import org.eclipse.jface.resource.ImageDescriptor;

/**
 * This action class responds to requests to save a file
 */
public class SaveAction extends Action {
  /**
   * SaveAction constructor
   */
```

```
  public SaveAction() {
    super("&Save@Ctrl+S", ImageDescriptor.createFromFile(SaveAction.class,
        "/images/save.gif"));
    setDisabledImageDescriptor(ImageDescriptor.createFromFile(SaveAction.class,
        "/images/disabledSave.gif"));
    setToolTipText("Save");
  }

  /**
   * Saves the file
   */
  public void run() {
    Librarian.getApp().saveFile();
  }
}
```

Listing 16-8. SaveAsAction.java

```
package examples.ch16;

import org.eclipse.jface.action.Action;
import org.eclipse.jface.resource.ImageDescriptor;

/**
 * This action class responds to requests to save a file as . . .
 */
public class SaveAsAction extends Action {
  /**
   * SaveAsAction constructor
   */
  public SaveAsAction() {
    super("Save As...", ImageDescriptor.createFromFile(SaveAsAction.class,
        "/images/saveAs.gif"));
    setDisabledImageDescriptor(ImageDescriptor.createFromFile(SaveAsAction.class,
        "/images/disabledSaveAs.gif"));
    setToolTipText("Save As");
  }

  /**
   * Saves the file
   */
  public void run() {
    SafeSaveDialog dlg = new SafeSaveDialog(Librarian.getApp().getShell());
    String fileName = dlg.open();
    if (fileName != null) {
      Librarian.getApp().saveFileAs(fileName);
    }
  }
}
```

Listing 16-9. ShowBookCount.java

```java
package examples.ch16;

import org.eclipse.jface.action.*;
import org.eclipse.jface.resource.ImageDescriptor;

/**
 * This action class determines whether to show the book count
 */
public class ShowBookCountAction extends Action {
  public ShowBookCountAction() {
    super("&Show Book Count@Ctrl+C", IAction.AS_CHECK_BOX);
    setChecked(true);
    setImageDescriptor(ImageDescriptor.createFromFile(ShowBookCountAction.class,
        "/images/count.gif"));
    setDisabledImageDescriptor(ImageDescriptor.createFromFile(
        ShowBookCountAction.class, "/images/disabledCount.gif"));
  }
}
```

The next sections illustrate creating menus, toolbars, coolbars, and a status line for an application window. Each section uses the action classes listed.

Creating Menus

Open virtually any GUI application, and you'll find a set of dropdown menus across the top of the window, right below the title bar. Menus have become *de rigueur* in graphical interfaces, providing commands that drive the application. Users, accustomed to these menus, orient themselves quickly in an unfamiliar application by exploring the menus. Conventions have sprung up, and most applications have a few standard menus: File, Edit, View, Window, and Help. As creatures of habit, users point and click to expected locations in the menu for certain commands. For example, when users want to open a file, they head to File ➤ Open. To see the application's About box, they look for Help ➤ About. Programs that deviate too far from these application mores can expect little usage, and likely quick deletion.

Adding a Menu Bar

The strip of menus across the top of the main window, commonly referred to as the menu bar, enjoys direct support from JFace's ApplicationWindow. To add a menu bar to your application, call ApplicationWindow.addMenuBar() before the actual window (Shell) is created. You'll usually do this in your derived class's constructor, like this:

```java
public class MyApplicationWindow extends ApplicationWindow {
  public MyApplicationWindow() {
    super(null);
```

```
    // Add a menu bar
    addMenuBar();
  }
}
```

This method calls createMenuManager(), which you should override to create the MenuManager object that describes the specific set of menus for your application. The signature for createMenuManager() is as follows:

```
protected MenuManager createMenuManager()
```

For example, the following code creates a menu with two commands: File ➤ Open and Help ➤ About:

```
protected MenuManager createMenuManager() {
  // Create the main menu manager
  MenuManager menuManager = new MenuManager();

  // Create the File menu and add it to the main menu
  MenuManager fileMenuManager = new MenuManager("File");
  menuManager.add(fileMenuManager);

  // Add the Open action
  fileMenuManager.add(openAction);

  // Create the Help menu and add it to the main menu
  MenuManager helpMenuManager = new MenuManager("Help");
  menuManager.add(helpMenuManager);

  // Add the About action
  helpMenuManager.add(helpAction);

  // Return the main menu
  return menuManager;
}
```

As this code demonstrates, you can construct a MenuManager with or without text. To use a menu manager, you usually construct a parent MenuManager, passing no parameters. Then, for each top-level menu (for example, File), you create another MenuManager instance, passing the text to display in the constructor. You add the top-level MenuManagers to the parent MenuManager by passing them, one by one, to calls to the parent's add() method, like this:

```
MenuManager parent = new MenuManager();
MenuManager topLevel = new MenuManager("Top Level");
parent.add(topLevel);
```

For each action that you wish to add to a menu, call that menu manager's add() method, passing the action. For example, the following code adds an instance of MyAction to the top level menu:

```
topLevel.add(new MyAction());
```

To create cascading menus, add a MenuManager to another MenuManager. You can then add actions to the cascading menu. In fact, you can also add other MenuManagers to it, cascading menus ad nauseum. This code creates the cascading menu displayed in Figure 16-9:

```
// Create the parent menu
MenuManager mm = new MenuManager();

// Create the File menu
MenuManager fileMenu = new MenuManager("File");
mm.add(fileMenu);

// Add the actions to the File menu
fileMenu.add(newAction);
fileMenu.add(openAction);
fileMenu.add(saveAction);
fileMenu.add(saveAsAction);

// Create the cascading menu
MenuManager cascadingMenu = new MenuManager("Cascading");
cascadingMenu.add(newAction);
cascadingMenu.add(openAction);
cascadingMenu.add(saveAction);
cascadingMenu.add(saveAsAction);
fileMenu.add(cascadingMenu);

// Create the More Cascading menu
MenuManager moreCascading = new MenuManager("More Cascading");
moreCascading.add(aboutAction);
cascadingMenu.add(moreCascading);

// Create the rest of File's actions
fileMenu.add(new Separator());
fileMenu.add(exitAction);
```

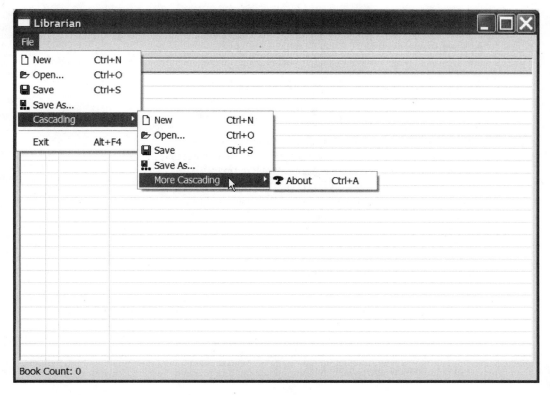

Figure 16-9. Cascading menus

Notice the penultimate line in that snippet:

```
fileMenu.add(new Separator());
```

Adding a separator to a menu creates a horizontal bar that separates menu items. You can add these to group like actions, separating them from dissimilar groups. For example, the preceding code separates actions taken on files (New, Open, Save, and so on) from the command to close the application.

Using a Menu in an Application

The Librarian application begins with just a menu for triggering the actions. The main class, Librarian, extends ApplicationWindow (see Listing 16-10). It creates instances of the preceding actions as member variables. In its constructor, it calls addMenuBar(), and overrides createMenuManager() to create the application-specific menus, adding the actions to the appropriate MenuManager instances.

Listing 16-10. `Librarian.java`

```java
package examples.ch16;

import java.io.IOException;
import java.lang.reflect.InvocationTargetException;

import org.eclipse.core.runtime.IProgressMonitor;
import org.eclipse.jface.action.*;
import org.eclipse.jface.dialogs.MessageDialog;
import org.eclipse.jface.operation.IRunnableWithProgress;
import org.eclipse.jface.operation.ModalContext;
import org.eclipse.jface.util.IPropertyChangeListener;
import org.eclipse.jface.util.PropertyChangeEvent;
import org.eclipse.jface.viewers.*;
import org.eclipse.jface.window.ApplicationWindow;
import org.eclipse.swt.SWT;
import org.eclipse.swt.layout.*;
import org.eclipse.swt.widgets.*;

/**
 * This class keeps track of your library, and who you've loaned books to
 */
public class Librarian extends ApplicationWindow {
  // A static instance to the running application
  private static Librarian APP;

  // Table column names/properties
  public static final String TITLE = "Title";
  public static final String CHECKED_OUT = "?";
  public static final String WHO = "By Whom";
  public static final String[] PROPS = { TITLE, CHECKED_OUT, WHO};

  // The viewer
  private TableViewer viewer;

  // The current library
  private Library library;

  // The actions
  private NewAction newAction;
  private OpenAction openAction;
  private SaveAction saveAction;
  private SaveAsAction saveAsAction;
  private ExitAction exitAction;
  private AddBookAction addBookAction;
  private RemoveBookAction removeBookAction;
  private AboutAction aboutAction;
  private ShowBookCountAction showBookCountAction;

  /**
   * Gets the running application
   */
```

```java
public static final Librarian getApp() {
  return APP;
}

/**
 * Librarian constructor
 */
public Librarian() {
  super(null);

  APP = this;

  // Create the data model
  library = new Library();

  // Create the actions
  newAction = new NewAction();
  openAction = new OpenAction();
  saveAction = new SaveAction();
  saveAsAction = new SaveAsAction();
  exitAction = new ExitAction();
  addBookAction = new AddBookAction();
  removeBookAction = new RemoveBookAction();
  aboutAction = new AboutAction();
  showBookCountAction = new ShowBookCountAction();

  addMenuBar();
  addCoolBar(SWT.NONE);
  addStatusLine();
}

/**
 * Runs the application
 */
public void run() {
  // Don't return from open() until window closes
  setBlockOnOpen(true);

  // Open the main window
  open();

  // Dispose the display
  Display.getCurrent().dispose();
}

/**
 * Configures the shell
 *
 * @param shell the shell
 */
protected void configureShell(Shell shell) {
  super.configureShell(shell);
```

```
    // Set the title bar text
    shell.setText("Librarian");
}

/**
 * Creates the main window's contents
 *
 * @param parent the main window
 * @return Control
 */
protected Control createContents(Composite parent) {
  Composite composite = new Composite(parent, SWT.NONE);
  composite.setLayout(new GridLayout(1, false));

  viewer = new TableViewer(composite, SWT.FULL_SELECTION | SWT.BORDER);
  Table table = viewer.getTable();
  table.setLayoutData(new GridData(GridData.FILL_BOTH));

  // Set up the viewer
  viewer.setContentProvider(new LibraryContentProvider());
  viewer.setLabelProvider(new LibraryLabelProvider());
  viewer.setInput(library);
  viewer.setColumnProperties(PROPS);
  viewer.setCellEditors(new CellEditor[] { new TextCellEditor(table),
      new CheckboxCellEditor(table), new TextCellEditor(table)});
  viewer.setCellModifier(new LibraryCellModifier());

  // Set up the table
  for (int i = 0, n = PROPS.length; i < n; i++)
    new TableColumn(table, SWT.LEFT).setText(PROPS[i]);
  table.setHeaderVisible(true);
  table.setLinesVisible(true);

  // Add code to hide or display the book count based on the action
  showBookCountAction.addPropertyChangeListener(new IPropertyChangeListener() {
    public void propertyChange(PropertyChangeEvent event) {
      // The value has changed; refresh the view
      refreshView();
    }
  });

  // Refresh the view to get the columns right-sized
  refreshView();

  return composite;
}

/**
 * Creates the menu for the application
 *
 * @return MenuManager
 */
```

```
protected MenuManager createMenuManager() {
    // Create the main menu
    MenuManager mm = new MenuManager();

    // Create the File menu
    MenuManager fileMenu = new MenuManager("File");
    mm.add(fileMenu);

    // Add the actions to the File menu
    fileMenu.add(newAction);
    fileMenu.add(openAction);
    fileMenu.add(saveAction);
    fileMenu.add(saveAsAction);
    fileMenu.add(new Separator());
    fileMenu.add(exitAction);

    // Create the Book menu
    MenuManager bookMenu = new MenuManager("Book");
    mm.add(bookMenu);

    // Add the actions to the Book menu
    bookMenu.add(addBookAction);
    bookMenu.add(removeBookAction);

    // Create the View menu
    MenuManager viewMenu = new MenuManager("View");
    mm.add(viewMenu);

    // Add the actions to the View menu
    viewMenu.add(showBookCountAction);

    // Create the Help menu
    MenuManager helpMenu = new MenuManager("Help");
    mm.add(helpMenu);

    // Add the actions to the Help menu
    helpMenu.add(aboutAction);

    return mm;
}

/**
 * Creates the toolbar for the application
 */
protected ToolBarManager createToolBarManager(int style) {
    // Create the toolbar manager
    ToolBarManager tbm = new ToolBarManager(style);
```

```
      // Add the file actions
      tbm.add(newAction);
      tbm.add(openAction);
      tbm.add(saveAction);
      tbm.add(saveAsAction);

      // Add a separator
      tbm.add(new Separator());

      // Add the book actions
      tbm.add(addBookAction);
      tbm.add(removeBookAction);

      // Add a separator
      tbm.add(new Separator());

      // Add the show book count, which will appear as a toggle button
      tbm.add(showBookCountAction);

      // Add a separator
      tbm.add(new Separator());

      // Add the about action
      tbm.add(aboutAction);

      return tbm;
    }

    /**
     * Creates the coolbar for the application
     */
    protected CoolBarManager createCoolBarManager(int style) {
      // Create the coolbar manager
      CoolBarManager cbm = new CoolBarManager(style);

      // Add the toolbar
      cbm.add(createToolBarManager(SWT.FLAT));

      return cbm;
    }

    /**
     * Creates the status line manager
     */
    protected StatusLineManager createStatusLineManager() {
      return new StatusLineManager();
    }

    /**
     * Adds a book
     */
    public void addBook() {
      library.add(new Book("[Enter Title]"));
      refreshView();
    }
```

```java
/**
 * Removes the selected book
 */
public void removeSelectedBook() {
  Book book = (Book) ((IStructuredSelection) viewer.getSelection())
      .getFirstElement();
  if (book != null) library.remove(book);
  refreshView();
}

/**
 * Opens a file
 *
 * @param fileName the file name
 */
public void openFile(final String fileName) {
  if (checkOverwrite()) {
    // Disable the actions, so user can't change library while loading
    enableActions(false);

    library = new Library();
    try {
      // Launch the Open runnable
      ModalContext.run(new IRunnableWithProgress() {
        public void run(IProgressMonitor progressMonitor) {
          try {
            progressMonitor.beginTask("Loading", IProgressMonitor.UNKNOWN);
            library.load(fileName);
            progressMonitor.done();
            viewer.setInput(library);
            refreshView();
          } catch (IOException e) {
            showError("Can't load file " + fileName + "\r" + e.getMessage());
          }
        }
      }, true, getStatusLineManager().getProgressMonitor(), getShell()
          .getDisplay());
    } catch (InterruptedException e) {} catch (InvocationTargetException e) {}
    finally {
      // Enable actions
      enableActions(true);
    }
  }
}

/**
 * Creates a new file
 */
public void newFile() {
  if (checkOverwrite()) {
    library = new Library();
    viewer.setInput(library);
  }
}
```

```java
/**
 * Saves the current file
 */
public void saveFile() {
  String fileName = library.getFileName();
  if (fileName == null) {
    fileName = new SafeSaveDialog(getShell()).open();
  }
  saveFileAs(fileName);
}

/**
 * Saves the current file using the specified file name
 *
 * @param fileName the file name
 */
public void saveFileAs(final String fileName) {
  // Disable the actions, so user can't change file while it's saving
  enableActions(false);

  try {
    // Launch the Save runnable
    ModalContext.run(new IRunnableWithProgress() {
      public void run(IProgressMonitor progressMonitor) {
        try {
          progressMonitor.beginTask("Saving", IProgressMonitor.UNKNOWN);
          library.save(fileName);
          progressMonitor.done();
        } catch (IOException e) {
          showError("Can't save file " + library.getFileName() + "\r"
              + e.getMessage());
        }
      }
    }, true, getStatusLineManager().getProgressMonitor(), getShell()
        .getDisplay());
  } catch (InterruptedException e) {} catch (InvocationTargetException e) {}
  finally {
    // Enable the actions
    enableActions(true);
  }
}

/**
 * Shows an error
 *
 * @param msg the error
 */
public void showError(String msg) {
  MessageDialog.openError(getShell(), "Error", msg);
}

/**
 * Refreshes the view
 */
```

```
public void refreshView() {
  // Refresh the view
  viewer.refresh();

  // Repack the columns
  for (int i = 0, n = viewer.getTable().getColumnCount(); i < n; i++) {
    viewer.getTable().getColumn(i).pack();
  }

  getStatusLineManager().setMessage(
      showBookCountAction.isChecked() ? "Book Count: "
          + library.getBooks().size() : "");
}

/**
 * Checks the current file for unsaved changes. If it has unsaved changes,
 * confirms that user wants to overwrite
 *
 * @return boolean
 */
public boolean checkOverwrite() {
  boolean proceed = true;
  if (library.isDirty()) {
    proceed = MessageDialog.openConfirm(getShell(), "Are you sure?",
        "You have unsaved changes--are you sure you want to lose them?");
  }
  return proceed;
}

/**
 * Sets the current library as dirty
 */
public void setLibraryDirty() {
  library.setDirty();
}

/**
 * Closes the application
 */
public boolean close() {
  if (checkOverwrite()) return super.close();
  return false;
}

/**
 * Enables or disables the actions
 *
 * @param enable true to enable, false to disable
 */
private void enableActions(boolean enable) {
  newAction.setEnabled(enable);
  openAction.setEnabled(enable);
```

```java
      saveAction.setEnabled(enable);
      saveAsAction.setEnabled(enable);
      exitAction.setEnabled(enable);
      addBookAction.setEnabled(enable);
      removeBookAction.setEnabled(enable);
      aboutAction.setEnabled(enable);
      showBookCountAction.setEnabled(enable);
    }

    /**
     * The application entry point
     *
     * @param args the command line arguments
     */
    public static void main(String[] args) {
      new Librarian().run();
    }
  }
```

The Librarian program uses the Book class, shown in Listing 16-11, to store each book. Each book maintains both its title and who has it checked out.

Listing 16-11. `Book.java`

```java
package examples.ch16;

/**
 * This class represents a book
 */
public class Book {
  private String title;
  private String checkedOutTo;

  /**
   * Book constructor
   * @param title the title
   */
  public Book(String title) {
    setTitle(title);
  }

  /**
   * Sets the title
   * @param title the title
   */
  public void setTitle(String title) {
    this.title = title;
  }

  /**
   * Gets the title
   * @return String
   */
```

```java
  public String getTitle() {
    return title;
  }

  /**
   * Check out
   * @param who the person checking this book out
   */
  public void checkOut(String who) {
    checkedOutTo = who;
    if (checkedOutTo.length() == 0) checkedOutTo = null;
  }

  public boolean isCheckedOut() {
    return checkedOutTo != null && checkedOutTo.length() > 0;
  }

  public void checkIn() {
    checkedOutTo = null;
  }

  /**
   * Gets who this book is checked out to
   * @return String
   */
  public String getCheckedOutTo() {
    return checkedOutTo;
  }
}
```

An instance of the Library class stores the Book instances, and provides the data model for the application (see Listing 16-12). A Library can both load itself from, and save itself to, a file.

Listing 16-12. Library.java

```java
package examples.ch16;

import java.io.*;
import java.util.*;

/**
 * This class holds all the books in a library. It also handles loading from and
 * saving to disk
 */
public class Library {
  private static final String SEP = "|";

  // The filename
  private String filename;
```

```java
// The books
private Collection books;

// The dirty flag
private boolean dirty;

/**
 * Library constructor. Note the signature. :-)
 */
public Library() {
  books = new LinkedList();
}

/**
 * Loads the library from a file
 *
 * @param filename the filename
 * @throws IOException
 */
public void load(String filename) throws IOException {
  BufferedReader in = new BufferedReader(new LineNumberReader(new FileReader(
      filename)));
  String line;
  while ((line = in.readLine()) != null) {
    StringTokenizer st = new StringTokenizer(line, SEP);
    Book book = null;
    if (st.hasMoreTokens()) book = new Book(st.nextToken());
    if (st.hasMoreTokens()) book.checkOut(st.nextToken());
    if (book != null) add(book);
  }
  in.close();
  this.filename = filename;
  dirty = false;
}

/**
 * Saves the library to a file
 *
 * @param filename the filename
 * @throws IOException
 */
public void save(String filename) throws IOException {
  BufferedWriter out = new BufferedWriter(new FileWriter(filename));
  for (Iterator itr = books.iterator(); itr.hasNext();) {
    Book book = (Book) itr.next();
    out.write(book.getTitle());
    out.write('|');
    out.write(book.getCheckedOutTo() == null ? "" : book.getCheckedOutTo());
    out.write('\r');
  }
  out.close();
  this.filename = filename;
  dirty = false;
}
```

```
/**
 * Adds a book
 *
 * @param book the book to add
 * @return boolean
 */
public boolean add(Book book) {
  boolean added = books.add(book);
  if (added) setDirty();
  return added;
}

/**
 * Removes a book
 *
 * @param book the book to remove
 */
public void remove(Book book) {
  books.remove(book);
  setDirty();
}

/**
 * Gets the books
 *
 * @return Collection
 */
public Collection getBooks() {
  return Collections.unmodifiableCollection(books);
}

/**
 * Gets the file name
 *
 * @return String
 */
public String getFileName() {
  return filename;
}

/**
 * Gets whether this file is dirty
 *
 * @return boolean
 */
public boolean isDirty() {
  return dirty;
}

/**
 * Sets this file as dirty
 */
public void setDirty() {
```

```
        dirty = true;
    }
}
```

The Librarian program displays the books in a TableViewer, which needs a content provider and a label provider. Listing 16-13 contains the content provider, and Listing 16-14 contains the label provider. Notice that the label provider uses images instead of text for the checked-out state. This allows the table to show a checked checkbox for a book that's checked out, and an unchecked checkbox for one that isn't.

Listing 16-13. LibraryContentProvider.java

```java
package examples.ch16;

import org.eclipse.jface.viewers.IStructuredContentProvider;
import org.eclipse.jface.viewers.Viewer;

/**
 * This class provides the content for the library table
 */
public class LibraryContentProvider implements IStructuredContentProvider {
  /**
   * Gets the books
   *
   * @param inputElement the library
   * @return Object[]
   */
  public Object[] getElements(Object inputElement) {
    return ((Library) inputElement).getBooks().toArray();
  }

  /**
   * Disposes any resources
   */
  public void dispose() {
// Do nothing
  }

  /**
   * Called when the input changes
   *
   * @param viewer the viewer
   * @param oldInput the old library
   * @param newInput the new library
   */
  public void inputChanged(Viewer viewer, Object oldInput, Object newInput) {
// Ignore
  }
}
```

Listing 16-14. `LibraryLabelProvider.java`

```java
package examples.ch16;

import org.eclipse.jface.viewers.ILabelProviderListener;
import org.eclipse.jface.viewers.ITableLabelProvider;
import org.eclipse.swt.graphics.Image;

/**
 * This class provides the labels for the library table
 */
public class LibraryLabelProvider implements ITableLabelProvider {
  private Image checked;
  private Image unchecked;

  /**
   * LibraryLabelProvider constructor
   */
  public LibraryLabelProvider() {
    // Create the check mark images
    checked = new Image(null, LibraryLabelProvider.class
        .getResourceAsStream("/images/checked.gif"));
    unchecked = new Image(null, LibraryLabelProvider.class
        .getResourceAsStream("/images/unchecked.gif"));
  }

  /**
   * Gets the column image
   *
   * @param element the book
   * @param columnIndex the column index
   * @return Image
   */
  public Image getColumnImage(Object element, int columnIndex) {
    // For the "Checked Out" column, return the check mark
    // if the book is checked out
    if (columnIndex == 1)
        return ((Book) element).isCheckedOut() ? checked : unchecked;
    return null;
  }

  /**
   * Gets the column text
   *
   * @param element the book
   * @param columnIndex the column index
   * @return String
   */
  public String getColumnText(Object element, int columnIndex) {
    Book book = (Book) element;
    String text = null;
```

```
      switch (columnIndex) {
      case 0:
        text = book.getTitle();
        break;
      case 2:
        text = book.getCheckedOutTo();
        break;
      }
      return text == null ? "" : text;
   }

   /**
    * Adds a listener
    */
   public void addListener(ILabelProviderListener listener) {
   // Ignore
   }

   /**
    * Disposes any resources
    */
   public void dispose() {
      if (checked != null) checked.dispose();
      if (unchecked != null) unchecked.dispose();
   }

   /**
    * Gets whether this is a label property
    *
    * @param element the book
    * @param property the property
    * @return boolean
    */
   public boolean isLabelProperty(Object element, String property) {
      return false;
   }

   /**
    * Removes a listener
    *
    * @param listener the listener
    */
   public void removeListener(ILabelProviderListener listener) {
   // Ignore
   }
}
```

To allow editing the books within the table, Librarian uses a cell modifier class called LibraryCellModifier, shown in Listing 16-15.

Listing 16-15. LibraryCellModifier.java

```java
package examples.ch16;

import org.eclipse.jface.viewers.ICellModifier;
import org.eclipse.swt.widgets.Item;

/**
 * This class is the cell modifier for the Librarian program
 */
public class LibraryCellModifier implements ICellModifier {
  /**
   * Gets whether the specified property can be modified
   *
   * @param element the book
   * @param property the property
   * @return boolean
   */
  public boolean canModify(Object element, String property) {
    return true;
  }

  /**
   * Gets the value for the property
   *
   * @param element the book
   * @param property the property
   * @return Object
   */
  public Object getValue(Object element, String property) {
    Book book = (Book) element;
    if (Librarian.TITLE.equals(property))
      return book.getTitle();
    else if (Librarian.CHECKED_OUT.equals(property))
      return Boolean.valueOf(book.isCheckedOut());
    else if (Librarian.WHO.equals(property))
      return book.getCheckedOutTo() == null ? "" : book.getCheckedOutTo();
    else
      return null;
  }

  /**
   * Modifies the element
   *
   * @param element the book
   * @param property the property
   * @param value the new value
   */
  public void modify(Object element, String property, Object value) {
    if (element instanceof Item) element = ((Item) element).getData();
```

```
      Book book = (Book) element;
      if (Librarian.TITLE.equals(property))
        book.setTitle((String) value);
      else if (Librarian.CHECKED_OUT.equals(property)) {
        boolean b = ((Boolean) value).booleanValue();
        if (b)
          book.checkOut("[Enter Name]");
        else
          book.checkIn();
      } else if (Librarian.WHO.equals(property)) book.checkOut((String) value);

      // Refresh the view
      Librarian.getApp().refreshView();

      // Set the library as dirty
      Librarian.getApp().setLibraryDirty();
  }
}
```

Run the program and choose Book ➤ Add Book, as shown in Figure 16-10, to add a book to your library. Figure 16-11 shows the added book. Click the Title to change it. Then click the checkbox to check the book out to someone. Figure 16-12 shows the book titled *Leveraging Lisp in Web Services* checked out to a strangely named individual.

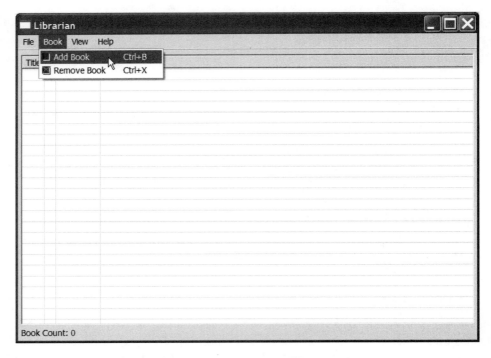

Figure 16-10. Adding a book to the Librarian application

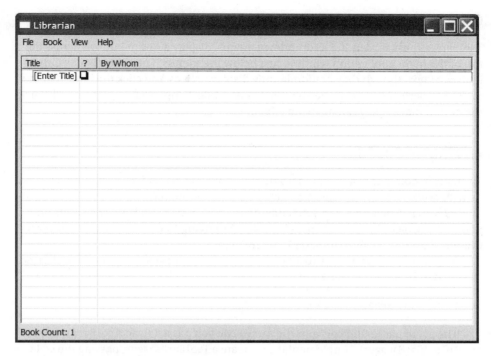

Figure 16-11. Book added to Library

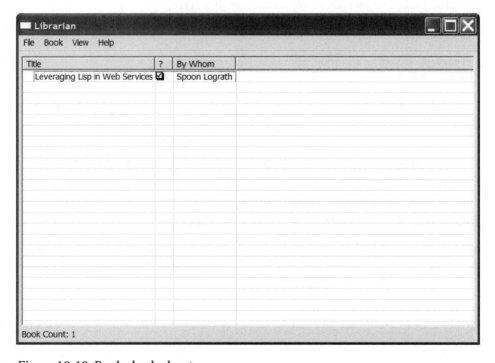

Figure 16-12. Book checked out

Creating ToolBars

Toolbars, almost as plentiful as dropdown menus, display a row of buttons across the top of the main application window, just below the menus. They can display either images or text, though they predominantly display images. You click the button in the toolbar to perform its associated action. For example, to open a file, users usually click the button that displays an open file folder.

Adding a ToolBar

To create a toolbar in JFace, call addToolBar() in your ApplicationWindow-derived class. As with addMenuBar(), you must call addToolBar() before the underlying Shell is created, so you'll usually call it in your constructor. addToolBar() takes a style as its only parameter, which is eventually passed to the underlying ToolBar constructor. Refer to Chapter 8 for more information on ToolBar styles.

You must also override createToolBarManager() in your ApplicationWindow-derived class. It has the following signature:

```
protected ToolBarManager createToolBarManager(int style)
```

The style parameter contains the same style you passed to addToolBar(). In your createToolBarManager() implementation, create a ToolBarManager, passing the style. Then, add your actions to the ToolBarManager. Your implementation might look like this:

```
protected ToolBarManager createToolBarManager(int style) {
  // Create the manager
  ToolBarManager manager = new ToolBarManager(style);

  // Add an action
  manager.add(myAction);

  // Return the manager
  return manager;
}
```

If your actions have images, the images will display on the toolbar buttons. Otherwise, their text will display.

Updating Librarian with a ToolBar

To add a toolbar to the Librarian application, add a call to addToolBar(SWT.FLAT) to Librarian's constructor, so that the constructor's code now looks like this:

```
/**
 * Librarian constructor
 */
public Librarian() {
  super(null);
  APP = this;
```

```
// Create the data model
library = new Library();

// Create the actions
newAction = new NewAction();
openAction = new OpenAction();
saveAction = new SaveAction();
saveAsAction = new SaveAsAction();
exitAction = new ExitAction();
addBookAction = new AddBookAction();
removeBookAction = new RemoveBookAction();
aboutAction = new AboutAction();
showBookCountAction = new ShowBookCountAction();

addMenuBar();
addToolBar(SWT.FLAT);
}
```

Then, add a `createToolBarManager()` implementation in the `Librarian` class that creates a `ToolBarManager` and adds the appropriate actions to it. It should look like this:

```
/**
 * Creates the toolbar for the application
 */
protected ToolBarManager createToolBarManager(int style) {
  // Create the toolbar manager
  ToolBarManager tbm = new ToolBarManager(style);

  // Add the file actions
  tbm.add(newAction);
  tbm.add(openAction);
  tbm.add(saveAction);
  tbm.add(saveAsAction);

   // Add a separator
  tbm.add(new Separator());

  // Add the book actions
  tbm.add(addBookAction);
  tbm.add(removeBookAction);

  // Add a separator
  tbm.add(new Separator());

  // Add the show book count, which will appear as a toggle button
  tbm.add(showBookCountAction);

  // Add a separator
  tbm.add(new Separator());

  // Add the about action
  tbm.add(aboutAction);

  return tbm;
}
```

Now when you run the Librarian application, you see a toolbar, as shown in Figure 16-13. Clicking any of the toolbar buttons performs the appropriate action. Because they run the exact same action classes that the menu runs, they perform just as the menu does.

Notice that the checkbox action—whether or not to show the count of books—that appears with or without a check in the menu appears in the toolbar as a toggle button.

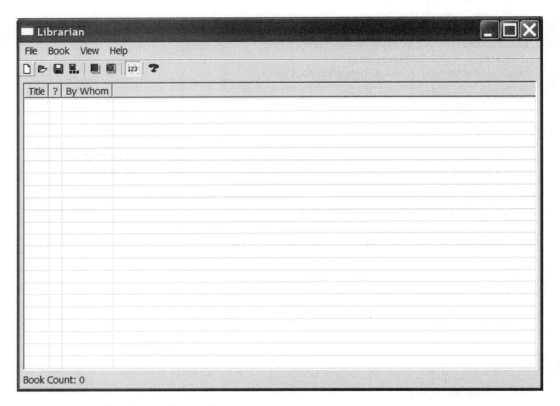

Figure 16-13. Librarian with a toolbar

Creating CoolBars

Your ApplicationWindow-derived JFace application can sport either a toolbar or a coolbar. See Chapter 8 for more information on coolbars. As of this writing, the ApplicationWindow code has a bug that allows you to have both a toolbar and a coolbar if you create the toolbar first. This hole, if not already plugged, soon will be.

Adding a CoolBar

To add a coolbar to an ApplicationWindow-derived class, call addCoolBar() before the Shell is created—usually in the constructor. addCoolBar() takes a style constant; refer to Chapter 8 for coolbar style constants. You also override createCoolBarManager(), which has the following signature:

```
protected CoolBarManager createCoolBarManager(int style)
```

The style parameter contains the style constant you passed to addCoolBar(). In your implementation of this method, you should create a CoolBarManager(). However, instead of adding actions directly to it, you should add a ToolBarManager to it that contains the actions. Review Chapter 8 on coolbars to understand the relationship between toolbars and coolbars.

The following code leverages an existing createToolBarManager() implementation to show a coolbar instead of a toolbar:

```
protected CoolBarManager createCoolBarManager(int style) {
  // Create the CoolBarManager
  CoolBarManager cbm = new CoolBarManager(style);

  // Add the toolbar that contains the actions
  cbm.add(createToolBarManager(SWT.NONE));

  // Return the manager
  return cbm;
}
```

Updating Librarian with a CoolBar

To swap Librarian's toolbar for a coolbar, change the call in the constructor from addToolBar(SWT.FLAT) to addCoolBar(SWT.NONE). Then, override createCoolBarManager() with this implementation:

```
/**
 * Creates the coolbar for the application
 */
protected CoolBarManager createCoolBarManager(int style) {
  // Create the coolbar manager
  CoolBarManager cbm = new CoolBarManager(style);

  // Add the toolbar
  cbm.add(createToolBarManager(SWT.FLAT));

  return cbm;
}
```

Be sure to leave in your createToolBarManager() implementation, as this createCoolBarManager() implementation relies on it.

The main window now looks like Figure 16-14. The buttons still work as before, as they still call the same action classes.

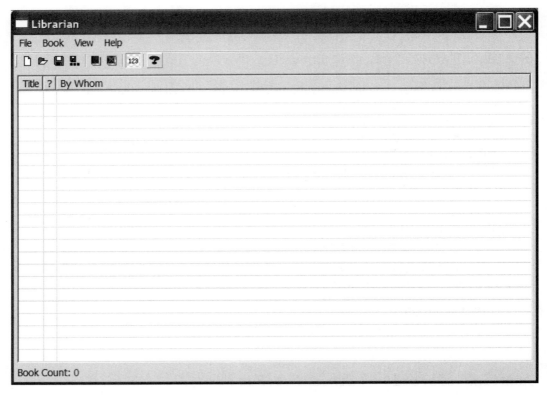

Figure 16-14. Librarian with a coolbar

Creating a Status Line

The status line, or status bar, represents another application window convention. Running across the bottom of the window, it provides an unobtrusive communication mechanism between the application and the user. The status line can display non-critical messages about the state of the application. It can display critical messages too, of course, but because status line messages do nothing to arrest the attention of the user, using them for critical communications would be ineffective.

Adding a Status Line

Call addStatusLine() in the constructor of your ApplicationWindow-derived class to create a status line. You must also override createStatusLineManager(), which has the following signature:

```
protected StatusLineManager createStatusLineManager()
```

In your implementation, you should create a StatusLineManager and return it. You can add actions to it, which create corresponding buttons to trigger the actions in the status line. See Figure 16-15; look at the lower right. This seems a little over the top, scattering buttons all over the interface. The application already has the actions in the menu and in the toolbar or coolbar, and having them in the status line might prove confusing. Although developers tend to believe that having more than one way to do things improves usability, studies show the opposite is true. Like Frank Gilbreth's (of *Cheaper by the Dozen* fame) "one best way," typical users want one best way to perform a task. They tolerate menus and buttons, but adding duplicate buttons confuses them and reduces usability. Nevertheless, feel free to defy this advice and add actions to your status lines.

The following code creates a status line, but doesn't add anything to it.

```
protected StatusLineManager createStatusLineManager() {
  // Create the status line manager
  StatusLineManager slm = new StatusLineManager();

  // Return it
  return slm;
}
```

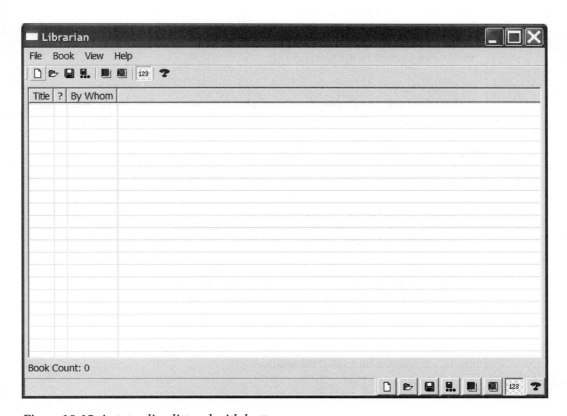

Figure 16-15. A status line littered with buttons

If you shouldn't add actions to the status line, what should you add? You can add messages to it by calling its setMessage() method, passing the method to add. Pass an empty string to setMessage() to clear the message. You can also add a progress bar to it to keep the user updated on lengthy operations. The next section incorporates status line messages and a progress bar into Librarian.

Updating Librarian with a Status Line

Until now, a Label has optionally displayed the book count. This seems just the sort of information to display in the status line. To add the status line and display the book count in it, first call addStatusLine() in Librarian's constructor. The last three lines of code in the constructor now look like this:

```
addMenuBar();
addCoolBar(SWT.NONE);
addStatusLine();
```

Next, override createStatusLineManager() to return an empty status line manager. The implementation looks like this:

```
protected StatusLineManager createStatusLineManager() {
  return new StatusLineManager();
}
```

Delete any reference to the bookCount label (still in Librarian.java). Then, change the refreshView() method to display the book count in the status line, like this:

```
public void refreshView() {
  // Refresh the view
  viewer.refresh();

  // Repack the columns
  for (int i = 0, n = viewer.getTable().getColumnCount(); i < n; i++) {
    viewer.getTable().getColumn(i).pack();
  }

  getStatusLineManager().setMessage(showBookCountAction.isChecked() ?
    "Book Count: " + library.getBooks().size() : "");
}
```

Now the window looks like Figure 16-16. Notice the book count displayed in the status line across the bottom of the window.

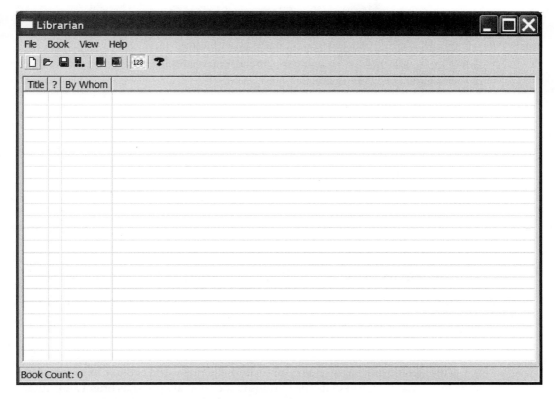

Figure 16-16. The book count displayed in the status line

Adding a progress monitor to the status line requires only a little more work. Call the status line's getProgressMonitor() method to get a reference to its progress monitor, like this:

```
IProgressMonitor pm = getStatusLineManager().getProgressMonitor();
```

You can then call the same progress monitor methods discussed in Chapter 15: beginTask(), work(), done(), and so on.

Opening and saving a file can potentially take a long time, and these make excellent candidates for progress monitors. This section adds a progress monitor to the status line for both opening and saving a file. The threading model presents a few hurdles. For the progress monitor to display and update during the open or save, the UI must remain responsive. However, if the UI remains responsive during the open or save, users can change the library file while it's being read from or written to disk. Somehow you must prevent the users from changing the library during open or save, yet keep the UI responsive.

Keeping the UI responsive entails spinning the save or open into its own thread. You can use ModalContext.run() for that. Its signature is as follows:

```
ModalContext.run(IRunnableWithProgress operation, boolean fork,
  IProgressMonitor monitor, Display display)
```

Enclose the save or open in operation, pass true for fork, pass the status line's progress monitor for monitor, and pass the current display for display.

Keeping the user from changing the library file while the thread runs involves disabling the actions before spawning the thread, and enabling them in the finally block, as this pseudo code demonstrates:

```
// Disable actions

// Spawn thread
try {
  ModalContext.run(...);
}
catch (...) {}
finally {
  // Enable actions
}
```

To disable the actions, you could try a shortcut by disabling the menu and the coolbar, like this:

```
getMenuBarManager().getMenu().setEnabled(false);
getCoolBarControl().setEnabled(false);
```

Although the preceding code disables both the menu and coolbar, as expected, it provides no visual clue of that. The buttons in the coolbar appear as bright and vibrant, ready to be clicked, as ever. Instead, you must disable the actions themselves. Write a convenience method that takes a boolean parameter and calls setEnabled() on each action, passing the boolean, like this:

```
private void enableActions(boolean enable) {
  newAction.setEnabled(enable);
  openAction.setEnabled(enable);
  saveAction.setEnabled(enable);
  saveAsAction.setEnabled(enable);
  exitAction.setEnabled(enable);
  addBookAction.setEnabled(enable);
  removeBookAction.setEnabled(enable);
  aboutAction.setEnabled(enable);
  showBookCountAction.setEnabled(enable);
}
```

Retrofit openFile() and saveFileAs() to disable the actions, spawn the thread, and enable the actions. openFile() should now look like this:

```
public void openFile(final String fileName) {
  if (checkOverwrite()) {
    // Disable the actions, so user can't change library while loading
    enableActions(false);
```

```
    library = new Library();
    try {
      // Launch the Open runnable
      ModalContext.run(new IRunnableWithProgress() {
        public void run(IProgressMonitor progressMonitor) {
          try {
            progressMonitor.beginTask("Loading", IProgressMonitor.UNKNOWN);
            library.load(fileName);
            progressMonitor.done();
            viewer.setInput(library);
            refreshView();
          } catch (IOException e) {
            showError("Can't load file " + fileName + "\r" + e.getMessage());
          }
        }
      }, true, getStatusLineManager().getProgressMonitor(),
      getShell().getDisplay());
    }
    catch (InterruptedException e) {}
    catch (InvocationTargetException e) {}
    finally {
      // Enable actions
      enableActions(true);
    }
  }
}
```

saveFileAs() should look like this:

```
public void saveFileAs(final String fileName) {
  // Disable the actions, so user can't change file while it's saving
  enableActions(false);

  try {
    // Launch the Save runnable
    ModalContext.run(new IRunnableWithProgress() {
      public void run(IProgressMonitor progressMonitor) {
        try {
          progressMonitor.beginTask("Saving", IProgressMonitor.UNKNOWN);
          library.save(fileName);
          progressMonitor.done();
        } catch (IOException e) {
          showError("Can't save file " + library.getFileName() + "\r"
              + e.getMessage());
        }
      }
    }, true, getStatusLineManager().getProgressMonitor(),
    getShell().getDisplay());
  }
```

```
      catch (InterruptedException e) {}
      catch (InvocationTargetException e) {}
      finally {
        // Enable the actions
        enableActions(true);
      }
  }
```

You must add the following imports to the top of Librarian.java:

```
import java.lang.reflect.InvocationTargetException;
import org.eclipse.core.runtime.IProgressMonitor;
import org.eclipse.jface.operation.IRunnableWithProgress;
import org.eclipse.jface.operation.ModalContext;
```

Now when you open or save a file, you see a progress monitor in the status line. Unless you're opening or saving a large file, or are using a slow computer, you won't see the progress monitor, as the open or save happens too fast. You can toss a call to Thread.sleep() into the IRunnableWithProgress.run() implementation to see the progress bar. Figure 16-17 shows the application saving a file. Note the progress monitor in the lower-right corner.

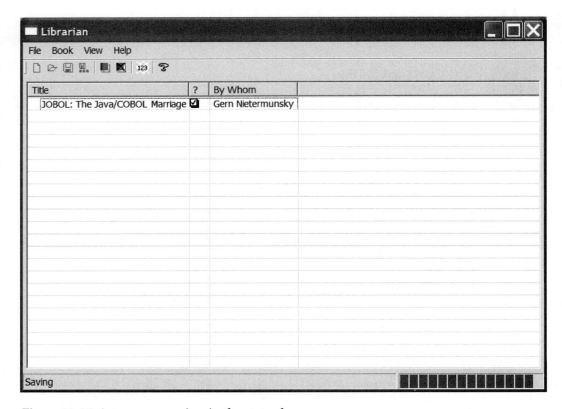

Figure 16-17. A progress monitor in the status bar

Summary

The JFace "action" concept encourages reuse and drives powerful interaction with users. By creating actions and adding them to various action containers, you achieve continuity and flexibility in your applications with little work. Menus, toolbars, coolbars, and status lines provide avenues for your actions, and allow users to get things done—which is why they use your applications.

CHAPTER 17

Using
Preferences

AS MARILYN MONROE and Jack Lemmon showed on the big screen, some like it hot. It follows, then, that some like it cold, some like it lukewarm, and some don't care what temperature it is. People prefer different things, and want to work with your applications in different ways. Your applications should not only accommodate different preferences, but also must plan for them by making preference specification integral to their interfaces.

When small programs that ran from the command line ruled the computing landscape, preferences were specified on the command line at each program invocation. Although syntax and semantics differed slightly across operating systems, the basics remained the same through all platforms: type the name of the program, specify terse flags that you'd memorized (or looked up on a reference sheet), and hit Enter. For example, to display the contents of the current directory in Unix, with everything sorted newest first, you'd type the following:

```
ls -alt
```

Under DOS or Windows, you'd type the following:

```
dir /o-d
```

However, as programs grew in complexity, and the number of preferences to configure grew exponentially, specifying all preferences at each invocation became too cumbersome. Then, as GUIs entered the mainstream, the practice of entering preferences on the command line became unworkable: programs were invoked not by typing in a command line, but by clicking an icon. Invoking a program in a GUI involves no typing at all, and hence no provision for specifying preferences.

To fill this void, complex programs offer interfaces from within the programs to specify preferences. Once you enter preferences, the programs store the preferences for use each time the program runs. They remember your customization preferences, so you can set up a program to run how you like it (within the bounds offered by the program), and you don't have to worry about customizing it again. Or, if you desire, you can go back into the familiar interface to alter the preferences anew. This chapter discusses the JFace preferences framework, found in package `org.eclipse.jface.preference`.

Persisting Preferences

One of the most divisive issues between Windows users and Unix users concerns the way programs store preferences. With the introduction of Windows 95, Windows migrated in full force from its text-based INI files to its binary Registry. The binary format enables quicker search and retrieval, but requires specialized tools such as regedit.exe to view and edit the preference data. Further, not only can a corrupted Registry keep your computer from booting, but it can become so corrupted that no tool can read it or allow you to edit it. Unix, on the other hand, stores preference data almost exclusively in text files, sacrificing some search-and-retrieval speed for transparency and ease of use. You can use any editor to view or edit Unix preference files, and their human-readable nature makes correcting corruption more likely.

Java reveals its Unix heritage with its properties files, which are text-based files listing name-value pairs. A sample properties file might look like this:

```
database.name=MyDB
sort=true
sort.order=ascending
```

Java uses the java.util.Properties class to load, retrieve, set, and store properties files.

JFace piggybacks atop properties files, using a preferences API to read and write the underlying properties file. The PreferenceStore class, which implements both IPreferenceStore and IPersistPreferenceStore, handles the properties file interaction. You can create a PreferenceStore instance either with or without an associated properties file using one of its two constructors:

- PreferenceStore()

- PreferenceStore(String filename)

For example, to create a PreferenceStore and associate it with the file foo.properties, use this code:

```
PreferenceStore preferenceStore = new PreferenceStore("foo.properties");
```

PreferenceStore supports two tiers of default values: a default value for a specified name, and a default value for a specified data type. If you attempt to retrieve a value for a configured name in your application, but the user hasn't yet set a value for it, the default value for the specified name is returned. However, if you attempt to retrieve a value for a name that hasn't been configured in your application, the default value for the specified data type comes back instead. Only user-specified preferences are stored.

For example, your application might have a property whose name is UserName. You've configured the default value for UserName to be "[Your Name Goes Here]." If the user has specified his or her name for this property, the properties file might look like this:

```
UserName=Jane Doe
```

Retrieving the value for UserName returns "Jane Doe."

If the user hasn't specified his or her name for the UserName property, retrieving the value for this property returns the default value for UserName, which is "[Your Name Goes Here]." However, trying to retrieve the value for an unspecified name such as UserAstrologySign returns the default value for the type, which in this case is an empty string.

Table 17-1 lists `PreferenceStore`'s methods.

Table 17-1. `PreferenceStore` *Methods*

Method	Description
void addPropertyChangeListener (IPropertyChangeListener listener)	Adds a listener to the notification list that's notified when a property changes.
boolean contains(String name)	Returns `true` if this preference store contains a value for the specified name, whether a user-specified value or a default value. Otherwise, returns `false`.
void firePropertyChangeEvent(String name, Object oldValue, Object newValue)	Fires a property change event when the value for the specified name changes. `PreferenceStore` calls this method automatically when a value changes.
boolean getBoolean(String name)	Returns the user-specified `boolean` value for the specified name.
boolean getDefaultBoolean(String name)	Returns the default `boolean` value for the specified name.
double getDefaultDouble(String name)	Returns the default `double` value for the specified name.
float getDefaultFloat(String name)	Returns the default `float` value for the specified name.
int getDefaultInt(String name)	Returns the default `int` value for the specified name.
long getDefaultLong(String name)	Returns the default `long` value for the specified name.
String getDefaultString(String name)	Returns the default `String` value for the specified name.
double getDouble(String name)	Returns the user-specified `double` value for the specified name.
float getFloat(String name)	Returns the user-specified `float` value for the specified name.
int getInt(String name)	Returns the user-specified `int` value for the specified name.
long getLong(String name)	Returns the user-specified `long` value for the specified name.
String getString(String name)	Returns the user-specified `String` value for the specified name.
boolean isDefault(String name)	Returns `true` if the user doesn't have a user-specified value for the specified name, but a default value does exist.
void list(PrintStream out)	Prints the contents of this preference store to the specified print stream.
void list(PrintWriter out)	Prints the contents of this preference store to the specified print writer.
void load()	Loads the associated properties file into this preference store. Throws an `IOException` if no file name has been specified, or if the file can't be loaded.

Table 17-1. PreferenceStore *Methods (continued)*

Method	Description
void load(InputStream in)	Loads the data from the specified input stream into this preference store.
boolean needsSaving()	Returns true if any values in this preference store have changed and not been saved.
String[] preferenceNames()	Returns the names of the preferences for which user-specified values have been set.
void putValue(String name, String value)	Sets the user-specified value for the specified name.
void removePropertyChangeListener (IPropertyChangeListener listener)	Removes the specified listener from the notification list.
void save()	Saves the user-specified preferences to the associated properties file. Throws an IOException if no file name has been specified, or if the file can't be saved.
void save(OutputStream out, String header)	Saves the user-specified preferences to the specified output stream, using the specified header.
void setDefault(String name, boolean value)	Sets the default value for the specified name.
void setDefault(String name, double value)	Sets the default value for the specified name.
void setDefault(String name, float value)	Sets the default value for the specified name.
void setDefault(String name, int value)	Sets the default value for the specified name.
void setDefault(String name, long value)	Sets the default value for the specified name.
void setDefault(String name, String value)	Sets the default value for the specified name.
void setFilename(String name)	Sets the name of the file to associate with this preference store.
void setToDefault(String name)	Sets the value for the specified name to the default value.
void setValue(String name, boolean value)	Sets the user-specified value for the specified name.
void setValue(String name, double value)	Sets the user-specified value for the specified name.
void setValue(String name, float value)	Sets the user-specified value for the specified name.
void setValue(String name, int value)	Sets the user-specified value for the specified name.
void setValue(String name, long value)	Sets the user-specified value for the specified name.
void setValue(String name, String value)	Sets the user-specified value for the specified name.

The PreferenceStoreTest application in Listing 17-1 creates a preference store, loads the file foo.properties, sets some defaults, and then prints the preferences.

Listing 17-1. PreferenceStoreTest.java

```
package examples.ch17;

import java.io.IOException;

import org.eclipse.jface.preference.PreferenceStore;

/**
 * This class demonstrates PreferenceStore
 */
public class PreferenceStoreTest {
  public static void main(String[] args) throws IOException {
    // Create the preference store
    PreferenceStore preferenceStore = new PreferenceStore("foo.properties");

    // Load it
    preferenceStore.load();

    // Set some defaults
    preferenceStore.setDefault("name1", true);
    preferenceStore.setDefault("name2", 42);
    preferenceStore.setDefault("name3", "Stack");

    // List the preferences
    preferenceStore.list(System.out);
  }
}
```

Say the contents of foo.properties are as follows:

```
name1=false
name3=House
```

Then the output from PreferenceStoreTest is as follows:

```
-- listing properties --
name3=House
name2=42
name1=false
```

Notice that the preference store uses one of the default values, 42 (for name2), but uses the two values specified in foo.properties for name1 and name3.

Receiving Notification of Preference Changes

When users change their preferences, you should respond to their desires immediately by updating your program's view and whatever else is appropriate. To respond to changed preferences, you obviously must know about them. The preference store takes care of notifying all interested parties each time any of the properties it manages changes.

To register your interest in property changes, create an IPropertyChangeListener implementation, which declares a single method:

```
void propertyChange(PropertyChangeEvent event)
```

The org.eclipse.jface.util package contains both IPropertyChangeListener and PropertyChangeEvent.

After creating an IPropertyChangeListener, register it with the preference store by passing it to IPreferenceStore.addPropertyChangeListener(). The preference store calls your propertyChange() method once for each property that changes, each time that it changes. The PropertyChangeEvent that it receives exposes three methods, getters for the three pieces of data it carries: the name of the changed property, the old value of the property, and the new value of the property. Table 17-2 lists PropertyChangeEvent's methods.

Table 17-2. PropertyChangeEvent *Methods*

Method	Description
Object getNewValue()	Returns the changed property's new value
Object getOldValue()	Returns the changed property's old value
String getProperty()	Returns the name of the property that changed

For example, suppose you have an ApplicationWindow-derived class that allows users to set the text in the title bar via preferences. The class might look something like this:

```
public class MyWindow extends ApplicationWindow
    implements IPropertyChangeListener {
  // The preference store
  private IPreferenceStore ps;

  /**
   * MyWindow constructor
   */
  public MyWindow() {
    super(null);

    // Create the preference store and register this window as a listener
    ps = new PreferenceStore("my.properties");
    ps.addPropertyChangeListener(this);
  }
```

```
/**
 * Called when a property changes
 * @param event the PropertyEvent
 */
public void propertyChange(PropertyChangeEvent event) {
  if ("title".equals(event.getProperty())) {
    getShell().setText((String) event.getNewValue());
  }
}
// The rest of the code goes here . . . .
}
```

Any time the user changes the preference for the "title" property, this window updates its title text to the new preferred text. Note that this code offers the user no means for changing the preferences. The balance of this chapter describes how to allow users to change preferences.

Displaying a Preference Dialog

Storing preferences in editable text-based files and offering no interface beyond a text editor might placate die-hard Unix users, who are probably wondering why your application isn't just part of Emacs anyway. Some people do prefer to use a text editor to view and edit preferences. However, those accustomed to GUIs—including Windows users, Mac OS X users, and even the latest crop of Linux users who boot directly into KDE or GNOME—demand graphical interfaces, launched from within your application, to view and set their preferences. JFace provides all the classes necessary to whip up a pretty face on a preference store.

The JFace preference interface displays a tree on the left. Each node in the tree, represented by an IPreferenceNode implementation, corresponds to a preference page, represented by an IPreferencePage implementation. Each preference page can display multiple controls to view and display preferences. Clicking the node in the tree displays the corresponding preference page on the right. Figure 17-1 shows the Eclipse preference interface. The Workbench node is highlighted on the left, and the Workbench property page is displayed on the right.

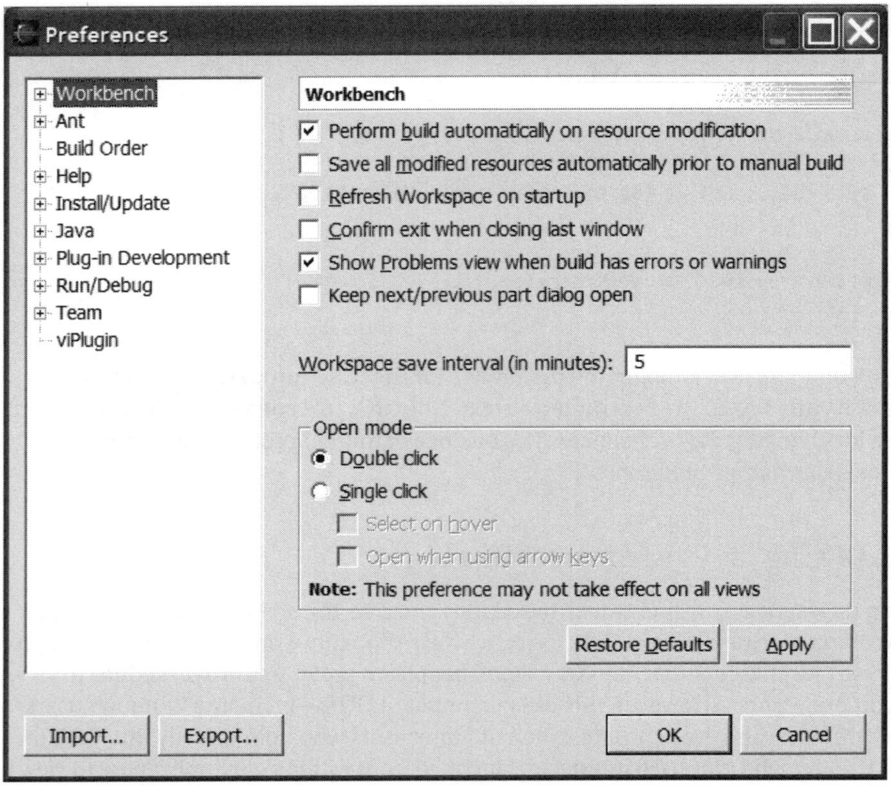

Figure 17-1. The Eclipse preference interface

To display a preference dialog, use the PreferenceDialog class as you would any other dialog class: construct one, then call its open() method. However, the PreferenceDialog constructor gets a little tricky, as it requires an instance of PreferenceManager. The constructor's signature looks like this:

```
PreferenceDialog(Shell parentShell, PreferenceManager manager)
```

You can display a preference dialog, then, with this code:

```
PreferenceDialog dlg = new PreferenceDialog(shell, manager);
dlg.open();
```

However, because passing null for the preference manager throws a NullPointerException, you must create a PreferenceManager. The next sections explain how to do that, beginning with the entities a preference manager ultimately manages: preference pages.

Creating a Page

A preference page displays the labels and entry fields that both display and afford editing of the user preferences. In the Eclipse preference dialog shown in Figure 17-1, the right side of the dialog displays a preference page with checkboxes, labels, a text box, and radio buttons.

A JFace preference page must implement the IPreferencePage interface, whose methods are listed in Table 17-3. However, instead of building a preference page from scratch and enduring the drudgery of implementing all the IPreferencePage methods, you'll probably rely on JFace's implementation, PreferencePage. To create a page, subclass PreferencePage and implement its one abstract method, createContents(), whose signature looks like this:

```
abstract Control createContents(Composite parent)
```

In your implementation of this method, you create the controls for the preference page, and return the containing Control, like this:

```
protected Control createContents(Composite parent) {
    Composite composite = new Composite(parent, SWT.NONE);
    composite.setLayout(new GridLayout(2, false));

    // Create a field for the workspace save interval
    new Label(composite, SWT.LEFT).setText("Workspace save interval:");
    Text interval = new Text(composite, SWT.BORDER);
    interval.setLayoutData(new GridData(GridData.FILL_HORIZONTAL));

    // Return the containing control
    return composite;
}
```

Table 17-3. IPreferencePage *Methods*

Method	Description
Point computeSize()	In this method, compute and return the size of this preference page.
boolean isValid()	In this method, return true if this preference page is in a valid state. Otherwise, return false.
okToLeave()	In this method, return true if it's OK to leave this preference page. Otherwise, return false.
boolean performCancel()	Called when the user clicks Cancel. In this method, perform any code in response to Cancel. Return true to allow the cancel, or false to abort the cancel.
boolean performOk()	Called when the user clicks OK. In this method, perform any code in response to OK. Return true to allow the OK, or false to abort the OK.
void setContainer (IPreferencePageContainer preferencePageContainer)	In this method, set the container (dialog) for this preference page to the specified container.
void setSize(Point size)	In this method, set the size for this preference page to the specified size.

Although you can create a fully functional preference page that blends perfectly with the preference framework by implementing only the createContents() method in your subclass, you can customize your preference page further by using different constructors or overriding additional methods. Table 17-4 lists PreferencePage's constructors, and Table 17-5 lists PreferencePage's methods.

Table 17-4. PreferencePage *Constructors*

Constructor	Description
protected PreferencePage()	Creates a preference page.
protected PreferencePage(String title)	Creates a preference page with the specified title. In the default behavior, the title displays in the preference dialog's tree, and at the top of the preference page.
protected PreferencePage(String title, ImageDescriptor image)	Creates a preference page with the specified title, and with the image created from the specified image descriptor. In the default behavior, the title displays in the preference dialog's tree and at the top of the preference page. The image doesn't display, although you can retrieve it by calling getImage().

Table 17-5. PreferencePage *Methods*

Method	Description
protected void applyDialogFont (Composite composite)	Applies the dialog font to the specified composite. Called from this preference page's createControl() method. Override to set a different font.
Point computeSize()	Computes the size of this preference page's control.
protected void contributeButtons (Composite parent)	Adds buttons to the row of buttons that defaults to Restore Defaults and Apply. Override to add any buttons. For each button you add, you must increment the number of columns in parent's grid layout, like this: ((GridLayout) parent.getLayout()) .numColumns++. Otherwise, the buttons will wrap.
protected abstract Control createContents(Composite parent)	Override this method to create your page's contents.
void createControl(Composite parent)	Creates the label at the top of the preference page and the Restore Defaults and Apply buttons at the bottom. It calls createContents() to create the contents. Override to alter the preference page's layout.
protected Label createDescription Label(Composite parent)	Creates a label at the top of the preference page that displays the description set by setDescription(). By default, the description is blank, so the default implementation does nothing. Override to change the label.
protected Composite createNote Composite(Font font, Composite composite, String title, String message)	Creates a composite using the specified font, with the specified composite as parent. The default implementation displays the specified title in bold, followed by the specified message. Override to change what displays. Note, however, that by default this method is never called.
protected Point doComputeSize()	Called by computeSize(). Override to change how the size is computed.

Table 17-5. `PreferencePage` *Methods (continued)*

Method	Description
`protected IPreferenceStore doGetPreferenceStore()`	Called by `getPreferenceStore()`. The default implementation returns `null`. Override to return a page-specific preference store, instead of using the container's preference store.
`protected Button getApplyButton()`	Returns the Apply button.
`IPreferencePageContainer getContainer()`	Returns the container for this preference page.
`protected Button getDefaultsButton()`	Returns the Restore Defaults button.
`IPreferenceStore getPreferenceStore()`	Returns this preference page's preference store.
`boolean isValid()`	Returns `true` if this page is valid. Otherwise, returns `false`.
`protected void noDefaultAnd ApplyButton()`	Suppresses the creation of the Restore Defaults and Apply buttons. To use, call this method from within your preference page's code before its controls are created. This usually means that you'll call it from within your constructor.
`boolean okToLeave()`	Returns `true` if it's OK to leave this page. Otherwise, returns `false`. The default implementation returns `isValid()`.
`protected void performApply()`	Called when the user clicks Apply. Override to perform any desired processing. The default implementation calls `performOk()`.
`boolean performCancel()`	Called when the user clicks Cancel. Returns `true` to close the preference dialog, or `false` to leave the preference dialog open. Override to change Cancel behavior.
`protected void performDefaults()`	Called when the user clicks Restore Defaults. Override to perform any desired processing.
`void performHelp()`	Called when the user requests help.
`boolean performOk()`	Called when the user clicks OK. Returns `true` to close the preference dialog, or `false` to leave the preference dialog open. Override to change OK behavior.
`void setContainer(IPreference PageContainer container)`	Sets the container for this preference page.
`void setErrorMessage(String newMessage)`	Sets the error message for this preference page.
`void setMessage(String newMessage, int newType)`	Sets the message for the type specified by `newType` to the text specified by `newMessage`. `newType` should be one of `IMessageProvider.NONE`, `IMessageProvider.INFORMATION`, `IMessageProvider.WARNING`, or `IMessageProvider.ERROR`.
`void setPreferenceStore (IPreferenceStore preferenceStore)`	Sets the preference store for this preference page.
`void setSize(Point uiSize)`	Sets the size of this preference page.
`void setTitle(String title)`	Sets the title for this preference page.
`void setValid(boolean valid)`	If `valid` is `true`, sets this preference page valid. Otherwise, sets it invalid.
`protected void updateApplyButton()`	Updates the Apply button, enabling or disabling it based on whether this preference page is valid.

If the default preference page implementation satisfies your requirements, all you must do in your derived class is define `createContents()` to create the fields for your page. You probably should override `performOk()` as well, so you can retrieve any values from the fields in the page and save them into the preference store. Finally, you should probably override `performDefaults()` to reset the fields to default values from the preference store. The `PrefPageOne` class in Listing 17-2 follows that pattern.

Listing 17-2 `PrefPageOne.java`

```
package examples.ch17;

import org.eclipse.jface.preference.*;
import org.eclipse.swt.SWT;
import org.eclipse.swt.layout.*;
import org.eclipse.swt.widgets.*;

/**
 * This class creates a preference page
 */
public class PrefPageOne extends PreferencePage {
  // Names for preferences
  private static final String ONE = "one.one";
  private static final String TWO = "one.two";
  private static final String THREE = "one.three";

  // Text fields for user to enter preferences
  private Text fieldOne;
  private Text fieldTwo;
  private Text fieldThree;

  /**
   * Creates the controls for this page
   */
  protected Control createContents(Composite parent) {
    Composite composite = new Composite(parent, SWT.NONE);
    composite.setLayout(new GridLayout(2, false));

    // Get the preference store
    IPreferenceStore preferenceStore = getPreferenceStore();

    // Create three text fields.
    // Set the text in each from the preference store
    new Label(composite, SWT.LEFT).setText("Field One:");
    fieldOne = new Text(composite, SWT.BORDER);
    fieldOne.setLayoutData(new GridData(GridData.FILL_HORIZONTAL));
    fieldOne.setText(preferenceStore.getString(ONE));
```

```
      new Label(composite, SWT.LEFT).setText("Field Two:");
      fieldTwo = new Text(composite, SWT.BORDER);
      fieldTwo.setLayoutData(new GridData(GridData.FILL_HORIZONTAL));
      fieldTwo.setText(preferenceStore.getString(TWO));

      new Label(composite, SWT.LEFT).setText("Field Three:");
      fieldThree = new Text(composite, SWT.BORDER);
      fieldThree.setLayoutData(new GridData(GridData.FILL_HORIZONTAL));
      fieldThree.setText(preferenceStore.getString(THREE));

      return composite;
   }

   /**
    * Called when user clicks Restore Defaults
    */
   protected void performDefaults() {
      // Get the preference store
      IPreferenceStore preferenceStore = getPreferenceStore();

      // Reset the fields to the defaults
      fieldOne.setText(preferenceStore.getDefaultString(ONE));
      fieldTwo.setText(preferenceStore.getDefaultString(TWO));
      fieldThree.setText(preferenceStore.getDefaultString(THREE));
   }

   /**
    * Called when user clicks Apply or OK
    *
    * @return boolean
    */
   public boolean performOk() {
      // Get the preference store
      IPreferenceStore preferenceStore = getPreferenceStore();

      // Set the values from the fields
      if (fieldOne != null) preferenceStore.setValue(ONE, fieldOne.getText());
      if (fieldTwo != null) preferenceStore.setValue(TWO, fieldTwo.getText());
      if (fieldThree != null)
          preferenceStore.setValue(THREE, fieldThree.getText());

      // Return true to allow dialog to close
      return true;
   }
}
```

Figure 17-2 shows the preference page created by the PrefPageOne class.

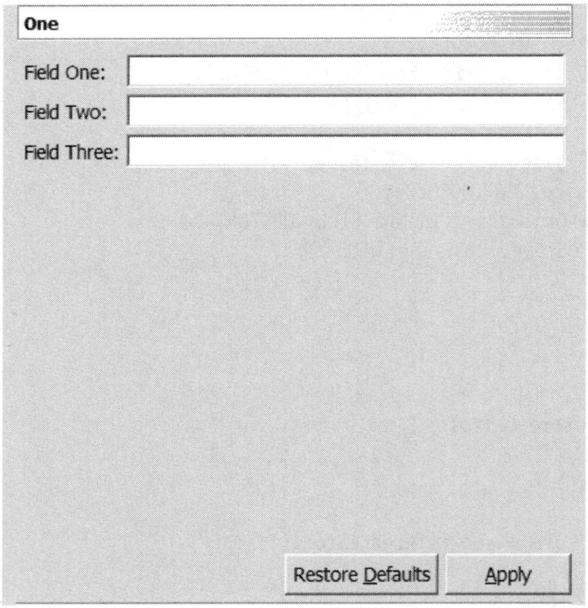

Figure 17-2. The `PrefPageOne` *preference page*

When requirements dictate that you deviate from the default look or behavior, override other `PreferencePage` methods as necessary. For example, the `PrefPageTwo` class implements the default constructor to set the title and the description (see Listing 17-3). It overrides the `contributeButtons()` method to add two buttons, Select All and Clear All, that select all and clear all the checkboxes on the page, respectively. It overrides `createDescriptionLabel()` to create a label that's right-aligned, and displays the description in all upper case. As with `PrefPageOne`, it overrides both `performDefaults()` and `performOk()` to reset the default values and to save the preferences to the preference store, respectively.

Listing 17-3. `PrefPageTwo.java`

```
package examples.ch17;

import org.eclipse.jface.preference.*;
import org.eclipse.swt.SWT;
import org.eclipse.swt.events.*;
import org.eclipse.swt.layout.*;
import org.eclipse.swt.widgets.*;

/**
 * This class creates a preference page
 */
public class PrefPageTwo extends PreferencePage {
```

```java
// Names for preferences
private static final String ONE = "two.one";
private static final String TWO = "two.two";
private static final String THREE = "two.three";

// The checkboxes
private Button checkOne;
private Button checkTwo;
private Button checkThree;

/**
 * PrefPageTwo constructor
 */
public PrefPageTwo() {
  super("Two");
  setDescription("Check the checks");
}

/**
 * Creates the controls for this page
 */
protected Control createContents(Composite parent) {
  Composite composite = new Composite(parent, SWT.NONE);
  composite.setLayout(new RowLayout(SWT.VERTICAL));

  // Get the preference store
  IPreferenceStore preferenceStore = getPreferenceStore();

  // Create three checkboxes
  checkOne = new Button(composite, SWT.CHECK);
  checkOne.setText("Check One");
  checkOne.setSelection(preferenceStore.getBoolean(ONE));

  checkTwo = new Button(composite, SWT.CHECK);
  checkTwo.setText("Check Two");
  checkTwo.setSelection(preferenceStore.getBoolean(TWO));

  checkThree = new Button(composite, SWT.CHECK);
  checkThree.setText("Check Three");
  checkThree.setSelection(preferenceStore.getBoolean(THREE));

  return composite;
}

/**
 * Add buttons
 *
 * @param parent the parent composite
 */
protected void contributeButtons(Composite parent) {
```

```
    // Add a select all button
    Button selectAll = new Button(parent, SWT.PUSH);
    selectAll.setText("Select All");
    selectAll.addSelectionListener(new SelectionAdapter() {
      public void widgetSelected(SelectionEvent event) {
        checkOne.setSelection(true);
        checkTwo.setSelection(true);
        checkThree.setSelection(true);
      }
    });

    // Add a clear all button
    Button clearAll = new Button(parent, SWT.PUSH);
    clearAll.setText("Clear All");
    clearAll.addSelectionListener(new SelectionAdapter() {
      public void widgetSelected(SelectionEvent event) {
        checkOne.setSelection(false);
        checkTwo.setSelection(false);
        checkThree.setSelection(false);
      }
    });

    // Add two columns to the parent's layout
    ((GridLayout) parent.getLayout()).numColumns += 2;
}

/**
 * Change the description label
 */
protected Label createDescriptionLabel(Composite parent) {
  Label label = null;
  String description = getDescription();
  if (description != null) {
    // Upper case the description
    description = description.toUpperCase();

    // Right-align the label
    label = new Label(parent, SWT.RIGHT);
    label.setText(description);
  }
  return label;
}

/**
 * Called when user clicks Restore Defaults
 */
protected void performDefaults() {
  // Get the preference store
  IPreferenceStore preferenceStore = getPreferenceStore();

  // Reset the fields to the defaults
  checkOne.setSelection(preferenceStore.getDefaultBoolean(ONE));
```

```
    checkTwo.setSelection(preferenceStore.getDefaultBoolean(TWO));
    checkThree.setSelection(preferenceStore.getDefaultBoolean(THREE));
  }

  /**
   * Called when user clicks Apply or OK
   *
   * @return boolean
   */
  public boolean performOk() {
    // Get the preference store
    IPreferenceStore preferenceStore = getPreferenceStore();

    // Set the values from the fields
    if (checkOne != null) preferenceStore.setValue(ONE, checkOne.getSelection());
    if (checkTwo != null) preferenceStore.setValue(TWO, checkTwo.getSelection());
    if (checkThree != null)
        preferenceStore.setValue(THREE, checkThree.getSelection());

    // Return true to allow dialog to close
    return true;
  }
}
```

Figure 17-3 shows the preference page that the PrefPageTwo class creates.

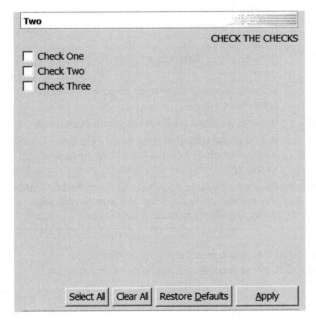

Figure 17-3. The PrefPageTwo *preference page*

Tying the Page to a Node

A preference manager doesn't manage preference pages directly. Instead, it manages preference nodes. Each preference page belongs to a preference node, and each preference node has a corresponding preference page. Preference nodes represent nodes in the tree on the left side of the preference dialog. As nodes in a tree, preference nodes can have child nodes, and the tree can be expanded or collapsed to show or hide child nodes.

Each preference node can display both an image and some text, in addition to the clickable plus or minus sign if the node has children. For management purposes, each node has an ID, which can't be null. You should make the IDs unique, although no check is performed to enforce this.

The IPreferenceNode interface represents a preference node. Table 17-6 lists IPreferenceNode's methods.

Table 17-6. IPreferenceNode *Methods*

Method	Description
void add(IPreferenceNode node)	Adds the specified node as a child of this node.
void createPage()	Creates the preference page associated with this preference node.
void disposeResources()	Disposes any resources associated with this preference node.
IPreferenceNode findSubNode (String id)	Returns the child node with the specified ID, or null if no child node has the specified ID.
String getId()	Returns this preference node's ID.
Image getLabelImage()	Returns the image associated with this preference node.
String getLabelText()	Returns the text associated with this preference node.
IPreferencePage getPage()	Returns the preference page associated with this preference node.
IPreferenceNode[] getSubNodes()	Returns the child nodes of this preference node.
boolean remove(IPreferenceNode node)	Removes the specified child node from this preference node. Returns true if the node was found. Otherwise, returns false.
IPreferenceNode remove(String id)	Removes the child node with the specified ID from this preference node. Returns the removed child node, or null if the node wasn't found.

The JFace preferences package contains a concrete implementation of IPreferenceNode called PreferenceNode. PreferenceNode offers three constructors, listed in Table 17-7.

Table 17-7. `PreferenceNode` *Constructors*

Constructor	Description
`PreferenceNode(String id)`	Creates a preference node with the specified ID.
`PreferenceNode(String id, IPreferencePage page)`	Creates a preference node with the specified ID and associates it with the specified preference page.
`PreferenceNode(String id, String label, ImageDescriptor image, String className)`	Creates a preference node with the specified ID, label, and image. When activated, loads the class specified by `className` and uses it as its preference page.

If you use the first constructor, you call `setPage()` to associate this node with a page, like this:

```
MyPreferencePage page = new MyPreferencePage();
PreferenceNode node = new PreferenceNode("node1");
node.setPage(page);
```

The second constructor creates the node and sets its associated preference page in one step, like this:

```
MyPreferencePage page = new MyPreferencePage();
PreferenceNode node = new PreferenceNode("node1", page);
```

Both of these constructors use the page's title for this node's label within the tree. However, the third constructor reverses control and not only uses the specified label for the label in the tree, but also uses it for the page. It also displays the specified image beside the label in the tree (and takes care of disposing it when appropriate), though you can pass `null` for no image. To use the third constructor, use code such as this:

```
PreferenceNode node = new PreferenceNode("node1", "My Node",
  ImageDescriptor.createFromFile(MyPreferencePage.class, "myImage.png",
  MyPreferencePage.class.getName());
```

To add a node to another node, making it a child, use the `add()` method like this:

```
PreferenceNode node1 = new PreferenceNode("node1", new PreferencePage1());
PreferenceNode node2 = new PreferenceNode("node2", new PreferencePage2());
node1.add(node2);
```

You can also use the preference manager to set node hierarchies, as the next section shows.

Managing the Nodes

The `PreferenceManager` class manages the preference nodes.

To create a preference manager, call one of its two constructors:

- `PreferenceManager()`

- `PreferenceManager(char separatorChar)`

The first constructor creates a preference manager with the default separator character, a period. If you use the second constructor, you can specify a different separator character. The separator character is used to separate the node IDs when specifying the full path to a node.

After you create a preference manager, you add nodes to it using the `addToRoot()` or `addTo()` methods, like this:

```
PreferenceManager mgr = new PreferenceManager();
mgr.addToRoot(node1);
mgr.addTo(node1.getId(), node2);
mgr.addTo("node1.node2", node3);
```

Table 17-8 lists `PreferenceManager`'s methods.

Table 17-8. `PreferenceManager` *Methods*

Method	Description
`boolean addTo(String path, IPreferenceNode node)`	Adds the specified node as a child of the node specified by the path. The path is composed of the IDs of the preference nodes, starting at the root node, separated by the separator character. Returns true if the path was found. Otherwise, returns `false`.
`void addToRoot(IPreferenceNode node)`	Adds the specified node to the root of the tree.
`IPreferenceNode find(String path)`	Finds the node that corresponds to the specified path. The path consists of the IDs of the ancestor nodes, beginning with the root node, separated by the separator character.
`List getElements(int order)`	Returns all preference nodes in this preference manager, sorted in the specified order. The valid values for order are `PreferenceManager.POST_ORDER`, which sorts children first, or `PreferenceManager.PRE_ORDER`, which sorts roots first.
`boolean remove(IPreferenceNode node)`	Removes the specified preference node. Returns true if the node was found and removed. Otherwise, returns `false`.
`IPreferenceNode remove(String path)`	Removes the preference node at the specified ID path. Returns the removed preference node, or `null` if the node specified by the path wasn't found.
`void removeAll()`	Removes all the preference nodes in this preference manager.

Displaying the Dialog

With a preference manager full of preference nodes, each with a preference page, you're ready to display a preference dialog. Construct a PreferenceDialog object, passing the parent shell and the preference manager. Set the preference store on the dialog using the setPreferenceStore() method. Then, call open(). Your code might look like this:

```
PreferenceDialog dlg = new PreferenceDialog(shell, preferenceManager);
dlg.setPreferenceStore(preferenceStore);
dlg.open();
```

The ShowPrefs program in Listing 17-4 displays a preference dialog that shows two pages: PrefPageOne and PrefPageTwo. It creates PrefPageTwo as a child of PrefPageOne. PrefPageOne displays an image in the tree, while PrefPageTwo doesn't. To keep the code focused, ShowPrefs doesn't create a main window; it just displays the preference dialog. Most applications will have a main window, and will display the preference dialog in response to a user action (for example, a menu selection).

Listing 17-4. ShowPrefs.java

```
package examples.ch17;

import java.io.IOException;

import org.eclipse.jface.preference.*;
import org.eclipse.jface.resource.ImageDescriptor;
import org.eclipse.swt.widgets.*;

/**
 * This class demonstrates JFace preferences
 */
public class ShowPrefs {
  /**
   * Runs the application
   */
  public void run() {
    Display display = new Display();

    // Create the preference manager
    PreferenceManager mgr = new PreferenceManager();

    // Create the nodes
    PreferenceNode one = new PreferenceNode("one", "One", ImageDescriptor
        .createFromFile(ShowPrefs.class, "/images/about.gif"), PrefPageOne.class
        .getName());
    PreferenceNode two = new PreferenceNode("two", new PrefPageTwo());

    // Add the nodes
    mgr.addToRoot(one);
    mgr.addTo(one.getId(), two);
```

```
   // Create the preference dialog
   PreferenceDialog dlg = new PreferenceDialog(null, mgr);

   // Set the preference store
   PreferenceStore ps = new PreferenceStore("showprefs.properties");
   try {
     ps.load();
   } catch (IOException e) {
     // Ignore
   }
   dlg.setPreferenceStore(ps);

   // Open the dialog
   dlg.open();

   try {
     // Save the preferences
     ps.save();
   } catch (IOException e) {
     e.printStackTrace();
   }
   display.dispose();
 }

 /**
  * The application entry point
  *
  * @param args the command line arguments
  */
 public static void main(String[] args) {
   new ShowPrefs().run();
 }
}
```

Figure 17-4 shows the preference dialog displaying the PrefsPageOne preference page. Figure 17-5 shows the same dialog, but with the tree expanded and PrefsPageTwo displaying.

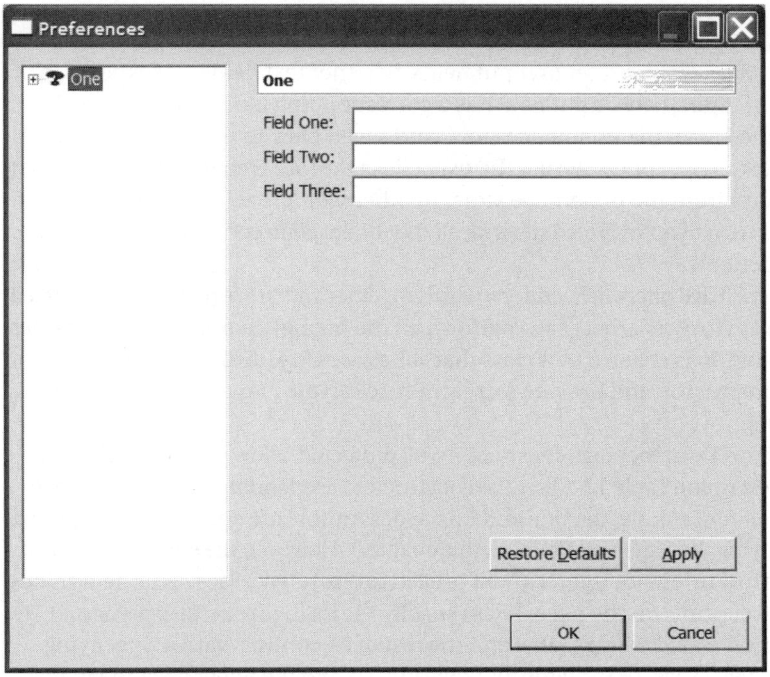

Figure 17-4. A preference dialog

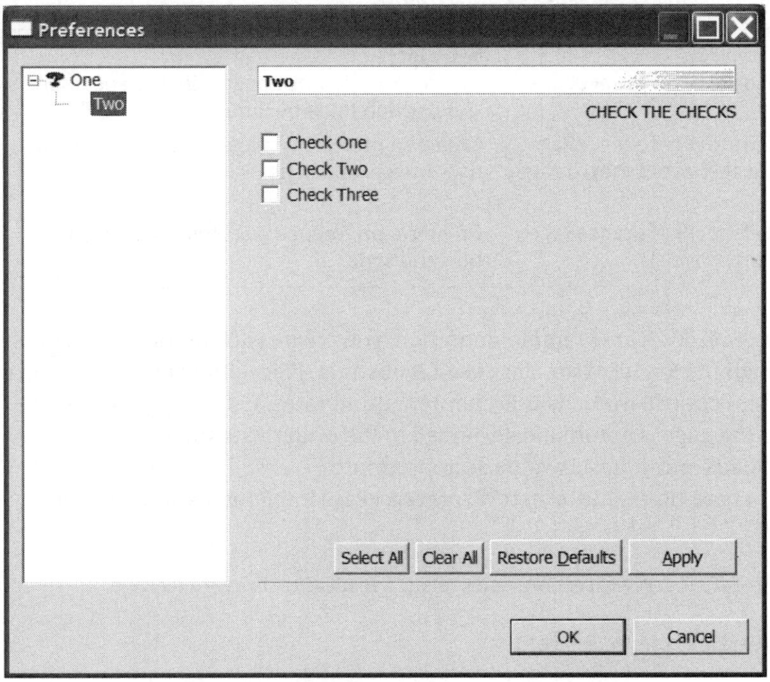

Figure 17-5. A preference dialog with the tree expanded

Using Field Editors

Most preference pages display a set of input fields, whether text fields, checkboxes, or some other type of input. Each input field has a corresponding label to identify it. The input fields are filled from the preference store, and saved back to the preference store when the user clicks Apply or OK. When the user clicks Restore Defaults, the fields reset to the default values from the preference store. In other words, each preference page is essentially the same, yet you're forced to write all that boilerplate code each time. Surely there must be a better way.

Luckily, there is. JFace offers field editors, which together with a PreferencePage-derived class called FieldEditorPreferencePage perform all the menial chores discussed earlier for you. All you must do is create a new class that subclasses FieldEditorPreferencePage, create a public constructor, and provide a createFieldEditors() method that creates all the field editors.

The FieldEditorPreferencePage constructors, all protected, allow you to specify a style, title, and image descriptor. Table 17-9 lists the constructors. Depending on how you create the associated preference node, the title and image descriptors are either used or ignored (see the section "Tying the Page to a Node" in this chapter). However, the style, which must be either FieldEditorPreferencePage.FLAT or FieldEditorPreferencePage.GRID, determines how to lay out the controls on the page. If you specify FieldEditorPreferencePage.FLAT, the division between a field editor's label and the rest of its controls varies. Specifying FieldEditorPreferencePage.GRID aligns that division, so that the left edge of the first control in each field editor on the page lines up.

Table 17-9. FieldEditorPreferencePage *Constructors*

Constructor	Description
protected FieldEditorPreferencePage (int style)	Creates a preference page with the specified style, which must be either GRID or FLAT
protected FieldEditorPreferencePage (String title, ImageDescriptor image, int style)	Creates a preference page with the specified title, image, and style
protected FieldEditorPreferencePage (String title, int style)	Creates a preference page with the specified title and style

In your createFieldEditors() implementation, you create each of the field editors on the page. Though the FieldEditor class itself is abstract, JFace offers numerous concrete field editors to choose from, as this chapter enumerates. Each field editor you create and add to the page is automatically linked to the underlying preference store, so automatically loads and stores its value as appropriate.

For example, a bare-bones FieldEditorPreferencePage implementation might look like this:

```
public class MyFieldEditorPreferencePage extends FieldEditorPreferencePage
{
  public MyFieldEditorPreferencePage()
  {
    super(GRID);
  }
```

```
  protected void createFieldEditors()
  {
    // Create and add the field editors here
  }
}
```

FieldEditor

The FieldEditor class anchors the field editor classes. As the superclass of all the field editors, it defines how to set up field editors: with a preference name, text for the label, and a parent composite. The preference name is used when storing the selected value in the preference store. The label displays on the preference page, adjacent to the entry field. The general form of the constructor is as follows:

```
FieldEditor(String name, String labelText, Composite parent)
```

You should always pass the composite returned by getFieldEditorParent() for parent. After you create the field editor, you add it to the preference page and underlying preference store by passing it to addField(). The structure for creating a field editor on your field editor preference page is as follows:

```
protected void createFieldEditors()
{
  // Note that this won't compile, as FieldEditor is abstract
  FieldEditor fieldEditor = new FieldEditor("myField", "Field:",
    getFieldEditorParent());
  addField(fieldEditor);
}
```

Some field editors have more configuration options, so require more constructor parameters. The following sections discuss each type of field editor, and highlight those that deviate from the preceding pattern.

BooleanFieldEditor

A BooleanFieldEditor displays a checkbox and a label, and stores a boolean value. You create a BooleanFieldEditor like this:

```
BooleanFieldEditor booleanFieldEditor = new BooleanFieldEditor("myBoolean",
  "Boolean Value", getFieldEditorParent());
```

This creates a field editor with the checkbox on the left and the label on the right. You can reverse the order of the two controls and display the label on the left and the checkbox on the right by using the constructor that also takes a style constant:

```
BooleanFieldEditor(String name, String label, int style, Composite parent)
```

Table 17-10 lists the possible style constants. For example, to create a boolean field editor with the controls reversed, use this code:

```
BooleanFieldEditor booleanFieldEditor = new BooleanFieldEditor("myBoolean",
  "Boolean Value", BooleanFieldEditor.SEPARATE_LABEL, getFieldEditorParent());
```

Table 17-10. BooleanFieldEditor *Style Constants*

Constant	Description
static int DEFAULT	Creates a BooleanFieldEditor with the checkbox on the left and the label on the right
static int SEPARATE_LABEL	Creates a BooleanFieldEditor with the label on the left and the checkbox on the right

ColorFieldEditor

A ColorFieldEditor displays a button and a label, and stores an RGB value. The color that corresponds to the stored RGB value paints the face of the button. Clicking the button displays the standard color selection dialog, from which you select a new color. You create a ColorFieldEditor like this:

```
ColorFieldEditor colorFieldEditor = new ColorFieldEditor("myColor",
  "Color:", getFieldEditorParent());
```

DirectoryFieldEditor

A DirectoryFieldEditor displays a label, a text box, and a Browse button. It stores a string that represents an existing directory. You can type a directory path into the text box, or you can click Browse to display the standard directory-selection dialog and navigate to the desired directory. The specified directory is validated, and you can't accept (via OK or Apply) a directory that doesn't exist. You create a DirectoryFieldEditor like this:

```
DirectoryFieldEditor directoryFieldEditor = new DirectoryFieldEditor("myDir",
  "Directory:", getFieldEditorParent());
```

If you don't want directory validation—if you want users to be able to enter a directory that doesn't exist—subclass DirectoryFieldEditor and override the doCheckState() method, which has the following signature:

```
protected boolean doCheckState()
```

Return true to accept the entered contents and allow the user to click Apply or OK, or false to reject the contents and disable the Apply and OK buttons. For example, to allow users to enter anything in the text box, use the following doCheckState() implementation:

```
protected boolean doCheckState()
{
  return true;
}
```

FileFieldEditor

Like DirectoryFieldEditor, FileFieldEditor validates that the file name you enter represents an existing file. It stores the full path of the file as a string. It also displays a label, a text box, and a Browse button. Clicking Browse opens the standard file selection dialog. You create a FileFieldEditor like this:

```
FileFieldEditor fileFieldEditor = new FileFieldEditor("myFile", "File:",
  getFieldEditorParent());
```

The file selection dialog, by default, uses no file extensions to filter which files to display. You can add filter extensions to the file selection dialog by calling FileFieldEditor's setFileExtensions() method, which takes an array of Strings. For example, to filter on the extensions *.java and *.txt, use code such as this:

```
FileFieldEditor fileFieldEditor = new FileFieldEditor("myFile", "File:",
  getFieldEditorParent());
fileFieldEditor.setFileExtensions(new String[] { "*.java", "*.txt" });
```

This sets the filter extensions on the file dialog. FileFieldEditor offers no way to set the filter names. See Chapter 7 for more information on filter extensions and filter names with the file selection dialog.

By default, the selected file can have a relative path. You can enforce an absolute path using FileFieldEditor's other constructor:

```
FileFieldEditor(String name, String labelText, boolean enforceAbsolute,
  Composite parent)
```

Passing true for enforceAbsolute requires that users enter an absolute path to the file, while false allows relative paths.

If you don't want FileFieldEditor to insist on an existing file, subclass it and override the checkState() method, which has the following signature:

```
protected boolean checkState()
```

Return true to accept what the user has entered, or false to reject it.

FontFieldEditor

A FontFieldEditor displays a label; the name, style, and height of the selected font; and a Change button. It stores the string representation of a FontData object that corresponds to the selected font. Clicking the Change button displays the standard font selection dialog. You create a FontFieldEditor like this:

```
FontFieldEditor fontFieldEditor = new FontFieldEditor("myFont", "Font:",
  getFieldEditorParent());
```

Although the name, style, and height of the font convey all the pertinent information about the selected font, it lacks the oomph that displaying the actual font packs. You can add a preview area to your FontFieldEditor just by using its other constructor and specifying some preview text. The other constructor looks like this:

```
FontFieldEditor(String name, String labelText, String previewAreaText,
  Composite parent)
```

For example, the following code creates a font field editor and displays the word "Preview" in the selected font:

```
FontFieldEditor fontFieldEditor = new FontFieldEditor("myFont", "Font:",
  "Preview", getFieldEditorParent());
```

FontFieldEditor offers one other customization opportunity: you can change the text of the button that launches the font selection dialog by calling the setChangeButtonText() method. For example, to make the button display "Change the Font," add the following code:

```
fontFieldEditor.setChangeButtonText("Change the Font");
```

IntegerFieldEditor

An IntegerFieldEditor displays a label and a text box. Although you can type any characters into the text box, an error message displays if you've entered invalid characters, and you can't click Apply or OK to accept the changes. Also, you can't enter just any digits; the value you enter must fall within the range 0 to 2,147,483,647, inclusive. You create an IntegerFieldEditor like this:

```
IntegerFieldEditor integerFieldEditor = new IntegerFieldEditor("myInteger",
  "Integer:", getFieldEditorParent());
```

You can change the field editor's acceptable range using its setValidRange() method, which takes a minimum value and a maximum value. Both values must be integers, and are inclusive to the range. For example, to change the range to allow integers between −100 and 100, use the following code:

```
integerFieldEditor.setValidRange(-100, 100);
```

IntegerFieldEditor limits the number of characters you can type in the text box, defaulting to ten characters. You can change this limit by using the other constructor:

```
IntegerFieldEditor(String name, String labelText, Composite parent,
  int textLimit)
```

The textLimit parameter defines the maximum number of characters the text box accepts.

To override or eliminate IntegerFieldEditor's validation, subclass it and override the checkState() method:

```
protected boolean checkState()
```

Return true to accept the input, and false to reject it.

PathEditor

PathEditor is visually the most complex of all the field editors, displaying a label, a list box, and four buttons: New, Remove, Up, and Down. Use this field editor to allow users to specify multiple directories and control their order. The preference store saves all the directory names in a single string, in the specified order.

Despite its visual complexity, PathEditor is no harder to create than any of the other field editors. To create one, use the following constructor:

```
PathEditor(String name, String labelText, String dirChooserLabelText,
  Composite parent)
```

The new parameter, dirChooserLabelText, specifies the label to use in the directory-selection dialog that displays when the user clicks the New button. For example, the following code creates a PathEditor:

```
PathEditor pathEditor = new PathEditor("myPath", "Paths:",  "Select a directory",
  getFieldEditorParent());
```

Each entry in the list box is a directory. To add a directory, click the New button, which displays the standard directory-selection dialog. To remove a directory, highlight it and click the Remove button. To move a directory in the list, select it and click the Up button to move it up, or Down to move it down.

RadioGroupFieldEditor

A RadioGroupFieldEditor displays a group of radio buttons. Each radio button has both a label and an associated value; the radio button displays the label, but saves the value in the preference store. The radio button is mutually exclusive: you can select only one radio button from the group. However, RadioGroupFieldEditor has a bug: if you specify multiple buttons with the same value, all buttons with that value will be selected when the preference page displays, as Figure 17-6 shows.

Figure 17-6. Specifying radio buttons with the same value

You control the number of columns RadioGroupFieldEditor uses to display its radio buttons, and also whether it surrounds the buttons with a group box. You specify this information in the constructor. In addition to the default constructor, RadioGroupFieldEditor offers two constructors:

```
RadioGroupFieldEditor(String name, String labelText, int numColumns,
   String[][] labelAndValues, Composite parent)
RadioGroupFieldEditor(String name, String labelText, int numColumns,
   String[][] labelAndValues, Composite parent, boolean useGroup)
```

The numColumns parameter specifies the number of columns to use for the radio buttons, and must be greater than zero. The useGroup parameter specifies whether to surround the radio buttons with a group box; the default is false.

The labelAndValues parameter carries a little more complexity (but not much). It's an array of string arrays. The size of the enclosing array determines how many radio buttons are created. Each string array within the enclosing array must contain exactly two strings: one for the label and one for the value, in that order.

To create a RadioGroupFieldEditor that displays six radio buttons in three columns, surrounded by a group box, use this code:

```
RadioGroupFieldEditor radioGroupFieldEditor = new RadioGroupFieldEditor(
   "myRadioGroup", "Radio Group", 3, new String[][] { { "Option 1", "1" },
   { "Option 2", "2" }, { "Option 3", "3" }, { "Option 4", "4" },
   { "Option 5", "5" }, { "Option 6", "6" } }, getFieldEditorParent(), true);
```

The radio button labels start with "Option," followed by the option number. Only the option number is stored in the preference store.

ScaleFieldEditor

Whereas IntegerFieldEditor allows users to enter an integer by typing it in a text box, ScaleFieldEditor allows users to enter an integer using a scale. Users can drag the thumb of the scale left or right to select the desired integer. ScaleFieldEditor only supports horizontal scales, not vertical scales. Its default range is zero to ten, in increments of one. You create a ScaleFieldEditor like this:

```
ScaleFieldEditor scaleFieldEditor = new ScaleFieldEditor("myScale", "Scale:",
   getFieldEditorParent());
```

You can change the range, the increment, and also the page increment (the amount of change in the value when the user presses Page Up or Page Down) by calling the appropriate ScaleFieldEditor methods listed in Table 17-11. Alternatively, you can pass these values in ScaleFieldEditor's other constructor:

```
ScaleFieldEditor(String name, String labelText, Composite parent, int min,
   int max, int increment, int pageIncrement)
```

The following code creates a ScaleFieldEditor with a range of 0 to 100 in increments of 5. Pressing Page Up or Page Down changes the value by 20.

```
ScaleFieldEditor scaleFieldEditor = new ScaleFieldEditor("myScale", "Scale:",
   getFieldEditorParent(), 0, 100, 5, 20);
```

Table 17-11. Methods to Set ScaleFieldEditor *Values*

Method	Description
void setIncrement(int increment)	Sets the increment
void setMaximum(int max)	Sets the maximum value in the range
void setMinimum(int min)	Sets the minimum value in the range
void setPageIncrement(int pageIncrement)	Sets the Page Up/Page Down increment

StringFieldEditor

A StringFieldEditor accepts a string of text. It displays a label and a text box. You create one like this:

```
StringFieldEditor stringFieldEditor = new StringFieldEditor("myString",
  "String:", getFieldEditorParent());
```

It allows no text, unlimited text, and everything in between. You can change the following:

- The width of the text box

- The maximum number of characters the text box allows (the text limit)

- Whether the text box allows an empty string

- The validation strategy to use (whether to validate each time the user presses a key, or to wait until the user leaves the text box)

- How to determine whether the entered text is valid

- The error message to display if the entered text isn't valid

StringFieldEditor directly supports most of these customizations, but changing what constitutes a valid string requires subclassing.

Table 17-12 lists methods for customizing StringFieldEditor. You can also change the width of the text box by using the following constructor:

```
StringFieldEditor(String name, String labelText, int width, Composite parent)
```

The width parameter specifies the width of the text box, which has no effect on the text limit. You can specify both the text box width and the validation strategy by using the following constructor:

```
StringFieldEditor(String name, String labelText, int width, int strategy,
  Composite parent)
```

The strategy parameter specifies the validation strategy, which must be either String-FieldEditor.VALIDATE_ON_KEY_STROKE, which validates each time a key is pressed, or StringFieldEditor.VALIDATE_ON_FOCUS_LOST, which validates when focus leaves the text box. The default setting validates on each keystroke.

Table 17-12. StringFieldEditor *Customization Methods*

Method	Description
void setEmptyStringAllowed(boolean allow)	If allow is true, allows an empty string. Otherwise, disallows an empty string. The default allows an empty string.
void setErrorMessage(String message)	Sets the error message to display if the entered string isn't valid.
void setStringValue(String value)	Sets the text in the text box.
void setTextLimit(int limit)	Sets the text limit (the maximum number of characters to allow in the text box).
void setValidateStrategy(int strategy)	Sets the validation strategy, which must be either StringFieldEditor.VALIDATE_ON_KEY_STROKE or StringEditor.VALIDATE_ON_FOCUS_LOST, for validating on each keystroke or validating when the text box loses focus, respectively.
void showErrorMessage()	Shows the configured error message. You'll probably only call this from a subclass's checkState() or doCheckState(), when the entered text isn't valid.

Changing the validation, which rejects empty strings if you've disallowed them, requires that you create a subclass of StringFieldEditor. To augment the validation, allowing it to validate your empty string setting in addition to your custom validation, override the doCheckState() method in your subclass. It has the following signature:

```
protected boolean doCheckState()
```

Return true for valid, false for invalid. To replace the validation, override checkState(), which has the following signature:

```
protected boolean checkState()
```

Again, return true for valid and false for invalid.

Seeing the FieldEditors

The ShowFieldPrefs application in Listing 17-5 creates two preference pages, each of which uses the FieldEditorPreferencePage class. The two preference pages show each of the types of field editors, some on the first page and some on the second. The first page uses the FLAT layout, while the second page uses the GRID layout. Listing 17-6 contains the code for the first page, and Listing 17-7 contains the code for the second page.

Listing 17-5. ShowFieldPrefs.java

```java
package examples.ch17;

import java.io.IOException;

import org.eclipse.jface.preference.*;
import org.eclipse.swt.widgets.*;

/**
 * This class demonstrates JFace preferences and field editors
 */
public class ShowFieldPrefs {
  /**
   * Runs the application
   */
  public void run() {
    Display display = new Display();

    // Create the preference manager
    PreferenceManager mgr = new PreferenceManager();

    // Create the nodes
    PreferenceNode one = new PreferenceNode("one", "One", null,
        FieldEditorPageOne.class.getName());
    PreferenceNode two = new PreferenceNode("two", "Two", null,
        FieldEditorPageTwo.class.getName());

    // Add the nodes
    mgr.addToRoot(one);
    mgr.addToRoot(two);

    // Create the preference dialog
    PreferenceDialog dlg = new PreferenceDialog(null, mgr);

    // Set the preference store
    PreferenceStore ps = new PreferenceStore("showfieldprefs.properties");
    try {
      ps.load();
    } catch (IOException e) {
      // Ignore
    }
    dlg.setPreferenceStore(ps);

    // Open the dialog
    dlg.open();

    try {
      // Save the preferences
      ps.save();
    } catch (IOException e) {
```

```
      e.printStackTrace();
    }
    display.dispose();
  }

  /**
   * The application entry point
   *
   * @param args the command line arguments
   */
  public static void main(String[] args) {
    new ShowFieldPrefs().run();
  }
}
```

Listing 17-6. `FieldEditorPageOne.java`

```
package examples.ch17;

import org.eclipse.jface.preference.*;

/**
 * This class demonstrates field editors
 */
public class FieldEditorPageOne extends FieldEditorPreferencePage {
  public FieldEditorPageOne() {
    // Use the "flat" layout
    super(FLAT);
  }

  /**
   * Creates the field editors
   */
  protected void createFieldEditors() {
    // Add a boolean field
    BooleanFieldEditor bfe = new BooleanFieldEditor("myBoolean", "Boolean",
        getFieldEditorParent());
    addField(bfe);

    // Add a color field
    ColorFieldEditor cfe = new ColorFieldEditor("myColor", "Color:",
        getFieldEditorParent());
    addField(cfe);

    // Add a directory field
    DirectoryFieldEditor dfe = new DirectoryFieldEditor("myDirectory",
        "Directory:", getFieldEditorParent());
    addField(dfe);
```

```
      // Add a file field
      FileFieldEditor ffe = new FileFieldEditor("myFile", "File:",
          getFieldEditorParent());
      addField(ffe);

      // Add a font field
      FontFieldEditor fontFe = new FontFieldEditor("myFont", "Font:",
          getFieldEditorParent());
      addField(fontFe);

      // Add a radio group field
      RadioGroupFieldEditor rfe = new RadioGroupFieldEditor("myRadioGroup",
          "Radio Group", 2, new String[][] { { "First Value", "first"},
              { "Second Value", "second"}, { "Third Value", "third"},
              { "Fourth Value", "fourth"}}, getFieldEditorParent(), true);
      addField(rfe);

      // Add a path field
      PathEditor pe = new PathEditor("myPath", "Path:", "Choose a Path",
          getFieldEditorParent());
      addField(pe);
  }
}
```

Listing 17-7. `FieldEditorPageTwo.java`

```
package examples.ch17;

import org.eclipse.jface.preference.*;

/**
 * This class demonstrates field editors
 */
public class FieldEditorPageTwo extends FieldEditorPreferencePage {
  public FieldEditorPageTwo() {
    // Use the "grid" layout
    super(GRID);
  }

  /**
   * Creates the field editors
   */
  protected void createFieldEditors() {
    // Add an integer field
    IntegerFieldEditor ife = new IntegerFieldEditor("myInt", "Int:",
        getFieldEditorParent());
    addField(ife);
```

```
    // Add a scale field
    ScaleFieldEditor sfe = new ScaleFieldEditor("myScale", "Scale:",
        getFieldEditorParent(), 0, 100, 1, 10);
    addField(sfe);

    // Add a string field
    StringFieldEditor stringFe = new StringFieldEditor("myString", "String:",
        getFieldEditorParent());
    addField(stringFe);
  }
}
```

Figure 17-7 shows the program displaying the first preference page, and Figure 17-8 shows the program displaying the second preference page.

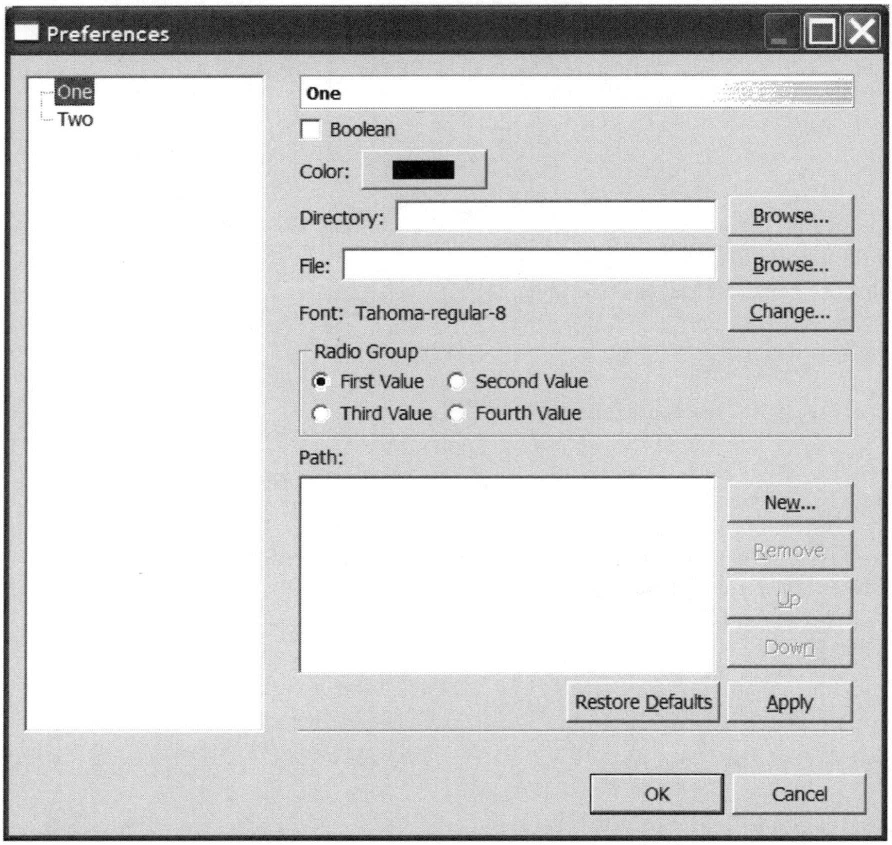

Figure 17-7. A field editor page

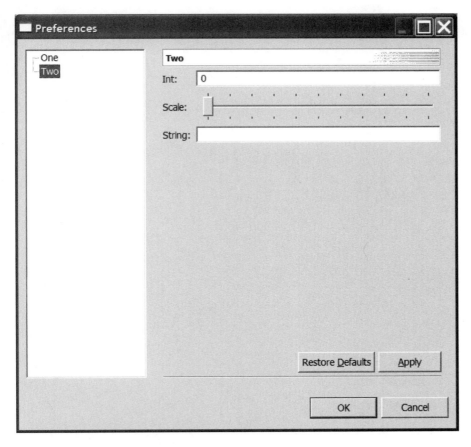

Figure 17-8. Another field editor page

Summary

Specifying configuration options often represents the drudgery in building applications, as it requires writing code, ancillary to the main focus of the application, that doesn't do anything "cool." Too many applications reflect a resentment to building the interface to display and edit program preferences. They display a crude, bolted-on interface, or even worse, they make users edit text files outside the application. JFace removes the toil from building an interface to user preferences, and makes building professional-looking and functioning interfaces quick and easy. Use PreferencePage to exert more control over your page layout, or FieldEditorPreferencePage for quicker development and standard layouts.

CHAPTER 18

Editing Text

As Chapter 11 explains, the StyledText widget receives a disproportionate amount of attention from SWT's developers, because it forms the core of Eclipse. As the *raison d'être* of Eclipse, it enjoys the preferential treatment usually reserved for star athletes, rock stars, or supermodels. Such a VIP could never be left to languish with only the raw widget interface that StyledText provides. Instead, JFace wraps StyledText with such an extensive MVC implementation that all the other widgets chafe with resentment. Sprawling across eight distinct packages, all of whose names begin with org.eclipse.jface.text, and all of which teem with both classes and interfaces, the text-editing framework in JFace would require tomes for complete coverage. To explore it fully would mean describing how to build an award-winning programmer's editor, which stretches far beyond the scope of this book. Instead, this book settles for a single chapter that covers the high points, but hits enough to prepare you to use JFace's text editing capabilities in your applications. It focuses on creating a single application—a simple Perl editor— but explains the various technologies it uses to create the program.

Getting into the Text Framework

The ITextViewer interface represents the view component for JFace's MVC text-editing framework. You can create your own ITextViewer implementation, but be forewarned that the size of the interface means that developing an implementation requires extensive time and effort. You'll probably use either TextViewer, which will likely meet all your text viewer needs, or its subclass, SourceTextViewer, which adds a vertical ruler along the left edge of the viewer, suitable for displaying annotations (for example, breakpoint markers, syntax error indicators, and so on). The documentation for both classes warns against subclassing either one, so if neither meets your needs, you should build from scratch.

Like ListViewer, TableViewer, and TreeViewer, TextViewer exposes a setInput() method to allow you to set the model for the viewer. However, you'll probably eschew setInput(), which takes an Object, as it merely passes through to the more specialized setDocument() method, which takes an IDocument instance. Instead, you'll call setDocument(), passing your IDocument. The IDocument interface represents the model, or data, for the text editing framework. You can create your own document class, implementing the IDocument interface, or you can use the robust Document class from the org.eclipse.jface.text package.

Table 18-1 lists ITextViewer's methods, while Table 18-2 lists IDocument's methods.

Table 18-1. `ITextViewer` *Methods*

Method	Description
`void activatePlugins()`	Activates the plug-ins that control undo operations, double-click behavior, automatic indentation, and hovering over text.
`void addTextInputListener (ITextInputListener listener)`	Adds a listener that's notified when the document associated with this viewer is replaced by a different document.
`void addTextListener (ITextListener listener)`	Adds a listener that's notified when the text in this viewer changes.
`void addViewportListener (IViewportListener listener)`	Adds a listener that's notified when the viewport (the visible portion of the underlying document) changes.
`void changeTextPresentation (TextPresentation presentation, boolean controlRedraw)`	Applies the color information from the specified `TextPresentation` to the text in this viewer. If `controlRedraw` is true, manages the redraw for the control.
`int getBottomIndex()`	Returns the zero-based line number of the line at the bottom of the viewport.
`int getBottomIndexEndOffset()`	Returns the zero-based character offset of the character at the bottom right corner of the viewport.
`IDocument getDocument()`	Returns the underlying document associated with this viewer.
`IFindReplaceTarget getFindReplaceTarget()`	Returns this viewer's find/replace target.
`Point getSelectedRange()`	Returns the current selection range.
`ISelectionProvider getSelectionProvider()`	Returns this viewer's selection provider.
`ITextOperationTarget getTextOperationTarget()`	Returns the target for any text operations.
`StyledText getTextWidget()`	Returns this viewer's underlying `StyledText` widget.
`int getTopIndex()`	Returns the zero-based line number of the line at the top of the viewport.
`int getTopIndexStartOffset()`	Returns the zero-based character offset of the character at the top left corner of the viewport.
`int getTopInset()`	Returns the number of pixels the first line of text displays below the top of this viewer.
`IRegion getVisibleRegion()`	Returns the visible region of the current document.
`void invalidateTextPresentation()`	Marks the current view as invalid.
`boolean isEditable()`	Returns true if the current document is editable. Otherwise, returns false.
`boolean overlapsWithVisibleRegion (int offset, int length)`	Returns true if the specified text range is visible, either wholly or in part. Otherwise, returns false.
`void removeTextInputListener (ITextInputListener listener)`	Removes the specified listener from the notification list.

Table 18-1. `ITextViewer` *Methods (continued)*

Method	Description
void removeTextListener (ITextListener listener)	Removes the specified listener from the notification list.
void removeViewportListener (IViewportListener listener)	Removes the specified listener from the notification list.
void resetPlugins()	Resets the installed plug-ins.
void resetVisibleRegion()	Resets the visible region of this viewer's document to the original region.
void revealRange(int offset, int length)	Scrolls the viewer as necessary to ensure that the specified range is visible.
void setAutoIndentStrategy (IAutoIndentStrategy strategy, String contentType)	Sets the strategy used for automatically indenting text.
void setDefaultPrefixes(String[] defaultPrefixes, String contentType)	Sets the default prefixes for lines of the specified content type.
void setDocument(IDocument document)	Sets the document for this viewer.
void setDocument(IDocument document, int visibleRegionOffset, int visibleRegionLength)	Sets the document for this viewer, scrolling as necessary to ensure that the specified range is visible.
void setEditable(boolean editable)	If editable is true, makes the current document editable. Otherwise, makes it read only.
void setEventConsumer (IEventConsumer consumer)	Sets the event consumer for this viewer, which can consume events before they reach this viewer.
void setIndentPrefixes(String[] indentPrefixes, String contentType)	Sets the prefixes to use for lines of the specified content type when they're indented (that is, the user performs a shift operation on them).
void setSelectedRange(int offset, int length)	Selects the text in the specified range.
void setTextColor(Color color)	Sets the selected text to the specified color.
void setTextColor(Color color, int offset, int length, boolean controlRedraw)	Sets the text in the specified range to the specified color. If controlRedraw is true, turns off redrawing during this operation.
void setTextDoubleClickStrategy (ITextDoubleClickStrategy strategy, String contentType)	Sets the double-click strategy for the specified content type.
void setTextHover(ITextHover textViewerHover, String contentType)	Sets the text hover for the specified content type.
void setTopIndex(int index)	Scrolls the viewer so that the zero-based line number specified by index is at the top of the viewport.
void setUndoManager(IUndoManager undoManager)	Sets the undo manager for this viewer.
void setVisibleRegion(int offset, int length)	Sets the specified region visible.

Table 18-2. IDocument *Methods*

Method	Description
void addDocumentListener(IDocument Listener listener)	Adds a listener that's notified when this document is about to change, and again after it changes.
void addDocumentPartitioningListener (IDocumentPartitioningListener listener)	Adds a listener that's notified when this document's partitioning changes.
void addPosition(Position position)	Adds a position to this document.
void addPosition(String category, Position position)	Adds a position for the specified category to this document.
void addPositionCategory(String category)	Adds a position category to this document.
void addPositionUpdater(IPosition Updater updater)	Adds a position updater to this document.
void addPrenotifiedDocumentListener (IDocumentListener listener)	Adds a listener that's notified when this document is about to change, and again after it changes. Listeners added using this method are notified before listeners added using addDocumentListener().
int computeIndexInCategory(String category, int offset)	Computes the zero-based index at which the position containing the specified offset would be inserted into the specified category.
int computeNumberOfLines(String text)	Returns the number of lines the specified text occupies.
ITypedRegion[] computePartitioning (int offset, int length)	Computes the partitioning of the document range starting at the specified offset and continuing for the specified length.
boolean containsPosition(String category, int offset, int length)	Returns true if this document contains the position in the specified category, at the specified offset, and with the specified length. Otherwise, returns false.
boolean containsPositionCategory (String category)	Returns true if this document contains the specified category.
String get()	Returns this document's text.
String get(int offset, int length)	Returns this document's text, beginning at the specified offset and continuing the specified length.
char getChar(int offset)	Returns the character at the specified offset.
String getContentType(int offset)	Returns the content type of the partition at the specified offset.
IDocumentPartitioner getDocument Partitioner()	Returns this document's partitioner.
String[] getLegalContentTypes()	Returns the legal content types of all the partitions in this document.
String[] getLegalLineDelimiters()	Returns the legal line delimiters.
int getLength()	Returns the number of characters in this document.

Table 18-2. `IDocument` *Methods (continued)*

Method	Description
`String getLineDelimiter(int line)`	Returns the line delimiter at the line specified by the zero-based index.
`IRegion getLineInformation(int line)`	Returns information about the line specified by the zero-based index.
`IRegion getLineInformationOfOffset (int offset)`	Returns information about the line containing the character at the specified offset.
`int getLineLength(int line)`	Returns the length of the line at the specified zero-based index.
`int getLineOffset(int line)`	Returns the offset of the first character in the specified line.
`int getLineOfOffset(int offset)`	Returns the line containing the character at the specified offset.
`int getNumberOfLines()`	Returns the number of lines in this document.
`int getNumberOfLines(int offset, int length)`	Returns the number of lines used by the text starting at the specified offset and continuing the specified length.
`ITypedRegion getPartition(int offset)`	Returns the partition containing the character at the specified offset.
`String[] getPositionCategories()`	Returns the position categories for this document.
`Position[] getPositions(String category)`	Returns the positions for the specified category.
`IPositionUpdater[] getPositionUpdaters()`	Returns the position updaters for this document.
`void insertPositionUpdater (IPositionUpdater updater, int index)`	Inserts the specified position updater at the specified index.
`void removeDocumentListener (IDocumentListener listener)`	Removes the specified listener from the notification list.
`void removeDocumentPartitioning Listener(IDocumentPartitioning Listener listener)`	Removes the specified listener from the notification list.
`void removePosition(Position position)`	Removes the specified position from this document.
`void removePosition(String category, Position position)`	Removes the specified position from the specified category.
`void removePositionCategory(String category)`	Removes the specified category from this document.
`void removePositionUpdater (IPositionUpdater updater)`	Removes the specified position updater from this document.
`void removePrenotifiedDocument Listener(IDocumentListener listener)`	Removes the specified listener from the notification list.
`void replace(int offset, int length, String text)`	Replaces the text beginning at the specified offset and continuing the specified length with the specified text.
`void set(String text)`	Sets the text for this document.
`void setDocumentPartitioner (IDocumentPartitioner partitioner)`	Sets the document partitioner for this document.

To create a minimal text editor, create a TextViewer and add a Document object to it, like this:

```
TextViewer viewer = new TextViewer(parent, SWT.NONE);
viewer.setDocument(new Document());
```

Those two lines of code create a text editor that competes with Windows Notepad, albeit without persistence or print support. The TextEditor program uses these two lines of code at its core, wrapping the two lines of code with just enough additional code to provide a window to house the editor (see Listing 18-1).

Listing 18-1. TextEditor.java

```
package examples.ch18;

import org.eclipse.jface.text.*;
import org.eclipse.jface.window.ApplicationWindow;
import org.eclipse.swt.SWT;
import org.eclipse.swt.widgets.*;

/**
 * This class demonstrates TextViewer and Document
 */
public class TextEditor extends ApplicationWindow {
  /**
   * TextEditor constructor
   */
  public TextEditor() {
    super(null);
  }

  /**
   * Runs the application
   */
  public void run() {
    setBlockOnOpen(true);
    open();
    Display.getCurrent().dispose();
  }

  /**
   * Configures the shell
   *
   * @param shell the shell
   */
  protected void configureShell(Shell shell) {
    super.configureShell(shell);
    shell.setText("Text Editor");
    shell.setSize(600, 400);
  }
```

```
/**
 * Creates the main window's contents
 *
 * @param parent the main window
 * @return Control
 */
protected Control createContents(Composite parent) {
  // Create the viewer
  TextViewer viewer = new TextViewer(parent, SWT.NONE);

  // Create the associated document
  viewer.setDocument(new Document());

  // Return the StyledText
  return viewer.getTextWidget();
}

/**
 * The application entry point
 *
 * @param args the command line arguments
 */
public static void main(String[] args) {
  new TextEditor().run();
}
}
```

You can type text, delete text, and even cut, copy, or paste text using the keyboard. Figure 18-1 shows the TextEditor program with its own code pasted in.

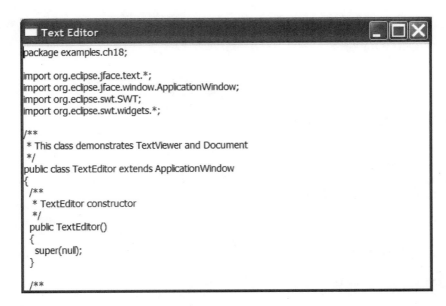

Figure 18-1. TextViewer *and document*

Because a `StyledText` widget—which you can retrieve by calling `getTextWidget()`—lies beneath the `TextViewer`, you can make some simple improvements to TextEditor, such as adding a vertical scrollbar and turning on word wrap, like this:

```
TextViewer viewer = new TextViewer(parent, SWT.V_SCROLL);
viewer.getTextWidget().setWordWrap(true);
```

The TextEditor2 program adds a vertical scrollbar and word wrap, and also adds printing (see Listing 18-2). To print the current document in TextEditor2 to the default printer, press Ctrl-P. The program uses the `StyledText.print()` method to do the printing.

Listing 18-2. `TextEditor2.java`

```
package examples.ch18;

import org.eclipse.jface.text.*;
import org.eclipse.jface.window.ApplicationWindow;
import org.eclipse.swt.SWT;
import org.eclipse.swt.custom.StyledText;
import org.eclipse.swt.events.KeyAdapter;
import org.eclipse.swt.events.KeyEvent;
import org.eclipse.swt.widgets.*;

/**
 * This class demonstrates TextViewer and Document. It adds a vertical scrollbar,
 * word wrap, and printing
 */
public class TextEditor2 extends ApplicationWindow {
  /**
   * TextEditor2 constructor
   */
  public TextEditor2() {
    super(null);
  }

  /**
   * Runs the application
   */
  public void run() {
    setBlockOnOpen(true);
    open();
    Display.getCurrent().dispose();
  }

  /**
   * Configures the shell
   *
   * @param shell the shell
   */
  protected void configureShell(Shell shell) {
```

```
    super.configureShell(shell);
    shell.setText("Text Editor 2");
    shell.setSize(600, 400);
  }

  /**
   * Creates the main window's contents
   *
   * @param parent the main window
   * @return Control
   */
  protected Control createContents(Composite parent) {
    // Create the viewer
    TextViewer viewer = new TextViewer(parent, SWT.V_SCROLL);

    // Get the StyledText
    final StyledText styledText = viewer.getTextWidget();

    // Turn on word wrap
    styledText.setWordWrap(true);

    // Add a listener to detect Ctrl+P
    styledText.addKeyListener(new KeyAdapter() {
      public void keyReleased(KeyEvent event) {
        if (event.keyCode == 'p' && (event.stateMask & SWT.CTRL) != 0) {
          // Ctrl+P pressed; print the document
          styledText.print();
        }
      }
    });

    // Create the associated document
    viewer.setDocument(new Document());

    // Return the StyledText
    return styledText;
  }

  /**
   * The application entry point
   *
   * @param args the command line arguments
   */
  public static void main(String[] args) {
    new TextEditor2().run();
  }
}
```

Figure 18-2 shows the TextEditor2 program with its source code pasted in. Notice the vertical scrollbar along the right edge of the window. Also notice that the first line of the source code has been modified to make it wider than the window, demonstrating that word wrap is on.

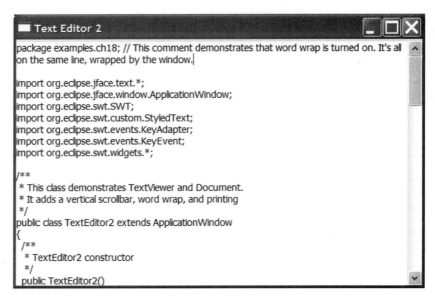

Figure 18-2. A `TextViewer` *with enhancements*

IDocument doesn't provide any built-in persistence methods, so you must build your own mechanism for writing your text to or reading it from files. Because you can get the IDocument's contents by calling its `get()` method, and set its contents by calling its `set()` method, you can persist to files using methods such as these:

```java
public void save(IDocument document, String filename) {
  FileWriter out = null;
  try {
    out = new FileWriter(filename);
    String text = document.get();
    out.write(text, 0, text.length());
  } catch (IOException e) {
    // Report the error
  } finally {
    if (out != null) { try { out.close(); } catch (IOException e) { } }
  }
}

public IDocument load(String filename) {
  IDocument document = null;
  FileReader in = null;
  try {
    in = new FileReader(filename);
    StringBuffer buf = new StringBuffer();
    int n;
    while ((n = in.read()) != -1) {
      buf.append((char) n);
    }
```

```
        document = new Document();
        document.set(buf.toString());
    } catch (IOException e) {
        // Report the error
    } finally {
        if (in != null) { try { in.close(); } catch (IOException e) { } }
    }
}
```

Add these methods, a menu, and just a little more plumbing to the TextEditor program, and you have a replacement for Windows Notepad, GNOME gnotepad+, or iNotePad. Using TextViewer and Document, you can create a powerful text editor with little original code.

Although a small effort produces big results, you won't confuse those results with professional-grade source code editors such as Vim, Emacs, or the editor that comes with Eclipse. Your small-effort editor doesn't have context coloring, code completion, line numbering, or any of a host of features that top-grade text editors offer. Adding those features to your editor requires using more of the JFace text editing framework. The balance of this chapter explores how to add more text editing features.

Undoing and Redoing

Computer software used to destroy data irrevocably on command. For example, if you deleted a file, you couldn't invoke some sort of "oops" clause to bring that file back. Text editing software would respond to everything you typed—even if you hit the Backspace key more times than you meant and you sent your latest novel into the ether. Today's software, however, trusts you less than the software from days of yore used to. It still responds to commands to delete files or text, but also allows you to repent from any hasty actions and undo the damage you've wreaked. In fact, any modern software without the capability to undo what it does retains little chance of success.

ITextViewer allows you to plug in an undo manager to manage undo and redo capabilities. The IUndoManager interface declares the methods that an undo manager must define to use with ITextViewer. Table 18-3 lists IUndoManager's methods.

Table 18-3. IUndoManager *Methods*

Method	Description
void beginCompoundChange()	Begins an undoable "transaction": all changes between this call and a call to endCompoundChange() are treated as a single change for undoing and redoing.
void connect(ITextViewer viewer)	Connects this undo manager to the specified text viewer.
void disconnect()	Disconnects this undo manager from its text viewer.
void endCompoundChange()	Ends the undoable "transaction." See beginCompoundChange().
void redo()	Redoes the most recently undone change.

Table 18-3. IUndoManager *Methods (continued)*

Method	Description
boolean redoable()	Returns true if a change can be redone. Otherwise, returns false.
void reset()	Clears the undo history.
void setMaximalUndoLevel(int undoLevel)	Sets the maximum number of changes this undo manager stores in its history.
void undo()	Undoes the most recent change.
boolean undoable()	Returns true if a change can be undone. Otherwise, returns false.

You can write your own IUndoManager class, or you can use the DefaultUndoManager provided. The DefaultUndoManager class has a single constructor that takes the maximum desired undo level as a parameter. For example, to create a text viewer with undo support, use code such as this:

```
ITextViewer textViewer = new TextViewer(parent, SWT.NONE);
IUndoManager undoManager = new DefaultUndoManager(500);
undoManager.connect(textViewer);
```

You also must provide mechanisms for users to invoke the undo manager's undo and redo methods. For example, you could have action classes that you add to a menu or toolbar to call the manager's undo() and redo() methods. Here are some example action classes to do that:

```
public class UndoAction extends Action {
  // Store the undo manager
  private IUndoManager undoManager;

  public UndoAction(IUndoManager undoManager) {
    super("&Undo@Ctrl+Z");
    this.undoManager = undoManager;
  }

  public void run() {
    // Undo the last action
    undoManager.undo();
  }
}

public class RedoAction extends Action {
  // Store the undo manager
  private IUndoManager undoManager;

  public RedoAction(IUndoManager undoManager) {
    super("&Redo@Ctrl+Y");
    this.undoManager = undoManager;
  }
```

```
  public void run() {
    // Redo the last action
    undoManager.redo();
  }
}
```

Finding and Replacing

Humans' searching abilities suffer sufficiently for us to have developed a vocabulary around failed searches:

- "It's as plain as the nose on your face."

- "If it were a snake, it would've bit you."

- "It's like trying to find a needle in a haystack."

Fortunately, computers don't suffer from the same myopia we humans do. When computers search for something, they never overlook their quarry. As long as what they seek is present, computers will find it.

 CAUTION *The API for finding and replacing has changed. Please refer to this book's site on the Web for more information and corrected source code.*

The JFace text framework has searching and replacing built in, using a class called FindReplaceDocumentAdapter. You must construct this class with the IDocument instance that it searches, like this:

```
FindReplaceDocumentAdapter frda = new FindReplaceDocumentAdapter(document);
```

FindReplaceDocumentAdapter's findReplace() method constitutes the heart of the find/replace engine. It takes several parameters to define the search, including where to begin searching, the search text, the replacement text, whether to search forward or backward, whether to ignore case while searching, whether to search only for whole words that match the search text, and whether the search text represents a regular expression. Most importantly, however, you must tell findReplace() which operation to perform: find the first match, find the next match, replace the current match, or replace the current match and find the next match. The FindReplaceOperationCode class contains constants representing those operations, as listed in Table 18-4.

Table 18-4. FindReplaceOperationCode *Constants*

Code	Description
FIND_FIRST	Finds the first match
FIND_NEXT	Finds subsequent matches
REPLACE	Replaces the current match
REPLACE_FIND_NEXT	Replaces the current match and finds the next match

The signature for findReplace() is as follows:

```
public IRegion findReplace(FindReplaceOperationCode operationCode,
    int startOffset,
    String findString,
    String replaceText,
    boolean forwardSearch,
    boolean caseSensitive,
    boolean wholeWord,
    boolean regExSearch)
    throws BadLocationException
```

Calling this method returns null if no match occurs, or an IRegion object that contains the offset and length of the matched text. Call getOffset() and getLength() to retrieve the offset and length, respectively. This method throws a BadLocationException if you specify a startOffset that's outside the range of this FindReplaceDocumentAdapter's document.

FindReplaceDocumentAdapter preserves the last operation used and the location of the last match. Passing FIND_FIRST for the operation resets the state. The other operations ignore the state parameters passed (such as startOffset) and use the internal state. The operations have temporal dependencies: you must perform a FIND_FIRST before you perform a FIND_NEXT. You must perform a FIND_FIRST or FIND_NEXT before performing a REPLACE or a REPLACE_FIND_NEXT. Calling operations out of order throws an IllegalStateException.

Another caveat to bear in mind: you can't search both on whole words and on regular expressions, or the code will trigger an assertion.

Table 18-5 lists FindReplaceDocumentAdapter's methods.

Table 18-5. FindReplaceDocumentAdapter *Methods*

Method	Description
char charAt(int index)	Returns the character in the associated document at the specified zero-based index.
IRegion findReplace(FindReplace OperationCode operationCode, int startOffset, String findString, String replaceText, boolean forwardSearch, boolean caseSensitive, boolean wholeWord, boolean regExSearch)	Performs a find/replace operation using the specified criteria.
int length()	Returns the length of the associated document.
IRegion replace(String text, boolean regExReplace)	Replaces the previous match with the specified text. If regExReplace is true, text represents a regular expression.
IRegion search(int startOffset, String findString, boolean forwardSearch, boolean caseSensitive, boolean wholeWord, boolean regExSearch)	Performs a "find first" using the specified criteria.
CharSequence subSequence(int start, int end)	Returns the text from the associated document between the offsets specified by start and end.
String toString()	Returns the associated document's contents.

For example, to perform a search for the text "foo," you could call this:

```
IRegion region = findReplaceDocumentAdapter.findReplace(
  FindReplaceOperationCode.FIND_FIRST, 0, "foo", null, true, true, false, false);
```

Or you could call this:

```
IRegion region = findReplaceDocumentAdapter.search(0, "foo", true, true, false,
  false);
```

To replace the matched text with "bar," you could call this:

```
IRegion region = findReplaceDocumentAdapter.findReplace(
  FindReplaceOperationCode.REPLACE, 0, null, "bar", true, true, false, false);
```

Or you could call this:

```
IRegion region = findReplaceDocumentAdapter.replace("bar", false);
```

The FindReplaceDialog class seen in Listing 18-3 provides a graphical interface to FindReplaceDocumentAdapter. It allows users to specify the search text, the replacement text, whether to do a case-sensitive search, whether to search on whole words, whether to search using regular expressions, and which direction to search. It manages the state transitions for performing legal operations by enabling and disabling the Replace buttons, as appropriate.

Listing 18-3. FindReplaceDialog.java

```java
package examples.ch18.perledit.ui;

import java.util.regex.PatternSyntaxException;

import org.eclipse.jface.dialogs.MessageDialog;
import org.eclipse.jface.text.*;
import org.eclipse.swt.SWT;
import org.eclipse.swt.events.*;
import org.eclipse.swt.layout.*;
import org.eclipse.swt.widgets.*;

/**
 * This class displays a find/replace dialog
 */
public class FindReplaceDialog extends Dialog {
  // The adapter that does the finding/replacing
  private FindReplaceDocumentAdapter frda;

  // The associated viewer
  private ITextViewer viewer;
```

```
// The find and replace buttons
private Button doFind;
private Button doReplace;
private Button doReplaceFind;

/**
 * FindReplaceDialog constructor
 *
 * @param shell the parent shell
 * @param document the associated document
 * @param viewer the associated viewer
 */
public FindReplaceDialog(Shell shell, IDocument document, ITextViewer viewer) {
  super(shell, SWT.DIALOG_TRIM | SWT.MODELESS);
  frda = new FindReplaceDocumentAdapter(document);
  this.viewer = viewer;
}

/**
 * Opens the dialog box
 */
public void open() {
  Shell shell = new Shell(getParent(), getStyle());
  shell.setText("Find/Replace");
  createContents(shell);
  shell.pack();
  shell.open();
  Display display = getParent().getDisplay();
  while (!shell.isDisposed()) {
    if (!display.readAndDispatch()) {
      display.sleep();
    }
  }
}

/**
 * Performs a find/replace
 *
 * @param code the code
 * @param find the find string
 * @param replace the replace text
 * @param forward whether to search forward
 * @param matchCase whether to match case
 * @param wholeWord whether to search on whole word
 * @param regexp whether find string is a regular expression
 */
protected void doFind(FindReplaceOperationCode code, String find,
    String replace, boolean forward, boolean matchCase, boolean wholeWord,
    boolean regexp) {
  // You can't mix whole word and regexp
  if (wholeWord && regexp) {
    showError("You can't search on both Whole Words and Regular Expressions");
```

```java
    } else {
      IRegion region = null;
      try {
        // Get the current offset (only used on FIND_FIRST)
        int offset = viewer.getTextWidget().getCaretOffset();

        // Make sure we're in the document
        if (offset >= frda.length()) offset = frda.length() - 1;

        // Perform the find/replace
        region = frda.findReplace(code, viewer.getTextWidget().getCaretOffset(),
            find, replace, forward, matchCase, wholeWord, regexp);

        // Update the viewer with found selection
        if (region != null) {
          viewer.setSelectedRange(region.getOffset(), region.getLength());
        }

        // If find succeeded, flip to FIND_NEXT and enable Replace buttons
        // Otherwise, reset to FIND_FIRST and disable Replace buttons
        // We know find succeeded if region is not null AND the operation
        // wasn't REPLACE (REPLACE finds nothing new, but still returns
        // a region).
        boolean succeeded = region != null
            && code != FindReplaceOperationCode.REPLACE;
        doFind.setData(succeeded ? FindReplaceOperationCode.FIND_NEXT
            : FindReplaceOperationCode.FIND_FIRST);
        enableReplaceButtons(succeeded);
      } catch (BadLocationException e) {
        // Ignore
      } catch (PatternSyntaxException e) {
        // Show the error to the user
        showError(e.getMessage());
      }
    }
  }
}

/**
 * Creates the dialog's contents
 *
 * @param shell
 */
protected void createContents(final Shell shell) {
  shell.setLayout(new GridLayout(2, false));

  // Add the text input fields
  Composite text = new Composite(shell, SWT.NONE);
  text.setLayoutData(new GridData(GridData.FILL_HORIZONTAL));
  text.setLayout(new GridLayout(3, true));

  new Label(text, SWT.LEFT).setText("&Find:");
  final Text findText = new Text(text, SWT.BORDER);
```

```
GridData data = new GridData(GridData.FILL_HORIZONTAL);
data.horizontalSpan = 2;
findText.setLayoutData(data);

new Label(text, SWT.LEFT).setText("R&eplace With:");
final Text replaceText = new Text(text, SWT.BORDER);
data = new GridData(GridData.FILL_HORIZONTAL);
data.horizontalSpan = 2;
replaceText.setLayoutData(data);

// Add the match case checkbox
final Button match = new Button(text, SWT.CHECK);
match.setText("&Match Case");

// Add the whole word checkbox
final Button wholeWord = new Button(text, SWT.CHECK);
wholeWord.setText("&Whole Word");

// Add the regular expression checkbox
final Button regexp = new Button(text, SWT.CHECK);
regexp.setText("RegE&xp");

// Add the direction radio buttons
final Button down = new Button(text, SWT.RADIO);
down.setText("D&own");

final Button up = new Button(text, SWT.RADIO);
up.setText("&Up");

// Add the buttons
Composite buttons = new Composite(shell, SWT.NONE);
buttons.setLayout(new GridLayout(1, false));

// Create the Find button
doFind = new Button(buttons, SWT.PUSH);
doFind.setText("Fi&nd");
doFind.setLayoutData(new GridData(GridData.FILL_HORIZONTAL));

// Set the initial find operation to FIND_FIRST
doFind.setData(FindReplaceOperationCode.FIND_FIRST);

// Create the Replace button
doReplace = new Button(buttons, SWT.PUSH);
doReplace.setText("&Replace");
doReplace.setLayoutData(new GridData(GridData.FILL_HORIZONTAL));

// Create the Replace/Find button
doReplaceFind = new Button(buttons, SWT.PUSH);
doReplaceFind.setText("Replace/Fin&d");
doReplaceFind.setLayoutData(new GridData(GridData.FILL_HORIZONTAL));
doReplaceFind.addSelectionListener(new SelectionAdapter() {
```

```
    public void widgetSelected(SelectionEvent event) {
      doFind(FindReplaceOperationCode.REPLACE_FIND_NEXT, findText.getText(),
          replaceText.getText(), down.getSelection(), match.getSelection(),
          wholeWord.getSelection(), regexp.getSelection());
    }
  });

  // Create the Close button
  Button close = new Button(buttons, SWT.PUSH);
  close.setText("Close");
  close.setLayoutData(new GridData(GridData.FILL_HORIZONTAL));
  close.addSelectionListener(new SelectionAdapter() {
    public void widgetSelected(SelectionEvent event) {
      shell.close();
    }
  });

  // Reset the FIND_FIRST/FIND_NEXT when find text is modified
  findText.addModifyListener(new ModifyListener() {
    public void modifyText(ModifyEvent event) {
      doFind.setData(FindReplaceOperationCode.FIND_FIRST);
      enableReplaceButtons(false);
    }
  });

  // Change to FIND_NEXT and enable replace buttons on successful find
  doFind.addSelectionListener(new SelectionAdapter() {
    public void widgetSelected(SelectionEvent event) {
      // Do the find, pulling the operation code out of the button
      doFind((FindReplaceOperationCode) event.widget.getData(), findText
          .getText(), replaceText.getText(), down.getSelection(), match
          .getSelection(), wholeWord.getSelection(), regexp.getSelection());
    }
  });

  // Replace loses "find" state, so disable buttons
  doReplace.addSelectionListener(new SelectionAdapter() {
    public void widgetSelected(SelectionEvent event) {
      doFind(FindReplaceOperationCode.REPLACE, findText.getText(), replaceText
          .getText(), down.getSelection(), match.getSelection(), wholeWord
          .getSelection(), regexp.getSelection());
    }
  });

  // Set defaults
  down.setSelection(true);
  findText.setFocus();
  doReplace.setEnabled(false);
  doReplaceFind.setEnabled(false);
  shell.setDefaultButton(doFind);
}
```

```
/**
 * Enables/disables the Replace and Replace/Find buttons
 *
 * @param enable whether to enable or disable
 */
protected void enableReplaceButtons(boolean enable) {
  doReplace.setEnabled(enable);
  doReplaceFind.setEnabled(enable);
}

/**
 * Shows an error
 *
 * @param message the error message
 */
protected void showError(String message) {
  MessageDialog.openError(getParent(), "Error", message);
}
}
```

FindReplaceDialog contains a FindReplaceDocumentAdapter instance, and calls
findReplace() inside the doFind() method. The button handlers determine the parameters to send to doFind(). To use this dialog, construct one, passing the shell, the document, and the viewer, and then call open(). The dialog is modeless, so you can move
back and forth between your main window and the dialog. Figure 18-3 shows the dialog when it first displays, and Figure 18-4 shows the dialog after a successful find. Note
that the Replace buttons are enabled.

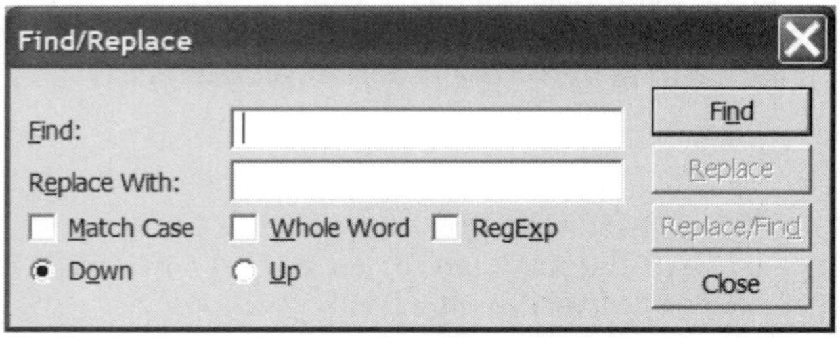

Figure 18-3. The FindReplaceDialog *class*

Figure 18-4. The FindReplaceDialog *with replacements enabled*

Use `FindReplaceDialog` in your code like this:

```
FindReplaceDialog dlg = new FindReplaceDialog(shell, document, viewer);
dlg.open();
```

Dividing Partitions

JFace documents rely on partitions, which divide documents into chunks of text. Like Lego bricks that, when snapped together, form a beautiful creation, partitions band together to form a document. Partitions have an offset and a length (in other words, they span a specific range of characters in the document), and also a content type. They never overlap. You can think of them as sections of a word-processing document that have specific styles. For example, in OpenOffice.org or Microsoft Word, each span of text can have a style that defines key characteristics about the text:

- What font it uses

- Whether it's normal, bolded, italicized, underlined, struck out, or some combination

- Whether it's bulleted, numbered, or not

- How far it's indented from the left margin

- How much space displays above and below it

Though by no means exhaustive, this list of style characteristics demonstrates ways that people use metadata about text to augment what would otherwise result in a drab display of data.

JFace partitions also adopt another key feature of word processor styles: their dynamic updating. Changing a word processor style updates all the ranges of text within the document with that style. Suppose, for example, that you're working on a document that has several stretches of text with the style "Heading 3." You decide to change the font for Heading 3 from Helvetica to Times Roman. Once you change it, any text with the Heading 3 style changes its font immediately (or at least as fast as your hardware and word processor can muster). Changes you make to JFace partitions share this universality—as you change the partition handling, all partitions of the changed type update.

 NOTE *Word processors typically support mixing fonts within a document. However, because SWT's* `StyledText` *widget forms the basis of JFace's* `TextViewer`, *JFace partitions all use the same font.*

However, unlike word processing documents, you don't directly define partitions in your JFace document. If you want some text in your word processor to sport the Heading 3 style, you must select the text and explicitly apply the style. The word processor has no way of deducing what style you want from the text. However, source code is different: it implicitly carries rules about itself that can be used to determine partitions. For example, if you're editing a Java source code file and insert a character sequence such as this, a Java-aware editor can deduce that this text constitutes a Javadoc comment:

```
/**
 * Do something important
 */
```

In fact, you wouldn't dream of using a text editor that didn't recognize that. Can you imagine having to use a source code editor that made you select your Javadoc comments and then explicitly apply a style from a dropdown? No, source code (unlike your term paper on mollusks) carries enough information intrinsically for editors to determine its styles or partitions.

In JFace, the responsibility for parsing source code and determining the partitions falls on a document partitioner, represented by an IDocumentPartitioner implementation. Each document partitioner corresponds to, or "is connected to" in JFace parlance, a JFace document (IDocument instance). IDocumentPartitioner declares the methods listed in Table 18-6. You can create your own IDocumentPartitioner class, but you'll usually use JFace's DefaultPartitioner class.

Table 18-6. IDocumentPartitioner *Methods*

Method	Description
ITypedRegion[] computePartitioning (int offset, int length)	In this method, you should compute the partitioning for the specified offset and length of the associated document.
void connect(IDocument document)	In this method, you should establish the relationship between this document partitioner and the specified document.
void disconnect()	In this method, you should break the relationship between this document partitioner and its associated document.
void documentAboutToBeChanged (Document event)	In this method, you should perform any appropriate processing before a change occurs to the associated document.
boolean documentChanged (DocumentEvent event)	In this method, you should respond to the change in the associated document, usually by recomputing the partitioning. You should return true if the document's partitioning changed, or false if it didn't.
String getContentType(int offset)	In this method, you should return the content type of the partition that contains the specified offset into the associated document.
String[] getLegalContentTypes()	In this method, you should return all the content types handled by this partitioner.
ITypedRegion getPartition(int offset)	In this method, you should return the partition that contains the specified offset into the associated document.

The DefaultPartitioner class performs all this work for you in a reasonable way. Obviously, however, you must customize DefaultPartitioner's behavior somehow, or all documents would be partitioned using the same rules. This would mean that C++ source code files, for example, could contain Javadoc partitions, which is certainly not desirable. Different languages require different rules to handle them. However, to customize DefaultPartitioner's behavior, you don't make any direct changes to it. Instead, you create a partition scanner and pass it, along with the partition types (content types) it handles, to your DefaultPartitioner's constructor, like this:

```
IDocumentPartitioner partitioner = new DefaultPartitioner(myPartitionScanner,
  myPartitionScannerTypes);
```

Note that partition scanners and partitions don't directly provide syntax code highlighting. For example, you shouldn't use them to try to identify each keyword in your source code. Instead, partition scanners simply identify sections of your documents, providing an infrastructure that you can add things to, such as syntax highlighting. For example, you might have a partition with type "code" that you later add syntax highlighting to. This chapter covers syntax highlighting, along with some other things you can do to partitions that your partition scanners identify.

Understanding partition scanners requires that you understand tokens and their relationship to partitions. The next section describes tokens.

Collecting Tokens

A token in JFace contains data that applies to a span of text in a document. It isn't the text itself, nor does it contain the text. It doesn't contain the offset of the text or its length. In fact, it has no intrinsic connection to the text it describes. Instead, it contains information about the span of text that other classes use when working with the text. For example, a partition scanner associates a token with each partition that contains the partition's type. Code scanners use tokens that contain the colors to use when displaying the text. Tokens are reusable across the document.

Scanning for Partitions

The IPartitionTokenScanner interface represents a partition scanner. The DefaultPartitioner class uses its IPartitionTokenScanner instance to scan through regions of the document and find its tokens, or partitions. IPartitionTokenScanner declares a single method:

```
void setPartialRange(IDocument document, int offset, int length,
  String contentType, int partitionOffset);
```

DefaultPartitioner calls this method when its associated document changes, requesting the scanner to scan the specified document region for partition information. However, because IPartitionTokenScanner extends ITokenScanner, you must also implement ITokenScanner's methods, listed in Table 18-7.

Table 18-7. `ITokenScanner` *Methods*

Method	Description
`int getTokenLength()`	In this method, you should return the length in characters of the last token (partition) that this scanner read
`int getTokenOffset()`	In this method, you should return the zero-based offset of the last token (partition) that this scanner read
`IToken nextToken()`	In this method, you should return the next token (partition) in the document
`void setRange(IDocument document, int offset, int length)`	In this method, you should configure your scanner to scan the specified document beginning at the specified zero-based offset and continuing the specified length of characters

However, instead of writing code to create your own partition scanner from the ground up, you'll usually use one of JFace's existing partition scanners as a basis for your partition scanner. For source code, or any text whose partitions can be derived from the data itself, subclass `RuleBasedPartitionScanner` as the basis for your partition scanner. In your subclass, define the rules governing your partitioning and add them to the scanner. Each recognized partition type requires a rule to recognize it. For example, a partition scanner for partitioning Java code likely recognizes partitions for Javadoc comments, partitions for multiline comments, and partitions for Java code. It therefore must have three rules, one for each of these partition types. Because partition scanners recognize a default partition, you just need two new partition types, with two rules to identify them.

JFace offers several rules, which you configure to identify a partition based on certain character sequences. When you create a rule instance, you tell it the character sequences to look for, and you give it the token that corresponds to the partition type that the rule identifies. When the rule detects a section of the document that it matches, it marks that section by returning its associated token. Table 18-8 lists the existing rule classes, and you can also create your own rules by implementing `IRule` or `IPredicateRule`.

Table 18-8. `JFace` *Rules*

Rule	Description
`EndOfLineRule`	Rule that matches a starting sequence of characters and continues to the end of the line. Example usage: single-line comments.
`MultiLineRule`	Rule that matches a starting sequence and an ending sequence of characters that may be separated by multiple lines. Example usage: multiline comments.
`NumberRule`	Rule that matches a sequence of digits.
`PatternRule`	Rule that matches a starting sequence and an ending sequence of characters, or may continue to the end of the line.
`SingleLineRule`	Rule that matches a starting sequence and an ending sequence of characters that may not span more than one line.

Table 18-8. JFace *Rules (continued)*

Rule	Description
WhitespaceRule	Rule that matches whitespace. Requires that you develop an IWhitespaceDetector implementation to determine what constitutes whitespace.
WordPatternRule	Rule that matches a starting sequence and an ending sequence of characters that must occur within a word. Requires that you develop an IWordDetector implementation to determine what constitutes a word.
WordRule	Rule that detects a word. Requires that you develop an IWordDetector implementation to determine what constitutes a word. Example usage: keywords.

Armed with these rules, you can build a Java partition scanner to handle partitions for Javadoc comments, multiline comments, and code. You might create tokens and rules for the Javadoc comments partitions and the multiline comments partitions, and leave the rest—the code—as the default partition type. The code might look like this:

```java
public class JavaPartitionScanner extends RuleBasedPartitionScanner {
  // Define the partitions
  public static final String JAVADOC = "Javadoc";
  public static final String MULTILINE_COMMENT = "Multi-line Comment";
  public static final String[] PARTITION_TYPES = { JAVADOC, MULTILINE_COMMENT };

  /**
   * JavaPartitionScanner constructor
   */
  public JavaPartitionScanner() {
    // Create the tokens to go with the partitions
    IToken javadoc = new Token(JAVADOC);
    IToken multilineComment = new Token(MULTILINE_COMMENT);

    // Add rules
    IPredicateRule[] rules = new IPredicateRule[2];

    // Javadoc rule: starts with /**, ends with */, has no escape character,
    // and breaks on EOF
    rules[0] = new MultiLineRule("/**", "*/", javadoc, (char) 0, true);

    // Multi-line comment rule: starts with /*, ends with */, has no escape
    // character, and breaks on EOF
    rules[1] = new MultiLineRule("/*", "*/", multilineComment, (char) 0, true);

    // Set the rules
    setPredicateRules(rules);
  }
}
```

The static PARTITION_TYPES member makes adding this scanner to a DefaultPartitioner simple, as this code demonstrates:

```
JavaPartitionScanner scanner = new JavaPartitionScanner();
IDocumentPartitioner partitioner = new DefaultPartitioner(scanner,
  JavaPartitionScanner.PARTITION_TYPES);
```

The preceding code creates a JavaPartitionScanner, then creates an IDocumentPartitioner. It tells the partitioner to use the created scanner for the partition types specified by JavaPartitionScanner.PARTITION_TYPES. However, until you associate the partitioner with a document, it has nothing to do, and sits idle. To put the partitioner to work scanning your document, pass the partitioner and its name to the document's setDocumentPartitioner(), like this:

```
document.setDocumentPartitioner("Java", partitioner);
```

The name you specify as the first parameter to setDocumentPartitioner() is also used in the SourceViewerConfiguration subclass that's used to configure the document's viewer, explained later in this chapter.

To consummate the relationship between document and partitioner, connect the partitioner to the document using the partitioner's connect() method, like this:

```
partitioner.connect(document);
```

We have a small confession: although source code generally contains enough self-describing information for partitioners to partition them correctly, not all text documents have sufficient information. When it proves impossible to create a partition scanner that can scan and partition the document it's connected to without external information, you can't use a rule-based partitioner. Instead, you must create an IDocumentPartitioner implementation and provide a means for it to gather the necessary information to perform its partitioning. This chapter doesn't cover non-rule-based partitioners.

Configuring the Viewer

A properly partitioned document provides plenty of information to a viewer designed to display the document. As a paragon of the separation between model and view, the partitions in the document contain no view-specific information. Instead, the viewer reads the partitions and interprets how to display and treat them. You tell the viewer how you want it to treat the partitions by configuring it using a subclass of SourceViewerConfiguration that you create.

The SourceViewerConfiguration class exposes an interface full of getter methods that associated classes call to get specific configuration information. Table 18-9 lists SourceViewerConfiguration's methods. In your subclass, override the methods for which you want to alter the default information, and leave the rest alone.

Table 18-9. `SourceViewerConfiguration` *Methods*

Method	Description
`IAnnotationHover getAnnotationHover (ISourceViewer sourceViewer)`	Returns the annotation hover, which displays text in a popup window when the mouse hovers.
`IAutoIndentStrategy getAutoIndentStrategy (ISourceViewer, String contentType)`	Returns the auto-indent strategy for the specified content type. The auto-indent strategy determines how to indent text.
`String[] getConfiguredContentTypes (ISourceViewer sourceViewer)`	Returns the content types that the viewer handles. These content types are the names of the partitions that the viewer corresponding to this configuration can act on.
`String getConfiguredDocumentPartitioning (ISourceViewer sourceViewer)`	Returns the partitioning name of the partitioner this configuration uses. This should be the name of the partitioner passed to the document's `setDocumentPartitioner()` method.
`int[] getConfiguredTextHoverStateMasks (ISourceViewer sourceViewer, String contentType)`	Returns the event state masks for which text hovering is configured, for the specified content type.
`IContentAssistant getContentAssistant (ISourceViewer sourceViewer)`	Returns the content assistant, which provides dynamic content completion.
`IContentFormatter getContentFormatter (ISourceViewer sourceViewer)`	Returns the content formatter, which formats the text in the document.
`String[] getDefaultPrefixes(ISourceViewer sourceViewer, String contentType)`	Returns the default prefixes for the specified content type.
`ITextDoubleClickStrategy getDouble ClickStrategy(ISourceViewer sourceViewer, String contentType)`	Returns the double-click strategy for the specified content type.
`String[] getIndentPrefixes(ISourceViewer sourceViewer, String contentType)`	Returns the indent prefixes for the specified content type.
`IInformationControlCenter getInformation ControlCenter(ISourceViewer sourceViewer)`	Returns a factory for creating information controls, which are controls that display textual information.
`IInformationPresenter getInformation Presenter(ISourceViewer sourceViewer)`	Returns the information presenter, which presents information about the current cursor position.
`IAnnotationHover getOverviewRuler AnnotationHover(ISourceViewer sourceViewer)`	Returns the annotation hover for the overview ruler.
`IPresentationReconciler getPresentation Reconciler(ISourceViewer sourceViewer)`	Returns the presentation reconciler, which is responsible for performing context highlighting.
`IReconciler getReconciler(ISourceViewer sourceViewer)`	Returns the reconciler, which reconciles differences between the document and the model of the document's content.
`int getTabWidth(ISourceViewer sourceViewer)`	Returns the number of characters to display for a tab.
`ITextHover getTextHover(ISourceViewer sourceViewer, String contentType)`	Returns the text hover for the specified content type. The text hover provides the text to display in a popup window when the mouse hovers.
`ITextHover getTextHover(ISourceViewer sourceViewer, String contentType, int stateMask)`	Returns the text hover for the specified content type, using the specified event state mask. The text hover provides the text to display in a popup window when the mouse hovers.
`IUndoManager getUndoManager(ISourceViewer sourceViewer)`	Returns the undo manager.

For example, the MinimalSourceViewerConfiguration class creates a source viewer configuration that shows two spaces for a tab, and relies on the defaults for everything else:

```
public class MinimalSourceViewerConfiguration extends SourceViewerConfiguration {
  public int getTabWidth(ISourceViewer sourceViewer) {
    return 2;
  }
}
```

To associate the configuration with the viewer, pass it to the viewer's configure() method. Make sure to call configure() before you call setDocument(), as the document uses the configuration for some initialization. For example, the following code creates a viewer, configures it, and associates it with a document:

```
SourceViewer viewer = new SourceViewer(parent, new VerticalRuler(10),
  SWT.V_SCROLL | SWT.H_SCROLL);
viewer.configure(new MinimalSourceViewerConfiguration());
viewer.setDocument(document);
```

The source viewer configuration provides some viewer functionality. This chapter examines one: syntax coloring.

Living in Color

Any programmers that pooh-pooh syntax coloring, also known as context highlighting, want attention. They desperately need you to feel intimidated by their mental prowess, and achieve validation by shunning anything that could be deemed a crutch. They eschew GUIs, too, and never let their hands touch a mouse. We can think of no good reason for anyone to ignore this powerful tool, and indeed can find few remaining in this withering camp. Syntax highlighting dramatically improves both code reading and code writing, and no serious code editor can flourish without it.

To incorporate syntax coloring in your text editor, you must create the following:

- A presentation reconciler

- Damager/repairer pairs for each partition type you want to color

- A rule-based scanner (*not* a partition scanner) for each partition type you want to color

To color text, JFace uses damagers and repairers, which aren't as drastic or foreboding as they sound. Damagers, represented by IPresentationDamager instances, "damage" a document only in the sense that they respond to user input (such as keystrokes) by changing the document. Repairers, represented by IPresentationRepairer instances, respond to this "damage" by readjusting the view as appropriate for the changed document. Damagers and repairers come in pairs, attached to a presentation reconciler, represented by IPresentationReconciler. A presentation reconciler can have several damager/repairer pairs, and each pair corresponds to a specific partition type. Damagers and repairers react to changes only in partitions that have the type they're configured for.

A damager/repairer pair also contains a scanner that scans all corresponding partitions. The scanner, usually derived from RuleBasedScanner, contains rules that the repairer applies to color the code appropriately. JFace offers a class, DefaultDamagerRepairer, that implements both IPresentationDamager and IPresentationRepairer. To use it, pass the scanner to its constructor, like this:

```
DefaultDamagerRepairer ddr = new DefaultDamagerRepairer(myRuleScanner);
```

After constructing the damager/repairer, pass it to your presentation reconciler twice: once to its setDamager() method and once to its setRepairer() method. Both methods take the partition type you're setting the damager or repairer for, as well. For example, to set the preceding damager/repairer into a presentation reconciler for the partition type "My Partition Type," use this code:

```
PresentationReconciler reconciler = new PresentationReconciler();
reconciler.setDamager(ddr, "My Partition Type");
reconciler.setRepairer(ddr, "My Partition Type");
```

To make your presentation reconciler handle more partition types, create a DefaultDamagerRepairer for each type, passing it the appropriate scanner for the partition type. Then call reconciler.setDamager() and reconciler.setRepairer(), passing the DefaultDamagerRepairer and the partition type to each.

The scanner configures how to color code by creating tokens containing TextAttribute instances and passing the tokens to rules. The TextAttribute class contains a foreground color, a background color, and a font style, all of which are applied to code that passes the associated rule. For example, to color a Java single-line comment green, use code such as this:

```
public class JavaCommentScanner extends RuleBasedScanner {
  public JavaCommentScanner() {
    // Create the token for green text
    IToken green = new Token(new TextAttribute(Display.getCurrent()
      .getSystemColor(SWT.COLOR_GREEN))); // Use defaults for background & style

    // Create the rule and set it
    setRules(new IRule[] { new EndOfLineRule("#", green) });
  }
}
```

To wire your presentation reconciler, with all its damager/repairer pairs, to your viewer, return it from the getPresentationReconciler() in your viewer's SourceViewerConfiguration class. As you change the text in your document, the viewer uses the presentation reconciler to color the text automatically according to the rules you've set.

Editing Perl

The PerlEditor program creates a full-blown text editor that can edit any text file. However, it shines when editing Perl code, as it uses syntax highlighting with Perl. It displays comments in one color, Perl keywords in another, and strings in yet another. However, it doesn't automatically obfuscate Perl code into the unreadable condition Perl programmers strive for; you'll have to do that yourself. You can download the full source code from the Downloads section of the Apress Web site (http://www.apress.com); some parts are highlighted here.

The program's document partitioner creates two partitions: one for comments, and the default partition for the rest of the code (see Listing 18-4). It uses an instance of CommentScanner for the comment partition, which indiscriminately makes all text green. For the default partition, it uses an instance of PerlCodeScanner, which makes Perl keywords cyan and bold, and strings red.

Listing 18-4. PerlPartitionScanner.java

```java
package examples.ch18.perledit.source;

import org.eclipse.jface.text.rules.*;

/**
 * This class scans a document and partitions it
 */
public class PerlPartitionScanner extends RuleBasedPartitionScanner {
  // Create a partition for comments, and leave the rest for code
  public static final String COMMENT = "comment";
  public static final String[] TYPES = { COMMENT};

  /**
   * PerlPartitionScanner constructor
   */
  public PerlPartitionScanner() {
    super();

    // Create the token for comment partitions
    IToken comment = new Token(COMMENT);

    // Set the rule--anything from # to the end of the line is a comment
    setPredicateRules(new IPredicateRule[] { new EndOfLineRule("#", comment)});
  }
}
```

The CommentScanner class turns all text in any "comment" partition green (see Listing 18-5). It doesn't need any rules to do this; it just creates a token for green text, and returns it as the default.

Listing 18-5. `CommentScanner.java`

```
package examples.ch18.perledit.source;

import org.eclipse.jface.text.TextAttribute;
import org.eclipse.jface.text.rules.*;

import examples.ch18.perledit.PerlEditor;

/**
 * This class scans comment partitions
 */
public class CommentScanner extends RuleBasedScanner {
  /**
   * CommentScanner constructor
   */
  public CommentScanner() {
    // Get the color manager
    ColorManager colorManager = PerlEditor.getApp().getColorManager();

    // Create the tokens
    IToken other = new Token(new TextAttribute(colorManager
        .getColor(ColorManager.COMMENT)));

    // Use "other" for default
    setDefaultReturnToken(other);

    // This scanner has an easy job--we need no rules. Anything in a comment
    // partition should be scanned as a comment.
  }
}
```

The `PerlCodeScanner` class works a little harder, though not much (see Listing 18-6). It adds rules for strings, for white space, and for keywords. For the keywords, it creates a `WordRule` instance, and calls its `addWord()` method repeatedly, passing each Perl keyword in turn.

Listing 18-6. `PerlCodeScanner.java`

```
package examples.ch18.perledit.source;

import java.util.*;

import org.eclipse.jface.text.TextAttribute;
import org.eclipse.jface.text.rules.*;
import org.eclipse.swt.SWT;

import examples.ch18.perledit.PerlEditor;
```

```
/**
 * This class scans through a code partition and colors it.
 */
public class PerlCodeScanner extends RuleBasedScanner {
  /**
   * PerlCodeScanner constructor
   */
  public PerlCodeScanner() {
    // Get the color manager
    ColorManager cm = PerlEditor.getApp().getColorManager();

    // Create the tokens for keywords, strings, and other (everything else)
    IToken keyword = new Token(
      new TextAttribute(cm.getColor(ColorManager.KEYWORD),
      cm.getColor(ColorManager.BACKGROUND), SWT.BOLD));
    IToken other = new Token(
      new TextAttribute(cm.getColor(ColorManager.DEFAULT)));
    IToken string = new Token(
      new TextAttribute(cm.getColor(ColorManager.STRING)));

    // Use "other" for default
    setDefaultReturnToken(other);

    // Create the rules
    List rules = new ArrayList();

    // Add rules for strings
    rules.add(new SingleLineRule("\"", "\"", string, '\\'));
    rules.add(new SingleLineRule("'", "'", string, '\\'));

    // Add rule for whitespace
    rules.add(new WhitespaceRule(new IWhitespaceDetector() {
      public boolean isWhitespace(char c) {
        return Character.isWhitespace(c);
      }
    }));

    // Add rule for keywords, and add the words to the rule
    WordRule wordRule = new WordRule(new PerlWordDetector(), other);
    for (int i = 0, n = PerlSyntax.KEYWORDS.length; i < n; i++)
      wordRule.addWord(PerlSyntax.KEYWORDS[i], keyword);
    rules.add(wordRule);

    IRule[] result = new IRule[rules.size()];
    rules.toArray(result);
    setRules(result);
  }
}
```

The PerlEditorSourceViewerConfiguration class in Listing 18-7 sets up the syntax coloring.

Listing 18-7. PerlEditorSourceViewerConfiguration.java

```java
package examples.ch18.perledit.source;

import org.eclipse.jface.text.IDocument;
import org.eclipse.jface.text.presentation.*;
import org.eclipse.jface.text.rules.*;
import org.eclipse.jface.text.source.ISourceViewer;
import org.eclipse.jface.text.source.SourceViewerConfiguration;

import examples.ch18.perledit.PerlEditor;

/**
 * This class provides the source viewer configuration
 */
public class PerlEditorSourceViewerConfiguration extends
    SourceViewerConfiguration {
  /**
   * Gets the presentation reconciler. This will color the code.
   */
  public IPresentationReconciler getPresentationReconciler(
      ISourceViewer sourceViewer) {
    // Create the presentation reconciler
    PresentationReconciler reconciler = new PresentationReconciler();
    reconciler.setDocumentPartitioning(
      getConfiguredDocumentPartitioning(sourceViewer));

    // Create the damager/repairer for comment partitions
    DefaultDamagerRepairer dr = new DefaultDamagerRepairer(new CommentScanner());
    reconciler.setDamager(dr, PerlPartitionScanner.COMMENT);
    reconciler.setRepairer(dr, PerlPartitionScanner.COMMENT);

    // Create the damager/repairer for default
    dr = new DefaultDamagerRepairer(PerlEditor.getApp().getCodeScanner());
    reconciler.setDamager(dr, IDocument.DEFAULT_CONTENT_TYPE);
    reconciler.setRepairer(dr, IDocument.DEFAULT_CONTENT_TYPE);

    return reconciler;
  }

  /**
   * Gets the configured document partitioning
   *
   * @return String
   */
  public String getConfiguredDocumentPartitioning(ISourceViewer sourceViewer) {
    return PerlEditor.PERL_PARTITIONING;
  }
}
```

```
/**
 * Gets the configured partition types
 *
 * @return String[]
 */
public String[] getConfiguredContentTypes(ISourceViewer sourceViewer) {
    return new String[] { IDocument.DEFAULT_CONTENT_TYPE,
        PerlPartitionScanner.COMMENT};
}
}
```

PerlEditor uses the find/replace dialog created in this chapter to do the finding
and replacing, as well as the SafeSaveDialog class to confirm overwriting existing files.
Figure 18-5 shows the PerlEditor with some Perl source code.

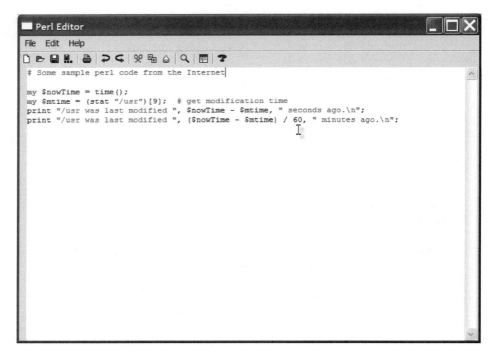

Figure 18-5. The PerlEditor

Summary

Though this chapter creates a fully featured text editor for creating and editing Perl files,
it only scratches the surface of JFace's text editing capabilities. Because text editing forms
the core of Eclipse, JFace's text editing capabilities not only outpace other parts of the library, both in breadth and depth, but also grow the fastest. With each new Eclipse release,
it seems, more text editing capabilities appear. Stay abreast of the Javadoc documentation for the latest developments in JFace text editing.

CHAPTER 19

Miscellaneous
Helper Classes

ANY CLASS LIBRARY contains a motley assemblage of unheralded classes and interfaces that don't submit readily to categorization. After careful consideration, class library designers gather up these recalcitrant classes and sweep them into one or more "utility" packages. Just as a utility tool belt carries a menagerie of tools that fulfill disparate purposes, a utility package holds an array of classes you can use to fill in the gaps left behind by the rest of the library. This chapter examines the utility packages that JFace offers.

Using ModalContext for Modal Operations

The Librarian example program in Chapter 16 uses ModalContext when saving or loading files. When you have long-running operations, you should run them in separate threads, as Librarian does with its disk access, so you don't tie up the UI. Running long operations inside the UI thread starves your program's ability to paint itself, confusing and even disgusting users.

You use ModalContext, found in the org.eclipse.jface.operation package, to run operations in separate threads. You can instantiate a ModalContext, but all its usable interface is static. Table 19-1 lists ModalContext's methods.

Table 19-1. ModalContext *Methods*

Method	Description
static boolean canProgressMonitorBeUsed (IProgressMonitor monitor1, IProgressMonitor monitor2)	Returns true if monitor1 and monitor2 refer to the same monitor. Also returns true if monitor1 wraps monitor2. Otherwise, returns false.
static void checkCanceled (IProgressMonitor monitor)	If the specified monitor has been cancelled, throws an InterruptedException.
static int getModalLevel()	Returns an int representing the nested modal level.
static boolean isModalContextThread (Thread thread)	Returns true if the specified thread is a ModalContextThread instance.
static void run(IRunnableWithProgress operation, boolean fork, IProgressMonitor monitor, Display display)	Runs the specified operation. If fork is true, runs the operation in a new thread. Otherwise, runs the operation in the same thread. Uses the specified monitor to display progress and accept cancellation requests. Uses the specified display to read and dispatch events.
static void setDebugMode(boolean debugMode)	If debugMode is true, turns on debugging messages. Otherwise, turns off debugging messages. When debugging is turned on, exceptions thrown when running operations are logged to stderr.

For example, to launch a long-running operation with a progress monitor in a separate thread, use code such as this:

```
class MyRunnable implements IRunnableWithProgress {
  public void run(IProgressMonitor monitor) {
    progressMonitor.beginTask("Performing operation", 100);
    for (int i = 0; i < 100; i++) {
      doSomething(i);
      progressMonitor.worked(1);
    }
    progressMonitor.done();
  }
}

. . .

try {
  ModalContext.run(new MyRunnable(), true, myProgressMonitor, display);
} catch (InterruptedException e) {
  // Do something
} catch (InvocationTargetException e) {
  // Do something
}
```

Creating Images Using ImageDescriptor

Image descriptors, used in actions, wizard pages, and anywhere else you need an image, possess the ability to create images. Think of them as image factories, churning out images on demand. They don't require a Display object to create images, either, making them indispensable for those situations in which you have no Display.

ImageDescriptor is an abstract class, housed in org.eclipse.jface.resource, that hides three concrete implementations: FileImageDescriptor, URLImageDescriptor, and MissingImageDescriptor. You can create your own ImageDescriptor implementation by subclassing ImageDescriptor and defining a getImageData() method. Usually, though, you'll use two of ImageDescriptor's static methods, createFromFile() and createFromURL(), to create ImageDescriptor instances that you pass to methods requiring them.

Reading from a File

To read an image from a file into an ImageDescriptor, use createFromFile(), which has the following signature:

```
static ImageDescriptor createFromFile(Class location, String filename)
```

If location is non-null, filename must represent an absolute path to the desired file. Otherwise, the implementation uses Class.getResourceAsStream() and its attendant rules to load the image. For example, if you have a class file called foo.Bar.class, and your image file lives in a directory called graphics that's a peer to the foo directory, you'll use this code:

```
ImageDescriptor id = ImageDescriptor.createFromFile(foo.Bar.class,
  "/graphics/myimage.png");
```

createFromFile() returns a FileImageDescriptor instance, which you treat as an ImageDescriptor instance because FileImageDescriptor isn't visible.

Loading from a URL

To load an image from a URL into an ImageDescriptor, use createFromURL(), which has this signature:

```
static ImageDescriptor createFromURL(URL url)
```

For example, to load an image from the Web, use code such as this:

```
ImageDescriptor id = null;
try {
  URL url = new URL("http://www.mydomain.com/myimage.png");
  id = ImageDescriptor.createFromURL(url);
} catch (MalformedURLException e) {
  // Do something
}
```

createFromURL() returns a URLImageDescriptor instance, which you treat as an ImageDescriptor because URLImageDescriptor isn't visible.

Using Resource Utilities

A GUI program often uses several graphical items, including fonts, images, and colors. The org.eclipse.jface.resource package contains classes that help you work with those items. Based on the concept of "registries," these classes store the graphical items by name, allowing you to retrieve them by name and use them in your applications.

Retrieving from JFaceResources

The JFaceResources class allows you to retrieve JFace-specific resources by name. Many of these resources are Eclipse specific; for example, the font Eclipse uses for banners. JFaceResources also stores the following registries:

- The color registry

- The font registry

- The image registry

- A resource bundle

You don't instantiate JFaceResources. Instead, you use its static methods, listed in Table 19-2.

Table 19-2. `JFaceResources` *Methods*

Method	Description
`static String format(String key, Object[] args)`	Returns the formatted string for the specified key from the resource bundle. Uses `java.text.MessageFormat` to do the formatting.
`static Font getBannerFont()`	Returns the font used for banners in Eclipse.
`static ResourceBundle getBundle()`	Returns the resource bundle.
`static ColorRegistry getColorRegistry()`	Returns the color registry.
`static Font getDefaultFont()`	Returns the default font.
`static Font getDialogFont()`	Returns the font used in dialogs.
`static Font getFont(String symbolicName)`	Returns the font that corresponds to the symbolic name. See Table 19-3 for the supported symbolic names.
`static FontRegistry getFontRegistry()`	Returns the font registry.
`static Font getHeaderFont()`	Returns the font used for headers in Eclipse.
`static Image getImage(String key)`	Returns the image from the image registry for the specified key.
`static ImageRegistry getImageRegistry()`	Returns the image registry.
`static String getString(String key)`	Returns the string from the resource bundle for the specified key.
`static String[] getStrings(String[] keys)`	Convenience method that returns the strings from the resource bundle for the specified keys.
`static Font getTextFont()`	Returns the text font.
`static void setFontRegistry(FontRegistry registry)`	Sets the font registry to the specified registry.

`JFaceResources` contains several static fields that correspond to symbolic names for fonts. You use these fields with the `getFont()` method to specify which font you want. Table 19-3 lists the fields.

Table 19-3. `JFaceResources` *Fields*

Field	Description
`static String BANNER_FONT`	Symbolic name for the banner font
`static String DEFAULT_FONT`	Symbolic name for the default font
`static String DIALOG_FONT`	Symbolic name for the dialog font
`static String HEADER_FONT`	Symbolic name for the header font
`static String TEXT_FONT`	Symbolic name for the text font

Painting with ColorRegistry

The ColorRegistry class maps names to colors. You fill the map with RGB values corresponding to names, and the color registry creates colors from the RGB values as requested. Because the color registry creates the colors, it, not you, carries the responsibility to dispose them. You put colors in and take them out with impunity.

To retrieve JFace's ColorRegistry from within your application, call JFaceResource.getColorRegistry(). You can also construct your own color registry using one of the following constructors:

- ColorRegistry()

- ColorRegistry(Display display)

The first constructor listed uses the current display. Table 19-4 lists ColorRegistry's methods.

Table 19-4. ColorRegistry *Methods*

Method	Description
void addListener(IPropertyChange Listener listener)	Adds a listener that's notified if any colors are added or changed.
Color get(String symbolicName)	Returns the color for the specified symbolic name.
RGB getRGB(String symbolicName)	Returns the RGB data for the specified symbolic name.
boolean hasValueFor(String colorKey)	Returns true if the color registry has a value for the specified key. Otherwise, returns false.
void put(String symbolicName, RGB colorData)	Stores the color data under the specified symbolic name for later retrieval.
void removeListener(IPropertyChange Listener listener)	Removes the specified listener from the notification list.

The following example code stores a color for the symbolic name "foo." Later, it attempts to retrieve that color to set on a control:

```
ColorRegistry colorRegistry = JFaceResources.getColorRegistry();
colorRegistry.put("foo", new RGB(255, 0, 0));

// Do some other stuff

Label label = new Label(composite, SWT.CENTER);
if (colorRegistry.hasValueFor("foo")) {
  label.setBackground(colorRegistry.get("foo"));
}
```

Writing with FontRegistry

The FontRegistry class performs for fonts what ColorRegistry performs for colors: it maps fonts to names, creates fonts, manages fonts, and disposes fonts. You can use JFace's font registry by calling JFaceResources.getFontRegistry(), or you can create one yourself. Table 19-5 lists FontRegistry's constructors.

Table 19-5. FontRegistry *Constructors*

Constructor	Description
FontRegistry()	Creates a font registry using the current display.
FontRegistry(Display display)	Creates a font registry using the specified display.
FontRegistry(String location)	Creates a font registry from the resource bundle specified by location.
FontRegistry(String location, ClassLoader loader)	Creates a font registry from the resource bundle specified by location. Currently, the specified class loader is ignored.

FontRegistry's methods mirror those offered by ColorRegistry, as Table 19-6 shows.

Table 19-6. FontRegistry *Methods*

Method	Description
void addListener(IPropertyChange Listener listener)	Adds a listener that's notified if any fonts are added or changed.
FontData[] bestDataArray(FontData[] fonts, Display)	Returns the first valid FontData in the array specified by fonts.
Font get(String symbolicName)	Returns the font for the specified symbolic name.
FontData[] getFontData(String symbolicName)	Returns the font data for the specified symbolic name.
boolean hasValueFor(String fontKey)	Returns true if the font registry has a value for the specified key. Otherwise, returns false.
void put(String symbolicName, FontData[] fontData)	Stores the font data under the specified symbolic name for later retrieval.
void removeListener(IPropertyChange Listener listener)	Removes the specified listener from the notification list.

The RegistryTest program demonstrates both ColorRegistry and FontRegistry. It displays a greeting and a button. Clicking the button puts random values for the background and foreground colors into the color registry, and a font with a random height in the font registry. Changing the values in those registries fires a property change notification. Because the RegistryTest class listens for those notifications, it sets the new values from the registry into the greeting (see Listing 19-1).

Listing 19-1. `RegistryTest.java`

```java
package examples.ch19;

import org.eclipse.jface.resource.*;
import org.eclipse.jface.util.*;
import org.eclipse.jface.window.ApplicationWindow;
import org.eclipse.swt.SWT;
import org.eclipse.swt.events.*;
import org.eclipse.swt.graphics.*;
import org.eclipse.swt.layout.*;
import org.eclipse.swt.widgets.*;

/**
 * This class tests the various JFace registries
 */
public class RegistryTest extends ApplicationWindow implements
    IPropertyChangeListener {
  // Keys for the registries
  private static final String FOREGROUND = "foreground";
  private static final String BACKGROUND = "background";
  private static final String FONT = "font";

  // The label to display the colors and fonts
  private Label label;

  // The color registry
  private static ColorRegistry CR;

  // The font registry
  private static FontRegistry FR;

  /**
   * RegistryTest constructor
   */
  public RegistryTest() {
    super(null);
  }

  /**
   * Runs the application
   */
  public void run() {
    setBlockOnOpen(true);
    open();
    Display.getCurrent().dispose();
  }
```

```java
/**
 * Creates the window's contents
 *
 * @param parent the parent composite
 * @return Control
 */
protected Control createContents(Composite parent) {
  Composite composite = new Composite(parent, SWT.NONE);
  composite.setLayout(new FillLayout(SWT.VERTICAL));

  // Set up the registries
  CR = new ColorRegistry();
  CR.addListener(this);

  FR = new FontRegistry();
  FR.addListener(this);

  // Create the label
  label = new Label(composite, SWT.CENTER);
  label.setText("Hello from JFace");

  // Create the randomize button
  Button button = new Button(composite, SWT.PUSH);
  button.setText("Randomize");
  button.addSelectionListener(new SelectionAdapter() {
    public void widgetSelected(SelectionEvent event) {
      CR.put(FOREGROUND, new RGB((int) (Math.random() * 255), (int) (Math
          .random() * 255), (int) (Math.random() * 255)));
      CR.put(BACKGROUND, new RGB((int) (Math.random() * 255), (int) (Math
          .random() * 255), (int) (Math.random() * 255)));
      FontData fontData = new FontData("Times New Roman",
          (int) (Math.random() * 72), SWT.BOLD);
      FR.put(FONT, new FontData[] { fontData});
    }
  });
  return composite;
}

/**
 * Called when any property changes
 *
 * @param event the event
 */
public void propertyChange(PropertyChangeEvent event) {
  // Properties have changed; set into label
  if (CR.hasValueFor(FOREGROUND)) label.setForeground(CR.get(FOREGROUND));
  if (CR.hasValueFor(BACKGROUND)) label.setBackground(CR.get(BACKGROUND));
  if (FR.hasValueFor(FONT)) label.setFont(FR.get(FONT));

  getShell().pack();
}
```

```
/**
 * The application entry point
 *
 * @param args the command line arguments
 */
public static void main(String[] args) {
    new RegistryTest().run();
}
}
```

Figure 19-1 shows the main window with some random color and font combinations.

Figure 19-1. Using color and font registries

Drawing with `ImageRegistry`

What `ImageRegistry` does for images approximates what `ColorRegistry` and `FontRegistry` do for colors and fonts, respectively. `ImageRegistry` manages images, associating them with names, creating them on demand, and disposing them when the associated display is disposed. However, it deviates slightly but significantly in how it reacts to duplicate keys. Both `ColorRegistry` and `FontRegistry` happily accept duplicate keys, replacing the previous color or font associated with that key. `ImageRegistry` accepts duplicate keys for entries for which the image descriptor has been specified, but the associated image hasn't yet been created. However, once `ImageRegistry` has created the image, it throws an `IllegalArgumentException` if you try to add a duplicate key.

You can use JFace's `ImageRegistry` by calling `JFaceResources.getImageRegistry()`, or you can create your own `ImageRegistry` using one of its constructors:

- `ImageRegistry()`

- `ImageRegistry(Display display)`

The empty constructor ties the image registry to the current display, while the second constructor ties it to the specified display. You can add either Image objects or

ImageDescriptor objects to an image registry. However, whatever you add to the registry becomes the registry's property. The registry disposes the image, even if you created it. You must not dispose it. Table 19-7 lists ImageRegistry's methods.

Table 19-7. ImageRegistry *Methods*

Method	Description
Image get(String key)	Returns the image for the specified key
ImageDescriptor getDescriptor(String key)	Returns the image descriptor for the specified key
void put(String key, Image image)	Stores the specified image under the specified key for later retrieval
void put(String key, ImageDescriptor)	Stores the specified image descriptor under the specified key for later retrieval

The ImageRegistryTest program creates an image registry and adds three images to it (see Listing 19-2). Its main window displays the three images, extracting them from the image registry.

Listing 19-2. ImageRegistryTest.java

```
package examples.ch19;

import org.eclipse.jface.resource.*;
import org.eclipse.jface.window.ApplicationWindow;
import org.eclipse.swt.SWT;
import org.eclipse.swt.layout.*;
import org.eclipse.swt.widgets.*;

/**
 * This class tests ImageRegistry
 */
public class ImageRegistryTest extends ApplicationWindow {
  // Keys for the registry
  private static final String ONE = "one";
  private static final String TWO = "two";
  private static final String THREE = "three";

  /**
   * ImageRegistryTest constructor
   */
  public ImageRegistryTest() {
    super(null);
  }

  /**
   * Runs the application
   */
```

```java
  public void run() {
    setBlockOnOpen(true);
    open();
    Display.getCurrent().dispose();
  }

  /**
   * Creates the window's contents
   *
   * @param parent the parent composite
   * @return Control
   */
  protected Control createContents(Composite parent) {
    Composite composite = new Composite(parent, SWT.NONE);
    composite.setLayout(new FillLayout());

    // Put the images in the registry
    ImageRegistry ir = new ImageRegistry();
    ir.put(ONE, ImageDescriptor.createFromFile(ImageRegistryTest.class,
        "/images/one.gif"));
    ir.put(TWO, ImageDescriptor.createFromFile(ImageRegistryTest.class,
        "/images/two.gif"));
    ir.put(THREE, ImageDescriptor.createFromFile(ImageRegistryTest.class,
        "/images/three.gif"));

    // Create the labels and add the images
    Label label = new Label(composite, SWT.NONE);
    label.setImage(ir.get(ONE));
    label = new Label(composite, SWT.NONE);
    label.setImage(ir.get(TWO));
    label = new Label(composite, SWT.NONE);
    label.setImage(ir.get(THREE));

    getShell().pack();

    return composite;
  }

  /**
   * The application entry point
   *
   * @param args the command line arguments
   */
  public static void main(String[] args) {
    new ImageRegistryTest().run();
  }
}
```

Figure 19-2 shows the program's main window. You can download the images or create your own.

Figure 19-2. Displaying images from an image registry

Accessing the Palette of JFaceColors

JFace uses certain colors to display various elements in the Eclipse interface, and the JFaceColors class stores the colors for easy access. JFaceColors exposes a number of static methods to retrieve the colors, listed in Table 19-8.

Table 19-8. JFaceColors Methods

Method	Description
static void clearColor(String colorName)	Removes the color for the specified color name from the cache.
static void disposeColors()	Disposes all the cached colors.
static Color getActiveHyperlinkText (Display display)	Returns the color used for active hyperlinks.
static Color getBannerBackground(Display display)	Returns the color used for banner backgrounds.
static Color getBannerForeground(Display display)	Returns the color used for banner foregrounds.
static Color getErrorBackground(Display display)	Returns the color used for error backgrounds.
static Color getErrorBorder(Display display)	Returns the color used for error borders.
static Color getErrorText(Display display)	Returns the color used for error text.
static Color getHyperlinkText(Display display)	Returns the color used for hyperlinks.
static void setColors(Control control, Color foreground, Color background)	Convenience method that sets the foreground and background colors for the specified control. Doesn't cache the specified colors.

Converting Values Using StringConverter

GUIs often require that you display primitive or other data types in human-readable form. The StringConverter class can help you with that. It offers static methods to convert values to strings, and vice versa. It contains support for the following value types:

- boolean

- double

- float

- int

- long

- FontData

- Point

- Rectangle

- RGB

Most of the methods have a counterpart that takes a default value that's returned if StringConverter has any problems converting the specified value. Table 19-9 lists StringConverter's methods.

Table 19-9. StringConverter *Methods*

Method	Description
static String[] asArray(String value)	Returns the words in the specified string, one word per array member. Uses a space delimiter to identify words.
static String[] asArray(String value, String[] dflt)	Returns the words in the specified string, one word per array member. Uses a space delimiter to identify words. If any data format problems occur, returns the default string array specified by dflt.
static boolean asBoolean(String value)	Returns true if the specified value is "t" or "true" (case insensitive). Returns false if the specified value is "f" or "false" (case insensitive). Otherwise, throws a DataFormatException.
static boolean asBoolean(String value, boolean dflt)	Returns true if the specified value is "t" or "true" (case insensitive). Returns false if the specified value is "f" or "false" (case insensitive). Otherwise, returns the value specified by dflt.
static double asDouble(String value)	Returns the double represented by the specified value. Throws a DataFormatException if the specified value doesn't represent a double.
static double asDouble(String value, double dflt)	Returns the double represented by the specified value. If the specified value doesn't represent a double, returns the value specified by dflt.
static float asFloat(String value)	Returns the float represented by the specified value. Throws a DataFormatException if the specified value doesn't represent a float.
static float asFloat(String value, float dflt)	Returns the float represented by the specified value. If the specified value doesn't represent a float, returns the value specified by dflt.

Table 19-9. `StringConverter` *Methods (continued)*

Method	Description
`static FontData asFontData(String value)`	Returns the `FontData` represented by the specified value. Throws a `DataFormatException` if the specified value doesn't represent a `FontData`.
`static FontData asFontData(String value, FontData dflt)`	Returns the `FontData` represented by the specified value. If the specified value doesn't represent a `FontData`, returns the value specified by `dflt`.
`static int asInt(String value)`	Returns the `int` represented by the specified value. Throws a `DataFormatException` if the specified value doesn't represent an `int`.
`static int asInt(String value, int dflt)`	Returns the `int` represented by the specified value. If the specified value doesn't represent an `int`, returns the value specified by `dflt`.
`static long asLong(String value)`	Returns the `long` represented by the specified value. Throws a `DataFormatException` if the specified value doesn't represent a `long`.
`static long asLong(String value, long dflt)`	Returns the `long` represented by the specified value. If the specified value doesn't represent a `long`, returns the value specified by `dflt`.
`static Point asPoint(String value)`	Returns the `Point` represented by the specified value. Throws a `DataFormatException` if the specified value doesn't represent a `Point`.
`static Point asPoint(String value, Point dflt)`	Returns the `Point` represented by the specified value. If the specified value doesn't represent a `Point`, returns the value specified by `dflt`.
`static Rectangle asRectangle(String value)`	Returns the `Rectangle` represented by the specified value. Throws a `DataFormatException` if the specified value doesn't represent a `Rectangle`.
`static Rectangle asRectangle(String value, Rectangle dflt)`	Returns the `Rectangle` represented by the specified value. If the specified value doesn't represent a `Rectangle`, returns the value specified by `dflt`.
`static RGB asRGB(String value)`	Returns the `RGB` represented by the specified value. Throws a `DataFormatException` if the specified value doesn't represent an `RGB`.
`static RGB asRGB(String value, RGB dflt)`	Returns the `RGB` represented by the specified value. If the specified value doesn't represent an `RGB`, returns the value specified by `dflt`.
`static String asString(boolean value)`	Returns the string representation of the specified value.
`static String asString(Boolean value)`	Returns the string representation of the specified value.
`static String asString(double value)`	Returns the string representation of the specified value.
`static String asString(Double value)`	Returns the string representation of the specified value.
`static String asString(float value)`	Returns the string representation of the specified value.
`static String asString(Float value)`	Returns the string representation of the specified value.
`static String asString(FontData value)`	Returns the string representation of the specified value.
`static String asString(int value)`	Returns the string representation of the specified value.
`static String asString(Integer value)`	Returns the string representation of the specified value.

Table 19-9. StringConverter *Methods (continued)*

Method	Description
static String asString(long value)	Returns the string representation of the specified value.
static String asString(Long value)	Returns the string representation of the specified value.
static String asString(Point value)	Returns the string representation of the specified value.
static String asString(Rectangle value)	Returns the string representation of the specified value.
static String asString(RGB value)	Returns the string representation of the specified value.
static String removeWhiteSpaces(String value)	Returns the string specified by value with all its white space removed. Any characters whose codes are less than or equal to the code for a space character (\u0020) are considered white space.

Converting strings to objects requires agreed-upon formats for the strings. Table 19-10 lists the expected formats for the different objects that StringConverter can create from strings.

Table 19-10. String Formats for Objects

Object	String Format
FontData	"fontname-style-height" where fontname is the name of a font, style is the style (regular, bold, italic, or bold italic), and height is an int
Point	"x,y" where x and y are ints
Rectangle	"x,y,width,height" where x, y, width, and height are ints
RGB	"red,green,blue" where red, green, and blue are ints

Using Other Utilities

The org.eclipse.jface.util package represents the final amalgam of utility classes. Searching for a common thread among these classes yields nothing. This package ranks as perhaps the ultimate hodgepodge of classes you'll find in JFace.

Asserting with Assert

When the Eclipse team began their quest to develop the ultimate IDE, Java had no assert mechanism. Since that time, however, Java added the assert keyword, rendering JFace's Assert class obsolete. You should use Java's assert and ignore this class.

Getting the Goods from Geometry

The Geometry class collects a bunch of static methods for working with SWT's geometric figures. Table 19-11 lists Geometry's methods.

Table 19-11. Geometry *Methods*

Method	Description
static Point add(Point point1, Point point2)	Returns the sum of the two specified points, added as two-dimensional vectors.
static Point centerPoint(Rectangle rect)	Returns the point at the center of the specified rectangle.
static Point copy(Point toCopy)	Returns a copy of the specified point.
static Rectangle copy(Rectangle toCopy)	Returns a copy of the specified rectangle.
static Rectangle createRectangle(Point position, Point size)	Returns a rectangle with the specified position and size.
static int distanceSquared(Point p1, Point p2)	Returns the square of the distance, in pixels, between the two specified points.
static int dotProduct(Point p1, Point p2)	Returns the dot product of the specified vectors (passed as Point objects).
static int getClosestSide(Rectangle boundary, Point toTest)	Returns the side of the specified rectangle that's closest to the specified point. The return value is one of SWT.LEFT, SWT.RIGHT, SWT.TOP, or SWT.BOTTOM, for left, right, top, or bottom, respectively.
static int getDimension(Rectangle rect, boolean width)	If width is true, returns the width in pixels of the specified rectangle. Otherwise, returns its height in pixels.
static Point getDirectionVector(int distance, int direction)	Returns a vector, represented as a point, with the specified distance in pixels and in the specified direction. direction should be one of SWT.TOP, SWT.BOTTOM, SWT.LEFT, or SWT.RIGHT.
static int getDistanceFromEdge(Rectangle rectangle, Point point, int edge)	Returns the distance in pixels of the specified point from the specified edge of the specified rectangle. edge should be one of SWT.TOP, SWT.BOTTOM, SWT.LEFT, or SWT.RIGHT.
static Rectangle getExtrudedEdge (Rectangle rectangle, int size, int orientation)	Returns a rectangular slice of the specified rectangle. This slice is taken from the side specified by orientation, which should be one of SWT.TOP, SWT.BOTTOM, SWT.LEFT, or SWT.RIGHT. The returned rectangle has the height or width, depending on the specified orientation, specified by size.
static Point getLocation(Rectangle toQuery)	Returns the position of the specified rectangle.
static int getOppositeSide(int swtDirectionConstant)	Returns the opposite side constant from the side constant specified by swtDirectionConstant. swtDirectionConstant should be one of SWT.TOP, SWT.BOTTOM, SWT.LEFT, or SWT.RIGHT. If SWT.TOP is specified, returns SWT.BOTTOM, and vice versa. If SWT.LEFT is specified, returns SWT.RIGHT, and vice versa.
static int getRelativePosition(Rectangle boundary, Point toTest)	Returns the relative position of the specified point to the specified rectangle. Imagine that the specified rectangle represents the center square in a standard tic-tac-toe board that extends infinitely in all directions. If the point lies in the upper-left square, this method returns SWT.LEFT | SWT.TOP. If in the top center square, it returns SWT.TOP, and so forth. If the point lies within the rectangle, this method returns zero.

Table 19-11. Geometry *Methods (continued)*

Method	Description
static Point getSize(Rectangle rectangle)	Returns the size of the specified rectangle as a point.
static int getSwtHorizontalOrVertical Constant(boolean horizontal)	If horizontal is true, returns SWT.HORIZONTAL. Otherwise, returns SWT.VERTICAL.
static boolean isHorizontal(int swtSideConstant)	Returns true if swtSideConstant is SWT.TOP or SWT.BOTTOM. Otherwise, returns false.
static double magnitude(Point point)	Returns the magnitude of the specified vector (passed as a Point).
static int magnitudeSquared(Point point)	Returns the square of the magnitude of the specified vector (passed as a Point).
static Point max(Point p1, Point p2)	Returns a point whose x coordinate is the maximum x coordinate of the two specified points, and whose y coordinate is the maximum y coordinate of the two specified points.
static Point min(Point p1, Point p2)	Returns a point whose x coordinate is the minimum x coordinate of the two specified points, and whose y coordinate is the minimum y coordinate of the two specified points.
static void moveRectangle(Rectangle rectangle, Point point)	Moves the specified rectangle the distance along the x and y axes specified by point.
static void normalize(Rectangle rectangle)	Normalizes the specified rectangle by converting any negative dimensions to positive dimensions, retaining the existing upper-left corner of the rectangle.
static void setLocation(Rectangle rectangle, Point newSize)	Moves the specified rectangle to the specified point. (Note: as of version 3.0 M8, this method has a bug—it sets the width, not the location.)
static void setSize(Rectangle rectangle, Point newSize)	Sets the size of the specified rectangle to the specified size.
static Point subtract(Point point1, Point point2)	Returns the difference between the specified points, subtracted as vectors.
static Rectangle toControl(Control coordinateSystem, Rectangle toConvert)	Converts the specified rectangle from display coordinates to coordinates relative to the specified control.
static Rectangle toDisplay(Control coordinateSystem, Rectangle rectangle)	Returns a rectangle that results from converting the specified rectangle from the coordinate system of the specified control to the display coordinate system.

Listing a ListenerList

A ListenerList, as its name implies, holds a list of listeners. It grows as necessary, and doesn't store duplicate listeners. JFace uses this class to store and notify registered listeners. Table 19-12 lists its constructors, and Table 19-13 lists its methods. You can use this class in your implementations any time you need to store listeners.

Table 19-12. `ListenerList` *Constructors*

Constructor	Description
`ListenerList()`	Creates a `ListenerList` with an initial capacity of one
`ListenerList(int capacity)`	Creates a `ListenerList` with the specified initial capacity

Table 19-13. `ListenerList` *Methods*

Method	Description
`void add(Object listener)`	Adds the specified listener to the notification list.
`void clear()`	Removes all listeners from the list.
`Object[] getListeners()`	Returns all the listeners in the list.
`boolean isEmpty()`	Returns `true` if the list is empty. Otherwise, returns `false`.
`void remove(Object listener)`	Removes the specified listener from the list.
`int size()`	Returns the number of listeners in the list.

Detecting Changes Using PropertyChangeEvent

The JFace framework notifies interested parties when internal properties change, so that the external parties can update their displays using the new values. It uses instances of `PropertyChangeEvent` to send these notifications. The registry programs in this chapter use `PropertyChangeEvent` in conjunction with `IPropertyChangeListener` to detect when properties change.

`IPropertyChangeListener` declares one method:

```
void propertyChange(PropertyChangeEvent event)
```

In your `propertyChange` implementations, you can examine the values in `Property-ChangeEvent` using the methods listed in Table 19-14.

Table 19-14. `PropertyChangeEvent` *Methods*

Method	Description
`Object getNewValue()`	Returns the new value for the property
`Object getOldValue()`	Returns the old value for the property
`String getProperty()`	Returns the name of the changed property

A possible `IPropertyChangeListener` implementation might look like this:

```
public class MyPropertyChangeListener implements IPropertyChangeListener {
  public void propertyChange(PropertyChangeEvent event) {
    // If the value for "myProperty" changes, we must update our view
    if ("myProperty".equals(event.getProperty())) {
      // update the view
      updateView();
    }
  }
}
```

Summary

The classes and interfaces described in this chapter carry a load that you'd have to carry yourself if these classes didn't exist. Learn to incorporate the utilities offered by the classes listed in this chapter, and you'll create leaner programs with fewer bugs. The registry classes, in particular, save you from the biggest gripe people have about SWT: the need to dispose what you create. By allowing the registry classes to manage your resources, you return to the garbage-collecting world of vanilla Java.

Creating
Wizards

DURING THE MID-1980s, a friend worked at a submarine sandwich shop. This restaurant offered a bewildering array of choices to construct a sandwich: different breads, cheeses, meats, vegetables, amounts, and temperatures. To assist customers in navigating the complex options, its menu consisted of a series of questions that began something like this:

- Would you like white or wheat bread?

- What kind of meats would you like?

- Would you like American, Swiss, or provolone cheese?

- Would you like your sandwich hot or cold?

- What vegetables would you like?

The questions continued until the customer had given enough information for the restaurant to build the sandwich. Why was this ordering system adopted? Instead of feeling swallowed by the entirety of the menu at once, customers could attack the menu one bite at a time, to arrive at their desired sandwich.

Wizards, the corollary to the sandwich menu in the software world, guide users through a series of questions to perform some action. Appearing inside a popup window, wizards display a sequence of "pages" that pose questions and receive input. Users can navigate forward and backward through the pages, and, in some cases, can finish the wizard before viewing or responding to some of the pages. Pages have an optional title, graphic, and description, reserving a large area for controls that you, as a programmer, define. Buttons marked Back, Next, Finish, and Cancel line the bottom of the window to provide navigation through the pages. Although not appropriate for all situations, the hand-holding help that wizards provide can enable operations that would stump users if presented in a more traditional format.

Launching Wizards

The wizard classes and interfaces, found in org.eclipse.jface.wizard, provide a solid foundation for building and launching wizards. The WizardDialog class found in this package supplies the core of wizardry. Derived from `TitleAreaDialog`, it creates the wizard window that contains the title, description, graphic, control area, and button bar. Figure 20-1 shows a vanilla `WizardDialog` that labels the various parts of the wizard: the title, description, control area, and image. If you don't specify an image, the wizard displays the three horizontal bars of different length shown in Figure 20-1.

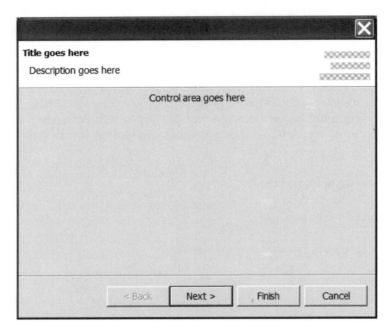

Figure 20-1. A WizardDialog

If you desire a different look or feel for your wizard, you can subclass `WizardDialog` to create your own implementation. Usually, though, you'll use the stock dialog. You construct a `WizardDialog`, passing the parent shell and the wizard (covered in the next section), then call `open()`. The `open()` method returns `IDialogConstants.OK_ID` if the user clicks Finish on the wizard. Otherwise, it returns `IDialogConstants.CANCEL_ID`. The code to create and open a wizard looks like this:

```
WizardDialog dlg = new WizardDialog(shell, myWizard);
int rc = dlg.open();
```

Conjuring Wizards

A JFace wizard relies on a nonvisual interface, `IWizard`, to manage the wizard pages and act as a liaison between the dialog and the pages. You can write your own `IWizard` implementation from scratch, writing definitions for all the `IWizard` methods listed in Table 20-1.

Table 20-1. IWizard *Methods*

Method	Description
void addPages()	Called immediately before the wizard displays. In this method, you should add any pages to your wizard.
boolean canFinish()	In this method, you should return true if the Finish button should be enabled. Otherwise, return false.
void createPageControls(Composite pageContainer)	In this method, you should create the controls for the control areas of all the pages.
void dispose()	In this method, you should dispose any resources you create.
IWizardContainer getContainer()	In this method, you should return this wizard's container.
Image getDefaultPageImage()	In this method, you should return the default image for the pages.
IDialogSettings getDialogSettings()	In this method, you should return the settings for this wizard's dialog.
IWizardPage getNextPage(IWizardPage page)	In this method, you should return the page that succeeds the specified page.
IWizardPage getPage(String pageName)	In this method, you should return the page that corresponds to the specified name.
int getPageCount()	In this method, you should return the number of pages in this wizard.
IWizardPage[] getPages()	In this method, you should return all the pages in this wizard.
IWizardPage getPreviousPage(IWizardPage page)	In this method, you should return the page that precedes the specified page.
IWizardPage getStartingPage()	In this method, you should return the first page in this wizard.
RGB getTitleBarColor()	In this method, you should return an RGB instance that represents the color used for the title bar of this wizard's dialog.
String getWindowTitle()	In this method, you should return the window title for this wizard.
boolean isHelpAvailable()	In this method, you should return true if help is available for this wizard. Otherwise, return false.
boolean needsPreviousAndNextButtons()	In this method, you should return true if this wizard should display Previous and Next buttons in the button bar (that is, if this wizard has more than one page). Otherwise, return false.
boolean needsProgressMonitor()	In this method, you should return true if this wizard should display a progress monitor. Otherwise, return false.
boolean performCancel()	Called when the user clicks Cancel. In this method, you should return true if the dialog should be dismissed. Otherwise, return false.
boolean performFinish()	Called when the user clicks Finish. In this method, you should return true if the dialog should be dismissed. Otherwise, return false.
void setContainer(IWizardContainer container)	In this method, you should store the specified container to use as this wizard's container.

If you think that implementing IWizard looks like a lot of work, you're right. Fortunately, the Eclipse team concurs, and provides an abstract IWizard implementation for you called Wizard that provides usable implementations for every IWizard method but one: performFinish(). To take advantage of the Eclipse team's work, subclass Wizard and provide an implementation for the abstract method performFinish(). Your class might look like this:

```
public class MyWizard extends Wizard {
    public boolean performFinish() {
        // Perform the work this wizard was designed to do
        // Return true to close the wizard
        return true;
    }
}
```

Wizard adds a few new methods not found in the IWizard interface, listed in Table 20-2. Use these methods to add pages, change the parent dialog's window title, or otherwise customize or interact with your wizard.

Table 20-2. Wizard *Methods Not in* IWizard

Method	Description
void addPage(IWizardPage page)	Adds the specified page to this wizard.
Shell getShell()	Returns this wizard's shell.
void setDefaultPageImageDescriptor (ImageDescriptor imageDescriptor)	Sets the default image for each page by using an image descriptor.
void setDialogSettings(IDialogSettings settings)	Sets the dialog settings for this wizard.
void setForcePreviousAndNextButtons (boolean force)	If force is true, forces the Previous and Next buttons to display, even if they normally wouldn't have been displayed. Otherwise, doesn't force the display of Previous and Next.
void setHelpAvailable(boolean helpAvailable)	If helpAvailable is true, sets help available. Otherwise, sets help unavailable.
void setNeedsProgressMonitor(boolean needs)	If needs is true, makes this wizard display a progress monitor while completing the action. Otherwise, doesn't display a progress monitor. Use this with WizardDialog.run() and IRunnableWithProgress. See Chapter 15 for more information.
void setTitleBarColor(RGB color)	Sets the RGB value to use for the title bar color. Although calling this method might seem to change the title bar color, in practice this does nothing. However, perhaps the implementation has not yet been completed.
void setWindowTitle(String newTitle)	Sets the title for the window.

Adding Wizard Pages

A wizard presents a series of pages that users work through sequentially to provide the necessary information for the wizard to perform its task. Each page displays a set of controls to elicit and receive input. The IWizardPage interface represents a page, and contains the methods listed in Table 20-3.

Table 20-3. IWizardPage *Methods*

Method	Description
boolean canFlipToNextPage()	In this method, you should return true if the user can click Next to go to the next page. Otherwise, return false.
String getName()	In this method, you should return a name for the page that's unique across the wizard. The wizard uses the page name as the page's key.
IWizardPage getNextPage()	In this method, you should return the page that the wizard should display when the user clicks Next.
IWizardPage getPreviousPage()	In this method, you should return the page that the wizard should display when the user clicks Back.
IWizard getWizard()	In this method, you should return the wizard that contains this page.
boolean isPageComplete()	In this method, you should return true if the information on this page is complete. Otherwise, return false. The wizard uses the completion status of all its pages to determine whether to enable the Finish button.
void setPreviousPage (IWizardPage page)	In this method, you should set the previous page (the one that displays when the user clicks Back) to the specified page.
void setWizard(IWizard wizard)	In this method, you should set the containing wizard to the specified wizard.

The list of methods seems reasonable enough to entice you to break out your editor and start coding an implementation. However, IWizardPage inherits from IDialogPage, so you must also implement IDialogPage's methods, listed in Table 20-4.

Table 20-4. IDialogPage *Methods*

Method	Description
void createControl(Composite parent)	In this method, you should create the controls for this page as children of a single control whose parent is the specified parent.
void dispose()	In this method, you should dispose any resources you create.
Control getControl()	In this method, you should return the parent control for the controls in this page.
String getDescription()	In this method, you should return the description for this page.

Table 20-4. IDialogPage *Methods (continued)*

Method	Description
String getErrorMessage()	In this method, you should return the error message for this page.
Image getImage()	In this method, you should return the image for this page.
String getMessage()	In this method, you should return the message for this page.
String getTitle()	In this method, you should return the title for this page.
void performHelp()	Called when the user requests help, usually by pressing F1 on the keyboard. In this method, you should display the help for this page. No help infrastructure is provided, so you're on your own for how to display help, whether you launch an HTML page, show a dialog box, or use some other method.
void setDescription(String description)	In this method, you should set the description for this page to the specified description.
void setImageDescriptor(Image Descriptor descriptor)	In this method, you should set the image descriptor for this page to the specified image descriptor.
void setTitle(String title)	In this method, you should set the title for this page to the specified title.
void setVisible(boolean visible)	In this method, you should set this page to visible if visible is true. Otherwise, set this page to hidden.

This much work tempts us to seek help. Again, the Eclipse team comes to the rescue, offering the WizardPage class that implements almost all the necessary methods for a page. You subclass WizardPage and provide, at a minimum, both a public constructor and a createControl() implementation. Your constructor should call one of the two WizardPage constructors, both of which are protected, listed in Table 20-5.

Table 20-5. WizardPage *Constructors*

Constructor	Description
WizardPage(String pageName)	Constructs a wizard page with the specified name
WizardPage(String pageName, String title, ImageDescriptor titleImage)	Constructs a wizard page with the specified name, title, and image

Your createControl() implementation should create the page's controls as children of a parent control. You must then pass that parent control to the page's setControl() method, or your wizard will throw an AssertionFailedException when launched.

CAUTION *You must call* setControl() *in your* createControl() *implementation, passing the parent control, or your wizard won't display.*

For example, your WizardPage class might look like this:

```
public class MyWizardPage extends WizardPage {
  public MyWizardPage() {
    super("My Wizard");
  }

  public void createControl(Composite parent) {
    // Create the parent control
    Composite composite = new Composite(parent, SWT.NONE);
    composite.setLayout(new GridLayout(2, false));

    // Create some controls
    new Label(composite, SWT.LEFT).setText("Field #1:");
    Text field1 = new Text(composite, SWT.BORDER | SWT.SINGLE);
    field1.setLayoutData(new GridData(GridData.FILL_BOTH));

    new Label(composite, SWT.LEFT).setText("Field #2:");
    Text field2 = new Text(composite, SWT.BORDER | SWT.SINGLE);
    field2.setLayoutData(new GridData(GridData.FILL_BOTH));

    // Important!
    setControl(composite);
  }
}
```

You can set an error message, a message, and a description in each page. However, unless you subclass WizardDialog and lay the dialog out differently, only one of the three displays. If an error message has been set for the page, WizardDialog shows it. If not, but a message has been set, the message displays. Finally, if no message has been set, but a description has, the description displays.

A typical page displays a title, description, and image. It also shows an error message if users input bad data. For example, the page in Listing 20-1 displays a page with a title, description, and image. It asks the user to type a string of consonants. If the user types a vowel, an error message displays. Finally, if the user requests help, a help message displays.

Listing 20-1. `ConsonantPage.java`

```java
package examples.ch20;
package examples.ch20;

import org.eclipse.jface.dialogs.MessageDialog;
import org.eclipse.jface.resource.ImageDescriptor;
import org.eclipse.jface.wizard.WizardPage;
import org.eclipse.swt.SWT;
import org.eclipse.swt.events.*;
import org.eclipse.swt.layout.*;
import org.eclipse.swt.widgets.*;

/**
 * This page requests a string of consonants
 */
public class ConsonantPage extends WizardPage {
  /**
   * ConsonantPage constructor
   */
  public ConsonantPage() {
    // Set the name, title, and image
    super("Consonant", "Consonant", ImageDescriptor.createFromFile(
        ConsonantPage.class, "/images/consonant.gif"));

    // Set the description
    setDescription("Enter a string of consonants");
  }

  /**
   * Creates the controls
   *
   * @param parent the parent composite
   */
  public void createControl(Composite parent) {
    Composite composite = new Composite(parent, SWT.NONE);
    composite.setLayout(new GridLayout(2, false));

    // Add the label and entry field
    new Label(composite, SWT.LEFT).setText("Consonants:");
    Text text = new Text(composite, SWT.BORDER);
    text.setLayoutData(new GridData(GridData.FILL_HORIZONTAL));

    // Add a listener to detect when text changes, so we can check for vowels
    text.addModifyListener(new ModifyListener() {
      public void modifyText(ModifyEvent event) {
```

```
        String s = ((Text) event.widget).getText().toUpperCase();
        if (s.length() > 0
              && (s.indexOf('A') != -1 || s.indexOf('E') != -1
              || s.indexOf('I') != -1 || s.indexOf('O') != -1 ||
              s.indexOf('U') != -1)) {
          setErrorMessage("You must enter only consonants");
        } else {
          setErrorMessage(null);
        }
      }
    });

    setControl(composite);
  }

  /**
   * Displays the help
   */
  public void performHelp() {
    MessageDialog.openInformation(getWizard().getContainer().getShell(),
        "Consonant Help", "Enter consonants in the text box");
  }
}
```

Figure 20-2 shows the consonant page. Figure 20-3 shows the same page, but with some vowels entered. Notice the error message that displays.

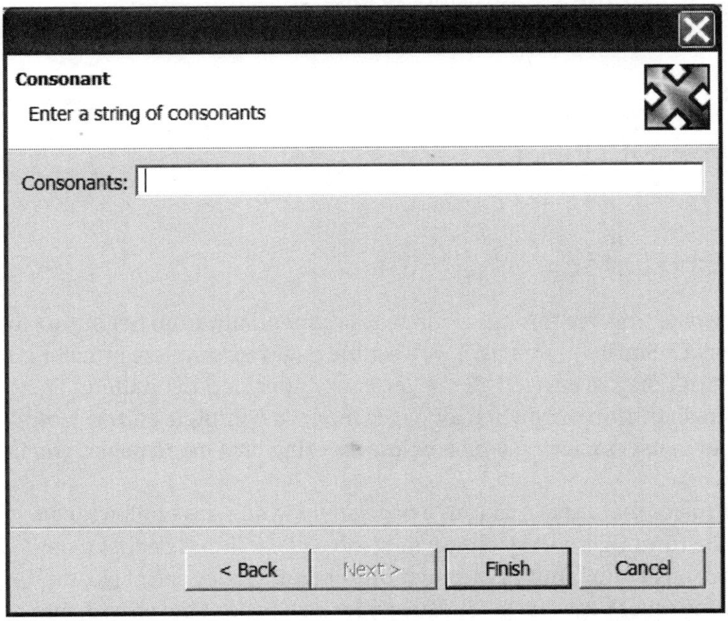

Figure 20-2. The consonant page

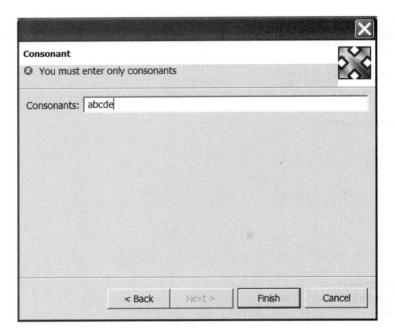

Figure 20-3. The consonant page with an error message

To add the pages to your wizard, call `Wizard.addPage()` in your wizard's constructor. The wizard maintains the pages in the same order you add them. For example, to add two pages to your wizard, use a constructor like this:

```
public MyWizard() {
    super("My Page");
    addPage(new FirstPage());
    addPage(new SecondPage());
}
```

Customizing Navigation

You might require users to traverse through your pages sequentially, from beginning to end, before they can click Finish. In that case, you set the pages incomplete by calling `setComplete(false)` until they've entered all the necessary information on them. The wizard enables its Finish button only when all pages report a complete status. However, if you can swallow a user's clicking Finish before entering data on all pages, you'll have to do no extra work.

In some cases, choices that users make on a page affect which page follows. For example, you might be running a survey concerning job satisfaction. The first page might ask if users have any complaints about their present job. If they select No, the wizard might bypass any other page and go directly to the final page of the wizard, one that thanks the user for participating in the survey. To change the page that displays next, override the getNextPage() method from IWizardPage. Your implementation might look like this:

```
public IWizardPage getNextPage() {
  if (hasComplaints) {
    // Go to the normal next page
    return super.getNextPage();
  }
  // No complaints? Get out!
  return getWizard.getPage("Thanks");
}
```

The Survey program uses this technique to skip the survey if the user has no complaints. Its first page asks if the user has any complaints. If so, it shows the second page, which gathers more information. Typical to many surveys, however, it jettisons any information the user types. If the user has no complaints, it skips to the final page.

The Survey program also demonstrates how to use a wizard as the main window of your program (see Listing 20-2). It creates a Shell instance to parent the wizard dialog, but never opens the shell.

Listing 20-2. Survey.java

```
package examples.ch20;

import org.eclipse.jface.wizard.WizardDialog;
import org.eclipse.swt.widgets.*;

/**
 * This class displays a survey using a wizard
 */
public class Survey {
  /**
   * Runs the application
   */
  public void run() {
    Display display = new Display();

    // Create the parent shell for the dialog, but don't show it
    Shell shell = new Shell(display);

    // Create the dialog
    WizardDialog dlg = new WizardDialog(shell, new SurveyWizard());
    dlg.open();

    // Dispose the display
    display.dispose();
  }
```

```
/**
 * The application entry point
 *
 * @param args the command line arguments
 */
public static void main(String[] args) {
  new Survey().run();
}
}
```

The SurveyWizard class in Listing 20-3 creates and adds the three pages. It does nothing when the user clicks Finish except close the wizard.

Listing 20-3. SurveyWizard.java

```
package examples.ch20;

import org.eclipse.jface.wizard.Wizard;

/**
 * This class shows a satisfaction survey
 */
public class SurveyWizard extends Wizard {
  public SurveyWizard() {
    // Add the pages
    addPage(new ComplaintsPage());
    addPage(new MoreInformationPage());
    addPage(new ThanksPage());
  }

  /**
   * Called when user clicks Finish
   *
   * @return boolean
   */
  public boolean performFinish() {
    // Dismiss the wizard
    return true;
  }
}
```

The first page in the wizard, ComplaintsPage, asks users if they have any complaints. It provides Yes and No radio buttons to gather the response. If the user selects Yes, the wizard proceeds normally. However, if the user selects No, the wizard bypasses the rest of the survey and jumps to the final page. You find the logic to accomplish this navigation trick in getNextPage(). Listing 20-4 contains the code.

Listing 20-4. ComplaintsPage.java

```java
package examples.ch20;

import org.eclipse.jface.wizard.IWizardPage;
import org.eclipse.jface.wizard.WizardPage;
import org.eclipse.swt.SWT;
import org.eclipse.swt.layout.*;
import org.eclipse.swt.widgets.*;

/**
 * This class determines if the user has complaints. If not, it jumps to the last
 * page of the wizard
 */
public class ComplaintsPage extends WizardPage {
  private Button yes;
  private Button no;

  /**
   * ComplaintsPage constructor
   */
  public ComplaintsPage() {
    super("Complaints");
  }

  /**
   * Creates the page controls
   */
  public void createControl(Composite parent) {
    Composite composite = new Composite(parent, SWT.NONE);
    composite.setLayout(new GridLayout(2, true));

    new Label(composite, SWT.LEFT).setText("Do you have complaints?");
    Composite yesNo = new Composite(composite, SWT.NONE);
    yesNo.setLayout(new FillLayout(SWT.VERTICAL));

    yes = new Button(yesNo, SWT.RADIO);
    yes.setText("Yes");

    no = new Button(yesNo, SWT.RADIO);
    no.setText("No");

    setControl(composite);
  }

  public IWizardPage getNextPage() {
    // If they have complaints, go to the normal next page
    if (yes.getSelection()) { return super.getNextPage(); }
    // No complaints? Short-circuit the rest of the pages
    return getWizard().getPage("Thanks");
  }
}
```

The second page, which constitutes the survey, asks the user to enter more information about any complaints. It does nothing with the information, but we've come to expect that. Listing 20-5 contains the code.

Listing 20-5. `MoreInformation.java`

```java
package examples.ch20;

import org.eclipse.jface.wizard.WizardPage;
import org.eclipse.swt.SWT;
import org.eclipse.swt.layout.*;
import org.eclipse.swt.widgets.*;

/**
 * This page gathers more information about the complaint
 */
public class MoreInformationPage extends WizardPage {
  /**
   * MoreInformationPage constructor
   */
  public MoreInformationPage() {
    super("More Info");
  }

  /**
   * Creates the controls for this page
   */
  public void createControl(Composite parent) {
    Composite composite = new Composite(parent, SWT.NONE);
    composite.setLayout(new GridLayout(1, false));

    new Label(composite, SWT.LEFT).setText("Please enter your complaints");
    Text text = new Text(composite, SWT.MULTI | SWT.BORDER | SWT.V_SCROLL);
    text.setLayoutData(new GridData(GridData.FILL_BOTH));

    setControl(composite);
  }
}
```

Finally, the `ThanksPage` class in Listing 20-6 displays the final page in the wizard. It thanks the user.

Listing 20-6. `ThanksPage.java`

```java
package examples.ch20;

import org.eclipse.jface.wizard.WizardPage;
import org.eclipse.swt.SWT;
import org.eclipse.swt.widgets.Composite;
import org.eclipse.swt.widgets.Label;
```

```
/**
 * This page thanks the user for taking the survey
 */
public class ThanksPage extends WizardPage {
  /**
   * ThanksPage constructor
   */
  public ThanksPage() {
    super("Thanks");
  }

  /**
   * Creates the controls for this page
   */
  public void createControl(Composite parent) {
    Label label = new Label(parent, SWT.CENTER);
    label.setText("Thanks!");
    setControl(label);
  }
}
```

Figure 20-4 shows the first page of the wizard. Figure 20-5 shows the second page—the page that's skipped when the user has no complaints. Figure 20-6 shows the wizard's final page, thanking the user for taking the survey.

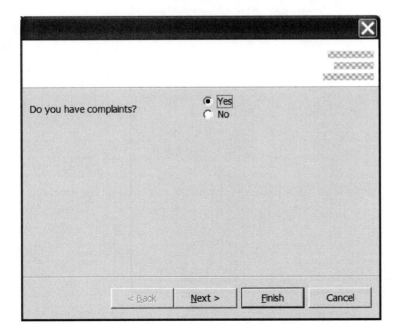

Figure 20-4. The Complaints page

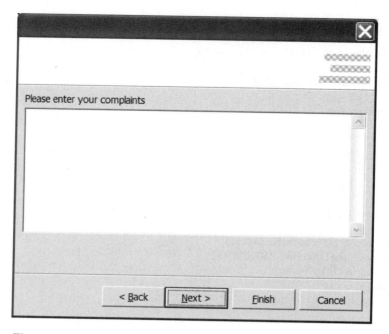

Figure 20-5. The More Information page. You won't see this page if you have no complaints.

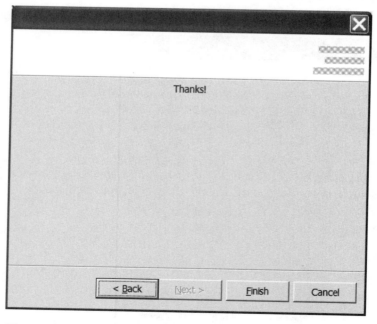

Figure 20-6. Thanking the user

Performing the Work

When the user clicks the Finish button, you should perform the work the wizard intends. Because WizardDialog.open() returns IDialogConstants.OK_ID only if the user clicks Finish, you can put the code to perform the wizard work in the code that launches the wizard, like this:

```
WizardDialog dlg = new WizardDialog(shell, myWizard);
int rc = dlg.open();
if (rc == IDialogConstants.OK_ID) {
  // User clicked Finish--perform the work
} else {
  // User clicked Cancel--do nothing
}
```

However, the wizard framework offers a better solution, one that encapsulates the wizard work within the wizard: IWizard's performFinish() method. The wizard framework calls this method, which returns true to dismiss the wizard or false to keep the wizard alive, when the user clicks Finish. Performing the work inside your IWizard implementation preserves the wizard work code with the rest of the wizard code. Besides, because you must implement performFinish() anyway, you might as well perform the work there.

Witnessing a Wizard

The AddressBook application displays a list of people and e-mail addresses. It uses a wizard to allow users to add address-book entries. To maintain focus on wizards, AddressBook omits functionality necessary for a usable application. For example, it incorporates no persistence, so any address-book entries you add drop into the bit bucket when the application closes. It has no menu, and provides no way to edit or delete an existing entry. In fact, it offers only one command: add an entry by launching the Add Entry wizard. To execute the command, click the plus sign in the toolbar.

The wizard class, AddEntryWizard, adds three pages in its constructor: a welcome page, a name entry page, and an e-mail address entry page. It also sets the dialog window's title. Its implementation of performFinish() creates an address-book entry, sets the input data into it, and adds it to the application. Listing 20-7 contains AddEntryWizard's code.

Listing 20-7. AddEntryWizard.java

```
package examples.ch20;

import org.eclipse.jface.wizard.Wizard;

/**
 * This class represents the wizard for adding entries to the address book
 */
```

```java
public class AddEntryWizard extends Wizard {
  // The pages in the wizard
  private WelcomePage welcomePage;
  private NamePage namePage;
  private EmailPage emailPage;

  /**
   * AddEntryWizard constructor
   */
  public AddEntryWizard() {
    // Create the pages
    welcomePage = new WelcomePage();
    namePage = new NamePage();
    emailPage = new EmailPage();

    // Add the pages to the wizard
    addPage(welcomePage);
    addPage(namePage);
    addPage(emailPage);

    // Set the dialog window title
    setWindowTitle("Address Book Entry Wizard");
  }

  /**
   * Called when the user clicks Finish. Creates the entry in the address book
   */
  public boolean performFinish() {
    // Create the entry based on the inputs
    AddressEntry entry = new AddressEntry();
    entry.setFirstName(namePage.getFirstName());
    entry.setLastName(namePage.getLastName());
    entry.setEmail(emailPage.getEmail());

    AddressBook.getApp().add(entry);

    // Return true to exit wizard
    return true;
  }
}
```

The first page in the wizard, WelcomePage, displays a welcome page that requests no information from the user (see Listing 20-8). It displays some descriptive text.

Listing 20-8. WelcomePage.java

```java
package examples.ch20;

import org.eclipse.jface.resource.ImageDescriptor;
import org.eclipse.jface.wizard.WizardPage;
import org.eclipse.swt.SWT;
import org.eclipse.swt.layout.FillLayout;
import org.eclipse.swt.widgets.*;
```

```
/**
 * This page displays a welcome message
 */
public class WelcomePage extends WizardPage {
  /**
   * WelcomePage constructor
   */
  protected WelcomePage() {
    super("Welcome", "Welcome", ImageDescriptor.createFromFile(WelcomePage.class,
        "/images/welcome.gif"));
    setDescription("Welcome to the Address Book Entry Wizard");
  }

  /**
   * Creates the page contents
   *
   * @param parent the parent composite
   */
  public void createControl(Composite parent) {
    Composite composite = new Composite(parent, SWT.NONE);
    composite.setLayout(new FillLayout(SWT.VERTICAL));
    new Label(composite, SWT.CENTER)
      .setText("Welcome to the Address Book Entry Wizard!");
    new Label(composite, SWT.LEFT)
      .setText("This wizard guides you through creating an Address Book entry.");
    new Label(composite, SWT.LEFT).setText("Click Next to continue.");
    setControl(composite);
  }
}
```

The second page in the wizard, NamePage, displays two text-entry fields: one for first name and one for last name. It doesn't allow users to advance to the next page until they enter first and last names. Listing 20-9 shows the code.

Listing 20-9. NamePage.java

```
package examples.ch20;

import org.eclipse.jface.resource.ImageDescriptor;
import org.eclipse.jface.wizard.WizardPage;
import org.eclipse.swt.SWT;
import org.eclipse.swt.events.*;
import org.eclipse.swt.layout.*;
import org.eclipse.swt.widgets.*;

/**
 * This page collects the first and last names
 */
public class NamePage extends WizardPage {
  // The first and last names
  private String firstName = "";
  private String lastName = "";
```

```java
/**
 * NamePage constructor
 */
public NamePage() {
  super("Name", "Name", ImageDescriptor.createFromFile(NamePage.class,
      "/images/name.gif"));
  setDescription("Enter the first and last names");
  setPageComplete(false);
}

/**
 * Creates the page contents
 *
 * @param parent the parent composite
 */
public void createControl(Composite parent) {
  Composite composite = new Composite(parent, SWT.NONE);
  composite.setLayout(new GridLayout(2, false));

  // Create the label and text field for first name
  new Label(composite, SWT.LEFT).setText("First Name:");
  final Text first = new Text(composite, SWT.BORDER);
  first.setLayoutData(new GridData(GridData.FILL_HORIZONTAL));

  // Create the label and text field for last name
  new Label(composite, SWT.LEFT).setText("Last Name:");
  final Text last = new Text(composite, SWT.BORDER);
  last.setLayoutData(new GridData(GridData.FILL_HORIZONTAL));

  // Add the handler to update the first name based on input
  first.addModifyListener(new ModifyListener() {
    public void modifyText(ModifyEvent event) {
      firstName = first.getText();
      setPageComplete(firstName.length() > 0 && lastName.length() > 0);
    }
  });

  // Add the handler to update the last name based on input
  last.addModifyListener(new ModifyListener() {
    public void modifyText(ModifyEvent event) {
      lastName = last.getText();
      setPageComplete(firstName.length() > 0 && lastName.length() > 0);
    }
  });

  setControl(composite);
}

/**
 * Gets the first name
 *
 * @return String
 */
```

```
  public String getFirstName() {
    return firstName;
  }

  /**
   * Gets the last name
   *
   * @return String
   */
  public String getLastName() {
    return lastName;
  }
}
```

The final page in the wizard, EmailPage, shows a single text field for entering the e-mail address for the entry (see Listing 20-10). It prevents users from finishing the wizard until they've entered an e-mail address.

Listing 20-10. EmailPage.java

```
package examples.ch20;

import org.eclipse.jface.resource.ImageDescriptor;
import org.eclipse.jface.wizard.WizardPage;
import org.eclipse.swt.SWT;
import org.eclipse.swt.events.*;
import org.eclipse.swt.layout.*;
import org.eclipse.swt.widgets.*;

/**
 * This page collects the e-mail address
 */
public class EmailPage extends WizardPage {
  // The e-mail address
  private String email = "";

  /**
   * EmailPage constructor
   */
  public EmailPage() {
    super("E-mail", "E-mail Address", ImageDescriptor.createFromFile(
        EmailPage.class, "/images/email.gif"));
    setDescription("Enter the e-mail address");

    // Page isn't complete until an e-mail address has been added
    setPageComplete(false);
  }

  /**
   * Creates the contents of the page
   *
   * @param parent the parent composite
   */
```

```
public void createControl(Composite parent) {
  Composite composite = new Composite(parent, SWT.NONE);
  composite.setLayout(new GridLayout(2, false));

  // Create the label and text box to hold e-mail address
  new Label(composite, SWT.LEFT).setText("E-mail Address:");
  final Text ea = new Text(composite, SWT.BORDER);
  ea.setLayoutData(new GridData(GridData.FILL_HORIZONTAL));

  // Add handler to update e-mail based on input
  ea.addModifyListener(new ModifyListener() {
    public void modifyText(ModifyEvent event) {
      email = ea.getText();
      setPageComplete(email.length() > 0);
    }
  });

  setControl(composite);
}

/**
 * Gets the e-mail
 *
 * @return String
 */
public String getEmail() {
  return email;
}
}
```

The AddressEntry class in Listing 20-11 contains the data for a single address-book entry: a first name, last name, and e-mail address. It provides corresponding accessors and mutators.

Listing 20-11. AddressEntry.java

```
package examples.ch20;

/**
 * This class contains an entry in the Address Book
 */
public class AddressEntry {
  private String lastName;
  private String firstName;
  private String email;

  /**
   * Gets the e-mail
   *
   * @return String
   */
  public String getEmail() {
    return email;
  }
```

```
/**
 * Sets the e-mail
 *
 * @param email The email to set.
 */
public void setEmail(String email) {
  this.email = email;
}

/**
 * Gets the first name
 *
 * @return String
 */
public String getFirstName() {
  return firstName;
}

/**
 * Sets the first name
 *
 * @param firstName The firstName to set.
 */
public void setFirstName(String firstName) {
  this.firstName = firstName;
}

/**
 * Gets the last name
 *
 * @return String
 */
public String getLastName() {
  return lastName;
}

/**
 * Sets the last name
 *
 * @param lastName The lastName to set.
 */
public void setLastName(String lastName) {
  this.lastName = lastName;
}
}
```

The application uses the AddEntryAction class from Listing 20-12 to launch the wizard. This action class creates a new AddEntryWizard instance, wraps it in a WizardDialog, and quickly gets out of the way so the wizard can do its work.

Listing 20-12. AddEntryAction.java

```
package examples.ch20;

import org.eclipse.jface.action.Action;
import org.eclipse.jface.resource.ImageDescriptor;
import org.eclipse.jface.wizard.WizardDialog;

/**
 * This class launches the add entry wizard
 */
public class AddEntryAction extends Action {
  /**
   * AddEntryAction constructor
   */
  public AddEntryAction() {
    super("Add Entry", ImageDescriptor.createFromFile(AddEntryAction.class,
        "/images/addEntry.gif"));
    setToolTipText("Add Entry");
  }

  /**
   * Runs the action
   */
  public void run() {
    WizardDialog dlg = new WizardDialog(AddressBook.getApp().getShell(),
        new AddEntryWizard());
    dlg.open();
  }
}
```

AddressBook displays the address book in a TableViewer. Listing 20-13 shows the TableViewer's content provider, AddressBookContentProvider, and Listing 20-14 shows the label provider, AddressBookLabelProvider.

Listing 20-13. AddressBookContentProvider.java

```
package examples.ch20;

import java.util.*;

import org.eclipse.jface.viewers.IStructuredContentProvider;
import org.eclipse.jface.viewers.Viewer;

/**
 * This class provides the content for the AddressBook application
 */
public class AddressBookContentProvider implements IStructuredContentProvider {
  /**
   * Gets the elements
   *
   * @param inputElement the List of elements
```

```
 * @return Object[]
 */
public Object[] getElements(Object inputElement) {
  return ((List) inputElement).toArray();
}

/**
 * Disposes any resources
 */
public void dispose() {
// Do nothing
}

/**
 * Called when the input changes
 *
 * @param viewer the viewer
 * @param oldInput the old input
 * @param newInput the new input
 */
public void inputChanged(Viewer viewer, Object oldInput, Object newInput) {
// Do nothing
}
}
```

Listing 20-14. AddressBookLabelProvider.java

```
package examples.ch20;

import org.eclipse.jface.viewers.ILabelProviderListener;
import org.eclipse.jface.viewers.ITableLabelProvider;
import org.eclipse.swt.graphics.Image;

/**
 * This class provides the labels for the Address Book application
 */
public class AddressBookLabelProvider implements ITableLabelProvider {
  /**
   * Gets the image for the column
   *
   * @param element the element
   * @param columnIndex the column index
   */
  public Image getColumnImage(Object element, int columnIndex) {
    return null;
  }

  /**
   * Gets the text for the column
   *
   * @param element the element
   * @param columnIndex the column index
   */
```

```java
public String getColumnText(Object element, int columnIndex) {
  AddressEntry ae = (AddressEntry) element;
  switch (columnIndex) {
  case 0:
    return ae.getFirstName();
  case 1:
    return ae.getLastName();
  case 2:
    return ae.getEmail();
  }
  return "";
}

/**
 * Adds a listener
 *
 * @param listener the listener
 */
public void addListener(ILabelProviderListener listener) {
// Do nothing
}

/**
 * Disposes any resources
 */
public void dispose() {
// Do nothing
}

/**
 * Returns true if changing the property for the element would change the label
 *
 * @param element the element
 * @param property the property
 */
public boolean isLabelProperty(Object element, String property) {
  return false;
}

/**
 * Removes a listener
 *
 * @param listener the listener
 */
public void removeListener(ILabelProviderListener listener) {
// Do nothing
  }
}
```

Lastly, the AddressBook application provides the entry point and launches the main window (see Listing 20-15).

Listing 20-15. `AddressBook.java`

```java
package examples.ch20;

import java.util.*;

import org.eclipse.jface.action.*;
import org.eclipse.jface.viewers.*;
import org.eclipse.jface.window.ApplicationWindow;
import org.eclipse.swt.SWT;
import org.eclipse.swt.widgets.*;

/**
 * This class displays an address book, using a wizard to add a new entry
 */
public class AddressBook extends ApplicationWindow {
  // The running instance of the application
  private static AddressBook APP;

  // The action that launches the wizard
  AddEntryAction addEntryAction;

  // The entries in the address book
  java.util.List entries;

  // The view
  private TableViewer viewer;

  /**
   * AddressBook constructor
   */
  public AddressBook() {
    super(null);

    // Store a reference to the running app
    APP = this;

    // Create the action and the entries collection
    addEntryAction = new AddEntryAction();
    entries = new LinkedList();

    // Create the toolbar
    addToolBar(SWT.NONE);
  }

  /**
   * Gets a reference to the running application
   *
   * @return AddressBook
   */
  public static AddressBook getApp() {
    return APP;
  }
```

```java
/**
 * Runs the application
 */
public void run() {
  // Don't return from open() until window closes
  setBlockOnOpen(true);

  // Open the main window
  open();

  // Dispose the display
  Display.getCurrent().dispose();
}

/**
 * Adds an entry
 *
 * @param entry the entry
 */
public void add(AddressEntry entry) {
  entries.add(entry);
  refresh();
}

/**
 * Configures the shell
 *
 * @param shell the shell
 */
protected void configureShell(Shell shell) {
  super.configureShell(shell);

  // Set the title bar text
  shell.setText("Address Book");
  shell.setSize(600, 400);
}

/**
 * Creates the main window's contents
 *
 * @param parent the main window
 * @return Control
 */
protected Control createContents(Composite parent) {
  // Create the table viewer
  viewer = new TableViewer(parent);
  viewer.setContentProvider(new AddressBookContentProvider());
  viewer.setLabelProvider(new AddressBookLabelProvider());
  viewer.setInput(entries);

  // Set up the table
  Table table = viewer.getTable();
  new TableColumn(table, SWT.LEFT).setText("First Name");
  new TableColumn(table, SWT.LEFT).setText("Last Name");
```

```
    new TableColumn(table, SWT.LEFT).setText("E-mail Address");
    table.setHeaderVisible(true);
    table.setLinesVisible(true);

    // Update the column widths
    refresh();

    return table;
  }

  /**
   * Creates the toolbar
   *
   * @param style the toolbar style
   * @return ToolBarManager
   */
  protected ToolBarManager createToolBarManager(int style) {
    ToolBarManager tbm = new ToolBarManager(style);

    // Add the action to launch the wizard
    tbm.add(addEntryAction);

    return tbm;
  }

  /**
   * Updates the column widths
   */
  private void refresh() {
    viewer.refresh();

    // Pack the columns
    Table table = viewer.getTable();
    for (int i = 0, n = table.getColumnCount(); i < n; i++) {
      table.getColumn(i).pack();
    }
  }

  /**
   * The application entry point
   *
   * @param args the command line arguments
   */
  public static void main(String[] args) {
    new AddressBook().run();
  }
}
```

Figure 20-7 shows the Welcome page in the wizard. Notice that the Finish button is disabled; you can't finish the wizard prematurely. You must enter first name, last name, and e-mail address. Figure 20-8 shows the Name page, which appears after the Welcome page. Until you enter something for both first and last name, you can't click Next. The E-mail page, shown in Figure 20-9, never enables the Next button, as it's the last page in the wizard. After you enter an e-mail address, click Finish to add the entry to the address book. Figure 20-10 shows the Address Book with the authors' names and e-mail addresses.

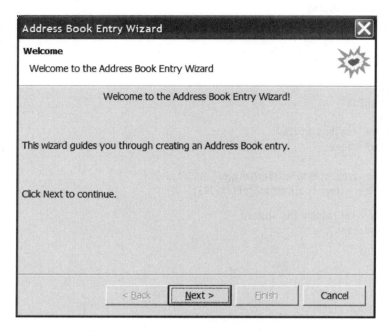

Figure 20-7. The Welcome page

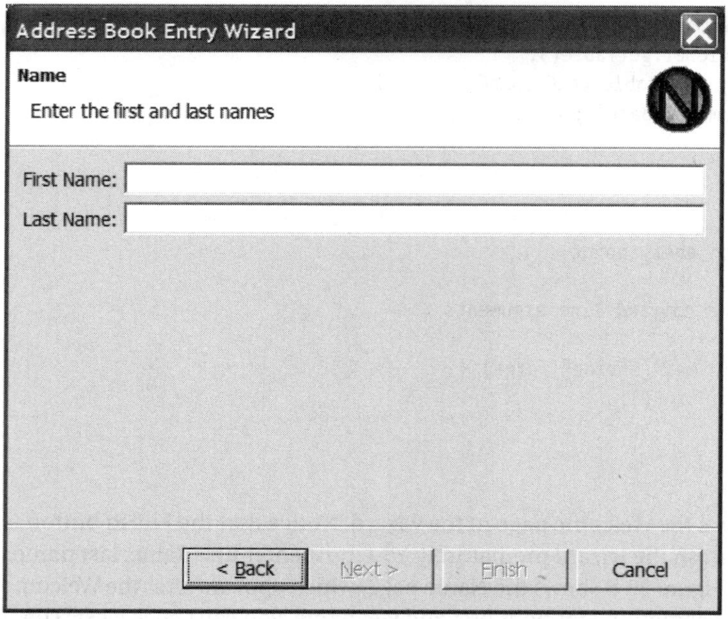

Figure 20-8. The Name page

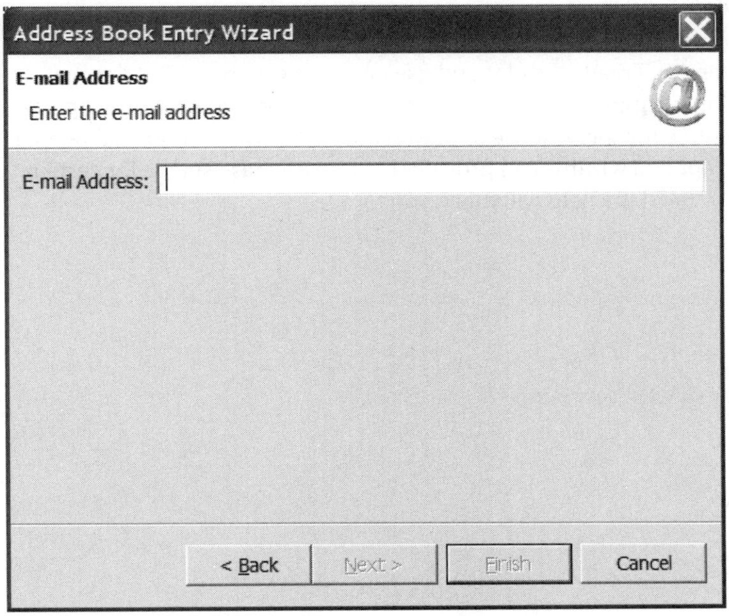

Figure 20-9. The E-mail page

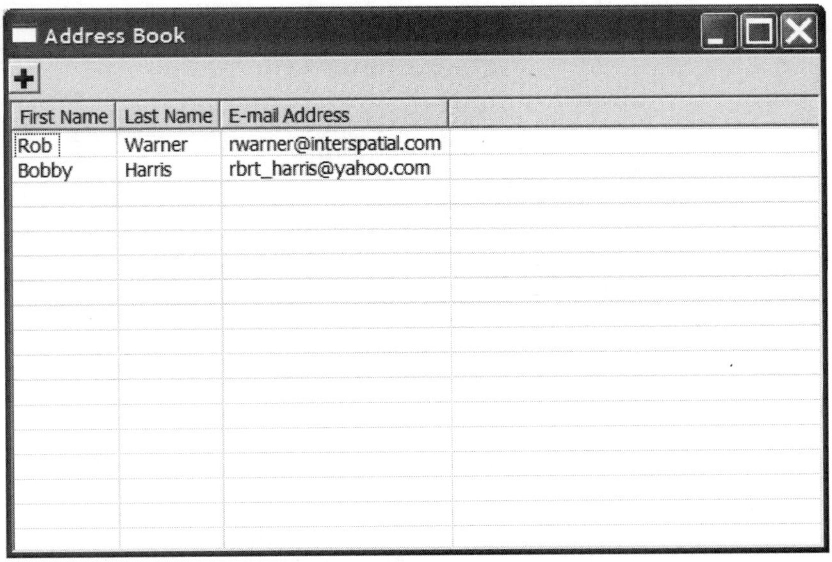

Figure 20-10. The Address Book

Summary

Computer jocks—those that read Slashdot and use nonwords such as 1337—scorn wizards. When developing applications for that crowd, remember to make any operations difficult, to preserve the jocks' sense of power and exclusivity. For normal people, however, judiciously applied wizards can provide the necessary assistance for certain operations. Users who need the help will thank you.

Index

G

forums.apress.com

JOIN THE APRESS FORUMS AND BE PART OF OUR COMMUNITY. You'll find discussions that cover topics of interest to IT professionals, programmers, and enthusiasts just like you. If you post a query to one of our forums, you can expect that some of the best minds in the business—especially Apress authors, who all write with *The Expert's Voice*™—will chime in to help you. Why not aim to become one of our most valuable participants (MVPs) and win cool stuff? Here's a sampling of what you'll find:

DATABASES
Data drives everything.

Share information, exchange ideas, and discuss any database programming or administration issues.

PROGRAMMING/BUSINESS
Unfortunately, it is.

Talk about the Apress line of books that cover software methodology, best practices, and how programmers interact with the "suits."

INTERNET TECHNOLOGIES AND NETWORKING
Try living without plumbing (and eventually IPv6).

Talk about networking topics including protocols, design, administration, wireless, wired, storage, backup, certifications, trends, and new technologies.

WEB DEVELOPMENT/DESIGN
Ugly doesn't cut it anymore, and CGI is absurd.

Help is in sight for your site. Find design solutions for your projects and get ideas for building an interactive Web site.

JAVA
We've come a long way from the old Oak tree.

Hang out and discuss Java in whatever flavor you choose: J2SE, J2EE, J2ME, Jakarta, and so on.

SECURITY
Lots of bad guys out there—the good guys need help.

Discuss computer and network security issues here. Just don't let anyone else know the answers!

MAC OS X
All about the Zen of OS X.

OS X is both the present and the future for Mac apps. Make suggestions, offer up ideas, or boast about your new hardware.

TECHNOLOGY IN ACTION
Cool things. Fun things.

It's after hours. It's time to play. Whether you're into LEGO® MINDSTORMS™ or turning an old PC into a DVR, this is where technology turns into fun.

OPEN SOURCE
Source code is good; understanding (open) source is better.

Discuss open source technologies and related topics such as PHP, MySQL, Linux, Perl, Apache, Python, and more.

WINDOWS
No defenestration here.

Ask questions about all aspects of Windows programming, get help on Microsoft technologies covered in Apress books, or provide feedback on any Apress Windows book.

HOW TO PARTICIPATE:
Go to the Apress Forums site at **http://forums.apress.com/**.
Click the New User link.